Structured
COBOL

Structured COBOL

GARY HAGGARD
University of Maine at Orono

WENDELL O. JONES
United States Military Academy

D. C. HEATH AND COMPANY

Lexington, Massachusetts   Toronto

Copyright © 1985 by D. C. Heath and Company.

Published simultaneously in Canada.

Printed in the United States of America.

International Standard Book Number: 0-669-06207-3

Library of Congress Catalog Card Number: 84-80294

Preface

COBOL has been a major programming language in commercial data processing for twenty-five years. Today, COBOL is still a vital part of most business data processing systems. Billions of dollars are invested in systems programmed in COBOL; and, although a number of new languages are now available, it is estimated that as much as eighty percent of all new applications are being written in COBOL. Needless to say, COBOL knowledge is destined to remain essential for years to come.

MAJOR FEATURES OF THE TEXT

American National Standard Orientation This text is designed for users of the 1974 ANS COBOL standard; however, other extensions such as WATBOL, and the earlier 1968 version can be used without difficulty. The new proposed ANS standard, referred to as COBOL 198X, is also discussed.

Structured Design and Program Logic Current structured design and development principles are an integral part of the text. Stepwise refinement, structured techniques, and the use of pseudocode are consistently emphasized and applied.

This text is intentionally designed to allow the student to focus on program design and logic from the outset. A special block of code called TEXTA is introduced to simplify understanding. It can easily be placed in the COPY library of a COBOL compiler or given to the student as a set of card images for placement at the beginning of a program. The student is freed from coding the IDENTIFICATION and ENVIRONMENT DIVISIONs and the FILE SECTION of the DATA DIVISION for the computing environment used by the text. TEXTA allows the use of files, utility programs, and peripheral devices early in the book without the student mastering interface complications. This block of code can be modified to adapt to any computing environment, and is found in Chapter 2.

Use of Real Files Throughout the Text An important feature is the use of the same files for all problems throughout the book. Once the files have been placed in the system library, they can be used by anyone with access to it. Using the same files for all problems provides realism, permits the use of COBOL's excellent file management capabilities, frees the user from entering data, and avoids the use of unrelated problems characteristic of other programming textbooks. Listings of the files are contained in Appendix C, D, E, and F.

Simple-to-Complex Presentation Using Models The text introduces features of COBOL by examining in detail programs that use the features. The problems are natural in the sense that the design and analysis of solutions are usually accomplished by working through some of the examples using pencil and paper. This simplification in approach allows the student to focus on the logic of programming solutions. Early in the text, a model is presented that can be used to overcome the problem of "How do I get started?" Subsequent models are refined versions of the first and give a general outline for most programming problems the student encounters.

Classroom Tested This text has been tested with students in a College of Business Administration who are required to take one COBOL course followed by a second that covers some advanced COBOL topics. Many of the students develop a genuine interest in computers and subsequently enroll in other computer science courses. COBOL need not be a difficult or frustrating language that "turns students off" to further study.

Rather than try to be a complete reference book that can confuse beginning students, this text presents new principles and concepts with complete programs that are clearly described. An easily understood style makes the book an excellent self-teaching source. Experience in classroom testing the manuscript has shown us that students find the book accessible.

Flexible Use For One- or Two-Term Courses This text can be used in a variety of courses. For the first semester (quarter) it is usually possible to cover Chapters 1–4 and 7. Parts of Chapter 5 can be included or excluded without having an impact on Chapter 7. Students who have already completed a computer programming or data processing course will find that Chapter 1 is an excellent review of introductory concepts. Chapter 13 is an effective bridge to more advanced study in an information systems curriculum.

Extensive Exercises, Problems, and Summary Material Each section of a chapter concludes with a combination of these important features: (1) a Syntax Summary of the important new features introduced; (2) Exercises designed for pencil and paper solutions to reinforce major teaching points; (3) Program Testing and Modification Exercises, which involve tracing execution or modifying program logic; and (4) Programming Problems, which apply concepts just introduced while building on earlier principles. In addition, each chapter concludes with a Summary and Test Yourself problems for student review.

Programming Problems Designed for Easy Modification The programming problems are intended as typical assignments that can be a model for other assignments using either a different file or different data elements. As a consequence, the instructor can easily modify a programming problem so that a different problem can be assigned each time the course is given. Because the same files are used for all the problems, student suggestions are a good source of additional problems as students become more familiar with the files.

Useful Appendices and Glossary In addition to complete files, a number of important subjects are treated in the appendices. These include flowcharting, the WATBOL system, differences between 1968 and 1974 ANS COBOL standards and the proposed 198X COBOL, and a complete COBOL glossary.

Acknowledgments

First, and most importantly, we owe a debt of gratitude to innumerable students who have participated in the stepwise refinement process used in developing this text. Special thanks must also be extended to those who helped with the process of creating the manuscript. These include Joan Lavoie, Mary Preble, and Melinda Westbrook. Mert Nickerson generously aided in making preliminary versions of the manuscript available for classroom use. It has been a pleasure working with the staff at D. C. Heath, in particular the Computer Science Editor Pam Kirshen and our Production Editor Peggy J. Flanagan.

Second, to our families who learned first hand the many days and long hours included in writing a text, we want to extend a special thank-you. Andrew, Henry, Grace, Dan, Brian, and Kimberly—thank you for your support and understanding.

Finally, we would like to ask instructors and students to communicate suggestions for improvement. Suggestions will be carefully considered for inclusion in revisions. It goes without saying that any errors in the manuscript are the responsibility of the authors, and any help in finding the last bug will be gratefully appreciated.

Gary Haggard
Wendell O. Jones

Contents

13. SUBPROGRAMS   358

Structured COBOL

1

Computers: People, Program Development, and Structured Programming

Chapter Objectives

After studying this chapter you should be able to

- describe the major components of a business computer system;
- define the various types of software and hardware in business computer systems, and the people who use them;
- explain the functional interrelationship of the parts of a central processing unit and input/output devices when executing a simple program;
- explain the program development process;
- explain the purpose and advantage of pseudocode for program design;
- identify the three flow-of-control structures used in structured programming.

Chapter Outline

1.1 Introduction to Business Computer Systems

It has been suggested that had the automobile and aviation industries progressed at the same rate as the computer industry, astronauts would have landed on the moon six months after the Wright brothers' flight at Kitty Hawk and a new automobile would cost $5 and would be capable of speeds up to 20,000 miles per hour. Computers are not only getting cheaper and more powerful every year, they are helping solve an ever wider range of human problems.

Today, the electronic computer is commonplace in business firms and government agencies. Virtually all of the scientific disciplines depend on the computer's speed and ability to deal with complex computational tasks. It is not rare to find computers in several academic departments of a university or college. Only a few short years ago, machine costs limited computer use to large organizations. Today, even a small business can make valuable use of this computational tool. The computer is even making impressive inroads in the home, where the microcomputer or personal computer is being used for education, games, household budgeting, and in a variety of other ways. Despite the impressive developments that have occurred during the past thirty years, some experts predict that the true impact of the computer on society is yet to be felt. Whether such predictions are accurate or not, there is no question that the demand for computer-literate personnel will steadily increase.

This book introduces you to computers and computer programming. This will equip you with knowledge about computers that will be valuable in any career field and will provide you with a solid foundation for further study of computer subjects.

Problem solving in the business environment is heavily dependent upon the computer. Payroll, billing, inventory control, and long-range planning are only a few of the many business activities that rely on the speed of the computer for problem solving because of the large amounts of data to process or the extensive computations required. Whether you will be involved with data processing and computer systems directly or will only use the output of computer systems in the decision process, you need to understand what is involved so you can make effective use of this valuable resource. Programming is one of the best ways to learn about computers.

The step-by-step instructions people write for a computer to solve problems are called a **computer program,** and the process people go through to create programs is called **programming.** Like any other human activity, fundamental principles of good programming practice apply to most *programming languages*. But, there is more to programming than writing the program code. You will learn what is involved in program development and how to program a computer to solve business problems using the COBOL programming language.

Introduction to COBOL

COBOL is an acronym taken from the words **CO**mmon **B**usiness **O**riented **L**anguage. As its name suggests, COBOL is a programming language designed to be used for typical business applications. Business applications are characterized by large volumes of input and output data, large files, and the need to produce output reports that require extensive editing and formatting of data. COBOL is a language designed for business data processing applications with these characteristics.

COBOL is an English-like language in that its vocabulary and grammar are based upon the clause, sentence, and paragraph structure of the English language. COBOL words such as FILE, DATA, MOVE, READ, WRITE, and others (called COBOL reserved words) have the same meaning as their English counterparts.

Unlike scientific-mathematical languages such as FORTRAN and Pascal, COBOL is essentially nonmathematical. Certainly, mathematical computations can be executed using COBOL, and FORTRAN can be used to solve business problems. Nevertheless, COBOL is better suited for business applications that involve repeating the same process for a large number of cases, and FORTRAN is more convenient and efficient for scientific problems such as complex mathematical computations.

First introduced in 1959, COBOL is one of the oldest programming languages. Just a few years after its introduction, COBOL established itself as one of the most widely used languages for business applications. It still is today.

In the late 1950s the United States Department of Defense (DOD) recognized that a common language was needed because of the many problems the DOD was experiencing at that time. Different computer manufacturers had different languages for each system. DOD auditors could not track contract costs without familiarity with the many different languages. As the single largest user of computers, training personnel for the variety of systems in the Department of Defense was also costly and virtually impossible. Due to equipment differences, no computer company's language could be used on other equipment and there was no existing higher-level language considered appropriate for commercial data processing.

With DOD encouragement, the Committee On DAta SYstems Language (CODASYL) was created in 1959 to address these problems. The committee included representatives of DOD, other government agencies, computer manufacturers, universities, and other computer users. Perhaps the most famous of these early pioneers is Commodore Grace Hopper of the United States Navy. She continues to play an important role in the field. CODASYL decided to develop a new language that would be common to all computers and would be easily understandable by people with limited computer training.

Results of the CODASYL conference were produced in 1960 with initial specifications for the language. Later revisions were made in 1963 and 1965. Meanwhile, each computer manufacturer added new implementations and took different approaches. Although all versions of COBOL were based on the same set of specifications, there were major differences between various computers systems. It was apparent that COBOL was fast becoming a language different from the original intent of the CODASYL. Consequently, in 1968 the American National Standards Institute (ANSI) approved a standard COBOL language. Versions of COBOL that conform to those ANSI standards are referred to as ANSI-68 COBOL. (Recently, ANSI COBOL has been shortened to ANS COBOL.)

The 1968 standards theoretically meant that one standard language would be used for all computers. In practice, however, each computer manufacturer added extensions to the language to meet capabilities wanted by various users. The 1968 standards allowed these extensions. In fact, manufacturers could refer to their versions as standard COBOL regardless of how many extensions were added. Needless to say, 1968 COBOL standards did not result in a truly standardized COBOL language.

In 1974 ANSI released a new set of standards that deleted some of the earlier standards, modified others, and added several new capabilities. COBOL versions based on the 1974 standards are usually referred to as 1974 ANS COBOL. In contrast to 1968 ANS COBOL, 1974 ANS COBOL for one computer is usually similar to the COBOL on another computer. Only a few minor revisions are normally required to convert from computer to computer. Nevertheless, extensions to the standard are still allowed. In the worst case, extensive changes may have to be made to an ANS 74 COBOL program to convert it from one computer to another. Fortunately, this is not a serious problem with the most widely used computers today. This book conforms to ANS 74 COBOL. COBOL continues to be reviewed and changed in response to the changing computing environment. In fact, one of the strengths of COBOL is that the language evolves in response to new computing developments.

Before you can understand the programming process in general and COBOL in detail, a few background ideas and some basic concepts of computer systems need to be examined.

Business Computer Systems

As its name suggests, a **business computer system** processes business-related data using a computer system. A **system** is a collection of components that interact and function to accomplish some purpose. Accordingly, a business computer system includes a computer and other components that interact to solve business data processing problems and satisfy an organization's information needs.

This book focuses on the development of COBOL programs that process data and solve relatively limited problems using a computer system. However, it is important to understand that a computer system consists of more than just machines. There are five important parts of a business computer system. These are *people, documentation, data, hardware,* and *software.* An appreciation for each of these integral components of a computer system is essential to place programming in its proper context.

People Who Use Business Computer Systems

The single most important component of a computer system is people. People bring together all the parts so that the entire system can achieve its purpose. Various categories of personnel are involved with computer systems: *systems analysts, programmers, operations personnel, users,* and *clients.*

System analysts design computer systems based on the data processing and information requirements of an organization. Effective system analysis and design are vital to development of efficient and effective computer systems, as well as individual programs. Many system analysis and design techniques are beyond the scope of this introductory programming text, where you will be dealing with essentially straightforward problems. However, it is important to realize that analysis and design of a business system usually precede the program development tasks learned using this text. Needless to say, a good system analyst should not only understand computers and the business environment, but also must be an effective communicator with people. Many system analysts are former computer programmers. Some are both and are called **programmer/analysts.**

Applications programmers analyze the specifications and requirements for a proposed system or program provided by the system analyst and develop the sequence of instructions that tell the computer how to accomplish the desired results. Applications programs are written to solve particular business data processing problems. They are commonly prepared for a computer-using organization as a system of programs for use in applications such as inventory control, payroll, or customer billing. COBOL programmers are applications programmers who use the COBOL language.

Applications programming can be divided into two types: development and maintenance programming. **Development programmers** work on new applications; **maintenance programmers** are concerned with modifying existing applications programs. In fact, data processing facilities typically organize their applications programmers into development and maintenance teams or sections. Even if programmers are not organized into separate teams, program modifications are almost always accomplished by someone other than the programmer who originally developed the program, because programmers typically complete one project and are then assigned to new projects. Often, the need for program changes results from changing business requirements. For example, a new contract for hourly employees can result in salary and benefit adjustments that in turn require modification of the payroll programs. Even the programmer who wrote the original payroll application may have a difficult time modifying the program unless careful attention was paid to documenting the design and structure of the program. Accordingly, the importance of developing correct programs and making sure that the program solutions are simple, straightforward, and easily understandable by other people cannot be overemphasized.

In addition to development and maintenance programmers, a third type is the system programmer. **System programmers** are not concerned with applications programming directly but instead, they work with the *system programs*. One important system program is the *operating system* that controls the operation and interaction of the computer resources of a computer center. System programs are discussed in a later section of this chapter.

Operations personnel are also involved in computer systems. Included in this category are personnel who actually operate the computer and other devices, perform data recording and data entry functions, and account for and distribute computer-produced reports to users.

Users are the people who use the computer system in the performance of their jobs. Examples are airline reservations agents working with computerized airline reservation systems and cash register clerks working with point-of-sale systems. **Clients** are a special category of users. Inventory managers, airline passengers, and bank tellers are some of the possible clients served by various business systems.

Documentation

Personnel and documentation go hand in hand. **Documentation** is the term broadly used to encompass all the written sets of instructions and procedures for people to follow in operating and using a computer system. User documentation explains user procedures, such as how to prepare input data for the system, how to interpret and use outputs produced by the system, and how to recover when errors are detected. Documentation for the computer operator involves directions for running the computer, sequencing various program jobs, and controlling operation of the equipment. Documentation for system programmers involves instructions for diagnosing and recovering from hardware malfunctions and interruptions.

External and Internal Documentation.   Applications programmers require both external and internal documentation. **External documentation** includes the written descriptions and explanations of how a program is designed and coded, and it consists of the program documentation that is not included in the program code. **Internal documentation,** on the other hand, refers to the comments and other descriptions that are written as part of the program code. Internal documentation is included so other people can read and more easily understand both the design decisions and the logic used in a program. Both external and internal program documentation are essential for effective program development and maintenance. This textbook will consistently emphasize the use of clear comments in your programs. Comments are inserted in a program to outline and communicate the structure and logic of a program to others and provide internal documentation inseparable from the program instructions.

Data

The basic raw material and finished product of a business computer system is data. A manufacturing system inputs raw materials and transforms them into a finished good. A computer system also transforms, or processes, raw data into information, as Figure 1.1.1 illustrates.

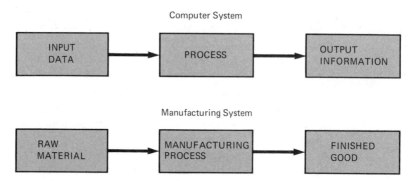

Figure 1.1.1 *Model of computing and manufacturing systems.*

Data is facts, figures, or unrelated messages for processing into information. Data, however, is not necessarily information. Information is data arranged in some ordered and useful way and produced to achieve specific purposes, solve problems, and/or enhance understanding.

Just as a finished product not put to a useful purpose by a consumer is of doubtful utility, a computer system that fails to meet the needs of its users is of little value. Not only must the business computer system be well designed by the system analysts, but also the application programmers must develop programs capable of correct execution.

Before a user need can be satisfied by a correct computer program, however, the data must be gathered. This is a special problem for computer systems, as all data must be captured on or converted into some machine-readable medium before it can be entered into the computer. Data may be typed directly into a computer from a key entry device, punched on cards and read by a card reader, recorded as magnetized spots on a reel of tape and read by a tape drive, or placed into any of several possible forms understandable by the computer. The term **medium** refers to the substance that the data is recorded on. The medium for this book is paper. Magnetic tape is a medium, as are punched cards. A **device** is a machine that uses the data carried on a medium. Keyboard terminals, card readers, tape drives, and optical scanners are some of the many devices used to enter data into a computer.

Hardware

The **hardware** component of a system consists of three major parts—an input device, a central processing unit, and an output device. Input devices accept data in some form from outside the computer system and transform it into an electronic form understandable by the computer. Such data is usually called **input data,** or simply **input.** One method of inputting data uses the punched card. Data is recorded on the cards by punching an appropriate pattern of holes. The input device (card reader) is designed to interpret the meaning of the holes punched in the card and transform the pattern of holes into an electronic representation understandable by the computer. Similarly, the symbols on a keyboard are directly transformed to machine-readable characters when keyed.

An **output** device performs the opposite function of an input device. An output device transforms data received from the computer into a form that can be used outside the computer system. This is called **output data,** or simply **output.** A common example is a printed report. To produce a report, the computer transmits data electronically to a printer (normally called **line printer** or **high-speed printer**). The printer then converts it into typed copy on paper. There are a variety of input and output devices available for modern computer systems. Some are shown in Figure 1.1.2.

(a)

(b)

(c)

Figure 1.1.2 *(a) A large computer system. (b) A minicomputer system. (c) A microcomputer system. Photos (a) and (c) courtesy of International Business Machines Corporation. Photo (b) courtesy of Digital Equipment Corporation.*

Between the input and output devices is the computer or central processing unit (CPU). Data is received in the CPU from an input device and stored internally in the CPU long enough to complete the processing specified by the computer program. The program is also stored in the CPU. Once the specified steps have been completed, information is then sent to some output device. To see how the CPU interprets its stored program and processes the data, let's look at how the three major units of a CPU interact.

A CPU consists of internal storage, arithmetic, and control units. Before the CPU can process data, its internal storage area must be loaded with all or certain parts of the applications program and the operating system. Together these sets of programs provide step-by-step instructions for the hardware to follow. In addition to storing application programs and operating system instructions, data read into and processed by the computer are stored in internal storage. Other terms frequently used for internal storage are *primary storage, core storage,* and *memory.* **Memory** will normally be used in this book when referring to internal storage.

The arithmetic unit in the CPU performs logical and arithmetic operations. Arithmetic operations are addition, subtraction, multiplication, and division. Logical operations involve comparing two numbers or words to determine if one is less than, greater than, or equal to another.

Operating under the overall direction of the operating system, the function of the control unit of the central processor is to interpret the program instructions and to tell other units in the system what to do. During processing, each instruction is brought from memory to the control unit. The control unit then issues commands to the other units based on what the program instruction tells it to do. Execution of an instruction may involve actions in any of the other units of the computer. After the first instruction is executed, the next instruction is brought to the control unit, and so on, until all instructions have been executed.

To better understand how the units of a CPU interact and function, let's assume we have a simple problem that has been programmed in some language (for purposes of this illustration, assume the language is English). The problem is to add two numbers and to produce a printed output that consists of the sum of the pair of numbers. The program would basically involve three instructions:

1. Read two numbers.
2. Add the two numbers.
3. Write the result.

These instructions would first have to be read into the computer from some medium such as punched cards through a card reader, or keyed by means of a keyboard terminal. The input device would send the program instructions to computer memory where the program would be stored.

On a signal to start, the first instruction in the program (Read two numbers.) would be sent to the control unit from memory. This instruction would result in the control unit sending a command to the input device to read the two numbers and send the values of the two numbers to memory. After that is accomplished, the second program instruction (Add the two numbers.) is brought to the control unit. This instruction would cause the control unit to send three messages: the first is to transfer the two numbers now in memory to the arithmetic unit; the second commands the arithmetic unit to add the numbers; and the third instructs the arithmetic unit to send the result to memory for storage. The last instruction (Write the result.) would cause the control unit to issue the command that the sum of the two numbers now in memory be sent to the output device and for the output device to write (print) the answer.

From this simplified description of how a computer would execute a program for adding two numbers, you may have noted that memory contains both the data to be processed, data awaiting transfer to an output device, and the program instructions. Any memory location has the capacity to store either data or instructions, but never both at the same time. It is sometimes useful to think of memory as having four different areas. We will call these "conceptual memory" areas as they are not physically separate sections of memory. Because they are conceptual, physical memory is partitioned with broken lines in Figure 1.1.3.

CPU

CONTROL UNIT	ARITHMETIC UNIT
INPUT (DATA)	SOFTWARE (PROGRAM)
TEMPORARY STORAGE	OUTPUT (DATA)

MEMORY

Figure 1.1.3 Conceptual memory areas.

Input memory stores data entered from an input device. **Temporary storage** is like a piece of scratch paper where the program holds data being processed as well as any intermediate results required for later processing. The *output* section contains processed information awaiting an output operation. The program instructions are in the *software* storage area.

Data read into memory is stored in the input area of memory until needed. Since actual processing of data occurs in the arithmetic unit, data moves from the input area of memory to the arithmetic unit, and intermediate results derived there are placed in the temporary area until needed later. In fact, data may move several times between temporary storage and the arithmetic unit, depending on what is required in any particular program. As noted earlier in this chapter, program instructions move from the software memory area to the control unit one at a time until the processing of the program is completed.

Memory can be visualized as mailboxes in the post office. A post office box is a storage location identified by a box number. For purposes of this analogy, assume that a mailbox only contains one thing at any one time. However, over time the box can hold different things such as a letter, a postcard, or a newspaper. Even though what is in the mailbox may change, the box and its number remain the same.

Computer memory also consists of "boxes" or "cells." Each cell has a numerical *address* and can hold either data or instructions encoded in the form of binary digits, 0's and 1's. One **binary digit** is a **bit.** The contents of the "boxes" are usually called **bytes,** because a byte is a grouping of bits treated as one logical unit of data. The "box number" is an **address.** This analogy with a post office box is appropriate if you keep in mind the fact that a computer memory location cannot hold more than one kind of data at any one time.

Figure 1.1.4 is a physical representation of a simplified computer memory with only nine memory locations. The computer can store data or instructions in the locations, and once placed there, the stored data remains unless new data is subsequently placed in the same location. New data would automatically "write over" and would therefore destroy the old data.

Suppose that the data shown in locations 1 and 2 of Figure 1.1.4 (a) are the hours worked and wage rate for one employee, and have been read into memory for subsequent processing (Figure 1.1.4 does not show the program instructions that would also occupy certain locations in memory). When the second employee's hours worked and wage rate are later read into the computer, new hours worked and wage rates would appear in the same locations. Figure 1.1.4 (b) shows the new contents of the two locations, assuming the second employee worked 36 hours and receives $5.80 per hour.

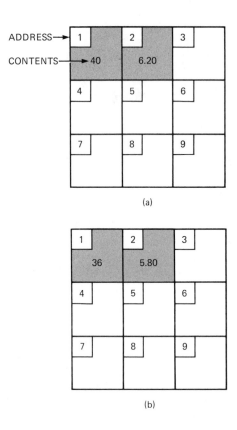

Figure 1.1.4 *Simplified model of computer memory. (a) Values at Stage 1; (b) values at Stage 2.*

The computer keeps track of storage locations by giving each a unique address. Fortunately, applications programmers do not normally have to write program instructions for memory addressing. Rather, they can refer to data elements such as "hours worked" and "wage rate" in the program without regard for whether "hours worked" is stored in location 1 or 5 and "wage rate" is in location 2 or 6. Bookkeeping tasks needed to keep track of locations are normally accomplished without any involvement of the programmer.

So far, we have discussed the central processor (CPU), input devices, and output devices. Input and output devices are part of a general category of hardware usually called peripheral devices and media. Another type of hardware is the auxiliary equipment. All three major categories of hardware are summarized in the following list.

1. **Central Processing Unit (CPU).** The CPU is composed of arithmetic, control, and memory units.

2. **Peripheral Devices and Media.** This hardware category includes all devices that are separate from the CPU, but are (or can be) online. **Online** means they are connected to and under control of the CPU. Peripherals include Input/Output devices, secondary storage devices, and data communications equipment.

3. **Auxiliary Equipment and Media.** This category includes equipment that is offline. **Offline** means a device is separate from and not under the control of the CPU. Examples of auxiliary equipment and media are input preparation devices such as keypunch machines, offline storage such as filing cabinets, paper, and other computer supplies.

Secondary storage on peripheral media and devices is important for business computer systems because business applications typically involve the storage and processing of files. For instance, a payroll application normally requires a file with a record for each employee in an organization. Each record would contain employee data such as the number of dependents used for computing income tax withholdings. Later, we will deal with files in more detail; for now, just remember that many types of peripherals can be used for input, output, and secondary storage of files. A reel of magnetic tape, for example, could be used as a medium to input data, output data, and store data for later processing. Applications programs are normally stored on tape, magnetic disk, or some other medium until they are needed. Most large programs are online during processing and only segments of the program are held in memory at any one time during actual processing. As needed, program instructions are read into memory from a secondary, online storage device.

Devices such as keyboard terminals enter data directly into a computer without the data being recorded on a medium. Terminals can directly display output on a TV-like screen. These are called **direct I/O devices** since no medium, like magnetic tape, is used for recording the data. Some purists, however, claim that "direct" is a misnomer as even the lines on the screen appear on a medium, namely the screen.

Many hardware devices can be used for input, output, and storage of data. Information about all the various types of devices and their uses is beyond the scope of an introductory programming course.

Software

Software is the general name given to all computer programs used to operate computer hardware and process data. Basically there are two broad categories: (1) applications programs and (2) system software. Recall that **applications programs** direct the processing of particular applications such as payroll, student registration, and customer billing. **System software,** on the other hand, consists of the computer programs that control and support the computer system. System programs are usually either supplied by the computer manufacturer or purchased from a software development firm. One major category of system software is the **operating system,** a set of integrated system programs that supervise the operations of the computer. The name "operating system" is used because the modern operating system performs many of the functions that were the responsibility of the computer operator in the first generation of computers.

In those early days of computers, programmers had to write application programs using machine codes that were specific to a particular computer. Such instructions typically consisted of strings of bits. These machine-specific languages are known as machine language. **Machine language** is what any computer actually understands. Each type of computer has its own machine language; since there are many different types of computers, there are many different machine languages. If an application program is written in a language like COBOL, it must be translated into machine language before the computer can execute the instructions. Today, therefore, a second major category of system software includes the language translators known as compilers. Figure 1.1.5 summarizes the major types of software.

Compilation.   Machine language is normally thought of as a low-level language because it is the basic language of a computer. Higher-level languages are closer to human language. COBOL is one of the many higher-level languages. All higher-level languages must be translated into machine language before the computer can follow the instructions. This translation process is called **compilation** because it is performed by a special system program called a **compiler.** After the programmer writes a program in COBOL, the COBOL compiler translates it into the appropriate machine language.

The program submitted for compilation is called a **source program** while the results of the compilation process are referred to as the **object program.** A source program is compiled and the object program is executed by the computer. The syntax of a language is the set of rules used to form correct statements in the language. The compiler checks the syntax of the source program before outputting an object program.

Syntax Errors.   The set of grammatical rules that govern how parts of a language may be legitimately used is called the **syntax** of the language. A program that adheres to the syntax of the language in which it is expressed is said to be syntactically correct. A deviation from the syntax of the language is called a **syntax error.** Spelling a word

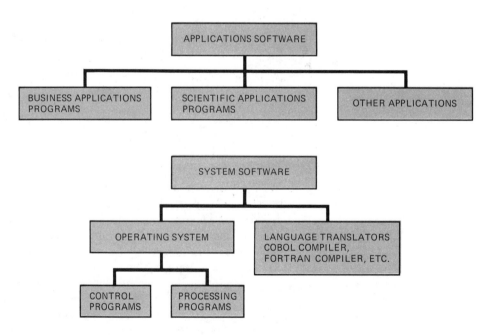

Figure 1.1.5 *Major types of computer software.*

incorrectly is an example of a syntax error. For example, the COBOL keyword READ has a specific meaning to the COBOL compiler. If the word is misspelled as RAED, most compilers would interpret this as an error and print a message that indicates where in the program it detected this strange word, RAED. Even though the compiler can locate an error, it usually cannot correct it. Therefore, the COBOL source program would not normally compile into an executable object program. If the compiler indicates that there are syntax errors, the programmer must then correct these specific lines of the program and again attempt to compile the source program.

Job Control Language.   When a program is submitted to a computer for compilation and execution, the program must be accompanied by special instructions for the operating system. These special instructions include who should be charged for the time and resources used, what compiler is required, and what part of the input is the instruction set and what part is the program's data. All this is accomplished with Job Control Language (JCL). There is not one standard JCL for all systems. The JCL depends on the computing environment used by the program.

A number of different COBOL compilers exist and are in use today, and Standard COBOL can be executed on a wide variety of machines. However, each COBOL program contains sections of code that depend on the hardware being used. Except for these minor parts of a COBOL program, the COBOL language was designed so that the code written is highly portable and can easily be used in different environments with little or no change to the source program. It is not unusual for the same computer installation to have more than one COBOL compiler. For example, one compiler might provide clearer error messages but have slower execution. This compiler would be used to compile during program or system development. Another compiler may have fewer of the possible capabilities of a complete COBOL compiler and may be used on a smaller computer, others may be better suited for student use, or have other advantages.

Once compilation is successful, the object program can then be loaded into computer memory and the data for processing read into the system for execution of the program. During execution, however, other errors may appear. These are called **execution time errors.** Detection of an execution time error usually causes the computer to print an error message and to terminate processing. An example is an attempt to divide a number by zero.

In addition to syntax and execution errors, there is a third type called **logic error.** A logic error can normally be detected only after compiling and executing a program. A logic error exists if the output from the program fails to agree with correct results. For example, if the correct action were to subtract one number from another, and the program told the computer to add the two numbers, erroneous results would be inevitable. During compilation and execution, the error would remain undetected, as the compiler understands what *add* means and does not know the programmer really wants to subtract. It is the programmer's responsibility to develop correct programs in the first place and to test these programs to detect and correct errors. In the jargon of the computer programmer, errors in programs are called **bugs** and the process of testing a program to find and correct bugs is called **debugging.**

Section 1.2 deals with some tools for the analysis and design of programs that are free of bugs (correct) and that are easily understood by other people (well-structured).

SUMMARY

In this section you have learned some basic concepts. You know that a computer system consists of more than a machine in that it takes skilled people to develop systems and programs and to operate and use computer systems. You know that the hardware component includes a computer or CPU that consists of arithmetic, control, and memory units. You also know that there are peripheral devices and media for input, output, and storage of data.

A computer can execute a set of instructions stored internally. The computer stores programs and data. In a business application program, memory locations usually store input data, output data, and temporary data. Each location in memory is assigned an address. However, the programmer need not know the address of a storage location but can let the system keep track of where the data is actually stored.

Today it is not necessary to code programs in machine language because a variety of higher-level languages like COBOL are available. The use of these languages requires translation of the source program into an object program of the machine language of the particular model computer being used. COBOL programs are translated into object programs in machine language using a COBOL compiler.

After a program has been freed of all syntax errors, such as misspelled words or missing punctuation marks, logic and execution errors are still possible. Therefore, programs must be tested to locate and remove these errors.

With this overview, we can now look at the tools of program analysis and design and the concepts of structured programming. Properly designed, well-structured programs can result in programs that are correct and easily understood.

EXERCISES

1. Briefly define each of the following terms.
   a. business computer system
   b. offline
   c. application program
   d. secondary storage
   e. external documentation
   f. system software
   g. internal documentation
   h. machine language
   i. operating system
   j. compiler
   k. central processing unit
   l. syntax error
   m. memory
   n. execution error
   o. address
   p. logic error
   q. online
2. A programmer has just completed compiling a program and remarks that it is bug free and ready for use. Would you doubt that statement? Why?
3. What is a computer program?
4. What does COBOL mean?
5. What are some of the advantages of COBOL?
6. What is a compiler?
7. What are the three major types of programming errors?

1.2 Introduction to Program Development and Structured Programming

As you learned in the preceding section, an application program consists of a set of instructions that tell a computer how to solve a problem. Inventory control, employee payroll, customer orders, and student registration are a few examples of business applications that are often processed on computers.

You may have thought that a computer was a brain. Nothing could be farther from the truth. The fact is that current computers are unable to perform calculations or solve any problems that people could not do by hand. What makes the computer such a valuable tool is not its superior intelligence; it can only do what people instruct it to do. Rather, the computer's great strength is its capacity to calculate and process data quickly and repetitively with essentially perfect accuracy. In order for the computer to achieve its potential, however, it must be correctly programmed.

Solving a problem and developing a computer program involve a sequence of orderly steps. As Figure 1.2.1 shows, program development can be considered as three general phases of nine basic steps.

```
Phase I    Analysis and Design
    Step 1    Analyze the problem and define a solution.
    Step 2    Design the solution.
Phase II   Development and Testing
    Step 3    Code the program.
    Step 4    Prepare the program for the computer.
    Step 5    Compile the program.
    Step 6    Correct errors and compile again.
    Step 7    Test and debug the program.
Phase III  Operation and Maintenance
    Step 8    Complete program documentation.
    Step 9    Implement, use, and maintain program.
```

Figure 1.2.1 Program development steps.

Program Development

The first phase includes planning the program. Novice programmers are far too often tempted to skip over the first two steps and immediately begin to code the program. For any but the most trivial problems, this is a mistake. *Good* programmers know that *good* programs result from first understanding what is needed, what approach to take, and how to organize the problem solution. The first two steps, therefore, should be accomplished effectively before proceeding to later stages. This section explains the overall program development process with emphasis on techniques that can help you analyze the problem, define a solution, and design the program.

The time spent on each of these nine steps will vary from program to program. A complex application might require hours of planning; a simple one could proceed to the third step in a few minutes. The various stages may also overlap. While analyzing the problem, for instance, you may simultaneously define some parts of the solution. In addition, you are documenting the program along the way rather than waiting to write all documentation after the program is running. Another point is that program development is not confined strictly to one step after the other. More commonly, you return to various steps as you proceed, particularly when testing reveals errors that require a redesign or other revisions of the program. With these general observations about the overall process, let's examine in detail what each step involves.

Step 1   Analyze the Problem and Define a Solution

The first step is to *analyze* and *understand* the problem. The problem statements in this book define the problem to some extent, and your instructor may choose to clarify further or extend some problems. However, you must still study the problem yourself to understand what is involved and required for a solution. In a real world situation, the extent of a programmer's analysis and design depends not only on the complexity of the proposed problem, but also on the degree of system analysis performed before the problem was turned over to the programmer.

Whether or not the proposed problem has already been subjected to extensive analysis, the programmer still must make a preliminary determination of what the program is to accomplish. If you understand that the pattern of most problem solutions is *input-process-output*, the initial analysis of your programming problems will seem rather straightforward. For example, suppose you need to manually process payroll checks for 50 employees in a company. You would first gather data such as hours worked and wage rate for one employee. Next you would multiply hours worked times wage rate to compute gross pay, subtract payroll deductions such as the various taxes, and then write a check for the net pay. You would then repeat the same steps for each of the remaining 49 employees.

In the analysis of a business computer problem, programmers normally think in terms of the same pattern—input, process, output, and repeat—until all the cases have been completed. Even if there were thousands of employees to pay, you would still input, process, output, and repeat until the last check is written. This pattern is so common, in fact, it is named the **input-process-output** (IPO) cycle and is depicted in Figure 1.2.2.

Although the IPO cycle says to analyze a proposed program in that order, experienced programmers usually approach the design of a program from the opposite direction; they start with the output. As specified by the system analyst or in consultation with the user, the user's output requirements are first specified and output formats are written by hand. Second, the inputs available to produce the desired outputs are determined. Third, the program's logic is designed. This reverse order is actually quite natural because the user almost always thinks of the application program in terms of its output.

In designing the output format, it is normally helpful to use a *print layout form*. On this form the programmer can show the format of the report to include report headings, data to be printed, spacing between elements, summary lines, totals, and other information. Figure 1.2.3 shows a blank print layout form.

The next action is to separate the input requirements from the output requirements. These might be listed on a sheet of paper or you may use a special form, such as the print layout form shown in Figure 1.2.3. The idea is to show the format and length of the data elements that will be input to the program and the resulting spacing between adjacent fields of the output.

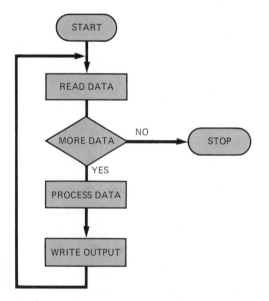

Figure 1.2.2 *The Input-Process-Output (IPO) cycle.*

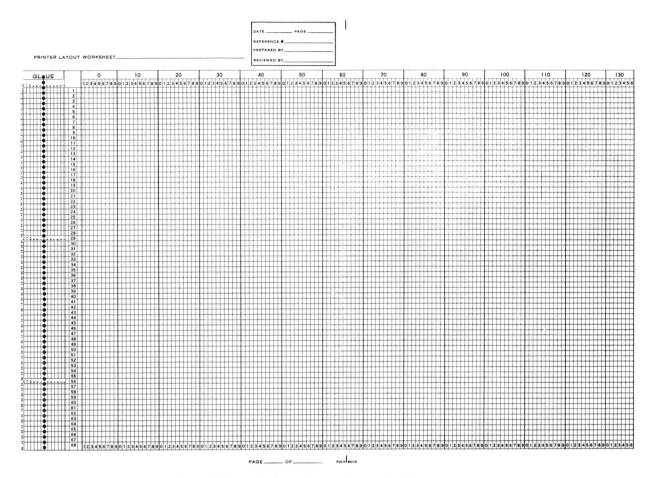

Figure 1.2.3 A blank print layout form (reduced in size).

Once output and input requirements are defined, the next action is to determine what processing must be performed. Processing in this sense means calculating (adding, multiplying, etc.), summarizing, and other actions that are performed on the input data to produce the desired output. To enhance your understanding, you may want to list the processing on a sheet of paper. With a basic understanding of the problem requirements, you can proceed to the second step.

Step 2   Design the Solution

In the first step you analyzed the problem and determined the requirements for output, input, and processing. Next, you must develop a detailed set of steps to solve the problem. These steps are known as an algorithm. An **algorithm** is a set of rules that solve a problem in a finite number of steps. The algorithm of a program is usually called the **program logic.**

Many tools and techniques are available for programmers to design program logic. The most common are

1. flowcharts
2. pseudocode
3. structure and hierarchy charts
4. decision tables
5. structured walkthroughs

A program **flowchart** is a graphical method of documenting the logic of a program by using specific symbols connected by flow lines to represent the various steps of the program logic. Figure 1.2.4 shows a program flowchart. **Pseudocode** uses English-like prose to describe the order of solution of an algorithm. A **structure chart** or **hierarchy chart** divides the problem into subparts and shows the subparts as modules comprising the whole problem. A **decision table** shows in tabular form the conditions and actions included in a problem solution. Decision tables are most powerful for defining complex program logic. A **structured walkthrough** is normally performed to catch design problems before proceeding to expend more time and effort on the program. A structured walkthrough, which may also be performed in later stages, is a technique of holding peer review to detect errors. Each review is typically initiated by the programmer whose work is to be reviewed.

Flowcharts as Program Design Tools.   Flowcharts have been in use for decades. There are two general types of flowcharts: system flowcharts and program flowcharts. A **system flowchart** is a diagram that shows a broad overview of the data flow and sequence of operations in a system. System flowcharts are normally prepared by system analysts. The emphasis is placed on showing the output reports, input documents, and flow of data through a system. Limited detail information is provided about how the computer actually solves the problem. Figure 1.2.4 (a) is an example of a system flowchart for processing customer bills. Figure 1.2.4 (b) shows how a program flowchart evolves from a system flowchart.

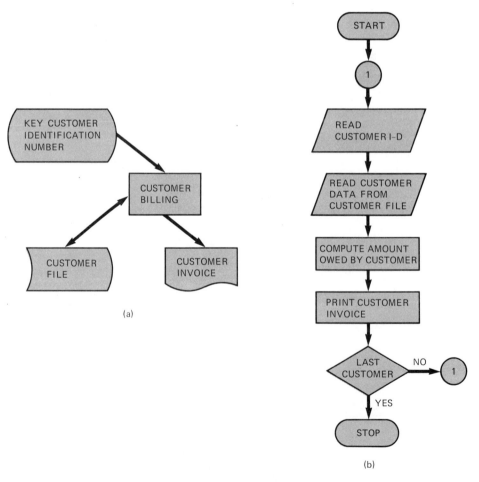

Figure 1.2.4 *(a) A system flowchart; (b) a program flowchart.*

A **program flowchart** expresses the logical correspondence of your solution to the sequence of instructions that will appear later in your program. You could consider a program flowchart as similar to a blueprint builders use to construct a house, or as a road map to reach a desired destination. Simple programs may not require a flowchart, but for most real world problems of any complexity, a flowchart is normally useful. Figure 1.2.5 (a) shows the most common symbols used for program flowcharts.

Since this book is concerned with programming, we will not assign problems that require you to draw system flowcharts. Figure 1.2.5 (b) depicts various system flowchart symbols.

A program flowchart is a graphical representation of the algorithmic solution. In other words, it shows how steps are performed within the machine to process the inputs into the desired outputs.

Appendix A provides a more detailed discussion of flowcharts.

Pseudocode as a Program Design Tool.   Another program design technique is **pseudocode**. *Pseudo* means imitation. *Code* refers to instructions written in a programming language. Thus, pseudocode is an imitation of actual computer instructions that are essentially abbreviated phrases written in a natural language.

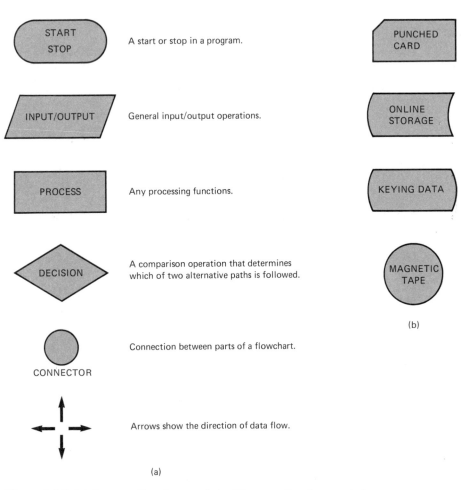

Figure 1.2.5 (a) Program flowchart symbols; (b) system flowchart symbols.

Figure 1.2.6 is an example of a program flowchart. Compare it to Figure 1.2.7, which is pseudocode for a grading program.

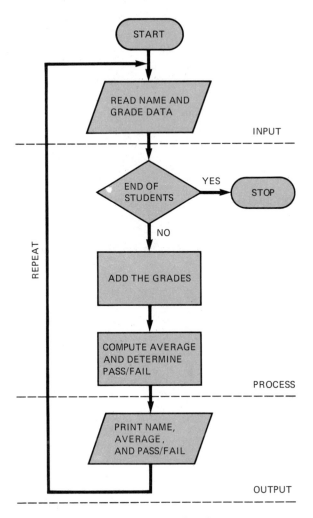

Figure 1.2.6 A grading program flowchart.

```
* START PROCESSING
* REPEAT UNTIL END OF DATA
*** READ STUDENT NAME AND GRADE DATA
*** COMPUTE STUDENT AVERAGE
*** PRINT STUDENT NAME, AVERAGE, AND EVALUATION
* END OF CODE REPEATED FOR EACH CASE
* TERMINATION PROCESSING
* STOP EXECUTION
```

Figure 1.2.7 Pseudocode for a grading program.

As you can see, pseudocode is compact, readable, and easy to revise. It uses full words and phrases rather than the graphic symbols of flowcharting. The absence of graphic symbols makes it easier to use meaningful names and removes the requirement to use cryptic statements tailored to fit within a small symbol. Some professional programmers prefer to use pseudocode rather than flowcharts when preparing a program plan.

Note that the flowchart and pseudocode both outline the major processing steps and data flow in a proposed program. Both also communicate to a reader the logic of the program. Using either the flowchart or the pseudocode as a first-level refinement (or outline) of the program, a programmer can proceed to further refine the logic into more specific subtasks until ready to write the program in a particular computer language. As a matter of fact, either design tool might be used at this first level of refinement with any programming language, since both the flowchart and pseudocode are a logical outline of the problem solution. An advantage of pseudocode is that it remains an integral part of the program itself by converting the English-like phrases into program comments.

Programmers sometimes continue to use pseudocode to express subtasks at each successive level of refinement and then directly convert each pseudocode statement to program code. In this textbook, however, we will normally deal with problems for which a first- or second-level outline in pseudocode suffices.

Each pseudocode line in Figure 1.2.7 is preceded by asterisks (*) because COBOL compilers treat a line beginning with an asterisk as a comment rather than a program instruction. The second and third asterisks are used to show indentation and have no special meaning here. This pseudocode outline is now ready to be prepared as COBOL comments. With each comment appearing as a description of what is to follow in the COBOL program, there exists a clear outline that people can read and easily understand.

Writing pseudocode in comment form and directly incorporating it into the program itself is a major advantage. Since flowchart symbols and arrows cannot be inserted into the program code, the program flowchart must be an external document. Accordingly, a person attempting to read, understand, and modify a program may have to refer to two separate documents—the program listing and the document containing the flowchart. Converting the pseudocode to comments *inside* the program, however, provides a ready-made source of internal documentation integral to the program listing. Updates that reflect changes in the program's logic are more apt to be made to pseudocode in a timely fashion. This usually means that the pseudocode actually reflects the logic of the program as it currently exists. This timeliness is harder to maintain with external documentation.

One final observation about the pseudocode example is appropriate at this time. Notice that using more than one asterisk makes it easy to read and discern which statements are tasks and which are subtasks. For example, even if the specific lines of COBOL code were filled in under each pseudocode statement, you could still see that the steps indented the same distance are all within a loop that will be repeated until an end-of-data condition is reached.

Step 3   Code the Program

After designing the program logic, the next step is writing or coding the COBOL program. Remember that the computer is not a brain. It must be programmed to do each task and there are a limited number of instructions that it can understand. For these reasons, precision and exactness are essential.

Using the sequence of symbols in the flowchart, or following the steps of the pseudocode solution, the programmer codes the COBOL instructions that correspond to the symbols or statements. Each COBOL statement must be written according to the rules of the language. The program statements might be written on a pad of paper, but generally a specifically designed *coding form* is used. Because of rules concerning the format requirements of each statement, the coding form is preferred over plain paper. Figure 1.2.8 (next page) is a COBOL coding form. Later you will learn the various format rules.

Step 4   Prepare the Program for the Computer

After writing the COBOL program, you are ready to prepare the source program in a medium that the computer can read. Depending upon the type of input equipment avail-

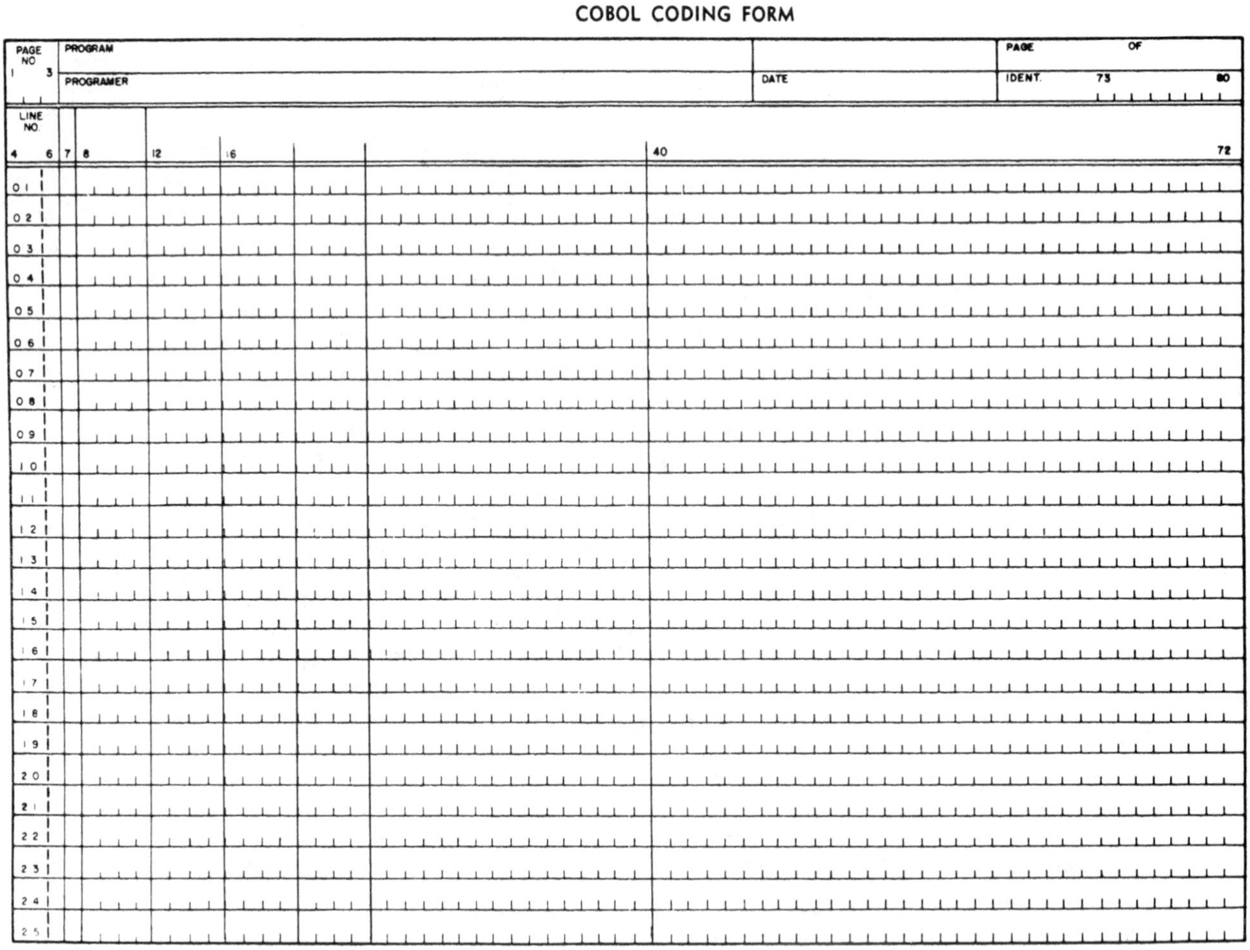

COBOL CODING FORM

Figure 1.2.8 A COBOL coding form (reduced in size).

able, the handwritten program is keyed to punched cards, magnetic tape, magnetic disk, or is entered from some other type of terminal or recording device.

In an academic environment, the most common methods used to put a program into a form acceptable to the computer are entry through a card reader and entry through a keyboard device. Let's briefly examine these methods to learn various terms and procedures.

COBOL statements may be punched into the common 80-column punched card using a keypunch machine or keyed a line at a time on a keyboard device. Each coded line on the coding form (Figure 1.2.8) is punched on one card or entered as one line at the keyboard.

Three different types of cards are normally required to prepare a COBOL program for the computer using punched cards:

1. COBOL source statement cards
2. Job Control Language (JCL) cards
3. Data cards

COBOL source statement cards are the instructions that make up your source deck. These cards must be arranged in the proper order for solving the problem.

JCL cards are needed to communicate various resource needs to the computer. Modern computers can process many files concurrently (known as multiprogramming). As Figure 1.2.9 illustrates, the typical JCL cards needed for a COBOL run are those that

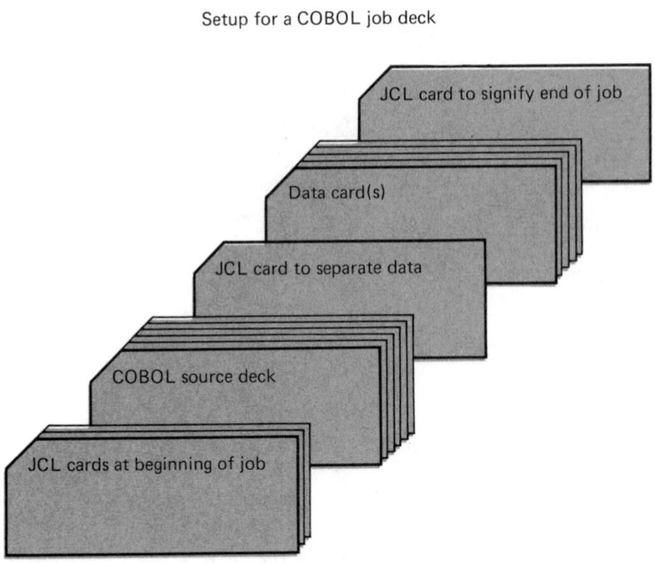

Setup for a COBOL job deck

JCL card to signify end of job

Data card(s)

JCL card to separate data

COBOL source deck

JCL cards at beginning of job

Figure 1.2.9 Typical Job Control Language (JCL) cards needed for a COBOL run.

indicate the beginning of a new job, signify the end of a job, and separate the COBOL source cards from the data cards. Since job control languages vary widely from system to system, detailed information on JCL will have to be provided by your instructor.

The **data cards** in Figure 1.2.9 are the actual data that the program is designed to process as input. If the data to be read is on some other medium such as tape or disk, data cards would obviously not be in your COBOL job deck. Processing of the type illustrated in Figure 1.2.9 is called **batch** processing.

In addition to punched cards, a second common method for entering a COBOL program is via a terminal or with the use of a microcomputer keyboard. Execution of programs entered in these ways is called **timesharing** or **interactive** processing.

The type of programming discussed in this text may be used for both batch processing and interactive processing. COBOL programming concepts and techniques are applicable to punched card or terminal input.

Terminals with keyboards allow the programmer to interact with the computer in a conversational mode. This mode of entering and executing your COBOL program will require you to learn how to log on and log off the system as well as to use the system commands for preparing programs for execution. We leave it to your instructor to tell you how to use the system in this mode. You will need similar instructions if you are using a microcomputer, because micros also have different system commands. Various microcomputers have different keyboards, COBOL compilers, and system software; therefore, you will have to learn separately how to use your particular personal computer.

Keying of the source program may be accomplished by a data-entry operator or terminal operator rather than the programmer, just as a report written by a manager may be typed by a clerk. Regardless of what is available, however, programmers usually key program corrections and modifications. (Student programmers usually have no alternative but to do their own keying of the original program and subsequent changes.) Once the program has been keyed, the next step is to run and compile the source program.

Step 5   Compile the Program

The steps of the compilation process are shown in Figure 1.2.10, on the following page. A program prepared in COBOL is called a **source program.** To translate a COBOL program into machine language, the COBOL compiler is read into the computer's memory. The

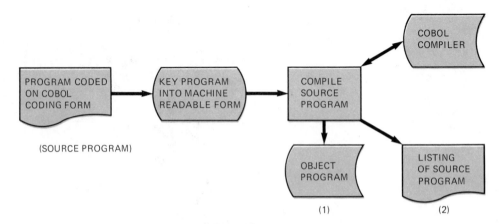

Figure 1.2.10 *Compilation of a COBOL program. (1) Object program is not produced if compiler finds syntax errors. (2) Compiler-produced syntax error messages are printed with source listing.*

compiler then takes control of the processing, reads the program, and translates it into machine language instructions. The resulting machine language program is called an **object program.**

After the coded program is entered into the computer from some input device, the computer is used to translate or compile the source program into an object (machine language) program. Recall that a computer can only execute a machine language program. The COBOL compiler attempts to translate the source program. If there are no syntax errors in the source program, the COBOL compiler produces an object program. Even if there are errors, it produces a printed listing of the source program along with error messages. Figure 1.2.11 depicts compilation and execution in both the card batch and interactive modes.

Step 6   Correct Errors and Compile Again

If errors are found, they must be corrected. These error messages are normally called **diagnostic messages** and the actual errors are called **compile-time errors** or **syntax errors.** Such errors occur because either the programmer or the person who keyed the program did not conform to the rules of the COBOL language. These errors must be corrected and the source program compiled again. A clean compile results when the compiler indicates no syntax errors. Once a clean compile is available, the next step is to run or execute the program with test data.

Step 7   Test and Debug the Program

In the vocabulary of professional programmers, this step is referred to as **testing** and **debugging.** The former means to execute the program on test data to verify accuracy of output results, and the latter refers to the process of locating and correcting the errors. When an error is found, the programmer corrects the program and continues to test further and to debug until all errors are eliminated.

As you may have experienced, an English composition can be free of grammatical errors but not be well written. Similarly, just because you obtain a clean compile does not mean the program will operate correctly. If you instructed the computer to multiply, for example, but the right action is to divide, the compiler has no way of knowing what you really meant the program to do. Incorrect answers will inevitably result because your program has a **logic error.** Other typical examples of logic errors are performing an operation in the wrong place or out of proper sequence, or omitting an action that is necessary. Human errors occur frequently in programs and seem to increase proportion-

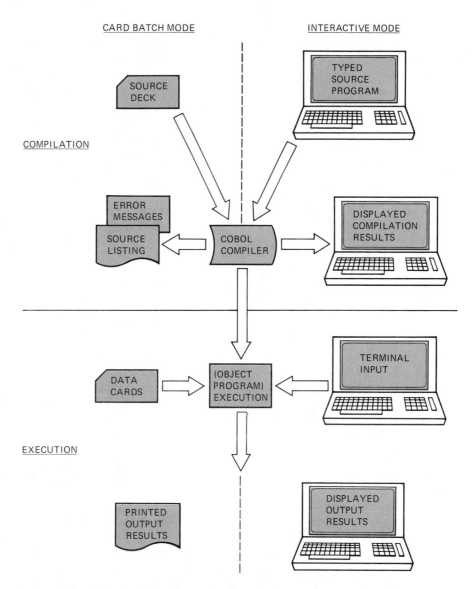

Figure 1.2.11 *Compilation and execution in card batch and interactive modes.*

ally to program size and complexity. Rarely does the novice programmer write an error-free program the first time. It is necessary, therefore, to thoroughly test your program by using test data that checks each path of logic in your program as well as test data with intentional errors to see if your program has taken care of all error conditions. Later you will learn more about methods for program testing and verification.

Remember that the COBOL compiler has no way of knowing what the programmer intended the program to do. Moreover, debugging can be especially difficult if a programmer has not used a style that makes it easy to trace through the program and to locate the cause of errors. We will have more to say about good style in subsequent sections.

Step 8   Complete Program Documentation

Although listed as Step 8, program documentation should be a part of each preceding step. In most modern organizations, staff turnover is common. Programmers are promoted, terminated, or transferred to other projects. Even if the same programmer is still present, the passage of time may make it difficult to recall details of a program developed weeks, months, or years earlier. Program documentation provides the continuity essential for the *maintenance* (upkeep) of programs over time. Program documentation consists of all the written records that explain how a program works. These documents should allow anyone unfamiliar with a program to understand it and make changes, called **program modifications.** Documentation not included in the program itself is called **external documentation.** Program flowcharts are one type of useful external documentation. In contrast, **internal program documentation** is the insertion of program comments in the source program. *You should use comments in your programs to provide a clear explanation of the program logic for both yourself and your instructor.*

Step 9   Implement, Use, and Maintain the Program

After testing and program documentation are completed, the program is usually ready for production runs. A **production run** refers to using real data for the intended problem solution. As examples, a payroll program may be used for production runs weekly, assuming employees are paid weekly; an airline reservation system would likely be operational almost constantly.

In the business environment, an acceptance test is conducted to prove to future users that a new system or program works and produces correct results. Your instructor will act as a user and evaluate your program by requiring you to use specific data to run your program. In this way, the instructor (or grader) knows what the output results should be for a correct program.

Students are not required to maintain programs over extended periods of time. Once you have completed Step 7 (testing and debugging), you make a final run and execute the program to produce correct output results. However, you should check the output to verify correctness again before submitting your work for grading.

We have now seen that the planning, design, and development of computer programs consists of three phases and nine steps. As a student solving problems that are relatively simple and not part of a complex system, you will likely find it more useful to view program development as six major activities. These activities are summarized in the following list.

1. Analysis of the problem
   a. Hand calculation of examples
   b. Design of a solution
2. Coding the solution
   Incorporating internal documentation (comments)
3. Compiling the code (Repeat until a successful compilation is obtained.)
4. Executing and testing the compiled code on test data
5. Refining the logic and improving internal documentation
6. Executing the final run

For most programs in this text, you should be able to understand the problem and figure out how to execute a hand-calculated solution. The hand calculations will often suggest a design for the solution that in many cases can be translated directly to COBOL code and internal documentation that clearly outline the steps of the solution process. You are then ready to enter the program into the computer and make as many corrections as necessary to compile the program. After compilation, you should run the program with test data to ensure that there are no execution or logic errors, while at the same time improving the internal documentation and style to make sure the program is easily understood. Finally, having ensured that the program is correct and understandable, you should be ready to make a final run and submit the program listing and output to your instructor.

Structured Programming

Structured programming techniques are used to develop programs that are easier to code, easier to understand, and less likely to contain any logic errors. The basic rules of structured programming require the programmer to restrict program statements to certain control-flow structures so that the logical structure of the program will be more understandable.

Before the introduction of structured methodologies in the mid-1970s, traditional programming practice relied on the creativeness of the programmer to write efficient programs. *Efficient* was interpreted to mean programs that used a minimum of the computer's memory space and processing time. This emphasis on creativity and efficiency, however, too often resulted in programs that were difficult for others to read and understand and costly for an organization to develop and maintain. Rather than creativity and efficiency, structured programming emphasizes standard program design methods that can reduce program complexity. The overall objectives of structured programming can be summarized as follows:

1. reduction of the time and cost of developing and maintaining programs;
2. elimination of program errors during development and better detection and correction of errors during testing;
3. simplification of programs by making them easier to code, read, correct, and maintain;
4. production of correct programs that fulfill the requirements of the user.

These goals are certainly important, given the accelerating costs of software development, declining costs of hardware, and the inevitable modifications of applications programs caused by changing needs of modern organizations. Because almost any program will likely require later modifications, it is essential to develop simply-structured programs.

Flow-of-Control Structures

The idea that only three flow-of-control structures should be used in structuring programs may soon seem obvious. Nonetheless, the role of these control structures has only recently been recognized as an effective guide for developing programs.

We can keep these control structures in mind by using a flowchart to indicate how they are executed by a program. The downward arrows indicate the natural order for sequencing the execution of computer statements.

Sequence is the first control structure of any program. The first command is executed, then the second command is executed, then the third command, and so on to the last command, unless one of the other control structures comes into play. A program that consists only of a sequence of commands is easy to understand. See Figure 1.2.12 (a) on the following page.

The **selection process,** the second control structure of a structured COBOL program, allows branching within the program. A condition is always evaluated as either TRUE or FALSE. Each possible result of evaluating a condition determines a different path for the flow of control in a program. This control structure in COBOL is implemented in the form

```
IF   condition

     THEN   (statements to execute
             if the condition is TRUE)

     ELSE   (statements to execute
             if the condition is FALSE).
```

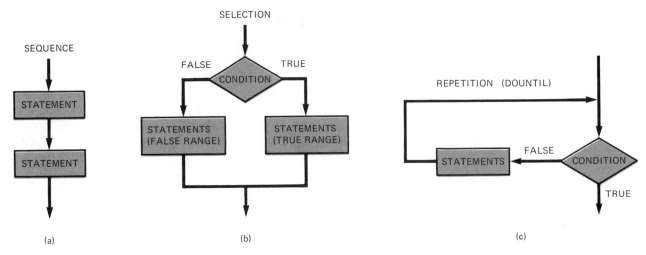

Figure 1.2.12 *Three flow-of-control structures: (a) a structure consisting only of a sequence of commands; (b) a structure that allows branching; (c) a structure that involves repetition.*

Notice that either the TRUE range (statements executed if the condition is TRUE) or the FALSE range (statements executed if the condition is FALSE) may include one or more statements and even other flow-of-control structures. See Figure 1.2.12 (b).

Repetition, the third control structure of a structured program, is particularly important in COBOL, since business applications usually involve the input-process-output-re-peat cycle. See Figure 1.2.12 (c). Typical examples are writing paychecks for each employee of a company or preparing mailing labels for a direct mail campaign. The mechanics of this third control structure are somewhat different than might be expected. When the condition is encountered, it is evaluated as either TRUE or FALSE. If the condition is FALSE, the routine is executed, and then control returns to test the condition again. As long as the condition evaluates as FALSE, the routine is repeated. As soon as the condition becomes TRUE, program control advances to the next sentence and rejoins the top-to-bottom logical flow of the program. The sequence of statements executed when the condition is FALSE must contain a statement that will eventually make the condition TRUE, or the program will be caught in an infinite loop. The form of the repeating command in COBOL is

```
PERFORM (some routine)
  UNTIL (condition to be tested.)
  —
  —
  —
(some routine).
  (commands)
```

A well-structured COBOL program will contain only these three control structures. By combining them, a programmer can create a complex logical structure, but it should always be possible to see how the final logical structure of the program was built by combining the three basic control structures.

Programs that solve business problems seldom remain unchanged. A new contract for hourly employees can result in salary and benefit adjustments that require payroll programs to be modified. Even the programmer who wrote the original application program may find it difficult to modify the program unless care and attention were devoted to documenting design decisions and the structural characteristics of the program. It is important to keep solutions simple and straightforward so that the logic can be understood by others. Careful adherence to structured programming rules will help. The problem remains, however, to make the program self-contained enough so that any programmer assigned the task of modifying the code can figure out what was done and how. Unfortunately, some programs are so poorly structured that it is easier to start over than to modify the existing program. Avoiding this costly result is an expected benefit of structured programming. Even simple habits, such as indenting code and using blank lines as separators, will make a program easier to read and understand. It is important to be consistent so that you as well as others recognize features of your programs more easily.

As we learned earlier, an effective method for making a program understandable to people involves incorporating *pseudocode* statements as comments in the body of the COBOL code. These comments do not result in any action by the COBOL compiler other than listing them in the source program. The compiler recognizes it as a comment line because of an asterisk (*). Comments can be read as an outline of the logic of the solution or as an explanation of any special features of the program when a person reads the printed source listing. A COBOL program usually involves input, processing, and output. By placing the comments in the program to indicate the sequencing of these operations, the first step in structuring a program can be accomplished. Each of these general functional requirements can have several identifiable subtasks. Incorporating more comments to indicate the subtasks, the programmer gradually refines the logic of the solution and brings the focus of the design process to the tasks that need special attention. Using this procedure for designing a solution provides an up-to-date description of the program. Thus, the design and internal documentation steps in program development are a single process.

The judicious use of indenting makes it clear how parts of the processing are related, in the same way the organization of a report is seen by examining its outline. When the logic is refined to the point that the COBOL coding needed becomes clear, the COBOL code is written and put in place. When programs are developed this way, the process is called **step-wise refinement.**

This book presents a series of Models to give you a good start on the process of designing solutions for problems. These Models show how blocks of code can be written to solve parts of common problems, and how effort can be focused on the real difficulties of the problem by completing several standard operations first. Each Model provides a pseudocode outline for a programming solution.

In cases where none of the developed Models seem helpful, think about problems similar to the one being posed to begin to see a path to solution. It is often the first efforts at modelling a problem that cause the most difficulty, and not the syntax of the language used in programming the solution. Usually the fundamental step needed to begin solving a problem involves doing some calculations by hand for a few examples. Hand calculations also give you something to use to check the output of the program. After solving a problem, you can often see ways of improving parts of the solution by looking back and asking if the logic is clear. It is also instructive to ask a classmate or friend to read your program to see if it really is clear.

Once a program has been written and is running, a question that should have been addressed during design and coding may still remain: Will the program execute correctly for all possible inputs? An exhaustive examination of cases is usually not possible. Testing with certain special cases can give some degree of confidence about the correctness of the program, but well-structured programs still give the programmer the best chance of choosing cases that will test all the branches of the program. Your goal is to design and develop well-structured programs that are correct.

SUMMARY

The program development process consists of three major phases. The first phase involves the steps of analyzing and defining solution requirements and designing the program solution. Adequate understanding of the problem and design of a solution are essential prerequisites to developing correct programs.

Programmers follow an orderly method of taking the problem specifications and analyzing the output, input, and processing requirements. Once the algorithm is defined, the programmer draws a flowchart, writes a pseudocode solution, or uses some other tool to design the program solution. A flowchart, which uses graphic symbols, is a common design tool. Pseudocode, which uses a narrative description of the solution, is a highly desirable tool.

Once one or more of the design tools result in an accurate expression of the program logic, the source program is coded in COBOL statements, keyed into a computer-readable medium, compiled into a machine language object program, and then tested and debugged to produce an error-free program for future use. Concurrently, the programmer writes documentation that completely and accurately describes the program in both program comments inside the program and external documents.

We concluded this section with a discussion of structured programming. We noted the importance of simple, understandable programs that are easy to modify. Use of only the three flow-of-control structures (sequence, selection, and repetition) along with clear and consistent style are necessary prerequisites to coding well-structured programs.

EXERCISES

1. Briefly define each of the following terms.
   a. system flowchart
   b. program flowchart
   c. internal documentation
   d. coding form
   e. logic error
   f. syntax error
   g. compiler
   h. source program
   i. object program
   j. pseudocode
2. Many computer programs are not designed, but created on the coding form or immediately keyed into the computer system. What do you expect from the first run of such a program?
3. Explain the process of program compilation.
4. Briefly describe the steps involved in developing computer programs.
5. What is a structured walkthrough? What is its purpose?
6. How are pseudocode and flowcharts helpful to programmers?
7. What are the most common tools and techniques used by programmers to design program logic?
8. Name the three flow-of-control structures and explain their functions.

Chapter Review

TEST YOURSELF

Instructions: For each of the following sentences and paragraphs, fill in the blank spaces with the appropriate word, words, or phrases.

A business computer system consists of five general parts: people, _____, documentation, _____, and _____. The various categories of people involved with computer systems include system analysts, _____, _____, _____, and clients. _____ design systems and _____ develop, code, test and maintain computer programs. There are two broad types of applications programmers: those who develop new applications and are called _____ programmers and those who modify existing programs and are called _____ programmers. In addition to applications programmers, another important type of programmer is the _____ programmer, a technical expert whose expertise includes knowledge of the operating system and other systems software.

All of the sets of instructions and procedures for people to follow in operating and using a computer system are collectively referred to as procedures or documentation. _____ documentation includes all of the written descriptions and explanations about how new programs are designed and used. _____ documentation refers to the comments written as part of the program code. Comments are an important part of good programs because they can help people read and understand the logic of a program.

Data read into a computer is called _____ data and data produced by a computer system is called _____ data. _____ is data that has been transformed in some ordered and useful way and produced to achieve specific purposes, solve problems, and/or enhance understanding. The term _____ refers to the substance on which data is recorded, and the term _____ is a machine that uses the data.

The hardware component of a computer system consists of _____ , _____ , and output device(s). The CPU stores program instructions and data and processes the data based on the program instructions. The various terms used to describe the area of a CPU where programs and data are stored are internal storage, primary storage, core storage, and _____ . In addition to internal storage, a CPU typically consists of an arithmetic-logic (A/L) element and _____ . A/L performs logical and arithmetic operations while the control unit interprets program instructions and sends instructions to other units in the system.

Some people find it instructive to visualize memory in a computer as consisting of four conceptual areas: input, temporary, output, and software storage areas. Program instructions and the system software are stored in the _____ storage area of memory.

There are two broad types of software: _____ and _____ . The former provides instructions on how to process specific applications like payroll, customer billing, and inventory while the latter type of software controls the functions of the entire computer system. One major category of system software is the _____ , a set of integrated programs that direct and supervise the operations of a computer.

There are a number of computer programming languages that one can use to program a computer. COBOL, FORTRAN, BASIC, Pascal, PL/I, and Ada are perhaps the best known. Programs written in a high-level language like COBOL must be translated into _____ language. This translation process is called _____ because it requires the use of a special system program called a COBOL _____ . The COBOL program is usually referred to as a source program and the program that results from the translation process is called an _____ . The set of grammar rules that govern how parts of a language may be used is called the _____ of a language. Spelling a word incorrectly is an example of a _____ error. Once a machine-language object program has been successfully compiled, the object program can then be executed with data. Errors detected when running a program are called _____ errors. A third type of possible errors in a program are called logic errors. Logic errors can normally be detected by testing and debugging a program on test data.

Solving a problem and developing correct programs involves a sequence of orderly steps. The first step is to analyze the problem. Once the problem is understood, the next step is to design a solution. This involves a detailed set of steps to be performed by the computer. These solution steps are usually called an _____ or program logic.

A program _____ is a graphical method of documenting the logic of a program by using specific symbols connected by flow lines. A structure chart or hierarchy chart divides the problem into subparts and shows the subparts or modules comprising the whole problem. In addition to these various tools and techniques to assist programmers designing program logic, a _____ is a technique that uses peer review to detect errors.

A _____ flowchart is a diagram that shows a broad overview of the data flow and sequence of operations in a system. A _____ flowchart expresses the logical correspondence of a program solution to the sequence of instructions that will later appear in the program.

_____ is another useful program design technique that involves abbreviated phrases written in an imitation code or a natural language like English. This imitation code can be converted to comments in a program. Therefore, not only is it a convenient way to design a solution, but the comments provide internal documentation that is integral to the program body. A programmer can then read and more easily understand the program logic by reading the program comments.

After designing the program logic, the next step is writing or _____ the COBOL program. The program statements might be written on a piece of paper, but a preferred method is to use a COBOL _____ form. Once the program has been written, it is now ready to be recorded on a medium that can be read into the computer. One way is to punch the statements on cards and another is to key in the program from a keyboard terminal. When cards are the medium used, two other types of cards are needed to comprise a COBOL job deck in addition to the COBOL source statement cards. The two other types of cards are _____ cards and _____ cards. Processing data with these three types of cards is usually called _____ processing.

In addition to card input for the program and data, a second, widely used method is to enter the program and the input data via a keyboard. Processing of this kind is typically called timesharing or _____ processing.

Once the program has been keyed, the next step is to enter the program and also have the compiler read into memory so the compiler can translate the COBOL instructions into machine language instructions. The resulting machine language program is called an object program, but it is produced only if there are no syntax errors in the COBOL source program. Even if there are syntax errors, the compilation attempt still produces a printed listing of the program and error _____. When errors exist, the programmer must find the errors, correct the appropriate program statements, and re-enter the program for another compilation attempt. A clean compile results when all _____ have been eliminated. The next step is to run or execute the program.

Two types of errors can still exist in the program even if it successfully compiles. These are called _____ errors and _____ errors. Instructing the computer to add two values when it should multiply is an example of a _____ error. The programmer tests and debugs the program to find and eliminate all of these errors.

Structured programming techniques are used to develop programs that are easier to code, easier to understand, and less likely to contain errors. Well-structured programs will contain only three _____ structures. The three are _____, _____, and _____. In addition, good programs will make use of comments to describe clearly the series of steps in a program and use indentation to help another programmer understand how various parts of a program are related.

Programs for Input and Output

Chapter Objectives

After studying this chapter you should be able to

- state the purpose of each division in a COBOL program;
- describe how a computer file is organized and formatted in COBOL;
- design and write a simple program to input and output records of a file;
- write record descriptions for input and output records;
- create headers for output reports;
- write a COBOL program that processes all records of a file using AT END clause for termination.

Chapter Outline

2.1   Introduction to Files

Coding a solution requires learning the syntax and semantics of a computer language. The syntax of COBOL includes the rules for forming names, sentences, and parts of the formal structure of a program. **Semantics** refers to the meaning given to well-formed sentences of the programming language. For example,

```
ADD variable1  variable2 GIVING variable3
```

is a correct sentence in COBOL if valid data names are supplied for variable1, variable2, and variable3.

The *syntax* for COBOL requires ADD to be followed by the names of two storage locations that contain numbers as well as GIVING to be followed by the name of another storage location. These names must be separated either by a blank space or by a comma followed by at least one blank. The *semantics* of the sentence is that the contents of the memory location named variable1 will be added to the contents of the memory location named variable2, and the answer will be put in the memory location named variable3. All these rules and the meanings attached to sentences form the building blocks for a sequence of operations that culminate in a solution to a problem using COBOL.

Once a solution has been incorporated into the proper sequence of COBOL commands, you will use the computer to translate the COBOL language into a language the computing machine understands. Machine language is very complicated, but it is the only language to which the computer will respond. As explained earlier, the translation is done by a program called a compiler.

The final step in getting the computer to work is to have the instructions that have been translated by the compiler actually executed by the computer. The time when this is done is called the program's **execution time.**

A program can run into snags at any step of the process. If the compiler is not able to complete its job, the computer will make no effort to execute the program. Even if the program is executed, you should always compare the machine's work with some hand calculations to verify that the answers are correct. By learning to develop a program skillfully, you will know that the logic is correct, and hence the results are correct at execution time.

Any business organization uses large amounts of information. This information may be customer names and addresses used in making mailing labels for an advertising campaign. It may be bills from suppliers who have to be paid or accounts of customers who must be billed. A collection of organized, related information is a **file.** The individual, organized components of a file are called **records.** The individual areas of information in a record are called **fields.** COBOL is the computer language especially designed for file processing.

In the programming examples that we will use to illustrate and introduce COBOL, two primary types of files will be used. The first contains the kind of information found in a business file, and the second contains the kind of information found in a college registrar's file. A listing of the records in each of these four files is located in Appendices C, D, E, and F.

We are going to solve some of the data processing problems of New-World-Airlines, Inc. Their main file concerns the customers who have charge privileges. The company has the following customer information stored somewhere. Our first task is to organize all this into a file.

CUSTOMER CHARGE IDENTIFICATION
EXPIRATION DATE OF CHARGE ACCOUNT
NAME
HOME ADDRESS
CITY OF RESIDENCE
STATE
LAST BILLING DATE
AMOUNT DUE
PAYMENT
CREDIT RATING

The information about each customer must be organized so that the same information is available in each record. Structuring a record requires two steps:

1. fixing an order in which the fields of information will appear in each record;
2. determining how many characters or symbols will be used to represent each piece of information.

The first task has been done already, since we have listed all the different fields of information available for a single customer. We have no reason to believe that the organization indicated is not satisfactory, so we will use it. The second task can only be accomplished by knowing more about the information itself.

The COBOL Character Set

The fields in a record can contain combinations of letters (A–Z), digits (0–9), or special characters. See Table 2.1.

The type of characters found in a field is important for programming. To identify the general characteristics of information fields, we will use an X to indicate that any character may appear and a 9 to indicate that only a digit may appear. When a field is indicated as an X-type, a number of the characters may be digits. A more careful description of the information in a customer record is given in Table 2.2.

TABLE 2.1   THE COBOL CHARACTER SET

Character	Meaning	Character	Meaning
0 through 9	digit	,	comma
A through Z	letter	;	semicolon
	space (blank)	.	period (decimal point)
+	plus sign	"	quotation mark
*	asterisk	(	left parenthesis
−	minus sign	)	right parenthesis
/	stroke (slash)	>	greater than symbol
=	equal sign	<	less than symbol
$	currency sign		

TABLE 2.2   DESCRIPTION OF THE INFORMATION IN A CUSTOMER RECORD

Information	Number of Characters of Information	Type of Information (9 = digits, X = character)
Customer Charge Identification	9	X
Expiration Date	6	9
Name	20	X
Home Address	20	X
City of Residence	20	X
State	2	X
Last Billing Date	6	9
Amount Due	5	9
Payment	5	9
Credit Rating	1	X

When these records become a file to be used in programs, we will need a way to store all the fields of each record so that we can access any of the individual fields as required. We do this in COBOL by writing a *record description* for a typical record in the file being processed. The NEW–WORLD–FILE will look like the following display, with the *simplifying assumption* that at this time we want to look at each field as a collection of symbols or characters and not look at any field as if it were a field of numbers. We will do arithmetic with fields containing numbers later. For now, let's consider all fields as collections of symbols. The computer stores each symbol in a basic storage unit called a byte. Thus, for the NAME field, we must set aside 20 bytes of storage. We will always identify a storage location with the name we assign to it in the record description to which it belongs. We can now look at what we will do in a program to prepare an area in memory for a record of this file.

```
01   CUSTOMER-INFO.
     05 CHARGE-NUMBER           PIC X(9).
     05 EXPIRATION-DATE         PIC X(6).
     05 NAME                    PIC X(20).
     05 HOME-ADDRESS            PIC X(20).
     05 CITY                    PIC X(20).
     05 STATE                   PIC X(2).
     05 LAST-BILLING-DATE       PIC X(6).
     05 AMOUNT-DUE              PIC X(5).
     05 PAYMENT                 PIC X(5).
     05 CREDIT-RATING           PIC X.
     05 FILLER                  PIC X(6).
```

Hierarchical Structure for Data

The level numbers, such as 01 and 05, indicate the position of a data item in a *hierarchical structure* for the data. The 01-level field is called a record. The numbers 02–49 are available for use as level numbers describing subdivisions of a record. Gaps are usually left between the level numbers used to allow for ease in modifying the record structure. The letters PIC are shorthand for PICTURE. Record descriptions require a 01-level item. For items that are part of a record, it is a good programming practice to use multiples of five for the level numbers.

Rules for Forming Data Names

A name assigned to a field is made up by the programmer using the following rule.

> 1. A *data name* is formed by using up to 30 characters, chosen from
>
>   A–Z (letters)
>   0–9 (digits)
>   –   (hyphen)
>
> 2. At least one character in a data name must be a letter, and no data name can begin or end with a hyphen.

Whenever we assign a name to a data field, we must use this rule. Notice that a space is not included in the set of characters that may be used in a data name. Sequences of words *must be hyphenated* if they are to represent a name for a single data field. Sequences of words joined by hyphens and used as data names can make it easier to understand the data and its role in the program. Data names made up by the programmer are **user-generated** names, while data names with a meaning defined by the compiler are **reserved words.**

The PICTURE Clause

The string PICTURE X(n), abbreviated to PIC X(n) and called the **picture clause,** assigns n consecutive bytes of storage to the field with the associated programmer-generated data name. The record name is assigned a storage area that has a length equal to the sum of all the lengths of individual fields subordinated to it if there are any (i.e., those with level numbers greater than 01). The extent of control of a data name, record name, or field name, representing a subdivided field is the collection of subfields immediately following it and having level numbers greater than it. A field that is not subdivided is called an elementary data item. Picture clauses occur only with elementary data items. In any case, the boundary of a field is determined by the next data name with the same or lower level number. For example, EXPIRATION–DATE consists of the 6 bytes beginning with byte 10 and ending with byte 15 of the area assigned to the record CUSTOMER–INFO. Notice that bytes 10–15 include 6 bytes. The number of bytes used by a field is calculated as:

Ending byte number − starting byte number + 1.

Without the +1, we would exclude the information contained in the last byte of the field!

The CUSTOMER–INFO record is 100 bytes in length. There is no space between fields, as the boundaries are carefully defined by the number of bytes in the picture clause and the position of this data name in the list of data names in the record. The first field named in a record has its information beginning in the first byte of storage assigned to the record. Any other field has its storage area beginning in the byte that immediately follows all the bytes assigned to fields preceding it in the record description.

FILLER

For the time being, we will consider the fields with digits just like fields with characters. Later, we will see how to use numerical information as numbers. In most files some space is left in each record for future expansion. Adding information to an unused portion of a record is always easier than redesigning a whole record. When first organizing a file, it is not uncommon to plan for adding information at a later date. This is the function of extra space in this record. The way COBOL reserves space in a record (or at least accounts for space unnecessary for a particular application) is to represent a field with the reserved word FILLER, which plays part of the role a data name plays. In any particular application, the word FILLER can be used to account for space in a record that does not currently hold information. We do not have to use data names for fields that will not be accessed in a particular application. A record may have different record descriptions in different programs depending on the fields a particular application uses.

Input Media

To use this information in a program, we must place the record on a medium the computing system can "read." If we use a data card, we will be limited to physical records of 80 bytes, because the standard data card is 80 columns or symbol positions wide. Although some computer systems have different size data cards, we will deal with the 80 column card when considering card entry of data. There is no such physical restriction on the size of a record stored on other media, such as magnetic tapes or disks. The records in the files listed in the Appendices are 100 bytes long, for instance.

With this introduction to the NEW–WORLD–FILE, we can introduce the second file, called REGISTRAR–FILE. It will be used as a change of pace from business applications, and contains information found in a university registrar's master file. The information is the type used for preparing end-of-semester grade reports. Table 2.3 on the following page is a listing of the fields in a record in this file.

TABLE 2.3   REGISTRAR–FILE

Information	Number of Characters of Information	Type of Information (9 = digits, X = character)
Social Security Number	9	X
Name	20	X
Sex	1	X
Class	2	X
Age	2	9
Math 13	1	X
English 2	1	X
Government 3	1	X
Geography 10	1	X
Philosophy 3	1	X
Cumulative GPA	3	9
Total Hours	3	9
Campus Address	20	X
Home State	2	X
Extra Space	33	X

A syntactically correct COBOL record description for a record in the REGISTRAR–FILE follows.

```
01   STUDENT-INFO.
     05 SOCIAL-SECURITY-NO       PIC X(9).
     05 NAME                     PIC X(20).
     05 SEX                      PIC X(1).
     05 CLASS                    PIC X(2).
     05 AGE                      PIC X(2).
     05 MATH-13                  PIC X(1).
     05 ENGLISH-2                PIC X(1).
     05 GOVERNMENT-3             PIC X(1).
     05 GEOGRAPHY-10             PIC X(1).
     05 PHILOSOPHY-3             PIC X(1).
     05 CUMULATIVE-GPA           PIC X(3).
     05 TOTAL-HOURS              PIC X(3).
     05 CAMPUS-ADDRESS           PIC X(20).
     05 HOME-STATE               PIC X(2).
     05 FILLER                   PIC X(33).
```

This record is 100 bytes long—the sum of the lengths of each of the 15 fields in the record. The fields with PICTURE clause X(1), X(2), and X(3) can be written X, XX, and XXX. Any character field of length 18 or less can be described by merely listing the appropriate number of X's in the PICTURE clause. So, it is at least as short to input an X followed by a number in parentheses if the field is of length 4 or more.

Additional files that will be used in examples and exercises are described and listed in the Appendices. You should review these files before beginning to write programs using them.

SYNTAX SUMMARY

In developing correct programs, you must write COBOL code that conforms to the syntax rules of the language. The new syntax features introduced in a section are recapped in the Syntax Summary. In addition, if the compilation process detects any syntactically incorrect sentences, the summary will help you eliminate the problems.

```
01 data-name
```

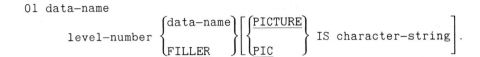

EXERCISES

1. Which of the following are correct COBOL names? *Hint:* Check the data name rules in this section and the list of reserved words found in Appendix G.

a. 913621	i. −KOUNT
b. H0961	j. KOUNT
c. HARRY	k. AMOUNT−DUE−CUSTOMER
d. MOVE	l. CUSTOMER−INFORMATION
e. COPY	m. CURRENT−DATE
f. DAY	n. CURRENT−DATES
g. C01	o. DIVIDES
h. KOUNT−	p. DATA−DATE

2. Which of the terms in Exercise 1 are COBOL reserved words?
3. Define the following terms:

a. file	e. compiler
b. record	f. semantics
c. field	g. byte
d. syntax	

4. What is meant by a hierarchical organization of a record? How are level numbers used to implement such an organization in data records?
5. What is an elementary data item?
6. For each of the following, write a COBOL record description using the listed fields from the STUDENT−FILE listed in Appendix C. (See Figure 2.1.1.)

STUDENT-RECORD

ID-NO	NAME	SEX	AGE	ALG	GEO	ENG	PHY	CHE	FILLER
1 4	5 22	23	24 25	26 28	29 31	32 34	35 37	38 40	41 100

Figure 2.1.1 Layout of record in STUDENT−FILE.

a. STUDENT−FILE   DATA−FIELDS
                                      ID−NO
                                      NAME
                                      SEX
                                      AGE
                                      ALGEBRA
                                      GEOMETRY
                                      ENGLISH
                                      PHYSICS
                                      CHEMISTRY

b. STUDENT−FILE   DATA−FIELDS
                                      ID−NO
                                      NAME
                                      PHYSICS
                                      CHEMISTRY

    c. STUDENT–FILE   <u>DATA–FIELDS</u>
                                 NAME
                                 SEX
                                 ALGEBRA
                                 ENGLISH

7. For each of the following, write a COBOL record description using the listed fields from the CUSTOMER–FILE listed in Appendix D. (See Figure 2.1.2.)

CUSTOMER–RECORD

ID-NO	NAME	STREET	CITY	EXPIRE	INVOICE	AMT DUE	REGION	C-LIMIT	FILLER
1 8	9 28	29 48	49 68	69 74	75 80	81 89	90	91	92 100

Figure 2.1.2 Layout of record in CUSTOMER–FILE.

    a. CUSTOMER–FILE   <u>DATA–FIELDS</u>
                                 CUSTOMER–NUMBER
                                 NAME
                                 STREET
                                 CITY
                                 EXPIRATION–DATE
                                 INVOICE–NO
                                 AMOUNT–DUE
                                 REGION–CODE
                                 CREDIT–LIMIT

    b. CUSTOMER–FILE   <u>DATA–FIELDS</u>
                                 NAME
                                 STREET
                                 CITY

    c. CUSTOMER–FILE   <u>DATA–FIELDS</u>
                                 AMOUNT–DUE
                                 REGION–CODE
                                 CREDIT–LIMIT

2.2   The Four Divisions of a COBOL Program

You should now have a general understanding of the program analysis and development process and may feel ready to write your first COBOL program.

Before we learn how to write a computer program using COBOL, it is necessary to know something about the four parts (*divisions*) of a complete COBOL program. The four divisions provide an overall description of the COBOL program, specify the hardware to be used to execute the program, define the format of the data to be processed, and provide a step-by-step set of instructions for solution of the problem. The COBOL divisions are

```
1. IDENTIFICATION DIVISION
2. ENVIRONMENT DIVISION
3. DATA DIVISION
4. PROCEDURE DIVISION
```

Figure 2.2.1 summarizes the functions of each of the four divisions of a complete COBOL program.

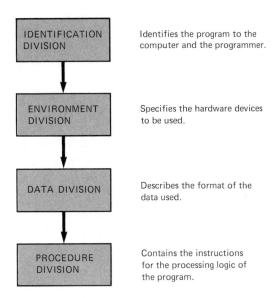

Figure 2.2.1 *The four divisions of a COBOL program.*

   The first three divisions define the hardware and software resources needed to execute the program. The PROCEDURE DIVISION contains the set of instructions for the computer to follow for solving the problem. The program logic or algorithm implementing a program flowchart or pseudocode appears in the PROCEDURE DIVISION.

   Each division may be further subdivided into *sections* and *paragraphs* as required. In this section of Chapter 2, we will discuss the first three divisions. Also, we will explain how to create an environment that can be used in solving a problem. Subsequent sections will deal with the commands that implement the plan developed for solving the problem.

The IDENTIFICATION DIVISION

The IDENTIFICATION DIVISION contains no sections, but is subdivided into various paragraphs. The format of the IDENTIFICATION DIVISION is shown in Figure 2.2.2.

```
IDENTIFICATION DIVISION.
PROGRAM-ID.  program-name.
[AUTHOR. [comment-entry]...]
[DATE-WRITTEN. [comment-entry]...]
[DATE-COMPILED. [comment-entry]...]
```

Figure 2.2.2 *IDENTIFICATION DIVISION format.*

The words IDENTIFICATION and DIVISION are underlined in Figure 2.2.2 because they are required COBOL reserved words. As noted earlier, words that have predefined meanings in the COBOL language are called **reserved words.** For example, when the COBOL compiler encounters the word PROGRAM–ID, the first paragraph in the IDEN-TIFICATION DIVISION, the compiler expects the words that follow to be the program's name. Notice too that a period follows the word DIVISION. If a period is shown in the format, it is required. Just as a period is required immediately following the word DIVI-SION, one space must occur between IDENTIFICATION and DIVISION.

PROGRAM–ID is the first paragraph of the IDENTIFICATION DIVISION. Note that all paragraph headers in the IDENTIFICATION DIVISION are underlined because they too are reserved words. After the paragraph header PROGRAM–ID, there is a period followed by the program name, which the programmer supplies. A name supplied by a programmer is called a **user-defined** or **user-generated word** in contrast to a reserved word.

Note that paragraph headers AUTHOR, INSTALLATION, DATE–WRITTEN, and DATE–COMPILED, are all enclosed in brackets and the headers with two words are separated by hyphens instead of spaces. The brackets mean these entries are optional in a COBOL program. The hyphens are required in paragraph headers as shown.

Most words in a COBOL program are either reserved words or user-defined words. However, certain entries in the IDENTIFICATION DIVISION are called comment-entries. A **comment-entry** is any combination of letters, numbers, and other characters.

Although AUTHOR, DATE–WRITTEN, and DATE–COMPILED listed in Figure 2.2.2 are not required in order for a program to compile and execute successfully, they nonetheless provide important information. The AUTHOR paragraph identifies who wrote the program. This information is quite helpful when we need to consult with the programmer at a later date about special characteristics of the program. Many program-ming managers and instructors require the programmer's name to appear here. The DATE–WRITTEN and DATE–COMPILED paragraphs can help ensure that we are working with the latest version of a program. As a matter of fact, we can leave the comment-entry for DATE–COMPILED blank in the source deck and let the compiler automatically insert the date when the program is compiled.

Types of COBOL Words

Thus far, three types of COBOL words have been introduced: reserved words, user-defined words, and comment-entries. Recall that reserved words have predefined mean-ings for the COBOL compiler. Therefore, reserved words cannot be used as user-defined words. A complete list of COBOL reserved words is found in Appendix G.

A user-defined word is created by the programmer but must conform to certain strict rules. In contrast to reserved words and user-defined words, a comment-entry may be any combination of characters. The term comment-entry should not be confused with a com-ment.

A **comment** is any line in the source program that has an asterisk in column seven and is followed by any text. A comment does not cause the compiler to do anything more than list the text at that point in the source listing. Comments are designed for the use of the programmer and others who will need to understand the code. A comment is always preceded by an asterisk.

Thus far we have learned that the first COBOL division (IDENTIFICATION DIVI-SION) consists of one required paragraph—PROGRAM–ID. The other paragraphs are optional but strongly recommended to identify and document the program.

The ENVIRONMENT DIVISION

The next COBOL division is the ENVIRONMENT DIVISION. Figure 2.2.3 shows the format of this division. The purpose of the ENVIRONMENT DIVISION is to specify which computer system will be used for compiling the program and which system will be used for executing the program. Recall that a program written in COBOL is called a **source program.** The machine cannot execute commands in COBOL. Therefore, we must first compile (translate) the COBOL source program into a machine language object program. The compilation process results in the COBOL compiler creating an **object program** that is in the machine language of the particular computer that will be used for execution of the program. Commonly, the object program is placed on a tape or disk after compilation.

The CONFIGURATION SECTION

Figure 2.2.3 shows that the ENVIRONMENT DIVISION consists of a CONFIGURA-TION SECTION and an INPUT–OUTPUT SECTION. The CONFIGURATION SEC-TION is another required entry that must end with a period. This section header is fol-lowed by two paragraph headers: SOURCE–COMPUTER and OBJECT–COMPUTER. Obviously, the SOURCE–COMPUTER paragraph identifies the computer that will be used for compilation of the COBOL program and the OBJECT–COMPUTER paragraph identifies the computer that will be used to execute the program after it has been success-fully compiled. It is not mandatory for a program to be compiled and executed on the same computer. That is why both the source and object computers must be specified in the ENVIRONMENT DIVISION. In this book, however, we will use IBM-370 for both entries. You will need to use paragraph entries applicable to the computer system on which your programs will be compiled and executed.

```
ENVIRONMENT DIVISION.
CONFIGURATION SECTION.
SOURCE-COMPUTER.  source-computer-entry.
OBJECT-COMPUTER.  object-computer-entry.
INPUT-OUPUT SECTION.
FILE-CONTROL.
        SELECT file name
             ASSIGN TO implementor-name
```

Figure 2.2.3 ENVIRONMENT DIVISION format.

The INPUT–OUTPUT SECTION

The next section in the ENVIRONMENT DIVISION is the INPUT–OUTPUT SEC-TION. This section defines the files used in the program as well as their external storage media. The paragraph in this section that we will use is the FILE–CONTROL paragraph. Let's look at the statements that make the card reader available to the program.

    SELECT CARD-READER ASSIGN TO UT-2540R-S-SYSIN.

The underlined words must occur in the order shown. The name CARD–READER is a user-defined name we have chosen to use for the file of cards to be processed by the card-reader. This name will be the program's logical representation of that physical file and the device used to process it. The string

    UT-2540R-S-SYSIN

specifies the card reader as a utility device (UT). The number used to identify it (2540R) appears on the name plaque of the device itself. The (S) entry indicates that the file is organized as a sequential file. Finally, SYSIN is the operating system's name for the card-reader. We identify CARD–READER and SYSIN so that when we write CARD–READER in the program, the operating system knows this is the card-reader device.

The general form of the SELECT statement varies depending on the operating system used. For purposes of this text, we use the following form.

```
SELECT   file-name    ASSIGN TO
(device class)-(device number)-S-(external name)
```

The notion of an external name needs more explanation. A computer system consists of many devices that communicate with the CPU by means of communication channels. The operating system is in charge of directing all the data flow in and out of the CPU. The operating system keeps track of the peripheral devices by giving them names. The programmer is allowed to refer to these same peripheral devices using names that are programmer generated. One function of the SELECT statement is to identify the programmer's names for a device—the file-name—with the operating system's name for the same device—external name. Since this identification is made when the program is compiled and only exists in the context of the particular program, the programmer is free to give descriptive names to the devices used. The operating system will use the identification established by the program to make sure data is transferred to or from the appropriate peripheral device.

The DATA DIVISION

The third division in a COBOL program is the DATA DIVISION. It is composed of five sections. For most programs in this text, we need to use only two of the five sections: FILE SECTION and WORKING–STORAGE SECTION. Two other sections will be examined later, when we discuss subroutines and report writing features.

The FILE SECTION is the first section of the DATA DIVISION and is formatted as shown in Figure 2.2.4.

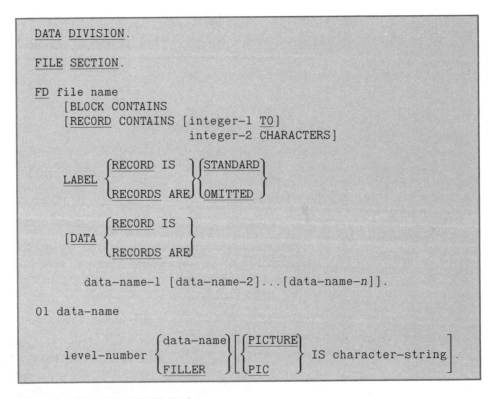

Figure 2.2.4 The FILE SECTION format.

Files used by COBOL programs can be viewed as having a physical organization and a logical organization. The physical organization describes how the data physically exists on the storage medium. The logical organization of the file describes how the programmer views the organization of the file as a set of records. The two organizations are not necessarily the same. It is the purpose of the FILE SECTION to describe both organizations so that the data transfer will be as the programmer expects. Each file defined in a SELECT statement in the ENVIRONMENT DIVISION also has an entry in the FILE SECTION of the DATA DIVISION. The form of the entry for a file in the FILE SECTION is

```
        FD    file name
              physical organization.
              logical organization.
```

where the file name is the same corresponding name as the programmer-generated name that occurs in the SELECT statement where the physical device is identified in the ENVIRONMENT DIVISION.

The following example is the physical and logical descriptions needed for the card reader.

```
FD   CARD-READER
     LABEL RECORDS ARE OMITTED.
01   CARD-IMAGE.
     05 FILLER PIC X(80).
```

This block of code is the file description (FD) for the 2540R card reader device. The name CARD-READER has already been explained. CARD-IMAGE is the name of the record associated with this file. Whenever this record name is used, it refers to a record from the file CARD-READER.

The LABEL RECORDS ARE OMITTED Clause

The clause LABEL RECORDS ARE OMITTED must be present for the card reader. This clause indicates that the file does not contain an identification label preceding the first record of the file nor an identification label following the last record. With a card reader, the first card in the data deck is the first to be processed. Tape and disk files, on the contrary, contain an identification label.

Now let's look at an example of this code for a file stored either on a tape or a disk. The example used is the CUSTOMER-FILE, which has 100-byte records.

```
FD   CUSTOMER-FILE
     BLOCK CONTAINS 34 RECORDS
     LABEL RECORDS ARE STANDARD.
01   CUSTOMER-FILE-RECORD.
     05 FILLER PIC X(100).
```

A standard label is one the operating system is programmed to supply automatically. Although a programmer may write label routines, this is usually relegated to the operating system.

The BLOCK CONTAINS Clause

The BLOCK CONTAINS clause needs explanation. Let's suppose we are creating a file containing three records. Each time we write a record, the end of the record is noted by the write mechanism by placing an end-of-record mark to separate that record from the next record. The last record in a file is followed by an end-of-file mark. The magnetic mark put at the end of each record takes up six tenths of an inch of the tape. If we had records that were not very long, we could imagine using more space for end-of-record marks than for storing records. We avoid this problem by telling the compiler to block records together before writing. In the CUSTOMER–FILE, the blocks consist of 34 records because we have the line BLOCK CONTAINS 34 RECORDS in the FD level indicator for this file. This way we save the space of 33 end-of-record marks.

When a physical record is accessed from the peripheral device containing the file, a block of records is brought into computer memory. The operating system then makes one record in the block available to the program at a time. When all the records in the block have been processed, another block is brought into the machine. When writing output records to a file on a peripheral device, the operating system fills up a block before actually physically outputting the entire block to the peripheral device. (This blocking process is not employed with the card reader or the line printer.)

The use of labels and blocking make the physical organization of a file different from the logical organization of the file. Logically a file is viewed as a set of records— unlabeled and having one record per block. In this way, we are able to use the available storage space on the tape or disk more efficiently by blocking the records while still permitting the programmer to view the data logically, as individual records.

Minimal COBOL Code

The following is the minimal COBOL code for the IDENTIFICATION, ENVIRON-MENT, and DATA divisions when using a card reader for input and a printer for output.

```
IDENTIFICATION DIVISION.
PROGRAM-ID.   CRDPRNTR.
ENVIRONMENT DIVISION.
CONFIGURATION SECTION.
SOURCE-COMPUTER.   IBM-370.
OBJECT-COMPUTER.   IBM-370.
INPUT-OUTPUT SECTION.
FILE-CONTROL.
    SELECT CARD-READER
        ASSIGN TO UT-2540-S-SYSIN.
    SELECT PRINTER
        ASSIGN TO UT-1403-S-SYSOUT.
DATA DIVISION.
FILE SECTION.
FD   CARD-READER
    LABEL RECORDS ARE OMITTED.
01   CARD-IMAGE.
    05 FILLER  PIC X(80).
FD   PRINTER
    LABEL RECORDS ARE OMITTED.
01   PRINT-LINE.
    05 FILLER  PIC X(133).
```

The WORKING–STORAGE SECTION

The WORKING–STORAGE SECTION of the DATA DIVISION is used to allocate temporary storage for a program. For now it suffices to say that any data items required by a program and not defined in FILE SECTION are described in the WORKING–STORAGE SECTION.

TEXTA

An important feature for most programs presented and assigned in this text is that you can use the appropriate files needed without having to write the code for the IDENTIFICATION, ENVIRONMENT, and DATA divisions every time. This is, in fact, a common practice in business organizations when a set of files is used by several programmers. Code is written to make the files available to all programs and each program simply accesses that block of code. If the hardware and/or its operating system are changed, another advantage is that this prewritten code can then be revised. All programs that used this code would then continue to execute correctly without having to modify each program individually. The block of code used in this book is called TEXTA. A complete listing of TEXTA follows, so you can see what code is included. Do not expect to understand it completely now. In due time the concepts involved will become familiar ones and you will be comfortable supplying all the code of a COBOL program.

Here is the complete listing of TEXTA.

```
IDENTIFICATION DIVISION.
PROGRAM-ID. GNRLPRGM.
ENVIRONMENT DIVISION.
CONFIGURATION SECTION.
SOURCE-COMPUTER. IBM-370.
OBJECT-COMPUTER. IBM-370.
INPUT-OUTPUT SECTION.
* HARDWARE CHARACTERISTICS OF THE FILES
* IN THIS COMPUTING ENVIRONMENT
FILE-CONTROL.
* SYSTEM SUPPLIED FILES
     SELECT CARD-READER
         ASSIGN TO UT-2540-S-SYSIN.
     SELECT PRINTER
         ASSIGN TO UT-1403-S-SYSOUT.
* READ-WRITE FILES AVAILABLE FOR TEMPORARY USE
     SELECT FILE1
         ASSIGN TO UT-3330-S-COBOL1.
     SELECT FILE2.
         ASSIGN TO UT-3330-S-COBOL2.
     SELECT FILE3
         ASSIGN TO UT-3330-S-COBOL3.
     SELECT FILE4
         ASSIGN TO UT-3330-S-COBOL4.
* READ ONLY FILES PREPARED FOR STUDENT USE
     SELECT CUSTOMER-FILE
         ASSIGN TO UT-3330-S-CONSUM3.
     SELECT STUDENT-FILE
         ASSIGN TO UT-3330-S-FILE03.
     SELECT NEW-WORLD-FILE
         ASSIGN TO UT-3330-S-PROJ2.
     SELECT REGISTRAR-FILE
         ASSIGN TO UT-3330-S-PROJ3.
DATA DIVISION.
FILE SECTION.
* SOFTWARE CHARACTERISTICS OF THE FILES
* IN THIS COMPUTING ENVIRONMENT
FD  CARD-READER
     LABEL RECORDS ARE OMITTED.
01  CARD-IMAGE.
     05 FILLER PIC X(80).
```

```
FD   PRINTER
     LABEL RECORDS ARE OMITTED.
01   PRINT-LINE.
     05 FILLER PIC X(133).
FD   FILE1
     BLOCK CONTAINS 34 RECORDS
     LABEL RECORDS ARE STANDARD.
01   FILE1-RECORD.
     05 FILLER PIC X(100).
FD   FILE2
     BLOCK CONTAINS 34 RECORDS
     LABEL RECORDS ARE STANDARD.
01   FILE2-RECORD.
     05 FILLER PIC X(100).
FD   FILE3
     BLOCK CONTAINS 34 RECORDS
     LABEL RECORDS ARE STANDARD.
01   FILE3-RECORD.
     05 FILLER PIC X(100).
FD   FILE4
     BLOCK CONTAINS 34 RECORDS
     LABEL RECORDS ARE STANDARD.
01   FILE4-RECORD.
     05 FILLER PIC X(100).
FD   CUSTOMER-FILE
     BLOCK CONTAINS 34 RECORDS
     LABEL RECORDS ARE STANDARD.
01   CUSTOMER-FILE-RECORD.
     05 FILLER PIC X(100).
FD   STUDENT-FILE
     BLOCK CONTAINS 34 RECORDS
     LABEL RECORDS ARE STANDARD.
01   STUDENT-FILE-RECORD.
     05 FILLER PIC X(100).
FD   NEW-WORLD-FILE
     BLOCK CONTAINS 34 RECORDS
     LABEL RECORDS ARE STANDARD.
01   NEW-WORLD-FILE-RECORD.
     05 FILLER PIC X(100).
FD   REGISTRAR-FILE
     BLOCK CONTAINS 34 RECORDS
     LABEL RECORDS ARE STANDARD.
01   REGISTRAR-FILE-RECORD.
     05 FILLER PIC X(100).
```

Figure 2.2.5 provides an overview of the files that TEXTA is designed to permit us to use. The files on the left in Figure 2.2.5 are the input files. The files STUDENT–FILE, CUSTOMER–FILE, REGISTRAR–FILE and NEW–WORLD–FILE have their records listed in the Appendices of this book. These files can be made available to a variety of programmers in a read only mode. This means that many programs can access the information, but the files are protected against a program modifying the contents of any of the records.

The files on the right in Figure 2.2.5 are the output files. The files named FILE1, FILE2, FILE3, and FILE4 can be used for either input or output. These files can be

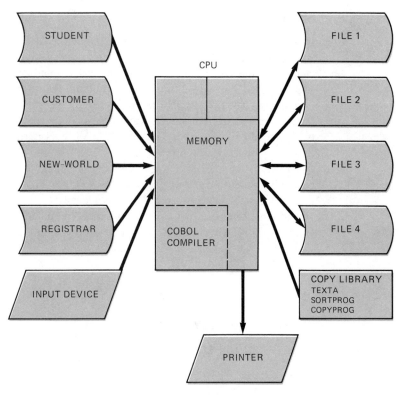

Figure 2.2.5 *General system model for TEXTA.*

viewed as a set of blank tapes or disks that can be used for reading or writing data. These scratch files are not normally permanent files, as are files like STUDENT–FILE, since scratch files used by a program while it is executing are then "erased" and made available to other programs. The line printer will be the output device used when a hard copy (paper) is required. Finally, the COPY library is a library of programs and partial programs that are made avilable for inclusion in a program by means of the COBOL verb COPY. The COPY verb merely copies the code from this library into the program that requests it.

TEXTA is found in the COPY library, so all we have to do is insert COPY TEXTA in the appropriate place in our COBOL program and thereby have TEXTA automatically inserted. In the first complete program, which follows shortly, you will see where to insert the command COPY TEXTA.

Later we will encounter problems for which TEXTA is not sufficient. At that time we will have no alternative but to write the needed code rather than rely on TEXTA. When we write our own code to substitute for TEXTA, we will write it for *only* the specific files needed at that time. Notice that TEXTA contains code to permit us to use all of the files described above. Until it is necessary to write the code that creates a particular programming environment, we have a ready-made block of code in TEXTA that provides us with a generalized computing environment. We can then use TEXTA for our specific programming problems without the need to code all COBOL divisions in their entirety each time.

The PROCEDURE DIVISION

The last COBOL division is the PROCEDURE DIVISION. In this division we implement the logic needed to solve problems. The remainder of this book focuses mainly on the features of COBOL used in this division.

SUMMARY

In Section 2.2 you have learned that a complete COBOL program consists of four divisions, which can be subdivided into sections and paragraphs as required. Some sections and paragraphs are required while others are optional. We noted that the IDENTIFICATION DIVISION is used to name the program and provide other important identifying information. The ENVIRONMENT DIVISION specifies the hardware to be used because there are many different models and types of computers on which a COBOL program can be compiled and executed. The DATA DIVISION defines the formats of the files and records to be used by the program.

Finally, we learned that many of the programs to be developed and coded in this book will not require you to write the IDENTIFICATION, ENVIRONMENT, and DATA divisions from scratch because TEXTA is available. In the next section you will learn, among other things, how to simply enter the command COPY TEXTA in your program and have TEXTA's code automatically inserted into your program.

SYNTAX SUMMARY

```
IDENTIFICATION DIVISION

    IDENTIFICATION DIVISION.
    PROGRAM-ID.  program-name

ENVIRONMENT DIVISION

    ENVIRONMENT DIVISION.
    CONFIGURATION SECTION.
    SOURCE-COMPUTER. computer-name.
    OBJECT-COMPUTER. computer-name.
    INPUT-OUPUT SECTION.
    FILE-CONTROL.
        {SELECT file-name
           ASSIGN TO system-name.}

DATA DIVISION

    DATA DIVISION.
    FILE SECTION.
    FD file name
        [BLOCK CONTAINS  integer-1 RECORDS]
        [RECORD CONTAINS [integer-1 TO]
                         integer-2 CHARACTERS]

        LABEL  {RECORD IS   } {STANDARD}
               {RECORDS ARE} {OMITTED }

        [DATA  {RECORD IS   }
               {RECORDS ARE}

            data-name-1 [data-name-2]...[data-name-n]].
```

EXERCISES

1. What is the purpose of each of the following:

   a. IDENTIFICATION DIVISION   c. PROCEDURE DIVISION
   b. DATA DIVISION   d. ENVIRONMENT DIVISION

2. List the order in which the four divisions appear in a COBOL program.
3. What occurs when an asterisk (*) is recorded in column 7 of a COBOL statement?
4. What is the purpose of TEXTA?
5. Which names in TEXTA are user-generated and which names in TEXTA are reserved words?
6. Explain why a file's logical organization is often different from its physical organization.
7. What is a COPY library as shown in the General System Model of Figure 2.2.5?
8. What are level numbers such as 01, 05, 10, . . .? Which level number is always used to indicate a record?
9. Write the minimal amount of TEXTA needed to execute a program using the following files:

   a. CUSTOMER–FILE
      PRINTER

   b. REGISTRAR–FILE
      CARD–READER
      PRINTER

   c. NEW–WORLD–FILE
      FILE3
      PRINTER

2.3 First Complete Program

In the preceding section we learned that a complete COBOL program consists of four divisions. Since we want to focus on the logic of the program in the PROCEDURE DIVISION, most of the programs in this text appear without explicitly showing the code for all four COBOL divisions. Instead, the block of prewritten code called TEXTA is used to supply the parts of the IDENTIFICATION, ENVIRONMENT, and DATA DIVISIONs not shown in the programs. This block of code is copied from the system's library to the place in a program where it belongs.

The first program we will examine is designed to create a listing of the contents of the first three records in the CUSTOMER–FILE. A listing of CUSTOMER–FILE is found in Appendix D. Conceptually, the program is very straightforward. Its steps (or algorithm) are

> **Repeat three times.**
> 1. Read the next record of the file into the computer.
> 2. Transfer this information to a storage location that looks like a printed line.
> 3. Send this pattern for a printed line to the line printer for printing.

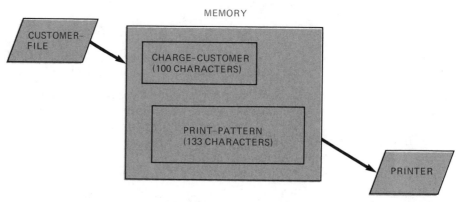

Figure 2.3.1 Diagram for first program.

We can obtain a better insight into this three-step algorithm by examining Figure 2.3.1, which represents the files for input, output, and the storage locations of main memory needed.

This figure shows that a file named CUSTOMER–FILE is to be read and that some output is to be written on the printer. As the first step of the algorithm in the preceding algorithm description, the first record on CUSTOMER–FILE is read into the computer. That record is placed in memory in an area 100 bytes wide called CHARGE–CUSTOMER. Then in the second step of the algorithm, the data in CHARGE–CUSTOMER is copied within memory to the area 133 bytes wide called PRINT–PATTERN. In the third step, the data in PRINT–PATTERN is written as one line of output on a line printer. These steps are repeated for the other records being processed.

CUSTOMER–FILE is an example of a file organized sequentially. A **sequential file** can be thought of as analogous to songs recorded on a stereo tape. Each song on the tape is recorded one after another. Similarly, each data record on the CUSTOMER–FILE is recorded in a sequential manner. You cannot play back the third song on the tape without advancing the stereo tape over the first and then the second song. In the same way, a sequentially organized computer file requires that the first record be read before the second and so on until the desired number of records are read. In this example, three records will be read since the steps are repeated three times.

Card files and magnetic tape files are examples of physical files that must be logically organized as sequential files because of their physical characteristics. A disk, on the other hand, can be used to store records sequentially or in other logical organizations discussed later. CUSTOMER–FILE is organized sequentially. The storage medium used to store this file could be a magnetic tape, a disk, or some other physical medium.

The following program is an example of a COBOL program for accomplishing the three steps of the algorithm discussed and then repeating these steps three times. To the left of each line in the program, we have inserted L1, L2, . . . , L26 to use as references for discussing each line of the program. Read carefully the explanation of each line as given following the program, as this provides you with important information about the first COBOL program you have encountered so far. As you read the explanations for L10 through L17, refer to the diagram in Figure 2.3.1.

```
L1    *
L2    * NAME:                ID:
L3    * PROGRAM-NUMBER: 2.3-1
L4    * DESCRIPTION: THE FIRST THREE RECORDS
L5    * OF THE CUSTOMER-FILE ARE TO BE LISTED BY
L6    * THE PRINTER.
L7    *
```

```
L8            COPY TEXTA.
L9        WORKING-STORAGE SECTION.
L10       01  CHARGE-CUSTOMER PICTURE X(100).
L11       01  PRINT-PATTERN   PICTURE X(133).
L12       PROCEDURE DIVISION.
L13           OPEN INPUT CUSTOMER-FILE
L14                OUTPUT PRINTER.

L15           READ CUSTOMER-FILE INTO CHARGE-CUSTOMER AT END.
L16           MOVE CHARGE-CUSTOMER TO PRINT-PATTERN.
L17           WRITE PRINT-LINE FROM PRINT-PATTERN.

L18           READ CUSTOMER-FILE INTO CHARGE-CUSTOMER AT END.
L19           MOVE CHARGE-CUSTOMER TO PRINT-PATTERN.
L20           WRITE PRINT-LINE FROM PRINT-PATTERN.
L21           READ CUSTOMER-FILE INTO CHARGE-CUSTOMER AT END.
L22           MOVE CHARGE-CUSTOMER TO PRINT-PATTERN.
L23           WRITE PRINT-LINE FROM PRINT-PATTERN.

L24           CLOSE CUSTOMER-FILE
L25                 PRINTER.
L26           STOP RUN.
```

With so many new things happening at once, let's go through each line of code and look at its function. The basic control structure used in the program is sequencing.

L1–L7   Any line that begins with an asterisk in column 7 is a comment. Comments are used to communicate information about the program to other possible users and other programmers. Although a program will run without any comment lines, the value and use of a program is enhanced by documenting the procedures in each program. Structured programs incorporate comments as an integral part of the design process. It cannot be emphasized enough that each program put into regular use will eventually be read and used by someone other than the original programmer. Modifications needed later will normally be incorporated into the program by someone other than the original programmer. The use of comments makes these tasks easier.

L8   Each COBOL statement or command begins with a verb. On this line, the verb is COPY. A COBOL compiler has a library of programs and partial programs associated with it. In this library, programmers can store often-used programs or pieces of programs. The command COPY TEXTA merely accesses the block of code stored in the COPY library called TEXTA and makes it part of the program being executed at the point in the program where the command is found. TEXTA includes certain sections of code that must be part of each COBOL program. By putting all these details in the COPY library, it is possible to avoid writing this code for each program. In addition, modifications can be made directly to the material in the COPY library, thereby ensuring that all affected programs will be properly modified. For now, TEXTA allows us to use certain files, including the CUS-TOMER-FILE and the STUDENT-FILE. Later in the text, we will write programs without using TEXTA so that you will be sure to learn what code is being replaced by TEXTA.

L9   The string of 15 characters called WORKING-STORAGE is the name of the section of a COBOL program through which space is allocated in the computer memory for all the fields and records not found in TEXTA.

L10   The record named CHARGE–CUSTOMER occupies 100 bytes of storage. These bytes are *contiguous* (physically, one after the other) in the computer memory. The record is just long enough to hold all the information in a typical record in CUSTOMER–FILE. Refer to Figure 2.3.1.

L11   This line of code defines a record named PRINT–PATTERN which occupies 133 bytes of storage. This record will be printed as a typical line by the IBM 1403 line printer. Other printers may have different sized print lines and would require other amounts of storage to be allocated at this point. Refer to Figure 2.3.1.

The two user-generated data names CHARGE–CUSTOMER and PRINT–PATTERN are formed using the rules outlined previously. You should review the rules for forming data names.

L12   PROCEDURE DIVISION announces to the compiler that the lines to follow are the actual instructions given to process the input file.

L13–14   The OPEN verb has as its general form:

```
        ⎧INPUT    file-name-1   [,file-name-2]⎫
  OPEN ⎨                                        ⎬ . . .
        ⎩OUTPUT   file-name-3   [,file-name-4]⎭
```

Before explaining this command a review of the meaning of the notation is needed. Any words or symbols enclosed in [   ] may or may not be used at that point of the command. These words and symbols are optional. Underlined words not found within [   ] are not optional. Any capitalized word underlined or contained in {   } must be present. In the case of file-name-1, an appropriate variable name of the program must be present. When words are stacked up, one of the list must be present at that point. The . . . at the end means the list can be as long as necessary. Now we can explain this sentence as a COBOL command. The function indicated by INPUT or OUTPUT is to identify if the file(s) whose name(s) follow are to be used for INPUT (reading) or OUTPUT (writing). If both input and output files are being defined, either two OPEN statements are needed or the pattern of L13–L14 can be used. The file names following INPUT will be opened for input operations only. The file names following OUTPUT will be opened for output operations only. Each file is either an input or an output file at any time during the execution of a program. Any file being processed in a program must be mentioned in an OPEN statement. Here we want to read records from CUSTOMER–FILE and write lines on the PRINTER. Notice that names have been attached to these files. The files themselves are not in the computer, but are being logically represented by names given to them. Ordinarily, we can make up any name we want for a file. Since naming takes place in the code TEXTA, however, we must use the supplied names until we write the code to replace TEXTA. The OPEN INPUT command prepares the hardware for acquisition of a record from a file by arranging for a suitable communication channel between the peripheral device containing the file and the computer itself. In the case of a tape or disk file, the READ head is positioned at the start of the first record. OPEN OUTPUT arranges for a suitable communication channel between the computer and the peripheral device on which a record will be written.

L15   One form of a READ command is

```
        READ file-name [INTO identifier] AT END.
```

In this problem, the file is called CUSTOMER–FILE and the storage area in which we want to put the information from the next customer record is called CHARGE–

CUSTOMER. The READ command causes information to pass from the file to the storage area in the computer. To help remember the syntax of the READ command, memorize: *read a file; write a record*. We follow READ with a file name, while we follow WRITE with a record name. The clause AT END is required for any READ from a sequential file. For the time being, the clause will just be included in all programs. A complete description of the AT END clause will be presented in Section 2.6.

L16   The MOVE command causes a copy of the information in CHARGE–CUSTOMER to be put in PRINT–PATTERN. The storage area CHARGE–CUSTOMER consists of 100 bytes of data, while PRINT–PATTERN has room for 133 bytes of information. The rule followed when a smaller field is moved into a larger field is that the information in the smaller field (CHARGE–CUSTOMER) will be put in the left-most positions of the larger field (PRINT–PATTERN). This is called *left justifying*. If all the area of PRINT–PATTERN is not filled, the remaining space will be filled with blanks. One form of this command is

```
MOVE data-name-1 TO data-name-2 [data-name-3,]...
```

Data-name-1 is called the *sending field*. Data-name-2 and any other data names that appear following data-name-2 are called the *receiving fields*. The content of storage location data-name-1 is copied into each of the storage locations whose names occur after the word TO.

L17   We now have filled a pattern for a printed line (L11), so we tell the computer to ship this pattern off to the line printer. One form of the WRITE command is

```
WRITE record-name FROM data-name
```

The record name used is associated with the file named PRINTER in TEXTA. Later, when we write the code to replace TEXTA, we can call the record associated with the printer whatever we want; but for now we must use the name PRINT–LINE. Remember, we WRITE a record and READ a file.

L18–L23   Repeat the code of L15–L17 twice. When the READ of L18 is executed, we will access the second record of the CUSTOMER–FILE for processing. This second record will be put in the storage area CHARGE–CUSTOMER and the current contents of the storage area will be lost to the program. When L21 is executed, we will access the third record of CUSTOMER–FILE for processing. In each case the record being read is put in the same internal storage location, replacing the previous record.

L24–25   The OPEN command is always paired with a CLOSE command. The CLOSE command surrenders the communication link between the file(s) named and the computer. The computer's operating system will then be free to assign these communication channels to the files of another program. The general form of the CLOSE command is

```
CLOSE file-name-1 [file-name-2]...
```

In the CLOSE command, there is no requirement to indicate whether the file was used for INPUT or OUTPUT. The machine is just instructed to surrender the communication link that has been reserved for the file.

L26   The command STOP RUN tells the machine to stop executing the program.

Listing all the records in a file would be a monumental task if processing each record required three lines of code. Just imagine what might be required in the case of an electric utility or telephone company wanting to bill all its customers. Fortunately, COBOL has another verb to help us. This verb is PERFORM. The first form of the verb we will use is

```
PERFORM paragraph-name number TIMES.
```

A paragraph name is a programmer-generated data name for a block of code. Paragraph names need not contain a letter, but normally are chosen to indicate the function of the paragraph. The word *number* represents the number of times we want to repeat the execution of the code in the paragraph named after PERFORM. All the code in such a block will be executed when control is passed to this paragraph. The control is passed by the PERFORM command. The PERFORM verb is the key to implementing the repetition control structure in COBOL. To see how this verb (PERFORM) manages the flow of control, we will carefully examine the following program. Rather than give every line of a program a number, the letters (A), (B), (C), . . . will be used to mark the parts of the programs that are to be explained in more detail.

```
*
* NAME:                               ID:
* PROGRAM-NUMBER: 2.3-2
* DESCRIPTION:  EACH RECORD IN THE CUSTOMER-FILE IS TO
*    BE LISTED BY THE PRINTER
*
      COPY TEXTA.
  WORKING-STORAGE SECTION.
  01  CHARGE-CUSTOMER  PICTURE X(100).
  01  PRINT-PATTERN    PICTURE X(133).
  PROCEDURE DIVISION.
      OPEN INPUT CUSTOMER-FILE
          OUTPUT PRINTER.
(A)   PERFORM LIST-RECORDS
          100 TIMES.
      CLOSE CUSTOMER-FILE
          PRINTER.
      STOP RUN.
(B) * PROCEDURE TO READ AND THEN WRITE A SINGLE
    * RECORD FROM THE CUSTOMER FILE
(C)   LIST-RECORDS.
      READ CUSTOMER-FILE INTO CHARGE-CUSTOMER AT END.
      MOVE CHARGE-CUSTOMER TO PRINT-PATTERN.
      WRITE PRINT-LINE FROM PRINT-PATTERN.
```

(A) When this line of code is executed, the machine passes control to the block of code named LIST-RECORDS. LIST-RECORDS contains

    1. a READ command;

    2. a MOVE command; and

    3. a WRITE command.

When control passes to this code, the commands in the block are executed. Once the WRITE statement has been executed, the program recognizes that this is also the end of the LIST-RECORDS paragraph. Control is then returned to the point in the program that called this paragraph, which is the line labeled (A). Since the PERFORM verb includes 100 TIMES as part of the sentence, a counter is set up by the compiler to keep track of how many times control has been passed to the LIST–RECORDS paragraph. If the counter has not passed 100, control is again returned to the block of code called LIST–RECORDS (C). In this way, the same block of code is repeated 100 times. The second time control is passed to this paragraph the READ command reads the second record of the file. Each time the READ is executed, the next record from the file is brought into computer memory for processing. In each case the record is put in the same storage location, replacing the previous record. When the counter that records how many times LIST–RECORDS has been executed passes 100, control is passed to the next sentence of the program following the PERFORM LIST–RECORDS 100 TIMES. PERFORM is the COBOL verb that implements the control structure.

(B)   The comments placed at this point in the program indicate how a particular record will be processed in the paragraph that follows. Comments can occur at any point in a program. As we know, comments should be included to help a person reading the program understand the logic and code.

(C)   This paragraph will be executed 100 times because 100 TIMES occurs as a clause in the PERFORM statement. Control is passed to this paragraph by the PERFORM sentence (A).

A program consists of a number of cards, or a number of card images if your input device is a terminal. Each card has 80 columns that the machine reads, and the COBOL language requires three *margins*. Margin A includes columns 8–11, Margin B includes columns 12–72. In addition, the * indicating a comment card appears in column 7. Columns 73–80 are not read as part of COBOL code. These columns are used for identification purposes. When writing COBOL code, we consider that the card ends with column 72. Code that is supposed to begin at Margin A must begin there. Any code not starting at Margin A can start any place after or including Margin B. Notice how OUTPUT is on the next line in the OPEN command of the previous program. This is done for display purposes and has no different effect than if the command appeared as

```
OPEN INPUT CUSTOMER-FILE OUTPUT PRINTER.
```

Now you have seen the code of a complete COBOL program that is ready for compiling and executing. However, in order to compile and execute it, certain Job Control Language (JCL) cards are required to tell the system what kind of job is being submitted and what files are required. The computer system you will use for compiling and executing programs has its own JCL. You must check with your instructor to learn how to prepare and sequence a complete set of JCL cards, if you are using a card batch processing system. If you are using a stand-alone microcomputer or terminal, you will have to learn the system commands for entering your COBOL program and any required JCL commands. Your instructor will have to provide this information also.

SYNTAX SUMMARY

```
CLOSE file-name-l [, file-name-2]...

MOVE data-name-l TO data-name-2 [data-name-3,]...

OPEN ⎰ INPUT    file-name-l [,file-name-2] ⎱ ...
     ⎱ OUTPUT   file-name-3 [,file-name-4] ⎰

PERFORM paragraph-name number TIMES.

READ file-name [INTO identifier] AT END.

STOP RUN

WRITE record-name FROM data-name
```

EXERCISES

1. Briefly define the following terms:

   a. margin A   d. object program

   b. margin B   e. JCL (Job Control Language)

   c. source program

2. What does it mean for a file to be organized and processed as a sequential file?
3. What are the rules for forming a paragraph name?
4. Write a valid MOVE statement that has as sending field NEW–INFO and receiving fields OLD–INFO and OUT–INFO.
5. Using the WORKING–STORAGE SECTION and the PROCEDURE DIVISION given below (assuming there are 100 records in the file) write the READ–WRITE–ROUTINE to accomplish the following:

   a. Print only the odd-numbered records (1st, 3rd, 5th, . . .);

   b. Print only the even-numbered records (2nd, 4th, 6th, . . .);

   c. Print two identical lines for each record read.

```
     COPY TEXTA.
 WORKING-STORAGE SECTION.
 01  CARD-RECORD  PICTURE X(80).
 01  PRINT-RECORD PICTURE X(133).
 PROCEDURE DIVISION.
     OPEN INPUT CARD-READER
         OUTPUT PRINTER.
     PERFORM READ-WRITE-ROUTINE
         _____ TIMES.
     CLOSE CARD-READER
         PRINTER.
     STOP RUN.
```

PROGRAM TESTING AND MODIFICATION EXERCISE

1. To test your understanding of the material so far, suppose that the following records are to be read as input:

   a. CARNER, JOANNE

   b. DI MAGGIO, JOE

   c. MANTLE, MICKEY

   d. BERRA, YOGI

   e. NAMATH, JOE

   f. EVERT–LLOYD, CHRIS

   Further, suppose that the program you are executing is the following:

```
*
* NAME:              ID:
* PROGRAM-NUMBER: 2.3-3
* DESCRIPTION:   THE LAST 3 RECORDS READ AS INPUT
*    ARE TO BE LISTED BY THE PRINTER.
*
     COPY TEXTA.
 WORKING-STORAGE SECTION.
 01  HERO         PICTURE X(80).
 01  PRINT-PATTERN PICTURE X(133).
```

```
PROCEDURE DIVISION.
    OPEN INPUT CARD-READER
         OUTPUT PRINTER.
    PERFORM SKIP-OVER
        3 TIMES.
    PERFORM LIST-RECORDS
        3 TIMES.
    CLOSE CARD-READER
          PRINTER.
    STOP RUN.

* PROCEDURE TO READ AND THEN WRITE A SINGLE RECORD
  LIST-RECORDS.
      READ CARD-READER INTO HERO AT END.
      MOVE HERO TO PRINT-PATTERN.
      WRITE PRINT-LINE FROM PRINT-PATTERN.
* ADVANCE TO NEXT RECORD IN CARD-READER.
  SKIP-OVER.
      READ CARD-READER INTO HERO AT END.
```

Indicate what each of the storage areas will contain at the end of executing the paragraphs as directed by the PERFORM sentences.

PARAGRAPH	HERO	PRINT-PATTERN
SKIP-OVER		
SKIP-OVER		
SKIP-OVER		
LIST-RECORDS		
LIST-RECORDS		
LIST-RECORDS		

PROGRAMMING PROBLEMS

1. Run PROGRAM-NUMBER 2.3-3 (Program Testing Exercise 1) on the computer. The records of the input file should be on separate data cards that are submitted with the program or entered from the terminal as separate data records.
2. Write a program that reads and prints the contents of the last 10 records in the CUSTOMER-FILE that is found in Appendix D. *Hint:* Use PROGRAM-NUMBER 2.3-3 as a model. Change the file name in that program to CUSTOMER-FILE (3 places). Use 90 and 10 in place of the occurrences of 3 in the source code. Also change the size of the input record description from 80 bytes to 100 bytes.

2.4   Horizontal and Vertical Spacing of Output

In Programming Problem 2 in Section 2.3 we described a record in CUSTOMER-FILE as a single field 100 bytes long. We would like, however, to deal with individual *fields,* such as those containing a NAME or a REGION-CODE. The various fields in a typical record in CUSTOMER-FILE are shown in Figure 2.4.1 on the next page.

We can take a record apart in any manner we like by using PICTURE clauses. If we want to consider two neighboring fields as one, or if we want to pick out a piece of a field, we simply give the compiler the appropriate record description. We don't have to use the same record description in different programs that use the same file. For instance, in one program we may be concerned with addresses and in another only with REGION–CODE. Different record descriptions can be written to conform to program specifications.

CUSTOMER-RECORD

ID-NO	NAME	STREET	CITY	EXPIRE	INVOICE	AMT DUE	REGION	C-LIMIT	FILLER
1 8	9 28	29 48	49 68	69 74	75 80	81 89	90	91	92 100

Figure 2.4.1 A typical record layout for a CUSTOMER–FILE.

The program that follows does not access the CUSTOMER–ID field and so that field is not given a user generated name. The space that field occupies in the record is accounted for by the reserved word FILLER with a PIC X(8) clause.

```
*
* NAME:            ID:
* PROGRAM-NUMBER: 2.4-1
* DESCRIPTION: PROCESS THE CUSTOMER-FILE AND PRINT A
*   MAILING LABEL FOR EACH CUSTOMER IN THE FILE.
*   PRINT ONLY THE NAME, STREET, AND CITY.
*
      COPY TEXTA.
   WORKING-STORAGE SECTION.

* INPUT RECORD
   01   CHARGE-CUSTOMER.
        05 FILLER PIC X(8).
        05 NAME   PIC X(20).
        05 STREET PIC X(20).
        05 CITY   PIC X(20).
        05 FILLER PIC X(32).

* OUTPUT RECORD
   01   PRINT-PATTERN PIC X(133).

   PROCEDURE DIVISION.

        OPEN INPUT CUSTOMER-FILE
             OUTPUT PRINTER.

        PERFORM MAKE-A-LABEL
             100 TIMES.

        CLOSE CUSTOMER-FILE
              PRINTER.
        STOP RUN.

* ACCESS A SINGLE RECORD AND LIST ON
* SUCCESSIVE LINES THE NAME FIELD,
* THE STREET FIELD AND THE CITY FIELD.
   MAKE-A-LABEL.
        READ CUSTOMER-FILE INTO CHARGE-CUSTOMER AT END.
```

(A)

(B)

(C)

(D)
```
        MOVE NAME   TO PRINT-PATTERN.
        WRITE PRINT-LINE FROM PRINT-PATTERN.
```
(E)
```
        MOVE STREET TO PRINT-PATTERN.
        WRITE PRINT-LINE FROM PRINT-PATTERN.
```
(F)
```
        MOVE CITY   TO PRINT-PATTERN.
        WRITE PRINT-LINE FROM PRINT-PATTERN.
```

(A)   We have identified three specific fields in the input record called CHARGE-
        CUSTOMER: NAME, STREET, and CITY. The other two areas in CHARGE-
        CUSTOMER have been assigned the name FILLER. FILLER accounts for the bytes
        occupied by data that is in the record, but not used in this program. The word FILLER is
        a COBOL reserved word. All COBOL reserved words cause the complier to react in a
        particular way each time they are encountered in a program. In this case, FILLER is used
        in place of a variable name. This allows a picture clause and some information to be
        accounted for at a particular point in the record. The customer's NAME actually begins in
        byte 9 of the record. If the sentence

                        05 FILLER PIC X(8)

        were omitted, we would be saying that the customer's NAME began in byte 1 of the
        record. In that case the first NAME would consist of the first 20 characters of the record
        which are

                        51900000WEINSMEIER C

        We can see that this is incorrect by checking the contents of NAME for the first record in
        CUSTOMER-FILE in Appendix D. The final

                        05 FILLER PIC X(32)

        accounts for bytes 69–100 of the record. It begins immediately following the bytes allo-
        cated in all the picture clauses that precede it. The lengths of these preceding picture
        clauses are 8, 20, 20, and 20 (8 + 20 + 20 + 20 = 68). Thus, the field FILLER begins at
        byte 69. The reserved word FILLER is used twice in this record description. We can use
        FILLER as often as needed to account for space in a record that is not accessed in a
        particular application. The information is still in the record. (See the remaining fields in
        the description (Appendix D) of a record of CUSTOMER-FILE that follow CITY).
        However, by using FILLER to describe 32 bytes, this program will account for the
        remaining bytes of the record even though they do not contain data that is needed for this
        application.

(B)   Remember, we are going to pass control to the paragraph called MAKE-A-LABEL one
        hundred separate times. Each time the complete block of code will be executed.

(C)   The comments preceding the paragraph name describe what task will be performed by that
        paragraph.

(D)   This sentence causes the machine to copy the information in the data area called NAME
        into the data area called PRINT-PATTERN and then send this pattern for a printed line
        off to be printed. The field called NAME is only 20 bytes long, so PRINT-PATTERN
        will have this information in its leftmost 20 bytes, followed by 113 bytes filled with
        spaces. We now have

                        WEINSMEIER CFR

        both in the storage location NAME and the storage location PRINT-PATTERN.

(E)   This second MOVE command copies the current contents of the storage location STREET over the current contents of the storage location PRINT–PATTERN. We have not read another record yet, because we want to use a second and a third piece of the first record as well. The current contents of the storage location PRINT–PATTERN are the characters

```
44 BERTA PLACE
```

(F)   After writing the STREET address we move CITY to PRINT–PATTERN, and then copy the contents of this storage location onto the next line of the printed output. While all these printed lines are being formed, the contents of CHARGE–CUSTOMER does not change.

Here again, two levels of organization exist within the program. The first, (B), ensures that each record in the file is processed. The second ensures that each individual record is processed by means of the code in the paragraph PRINT–A–LABEL.

Unfortunately, the first three lines of output are

```
EINSMEIER CFR
4 BERTA PLACE
ORONTO ONT
```

It will not do to have the first letter of a person's NAME, the first digit of the ADDRESS, and the first letter of the CITY disappear somewhere between PRINT–PATTERN and the printed line. We can easily fix this once we understand that the first byte of any record sent to the *line printer* for printing is used by the printer (a mechanical device) as a signal to advance the paper a number of lines. We must be resigned to allow the first byte of the print line to be used as a *carriage control signal*. We can reserve this byte for carriage control by making the first field in any record that is a pattern for a printed line.

```
05 FILLER PIC X.
```

Now instead of having a record name with a picture clause attached to the 01-level name we must subdivide PRINT–PATTERN into (at least) two fields. At the 05-level we allocate one byte for carriage control. The remaining 132 bytes are the real print positions that are available.

```
01  PRINT-PATTERN.
    05 FILLER         PIC X.
    05 REALLY-PRINTED PIC X(132).
```

The data field

```
05 FILLER PIC X
```

is only required when the output device is the line printer. For other output devices and input devices, the first byte of the record contains information. With this minor change in the previous program, we obtain

---

```
*
* NAME:                    ID:
* PROGRAM-NUMBER: 2.4-2
* DESCRIPTION: PROCESS THE CUSTOMER-FILE AND PRINT
*   A MAILING LABEL FOR EACH CUSTOMER IN THE FILE.
*
    COPY TEXTA.
  WORKING-STORAGE SECTION.
```

```
* INPUT RECORD
 01   CHARGE-CUSTOMER.
         05 FILLER PIC X(8).
         05 NAME   PIC X(20).
         05 STREET PIC X(20).
         05 CITY   PIC X(20).
         05 FILLER PIC X(32).

 * OUTPUT RECORD
 01   PRINT-PATTERN.
         05 FILLER            PIC X.
         05 REALLY-PRINTED PIC X(132).

 PROCEDURE DIVISION.

         OPEN INPUT CUSTOMER-FILE
              OUTPUT PRINTER.

         PERFORM MAKE-A-LABEL
              100 TIMES.

         CLOSE CUSTOMER-FILE
               PRINTER.
         STOP RUN.

 *
 * ACCESS A SINGLE RECORD AND LIST ON SUCCESSIVE
 *  LINES THE NAME, STREET, AND CITY OF THE CUSTOMER.
 *
 MAKE-A-LABEL.
         READ CUSTOMER-FILE INTO CHARGE-CUSTOMER AT END.
         MOVE NAME     TO REALLY-PRINTED.
         WRITE PRINT-LINE FROM PRINT-PATTERN.
         MOVE STREET   TO REALLY-PRINTED.
         WRITE PRINT-LINE FROM PRINT-PATTERN.
         MOVE CITY     TO REALLY-PRINTED.
         WRITE PRINT-LINE FROM PRINT-PATTERN.
```

(A) beside `01 PRINT-PATTERN.`
(B) beside `MAKE-A-LABEL.`

(A)   We have incorporated the minor adjustments needed to keep the printer from swallowing the first byte.

(B)   This paragraph differs from the previous MAKE–A–LABEL only in that the receiving field for the MOVE statement is the field REALLY–PRINTED; that is, the final 132 bytes of PRINT-PATTERN. The output for the first record is now correct.

```
                    WEINSMEIER CFR
                    44 BERTA PLACE
                    TORONTO ONT
```

In this last example, we printed the NAME, STREET, and CITY on successive lines. We often need a report that contains all this information on a single line. As well as accessing different fields in an input record, we can fill different fields in an output record. For an example we will subdivide the print line's pattern so that the NAME is printed on the left, the STREET is printed beginning with print position 50 and the CITY is printed beginning with print position 100. This *format* requirement for output is met as follows:

```
01  PRINT-PATTERN.
    05 FILLER                PIC X.
    05 PLACE-TO-WRITE-NAME   PIC X(48).
    05 PLACE-TO-WRITE-STREET PIC X(50).
    05 PLACE-TO-WRITE-CITY   PIC X(34).
```

The size of the various picture clauses depends on what layout is required for the output line. To fill these fields, we need a paragraph such as

```
*
* ACCESS A RECORD AND DISPLAY NAME, STREET,
*  AND CITY FIELDS ON A SINGLE LINE.
*
 MAKE-A-HORIZONTAL-LABEL.
      READ CUSTOMER-FILE INTO CHARGE-CUSTOMER.
      MOVE NAME   TO PLACE-TO-WRITE-NAME.
      MOVE STREET TO PLACE-TO-WRITE-STREET.
      MOVE CITY   TO PLACE-TO-WRITE-CITY.
      WRITE PRINT-LINE FROM PRINT-PATTERN.
```

The three MOVE statements must be executed before the single WRITE statement, since we want all the information to be printed on a single line. If we try to write before the three MOVE commands are executed, inaccurate data will be printed. Some compilers will cause double quote marks or other characters to be printed to signify that a field was not supplied with a value before the record was printed.

This last paragraph and the associated PRINT–PATTERN are one way of solving this problem. In COBOL the same data name may occur in different records—input and output. This is desirable because anyone reading the program normally assumes that information is being displayed, but not modified. There is a price to pay for this convenience, but first let's write the input and output record that allows this.

```
* INPUT RECORD
 01  CHARGE-CUSTOMER.
     05 FILLER PIC X(8).
     05 NAME   PIC X(20).
     05 STREET PIC X(20).
     05 CITY   PIC X(20).
     05 FILLER PIC X(32).
* OUTPUT RECORD
 01  PRINT-PATTERN.
     05 FILLER PIC X.
     05 NAME   PIC X(48).
     05 STREET PIC X(50).
     05 CITY   PIC X(34).
```

We now see the price we must pay when considering the following command.

```
MOVE NAME TO NAME.
```

Which record contains the sending field and which contains the receiving field? The compiler becomes hopelessly confused because this data name (NAME) occurs in two different records. The solution is to qualify the identical data names by telling the compiler which record contains the sending field and which record contains the receiving field. The command now becomes

```
MOVE NAME IN CHARGE-CUSTOMER TO
     NAME IN PRINT-PATTERN.
```

Since the amount of code has increased so much, it hardly seems worth the trouble to use identical names. Again, however, COBOL comes to the rescue with the following code.

```
MOVE CORRESPONDING CHARGE-CUSTOMER
        TO PRINT-PATTERN.
```

This single sentence will cause the following three commands (called *qualified moves*) to be executed.

```
MOVE NAME   IN CHARGE-CUSTOMER TO NAME   IN PRINT-PATTERN
MOVE STREET IN CHARGE-CUSTOMER TO STREET IN PRINT-PATTERN
MOVE CITY   IN CHARGE-CUSTOMER TO CITY   IN PRINT-PATTERN
```

The MOVE CORRESPONDING command determines if a data name in the first record also occurs in the second record. Whenever identical names are found, the qualified move is executed. This variation of the MOVE command should be used only in cases where the input information is directly moved to an output record and then printed but not used in any other way by the program.

SYNTAX SUMMARY

$$\underline{\text{MOVE}} \left\{ \begin{array}{l} \text{identifier-1} \\ \text{literal} \end{array} \right\} \underline{\text{TO}} \text{ identifier-2 [identifier-3]} \ldots$$

The MOVE statement allows multiple receiving fields for a single sending field. The MOVE CORRESPONDING statement is not often used, but has the form

$$\underline{\text{MOVE}} \left\{ \begin{array}{l} \text{CORRESPONDING} \\ \text{CORR} \end{array} \right\} \text{ identifier-1 } \underline{\text{TO}} \text{ identifier-2}$$

EXERCISES

1. Briefly define the following terms.

   a. carriage control   c. reserved word
   b. qualified move   d. output format

2. Write a correct MOVE statement if the sending field in the record ᴧCE-SUPPLY is called NAME and the receiving field in the record PRINT-PATTERN is called NAME.

3. The Helpful Loan Company has a record for each of its customers. To plan for an orderly expansion of 200% in six months, the chief loan officer would like some reports for study. In the following exercises, the input file is described and the output requirements are listed. Write record descriptions for the input record and each of the output line patterns. The record in the HELPFUL-LOAN-COMPANY file is 269 bytes long.

a. Input record:

Information	Beginning Byte	Length
Name	1	30
Credit Rating	37	2
Street Address	68	26
Zip Code	96	5
Current Balance	158	12
Percent Interest	199	3
Last Loan	212	10
Length of Loan	250	5

Output records:

b. NAME, ZIP–CODE, and CURRENT–BALANCE
c. CREDIT–RATING, CURRENT–BALANCE, and PERCENT–INTEREST
d. NAME, CURRENT–BALANCE, LAST–LOAN, and LENGTH–OF–LOAN

PROGRAMMING PROBLEMS

1. Modify PROGRAM–NUMBER 2.4-1 by including the CUSTOMER–NUMBER and EXPIRATION–DATE on the same line, to the right of the listing of NAME, STREET, and CITY.
2. Modify PROGRAM–NUMBER 2.4-2 so that similar results are printed for the NEW–WORLD–FILE.
3. Prepare a report that lists the NAME, AGE, and SEX of the first 25 students in the STUDENT–FILE.
4. Prepare a report listing the NAME and the GRADEs of every fourth student in the REGISTRAR–FILE.
5. List the NAME, AMOUNT–DUE, and PAYMENT for the last 20 customers in the NEW–WORLD–FILE.

2.5 Print Patterns for Output

We have seen how to define input records to gain access to individual fields of information. We have also seen how to arrange output information so that it will be printed properly. The next step to learn in presenting information is how to print *headers* for reports. We will consider two kinds of headers. The first identifies the information in the report itself. The second identifies the printed information from an individual record. Both types of headers use the COBOL feature that allows both fields and records to be assigned initial values at compile time.

The first example shows us the MOVE CORRESPONDING feature in an actual program. We also see how to design and use a header line to label the required information from each record.

```
*
* NAME                    ID:
* PROGRAM-NUMBER: 2.5-1
* DESCRIPTION: WRITE A REPORT USING THE RECORDS
*    OF THE CUSTOMER-FILE.  FOR EACH RECORD LIST
*    THE CUSTOMER NUMBER, NAME, STREET, AND CITY FIELDS.
*
     COPY TEXTA.
 WORKING-STORAGE SECTION.
```

```
* INPUT RECORD
  01  CHARGE-CUSTOMER.
      05 CUSTOMER-NUMBER PIC X(8).
      05 NAME            PIC X(20).
      05 STREET          PIC X(20).
      05 CITY            PIC X(20).
      05 FILLER          PIC X(32).

* OUTPUT RECORD
  01 PRINT-PATTERN.
      05 FILLER          PIC X.
      05 CUSTOMER-NUMBER PIC X(18).
      05 NAME            PIC X(30).
      05 STREET          PIC X(30).
      05 CITY            PIC X(54).

* SET UP COLUMN HEADERS AT COMPILE TIME
```
(A)
```
  01  HEADING-LINE.
      05 FILLER PIC X.
      05 FILLER PIC X(6)  VALUE IS 'NUMBER'.
      05 FILLER PIC X(12) VALUE IS SPACES.
      05 FILLER PIC X(4)  VALUE IS 'NAME'.
      05 FILLER PIC X(26) VALUE IS SPACES.
      05 FILLER PIC X(6)  VALUE IS 'STREET'.
      05 FILLER PIC X(24) VALUE IS SPACES.
      05 FILLER PIC X(4)  VALUE IS 'CITY'.
      05 FILLER PIC X(50) VALUE IS SPACES.

  PROCEDURE DIVISION.

      OPEN INPUT CUSTOMER-FILE
           OUTPUT PRINTER.

* PRINT THE HEADING LINE ONCE
```
(B)
```
      WRITE PRINT-LINE FROM HEADING-LINE.

* PROCESS THE FILE
      PERFORM READ-WRITE-ROUTINE
          100 TIMES.

* CLOSE UP SHOP AND CALL IT A DAY
      CLOSE CUSTOMER-FILE
            PRINTER.
      STOP RUN.

* PROCESS AN INDIVIDUAL RECORD
  READ-WRITE-ROUTINE.
      READ CUSTOMER-FILE INTO CHARGE-CUSTOMER AT END.
```
(C)
```
      MOVE CORRESPONDING CHARGE-CUSTOMER
          TO PRINT-PATTERN.
      WRITE PRINT-LINE FROM PRINT-PATTERN.
```

(A)   As noted earlier, the printed line is 133 print positions wide. The report being written will have four columns of information. We will label the top of each column to tell the user of the report the kind of information it contains. The VALUE clause causes the compiler to put the information enclosed in quotes following VALUE IS into the memory locations allocated by the PICTURE clauses. A string of characters is always indicated by being enclosed in quote marks. Without the quotes the compiler would think the string of characters, called a *nonnumeric literal constant,* was a variable name. As a matter of convenience, the word IS may be omitted without consequence. (This is much like shortening PICTURE to PIC.) The VALUE clause causes the information in quotes to be put in the memory location at compile time. Since we want to set up a header that will not change or be accessed at execution time (except as a complete line), we can use FILLER instead of a data name. We will not need to access this information except as a complete line ready to be printed. The spacing for the words that will be printed is determined by the size of the fields of information to be printed and the spacing needed to make the report readable. SPACES is the reserved word used to represent a blank space.

(B)   This statement causes the information put into the 133 bytes of the storage area called HEADING–LINE to be printed on the next line available to the line printer. This line of code is only executed once, since the code is not part of the repeated paragraph. After execution, control passes to the sentence beginning with PERFORM.

(C)   The MOVE CORRESPONDING causes all the following:

```
MOVE CUSTOMER-NUMBER IN CHARGE-CUSTOMER
    TO CUSTOMER-NUMBER IN PRINT-PATTERN.
MOVE NAME IN CHARGE-CUSTOMER
    TO NAME IN PRINT-PATTERN.
MOVE STREET IN CHARGE-CUSTOMER
    TO STREET IN PRINT-PATTERN.
MOVE CITY IN CHARGE-CUSTOMER
    TO CITY IN PRINT-PATTERN.
```

We now have some idea about how to put headings on columns of information. Often it is necessary to display several lines of information as a header for a report. The unfortunate part of header information is that each different pattern for a printed line requires a different record description. Much of the WORKING–STORAGE SECTION of any COBOL program is taken up by different patterns for print lines. Most of our difficulty lies in adjusting the size of the fields so that the result looks nice. The following example will help you handle that problem. Let's make a heading for the program we just examined. Suppose we want the report header to be formatted as in Figure 2.5.1.

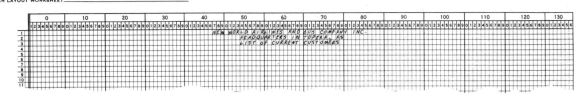

Figure 2.5.1 Sample printer layout.

We will need to define three print records because each of these lines is different. The line printer has 133 print positions with the first one taken for carriage control. As a result, we only see 132 print positions. The first line uses 39 print positions (as seen by counting each character space).

```
NEW-WORLD AIRLINES AND BUS COMPANY INC.
```

Therefore, 93 print positions remain on the line (132–39). We can split these in half so that the line has an equal amount of space on each side. The line can be described as

	blank space	text	blank space
1	46	39	47

The record description for this line is:

```
01  PRINT-PATTERN-2.
    05 FILLER PIC X.
    05 FILLER PIC X(46) VALUE SPACES.
    05 FILLER PIC X(39) VALUE 'NEW-WORLD AIRLIN...
    05 FILLER PIC X(47) VALUE SPACES.
```

We encounter a problem trying to put the company name in the appropriate storage location using the VALUE clause. The data card isn't wide enough! Again, for convenience, COBOL allows us to use more than one line for a *literal constant* (letters/symbols) of this kind.

The procedure is

1. Type the characters of the string in the form required up to and including column 72.
2. Type a hyphen in column 7 of the next line.
3. Type a single quote in margin B or beyond.
4. Continue the literal in the space immediately following the single quote.
5. Repeat steps 2, 3, and 4 until the complete string has been entered.
6. Following the last character of the string, enter a single quote to indicate the end of the string and then a period to indicate the end of the field description.

Assuming NEW–WORLD ends in column 72, the record description becomes

```
01  PRINT-PATTERN-2.
    05 FILLER PIC X.
    05 FILLER PIC X(46) VALUE SPACES.
    05 FILLER PIC X(39) VALUE 'NEW-WORLD
      'AIRLINES AND BUS COMPANY INC.'.
    05 FILLER PIC X(47) VALUE SPACES.
```

There is a second way to complete the record description for PRINT-PATTERN-2 without using the line continuation feature just described. Rather than think of the header as one long string of characters, view it as a set of smaller strings joined together one after another. For example, if the 39 characters in the header are viewed as three strings of length 13, the record description needed can be written without using the continuation feature.

```
01  PRINT-PATTERN-2.
    05 FILLER PIC X.
    05 FILLER PIC X(46) VALUE SPACES.
    05 FILLER PIC X(13) VALUE 'NEW-WORLD AIR'.
    05 FILLER PIC X(13) VALUE 'LINES AND BUS'.
    05 FILLER PIC X(13) VALUE 'COMPANY INC.'.
    05 FILLER PIC X(47) VALUE SPACES.
```

Either of the methods described works. You should choose the one that seems more convenient.

With this detailed examination of how to write a record description for the first line of the header, we can easily complete the other two record descriptions with the aid of the following diagrams:

HEADQUARTERS IN TOPEKA, KS

P-3	blank space	TEXT	blank space
1	53	26	53

LIST OF CURRENT CUSTOMERS

P-4	blank space	TEXT	blank space
1	53	25	54

It cannot be stressed enough how important the visual impact of printed output is. Fortunately, the information to be displayed in this case can be coded in the straightforward way explained here. We must now tell the computer to send these fixed print line patterns out to the line printer before the individual records of the file are processed. If these three lines are called PRINT–PATTERN–2, P-3, and P-4, the code we need is

```
* PRINT THE HEADER
        WRITE PRINT-LINE FROM PRINT-PATTERN-2.
        WRITE PRINT-LINE FROM P-3.
        WRITE PRINT-LINE FROM P-4.
```

For convenience, we can abbreviate the names of the records used. We must use different names for different records, but selecting those names is left up to us so long as we do not use reserved words and we follow the rules learned earlier.

This next program, called STUDENT–DISPLAY, will show how one designs a layout consisting of several different lines of output for a single record.

For each of the records 6–29 and 80–91 of the STUDENT-FILE, print six lines in the following pattern:

L1   all print positions should contain the symbol :
L2   centered on the page should be the student's name
L3   centered on the page should be the student's number
L4   equally spaced across the page, the set of three symbols should appear
         ALG, PHY, GEO, CHE, ENG (in this order)
L5   under the appropriate symbols in line 4, the corresponding symbols in the record
         should be printed
L6   all print positions should contain the symbol /

To understand this problem, lay out what the output for a typical record will look like before doing any coding. This is done in the following example.

```
:  :  :  :  :  :  :  :  :  :  :  :  :  :  :  :  :  :  :  :  :  :  :  :  :  :  :  :  :  :
                              STEVENS TK
                                 0110
ALG              PHY              GEO              CHE              ENG
065              056              063              076              085
 /  /  /  /  /  /  /  /  /  /  /  /  /  /  /  /  /  /  /  /  /  /  /  /  /  /  /  /  /  /
```

You might try this with your name being the pattern rather than : or / being the repeated pattern.

Once we understand what the output will look like, the next step is to layout the storage areas needed to represent the input file being processed, as well as the various printed patterns that will be used. Figure 2.5.2 gives us an overview of the storage allocations we need to make in the WORKING–STORAGE SECTION of the program.

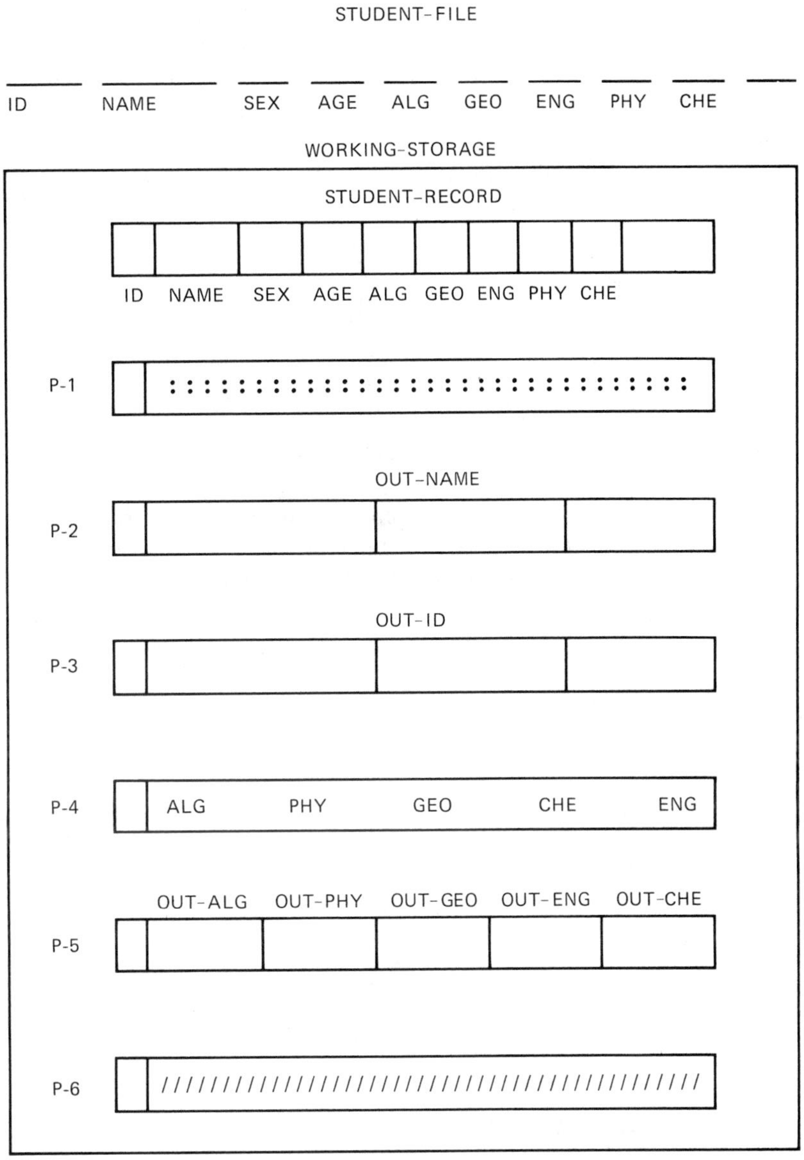

STUDENT-FILE

| ID | NAME | SEX | AGE | ALG | GEO | ENG | PHY | CHE |

WORKING-STORAGE

STUDENT-RECORD

ID NAME SEX AGE ALG GEO ENG PHY CHE

P-1 :::

OUT-NAME

P-2

OUT-ID

P-3

P-4 | ALG | PHY | GEO | CHE | ENG |

OUT-ALG OUT-PHY OUT-GEO OUT-ENG OUT-CHE

P-5

P-6 //

Figure 2.5.2 Record layout in memory for STUDENT-DISPLAY.

The relationship between storage locations and output lines can be further clarified again by laying out a typical record's output. On the printer layout form we put an X in any place where information will be inserted by the MOVE commands in the program. This is pictured in Figure 2.5.3.

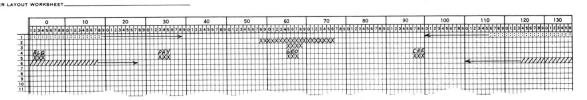

Figure 2.5.3 Printer layout for STUDENT-DISPLAY.

It is helpful not to skip any of these steps, even with simple programs. The use of graphics often makes the problem much more understandable. One final thing we must do to create these output lines is to ask the computer to repeat a pattern of characters as many times as possible within a storage area. The problem we have just examined asks that one line be filled entirely with the colons. Clearly, the VALUE IS clause and enough continuation lines for this string (of length 132) will accomplish this. However, we can describe the field as

```
05 FILLER PIC X(132) VALUE ALL ':'.
```

The machine puts this pattern (:) in the first byte of the storage area, and then asks itself if there are any bytes in the area remaining to be filled. In this case, there are still 131 bytes left, so the machine repeats the pattern beginning with the next available byte, which is byte 2 of this area. After repeating this process 132 times, there is no room left. Each byte has been filled with a colon. If the string of symbols were longer than one character, the process is the same; however, it would obviously not be repeated 132 times but some lesser number of times. If the length of the pattern does not evenly divide the size of the field being filled, the process ends with the character of the pattern that fits into the last byte of the field. For example, if 'HELLO' were being used as the pattern to fill an 8-byte field, then the contents of the field would be 'HELLOHEL'. You might try this in a program with the character string that consists of the letters in your own name.

One more hint should make this problem a bit easier. Let's design the record description for the line called P-2 in Figure 2.5.3.

	blank space	NAME	blank space
P-2 1	57	18	57

Since information from the input record must be put in bytes 59–76 of P-2, we need a data name to represent this field, so it can be the receiving field of a MOVE command. The record description can be

```
01  P-2
    02 FILLER   PIC X.
    02 FILLER   PIC X(57) VALUE SPACES.
    02 OUT-NAME PIC X(18).
    02 FILLER   PIC X(57) VALUE SPACES.
```

SYNTAX SUMMARY

$$
\text{level number } \left\{ \begin{matrix} \text{data-name-1} \\ \text{FILLER} \end{matrix} \right\} \left\{ \begin{matrix} \underline{\text{PICTURE}} \\ \text{PIC} \end{matrix} \right\} \text{ IS character-string}
$$

$$
\left[\begin{matrix} \underline{\text{VALUE}} \text{ IS literal-1} \\ \\ \text{VALUE ALL IS literal-2} \end{matrix} \right]
$$

EXERCISES

1. Briefly define the following terms.

   a. nonnumerical literal constant   c. literal constant
   b. compile time   d. line continuation procedure

2. At what point of program development is a print layout form most useful? What is its purpose at that time?

3. What is the difference between the

```
05 FILLER  PIC X(12) VALUE 'XYZ'.
05 FILLER  PIC X(12) VALUE ALL 'XYZ'.
```

4. What is a report header? A detail line header? A page header? A recap header?

PROGRAM TESTING AND MODIFICATION EXERCISES

1. Modify the following program as described in a, b, and c.

```
      COPY TEXTA.
    WORKING-STORAGE SECTION.

  * INPUT RECORD
    01  CUSTOMER-RECORD.
        05   CUSTOMER-NUMBER PIC X(8).
        05   NAME            PIC X(20).
        05   STREET          PIC X(20).
        05   CITY            PIC X(20).
        05   FILLER          PIC X(32).

  * OUTPUT RECORD
    01  PRINT-RECORD.
        05   FILLER          PIC X.
        05   OUT-NAME        PIC X(30).
        05   OUT-STREET      PIC X(30).
        05   OUT-CITY        PIC X(72).

    PROCEDURE DIVISION.

        OPEN INPUT CUSTOMER-FILE
             OUTPUT PRINTER.

        PERFORM READ-WRITE-ROUTINE
            100 TIMES.

        CLOSE CUSTOMER-FILE
              PRINTER.
        STOP RUN.

    READ-WRITE-ROUTINE.
        READ CUSTOMER-FILE INTO CUSTOMER-RECORD AT END.
        MOVE NAME   TO OUT-NAME.
        MOVE STREET TO OUT-STREET.
        MOVE CITY   TO OUT-CITY.
        WRITE PRINT-LINE FROM PRINT-RECORD.
```

   a. Modify the program so that the CUSTOMER-NUMBER is included on the listing with appropriate spacing. The CUSTOMER-NUMBER should appear on the left.
   b. Further modify the program so that appropriate headers are placed over each field.
   c. Change the record description for the print record so that the MOVE CORRESPONDING command can be used. Change the code in the READ-WRITE-ROUTINE to use that command.

2. Modify PROGRAM-NUMBER 2.5-1 so that the CUSTOMER-NUMBER is not printed.

PROGRAMMING PROBLEMS

1. Prepare a report that lists the NAME, the CUMULATIVE–GPA and the code for the HOME–STATE of the first 25 students in the REGISTRAR–FILE. The records of REGISTRAR–FILE are listed in Appendix E.
2. Prepare a report that lists the NAME, AGE, and SEX of every fifth student in the STUDENT–FILE. Include a heading for the columns of information printed.
3. Complete the program DISPLAY–STUDENT. Substitute your own name for the single character pattern ':' that is printed as the first line of output for each printed record.
4. For each of the records 25 through 50 of the REGISTRAR–FILE, print six lines in the following pattern:

   line 1: all print positions contain the pattern ICS.
   line 2: centered on the page—the name;
   line 3: centered on the page—dorm address;
   line 4: equally spaced—with the letters PH in columns 2 and 3 and the letters MT in columns 132 and 133:

                         PH EN GO GE MT

   line 5: under the appropriate title the grade;
   line 6: all print positions should contain the pattern 1984.

5. For each of the records 50 through 75 of the REGISTRAR–FILE, print six lines in the following pattern:

   line 1: all print positions contain the pattern COMPUTER;
   line 2: centered on the page—the name;
   line 3: centered on the page—the social security number.
   line 4: equally spaced—with the letters MT in columns 2 and 3 and the letters GO in columns 132 and 133:

                         MT PH GE EN GO

   line 5: under the appropriate title the grade;
   line 6: all print positions should contain the pattern PROGRAM.

2.6   End of File

The programs seen so far have involved a sentence of the form

```
PERFORM paragraph-name integer TIMES.
```

We have had to know in advance how many records are in the file so that paragraph-name would be executed once for each record in the file. This creates a lot of difficulty, since every time the file changes through addition or deletion of one or more records, we have to modify the programs being used with that file. It is not hard to imagine a program being run with the wrong number being used, so it is important to view a file as a dynamic rather than a static entity. For example, suppose a file consists of the names of all the students who attended the first class of this course. Considering the typical drop and add activity that affects each class, you know that by the start of the second week this list would be useless without many additions to and deletions from the file. Therefore, we need a way to process a file without worrying about how many records are currently in the file. There are two different ways to face this problem, and we shall examine both.

When a file is being processed, a very important record is the last one. If the program could identify the last record, it would know when the file had been completely processed.

In the case of the STUDENT–FILE, we can check the listing in Appendix C to know that the name of the last student in the file is CALLINGHAM. Let's write a program that keeps asking if the record just processed was CALLINGHAM's. We also want the program to stop when the answer to that question is YES.

```
*
* NAME:                      ID:
* PROGRAM-NUMBER: 2.6-1
* DESCRIPTION: LIST THE NAMES OF THE STUDENTS IN THE
*   STUDENT-FILE.  HAVE THE PROGRAM STOP AFTER
*   CALLINGHAM'S RECORD HAS BEEN PROCESSED - THIS
*   IS THE LAST RECORD IN THE FILE.
*
      COPY TEXTA.
 WORKING-STORAGE SECTION.

* INPUT RECORD
 01   STUDENT-INFO.
      05 FILLER PIC X(4).
      05 NAME   PIC X(18).
      05 FILLER PIC X(78).

* OUTPUT RECORD
 01   PRINT-PATTERN.
      05 FILLER     PIC X.
      05 NAME-OUT   PIC X(132).

 PROCEDURE DIVISION.

      OPEN INPUT STUDENT-FILE
           OUTPUT PRINTER.
```

(A)
```
      MOVE 'ANY STRING' TO NAME IN STUDENT-INFO.
      PERFORM LIST-NAME
          UNTIL NAME
                = 'CALLINGHAM        LO'.
      CLOSE STUDENT-FILE
            PRINTER.
      STOP RUN.

* PROCESS A SINGLE RECORD
 LIST-NAME.
```
(B)
```
      READ STUDENT-FILE INTO STUDENT-INFO AT END.
      MOVE NAME TO NAME-OUT.
      WRITE PRINT-LINE FROM PRINT-PATTERN.
```

(A)   The PERFORM statement contains an UNTIL clause. This is a form of the PERFORM command that is used in COBOL to implement the control structure of repetition. The sentence that contains it has two parts: a PERFORM part and an UNTIL part. The order in which these are executed is very important for understanding this sentence. In fact, the clause

```
            UNTIL NAME = 'CALLINGHAM        LO'
```

is executed first. The computer first determines whether or not the condition expressed following UNTIL is TRUE or FALSE. Any condition written there must be able to be evaluated as TRUE or FALSE. Since there has been no READ command yet in the program and we are asking the machine to compare the current contents of NAME with the string of characters 'CALLINGHAM   LO', we must give an initial value to NAME. This is the purpose of

```
MOVE 'ANY STRING' TO NAME IN STUDENT-INFO
```

This line of code allows the UNTIL clause to come up with TRUE (there is a match) or FALSE (there is not a match). What we put in STUDENT-INFO initially is immaterial, provided we assign that storage location some value not equal to the test value. When the UNTIL clause is false, PERFORM LIST-NAME is executed. When the UNTIL clause is true, control passes to the next sentence, which in this case is

```
CLOSE STUDENT-FILE
      PRINTER.
```

The UNTIL clause will be FALSE until the last record's NAME field is encountered and we match

```
'CALLINGHAM      LO'
```

We can process the file one record at a time *provided* we have a READ command someplace in LIST-NAME.

(B)   The first time LIST-NAME is entered, the only field in STUDENT-INFO which contains anything is NAME, and it contains 'ANY STRING'. Therefore, the READ is executed before the MOVE and WRITE in order to list the NAME of the first student. After these three sentences are executed, control is returned to the PERFORM...UNTIL that caused this paragraph to be executed. Now when the

```
PERFORM...UNTIL
```

is encountered, the NAME field contains

```
STEVENS        TK
```

and it is this value that is compared with

```
CALLINGHAM     LO.
```

Since there is still no match, control is returned to the paragraph where

```
WAGNER        YL
```

is the student NAME listed. This process continues as long as there is not a match between the contents of the NAME field in STUDENT-INFO and

```
CALLINGHAM     LO.
```

To further clarify this process, let's suppose LIST-NAME is being entered and the READ command brings in the record with the NAME

```
DUNKLEY        RS
```

After printing this NAME, control is returned to the PERFORM...UNTIL, where it is again found that the condition being tested is FALSE. Away we go to LIST-NAME again. This time, however, we READ and WRITE

```
CALLINGHAM     LO.
```

Now when we return to test the UNTIL condition the machine finds that the UNTIL clause contains a TRUE condition. Consequently, control is not returned to LIST-NAME, but passes to the next sentence which is a CLOSE command.

Our second procedure for processing a file is a slight variation of the one just examined. Realizing the dynamic nature of a file, it is unrealistic to expect the same record to be at the end of the file forever. To handle this situation, especially in the case where the file is a set of punched cards, we could put a DUMMY RECORD at the end of the data. In this DUMMY RECORD we use one field as the test field for the UNTIL clause and assign those columns a value that can *not* occur in a valid input record. This is seen in the next program, which looks surprisingly like the previous one. There is, however, a critical difference as you will shortly see.

```
*
* NAME:                    ID:
* PROGRAM-NUMBER: 2.6-2
* DESCRIPTION:  LIST THE NAMES OF THE STUDENTS IN
*    A CARD FILE.  DO NOT PROCESS THE DUMMY RECORD.
*
      COPY TEXTA.
   WORKING-STORAGE SECTION.

* INPUT RECORD
   01   STUDENT-INFO.
        05 FILLER PIC X(4).
        05 NAME   PIC X(18).
        05 FILLER PIC X(58).

* OUTPUT RECORD
   01   PRINT-PATTERN.
        05 FILLER   PIC X.
        05 OUT-NAME PIC X(132).

   PROCEDURE DIVISION.

        OPEN INPUT CARD-READER
             OUTPUT PRINTER.

* FILE PROCESSING PAIR
        READ CARD-READER INTO STUDENT-INFO AT END.
        PERFORM LIST-NAME
            UNTIL NAME = 'DUMMY RECORD'.

        CLOSE CARD-READER
              PRINTER.
        STOP RUN.

* THIS TIME WHEN WE ENTER LIST-NAME WE HAVE
* A RECORD IN MEMORY TO PROCESS
   LIST-NAME.
        MOVE NAME TO OUT-NAME.
        WRITE PRINT-LINE FROM PRINT-PATTERN.
        READ CARD-READER INTO STUDENT-INFO AT END.
```

(A)

(B)

(A)   Instead of using an artificial value to initialize NAME so that the comparison in the
UNTIL clause can be made, we immediately input the first record. The UNTIL clause is
not concerned with the contents of the fields which do not enter into the condition, as long
as the tested field has a value. The big difference appears in LIST–NAME.

(B)   When we enter LIST–NAME the first time, there is already a valid record in STUDENT–
INFO. Therefore, we want to execute the MOVE and WRITE immediately—not the
READ. By executing a READ as the first sentence in LIST–NAME, the record put in
STUDENT–RECORD by (A) would be replaced by the next record in the file. The
NAME in the initial record would not be listed. Since this is not what we want, we list the
NAME in the record already in the machine, and then access the next record before
returning to the PERFORM statement that sent us to LIST–NAME. It is important to
realize that the NAME that will be compared with 'DUMMY RECORD' is the NAME on
the second record of the file. We are *testing before processing*. Now when the last record
is read, we will test it and find that the UNTIL clause is true. This will cause control to
pass to the CLOSE statement. We will not print DUMMY RECORD as the last NAME on
the list we are making. With this model in mind, we can see that changes in the number of
valid records will not require changes in the program, since we can use the same artificial
record at the end of the modified file of valid records.

In the case of a tape file or a disk file, in contrast to a card file, we cannot either
determine the last record in a file or place a dummy record at the end of the file just before
processing the file. It is possible that the program is being submitted some distance from
the physical location of the file. We could live dangerously and assume that if a given
record were at the end of the file for one run of the program that this record would be at
the end of the file for all subsequent runs. But files normally change from day to day.
Because this is such a familiar problem in file processing, the COBOL language comes to
our aid with a special feature to solve our problem. We will see the solution in the next
program.

```
*
* NAME:                    ID:
* PROGRAM-NUMBER: 2.6-3
* DESCRIPTION:  LIST THE NAMES OF THE STUDENTS IN
*   STUDENT-FILE.
*
     COPY TEXTA.
 WORKING-STORAGE SECTION.

* INPUT RECORD
 01  STUDENT-INFO.
     05 FILLER PIC X(4).
     05 NAME    PIC X(18).
     05 FILLER PIC X(78).

* OUTPUT RECORD
 01  PRINT-PATTERN.
     05 FILLER   PIC X.
     05 OUT-NAME PIC X(132).

 PROCEDURE DIVISION.

     OPEN INPUT STUDENT-FILE
          OUTPUT PRINTER.
```

```
       * INITIALIZATION FOR UNTIL CLAUSE
(A)         PERFORM READ-RECORD.
       * MECHANISM TO PROCESS THE FILE.
(B)         PERFORM LIST-NAME
               UNTIL NAME = HIGH-VALUES.


       * CLOSE UP SHOP
            CLOSE STUDENT-FILE
                 PRINTER.
            STOP RUN.


       * PROCESS A RECORD AND ACCESS THE NEXT ONE
         LIST-NAME.
(C)         MOVE NAME TO OUT-NAME.
            WRITE PRINT-LINE FROM PRINT-PATTERN.
            PERFORM READ-RECORD.


       * THE INPUT FUNCTION IS MADE A SEPARATE PARAGRAPH
(D)      READ-RECORD.
            READ STUDENT-FILE INTO STUDENT-INFO
               AT END MOVE HIGH-VALUES TO NAME.
```

(A)   We have an unconditional PERFORM. At this point control is passed to the paragraph READ-RECORD. When that paragraph has been executed, control is returned to the PERFORM READ-RECORD sentence. Since the sentence asks for READ-RECORD to be executed once, the sentence has been satisfied, and control passes to the next sentence. We will examine what happens in READ-RECORD in (D), but assume for now that the first record is read and put in STUDENT-INFO.

(B)   We have not changed the form of this sentence from that used in the previous program. A complete discussion of the reserved word HIGH-VALUES that is assigned a value by the compiler is more appropriate when we discuss READ-RECORD.

(C)   Again this is patterned after the previous program. This time, however, we pass control to a second paragraph. We are in LIST-NAME when the

                          PERFORM READ-RECORD

is encountered. This causes the program to transfer control to the paragraph and to execute whatever code is there. When READ-RECORD is finished, control returns to this PER-FORM statement in LIST-NAME (where the program was when control was transferred to READ-RECORD) and the paragraph LIST-NAME has the rest of its code executed before returning to (B). This time the end of LIST-NAME is the line of code

                          PERFORM READ-RECORD

but this need not always be the case.

   The comments in (A) and (C) primarily have been concerned with the flow of control from one paragraph to another. We must still examine the paragraph READ-RECORD (D).

(D)   There are two parts to the sentence in the READ-RECORD paragraph. The first part

                  READ STUDENT-FILE INTO STUDENT-INFO

is familiar, and merely brings the next record in the STUDENT-FILE into the computer memory area called STUDENT-INFO. The unfamiliar part is

                  AT END MOVE HIGH-VALUES TO NAME.

Each time the machine is directed to access a new record from a file, the operation can either be completed successfully or not. If the operation is successfully completed, the code following AT END is not executed, and the sentence is treated as if it were

```
READ STUDENT-FILE INTO STUDENT-INFO.
```

If the operation is not successfully completed, a new record is not brought into memory. An error condition is noted by the operating system. The operating system has two choices:

1. signal an error condition and terminate the program; or
2. use this signal to cause something to be done in the program.

The AT END clause tells the operating system that when the input error condition caused by running out of records occurs, that the code

```
MOVE HIGH-VALUES TO NAME
```

should be executed instead of terminating the program.

A description of the processing of a tape or sequential disk file will help one to understand how this error occurs. Figure 2.6.1 is an illustration of a sequential tape file consisting of three records. There are seven identifiable parts to this file. Parts 1, 3, and 5 are the three records in the file. Parts 2 and 4 are the special marks used to signify the end of one record and the beginning of the next. These are *separators* that guarantee each time you READ you access only one record. The area called *label* at the beginning is used to identify the file as well as to supply the operating system with other needed information about the file. Area 6 is a special mark put on the tape or the disk to signify the physical end of the file. If we tried to read four records from this file, the fourth READ would attempt to interpret area six as a record. This attempt to read an end-of-file mark as if it were a record creates the error condition that causes the code following the AT END clause to be executed. Finally, this means we don't have to worry about any characteristic of the last record in the file when processing a file. We continue to READ until this special mark is encountered. When it is, we make the UNTIL clause of (B) true. The reserved word HIGH-VALUES is called a **figurative** or **compiler-generated constant.** Its value is a special bit configuration that does not represent any printable symbol, and so could never be confused with the contents of a real data field. The picture clause for HIGH-VALUES is of the X-kind, and we must move this to a field with PIC X(n), whatever n is. HIGH-VALUES can be any length you want.

From now on, we will terminate the processing of a sequential file by using the AT END clause with the READ command. The AT END clause relies on the operating system to determine whether the READ was successfully executed or not.

Figure 2.6.1 *File organization on magnetic tape.*

SYNTAX SUMMARY

```
PERFORM paragraph-name
     UNTIL condition-1
```

The order of execution of clauses in this sentence is as follows:

1. The condition is evaluated to be TRUE or FALSE.
2. If the condition is TRUE, control passes to the next sentence in the program.
3. If the condition is FALSE, the paragraph named following PERFORM is executed.

This order of execution is followed both when the sentence is first executed and each time control returns to this sentence from the paragraph named following PERFORM.

```
READ file-name INTO identifier
     AT END imperative statement
```

EXERCISES

1. What lines of code from TEXTA are required by PROGRAM-NUMBER 2.6-3?
2. Explain the syntax and semantics of the sentence

```
PERFORM REPORT-PAST-DUE
     UNTIL CUST-ID = HIGH-VALUES.
```

3. Explain the syntax and semantics of the sentence

```
READ ACE-FILE INTO CUSTOMER-INFO
     AT END MOVE HIGH-VALUES TO CUST-ID.
```

4. Briefly define the following terms:

   a. HIGH-VALUES   c. end-of-file mark
   b. end-of-record mark   d. figurative constant

5. Explain the order of execution for the clauses of:

```
PERFORM BILLING
     UNTIL NAME = HIGH-VALUES.
```

PROGRAM TESTING AND MODIFICATION EXERCISES

1. Indicate how to modify PROGRAM-NUMBER 2.6-1 to include a report heading as well as a heading for the information listed.
2. Use the following program to practice tracing the execution steps of a program. Each time a WRITE statement is encountered, list what would be listed by the printer.

```
     COPY TEXTA.
 WORKING-STORAGE SECTION.
 * EXERCISE USING END OF FILE FEATURE

 * INPUT RECORD
 01  CUSTOMER-INFO.
     05  CUST-NO PIC X(4).
     05  NAME    PIC X(20).
     05  FILLER  PIC X.
```

```
* OUTPUT RECORD
 01  PRINT-IT.
     05  FILLER      PIC X.
     05  INFORMATION PIC X(132).

 PROCEDURE DIVISION.

     OPEN INPUT HELPFUL-INFO
          OUTPUT PRINTER.

* PROCESS THE FILE
     MOVE '0000' TO CUST-NO.
     PERFORM READ-WRITE
         UNTIL CUST-NO EQUALS '9999'.

     CLOSE HELPFUL-INFO
           PRINTER.
     STOP RUN.
 READ-WRITE.
     READ HELPFUL-INFO INTO CUSTOMER-INFO AT END.
     MOVE CUST-NO TO INFORMATION.
     WRITE PRINT-LINE FROM PRINT-IT.
     MOVE NAME TO INFORMATION.
     WRITE PRINT-LINE FROM PRINT-IT.

        DATA
    1234  ABLE
    1243  CAIN
    9999  ERROR
```

OUTPUT FOR PROGRAM

3. Use the following program below to practice tracing the execution steps of a program. Each time a WRITE statement is encountered, list what would be listed by the printer.

```
     COPY TEXTA.
 WORKING-STORAGE SECTION.

* INPUT RECORD
 01  CUSTOMER-INFO.
     05  CUST-NO PIC X(4).
     05  NAME    PIC X(20).
     05  FILLER  PIC X.

* OUTPUT RECORD
 01  PRINT-IT.
     05  FILLER      PIC X.
     05  INFORMATION PIC X(132).

 PROCEDURE DIVISION.

     OPEN INPUT HELPFUL-INFO
          OUTPUT PRINTER.

* PROCESS THE FILE
     READ HELPFUL-INFO INTO CUSTOMER-INFO
         AT END MOVE HIGH-VALUES CUST-NO.
     PERFORM READ-WRITE
         UNTIL CUST-NO EQUALS HIGH-VALUES.
```

```
        CLOSE HELPFUL-INFO
              PRINTER.
        STOP RUN.
     READ-WRITE.
        MOVE CUST-NO TO INFORMATION.
        WRITE PRINT-LINE FROM PRINT-IT.
        MOVE NAME TO INFORMATION.
        WRITE PRINT-LINE FROM PRINT-IT.
        READ HELPFUL-INFO INTO CUSTOMER-INFO
             AT END MOVE HIGH-VALUES TO CUST-NO.

          DATA
     1234  ABLE
     1243  CAIN
```

PROGRAMMING PROBLEMS

1. List the NAME, AGE, and CHEMISTRY grade for each student in the STUDENT–FILE. Include appropriate headings.
2. List the NAME, CREDIT–LIMIT, and REGION of each customer in the CUS–TOMER–FILE. Include appropriate headings.
3. List the NAME and each of the GRADEs of each student in the REGISTRAR–FILE. Provide a heading to identify the information.
4. Modify Problem 3 so that the number of TOTAL–HOURS is listed as the left-most field in the output.
5. List the NAME, HOME–ADDRESS, STATE, and CREDIT–RATING of each customer in the NEW–WORLD–FILE. Include an appropriate heading for the listed information.

Chapter Review

SUMMARY

The construction of a correct program requires several interrelated components. The components include files, hardware, and instructions that embody the logic of the problem's solution.

Files are composed of records that are organized in a hierarchical fashion. Level numbers are used to show the relationship between fields of a record. Records are identified by the use of an 01-level indicator and fields use higher level numbers such as 05.

The hardware needed includes the devices used for input and output. Rather than have a group of programmers, who use a common subset of an installation's resources, write the code for each of their programs that is needed to describe these resources, a block of code available to all programmers is included in the COBOL compiler's COPY library. This common block of code supplies the needed information for using hardware resources for a number of programs. Any modifications to the hardware configuration can be easily reflected by changing this block of code. In this fashion, all the individual programs will continue to execute correctly and not have to be modified to reflect the hardware changes.

In the first program examined, the OPEN, READ, MOVE, WRITE, CLOSE, and STOP verbs were introduced. The second program introduced the PERFORM verb. The

PERFORM verb is used to implement repetition in a COBOL program. Much of the programming throughout this book depends on the use of these seven verbs.

After examining a simple program that demonstrated flow of control, the specific problem of learning how to make the printed output more useful was discussed. Adding headings for reports and detail lines using the VALUE clause was demonstrated. Extensive reports were developed in a line-by-line fashion.

Finally, the AT END clause was introduced as the appropriate approach to detect the end of a file. This feature allows the program to process the records of a file one after another until the physical end of the file is encountered. The AT END feature is different from most other syntax features because it depends on an interaction between the program and the operating system at execution time.

TEST YOURSELF

1. Which verbs are used to allocate and release links to peripheral devices?
2. Which verb is used to copy data from one storage location to another?
3. Which verb is used to bring data into memory and which verb is used to send information from memory to the printed page?
4. Which verb is used to halt execution?
5. Explain the syntax and the semantics of the verbs identified in Questions 1 to 4.
6. What is the function of the first byte of a record sent to the line printer?
7. How are initial values given to storage locations at compile time?
8. What is a nonnumeric literal? A figurative constant? Give examples of each.
9. Explain the syntax and the semantics of the VALUE ALL clause.
10. How are records separated on a physical storage medium?
11. How does the read mechanism recognize the end of a record? The end of a file?
12. Explain the syntax and the semantics of a READ command with an AT END clause.

The Selection Process

Chapter Objectives

After studying this chapter you should be able to

- describe the COBOL collating sequence for characters;
- describe how words are compared in COBOL using the collating sequence and simple conditions;
- write programs that select certain records of a file for a written report;
- write a program that uses the IF...THEN...ELSE statement to perform two kinds of processing depending on whether a condition is true or false;
- write a program that uses a nested IF statement to provide for multi-way selection of different courses of action;
- write a program that makes a selection based on a condition formed by combining conditions using the logical operators AND, OR, and NOT;
- after analysis of a problem, select Model I or Model II as the appropriate pseudocode outline for further program development;
- write a program using multiple record descriptions for a given file.

Chapter Outline

3.1   Using the Collating Sequence

Dictionary Ordering

When we look up two words in a dictionary, it is easy to determine which word occurs first. We can say that for any two words in a dictionary, the one occurring first is smaller than the one occurring later. For example, CAT is smaller than MOUSE. We can also say that one word is larger or greater than another. In this case, MOUSE is greater than CAT. In the case of the words CAT and CATCH, the determination of larger and smaller is usually done without thinking about the process that actually determines the difference. When we compare two words, we look at the first letter of each word. If the letters are different, we go to the alphabet to determine which word's initial letter occurs first. That word is then *smaller* than the other one. When two words have the same first letter, this same procedure is then applied to the second letters. We continue this process until we find different letters at the same place in each word. For example CAT and CAP have the same two first letters, C and A. In this case, we can't determine which word is smaller until we get to the third letters which are T and P. We see that P occurs first in the alphabet, so CAP is less than CAT. In this process the length of the word or the number of letters in the word is not used to determine which word is larger or smaller. For example, COMPUTER is larger than COMPUTATION. Here we must move to the seventh letter in each word, E in COMPUTER and A in COMPUTATION, before determining that

$$\text{'COMPUTATION'} < \text{'COMPUTER'}$$

The COBOL Alphabet

We must now relate this information to the computer and COBOL. When we want to compare two strings of characters in COBOL, we ask the computer to use the current contents of the storage locations mentioned and to perform this DICTIONARY ORDER-ING process on the two strings of characters. One of the differences is that the alphabet used in COBOL is longer. There are 51 characters in the COBOL alphabet. Three widely used codes for storing these symbols in a computer are (1) BCD (Binary Coded Decimal); (2) EBCDIC (Extended BCD Interchange Code); and (3) ASCII (American Standard Code for Information Interchange). In the BCD code, numbers are "smaller" than letters, whereas in EBCDIC the numbers are "larger" than letters. The material presented in this text assumes an EBCDIC code for representing characters.

Types of Characters

The characters are split into three kinds of symbols.

1. *Special Characters in the Order*:

   space + − * / = $, ; . ' ( ) > <

2. *Letters of the Alphabet in the Order*:

   A B C D E F G H I J K L M N O P Q R S T U V W X Y Z

3. *Digits in the Order*:

   0 1 2 3 4 5 6 7 8 9

The EBCDIC ordering is linear. It begins with special characters, followed by letters, followed by digits. The computer uses this ordering to determine that

```
          'A3 (*'   is greater than   '/ZZ'
```

When a string of characters is in quotation marks, it signifies a value and not the name of a storage location. We don't contend that all the "words" in this language make sense. Nevertheless, these strings of characters are words in COBOL's alphabet, and are ordered according to the linear ordering indicated. These 51 characters listed in the order used for determining less than, greater than, or equal is called the **collating sequence.**

Before we study how COBOL uses this ordering (Sections 3.2–3.5), let's return to the two words, CAT and CATCH, and see how COBOL determines which is larger. Suppose that these words are stored as follows:

```
05  WORD1 PIC X(3) VALUE 'CAT'.
05  WORD2 PIC X(5) VALUE 'CATCH'
```

When required to compare these two words, the machine will assume that WORD1 and WORD2 are the same length, by adding two spaces at the end of CAT in order to compare two words of equal length. That is

          CAT__   with   CATCH

A space is the smallest character, so when the machine comes to the fourth letters of each of these words it will compare the machine representation for a space with the machine representation for the letter C and use the result of that comparison to determine that the word whose next character is a space is smaller than the word whose next character is C. The result is

          WORD1 < WORD2

because

          'CAT' < 'CATCH'

The computer has determined that the word in storage location WORD1 is less than the word in storage location WORD2. Notice that the contents of a storage location with a PIC X(n) description are written in quotes while the name of the storage location is not.

EXERCISES

1. According to the collating sequence, the letter A is less than the letter C. In the REGISTRAR–FILE each record contains a sequence of letter grades for courses completed by the student. In schools the grade of A is better than a grade of C. How are the two orderings of A,B,C,D and E reconciled in an application that wants to identify all students in the file who received a grade better than a C in the GOVERNMENT–3 course?

2. Practice using the collating sequence to determine if one word is less than another by using the file of records listed in the following table.

Name	ID	Rating	City
Engle JC	818591641	4	Amherst
Eisner WL	863532076	5	Acton
Borden KR	873067780	3	Auburn
Carr GA	828275050	2	Andover
Ashby RE	896592747	3	Alfred
Bean CD	842583678	2	Antrim

a. List the NAMEs in increasing order.
b. List the IDs in increasing order.

c. List the RATINGs in increasing order. Together with the RATING, list the NAME belonging to the record. Break ties by listing NAMEs in increasing order among records with the same value of RATING.

d. Set up a table like the one shown in this exercise and list the records in order, as determined by the ordering of the field CITY. That is, the record with the smallest value for CITY is listed first, followed by the record with the second smallest value for CITY, and so on.

e. Repeat Part d, but use the value of the field RATING for purposes of ordering the records. List at least two ways to handle ties and indicate what was done in the case of ties.

3.2   IF...Statements

An **exception report** is a key management tool. Such a report signals to management trouble spots or potential trouble spots in an organization's operation. It is not usually as useful to know if a warehouse has a sufficient inventory of snow shovels as it is to know whether or not the current inventory level of an item is adequate to handle the usual demand between now and the time when a reorder process can be accomplished. A good exception report would alert management to reorder at a proper time. Another example of an exception report is the listing of all the overtime pay for a group of employees. Since we may have already budgeted the normal payroll amounts, the fact that this normal allocation has been used is not of much concern. However, a report of missed deadlines and overtime hours may be an important management tool.

Evaluating Conditions as True or False

Both examples of an exception report involve processing a file and picking out records that require special attention. Up to this point, we have been unable to pick out special records in a file. We have had to treat all the records alike. In COBOL we can differentiate among records in a file by asking if a condition about them is true or false. For example

```
IF SHOVEL-BRAND = 'PIEDMONT'    or    IF NAME > 'C'
```

The first condition can be evaluated by COBOL as either TRUE or FALSE by using the dictionary ordering process to compare the current contents of the data field SHOVEL-BRAND with the eight character string 'PIEDMONT'. In the second case, the condition is TRUE if the current contents of the storage location NAME consist of a character greater than 'C' or at least two nonblank characters if the first character is 'C'.

In addition to evaluating whether conditions are TRUE or FALSE, we can act on this information. For example

```
IF SHOVEL-BRAND = 'PIEDMONT'
   PERFORM EXCEPTION-REPORT
```

will have the paragraph EXCEPTION-REPORT executed only if the condition

```
SHOVEL-BRAND = 'PIEDMONT'
```

is TRUE. The statement or statements executed only when the condition is TRUE are called the *true range* of the condition. If the condition is FALSE, control will pass to the next sentence, and this PERFORM will not be executed. Here, then, is the ability to act depending on the contents of a data field.

A Program Using IF...

The next example shows how a program can incorporate this feature.

```
*
* NAME:
* PROGRAM-NUMBER: 3.2-1
* DESCRIPTION: LIST THE ALGEBRA GRADE AND THE
*    AGE OF EACH FEMALE STUDENT IN STUDENT-FILE
*
      COPY TEXTA.
   WORKING-STORAGE SECTION.

* INPUT RECORD
   01  STUDENT-INFO.
         05 FILLER        PIC X(4).
         05 NAME          PIC X(18).
         05 SEX           PIC X.
         05 AGE           PIC XX.
         05 ALGEBRA       PIC X(3).
         05 FILLER        PIC X(72).

* OUTPUT LINE
   01  PRINT-PATTERN.
         05 FILLER        PIC X.
         05 OUT-AGE       PIC X(10).
         05 OUT-ALGEBRA   PIC X(122).
* HEADER LINE
   01  HEADER.
         05 FILLER PIC X.
         05 FILLER PIC X(8)   VALUE 'AGE'.
         05 FILLER PIC X(124) VALUE 'ALGEBRA'.

   PROCEDURE DIVISION.
         OPEN INPUT STUDENT-FILE
              OUTPUT PRINTER.

* INITIALIZATION
* PRINT THE HEADER
         WRITE PRINT-LINE FROM HEADER.

* INITIALIZE NAME FOR THE UNTIL CLAUSE
* AND PROCESS THE FILE-USING THE FILE PROCESSING PAIR
         PERFORM READ-NEXT-RECORD.
         PERFORM SELECTION
              UNTIL NAME = HIGH-VALUES.

* TERMINATION ACTIVITY
         CLOSE STUDENT-FILE
               PRINTER.
         STOP RUN.

* INPUT PROCEDURE
   READ-NEXT-RECORD.
         READ STUDENT-FILE INTO STUDENT-INFO
              AT END MOVE HIGH-VALUES TO NAME.
```

(A)

(B)

(C)

```
      * SELECT RECORDS HAVING A VALUE 'F' IN THE DATA FIELD
      * SEX AND SHIP THEM OFF TO THE PARAGRAPH LIST-INFO
      * FOR FURTHER PROCESSING.  IN ANY CASE, WHETHER THE
      * RECORD IS SELECTED FOR FURTHER PROCESSING OR NOT,
      * GET THE NEXT RECORD AFTER THE SELECTION PROCESS AND
      * ITS CONSEQUENCES HAVE BEEN COMPLETED.
      *
(D)     SELECTION.
            IF SEX = 'F'
                PERFORM LIST-INFO.
            PERFORM READ-NEXT-RECORD.

      * LIST THE AGE AND ALGEBRA GRADE FOR ANY
      * RECORD REACHING THIS PARAGRAPH.
(E)     LIST-INFO.
            MOVE AGE      TO OUT-AGE.
            MOVE ALGEBRA TO OUT-ALGEBRA.
            WRITE PRINT-LINE FROM PRINT-PATTERN.
```

(A) In this case, only three of the data fields in each record of STUDENT-FILE are needed. We have accounted for the other information using FILLER, so we will look in the right place for the information needed.

(B) This record gives us titles for the columns of information we print. Notice it is only printed once, since we don't want to label each selected record's information. (Try moving this line of code down into the LIST-INFO paragraph to see what happens.)

(C) We are starting to get used to this pair of statements:

```
            PERFORM READ-NEXT-RECORD.
            PERFORM SELECTION
                UNTIL NAME = HIGH-VALUES.
```

We call these statements the *file processing pair*. We use these statements with one statement in SELECTION to make each record in the file pass by for processing. This is the main way repetition is implemented in structured programming.

(D) This paragraph is written to structure the program's action. This is a typical use of the control structure called selection. We are still not processing any records. We are just selecting records to be processed further and completing the code necessary to make sure every record in the file is considered. Notice how the program improves in clarity when we take this intermediate step before processing selected records. Further, the code so far has been easy to write. We have pushed our real coding problem to complete this program to the paragraph LIST-INFO. At least in LIST-INFO we know that all we have to do is take the records selected and list certain of their data fields on the printer. Already this doesn't sound like an insurmountable task.

(E) What we have gained by including an intermediate step for selecting records for processing is the realization that *all* we need to complete this program is to MOVE two data fields to the output area, and then print the detail line we have composed. This organization for a program is the first design key we should keep in mind since so many problems follow this model.

The Relational Test

There are six different relations that can be used in COBOL for testing purposes:

1. EQUAL   4. NOT LESS THAN
2. NOT EQUAL   5. GREATER THAN
3. LESS THAN   6. NOT GREATER THAN

There is no direct way to test greater than or equal, so NOT LESS THAN is used. Similarly, NOT GREATER THAN is just less than or equal. In place of the word EQUAL the use of = is permitted with some COBOL compilers. For GREATER THAN and LESS THAN the symbols > and <, respectively, can often be used.

Suppose the TRUE range of a condition consists of a sequence of commands such as the following:

```
IF AGE > '17'
      MOVE NAME    TO NAME-OUT
      WRITE PRINT-LINE FROM PRINT-PATTERN.
```

It is easy to see the difference between a COBOL statement and a COBOL sentence. Each MOVE and WRITE command is a statement and all the code from the IF to the next occurring period is a sentence. Sentences are always terminated by a period.

SYNTAX SUMMARY

```
IF  {data-name-1}  IS [NOT]  {EQUAL         }{data-name-2}
    {literal-1   }           {LESS THAN     }{literal-2   }
                             {GREATER THAN  }

         THEN imperative statements.
```

The conditions EQUAL, LESS THAN, and GREATER THAN can be represented by the symbols =, <, and > provided these symbols occur in the symbol set of the version of COBOL that is being used.

EXERCISES

1. What lines of code in TEXTA are required by PROGRAM-NUMBER 3.2-1?
2. What code in PROGRAM-NUMBER 3.2-1 is identified as the file processing pair? Why is an additional statement required in the record processing to guarantee that every record in the file is processed?
3. What are the six different relations that can be used in forming simple conditions?
4. The students listed in the REGISTRAR-FILE with last names beginning with one of the letters A–M are to be invited to a reception with the president. What condition could be used to select these students?

PROGRAM TESTING AND MODIFICATION EXERCISE

1. Using the code of PROGRAM-NUMBER 3.2-1, list the contents of the two printed fields of PRINT-PATTERN and the input record field NAME the first ten times the sentence:

```
PERFORM SELECTION
      UNTIL NAME = HIGH-VALUES.
```

is executed. Set up a table using TIME EXECUTED, OUT–AGE, OUT–ALGEBRA, and NAME. Remember that the statement is executed before a particular record is sent to SELECTION for processing. The purpose of this exercise is to give you a model for debugging activities. Since the PERFORM...UNTIL...statement is executed before each record is processed, it is a good place to check the values of certain variables to see if everything is as expected. We call this activity 'taking a snapshot of memory.'

PROGRAMMING PROBLEMS

1. Modify PROGRAM–NUMBER 3.2-1 so that the AGE and ALGEBRA grades are listed for records with 'M' as the code for SEX.
2. Prepare a report listing all 16-year-olds in the STUDENT–FILE. Include appropriate headings.
3. List the NAME and GRADEs for each student in REGISTRAR–FILE with MATH–13 grade at least a 'B'. Include an appropriate heading.
4. List the NAME, STREET, and CITY of all Canadian customers in the CUSTOMER–FILE. Include an appropriate heading.
5. List the NAME and GRADEs of each student in the STUDENT–FILE with an ALGEBRA grade at least as high as the ENGLISH grade. Include an appropriate heading.
6. List the NAME, CLASS, and GRADEs of each student in REGISTRAR–FILE for whom the GEOGRAPHY–10 grade is lower than the ENGLISH–2 grade. Include an appropriate heading.
7. List the NAME, STREET, CITY, CREDIT–LIMIT, and EXPIRATION–DATE for all customers in CUSTOMER–FILE who have value 'B' for REGION–CODE.
8. List the NAME, AMOUNT–DUE, and INVOICE–NUMBER for each customer in CUSTOMER–FILE with CREDIT–LIMIT greater than two. The AMOUNT–DUE will be displayed as a string of characters that happen to be digits. Later it will be possible to display numbers as numbers.

Model I   Process a File and Stop

Acquiring the ability to work independently and proceed from the design steps of a data processing problem to a finished, correct program that solves the problem is not easy. This ability can be developed less painfully if you develop good programming habits from the very beginning. A step in the right direction involves establishing objectives for solving problems. Every programmer has as an objective to write correct and well-structured programs that compile the first time they are run. To meet this objective, the first run to catch spelling and typing errors should not be counted. You should also try to simplify the programming problem and be satisfied on the first run with a no frills form of the output. At this point there may not seem to be any simple parts to a program. There is, however, a common thread in all the problems we have considered so far. It is the notion of taking an input file and processing it to create an output file. This points to a need for a description of both the input record and the output record. In the beginning it is best to keep the output record simple. It is easy to add headings and adjust spacing once the required information is displayed by a correct program.

We have already described some major tasks that help to give structure to our programs. We include these tasks as part of an outline for a file processing program.

```
        COPY TEXTA.
      WORKING-STORAGE SECTION.
      *** DESCRIPTION OF THE INPUT RECORD

      *** DESCRIPTION OF THE OUTPUT RECORD


      PROCEDURE DIVISION.
      ***   OPEN ALL FILES


      ***   THE FILE PROCESSING PAIR
      ****** THIS IS THE REPETITION CONTROL STRUCTURE


      ***   TERMINATION ACTIVITY
      ***   CLOSE THE FILES AND STOP THE RUN.
```

In many instances, once we have filled in the needed code indicated by the comments, we may have completed over half the program.

Our next step is to decide what field will be used to indicate the end-of-file condition, and to decide on a name for the paragraph that actually processes the individual records. This will allow us to fill in the code for

```
      ***   CODE THE FILE PROCESSING PAIR
            PERFORM para-name-1.
            PERFORM para-name-2
                UNTIL end-of-file-flag = HIGH-VALUES.
```

The paragraph called para-name-1 is easy to write, as it is of the form

```
      para-name-1.
           READ input file INTO input record
                AT END MOVE HIGH-VALUES TO end-of-file-flag.
```

The paragraph called para-name-2 can be broken down into two parts as described here.

```
           para-name-2.
           *** PROCESS THE RECORD CURRENTLY IN MEMORY



           *** GET THE NEXT RECORD
               PERFORM para-name-1.
```

We have developed a very simple program model for which we have only one coding problem: Supply the code for para-name-2 that processes the record currently in memory. This may require simple code or certain other paragraphs of code, but our efforts are focused there.

The next step in building a framework for approaching a programming problem involves including a selection process as part of the processing of a record. The paragraph para-name-2 then becomes

```
           para-name-2.
      ***   SELECT RECORDS FOR FURTHER PROCESSING
            IF condition  THEN
                PERFORM para-name-3.
      *** GET THE NEXT RECORD
            PERFORM para-name-1.

      para-name-3.
      ***   NOW WE FACE THE RECORD PROCESSING
```

Before seeing how this MODEL can be used to solve a variety of problems, let's put all the pieces together so that the MODEL will be easier to use.

```
            COPY TEXTA.
      WORKING-STORAGE SECTION.
      *** DESCRIPTION OF THE INPUT RECORD

      *** DESCRIPTION OF THE OUTPUT RECORD


       PROCEDURE DIVISION.
      ***   OPEN ALL FILES

      ***   FILE PROCESSING PAIR
            PERFORM para-name-1
            PERFORM para-name-2
                UNTIL end-of-file-flag = HIGH-VALUES.

      ***   TERMINATION ACTIVITY
      *     CLOSE FILES AND STOP RUN.

      *   INPUT PROCEDURE
       para-name-1.
            READ input file INTO input record
                AT END MOVE HIGH-VALUES TO end-of-file-flag.

      *   RECORD PROCESSING
       para-name-2.
      ***   PROCESS THE RECORD IN MEMORY


      ***   GET NEXT RECORD
            PERFORM para-name-1.
```

This Model can be used to solve each of the following problems dealing with the STU-DENT-FILE.

1. Write a report that lists the grades of each male student.
2. Write a report that lists all the female students.
3. List all students with an ALGEBRA grade less than '060'.
4. List the name of each student who is less than 18 years old.

For Problem 4, let's carry out the steps given in the program outline.

```
*
* NAME:                        ID:
* PROGRAM-NUMBER: MODEL-1
* DESCRIPTION:  LIST THE NAME OF EACH STUDENT WHO IS
*    LESS THAN 18 YEARS OLD.
*
      COPY TEXTA.
  WORKING-STORAGE SECTION.
```

```
***    DESCRIPTION OF THE INPUT RECORD
 01    STUDENT-RECORD.
         05 FILLER     PIC X(4).
         05 NAME       PIC X(18).
         05 FILLER     PIC X.
         05 AGE        PIC XX.
         05 FILLER     PIC X(75).

***    DESCRIPTION OF THE OUTPUT RECORD
 01    PRINT-RECORD.
         05 FILLER     PIC X.
         05 NAME-OUT   PIC X(30).
         05 AGE-OUT    PIC X(102).

   PROCEDURE DIVISION.
 * MODEL-I

***    OPEN ALL THE FILES TO BE USED
       OPEN INPUT STUDENT-FILE
            OUTPUT PRINTER.

***    CODE THE FILE PROCESSING PAIR
       PERFORM READ-STUDENT-FILE.
       PERFORM AGE-CHECK
            UNTIL NAME = HIGH-VALUES.

***    TERMINATION ACTIVITY
***    CLOSE THE FILES AND STOP THE RUN
       CLOSE STUDENT-FILE
             PRINTER.
       STOP RUN.

***    INPUT PROCEDURE
   READ-STUDENT-FILE.
       READ STUDENT-FILE INTO STUDENT-RECORD
            AT END MOVE HIGH-VALUES TO NAME.

***    RECORD PROCESSING
   AGE-CHECK.
***    SELECT RECORDS FOR FURTHER PROCESSING
       IF AGE < '18'
            PERFORM LIST-IT.
***    GET THE NEXT RECORD
       PERFORM READ-STUDENT-FILE.
***
   LIST-IT.
***    NOW WE FACE THE RECORD PROCESSING
       MOVE NAME TO NAME-OUT.
       MOVE AGE  TO AGE-OUT.
       WRITE PRINT-LINE FROM PRINT-RECORD.
```

This discussion of MODEL I has shown us two concepts. First, we have seen a generalized structured program outline that is a framework for many of the problems we will solve. Second, we have isolated blocks of code and common tasks that are easy to code, so that efforts can be focused on the difficult parts of the problem. By always using this outline, when applicable to structure coding efforts, programs should be completed and compiled very soon after beginning the coding process. There is no glory and very little learning involved in submitting a program for execution many times. The reason for learning to use a programming language is to solve problems and to get a program to compile correctly so that test data can be processed and the logic can be checked and refined.

This discussion has also shown us the advantage of breaking down big problems into their basic components using top-down programming methods. Once the basics are working, we can add features one at a time until the original problem is solved. This act of refining an initial programming effort allows us to see at each stage that the problems appearing in the program are a result of the *current* refinement. We don't worry about the whole program, just the part that has been added for the current run. Remember that before the additions of the current run, everything in the program worked correctly so that if any error occurs we know what caused it since we could always back up one step to a correct program. The final solution to any problem thus becomes the result of several stages of refining a basic program that solves the major tasks of the original problem.

EXERCISES

1. Explain how the stepwise refinement procedure was used in developing the final form of Model I.
2. What is the purpose of the pseudocode outline given in this section? What parts of the outline will require similar code for many application programs?
3. What changes would be required in the program Model I to list NAME and AGE of each 14-year-old student? Each female student? Each student with an ALGEBRA grade greater than '070'?

3.3   IF...THEN...ELSE   Statements

The selection process we studied in the last section allowed us to choose records for use in a report. In a more general setting two additional requirements arise.

1. Perform different kinds of processing depending on the different values of a variable.
2. Perform processing of a record depending on whether or not the variables of the record satisfy more complex conditions.

In the first case, we might, for example, want to print a code to indicate each customer's CREDIT–LIMIT in the printed output for the selected records. The variable CREDIT–LIMIT has five different values, and we must have a different code for each of these values. In the second case, we might want a more general selection criterion, such as AGE equals '18', or ALGEBRA grade greater than '065'. The programming technique that will allow different kinds of processing depending on the different values of a variable will be discussed in this section. In Section 3.5 we will learn how to ask more complex questions about the contents of a record.

The first problem we will consider involves creating a list of all the students in the STUDENT–FILE. More specifically, we want to list the ALGEBRA grade and GEOMETRY grade for male students, and list the ALGEBRA grade and CHEMISTRY grade for female students. Each record in the STUDENT–FILE contains a variable called SEX, which has either the value 'F' or the value 'M'. Once we know the value of this variable in a particular record, we can determine what kind of processing must be performed. We can look at this another way and ask if SEX has the value 'F'. Whenever this condition is FALSE, we know that the variable has a value 'M'. Figure 3.3.1 illustrates this with the picture of the flow of control in a program.

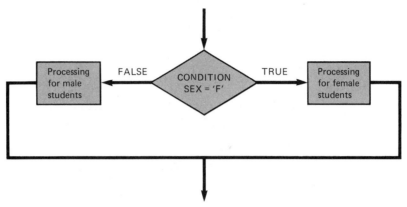

Figure 3.3.1 *Model for IF...THEN...ELSE statement.*

A Model for IF...THEN...ELSE Statements

The COBOL syntax that allows this two-way branching is

```
IF condition
        processing for male students
ELSE
        processing for female students.
```

When the condition is evaluated as TRUE, the statements following the condition and preceding the ELSE are executed. These statements are called the *true range* of the condition. When the condition is FALSE, the statements following ELSE and preceding the next appearing period are executed. These statements are called the *false range* of the condition. In any case, after one of these sets of statements is executed, control passes to the next sentence—the first command following the period that delineates the processing that is executed when the condition is FALSE.

The logic of the next program will be clearer after examining some typical output lines. TABLE 3.1 contains the output for the first four records of the STUDENT–FILE. Notice that not every record has a Geometry grade printed and that not every record has a Chemistry grade printed. The programming problem will be to make sure that only the correct grade is printed in each case.

TABLE 3.1

Name		Sex	Algebra	Geometry	Chemistry
Stevens	TK	M	065		076
Wagner	YL	M	065		074
Rancourt	FU	F	075	072	
Wagner	DT	M	070		083

Regardless of whether the student is a male or a female, all five fields must be given a value each time a record is processed. This is required because the WRITE command only copies the contents of a record onto the printed line. We must make sure that a Geometry grade is not printed when a male student's record is processed and that a Chemistry grade is not printed when a female's record is processed. Notice that the '074' in the Chemistry field for Wagner is replaced by spaces before the record of Rancourt is printed. We can manage this blanking out process and the filling of the special grade field using the IF...THEN...ELSE construction as seen in the next program.

```
*
* NAME:                        ID:
* PROGRAM-NUMBER: 3.3-1
* DESCRIPTION: LIST THE NAME AND SEX OF EACH
*   STUDENT IN THE STUDENT-FILE, LIST ALGEBRA
*   AND CHEMISTRY GRADES FOR MALES AND ALGEBRA
*   AND GEOMETRY GRADES FOR FEMALES.
*
      COPY TEXTA.
WORKING-STORAGE SECTION.

* INPUT RECORD
 01   STUDENT-INFO.
      05 FILLER              PIC X(4).
      05 NAME                PIC X(18).
      05 SEX                 PIC X.
      05 FILLER              PIC XX.
      05 ALGEBRA             PIC X(3).
      05 GEOMETRY            PIC X(3).
      05 FILLER              PIC X(6).
      05 CHEMISTRY           PIC X(3).
      05 FILLER              PIC X(60).

* OUTPUT RECORD
 01   PRINT-PATTERN.
      05 FILLER              PIC X.
      05 NAME-OUT            PIC X(30).
      05 SEX-OUT             PIC X(10).
      05 ALGEBRA-GRADE-OUT   PIC X(10).
      05 GEOMETRY-GRADE-OUT  PIC X(10).
      05 CHEMISTRY-GRADE-OUT PIC X(72).
* DETAIL LINE HEADER INFORMATION
 01   DETAIL-HEADER
      05  FILLER             PIC X.
      05  FILLER             PIC X(29) VALUE 'NAME'.
      05  FILLER             PIC X(8)  VALUE 'SEX'.
      05  FILLER             PIC X(10) VALUE 'ALGEBRA'.
      05  FILLER             PIC X(10) VALUE 'GEOMETRY'.
      05  FILLER             PIC X(72) VALUE 'CHEMISTRY'.

 PROCEDURE DIVISION.

      OPEN INPUT STUDENT-FILE
           OUTPUT PRINTER.
*   PRINT THE HEADER
      WRITE PRINT-LINE FROM DETAIL-HEADER.
* FILE PROCESSING PAIR
      PERFORM READ-STUDENT.
      PERFORM LIST
          UNTIL NAME = HIGH-VALUES.
```

```
* TERMINATION ACTIVITY
      CLOSE STUDENT-FILE
            PRINTER.
      STOP RUN.

* INPUT PROCEDURE
 READ-STUDENT.
      READ STUDENT-FILE INTO STUDENT-INFO
          AT END MOVE HIGH-VALUES TO NAME.

*  RECORD PROCESSING
 LIST.
* IN ANY CASE CERTAIN FIELDS WILL BE PRINTED
* MOVE THESE FIELDS BEFORE DOING ANY PROCESSING
* THAT DEPENDS ON THE EVALUATION OF A CONDITION
      MOVE NAME          TO NAME-OUT.
      MOVE SEX           TO SEX-OUT.
      MOVE ALGEBRA       TO ALGEBRA-GRADE-OUT.
      IF SEX = 'F'
          MOVE GEOMETRY  TO GEOMETRY-GRADE-OUT
          MOVE SPACES    TO CHEMISTRY-GRADE-OUT
      ELSE
          MOVE SPACES    TO GEOMETRY-GRADE-OUT
          MOVE CHEMISTRY TO CHEMISTRY-GRADE-OUT.
      WRITE PRINT-LINE FROM PRINT-PATTERN.
      PERFORM READ-STUDENT.
```

(A)
(B)
(C)
(D)
(E)
(F)
(G)

(A)   The condition asks if the current content of the field called SEX is the symbol 'F'. If the condition is TRUE, the lines of code labeled (B) and (C) are executed. If the condition is FALSE, the lines of code labeled (E) and (F) are executed. In either case, after this processing, the next line of code to be executed is (G). Lines (B) and (C) are the *true range* of the condition, and lines (E) and (F) are the *false range* of the condition. Notice that ELSE (D) and the period at the end of (F) act like barriers to separate blocks of code. We also assume there are no values but 'F' and 'M' in the SEX field. We assume that the file has been preprocessed to discover any errors of that sort in the data.

The difference between a COBOL *statement* and a COBOL *sentence* is illustrated in PROGRAM-NUMBER 3.3-1. A **statement** is a syntactically valid combination of words and symbols written in the PROCEDURE DIVISION beginning with a verb. On the other hand, a **sentence** is a sequence of one or more statements, the last of which is terminated by a period followed by a space. Condition (A) in PROGRAM-NUMBER 3.3-1 has two statements to execute as its true range and a different two statements to execute as its false range. These statements together with the condition and the ELSE comprise one sentence.

Reusing a File in a Program

The output of this program would be more effective if all the records of female students were listed before all the records of male students. To do this we must go through the file two separate times to produce first a list of all records of the female students, and then the second time to produce a list of all the records of the male students. The following code is just what is needed to read the file twice. The paragraphs OUT and OUTT will supply the required listings.

```
        PROCEDURE DIVISION.
(A)         OPEN INPUT STUDENT-FILE
                OUTPUT PRINTER.

        * FILE PROCESSING PAIR
            PERFORM READ-STUDENT.
(B)         PERFORM LIST-FEMALES
                UNTIL NAME = HIGH-VALUES.

        * TERMINATION ACTIVITY
(C)         CLOSE STUDENT-FILE.

        * START ALL OVER AGAIN
(D)         OPEN INPUT STUDENT-FILE.

        * FILE PROCESSING PAIR
            PERFORM READ-STUDENT.
(E)         PERFORM LIST-MALES
                UNTIL NAME = HIGH-VALUES.

        * TERMINATION ACTIVITY
(F)         CLOSE STUDENT-FILE
                    PRINTER.
            STOP RUN.

        * RECORD PROCESSING
        LIST-FEMALES.
            IF SEX = 'F'
                PERFORM OUT.
            PERFORM READ-STUDENT.
        LIST-MALES.
            IF SEX = 'M'
                PERFORM OUTT.
            PERFORM READ-STUDENT.
```

(A)–(C) and (D)–(F) The STUDENT–FILE must be prepared for use so we can select the records with 'F' as a value for SEX. In (B) we have finished the listing of the female students (C) and CLOSEd the file. We know we can't read any more records at this time, because we have come to the end of the file. Therefore, we must "rewind" the file and reposition the read head at the beginning of the first record. This is accomplished by (D). In (E) we process the file a second time. Now when we come to the end of the file (F), we want to close both of the files we used and stop execution. The PRINTER file is not closed until the very end, since we must pass through the STUDENT–FILE twice, before generating all the lines to be printed. At any point in a program the files in use must act under an OPEN command. As we have seen in this example, this does not mean we only OPEN a file at the beginning of a program and only CLOSE it at the end of the program. Files can be opened and closed as they are needed.

Two-Across Mailing Labels

The next program involves a new approach to solving a problem. We will use a special value for a data field to indicate the processing required. Suppose we want to list all the

17-year-old students' names having two such names appear on each output line. We can illustrate the output line as follows:

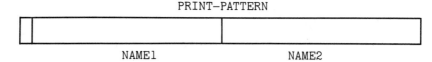

The problem that arises when we find the record of a 17-year-old student is deciding whether this NAME should be moved to NAME1 or to NAME2. We can easily solve this problem using hand calculations. If the first area of a line is filled, we will put the name in the second area, NAME2. We consider the next line on the page as having both the first and the second name areas blank, so the next name naturally goes in the first area, NAME1. What we are asking is whether or not the line is blank. If the answer is yes, we put the name in the first area, since the line will be filled only when a name has not already been put into NAME1. If the answer is no, we put the name in the second area, and then move on to the next line. Now let's find a simple computer solution to this problem. Suppose we have the following command right after we open our files.

```
MOVE SPACES TO PRINT-PATTERN
```

This, in effect, gives us a blank line. Now when processing a record of a 17-year-old student, if we ask

```
IF NAME1 = SPACES
```

and this condition is TRUE, we know we want to put the student's NAME in the area called NAME1. If the condition is FALSE, the NAME1 area is filled, and the student's NAME is put into NAME2. After filling NAME2 we are ready for

```
WRITE PRINT-LINE FROM PRINT-PATTERN.
```

This fills a line on the output page with two names. As we continue through the file, we want to simulate moving to the next line of the hand-calculated output. In the computer we don't have an endless supply of lines, we only have PRINT-PATTERN. To make this record look like the next line in the hand calculation model, we again

```
MOVE SPACES TO PRINT-PATTERN
```

This simulates the procedure of moving to the next line when you are solving this problem by hand. We can now repeat the procedure for deciding whether to put a name in NAME1 or NAME2 again and again, until the file is processed.

There is only one difficulty left to be resolved. When the end of file is encountered, a name may still be in the data field NAME1. How do we cause the computer to write this last name? We know that both NAME1 and NAME2 cannot contain student names, since complete lines are printed. In addition, if a complete line has been printed just before executing the READ statement that triggers the AT END option, the PRINT-PATTERN area will only contain blanks. Therefore, after control passes from the sentence

```
PERFORM para-name-2
      UNTIL end-of-file-flag = HIGH-VALUES
```

we must ask if anything but SPACES is in NAME1. If so, we must print this line with the one remaining NAME before performing the CLOSE tasks. If not, we can perform the CLOSE tasks directly.

Simulating hand calculations with COBOL code will become easy as we examine more programs. Now let's examine how this discussion fits into a complete program.

```
*
* NAME:                         ID:
* PROGRAM-NUMBER:  3.3-2
* DESCRIPTION: LIST THE NAME OF EACH 17
*   YEAR-OLD STUDENT. PUT TWO NAMES ON
*   EACH OUTPUT LINE.
*
        COPY TEXTA.
    WORKING-STORAGE SECTION.

* INPUT RECORD
    01  STUDENT-INFO.
        05 FILLER PIC X(4).
        05 NAME   PIC X(18).
        05 FILLER PIC X.
        05 AGE    PIC XX.
        05 FILLER PIC X(75).

* OUTPUT RECORD
    01  PRINT-PATTERN.
        05 FILLER PIC X.
        05 NAME1  PIC X(25).
        05 NAME2  PIC X(107).



    PROCEDURE DIVISION.

        OPEN INPUT STUDENT-FILE
             OUTPUT PRINTER.

* INITIALIZATION
        MOVE SPACES TO PRINT-PATTERN.

* FILE PROCESSING PAIR
        PERFORM READ-A-RECORD.
        PERFORM TWO-ACROSS
            UNTIL NAME = HIGH-VALUES.

* TERMINATION ACTIVITY
        IF NAME1 = SPACES
            NEXT SENTENCE
        ELSE
            WRITE PRINT-LINE FROM PRINT-PATTERN.
        CLOSE STUDENT-FILE
              PRINTER.
        STOP RUN.

* INPUT PROCEDURE
    READ-A-RECORD.
        READ STUDENT-FILE INTO STUDENT-INFO
            AT END MOVE HIGH-VALUES TO NAME.

* RECORD PROCESSING
    TWO-ACROSS.
        IF AGE = '17'
            PERFORM FILL.
        PERFORM READ-A-RECORD.
```

(A)

(B)

(C)

(D)
```
      FILL.
          IF NAME1 = SPACES
              MOVE NAME TO NAME1
          ELSE
              MOVE NAME TO NAME2
              WRITE PRINT-LINE FROM PRINT-PATTERN
              MOVE SPACES TO PRINT-PATTERN.
```

(A) We start the PRINT–PATTERN as if it were a blank line. The process of giving a value to a field before a particular processing can be completed is called **initialization.** This command is needed to make PRINT–PATTERN look like a blank line on a piece of paper. This is the key for determining whether a NAME is to be put in NAME1 or NAME2.

(B) After the file is processed, there may or may not be a value in NAME1. The condition shown here is TRUE when no NAME is in NAME1 (and consequently, no NAME is in NAME2) and FALSE when a NAME does exist in NAME1 (but not in NAME2). When the condition is TRUE we are ready to stop. When the condition is FALSE, we must print one more line. The condition generates these options. The NEXT SENTENCE command in the TRUE range merely passes control to the next sentence in the program, which, in this case, is

```
              CLOSE STUDENT-FILE
                    PRINTER.
```

The question we ask does not require any action when the condition is TRUE. Action is required *only* when this condition is FALSE. This construction simplifies the logic needed at this point in the program. The reserved words NEXT SENTENCE are the way we say *do nothing* but go on to the next sentence in the program if the condition is TRUE. The use of NEXT SENTENCE as the true range of the condition makes it possible to ask the natural question at this point rather than its negation. We do not MOVE SPACES to PRINT–PATTERN after printing this remaining NAME, since all the records are now processed, and we are ready to stop execution.

(C) This paragraph selects for further processing the records that satisfy the required condition. After the record is either selected and processed or not selected, we access the next record in the file. The problem remaining is how to fill in PRINT–PATTERN when a record is selected for further processing.

(D) When a record is selected for processing, we must decide whether the current contents of NAME are to be put in NAME1 or NAME2. Whenever we come to this paragraph and PRINT–PATTERN looks like a blank line, the condition is TRUE, and we put NAME in NAME1. When the condition is FALSE, a value exists in NAME1, so we put NAME in NAME2. In this latter case, we have a complete line of output. Therefore, we print the line and move SPACES to PRINT–PATTERN again. The next time we come to this paragraph, we will put a NAME in NAME1.

SYNTAX SUMMARY

$$
\text{IF} \begin{Bmatrix} \text{data-name-1} \\ \text{literal-1} \end{Bmatrix} \text{IS [\underline{NOT}]} \begin{Bmatrix} \underline{\text{EQUAL}} \\ \underline{\text{LESS}} \text{ THAN} \\ \underline{\text{GREATER}} \text{ THAN} \end{Bmatrix} \begin{Bmatrix} \text{data-name-2} \\ \text{literal-2} \end{Bmatrix}
$$

$$
\text{THEN} \begin{Bmatrix} \text{statements-1} \\ \underline{\text{NEXT}} \text{ SENTENCE} \end{Bmatrix}
$$

$$
\text{ELSE} \begin{Bmatrix} \text{statements-2} \\ \underline{\text{NEXT}} \text{ SENTENCE} \end{Bmatrix} .
$$

EXERCISES

1. What code in TEXTA is actually needed by PROGRAM–NUMBER 3.3-1?
2. Briefly explain the following terms:

   a. sentence   c. true range
   b. statement   d. false range

3. What is the semantics of the statement

   NEXT SENTENCE

   Is there any difference in the semantics of the following two sentences:

   ```
   a. IF NAME > 'N'
          NEXT SENTENCE
      ELSE
          PERFORM OUT-RTN.

   b. IF NAME NOT > 'N'
          PERFORM OUT-RTN.
   ```

4. Why solve a problem for a few typical cases before writing any code?
5. Rewrite the following sentences using an IF...THEN...ELSE construction:

   ```
   IF NAME > 'M'
           PERFORM SECOND-HALF.
   IF NAME NOT > 'M'
           PERFORM FIRST-HALF.
   ```

PROGRAM TESTING AND MODIFICATION EXERCISE

1. For the following program, list the order in which the statements are executed. Use the numbers on the left for listing purposes. Also indicate what will be printed if the first eleven records of CUSTOMER–FILE are processed.

```
        COPY TEXTA.
    WORKING-STORAGE SECTION.
    * INPUT RECORD
      01  CUSTOMER-RECORD.
          05  CUSTOMER-NUMBER  PIC X(8).
          05  NAME            PIC X(20).
          05  FILLER          PIC X(52).
          05  AMOUNT-DUE      PIC X(9).
          05  REGION-CODE     PIC X.
          05  CREDIT-LIMIT    PIC X.
          05  FILLER          PIC X(9).

1     01  BLANK-LINE          PIC X(133) VALUE SPACES.

    * OUTPUT RECORD
      01  PRINT-RECORD.
          05  FILLER          PIC X.
          05  CUSTOMER-NUMBER PIC X(20).
          05  NAME            PIC X(30).
          05  AMOUNT-DUE-FIELD PIC X(82).

2     PROCEDURE DIVISION.

3         OPEN INPUT CUSTOMER-FILE
                OUTPUT PRINTER.
```

```
         * FILE PROCESSING PAIR
4              PERFORM READ-CUSTOMER-RECORD.
5              PERFORM LISTING
                   UNTIL CUSTOMER-NUMBER IN CUSTOMER-RECORD
                                       = HIGH-VALUES.
         * TERMINATION ACTIVITY
6              CLOSE CUSTOMER-FILE
                     PRINTER.
7              STOP RUN.


         * INPUT PROCEDURE
         READ-CUSTOMER-RECORD.
8              READ CUSTOMER-FILE INTO CUSTOMER-RECORD
9                  AT END MOVE HIGH-VALUES TO
                       CUSTOMER-NUMBER IN CUSTOMER-RECORD.


         * RECORD PROCESSING
         LISTING.
10             IF REGION-CODE EQUALS 'A'
11                 PERFORM OUTT.
12             PERFORM READ-CUSTOMER-RECORD.
         *

         *
         OUTT.
13             MOVE CORRESPONDING CUSTOMER-RECORD TO
                       PRINT-RECORD.
15             IF CREDIT-LIMIT GREATHER THAN '2'
16                 MOVE AMOUNT-DUE TO AMOUNT-DUE-FIELD
               ELSE
17                 MOVE '***'      TO AMOUNT-DUE-FIELD.
18             WRITE PRINT-LINE FROM PRINT-RECORD.
19             WRITE PRINT-LINE FROM BLANK-LINE.
```

Number	Name	Amt-Due	Region	C-Limit
51900000	Weinsmeier CFR	000000123	A	2
51900100	Menzies RG	000001254	A	2
51900200	Bayless GF	000000432	A	2
51900300	Gray MJ	000154374	A	4
51900400	Mathews B	000015435	A	3
51900500	Battistas LB	000002323	A	2
61900500	Samuels HR	000056782	A	3
51900700	Mitchell JE	000567845	A	4
51900800	Cooper RH	000056745	A	3
51900900	Graham JW	000043567	A	3
51901000	Dyck TA	00000456P	C	2

PROGRAMMING PROBLEMS

1. Modify PROGRAM-NUMBER 3.3-1 to include appropriate headings. Also modify
   the code so that a MOVE CORRESPONDING statement can be used for NAME,
   SEX, and ALGEBRA grade.
2. Modify PROGRAM-NUMBER 3.3-2 so that information is printed before the first
   label to identify the output to follow. This should be the kind of information you
   expect to find on the title page of a report.
3. Using the NEW-WORLD-FILE for input, list the NAME, HOME-ADDRESS, and
   CITY for all customers from Maine or New York. List all the New York customers
   before all the Maine customers.

4. Using the REGISTRAR–FILE for input, list the NAME of each student with at least 100 as a value for TOTAL–HOURS. List two names on each line of output.
5. Using CUSTOMER–FILE for input, prepare a report that lists the NAME, STREET, and CITY for customers with EXPIRATION–DATE before January 1, 1985. For all other customers list NAME and YEAR of EXPIRATION–DATE.
6. List the AGE, SEX, and PHYSICS grade of each student in STUDENT–FILE with ALGEBRA grade less than PHYSICS grade. List the AGE, SEX, and ALGEBRA grade for all other students.
7. List the NAME and CLASS for students in the REGISTRAR–FILE with TOTAL–HOURS greater than 100. For all other students list NAME and CAMPUS–ADDRESS.

Model II   Cleaning Up After End of File

In the mailing label problem examined in the previous section, the pseudocode outline of Model I did not really fit. There were two kinds of processing required by that problem that do not occur in a problem that can use the pseudocode outline of Model I. The first difference was that we needed to initialize some storage areas in the mailing label problem before the first record was processed. This was done before the file processing pair was executed. This activity is called

```
***   INITIALIZATION
```

The second difference is that after the file was processed, there was still the possibility that one label needed was still in memory. To take care of this possibility, we include a command after the program detected that the file had been processed and before the files were CLOSED. This is called

```
***   TERMINATION ACTIVITY
```

By adding these two activities to the pseudocode outline of Model I, we get a different program model, Model II.

A listing of the pseudocode outline for developing programs of the type characterized as Model II is shown at the top of the next page. The key to deciding if this is the appropriate model to use is that the solution of the problem requires some action after the end–of–file condition has been triggered.

This refinement process that a program undergoes suggests another objective for us to keep in mind.

Objective

Write correct programs that compile the first time they are run by testing each step of the refinement process with hand calculations and with test data.

This Model will be even more useful when we have introduced the arithmetic commands. The problem of totaling the value for the sum of the amount due for all records in a file is a typical application of this Model. Another problem of this sort is printing mailing labels on special forms such as the ones shown on the next page.

```
        COPY TEXTA.
    WORKING-STORAGE SECTION.
*** RECORD DESCRIPTION OF INPUT RECORD

*** RECORD DESCRIPTION OF OUTPUT RECORD

 PROCEDURE DIVISION

*** OPEN FILES

*** INITIALIZE VARIABLES

*** FILE PROCESSING PAIR
        PERFORM para-name-1.
        PERFORM para-name-2
            UNTIL end-of-file-flag = HIGH-VALUES.
*** TERMINATION ACTIVITY

*** CLOSE FILES & STOP RUN

*** INPUT PROCEDURE
 para-name-1.
        READ input file INTO input record
            AT END MOVE HIGH-VALUES TO end-of-file-flag.


 para-name-2.
*** PROCESS THE RECORD IN MEMORY

*** ACCESS THE NEXT RECORD.
        PERFORM para-name-1.
```

When the last record in a file has been processed, only some of the labels in a row may be filled up as pictured. These last labels need to be printed, and the code to do this is executed after the file has been processed.

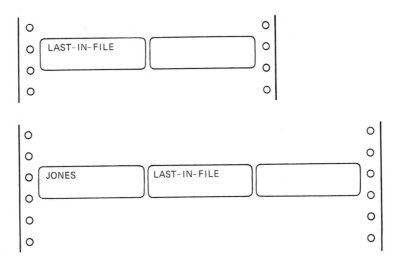

EXERCISES

1. What is the role of INITIALIZATION statements in a program?
2. What is the role of TERMINATION ACTIVITY statements in a program?
3. What are the major differences between Model I and Model II?
4. Can Model II be viewed as a stepwise refinement of Model I? Explain your answer.

3.4   Nested IF Statements

The ability to differentiate between two possibilities by means of an IF...THEN...ELSE statement is a first step toward understanding all the capabilities of COBOL to ask questions about the contents of memory locations. However, we are still not conveniently able to differentiate among three or more possibilities. For example, the region code in the customer information file will be one of the three symbols 'A', 'B', or 'C'. If each of these values of REGION–CODE is to trigger different kinds of processing, we can approach the solution as follows:

```
IF REGION-CODE = 'A'
    PERFORM A-OUT.
IF REGION-CODE = 'B'
    PERFORM B-OUT.
IF REGION-CODE = 'C'
    PERFORM C-OUT.
```

These three sentences will certainly solve the problem. We can see right away that this is a general solution for the problem. Three cases or thirty cases can be differentiated by an appropriate number of such sentences. Notice, however, that if the first condition is true, then the second and third conditions will still be evaluated, even though they are false. A more sophisticated solution involves nesting the IF statements. Let's look again at the form of the IF...THEN...ELSE statement.

```
IF condition
    true range
ELSE
    false range.
```

Nothing prohibits our making the false range of the condition another IF...THEN...ELSE statement. This is an instance of combining basic control structures in a structured way to handle more complex logical problems. Let's look at our example with the region code this way:

```
IF REGION-CODE = 'A'
    PERFORM OUT-A
ELSE
    IF REGION-CODE = 'B'
        PERFORM OUT-B
    ELSE
        IF REGION-CODE = 'C'
            PERFORM OUT-C.
```

The false range of REGION–CODE = 'A' is the second IF...THEN...ELSE statement and it differentiates between the remaining two cases. Clearly, if control were passed to the false range of the first condition we would know that REGION–CODE is not equal to 'A', so it must be either 'B' or 'C'. These two possibilities are differentiated by the IF...THEN...ELSE statement that begins with

```
IF REGION-CODE = 'B'
```

The indentation used shows how the true and false ranges of a complex condition are related. The COBOL language will pair the false range to the first preceding condition. In this case

```
IF REGION CODE = 'C'
    PERFORM OUT-C
```

is the false range of the condition

```
IF REGION-CODE = 'B'
```

and the condition

```
IF REGION-CODE = 'B'
    PERFORM OUT-B
ELSE
    IF REGION-CODE = 'C'
        PERFORM OUT-C
```

is the false range of the condition

```
IF REGION-CODE = 'A'
```

The advantage of this construction is that unnecessary conditions will not be evaluated. For example, if

```
REGION-CODE = 'A'
```

is true, then

```
PERFORM OUT-A
```

will be executed, and control will pass to the sentence that begins after the period following OUT–C. If

```
REGION-CODE = 'B'
```

is true, then after executing

```
PERFORM OUT-B
```

control passes to the next sentence that begins after the period following OUT–C. If

```
REGION-CODE = 'C'
```

is true, we would have evaluated all three conditions before finding one that is true. In each of the other cases, we only test conditions until we find one that is true. The program then continues at the next sentence, ignoring conditions for which we already have an answer. Again, the logic used can be different than we expected if the IF's and ELSE's are not properly nested. The habit of indenting or nesting to show the logical relationship between IF's and ELSE's is a good programming habit to acquire. We will now see how this concept is used in a program.

```
*
* NAME:                              ID:
* PROGRAM-NUMBER: 3.4-1
* DESCRIPTION:  PRINT A MAILING LABEL FOR EACH RECORD
*   IN CUSTOMER-FILE AND INDICATE ON THE LABEL THE
*   REGION OF THE CUSTOMER.
*
     COPY TEXTA.
WORKING-STORAGE SECTION.


* INPUT RECORD
01   CHARGE-CUSTOMER.
     05 FILLER       PIC X(8).
     05 NAME         PIC X(20).
     05 STREET       PIC X(20).
     05 CITY         PIC X(20).
     05 FILLER       PIC X(21).
     05 REGION-CODE  PIC X.
     05 FILLER       PIC X(10).


* OUTPUT RECORD
01   PRINT-PATTERN.
     05 FILLER       PIC X.
     05 GOOD-INFO  PIC X(30).
     05 KEY-MARK   PIC X(102).


PROCEDURE DIVISION.
* MODEL-I.
     OPEN INPUT CUSTOMER-FILE
          OUTPUT PRINTER.


* FILE PROCESSING PAIR
     PERFORM READ-A-RECORD.
     PERFORM LABEL-AND-TAG
          UNTIL NAME = HIGH-VALUES.


* TERMINATION ACTIVITY
     CLOSE CUSTOMER-FILE
          PRINTER.
     STOP RUN.


* INPUT PROCEDURE
READ-A-RECORD.
     READ CUSTOMER-FILE INTO CHARGE-CUSTOMER
          AT END MOVE HIGH-VALUES TO NAME.


* RECORD PROCESSING
* PRINT A MAILING LABEL WITH THE REGION
* IDENTIFIED. THEN GET THE NEXT RECORD
LABEL-AND-TAG.
     MOVE NAME TO GOOD-INFO.
```

(A)
```
IF REGION-CODE = 'A'
    MOVE '*' TO KEY-MARK
ELSE
    IF REGION-CODE = 'B'
        MOVE '**' TO KEY-MARK
    ELSE
        IF REGION-CODE = 'C'
            MOVE '***' TO KEY-MARK.
WRITE PRINT-LINE FROM PRINT-PATTERN.
MOVE STREET TO GOOD-INFO.
MOVE SPACES TO KEY-MARK.
WRITE PRINT-LINE FROM PRINT-PATTERN.
MOVE CITY   TO GOOD-INFO.
WRITE PRINT-LINE FROM PRINT-PATTERN.
PERFORM READ-A-RECORD.
```
(B)

(A)
The mark on the mailing label distinguishing the REGION–CODE is not for use by the addressee. The mark is for internal use, to help in handling the mail going out or the mail being returned. The labels may be separated by REGION–CODE and sent some place else for use. In any case, this differentiation is accomplished by a Nested IF construction. This sentence has the same effect as the following three sentences.

```
IF REGION-CODE = 'A'
    MOVE '*'   TO KEY-MARK.
IF REGION-CODE = 'B'
    MOVE '**'  TO KEY - MARK.
IF REGION-CODE = 'C'
    MOVE '***' TO KEY-MARK.
```

Remember that with the Nested IF construction we may evaluate fewer conditions. It may be useful to determine which value of REGION–CODE occurs most often so that, as often as possible, the first question is the only one asked. Many of the program efficiencies we employ depend on a better knowledge about patterns that occur in the records of the file being processed. We can't always determine if some feature of the code will lead to efficiencies in all cases, or if the efficiency proposed for one file can be improved differently for other files. This is why programming must always keep in touch with the files being processed. We can learn general guidelines for writing programs, however we should expect that each generalization will be modified when applied to a particular programming task.

(B)
The current content of the storage location KEY–MARK is either '*' or '**' or '***'. This information is needed on the line with the customer's NAME but not needed on either of the other two lines. Therefore, we blank out this field before loading and printing the STREET and the CITY. An interesting alternative to this requires a modification of the PRINT–PATTERN. If we replace

```
05 GOOD-INFO   PIC X(30).
05 KEY-MARK    PIC X(102)
```

by the following:

```
05 GOOD-INFO.
    10 FILLER   PIC X(30).
    10 KEY-MARK PIC X(102).
```

we can now omit the line of code labeled (B), since the statement

```
MOVE STREET TO GOOD-INFO
```

automatically puts blanks in the 132 byte field GOOD–INFO after the information in STREET has been moved to the left-most 20 bytes of this 132-byte field.

The technique of viewing a storage location as having two different logical organizations within a single program is very helpful. The EXPIRATION–DATE field of NEW–WORLD–FILE is of the form day/month/year. Suppose at one point of a program it is required to print this field whenever the year represents 1981. In this case a useful description of the field would be

```
05  EXPIRATION-DATE.
    10  EXPIRE-DAY     PIC XX.
    10  EXPIRE-MONTH   PIC XX.
    10  EXPIRE-YEAR    PIC XX.
```

Other references in the program to the field EXPIRATION–DATE could use six bytes of information. The 05-level entry does not contain a picture clause because it is further subdivided into three 10-level fields. The 10-level fields contain a picture clause because they are not further subdivided. A field that is not subdivided is called an **elementary item.** Each elementary item must have a picture clause describing it.

EXERCISES

1. Explain the rule for determining how the IFs and ELSEs are paired in a Nested IF construction.

2. Why is indentation a useful design tool, especially in the case of the Nested IF construction?

3. The ACE SUPPLY CO. has a file with a coded field that takes on one of 'X', 'Z', or '99' as a value. If it is known that there are more records with the coded value 'X' than records with any other value, what would be the most efficient way to write a Nested IF construction so that different processing could be accomplished for each different code value? What would your answer be if it were also known that there are more records with a code value of 'Z' than records with a code value of '99'?

4. Using the values for G1, G2, G3, G4, and G5 found in Record1–Record6 list the value that will be in the storage location G1 after each of the blocks of code a, b, and c has been executed.

	G1	G2	G3	G4	G5
RECORD1	065	063	085	056	076
RECORD2	065	086	085	084	074
RECORD3	075	072	070	068	065
RECORD4	070	058	083	064	090
RECORD5	080	080	075	074	085
RECORD6	072	074	075	075	075

a.
```
IF G1 > G2
    NEXT SENTENCE
ELSE
    MOVE G2 TO G1.
IF G1 > G3
    NEXT SENTENCE
ELSE
    MOVE G3 TO G1.
IF G1 > G4
    NEXT SENTENCE
ELSE
    MOVE G4 TO G1.
IF G1 > G5
    NEXT SENTENCE
ELSE
    MOVE G5 TO G1.
```
b.
```
IF NOT (G1 > G2)
    MOVE G2 TO G1
ELSE
    IF NOT (G1 > G3)
        MOVE G3 TO G1
    ELSE
        IF NOT (G1 > G4)
            MOVE G4 TO G1
        ELSE
            IF NOT (G1 > G5)
                MOVE G5 TO G1.
```
c.
```
IF G2 > G1
    MOVE G2 TO G1
ELSE
    IF G3 > G1
        MOVE G3 TO G1
    ELSE
        IF G4 > G1
            MOVE G4 TO G1
        ELSE
            IF G5 > G1
                MOVE G5 TO G1.
```

5. Write a record description for REGISTRAR–FILE that would allow a program to reference the student by first name, or last name, or both names with the last name appearing first.

PROGRAMMING PROBLEMS

1. Prepare three-across mailing labels for customers in CUSTOMER–FILE who live in the United States. Each label should include the customer's NAME, STREET, and CITY, as well as the REGION–CODE. Place the REGION–CODE to the right of the NAME.

2. Prepare three-across mailing labels using the STUDENT–FILE. List the NAME on one line, the SEX, AGE, and IDENTIFICATION–NUMBER on a second line, and

the GRADEs on the third line. Do this for all students with a CHEMISTRY grade greater than the PHYSICS grade.

3. Prepare a list of the NAMEs of all students in STUDENT–FILE. Print '*' after the NAME if ENGLISH is greater than PHYSICS, '**' after the NAME if ENGLISH is equal to PHYSICS, and '***' otherwise.

4. Prepare a report that lists the NAME of each customer in the CUSTOMER–FILE and a 3-character code indicating the year the credit card expires. Use 'X' for 1984, 'Y' for 1985, and 'Z' for 1986. This coding will allow the Helpful Loan Co. to determine from your list which customers should apply for their credit card rather than renew with NEW–WORLD.

5. Using the STUDENT–FILE for input, prepare a report that lists (1) the NAME and ALGEBRA grade for 14- and 15-year-olds; (2) the NAME and CHEMISTRY grade for 16-year-olds; and (3) the NAME and both ALGEBRA and CHEMISTRY grades for 17-, 18-, and 19-year-olds. Include appropriate headings.

6. For 16-year-old students in STUDENT–FILE, display the NAME, ALGEBRA, and GEOMETRY grades if ENGLISH is greater than PHYSICS. In case the PHYSICS grade is greater than the ENGLISH grade, display the NAME and the ENGLISH grade. In the case of equality, display the NAME and all the grades.

7. Using the STUDENT–FILE for input and a Nested IF construction, test the following conditions in the order they are listed:

   a. ENGLISH   > PHYSICS
   b. PHYSICS   > GEOMETRY
   c. GEOMETRY > CHEMISTRY
   d. CHEMISTRY > ALGEBRA

If all the conditions are false, print the largest grade. Otherwise, at the time a true condition is found, print the largest grade so far encountered in the record being processed. If condition a is false, then

$$\text{PHYSICS NOT LESS THAN ENGLISH}$$

If condition a is false and condition b is true, then PHYSICS is the largest grade encountered at that point.

3.5   Compound Conditions

It is necessary to see how COBOL differentiates cases when processing depends on multiple or compound conditions. Suppose we must list 14-year-old male students with high ALGEBRA grades and 16- or 17-year-old female students with high PHYSICS grades. The conditions we have seen so far have required only one condition to be tested. In COBOL we can put a series of simple conditions together using the logical connectives AND and OR. In this example, the simple conditions are

```
SEX = 'M'
AGE = '14'
AGE = '16'
AGE = '17'
SEX = 'F'
```

Our task is to put these five conditions together, so that the end result is true or false appropriately. The condition for the male students is that the first two simple conditions be true at the same time. We write them as

```
(1)    SEX = 'M' AND AGE = '14'
```

These two conditions, joined by AND, will be true if, and only if, each of the individual conditions is true. The compound condition for females is a bit different, since two of the conditions cannot be simultaneously true. In fact, we will only ask that one of the two age conditions be true. This is done by joining the two age conditions by OR, as follows:

```
AGE = '16' OR AGE = '17'.
```

The combination of two conditions joined by OR is true if at least one of the conditions is true. We now want to treat this as a single condition and join it to the condition SEX = 'F' by the logical operator AND. We write

```
(2)    SEX = 'F' AND (AGE = '16' OR AGE = '17').
```

The parentheses guarantee that the age conditions will be evaluated as a unit whose logical value (true or false) will be used as one of the operands for AND. The condition we were evaluating originally was that either (1) or (2) be true. Therefore, if we join the two compound conditions by an OR, we will have the condition we want

```
(SEX = 'M' AND AGE = '14') OR
(SEX = 'F' AND (AGE = '16' OR AGE = '17'))
```

We have included a pair of parentheses around each of the conditions to ensure that these conditions are first evaluated separately, and then put together using OR.

Evaluation of Logical Expressions

The compiler follows rules when evaluating logical expressions. The rules are executed in the following order.

1. Evaluate the expressions in parentheses starting with the innermost pair and working out.
2. Evaluate the AND operators in the order of occurrence proceeding from left to right.
3. Evaluate the OR operators in the order of occurrence proceeding from left to right.

A **compound condition** is defined to be a condition in which one or more of the operators AND and OR are used in the same IF statement. There is also a NOT operator that merely reverses the logical value of the condition or expression on which it acts. The NOT operator is executed before any AND or OR operators in an expression.

Table 3.2 summarizes the way COBOL evaluates conditions depending on the truth values of the simple conditions.

TABLE 3.2

P	Q	NOT P	P AND Q	P OR Q
TRUE	TRUE	FALSE	TRUE	TRUE
TRUE	FALSE	FALSE	FALSE	TRUE
FALSE	TRUE	TRUE	FALSE	TRUE
FALSE	FALSE	TRUE	FALSE	FALSE

Now let's look at the logic in action.

```
      *
      * NAME:                        ID:
      * PROGRAM-NUMBER: 3.5-1
      * DESCRIPTION: LIST THE GRADES OF ANY STUDENTS WITH
      *   ALGEBRA, PHYSICS, AND CHEMISTRY GRADES EACH GREATER
      *   THAN '070' OR ENGLISH, ALGEBRA, AND CHEMISTRY
      *   GRADES EACH GREATER THAN '075'.
      *
            COPY TEXTA.
        WORKING-STORAGE SECTION.


      * INPUT RECORD
(A)     01  STUDENT-INFO.
            05 FILLER     PIC X(4).
            05 NAME       PIC X(18).
            05 FILLER     PIC X(3).
            05 ALGEBRA    PIC X(3).
            05 GEOMETRY   PIC X(3).
            05 ENGLISH    PIC X(3).
            05 PHYSICS    PIC X(3).
            05 CHEMISTRY  PIC X(3).
            05 FILLER     PIC X(60).



      * OUTPUT RECORD
        01  PRINT-PATTERN.
            05 FILLER        PIC X.
            05 NAME-OUT       PIC X(35).
            05 PHYSICS-OUT    PIC X(10).
            05 ALGEBRA-OUT    PIC X(10).
            05 CHEMISTRY-OUT  PIC X(10).
            05 ENGLISH-OUT    PIC X(10).
            05 GEOMETRY-OUT   PIC X(57).
      * HEADER
(B)     01  HEADER.
            05 FILLER PIC X.
            05 FILLER PIC X(33)  VALUE 'NAME'.
            05 FILLER PIC X(112) VALUE
            'PHYSICS  ALGEBRA  CHEMISTRY  ENGLISH  GEOMETRY'.



        PROCEDURE DIVISION.
      * MODEL-I.
            OPEN INPUT STUDENT-FILE
                OUTPUT PRINTER.


      * INITIALIZATION
            WRITE PRINT-LINE FROM HEADER.


      * FILE PROCESSING PAIR
            PERFORM READ-A-RECORD.
            PERFORM MAKE-LIST
                UNTIL NAME = HIGH-VALUES.
```

```
* TERMINATION ACTIVITY
      CLOSE STUDENT-FILE
            PRINTER.
      STOP RUN.

* INPUT PROCEDURE
  READ-A-RECORD.
      READ STUDENT-FILE INTO STUDENT-INFO
          AT END MOVE HIGH-VALUES TO NAME.

* RECORD PROCESSING
  MAKE-LIST.
      IF (ALGEBRA > '070' AND PHYSICS > '070'
          AND CHEMISTRY > '070')   OR
          (ENGLISH > '075' AND ALGEBRA > '075'
            AND CHEMISTRY > '075')
          PERFORM OUT-INFO.
      PERFORM READ-A-RECORD.
  OUT-INFO.
      MOVE NAME       TO NAME-OUT.
      MOVE ALGEBRA    TO ALGEBRA-OUT.
      MOVE CHEMISTRY  TO CHEMISTRY-OUT.
      MOVE GEOMETRY   TO GEOMETRY-OUT.
      MOVE PHYSICS    TO PHYSICS-OUT.
      MOVE ENGLISH    TO ENGLISH-OUT.
      WRITE PRINT-LINE FROM PRINT-PATTERN.
```

(C)

(D)

(A)   Several fields in each record of the STUDENT-FILE are not used in this program. We account for them by using FILLER instead of data names. We must account for the space so that the data names used correspond to the needed information in the record.

(B)   The header line is set up at compile time. Values can be put in storage locations at compile time by using the VALUE clause. When the information we are putting in a storage location cannot be written on a single line we use the *continuation* feature for nonnumeric literals (strings of characters). This feature is complicated enough that it bears repeating at this point even though we do not need it for this literal. The COBOL syntax requires using all the columns of the line, up to and including column 72. On the next line we need a hyphen in column 7 and an opening quote in column 12 or beyond. The character string is continued after this quote just as if the character were being put in column 73 of the previous card. If additional lines are needed, this procedure may be repeated until the string is completed. The pattern used for the heading was

```
--PHYSICS---ALGEBRA--CHEMISTRY--ENGLISH---GEOMETRY
   XXX        XXX        XXX       XXX        XXX
```

The hyphens are included to indicate how the output will be spaced on the printed line. These hyphens will not appear as part of the output. The XXX patterns indicate where the characters in the data fields of the input record will be printed. We then count spaces to ensure that this pattern is correct.

(C)–(D)   It would be nice to have the condition and then in OUT-INFO use a MOVE CORRE-SPONDING. However, that would require qualifying each data name in the condition—too great a price to pay.

SYNTAX SUMMARY

CONDITION

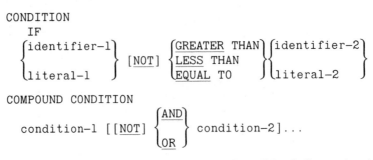

COMPOUND CONDITION

```
            (AND)
condition-1 [[NOT] {   } condition-2]...
            ( OR )
```

The formalism used to describe a compound condition indicates that the syntax contained in the outer pair of square braces can be repeated as many times as needed.

EXERCISES

1. Define the following:

   a. simple condition   c. continuation of nonnumeric literal
   b. compound condition   d. logical operator

2. What truth values can be assigned to the simple conditions A and B so that:

   a. A AND B is TRUE   c. A OR B is FALSE
   b. A OR B is TRUE   d. A OR NOT B is TRUE

3. Which of the following have the same truth values regardless of which truth values are assigned to the simple conditions A and B?

   a. NOT (A OR B)   c. NOT A AND NOT B
   b. NOT (A AND B)   d. NOT A OR NOT B

   Evaluate each of these expressions for the first five records of the STUDENT–FILE if

$$AGE > '14' \quad and \quad SEX = 'M'$$

   are the simple conditions A and B, respectively.

For each of the following logical expressions, find the first five records in the STUDENT–FILE that satisfy the expression. Indicate the five records by listing the record's STUDENT–NUMBER.

4. STUDENT–NUMBER > '2725'
       AND NAME < 'B'
       AND ALGEBRA NOT GREATER THAN PHYSICS

5. NOT (STUDENT–NUMBER > '2725'
       AND NAME < 'B')
       OR ALGEBRA NOT GREATER THAN PHYSICS

6. ALGEBRA > CHEMISTRY AND
       (PHYSICS < ENGLISH OR GEOMETRY < '080'
       AND SEX = 'F')

7. ALGEBRA > CHEMISTRY AND PHYSICS < ENGLISH
       OR GEOMETRY > '080' AND SEX = 'F'

8. ALGEBRA > CHEMISTRY AND
       PHYSICS < ENGLISH
       OR (GEOMETRY < '080' AND SEX = 'F')

```
9. NOT (ALGEBRA > CHEMISTRY
        AND PHYSICS > ENGLISH)
```

For each of the following logical expressions, find the first five records in the REG-ISTRAR–FILE that satisfy the expression. Indicate the five records by listing the student's NAME.

```
10. NOT (MATH-13 > PHILOSOPHY-3 AND GOVERNMENT - 3 > ENGLISH-2)
```

```
11. NOT (PHILOSOPHY-3 > ENGLISH-2 AND GEOGRAPHY-10 > MATH-13)
```

PROGRAMMING PROBLEMS

1. List the NAME and each of the five GRADEs for any student in REGISTRAR–FILE who received either an A in both MATH–13 and GEOGRAPHY–10 or at least a B in GOVERNMENT–3 and ENGLISH–2.
2. Prepare a report listing customers of NEW–WORLD–FILE who live in Maine or California and have a CREDIT–RATING of 2, 4, or 5. Include appropriate headings both for the report and the listed information.
3. List the students in the file REGISTRAR–FILE who are at least 21 years old and have a CUMULATIVE–GPA of at least 3.00. Also list all students who are less than 18 years old. *Hint:* The GPA condition should be tested as GPA > '300'.
4. List the customers in CUSTOMER–FILE who have an EXPIRATION–DATE of 1985 and an AMOUNT–DUE of less than $600.00 or any customers with an AMOUNT–DUE of more than $1,000.00. First try this with the compound condition of the form (condition–1 and condition–2 or condition–3). Then try the same program with the compound condition written as (condition–1 and (condition–2 or condition–3)). *Hint:* $600 is represented as '000060000' in CUSTOMER–FILE.
5. Prepare three-across mailing labels for all customers in CUSTOMER–FILE who do not live in Canada and who owe at least $500.00 or who have CREDIT–LIMIT at least 3. Try this first with the compound condition of the form:

```
        (REGION = 'A' AND AMOUNT-DUE > '000050000')
                    OR CREDIT-LIMIT > '2'
```

Then try the same program with the condition:

```
                REGION = 'A' AND
        (AMOUNT-DUE > '000050000' OR CREDIT-LIMIT > '2')
```

Are the answers the same?

3.6   Multiple Record Descriptions

TEXTA is very helpful for freeing the programmer to focus on the logic of the solution of the problem at hand. There are, however, important business applications that require the programmer to write this portion of a COBOL program. One such application involves files that have records with different record descriptions. For example, a file may contain one type of record for all transactions by a customer in a billing period together with another type of record giving the customer's mailing address. Following the description of the problem we want to solve and before examining the code needed, we examine an alternate form of the READ and WRITE statements that will be used in this application.

Files with Multiple Record Descriptions

The problem we want to solve can be understood better by examining some typical input records and the output they produce. Simply stated, the problem is to list all the charges made by a customer in one billing period. The input will consist of records needed to identify the customer and records containing information about the items charged. All the information for a single customer will not be contained on a single input record but we will have a record with the customer's name, address, and identification number followed by a series of records, each of which represents a different item charged by that customer. The end of one customer's charges will be indicated by the next customer's name, address, and identification number.

```
┌─────────────────────────────────────────────────────────────────────┐
│                              INPUT                                    │
│        A3187694176JAMES   ROBERT   JONES361BIRCHBANGORME04401          │
│        B3187694176HAMMER              318615                           │
│        B3187694176CHISEL              319198                           │
│        A4256143814WILLIAM EDWARD SMITH12 OAK   BREWERME04401           │
│        B4256143814WHEEL BARROW        816715                           │
│        B4256143814WRENCH              923315                           │
│        B4256143814PULLEY              726315                           │
│                             OUTPUT                                    │
│        3187694176  JAMES ROBERT JONES      BANGOR                      │
│            HAMMER            318615                                    │
│            CHISEL            319198                                    │
│        4256143814  WILLIAM EDWARD SMITH   BREWER                       │
│            WHEEL BARROW      816715                                    │
│            WRENCH            923315                                    │
│            PULLEY            726315                                    │
└─────────────────────────────────────────────────────────────────────┘
```

It is important to understand how a file consisting of records with different formats can be processed by a COBOL program. The memory allocated to a file when the file is OPENed should be thought of as a physical entity—some number of bytes of memory. The description of that physical area by a record description is a logical description of the physical area. Since the description is only a logical description, COBOL allows a programmer to incorporate more than one possible logical description of a given physical area allocated to an area defined in the FILE SECTION. In contrast, in the WORKING–STORAGE SECTION each record normally describes a different physical area. The solution to this multiple record type file should now be easier to understand. The programmer just defines different logical descriptions of a storage area and leaves it to the logic of the program to determine the type of the particular record in memory. If you examine the preceding input file, you will notice that the first byte of each input record contains an 'A' or a 'B'. The program will determine which letter occurs in the first byte and then process the record using the appropriate record description for that type record.

More Syntax for READ and WRITE Verbs

The two commands we have used in programs that involve memory in the FILE SECTION are

```
READ file-name INTO identifier
     AT END statement

WRITE record-name FROM data-name
```

These two statements were used to bring the next record of a file into a storage area defined in the WORKING–STORAGE SECTION or to make a copy of a record in the WORKING–STORAGE SECTION be the next record in some output file.

When a file is read, the next record does not come directly from the external device to a storage area in the WORKING–STORAGE SECTION. There are really two actions. The first is to bring the next record from the external file into the storage area associated with the file in the FILE SECTION. The second action is to move the record to the storage area in the WORKING–STORAGE SECTION. There are then actually two copies of the record in memory. The storage area for a file as defined in the FILE SECTION is not allocated to the program at compile time, but only at execution time when the file is OPENed. When the AT END clause is triggered in association with the READ from a file, the operating system releases the storage area in the FILE SECTION that was allocated when the file was OPENed. Thus, memory defined in the FILE SECTION is not assigned to a program from compile time until the end of execution time.

This is a major difference from the way storage is allocated in the WORKING–STORAGE SECTION. In the WORKING–STORAGE SECTION any field or record defined is allocated storage at compile time and that storage is not released until the program terminates execution.

When a program executes a statement of the form

<pre>   WRITE RECORD-NAME FROM STORAGE-NAME</pre>

the result is the execution of two commands. First, the storage area STORAGE–NAME has its contents copied into the storage area called RECORD–NAME. The information to be output is now in the record area associated with the device that is used for the output operation. At this point the WRITE verb is executed. If the record area associated with the output device is subdivided into a number of fields, these storage areas could be filled as a result of the execution of commands in the PROCEDURE DIVISION. In such a case, we can simply

<pre>   WRITE RECORD-NAME</pre>

since there will be no need to copy the contents of another storage area into this area before the output operation.

The new form of the READ and WRITE verbs that we use when the record areas in the FILE SECTION are involved are

<pre>   READ file-name
                        WRITE record-name</pre>

It is this form of the READ and WRITE that we use in the next application since files with different kinds of records will have record descriptions for each kind of record occurring after the FD level indicator for the file.

Programs with Multiple Record Descriptions

We can now examine the coding that solves the multiple record description problem presented earlier.

```
*
* NAME:            ID:
* PROGRAM-NUMBER: 3.6-1
* DESCRIPTION:   A COMPLETE PROGRAM WITHOUT TEXTA.
*    DIFFERENT RECORD DESCRIPTIONS ARE USED FOR
*    THE SAME FILE.  THE PROGRAM LISTS ITEMS
*    CHARGED TO AN ACCOUNT DURING A BILLING PERIOD.
*
 IDENTIFICATION DIVISION.
 PROGRAM-ID. MLTPLS.
```

```
                    ENVIRONMENT DIVISION.
                    CONFIGURATION SECTION.
                    SOURCE-COMPUTER.  IBM-370.
                    OBJECT-COMPUTER.  IBM-370.
                    INPUT-OUTPUT SECTION.
                    FILE-CONTROL.
                        SELECT CHARGE-FILE
                            ASSIGN TO UT-2540-S-SYSIN.
                        SELECT LINE-PRINTER
                            ASSIGN TO UT-1403-S-SYSOUT.
                    DATA DIVISION.
                    FILE SECTION.
                    FD  CHARGE-FILE
                        LABEL RECORDS ARE OMITTED
                        DATA RECORDS ARE MASTER-RECORD
                                        ITEM-CHARGED.

                * INPUT RECORDS
         (A)        01  MASTER-RECORD.
                        05  M-CODE              PIC X.
                        05  NUMBER1             PIC X(10).
                        05  NAME.
                            10  FIRST1          PIC X(8).
                            10  MIDDLE          PIC X(8).
                            10  LAST1           PIC X(12).
                        05  ADDRESS1.
                            10  STREET          PIC X(12).
                            10  CITY            PIC X(12).
                            10  STATE           PIC X(4).
                            10  ZIP             PIC X(5).
                        05  FILLER              PIC X(8).
                    01  ITEM-CHARGED.
                        05  N-CODE              PIC X.
                        05  FILLER              PIC X(10).
                        05  ITEM-DESCRIPTION    PIC X(20).
                        05  ITEM-STOCK-NO       PIC X(6).
                        05  FILLER              PIC X(43).
                    FD  LINE-PRINTER
                        LABEL RECORDS ARE OMITTED
                        DATA RECORDS ARE OUT-NAME
                                        OUT-ITEM.
                * OUTPUT RECORDS
         (B)        01  OUT-NAME.
                        05  FILLER              PIC X.
                        05  CHARGE-ACCT-NO      PIC X(10).
                        05  FILLER              PIC X(5).
                        05  NAME-OUT            PIC X(28).
                        05  FILLER              PIC X(5).
                        05  CITY-OUT            PIC X(41).
                        05  FILLER              PIC X(43).
                    01  OUT-ITEM.
                        05  FILLER              PIC X.
                        05  FILLER              PIC X(4).
                        05  ITEM-NAME           PIC X(20).
                        05  FILLER              PIC X(5).
                        05  ITEM-STOCK-NO-OUT   PIC X(9).
                        05  FILLER              PIC X(94).
                    WORKING-STORAGE SECTION.
         (C)        77  END-OF-FILE PIC X(6) VALUE SPACES.
```

```
      PROCEDURE DIVISION.
      * MODEL-I.
            OPEN INPUT CHARGE-FILE
                  OUTPUT LINE-PRINTER.


      * FILE PROCESSING PAIR
            PERFORM READ-A-RECORD.
            PERFORM LIST
                  UNTIL END-OF-FILE = HIGH-VALUES.


      * TERMINATION ACTIVITY
            CLOSE CHARGE-FILE
                  LINE-PRINTER.
            STOP RUN.


      * INPUT PROCEDURE
        READ-A-RECORD.
            READ CHARGE-FILE
                  AT END MOVE HIGH-VALUES TO END-OF-FILE.


      * RECORD PROCESSING
        LIST.
            IF M-CODE = 'A'
                  PERFORM MASTER-OUT
            ELSE
                  IF M-CODE = 'B'
                        PERFORM CHARGE-OUT.
            PERFORM READ-A-RECORD.
        MASTER-OUT.
            MOVE SPACES     TO OUT-NAME.
            MOVE NUMBER1    TO CHARGE-ACCT-NO.
            MOVE NAME       TO NAME-OUT.
            MOVE CITY       TO CITY-OUT.
            WRITE OUT-NAME.
        CHARGE-OUT.
            MOVE SPACES              TO OUT-ITEM.
            MOVE ITEM-DESCRIPTION TO ITEM-NAME.
            MOVE ITEM-STOCK-NO     TO ITEM-STOCK-NO-OUT.
            WRITE OUT-ITEM.
```

(D)

(E)

(A)   The file CHARGE-FILE contains a record with information about a customer followed by records giving that customer's charges during the current billing period. We can't predict how many charges a customer will make in a period, so we reserve one byte of the input record to identify the kind of information in that record. Both MASTER-RECORD and ITEM-CHARGED are record descriptions for CHARGE-FILE. We will know how the record currently in memory is organized by determining the value of the variable M-CODE. Note that M-CODE and N-CODE each represent the first byte of the record. The machine will not allocate two storage areas for the records. Rather, we should think of the two record descriptions as different ways of looking at the same 80-byte storage area. The value we put in the first byte of the record will tell us whether to deal with this record as one of the form of MASTER-RECORD or as one of the form ITEM-CHARGED. Notice that the identification number occurs on each type record so that the records are processed correctly. See Figure 3.6.1 on the next page.

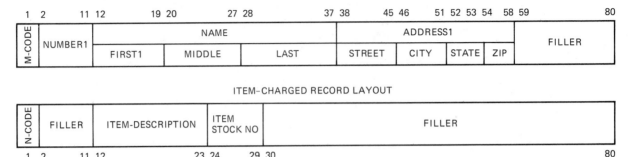

MASTER-RECORD RECORD LAYOUT

M-CODE	NUMBER1	NAME			ADDRESS1				FILLER
		FIRST1	MIDDLE	LAST	STREET	CITY	STATE	ZIP	

1 2   11 12   19 20   27 28   37 38   45 46   51 52 53 54   58 59   80

ITEM-CHARGED RECORD LAYOUT

N-CODE	FILLER	ITEM-DESCRIPTION	ITEM STOCK NO	FILLER

1 2   11 12   23 24   29 30   80

Figure 3.6.1 Record layout for CHARGE–FILE.

(B)   Both OUT–NAME and OUT–ITEM are patterns for a printed line. We will use OUT–NAME when we have a record of the form MASTER–RECORD in memory and OUT–ITEM when the record in memory is of the form ITEM–CHARGED. Again, it is important to understand that there is just one record area for LINE–PRINTER, but that we have two different ways of looking at it.

(C)   The END–OF–FILE field cannot be a variable in the FILE SECTION, as these variables are no longer available to the program after the end of file is encountered. The variables in the WORKING–STORAGE SECTION are allocated at compile time and remain available to the program until execution is stopped. Since the END–OF–FILE field is needed after the record area associated with the file is released by the compiler, this field is defined as an auxiliary storage location field in the WORKING–STORAGE SECTION using a 77-level designation. Such an auxiliary storage location is dealt with in the same manner as any other storage area. The difference is that such fields are needed while the program is executing, but are not part of either an input record or an output record. Often the program will need several auxiliary storage locations for related purposes. In such cases it is good programming practice to group these fields as subdivisions of a record.

(D)   By determining the value in M–CODE (which is the same storage location as N–CODE), we know whether or not the record currently in memory is of the form MASTER–RECORD or of the form ITEM–CHARGED. When the first byte of a record in CHARGE–FILE is the letter A, the record is of the form of MASTER–FILE. When this first byte contains the letter B, the record is of the form of ITEM–CHARGED. We assume here that the code field contains only an A or a B, that is, a preprocessing routine has scrubbed the data clean.

(E)   The paragraph MASTER–OUT moves and prints the information in a record. See Figure 3.6.2. If the record is of the form MASTER–RECORD it uses the output record descrip-

OUT-NAME RECORD LAYOUT

	CHARGE ACCT NO	FILLER	NAME-OUT	FILLER	ADDRESS-OUT	FILLER

1 2   11 12   16 17   44 45   49 50   59 60   133

OUT-ITEM RECORD LAYOUT

FILLER	ITEM-NAME	FILLER	ITEM STOCK NO-OUT	FILLER

1 2   5 6   25 26   30 31   39 40   133

Figure 3.6.2 Record layout for line printer.

tion OUT–NAME. The paragraph CHARGE–OUT moves and prints the information in a record of the form ITEM–CHARGED. This paragraph uses the output record description OUT–ITEM.

SYNTAX SUMMARY

```
01 data-name
           level-number  {data-name}  [{PICTURE}  character-string].
                         {FILLER   }   {PIC    }
```

EXERCISES

1. Briefly define the following terms.

   a. logical record   d. execution time storage allocation
   b. physical record   e. compile time storage allocation
   c. multiple record descriptions

2. When is the storage defined in the FILE SECTION actually allocated to a program? When is such storage released from program control?

3. Why is it invalid to use a VALUE clause in the FILE SECTION?

4. For each of the following blocks of code write a single semantically equivalent sentence.

   a. READ STUDENT–FILE.
      MOVE STUDENT–FILE–RECORD INTO STUDENT–INFO.
   b. MOVE STUDENT–INFO TO PRINT–LINE.
      WRITE PRINT–LINE.

5. When a file has multiple logical record descriptions, what mechanism can a program use to distinguish them?

6. Write the IDENTIFICATION, ENVIRONMENT, and DATA DIVISIONs for a program that uses the STUDENT–FILE and the PRINTER. The record descriptions for the files should appear in the FILE SECTION. Assume that the NAME and the GRADEs for each student are to be listed.

PROGRAMMING PROBLEM

1. The file used in making class lists has three kinds of records. Each type of record consists of 80 bytes of information, but each type of record has a different organization. The first few records of the file look like this:

   ```
   MATHEMATICS 26 SPRING SEMESTER 1985              1
   DR. IRMA GANNON                  313 BOARD HALL  2
   003165896 JONES, TIM     A&S JR  078096085       3
   086519439 SMITH, ROGER   E&S SO  077062075       3
   861549586 LANE, PETER    A&S JR  086088091       3
   ```

   The additional records for this class give information about the other students in the class. Each class may have a different number of students. The main difficulty in processing this file is figuring out what pattern exists on the card just read. Using the idea from PROGRAM–NUMBER 3.6-1, write a program that will process a file consisting of a number of classes with the kind of heading information given in the example. You should have no difficulty in creating a card file for three or four classes. (You might volunteer to prepare up-to-date class lists for your instructor's other classes!)

When a problem of this sort is given, it is likely that the types of cards will be described as in Table 3.3.

TABLE 3.3   FORM OF INPUT INFORMATION FOR EACH CLASS.

	Information	Begins In Byte	Length
Card 1	A heading that identifies the course (not all the bytes must contain information)	1	79
	A code of 1 indicating that this is the first heading card	80	1
Card 2	Name of the Instructor	1	30
	Location of class meeting place	34	30
	A code of 2 indicating this is the second heading card	80	1
Card 3	(One card of this type for each student in the class)		
	Student Id Number	1	9
	Name of the student	10	16
	College of the student	26	3
	A&S: Arts		
	E&S: Engineering		
	B: Business		
	Class of the student (FR, SO, JR, or SR)	30	2
	Scores for each of the three	34	3
	course exams (each is a	37	3
	number between 0 and 100)	40	3
	A code of 3 indicating this is a student's information	80	1

Write a program that reads and then prints such a file.

Chapter Review

SUMMARY

This chapter introduced and applied the selection feature of structured programming. The IF... construction can be used to test conditions and alter the flow of control in a program's logic. If the condition is true, then the statements following the condition are executed. An IF...THEN...ELSE construction is appropriate when one block of code is to be executed when a condition is true and another block when the condition is false. In addition to these two selection statements, the Nested IF construction allows one or more IF statements to be contained within an initial IF statement. This nesting of IF statements permits a series of cases to be distinguished more efficiently than coding a number of simple IF statements. In addition, with appropriate indentation of the Nested IF statements, the program's logic can be easily understood. Two or more simple conditions can also be utilized to form a compound condition in which each condition is tested separately before being joined by the logical operators AND and OR. The logical operator NOT can also be used to negate conditions. Logical operators allow more complex conditions to be tested.

In addition to IF statements and logical operators, this chapter introduced two models that will be useful for subsequent programming problems. Both models are used to facilitate program development. Pseudocode of a model can be inserted in the program as comments and can provide a first development step. Some sections of each model are more straightforward and should be completed first. Completing parts of a model's outline provides a way to progress toward the solution of a problem. It also allows parts of the problem to be dealt with independently of those already considered. The first model describes a program in which each record of a file generates a line of output. The second model is used when processing is required after the end of a file has been reached. This type of processing is called TERMINATION ACTIVITY. Assigning a field value to signal this condition is a way to build in the logic necessary for termination processing.

TEST YOURSELF

1. Which syntax features are used to implement the selection process?
2. What is a simple condition?
3. What are the relational tests used in simple conditions?
4. Explain the syntax and the semantics of the IF...THEN...ELSE construction.
5. What is the true range of a condition? The false range of a condition?
6. In an IF...THEN...ELSE statement, how is the true range identified? The false range?
7. What is a Nested IF construction?
8. What is the advantage of using a Nested IF construction?
9. What is a compound condition?
10. Name the logical operators?
11. For simple conditions A and B, what truth values for each will make A AND B true? A OR B true? NOT A true?
12. What is a physical record? A logical record?
13. How can one describe different logical organizations for the records of a single file?

4

Arithmetic Operations

Chapter Objectives

After studying this chapter you should be able to

- use the COBOL verbs ADD, SUBTRACT, MULTIPLY, DIVIDE, and COMPUTE;
- write a program that uses arithmetic operations;
- write a program that uses arithmetic operations and includes numeric editing features of COBOL;
- write a program that checks for the correctness of the data being processed by using range and digit checks.

Chapter Outline

4.1   Arithmetic Statements

Business data processing requires the use of arithmetic operations. Accounts receivable, accounts payable, payroll, and inventory systems are just a few of the applications that require arithmetic operations. The arithmetic operations available in COBOL are

1. addition
2. subtraction
3. multiplication
4. division
5. exponentiation

This list gives an approximate order of the operations by frequency of use. Exponentiation, which is listed last, is used least. We will, however, deal with problems calculating loan payments and the future value for an annuity where exponentiation is essential.

Each of these arithmetic operations requires four parts for computer implementation. They are (1 and 2) the two numbers to be operated on; (3) the operation to be performed; and (4) a name of a location for storing the answer. Before executing an arithmetic operation, the special part of a CPU called the *arithmetic unit* must be told

1. number 1
2. number 2
3. operation to be performed
4. a location for storing the answer

The storage location for the answer in memory may or may not have a value currently stored in it. However, after the operation is performed, the result of the operation will be stored there.

The syntax for each COBOL arithmetic operation gives implicit or explicit reference to each of the four parts listed. For example, one form of the addition command is

```
ADD  identifier-1  identifier-2 GIVING identifier-3.
```

The semantics (meaning) of this statement are

1. Send the current numeric contents of the storage location named identifier–1 and the current numeric contents of the storage location named identifier–2 to the arithmetic unit.
2. Send the message to the arithmetic unit that these two numbers are to be added together.
3. Indicate that the answer is to be placed in the storage location named identifier–3.

Tables 4.1 and 4.2 indicate the contents of the storage locations used in the command before and after the command is executed.

TABLE 4.1

DATA NAME	ADD SALE1 SALE2 GIVING TOTAL-SALE. BEFORE	AFTER
SALE1	5	5
SALE2	9	9
TOTAL-SALE	immaterial	14

The value of TOTAL–SALE before the operation is performed is immaterial because it does not enter into the computation. In fact, there need not be a value currently in the storage location TOTAL–SALE, since it is the receiving field for a MOVE of the form

```
MOVE answer TO TOTAL-SALE.
```

We can now generalize the syntax a bit, since we can add a constant to the current contents of a storage location.

TABLE 4.2

DATA NAME	ADD 17 COST GIVING SALE–TOTAL. BEFORE	AFTER
COST	18	18
	17	17
SALE–TOTAL	immaterial	35

We need not restrict ourselves to adding two terms. A more general syntax for ADD is

$$\underline{ADD} \left\{ \begin{array}{l} \text{identifier--1} \\ \text{literal--1} \end{array} \right\} \left\{ \begin{array}{l} \text{, identifier--2} \\ \text{literal--2} \end{array} \right\} \left[\begin{array}{l} \text{, identifier--3} \\ \text{, literal--3} \end{array} \right] \ldots$$

$$\underline{GIVING} \text{ identifier--4.}$$

The { } contain names of two kinds of elements. In COBOL syntax, these brackets indicate that some of the kinds of elements listed within the brackets must occur at that point in the COBOL statement. Here we need two elements, because we are going to ADD. The [ ] indicate that elements of the kind listed in the square brackets may occur if appropriate. If such elements are part of the command, we send a list of items to the arithmetic unit to be added together. The list can be longer than two elements. The . . . after identifier–3 indicates the list can be continued as long as needed. In any case, the answer will be put in the storage location called identifier–4. Here there are no brackets because we are allowed no choice. The answer generated by the addition must be put in some storage location. A storage location is identified by the name assigned to it. The underlined words must occur, spelled as indicated, at those particular places in the statement. An identifier is a data name, followed, as required, by the combination of qualifiers necessary to make a unique reference to a data name. A data name that does not occur in more than one record is an identifier.

We have spent time explaining ADD since it shows the basic pattern for all arithmetic operations using GIVING. We will just list the others and examine typical cases.

$$\underline{SUBTRACT} \left\{ \begin{array}{l} \text{identifier--1} \\ \text{literal--1} \end{array} \right\} \left[\begin{array}{l} \text{, identifier--2} \\ \text{, literal--2} \end{array} \right] \ldots$$

$$\underline{FROM} \left\{ \begin{array}{l} \text{identifier--3} \\ \text{literal--3} \end{array} \right\} \underline{GIVING} \text{ identifier--4.}$$

TABLE 4.3

DATA NAME	SUBTRACT COMMISSION FROM COST GIVING NET. BEFORE	AFTER
COMMISSION	9	9
COST	16	16
NET	31	7

In Table 4.3 the before value (31) of NET is replaced by seven. In this case, the previous value of NET is "lost." Note also that the variables COMMISSION and COST are unchanged by this operation just as the values were unchanged by the ADD command. When more than a single variable follows SUBTRACT, the values of all these variables are first added together and then this sum is subtracted from the value in the storage location whose name occurs following FROM. Table 4.4 illustrates this process.

TABLE 4.4

SUBTRACT TAX1 TAX2 TAX3 FROM SALE GIVING NET–AMT.		
DATA NAME	BEFORE	AFTER
TAX1	3	3
TAX2	8	8
TAX3	17	17
SALE	76	76
NET–AMT	82	48

The multiplication and division commands are easy to interpret once you understand addition and subtraction. See Table 4.5.

$$\underline{\text{MULTIPLY}} \begin{Bmatrix} \text{identifier-1} \\ \text{literal-1} \end{Bmatrix} \underline{\text{BY}} \begin{Bmatrix} \text{identifier-2} \\ \text{literal-2} \end{Bmatrix}$$

$$\underline{\text{GIVING}}\ \text{identifier-3}.$$

TABLE 4.5

MULTIPLY COST BY NO–ITEMS GIVING INV–VALUE.		
DATA NAME	BEFORE	AFTER
COST	7	7
NO–ITEMS	14	14
INV–VALUE	29	98

The DIVIDE command has two options. We can think of division as being represented by a fraction A/B. The term A is called the dividend, and B is called the divisor. COBOL has two commands for division, depending on whether the programmer wants to list the dividend first or the divisor first.

$$\underline{\text{DIVIDE}} \begin{Bmatrix} \text{identifier-1} \\ \text{literal-1} \end{Bmatrix} \begin{Bmatrix} \underline{\text{INTO}} \\ \underline{\text{BY}} \end{Bmatrix} \begin{Bmatrix} \text{identifier-2} \\ \text{literal-2} \end{Bmatrix}$$

$$\underline{\text{GIVING}}\ \text{identifier-3}.$$

The INTO and BY options in division can be misunderstood. The meanings are

$$\text{DIVIDE A INTO B is the same as } \frac{B}{A}$$

$$\text{DIVIDE A BY B is the same as } \frac{A}{B}$$

Either form will work. A different answer will be computed using the same values of two variables if INTO and BY are mixed up. Therefore, be careful when coding the DIVIDE command. See Tables 4.6 and 4.7.

TABLE 4.6

| DIVIDE NO–UNITS INTO SALES GIVING COST–UNIT. | | |
DATA NAME	BEFORE	AFTER
NO–UNITS	13	13
SALES	52	52
COST–UNIT	17	4

TABLE 4.7

| DIVIDE SALES BY NO–UNITS GIVING COST–UNIT. | | |
DATA NAME	BEFORE	AFTER
SALES	52	52
NO–UNITS	13	13
COST–UNIT	17	4

ADD with TO

We have seen the basic arithmetic commands for a situation where the result is put in a storage location whose value does not enter into the computation. There is another important option in the syntax which the following example explains.

Let ACCOUNTS–PAYABLE be a file in which each record contains a four-digit dollar amount. At the end of the year we must total the amounts due. We would like to have one variable called TOTAL that ends up having as its value the sum of the amount due from all the records. Let's suppose the amount on a record is put in a storage location called AMT–DUE when a record is read.

```
                        ACCOUNTS–PAYABLE
            Record1: _____ 8600 _____
            Record2: _____ 1900 _____
            Record3: _____ 2100 _____
```

RECORD1

data name	before	after
AMT–DUE	8600	8600
TOTAL	0	8600

RECORD2

data name	before	after
AMT–DUE	1900	1900
TOTAL	8600	10500

RECORD3

data name	before	after
AMT–DUE	2100	2100
TOTAL	10500	12600

The essential difference between this process and the one we examined previously is that the arithmetic unit must add the current contents of AMT–DUE and TOTAL, and then put the result back in TOTAL. TOTAL must, therefore, have the value ZERO before it is used in the first addition process. We can't put the answer in a storage location that is not used in the computation or the final answer will not be correct. The syntax for this form of the arithmetic statements is accomplished by removing the GIVING clause and using TO as a separator. The machine understands, in this instance, that it must use the second data name for two purposes.

1. Its current value is used in the operation.
2. The answer is to be put in the storage location represented by the second data name.

The following examples should clarify this situation.

$$
\underline{ADD} \begin{Bmatrix} \text{identifier--1} \\ \text{literal--1} \end{Bmatrix} \begin{bmatrix} , & \text{identifier--2} \\ , & \text{literal--2} \end{bmatrix} \ldots
$$
$$
\underline{TO} \ \text{identifier--3.}
$$

TABLE 4.8

	ADD SALE1 SALE2 TO SALES–TO–DATE	
DATA NAME	BEFORE	AFTER
SALE1	3	3
SALE2	5	5
SALES–TO–DATE	9	17

$$
\underline{SUBTRACT} \begin{Bmatrix} \text{identifier--1} \\ \text{literal--1} \end{Bmatrix} \begin{bmatrix} , & \text{identifier--2} \\ , & \text{literal--2} \end{bmatrix} \ldots
$$
$$
\underline{FROM} \ \text{identifier--3.}
$$

TABLE 4.9

	SUBTRACT REFUND 10 FROM TOTAL–SALES.	
DATA NAME	BEFORE	AFTER
REFUND	3	3
	10	10
TOTAL–SALES	17	4

$$
\underline{MULTIPLY} \begin{Bmatrix} \text{identifier--1} \\ \text{literal--1} \end{Bmatrix} \underline{BY} \ \text{identifier--2}
$$

TABLE 4.10

	MULTIPLY NO–UNITS BY PRICE.	
DATA NAME	BEFORE	AFTER
NO–UNITS	3	3
PRICE	8	24

$$
\underline{DIVIDE} \begin{Bmatrix} \text{identifier--1} \\ \text{literal--1} \end{Bmatrix} \underline{INTO} \ \text{identifier--2}
$$

TABLE 4.11

DATA NAME	DIVIDE NO–UNITS INTO PRICE. BEFORE	AFTER
NO–UNITS	3	3
PRICE	15	5

Since there are two different formats for each of the arithmetic verbs, you should study the differences to understand the advantages and disadvantages of each. We have seen an example where, to accumulate some numbers, the second format was preferable. If, however, the before values used in the computation had been required later in the program, the first format would have been preferable so that none of the storage locations containing values used in the computation would have been altered.

The COMPUTE Statement

There is one more command that can be used for arithmetic computations. You will notice that we have not mentioned exponentiation yet. There is no COBOL verb for this operation. However, exponentiation can be done using the verb COMPUTE. Business data processing uses exponentiation. Two examples of this are the calculation of interest over many compounding periods and the calculation of uniform mortgage payments for each payment of a contract. The operation of exponentiation is denoted by ** and multiplication is denoted by *. The command used for exponentiation is

$$\text{COMPUTE identifier-1} = \begin{Bmatrix} \text{identifier-2} \\ \text{literal-1} \\ \text{arithmetic} \\ \quad \text{expression} \end{Bmatrix}$$

TABLE 4.12

DATA NAME	COMPUTE X = Y ** 3 BEFORE	AFTER
Y	9	9
X	no value	729

TABLE 4.13

DATA NAME	COMPUTE X = (Y ** 2 + 2 * Y + 4) / Y BEFORE	AFTER
Y	4	4
X	5	7

The important feature for you to remember about COMPUTE is that the variable name on the left of the equal sign is the name of the storage location that will receive the result of the computation being performed on the right of the equal sign. We are not limited to using COMPUTE with the exponentiation operator, but we may use it with any appropriate combination of arithmetic operations as we saw in Table 4.13. COMPUTE is especially helpful when a calculation involves more than a single arithmetic operation.

Unless the arithmetic expression involves a combination of operations, the COMPUTE statement is not usually used. Normally the arithmetic operations that occur in a COBOL program should be limited to ADD, SUBTRACT, MULTIPLY, or DIVIDE verbs.

As with the logical operators AND, OR, and NOT, we need to know the order of execution for expressions in COMPUTE commands that involve more than a single operation.

Order of Execution

The hierarchy for arithmetic operators that determines the order of execution is given in decreasing order as

1. unary plus or minus
2. exponentiation
3. multiplication and division
4. addition and subtraction

This order leads to the following order of execution rules.

> 1. Parenthetical expressions are evaluated first, from the innermost pair to the outermost pair.
> 2. The unary plus or minus operations are performed.
> 3. Exponentiation operations are processed left to right as they occur.
> 4. Multiplication and division calculations are processed left to right as they occur.
> 5. Addition and subtraction calculations are processed left to right as they occur.

When two or more operators at the same level of the hierarchy are present, the order of execution is always from left to right in the order of occurrence. The operators $+$ and $-$ can be written either as a unary operator (taking one argument as in $+x$ or $-x$) or as a binary operator (taking two arguments as in $x + y$ or $x - y$). With addition and subtraction the operators are usually binary operators.

SYNTAX SUMMARY

The syntax for arithmetic statements is given in this section. At this point we will just review the key words used in the statements explained.

```
ADD ... GIVING ...
ADD ... TO ...
COMPUTE ...
```

$$\text{DIVIDE} \ldots \begin{Bmatrix} \underline{\text{INTO}} \\ \underline{\text{BY}} \end{Bmatrix} \ldots \text{GIVING} \ldots$$

```
DIVIDE ... INTO ...
MULTIPLY ... BY ... GIVING ...
MULTIPLY ... BY ...
SUBTRACT ... FROM ... GIVING ...
SUBTRACT ... FROM ...
```

With the addition of the arithmetic commands, a more general form of a condition can be used. A condition can be any statement of the following form.

$$\text{IF} \begin{Bmatrix} \text{data-name-1} \\ \text{literal-1} \\ \text{expression-1} \end{Bmatrix} \text{IS [NOT]} \begin{Bmatrix} \text{EQUAL} \\ \text{LESS THAN} \\ \text{GREATER THAN} \end{Bmatrix} \begin{Bmatrix} \text{data-name-2} \\ \text{literal-2} \\ \text{expression-2} \end{Bmatrix}$$

$$\text{THEN} \begin{Bmatrix} \text{statements-1} \\ \text{NEXT SENTENCE} \end{Bmatrix}$$

$$\text{ELSE} \begin{Bmatrix} \text{statements-2} \\ \text{NEXT SENTENCE} \end{Bmatrix}$$

EXERCISES

Indicate the contents of all storage locations after the execution of the following statements:

1. ADD EQ–RENTAL DEPRECIATION GIVING DEDUCTIBLE.

DATA NAME	BEFORE	AFTER
EQ–RENTAL	95.5	
DEPRECIATION	83.1	
DEDUCTIBLE	441.3	

2. SUBTRACT ENTERTAINMENT FROM SALARY GIVING TROUBLE.

DATA NAME	BEFORE	AFTER
ENTERTAINMENT	385.12	
SALARY	4613.12	
TROUBLE	8351.4	

3. MULTIPLY HOURS BY RATE GIVING WAGES–GROSS.

DATA NAME	BEFORE	AFTER
HOURS	39.75	
RATE	4.18	
WAGES–GROSS	316.54	

4. DIVIDE TOTAL–SALES BY NO–SALES GIVING AVG–SALES.

DATA NAME	BEFORE	AFTER
TOTAL–SALES	318514.12	
NO–SALES	319	
AVG–SALES	86.71	

5. ADD EQ–RENTAL TO DEPRECIATION.

DATA NAME	BEFORE	AFTER
EQ–RENTAL	95.5	
DEPRECIATION	83.1	

6. SUBTRACT ENTERTAINMENT FROM SALARY.

DATA NAME	BEFORE	AFTER
ENTERTAINMENT	385.12	
SALARY	4613.12	

7. MULTIPLY HOURS BY RATE.

DATA NAME	BEFORE	AFTER
HOURS	39.75	
RATE	4.18	

8. DIVIDE NO–SALES INTO TOTAL–SALES.

DATA NAME	BEFORE	AFTER
NO–SALES	319	
TOTAL–SALES	318514.12	

9. Using the verbs ADD, SUBTRACT, MULTIPLY, and DIVIDE with the GIVING option and X1, X2, X3, and X4 as storage locations for the intermediate and final results, as needed, write the code needed to calculate values for the following expressions:

a. B + C * D
b. (C − D) * B
c. (B + C) / D − E * 4

10. Using the verbs ADD, SUBTRACT, MULTIPLY, and DIVIDE without the GIVING option and using no additional storage locations, write the code needed to calculate values for the following expressions:

a. B + C * D + 5
b. B * (C − D + 7)
c. (B + C) / (D − E * 4)

4.2 Description of Storage for Numeric Fields

Numeric Data

Our discussion of the syntax and semantics of the arithmetic commands confronted one of the problems with which we have to deal. We intentionally did not worry about how the program itself recognizes that a variable is to be used in an arithmetic statement. It makes no sense to add the character 'A' to the character 'B'. Our picture clauses with X(n) have treated the contents of each storage location as collections of characters. Therefore, to allow the contents of a storage location to be treated as numeric data, we must give a different message to the compiler with the picture clause. In COBOL, numeric data is signified by using a 9 in place of an X in the picture clause. For example:

(a) PIC 999
(b) PIC 9(4)

signify a three-digit (a) and a four-digit numeric field (b). The compiler expects to find a digit in each byte of a storage location that is defined by a picture clause of the form 9(n).

Numeric data is right-justified in a storage location, whereas character data is left-justified. For example, the number 315 in a field described as

PIC 9(5)

would be stored as   00315

Each byte of a numeric field will have a digit stored in it, one of 0, 1, 2, . . . , 9. If there are fewer digits than spaces, the compiler automatically will pad to the left of the most significant digit with zeros when necessary. The same number (315) in a field described as

PIC 99

would result in

15

with the leading digit discarded, since there was no storage location for it. In this case, the program would not recognize this as an error that should cause execution to cease unless special coding features are used. A numeric picture clause may have up to 18 digits. In any problem the programmer will have to estimate the size of the field needed to ensure that significant digits are not discarded. This requires an understanding of the problem more than an understanding of COBOL. It is at a point like this that you begin to see how the real problem and the program should properly mirror each other. There are no COBOL rules for determining the size of a field. All the variables used in arithmetic operations must have numeric picture clauses, however.

```
*
* NAME:                    ID:
* PROGRAM-NUMBER: 4.2-1
* DESCRIPTION: SHOW HOW NUMERIC VARIABLES
*    ARE DEFINED IN THE WORKING-STORAGE SECTION.
*    HAVE THE PROGRAM USE THE ARITHMETIC STATEMENTS.
        COPY TEXTA.
   WORKING-STORAGE SECTION.
* AUXILIARY STORAGE LOCATIONS
(A)  77   SAMPLE-NO-1 PIC 9(4) VALUE 65.
     77   SAMPLE-NO-2 PIC 9(4) VALUE 13.

* OUTPUT RECORD
(B)  01   PRINT-PATTERN.
          05 FILLER      PIC X.
          05 ANSWER-ADD  PIC 9(8).
          05 ANSWER-SUBT PIC 9(8).
          05 ANSWER-MULT PIC 9(8).
          05 ANSWER-DIV  PIC 9(8).
          05 FILLER      PIC X(100) VALUE SPACES.

   PROCEDURE DIVISION.

       OPEN OUTPUT PRINTER.

       ADD SAMPLE-NO-1 SAMPLE-NO-2
           GIVING ANSWER-ADD.
       SUBTRACT SAMPLE-NO-2 FROM SAMPLE-NO-1
           GIVING ANSWER-SUBT.
       MULTIPLY SAMPLE-NO-1 BY SAMPLE-NO-2
           GIVING ANSWER-MULT.
       DIVIDE SAMPLE-NO-2 INTO SAMPLE-NO-1
           GIVING ANSWER-DIV.
(C)    WRITE PRINT-LINE FROM PRINT-PATTERN.

       CLOSE PRINTER.
       STOP RUN.
```

(A)   This line of code contains three new features. First, the *level number* 77 is used. Every variable in a COBOL program must be defined and associated with an appropriately described storage location in the DATA DIVISION. Variables that are part of input and output records have been dealt with before. Here we have a variable that only exists in the context of the program. The variables SAMPLE–NO–1 and SAMPLE–NO–2 are not read into the program and are not sent to the printer. They are, however, variables in the program. Variables of this type can be defined as 77-level variables or grouped as fields in a record. All 77-level variables so defined occur in the WORKING–STORAGE SEC-TION. The second new feature is variables with numeric values. These variables have the picture clause 9(4). The 9 is written in place of the X in a picture clause to indicate that the field will only contain digits. Third, in assigning values to these variables at compile time, we use VALUE, a word we are familiar with. The difference here is that the value itself is written as an ordinary number. There are no quotes around 65 or 13, because they are numbers and are not treated as two-letter words composed of symbols that happen to be digits.

(B)   The pattern for the printed line consists of 133 bytes, 32 of which are reserved for numeric values. These four eight-byte numeric fields will be given values in the PROCEDURE DIVISION. Each of these fields will be the receiving field for the result generated by an arithmetic command.

(C)   To motivate some of the additional features we will introduce, let's display the 32 characters that will be printed in the parts of PRINT–PATTERN that receive results of arithmetic operations.

0000007800000052000008450000005

Numeric Editing

In the output displayed, we have a picture of the contents of the 32 bytes of storage that are reserved for the results of the operations. Needless to say, the leading zeros are a nuisance. Just imagine a year-end budget report in which 2180 was printed as 00002180. Since displaying numbers in meaningful ways is an objective for any numeric report, COBOL has a built-in feature that automatically eliminates leading zeros. Consider

05 ANSWER–ADD PIC Z(8).

This picture clause is a **numerically edited picture clause.** The Z in place of 9 tells the compiler that when a number is sent to this storage location, the zeros (if any) found to the left of the most significant digit should be replaced by blanks. Now when the record description is

```
01   PRINT-PATTERN.
     05 FILLER       PIC X.
     05 ANSWER-ADD   PIC Z(8).
     05 ANSWER-SUBT  PIC Z(8).
     05 ANSWER-MULT  PIC Z(8).
     05 ANSWER-DIV   PIC Z(8).
     05 FILLER       PIC X(100) VALUE SPACES.
```

and the code is the same, the following output will be shown. (The underscores indicate spaces on the printed line that will be blank.)

_____78_____52_____845_____5

This is what we wanted in the first place.

When doing arithmetic operations using an identifier, COBOL requires that the picture clause of that identifier be strictly numeric, *not* numerically edited. If we try doing arithmetic with a numerically edited field we will get an ERROR message at execution time. The machine indicates that it was expecting one kind of data in the storage location it accessed and found another kind instead. The dollar sign included in a numeric field would cause such an error. Numerically edited fields may only be *receiving fields* for the result of an arithmetic operation or the receiving field for a MOVE command.

The Decimal Point

We have only looked at numeric fields that have no digits to the right of the decimal point. The decimal point is handled in two different ways, depending on whether the field is numeric or numerically edited.

A numeric field has a picture clause that may contain 9's to signify digits and a V to signify the position where a decimal point would exist. A numeric field cannot physically contain a decimal point, because arithmetic operations can only be performed using fields that are purely numeric. **The V in the picture clause signifies the implied position of the decimal point.** This position is remembered and accounted for automatically by the compiler. When one numeric field is moved to another numeric field, the positions of the implied decimal points are aligned, and then digits are moved to the left and right of that point until the sending field runs out of digits. Any spaces left unfilled in the receiving field are loaded with zeros. Extra digits in the sending field are ignored. To assign a value to a numeric field using VALUE, we write the number with a decimal point. The compiler remembers the position of the decimal point, but does not put a decimal point in a storage location. Let's look at Table 4.14 for some examples.

TABLE 4.14

VALUE	PICTURE	STORAGE
36.8	99V999	36800
512	9(6)V9	0005120
21.52	9V99	152

For output, the procedure is very simple. Just put the decimal point where you want it in the printed line. This makes the field a numerically edited field—normally the receiving field for the result of an arithmetic operation. Such a field is intended for printing and may not be used in subsequent arithmetic operations. Suppose, however, we want to both display an answer and use it in another arithmetic operation. We will need two storage locations. One might be described as a 77-level variable, and the other as part of an output record. This seems a bit clumsy, but again it is the procedure COBOL requires.

TABLE 4.15

STORAGE CONTENTS	SENDING FIELD PICTURE	RECEIVING FIELD PICTURE	OUTPUT
368	99V9	9(3).9	036.8
512	9(3)	9(2).9(2)	12.00
2152	9(2)V9(2)	9(5).9(3)	00021.520

The ROUNDED Phrase

If, after decimal point alignment, the number of places to the right of the decimal point in the storage location for the answer for an arithmetic operation is less than the number of places to the right of the decimal point in the answer itself, either truncation or rounding will occur. If no option is explicitly chosen, the answer will be truncated as soon as all the decimal digits in the storage location for the answer are filled. The syntax for each of the arithmetic commands allows the name of the storage location for the answer to be followed by the word ROUNDED. In the case the ROUNDED option is used, the last digit of the result is increased by one whenever the first unused digit is five or larger. An example is given in Table 4.16.

TABLE 4.16

	MULTIPLY AMT	BY RATE	GIVING TOTALS
FIELD	AMT	RATE	TOTALS
PICTURE	99V9	99V999	9999V99
VALUES	389	41321	160739
	986	38486	379472
	837	06713	056188

Negative Numbers

Our discussion of numbers needs some mention of negative numbers. For input, any numeric field that has an S preceding the first 9 of the picture clause will be handled as a negative number when appropriate. Without the S, the compiler would treat all numbers as positive. The output of a signed number can be accomplished by putting a − in front of the picture clause of the output field. This accounts for one more print position and is replaced by a blank when the number is positive.

This discussion of numbers prepares us for additional programming options.

```
*
* NAME:                    ID:
* PROGRAM-NUMBER: 4.2-2
* DESCRIPTION: DISPLAY EACH STUDENT'S NAME
*    AND GRADES AS WELL AS THE AVERAGE OF THE
*    FIVE GRADES.  THE INPUT FILE IS STUDENT-FILE
*    AND THE OUTPUT FILE IS THE PRINTER.
*
      COPY TEXTA.
 WORKING-STORAGE SECTION.
* AUXILIARY STORAGE LOCATION
   77  SUM-UP PIC 9(5).

* INPUT RECORD
  01   STUDENT-INFO.
       05 FILLER    PIC X(4).
       05 NAME      PIC X(18).
       05 FILLER    PIC X(3).
       05 ALGEBRA   PIC 9(3).
       05 GEOMETRY  PIC 9(3).
       05 ENGLISH   PIC 9(3).
       05 PHYSICS   PIC 9(3).
       05 CHEMISTRY PIC 9(3).
       05 FILLER    PIC X(60).

* OUTPUT RECORD
  01   PRINT-PATTERN.
       05 FILLER    PIC X.
       05 NAME-OUT  PIC X(20).
       05 ALG       PIC Z(6).
       05 GEO       PIC Z(6).
       05 ENG       PIC Z(6).
       05 PHY       PIC Z(6).
       05 CHE       PIC Z(6).
       05 AVG       PIC Z(6).99.
       05 FILLER    PIC X(73) VALUE SPACES.
```

```
          PROCEDURE DIVISION.
        * MODEL-I

                OPEN INPUT STUDENT-FILE
                     OUTPUT PRINTER.


        * FILE PROCESSING PAIR
(B)             PERFORM READ-A-RECORD.
(B)             PERFORM AVERAGE
                     UNTIL NAME = HIGH-VALUES.


        * TERMINATION ACTIVITY
                CLOSE STUDENT-FILE
                      PRINTER.
                STOP RUN.


        * INPUT PROCEDURE
          READ-A-RECORD.
                READ STUDENT-FILE INTO STUDENT-INFO
                     AT END MOVE HIGH-VALUES TO NAME.


        * RECORD PROCESSING
          AVERAGE.
                MOVE NAME       TO NAME-OUT.
(C)             MOVE ALGEBRA    TO ALG.
                MOVE GEOMETRY   TO GEO.
                MOVE ENGLISH    TO ENG.
                MOVE PHYSICS    TO PHY.
                MOVE CHEMISTRY  TO CHE.
(D)             ADD ALGEBRA
                    GEOMETRY
                    ENGLISH
                    PHYSICS
                    CHEMISTRY GIVING SUM-UP.
(E)             DIVIDE SUM-UP BY 5 GIVING AVG.
(F)             WRITE PRINT-LINE FROM PRINT-PATTERN.
        * GET THE NEXT RECORD
(B)             PERFORM READ-A-RECORD.
```

(A)   The zero suppression feature is used to our advantage. We know the first three or four bytes of each of the numeric fields will contain zeros when these fields are filled. The Z feature replaces these zeros with blanks, and consequently gives us a more readable printed line. We don't need VALUE SPACES until the end of the record, since the Z causes blanks to be inserted.

(B)   The three sentences labeled (B) are the familiar FILE PROCESSING PAIR and their partner.

(C)   We cannot use MOVE CORRESPONDING unless we want to qualify the fields summed in (D). The qualified form of the sentence would be

```
          ADD ALGEBRA   IN STUDENT-INFO
              GEOMETRY  IN STUDENT-INFO
              ENGLISH   IN STUDENT-INFO
              PHYSICS   IN STUDENT-INFO
              CHEMISTRY IN STUDENT-INFO
                  GIVING SUM-UP.
```

(D)   We will add all five of the student's GRADEs and put that number in SUM–UP. The next record will cause a new value to be put in SUM–UP, and the old value will be lost. Notice that the contents of SUM–UP are not used in the addition operation. Also notice that SUM–UP is purely numeric, since it is used in a subsequent arithmetic operation.

(E)   The average is just the sum of the student's GRADEs divided by 5.

(F)   The first and last line of output will be

```
STEVENS      TK  65  63  85  56  76  69.00
CALLINGHAM LO   68  69  69  69  68  68.60
```

SYNTAX SUMMARY

Valid symbols in a PICTURE clause.

S   The symbol S is used in a PICTURE character string to indicate the presence of an operational sign, and must be written as the leftmost character in the PICTURE clause. An operational sign indicates whether the value of an item involved in an operation is positive or negative. The symbol S is not counted in determining the size of the elementary item.

Z   Each Z in the character string represents a leading numeric character position; when that position contains a zero, the zero is replaced by a space character. Each Z is counted in the size of the item.

9   Each 9 in the character string represents a character position that contains a numeral and is counted in the size of the item.

        When a period appears in the character string, it is an editing symbol that represents the decimal point for alignment purposes. In addition, it represents a character position into which a period will be inserted. This character is counted in the size of the item.

V   The V is used in a character string to indicate the location of the assumed decimal point and may appear only once in a character string. The V does not represent a character position and, therefore, is not counted in the size of the elementary item.

EXERCISES

1. Briefly define the following terms.
   a. 77-level entry
   b. numeric field
   c. numerically edited field
2. Can values stored in numerically edited fields be used in arithmetic operations?
3. What must be included in a picture clause to represent a credit as a credit?
4. List the editing symbols introduced in this section and explain the purpose of each.
5. Indicate the contents of storage location B after the following statement:

```
MOVE A TO B
```

VALUE A	PICTURE A	PICTURE B	VALUE B
0123	99V99	ZZ.9	
45678	S9(3)V99	–ZZZZ.9	
90123	9(5)	Z(5)	
567891	99V9(4)	Z9.9(2)	
234	99V9	ZVZ	
5678	9(3)V9	ZZ	
9012	V9(4)	.9(4)	
34567	V9(5)	.9(5)	

6. Fill in the values of the variables after the indicated operation:

a. ADD EQ–RENTAL DEPRECIATION GIVING DEDUCTIBLE

DATA NAME	PICTURE	BEFORE	AFTER
EQ–RENTAL	S999V9	0955	
DEPRECIATION	S999V9	0831	
DEDUCTIBLE	S9(4)V9	04413	

b. SUBTRACT ENTERTAINMENT FROM SALARY GIVING TROUBLE

DATA NAME	PICTURE	BEFORE	AFTER
ENTERTAINMENT	S999V99	38512	
SALARY	S9(4)V99	461312	
TROUBLE	S9(5)V9	83514	

c. MULTIPLY HOURS BY RATE GIVING WAGES–GROSS

DATA NAME	PICTURE	BEFORE	AFTER
HOURS	99V99	3975	
RATE	99V99	0418	
WAGES–GROSS	9(3)V99	81423	

d. DIVIDE TOTAL–SALES BY NO–SALES GIVING AVG–SALES

DATA NAME	PICTURE	BEFORE	AFTER
TOTAL–SALES	9(6)V99	31851412	
NO–SALES	9(3)	319	
AVG–SALES	9(4)V99	816243	

PROGRAMMING PROBLEMS

1. Modify PROGRAM–NUMBER 4.2-2 so that it contains headings for the columns of information printed.
2. Modify PROGRAM–NUMBER 4.2-2 so any course grade that is greater than '080' is printed with '*' following the GRADE.
3. Modify PROGRAM–NUMBER 4.2-2 so that the information is only printed for 17- or 18-year-old male students or 16- or 17-year-old female students.
4. Using the REGISTRAR–FILE for input, calculate the semester average for each student. You must translate the letter GRADEs into numeric equivalents before calculating an average (A = 4; B = 3; C = 2; D = 1; E = 0). Each course is three hours.

```
Hint:    MOVE ZERO      TO COUNT.
         PERFORM CHANGE-TO-NUMBER.
         DIVIDE COUNT BY 15 GIVING AVERAGE.
   CHANGE-TO-NUMBER.
 *    MULTIPLY VALUE OF GRADE BY 3 BEFORE ADDING TO
 *    COUNT AS EACH COURSE IS A 3 HOUR COURSE.
       IF LETTER-GRADE = 'A'
          ADD 12 TO COUNT
       ELSE
          IF LETTER-GRADE = 'B'
             ADD 9 TO COUNT
          ELSE
             IF LETTER-GRADE = 'C'
                ADD 6 TO COUNT
             ELSE
                IF LETTER-GRADE = 'D'
                   ADD 3 TO COUNT.
```

5. Calculate the average grade in ALGEBRA for all the students in STUDENT–FILE. List the NAME and ALGEBRA grade for all students with an ALGEBRA grade greater than the class average. You will have to process the STUDENT–FILE twice to accomplish this. The first time you can accumulate information to use in calculating the average, and the second time you can compare this average to the ALGEBRA grade of each student to determine whether or not that student will be listed.

4.3   Input and Output of Numeric Data

Report Editing Features

It is a luxury to have the data for a program not only available, as in the case of files such as CUSTOMER–FILE, but also "clean" or error free. The next program we examine may have problems caused by "dirty" data.

The rules for numeric data seem straightforward when considered in the abstract. When we actually key numbers on the input record, we must, however, remember two important rules.

1. No editing symbol may appear in the columns of the input record that are the columns of a numeric field.
2. All numbers must be right-justified in the columns that represent the numeric field.

Let's suppose columns 21–27 of the input record represent a numeric field that can have any of the picture clauses we will list. Furthermore, the numeric value that is to be in this field is $3,819.56. Let's see what these columns of the record will look like.

```
(i)   PIC 9(4)V9(3)      3  8  1  9  5  6  0
                        21 22 23 24 25 26 27

(ii)  PIC 9(5)V99        0  3  8  1  9  5  6
                        21 22 23 24 25 26 27

(iii) PIC 9(6)V9         0  0  3  8  1  9  5
                        21 22 23 24 25 26 27
```

Case (i) illustrates that we cannot leave column 27 blank, or we will get an execution-time error. COBOL expects a digit in each of the positions in a numeric field. Some COBOL compilers allow leading zeros to be omitted, such as column 21 in case (ii) and columns 21 and 22 in case (iii), but never trailing zeros such as in column 27. When a character such as a blank is found in a storage location that is supposed to contain a digit, the execution time error indicated is called a **data exception.** Notice that all the editing symbols —the dollar sign, the comma, and the decimal point—have been removed. The implied position of the decimal point is represented by the position of the V in the picture clause.

The next problem arises when we try putting all these editing features back in the output. The features we use act much like the Z editing symbol in that the digits are "almost" left alone until the most significant digit is encountered. At that point special symbols are put in the remaining positions up to the left boundary of the field.

The Dollar Sign

In preparing reports it is often necessary to have the dollar sign printed. To do this, make the dollar sign the left-most character of the appropriate picture clause. This causes the dollar sign to be printed in this print position. For example:

```
                          OUTPUT FIELD
          STORAGE          PICTURE               PRINTED
          00123456         $9(6).99              $001234.56
```

Zero Suppression

We can easily get rid of the leading zeros.

```
                          OUTPUT FIELD
          STORAGE          PICTURE               PRINTED
          00123456         $Z(6).99              $__1234.56
```

This looks a little better, but the space between $ and 1 is awfully inviting to someone who comes along and wants to insert a digit or two. To eliminate this space, we *float* the dollar sign, just as we did Z.

```
                          OUTPUT FIELD
          STORAGE          PICTURE               PRINTED
          00123456         $(6).99               _$1234.56
```

As soon as the most significant digit is printed, the next position to the left has a $ printed in it. The remaining print positions to the left are blanked out.

We've made lots of progress. We still need to insert the comma that should appear between every three digits to the left of the decimal point. This is accomplished as follows:

```
                          OUTPUT FIELD
          STORAGE          PICTURE               PRINTED
          00123456         $$$,$$$.99            $1,234.56
```

As long as there is a digit to be placed to the left of the comma, the comma is inserted. As soon as the most significant digit is encountered, a dollar sign is printed in the next print position to its left. The remaining print positions to the left of the $ are filled with blanks. If the picture clause is not able to hold all the digits to the left of the decimal point and the $ sign, the dollar sign will be put in the left-most print position of the field in preference to a significant digit! We will examine one more feature here, and leave other similar features for the exercises.

Check Protection Symbol

Checks are often printed with the amount appearing in the form

```
          $***3,856.91
```

How do we get the check protection symbol between the most significant digit and the dollar sign? Easy. Put them in the picture clause, and let the machine determine how many check protection symbols to print.

```
                          OUTPUT FIELD
          STORAGE          PICTURE               PRINTED
          000385691        $***,***.99           $**3,856.91
```

We can now line up a column of dollar signs on a column of numbers.

COBOL contains many features for displaying output. Editing features for business reports are designed to be easy for the programmer to use.

```
      *
      * NAME:                          ID:
      * PROGRAM-NUMBER: 4.3-1
      * DESCRIPTION:  CALCULATE THE PAY FOR HOURLY
      *    EMPLOYEES OF THE NEW-WORLD CO.
      *    ASSUME THE INCOME TAX RATE IS 16% FOR ALL
      *    EMPLOYEES. ALSO ASSUME THAT THE EMPLOYEES'
      *    CONTRIBUTION TO SOCIAL SECURITY IS 6.5%
      *    OVERTIME (40 + HRS) IS PAID AT TIME AND A HALF.
      *    THE INPUT FILE IS A CARD FILE AND THE OUTPUT
      *    FILE IS THE PRINTER.
      *
            COPY TEXTA.
        WORKING-STORAGE SECTION.
      *   AUXILIARY STORAGE LOCATIONS
        77  GROSS-PAY1     PIC 9(4)V99.
(A)     77  SOC-SEC-DED1   PIC 9(4)V99.
        77  INCOME-TAX1    PIC 9(4)V99.


      * INPUT RECORD
        01  EMPLOYEE.
(B)         05 SOC-SEC-NO    PIC X(9).
            05 NAME          PIC X(20).
            05 DEPT          PIC XX.
            05 PAY-RATE      PIC 9V99.
            05 HOURS-WORKED  PIC 99V99.
            05 FILLER        PIC X(42).


      * OUTPUT RECORD
        01  PRINT-PATTERN.
            05 FILLER          PIC X.
            05 DEPT-PP         PIC X(5).
            05 NAME-PP         PIC X(40).
            05 HOURS-PP        PIC ZZ.99.
            05 GROSS-PAY-PP    PIC $$$,$$$.99.
            05 SOC-SEC-DED-PP  PIC $$,$$$.99.
            05 INCOME-TAX-PP   PIC $$$,$$$.99.
            05 NET-PAY-PP      PIC $$$,$$$.99.
            05 FILLER          PIC X(43) VALUE SPACES.


        PROCEDURE DIVISION.
      * MODEL-I

            OPEN INPUT CARD-READER
                 OUTPUT PRINTER.


      * FILE PROCESSING PAIR
            PERFORM GET-A-RECORD.
            PERFORM PAYROLL
                UNTIL NAME = HIGH-VALUES.


      * TERMINATION ACTIVITY
            CLOSE CARD-READER
                  PRINTER.
            STOP RUN.
```

```
* INPUT PROCEDURE
  GET-A-RECORD.
        READ CARD-READER INTO EMPLOYEE
             AT END MOVE HIGH-VALUES TO NAME.

* RECORD PROCESSING
  PAYROLL.
        MOVE DEPT          TO DEPT-PP.
        MOVE NAME          TO NAME-PP.
        MOVE HOURS-WORKED TO HOURS-PP.
        IF HOURS-WORKED NOT GREATER THAN 40
             MULTIPLY HOURS-WORKED BY PAY-RATE
                  GIVING GROSS-PAY1
        ELSE
             COMPUTE GROSS-PAY1 = 40 * PAY-RATE
                 + 1.5 * PAY-RATE * (HOURS-WORKED - 40).
        MULTIPLY GROSS-PAY1 BY .065 GIVING SOC-SEC-DED1.
        MULTIPLY GROSS-PAY1 BY .16 GIVING INCOME-TAX1.
        SUBTRACT SOC-SEC-DED1 INCOME-TAX1
             FROM GROSS-PAY1 GIVING NET-PAY-PP.
        MOVE GROSS-PAY1    TO GROSS-PAY-PP.
        MOVE SOC-SEC-DED1 TO SOC-SEC-DED-PP.
        MOVE INCOME-TAX1   TO INCOME-TAX-PP.
        WRITE PRINT-LINE FROM PRINT-PATTERN.
        PERFORM GET-A-RECORD.
```

TYPICAL INPUT RECORDS

(C)   534375918GEORGE M. COHAN_____364184000
         269342518JAMES SMITH   285123975

(A)   These auxiliary storage locations are needed, since the numbers they represent will be used in more than one arithmetic statement.

(B)   The record description says that the input records contain

DATA	COLUMNS OF RECORDS CONTAINING
Social Security number	1–9
Name	10–29
Department	30–31
Pay rate	32–34
Hours worked	35–38
Extra space	39–80

(C)   The input record should be keyed exactly as described in (B). Notice that in the first input record the hours worked are represented by 4000. There is no decimal point included since it is implied by the picture clause to be between the second and the third zero (counting back from the right-most column of the field). Also notice that even though there are no decimal digits, the storage locations of the decimal digits include zero. If this value were punched as 40__, the program would halt when the value of this field was first accessed because not every byte contains a digit as expected. The compiler *expects* a digit in each column of the numeric field to the right of the most significant digit. Some compilers require padding with zeros both to the right and to the left. Other COBOL compilers, for example, allow the padding with blanks to the left of the most significant digit.

A Payroll Program

The last program had rather simple output for a payroll routine. Let's improve it while reviewing some of the output features available in COBOL. A payroll program should produce a paycheck as its output, or at least a statement if a direct deposit service is available. Let's suppose we want the output for Cohan to contain the information shown in Figure 4.3.1. It looks like 13 separate print records must be defined in the WORKING–STORAGE SECTION, so all the features of the check are printed. In practice, much of the material in the check would be preprinted. The preprinted form might look like the one in Figure 4.3.2. The form would be mounted on a printing device and we would only have to fill in the blanks with computer-generated output.

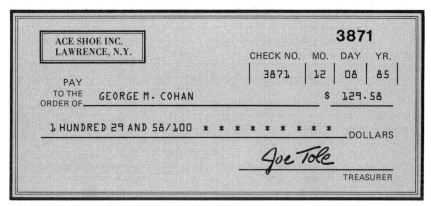

Figure 4.3.1 *Sample printed paycheck.*

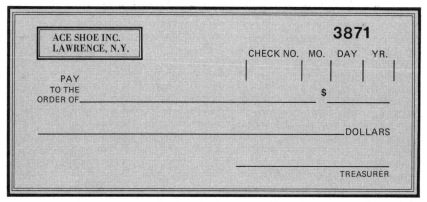

Figure 4.3.2 *Sample preprinted paycheck form.*

One rather interesting feature of this involves figuring out how to isolate the number of hundreds of dollars, the number of dollars less than a hundred, and the number of cents in the field with value $129.58. We will need some auxiliary storage locations, described as follows:

```
GROSS—PAY1          PIC 999V99.
HUNDREDS            PIC 9.
LESS—THAN—HUNDREDS  PIC 99.
CENTS               PIC V99.
```

The code we need is given now.

```
      DIVIDE GROSS-PAY1 BY 100 GIVING HUNDREDS.
      COMPUTE LESS-THAN-HUNDREDS =
            GROSS-PAY1 - 100 * HUNDREDS.
      COMPUTE CENTS =
            GROSS-PAY1 - 100 * HUNDREDS
                       - LESS-THAN-HUNDREDS.
```

Trace the execution of this code if GROSS-PAY1 represents $826.51. This example should help clarify what is happening.

We won't deal with special forms in our output. However, business applications do include special forms, such as checks and mailing labels. There is no difficulty dealing with these once the programmer knows how many output lines each contains and how many spaces are available for each of the output lines. Normally, special form output is relegated to off hours for printing to make the computing equipment readily available to daytime users.

Printing a Check

To illustrate the use of output features, the next program actually prints a check, given the amount, the payee, and the payer. We have incorporated the feature of isolating the dollars and cents of an amount as independent pieces of data.

```
*
* NAME:            ID:
* PROGRAM-NUMBER: 4.3-2
* DESCRIPTION:  USE SOME EDITING FEATURES TO
*   PRINT A CHECK.  THE INPUT IS A CARD FILE
*   OF THE FOLLOWING FORM:
*   COL 1-4:     CHECK NUMBER          PIC XXXX
*   COL 5-24     NAME OF RECEIVER      PIC X(20)
*   COL 25-30    DATE OF ISSUE         PIC 99
*                   FORM MMDDYY        PIC 99
*                                      PIC 99
*   COL 31-50    NAME OF SIGNER        PIC X(20)
*   COL 51-55    AMOUNT OF CHECK       PIC 999V99
*
      COPY TEXTA.
  WORKING-STORAGE SECTION.
* AUXILIARY STORAGE LOCATIONS
  77  HUNDREDS-TEMP     PIC 999.
  77  DOLLARS-TEMP      PIC 999.
  77  CENTS-TEMP        PIC V99.
* INPUT RECORD
  01  CARD-INFO.
      05  CHECK-NO           PIC X(4).
      05  NAME-OUT           PIC X(20).
      05  DATE-OF-CHECK.
          10 DAY-OF-WRITING  PIC 99.
          10 MONTH           PIC 99.
          10 YEAR            PIC 99.
      05  NAME-IN            PIC X(20).
      05  AMOUNT-OF-CHECK    PIC 999V99.
      05  FILLER             PIC X(25).
```

```
* OUTPUT RECORDS
 01   LINE-1.
        05    FILLER        PIC X.
        05    FILLER        PIC XX     VALUE '* '.
        05    FILLER        PIC X(48) VALUE SPACES.
        05    FILLER        PIC X(4)  VALUE 'NO. '.
        05    CHECK-NUMBER PIC X(4).
        05    FILLER        PIC XX     VALUE ' *'.
 01   LINE-2.
        05    FILLER        PIC X.
        05    FILLER        PIC XX     VALUE '* '.
        05    FILLER        PIC X(46) VALUE SPACES.
        05    DAY-WRIT      PIC Z9.
        05    FILLER        PIC X      VALUE '/'.
        05    MONTH-WRIT    PIC Z9.
        05    FILLER        PIC XXX    VALUE ' 19'.
        05    YEAR-WRIT     PIC 99.
        05    FILLER        PIC XX     VALUE ' *'.
 01   LINE-3.
        05    FILLER        PIC X.
        05    FILLER        PIC XX     VALUE '* '.
        05    FILLER        PIC X(10) VALUE 'PAY TO    '.
        05    NAME-PLACE PIC X(35).
        05    AMOUNT-CK  PIC $***,***.99.
        05    FILLER        PIC XX     VALUE ' *'.
 01   LINE-4.
        05    FILLER  PIC X.
        05    FILLER  PIC XX     VALUE '* '.
        05    HUNDREDS PIC ZZ.
        05    FILLER  PIC X(10) VALUE ' HUNDRED'.
        05    DOLLARS  PIC Z9.
        05    FILLER  PIC X(5)  VALUE ' AND '.
        05    CENTS    PIC 99.
        05    FILLER  PIC X(4)  VALUE '/100'.
        05    FILLER  PIC X(24) VALUE ALL '*'.
        05    FILLER  PIC X(7)  VALUE 'DOLLARS'.
        05    FILLER  PIC XX     VALUE ' *'.
 01   LINE-5.
        05    FILLER              PIC X.
        05    FILLER              PIC XX     VALUE '* '.
        05    FILLER              PIC X(36) VALUE SPACES.
        05    NAME-WRITING-CHECK PIC X(20).
        05    FILLER              PIC XX     VALUE ' *'.
 01   LINE-6.
        05    FILLER PIC X.
        05    FILLER PIC X(58) VALUE '*'.
        05    FILLER PIC XX     VALUE ' *'.
 01   LINE-7.
        05    FILLER PIC X.
        05    FILLER PIC X(60) VALUE ALL '*'.


 PROCEDURE DIVISION.
* MODEL-I


        OPEN INPUT CARD-READER
             OUTPUT PRINTER.
```

```
* FILE PROCESSING PAIR
      PERFORM READ-IN.
      PERFORM WRITE-CHECK
          UNTIL NAME-OUT = HIGH-VALUES.


* TERMINATION ACTIVITY
      CLOSE CARD-READER
            PRINTER.
      STOP RUN.


* INPUT PROCEDURE
 READ-IN.
      READ CARD-READER INTO CARD-INFO
          AT END MOVE HIGH-VALUES TO NAME-OUT.


* RECORD PROCESSING
 WRITE-CHECK.
      MOVE CHECK-NO        TO CHECK-NUMBER.
      MOVE MONTH           TO MONTH-WRIT.
      MOVE DAY-OF-WRITING  TO DAY-WRIT.
      MOVE YEAR            TO YEAR-WRIT.
      MOVE NAME-OUT        TO NAME-PLACE.
      MOVE AMOUNT-OF-CHECK TO AMOUNT-CK.
      MOVE NAME-IN         TO NAME-WRITING-CHECK.
      DIVIDE AMOUNT-OF-CHECK BY 100 GIVING
            HUNDREDS-TEMP.
      COMPUTE DOLLARS-TEMP =
          AMOUNT-OF-CHECK - 100 * HUNDREDS-TEMP.
      COMPUTE CENTS-TEMP =
          AMOUNT-OF-CHECK - 100 * HUNDREDS-TEMP
                          - DOLLARS-TEMP.
      *
      *   MOVE THE BREAKDOWN OF THE AMOUNT TO THE
      *     OUTPUT RECORD
      *
      MOVE HUNDREDS-TEMP TO HUNDREDS.
      MOVE DOLLARS-TEMP  TO DOLLARS.
      MULTIPLY CENTS-TEMP BY 100 GIVING CENTS.
      *
      WRITE PRINT-LINE FROM LINE-7
          AFTER ADVANCING 5 LINES.
      WRITE PRINT-LINE FROM LINE-1 AFTER 1.
      WRITE PRINT-LINE FROM LINE-6 AFTER 1.
      WRITE PRINT-LINE FROM LINE-2 AFTER 1.
      WRITE PRINT-LINE FROM LINE-6 AFTER 1.
      WRITE PRINT-LINE FROM LINE-3 AFTER 1.
      WRITE PRINT-LINE FROM LINE-6 AFTER 1.
      WRITE PRINT-LINE FROM LINE-4 AFTER 1.
      WRITE PRINT-LINE FROM LINE-6 AFTER 1.
      WRITE PRINT-LINE FROM LINE-5 AFTER 1.
(A)   WRITE PRINT-LINE FROM LINE-7
            BEFORE ADVANCING 5 LINES.
* GET THE NEXT RECORD
      PERFORM READ-IN.
```

(A) To this point we have not discussed how the printed output can have blank lines for spacing purposes. Two features of COBOL that facilitate this are

   (1) WRITE record-name FROM data-field AFTER ADVANCING integer LINES.
   (2) WRITE record-name FROM data-field BEFORE ADVANCING integer LINES.

The only required entries for the BEFORE and AFTER clauses are the words BEFORE and AFTER and an integer value indicating the number of lines involved. The difference is merely whether the current line is printed before or after the printer advances the carriage control an integer number of lines. COBOL compilers require the use of the AFTER or BEFORE clauses with *every* WRITE statement or with *none* of the WRITE statements. An additional option for accomplishing the spacing between lines of output is to define a record like

```
01  BLANK-LINE  PIC X(133) VALUE SPACES.
```

Whenever a space is needed the program can just execute the sentence

```
WRITE PRINT-LINE FROM BLANK-LINE
```

If more than one space is needed, this sentence can be executed under the control of a PERFORM---*n* TIMES.

To understand the program better, trace the execution if the input record is

```
1234JOHN J. MIRALLE      092185A.K. HONEYMAN        83835
1    5                   2    3                     5
                         5    1                     1
```

and see that the check pictured here is the output:

```
*****************************************************************
*                                                   NO. 1234 *
*                                                             *
*                                                   9/21 1985 *
*                                                             *
* PAY TO    JOHN J. MIRALLE                   $****838.35 *
*                                                             *
*  8 HUNDRED   38 AND 35/100********************DOLLARS *
*                                                             *
*                                           A. K. HONEYMAN *
*****************************************************************
```

SYNTAX SUMMARY

Valid symbols in a PICTURE CLAUSE.

B, 0   Each B in the character string represents a character position into which the space character will be inserted. A similar result occurs in each field that contains a 0.

+, −

CR, DB   These symbols are used as editing sign control symbols. When used, each represents the character position into which the editing sign control symbol will be placed. The symbols are mutually exclusive in one character string. Each character used in the symbol is counted in determining the size of the data item.

*   Each asterisk in the character string represents a leading numeric character position into which an asterisk will be placed when that position contains a zero. Each * is counted in the size of the item.

\$ The currency symbol in the character string represents a character position into which a currency symbol is to be placed. The currency symbol is counted in the size of the data item.

EXERCISES

1. List the editing symbols introduced in this section and explain the purpose of each.
2. Are values stored in numeric fields right justified or left justified?
3. What would the clause AFTER 2 cause to happen in a WRITE statement?
4. Explain the difference between an AFTER ADVANCING clause and a BEFORE ADVANCING clause.
5. In each case determine what the edited output will be if the information in the sending field is moved to the receiving field in the table below. The minus to the right of a number indicates that the number in storage is negative. For the floating minus, a sign

SENDING FIELD		RECEIVING FIELD	
PICTURE CLAUSE	DATA	PICTURE CLAUSE	EDITED RESULT
a. S999V99	14897	ZZZ.99	
S999V99	19071	ZZZ.99	
S999V99	76934−	ZZZ.99	
b. S9(4)V99	300780	Z,ZZZ.99	
S9(4)V99	080983−	Z,ZZZ.99	
S9(4)V99	230483	Z,ZZZ.99	
c. S9(4)V99	021284	$$,$$$.99	
S9(4)V99	090981−	$$,$$$.99	
S9(4)V99	180784	$$,$$$.99	
S99V99	5020	$$$.99	
S99V99	7983	$$$.99	
d. S9(4)V99	010980	$*,***.99	
S9(4)V99	280781−	$*,***.99	
S9(4)V99	060683	$*,***.99	
S9(5)V99	1220285	$*,***.99	
e. S9(6)	300380	ZZZ,ZZZCR	
S9(6)	070185	ZZZ,ZZZCR	
S9(4)V99	290685−	Z,ZZZ,ZZZCR	
S9(4)V99	240180	$$,$$$.99CR	
S9(4)V99	060281−	$$,$$$.99CR	
f. S9(4)V99	401708	++,+++.99	
S9(4)V99	690262−	++,+++.99	
S9(4)V99	285729	++,+++.99	
S9(4)V99	466903−	++,+++.99	
S9(4)V99	346348	++,+++.99	
S9(5)V99	1244510	++,+++.99	
g. S9(4)V99	003154−	−−,−−−.99	
S9(4)V99	053997	−−,−−−.99	
S99V99	6648−	−−−.99	
S99V99	0811	−−−.99	
h. S9(4)	7811	ZZZ,Z00	
S9(4)	0180	++,+++.00	
S9(4)	3072−	ZZZ,Z00CR	
S9(4)	4345	$$,$$$.00	
i. S9(6)	000982−	ZZZZBCR	
S9(6)	111281	99B99B99	
S9(6)	318542	ZZZB999	

will be printed only when the number is negative. For the floating plus sign there will be either a + or a − printed. The CR used in (e) will be printed following the numeric value whenever the value is a credit and not a debit. In any case the picture clause allows 2 spaces. In Parts h and i, the characters 0 and blank will be printed whenever 0 and B occur. This inclusion of extra characters improves readability in many cases. Also, units for large numbers in computations may be thousands of dollars while the printed output needs the actual amounts.

PROGRAMMING PROBLEMS

You have probably at some time received a computer-generated letter. You can see how the letter has been personalized by examining the use of your name and address. Often your name is also used at various points in the letter to reinforce the personal attention theme. The program assignments in this section will allow you to exercise your ingenuity in writing a computer-generated letter. The parts of the text that depend on information about the addressee such as state of residence, credit worthiness, or highest grade, can be tailored by asking questions about the contents of various data fields in the input record. You should design this letter so that very few words will be different in any particular letter produced.

1. You have just been promoted to Chief-Assistant-Associate-Vice Loan Officer of the New World Loan Co. You have been asked to design and implement a program that can be used to inform potential customers what their monthly payments will be for a loan if the true annual interest rate is ANNUAL–INT and the payments are the same each month. The formula for the payment is

> PAYMENT = AMOUNT-BORROWED * PERIODIC-INTEREST *
>   (1 + PERIODIC-INTEREST) ** NO-PAYMENTS /
>   ((1 + PERIODIC-INTEREST) ** NO-PAYMENTS − 1).
> NO–PAYMENTS will be measured in terms of months
> PERIODIC–INTEREST = (1 + ANNUAL–INT) ** (1 / 12) − 1.
> ANNUAL–INT will be the true annual interest rate

In the program you must make the interest rate depend on the purpose of the loan. The letter to the customer should have at least one clause depend on some information in the record.

    Create a file with six to eight records to be used as data with the program.

INPUT REQUIRED	OUTPUT REQUIRED
Name	(to be incorporated
Street	in the letter to
City	the customer)
Zip	monthly payment
Purpose of loan	annual interest rate
Amount requested	total interest costs
Requested length	amount borrowed
of loan	total number of payments

2. The formula for the value of an annuity after NO–PAYMENTS yearly payments of ANN–PAY dollars with INT–RATE is

a. ANN–VALUE = ANN–PAY *
   ((1 + INT–RATE) ** NO–PAYMENTS − 1)
   / INT–RATE.

Rather than make annual payments for an annuity, it is sometimes desirable to pay a lump sum of money knowing that for the next NO–YRS years an annual payment of ANN–PAY dollars will be made. The formula is

```
b. ANNUITY-START = ANN-PAY *
   (1 - (1 + INT-RATE) ** (- NO-YRS)) / INT-RATE.
```

Write a computer-generated letter answering customer inquiries about an annuity. The customers supply you with information to indicate whether they want an annuity purchased with NO–YRS annual payments of ANN–PAY dollars (Formula a) or, instead, a lump sum payment (Formula b) so that the value would be equivalent to a paid up annuity purchased with NO–YRS payments of ANN–PAY dollars. Determine the interest you will offer by including a coded field in the input record that can take on one of three values and then assign, in the program, 12%, 14%, or 16% to INT–RATE depending on the value of this code.

Include the values of INT–RATE, ANN–PAY, NO–YRS and either ANNUITY–START or ANN–VALUE in the letter you write. Phrase the letter so that nearly the same format can be used whether Formula a or Formula b is used.

Create a file with six to eight records to be used as data for the program.

4.4   Data Verification

When implementing computer solutions for file processing problems, the verification of the input data is a first step in completing a program. In this section we will discuss some of the ways data verification can be implemented.

Types of Data Verification

Data verification can be thought of at three different levels. On one level, the verification may be concerned with how the data is represented on an external storage medium such as a magnetic tape or disk.

At another level one can keep information about a file, such as the number of records or the total value of one field for all the records. When a file is processed again, the same information can be recalculated and then the result compared with the original calculation. Any discrepancy will indicate an error involving one or more of the records of the file.

A third way of verifying totals is to batch the records of a file and calculate the total for each batch and then add these partial totals to find a total for the file itself. If the records are consistently batched in a specific way, any error at the file level can be quite easily traced to an error in a particular batch of records.

Reasonableness and Range Checks

We are really more concerned with the validity of individual fields of each record of a file. Once we understand that we cannot guarantee that the information is correct in all cases, but only that the information has a valid form or takes on a reasonable value, we see that validation is primarily possible in the following two ways. First, we can verify whether or not a field contains only the right kind of characters. This is called a **reasonableness check.** Secondly, we can verify whether or not a field has a value in an acceptable range for values of that field. For example, if a field represents the number of hours an employee works in a given week, the two checks would consist of first verifying that each character in the field is a digit and then that the value of the digits was a number between zero and sixty. Again the data cannot be guaranteed to be correct, but it can be ascertained that the value is reasonable. A check of this type is called a **range check.**

Checking a Commonly Used Code

A second type of data check that occurs often involves checking the values of a commonly used code. For example, if an address of a customer contains a two-letter state abbreviation, it can be checked that the two letters correspond to one of the 50 valid state abbreviations. This involves comparing the value in a field to a list of all possible values for the code. Other similar cases occur if three-letter abbreviations are used for the names of months or if one wants to verify that telephone area codes are valid. One could even ask to check that a zip code actually represents an area in the state indicated in the address.

Another defensive strategy used with programming that involves selecting records by means of a value of a code was seen in Section 3.3. In that section the following sentence occurred as part of the record processing paragraph.

```
IF REGION-CODE = 'A'
    PERFORM OUT-A
ELSE
    IF REGION-CODE = 'B'
        PERFORM OUT-B
    ELSE
        IF REGION-CODE = 'C'
            PERFORM OUT-C.
```

By examining Appendix D we find that the values for REGION-CODE are one of the letters 'A', 'B', or 'C'. It is reasonable to ask why the condition

```
IF REGION-CODE = 'C'
```

is included in this code since at execution time the only way to arrive at this condition is if the record does have a value of 'C' for REGION-CODE. While this seems redundant, there are, however, at least two very good reasons for including this condition in the code. The first is that this statement makes it clear that the program is interested in processing records with one of the values 'A', or 'B', or 'C' for REGION-CODE and no other records in the file. Another programmer may not know that there are no other values for REGION-CODE in the file or the file may change by having one or more new values for REGION-CODE incorporated. In this latter case the code

```
IF REGION-CODE = 'A'
    PERFORM OUT-A
ELSE
    IF REGION-CODE = 'B'
        PERFORM OUT-B
    ELSE
        PERFORM OUT-C.
```

would not deal only with records having a value of 'A' or 'B' or 'C' for REGION-CODE. Thus the second reason for including this extra condition is so we do not write a program to process records with REGION-CODE having a value in one of the three categories: (1) value 'A'; (2) value 'B'; (3) any other value. We make the code clearer and we improve the chances of writing a correct program if we do not make assumptions about the data that do not have to be made.

ON SIZE ERROR

Certainly the first step in developing a system that works correctly for all possible inputs is to create an input file that is as free of errors as possible. Once the data enters the system, however, there are other difficulties that need to be prevented. One error that can go undetected can arise when moving one numeric field to another where there are fewer significant digits in the receiving field than in the sending field. As an example, consider the code below.

```
                      MOVE A TO B

       Data Name     Picture    Before    After
           A         999V99     31876     31876
           B          99V99     _ _ _ _    1876
```

A MOVE statement of this sort will not cause an error condition. The compiler is willing to continue executing the program using the erroneous value of B as if it were valid. A set of commands that can also give rise to a similar occurrence is the set of arithmetic commands. The error condition arises when the receiving field cannot hold all the significant digits of the number that is the result of the computation. For example, consider

```
                    MULTIPLY A BY B

       Data Name     Picture    Before    After
           A         999V99     31876     31876
           B          99V99      4126      5203
```

In this case the actual answer is 13152.0376 which is quite different from the value stored in B.

There is no feature in COBOL that can be used to detect this error associated with the MOVE statement. In the case of arithmetic statements, there is a COBOL feature that checks for this kind of error at execution time. The syntax is

```
                  arithmetic statement
              ON SIZE ERROR imperative statement
```

As long as the receiving field for the arithmetic statement is large enough to hold all the significant digits of the number resulting from the operation, the imperative statement following ON SIZE ERROR is not executed. Whenever the receiving field is not large enough to hold all the significant digits, the imperative statement following ON SIZE ERROR will be executed. Typically, the imperative statement will cause an error message to be printed and execution to continue from a point that prevents this erroneous value being used to compound the problems.

Checking for Numeric or Alphabetic Characters

In applications that involve using the result of merging a number of files, it can happen that non-numeric information can be mistaken for numeric information. It is possible to check a whole field at execution time to determine whether or not all the characters stored in the field are or are not numeric (0–9) or alphabetic (A–Z or space). The syntax uses the IF construction with a special way of writing the condition.

```
      IF   identifier   [NOT]  {NUMERIC   }
                               {ALPHABETIC}

            statement
```

The condition is TRUE just in the case where the contents of the identifier contains the expected kind of characters. One often poses this condition so that it is only true when an error condition exists. In such a case, the statement may cause an appropriate message to be printed and the flow of control resumed at some point that will not depend on the erroneous value. This condition really causes the compiler to generate code to check each byte of the field. Notice that the conditions allowed do not check special characters (other than a space in the case of ALPHABETIC) or any field that contains a mixture of character types.

It is always the programmer's responsibility to include any error-detecting code that is appropriate to ensure correct execution. When the data is incorrect, the program should both detect the error and continue execution in a way that does not depend on the incorrect data that was found.

A Data Verification Program

We now see how these techniques can be incorporated into a data verification program.

```
*
* NAME:                    ID:
* PROGRAM-NUMBER: 4.4-1
* DESCRIPTION:  CREATE A FILE OF RECORDS THAT
*   HAVE A CODE-VALUE OF 'A' OR 'B' AND AT
*   THE SAME TIME HAVE AN AMT-DUE IN THE
*   A SPECIFIED RANGE
*
       COPY TEXTA.
   WORKING-STORAGE SECTION.
* INPUT RECORD
   01  CARD-RECORD.
       05  SOC-SEC-NO        PIC X(9).
       05  NAME             PIC X(20).
       05  AMT-DUE          PIC 9(5)V99.
       05  CODE-VALUE       PIC X.
       05  FILLER           PIC X(43).
* OUTPUT RECORDS
   01  GOOD-RECORD.
       05  FILLER           PIC X.
       05  GOOD-RECORD-AREA PIC X(132).
   01  INVALID-RECORDS.
       05  FILLER           PIC X.
       05  CODE-VALUE-IN    PIC X(5).
       05  CARD-RECORD-IN   PIC X(85).
       05  AMT-DUE-IN       PIC 9(5)V99.
       05  FILLER           PIC X(45).
           VALUE 'CODE OR AMOUNT INCORRECT'.
   01  VALUES-WRONG.
       05  FILLER           PIC X.
       05  CODE-VALUE-VA    PIC X(5).
       05  CARD-RECORD-VA   PIC X(85).
       05  AMT-DUE-VA       PIC 9(5)V99.
       05  FILLER           PIC X(45)
           VALUE 'AMOUNT TOO LARGE FOR CODE'.

   PROCEDURE DIVISION.
* MODEL-I
       OPEN INPUT CARD-READER
            OUTPUT PRINTER.
```

```
* FILE PROCESSING PAIR
      PERFORM READ-A-RECORD.
      PERFORM VALIDATION
         UNTIL NAME = HIGH-VALUES.


* TERMINATION ACTIVITY
      CLOSE CARD-READER
           PRINTER.
      STOP RUN.


* INPUT PROCEDURE
 READ-A-RECORD.
      READ CARD-READER INTO CARD-RECORD
         AT END MOVE HIGH-VALUES TO NAME.


* RECORD PROCESSING
 VALIDATION.
      IF CODE-VALUE NOT ALPHABETIC
        OR AMT-DUE NOT NUMERIC
           PERFORM INPUT-ERROR-RTN
      ELSE
           PERFORM RANGE-CHECK.
      PERFORM READ-A-RECORD.
 RANGE-CHECK.
      IF CODE-VALUE = 'A'
        AND AMT-DUE GREATER THAN 300
           PERFORM AMOUNT-TOO-LARGE
      ELSE
           IF CODE-VALUE = 'B'
             AND AMT-DUE GREATER THAN 150
                PERFORM AMOUNT-TOO-LARGE
           ELSE
                IF CODE-VALUE = 'A'
                  OR CODE-VALUE = 'B'
                     MOVE CARD-RECORD TO GOOD-RECORD-AREA
                     WRITE PRINT-LINE FROM GOOD-RECORD
                ELSE
                     PERFORM INPUT-ERROR-RTN.
 INPUT-ERROR-RTN.
      MOVE CODE-VALUE  TO CODE-VALUE-IN.
      MOVE CARD-RECORD TO CARD-RECORD-IN.
      MOVE AMT-DUE     TO AMT-DUE-IN.
      WRITE PRINT-LINE FROM INVALID-RECORDS.
 AMOUNT-TOO-LARGE.
      MOVE CODE-VALUE  TO CODE-VALUE-VA.
      MOVE CARD-RECORD TO CARD-RECORD-VA.
      MOVE AMT-DUE     TO AMT-DUE-VA.
      WRITE PRINT-LINE FROM VALUES-WRONG.
```

(A) next to IF CODE-VALUE NOT ALPHABETIC line.
(B) next to IF CODE-VALUE = 'A' line.

(A)   This check verifies that the correct kind of characters occur in the fields CODE-VALUE and AMT-DUE. This check in itself is not completely satisfactory. It does, however, allow a more refined check at the next level of the program's logic.

(B)   The program first identifies records with valid codes, but AMT–DUE fields with invalid amounts. The next level of logic will find all valid records. Finally, those records with a CODE–VALUE other than 'A' or 'B' are found to be invalid regardless of the value in the AMT–DUE field. Valid records are just listed by the line printer. Invalid records are listed by the line printer with an appropriate notation.

In a large commercial programming shop one is beginning to see a separation between data verification and record processing. When several users depend on the same data, it makes sense to have a core of programs that do all the data verification before any user is allowed to write an application program with that data being used. This central cleaning of the input file makes the programming task much easier since not every program must verify the correctness of the data before using it. The read only files used with this text are an example of this process.

SYNTAX SUMMARY

```
CONDITION
                        ⎧NUMERIC   ⎫
   IF identifier [NOT]  ⎨          ⎬
                        ⎩ALPHABETIC⎭
```

EXERCISES

1. Why is data verification important?
2. What is a range check?
3. What are batch totals? What purpose do they serve in data verification? How are batch totals and file totals related?
4. Write a COBOL sentence that selects for special processing the customers in NEW–WORLD–FILE who have a CREDIT–RATING of 1, 3, or 5. The special processing for each category of customers is different.
5. Write a COBOL sentence that selects for special processing the students in REGISTRAR–FILE who have either an 'A' or a 'B' as the value for GEOGRAPHY–10. The special processing for each category of students is different.
6. Write the code needed to discover any customer in CUSTOMER–FILE who owes more money than what is allowed for the CREDIT–LIMIT the customer has. See Appendix D for the permissible range for each value of CREDIT–LIMIT.

PROGRAMMING PROBLEMS

1. Using the CUSTOMER–FILE for input, write a program that lists for each record in the file the NAME, CREDIT–LIMIT, and AMOUNT–DUE fields as well as the amount of credit still available to the customer.
2. Using the NEW–WORLD–FILE for input, write a program that lists the NAME of each customer and a code that indicates whether AMT–DUE–PAYMENT is in excess of the amount allowed for the CREDIT–RATING of the customer.
3. Using the REGISTRAR–FILE for input, write a program that creates a temporary file that includes all records for which the grade fields are each in the range 'A'–'D'.
4. Using the NEW–WORLD–FILE for input, write a program that verifies that each record contains a permissible value in HOME–STATE.

Chapter Review

SUMMARY

This chapter introduced and used the verbs ADD, SUBTRACT, MULTIPLY, DIVIDE, and COMPUTE. Applications such as calculating totals for the amounts stored in a field in each record or processing payroll checks depend on arithmetic calculations.

The syntax of arithmetic statements have two forms. One form is used when the answer for the calculation is stored in a field that did not contain one of the values used in the calculation. The other form uses the value in a storage location in the calculation and then puts the answer for the computation back in that storage location.

The storage allocation problem for numeric values differentiate between two kinds of fields: numeric and numerically edited. Numeric fields consist only of digits with features such as the placement of the decimal point and the presence of a sign managed by the compiler. Numeric fields are used in arithmetic operations. Only numeric fields can be operands in arithmetic operations. Numerically edited fields contain editing symbols as well as digits. These fields are used for output purposes so that reports have the edited form the user expects. Numerically edited fields may not be used as operands for arithmetic operations.

The input of numeric values must be carefully done since any error may have a serious impact on the execution of the program. The problems associated with the input of numeric values lead to consideration of programming techniques that can be used to ensure that programs use correct, or at least reasonable values. Checks on whether a field contains only digits or letters are typical. More sophisticated checks include range checks, batch and run totals, and checks for overflow during arithmetic operations.

TEST YOURSELF

1. How is a decimal point represented in a numeric field? In a numerically edited field?
2. What is meant by a floating editing symbol?
3. What is the order of execution for operations in an arithmetic expression involving more than a single operator?
4. What kinds of fields may be used in an arithmetic operation?
5. What is a numeric field?
6. What is a numerically edited field?
7. What are the symbols that can be used in a picture clause for a numeric field? A numerically edited field?
8. What is a data exception?
9. What are the two forms of the ADD, SUBTRACT, MULTIPLY, and DIVIDE verbs?
10. How many digits may a numeric field contain?
11. What are the COBOL verbs for doing arithmetic operations?
12. Explain the syntax and the semantics of the verbs identified in Question 11.
13. What is a range check?
14. Which verb is used for the evaluation of expressions using exponentiation?
15. Why is data verification important for files with many users?
16. What does it mean to say that data is reasonable but it may not be correct? Give an example of a value that could be reasonable but incorrect.

Sequential File Processing— SORT, MERGE, and File Update

Chapter Objectives

After studying this chapter you should be able to

- create a temporary file with selected records from a permanent file;
- produce a listing of selected fields in a record using a utility program;
- use the COBOL SORT verb to sort a file;
- use the COBOL MERGE verb to merge files;
- write a program to update a file by adding, deleting, or modifying records.

Chapter Outline

5.1   Utility Files

If a business firm wanted to use direct mail marketing, it would be important to use mailing lists of people most likely to respond. In fact, it has become a big business to sell files of mailing lists for which each record has an identifiable characteristic important to the firm doing the mailing. However, the important characteristics are not always predictable, so files are created in such a way that each record has many different characteristics. When a mailing list is requested, a search of the master file is performed to select records with the required properties and then a new file is created with only the selected records. Since the new file typically will be stored on disk or magnetic tape, a hard copy listing of the new file is usually created for direct use. This backup copy also gives some protection against the possibility that the file may become partially or completely destroyed.

The application described in this section involves two distinct job steps. The first is file-to-file processing that creates a new file from an existing file. The second step is to make a hard copy listing of the new file. This hard copy listing can be used both as a backup and as a ready reference to the contents of the file.

Creating a Utility File

When examining the structure of the CUSTOMER–FILE, we see data fields that can be used to divide the records into related groups. For example, the CREDIT–LIMIT field naturally splits the file into five categories as determined by its five possible values 1, 2, 3, 4, and 5, each containing all the records with the same value in this field. Likewise, the REGION–CODE field naturally splits the file into three pieces as determined by its three possible values A, B, and C.

Targeted mailings usually require selecting part of a file for use depending on certain characteristics that make these customers more likely to respond. In a large organization, mailings may be needed for customers in a particular region. These examples point to a need to access various records of a file independently of other records in the file. We can certainly write a program that selects records with the required characteristics. We do not, however, want to process the file each time we use these records. Instead, we want to create another tape or disk file containing only the special records. To facilitate this process, some blank tapes or empty disk file area is made available to the programmer. These special files are called **utility,** or **scratch, files.** Utility files are available to any programmer for use, and they should be thought of as empty tapes or disks available upon request. In our programming environment the names of these files are

```
FILE1
FILE2
FILE3
FILE4
```

Their associated records as defined in TEXTA are

```
FILE1-RECORD
FILE2-RECORD
FILE3-RECORD
FILE4-RECORD
```

These files are OPENed and CLOSEd in the same manner as any other file we use. We write on them using the record names they are assigned in TEXTA. We READ from them after they are loaded using their file names, just as we have READ from CUSTOMER–FILE to this point.

In the next example we partition the CUSTOMER–FILE into three separate files. Each file will contain all the customers from a particular region. The process is shown in Figure 5.1.1.

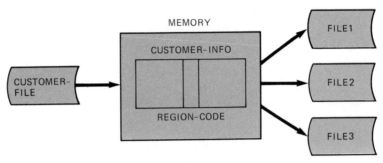

Figure 5.1.1. *Separating customers by region.*

We now examine the program that implements the procedure of creating three files from the CUSTOMER–FILE with each file containing all the records that belong to the customers from one region.

```
        IDENTIFICATION DIVISION.
        PROGRAM-ID.   CREATE.
        *
        * NAME:                          ID:
        * PROGRAM-NUMBER: 5.1-1
        * DESCRIPTION: FORM THREE NEW FILES WITH THE
        *    RECORDS OF CUSTOMER-FILE SEPARATED BY THE VALUE
        *    OF THE REGION-CODE.
        *
        ENVIRONMENT DIVISION.
        CONFIGURATION SECTION.
        SOURCE-COMPUTER.   IBM-370.
        OBJECT-COMPUTER.   IBM-370.
        INPUT-OUTPUT SECTION.
        FILE-CONTROL.
(A)          SELECT FILE1
                 ASSIGN TO UT-3330-S-COBOL1.
             SELECT FILE2
                 ASSIGN TO UT-3330-S-COBOL2.
             SELECT FILE3
                 ASSIGN TO UT-3330-S-COBOL3.
             SELECT CUSTOMER-FILE
                 ASSIGN TO UT-3330-S-CONSUM3.
        DATA DIVISION.
        FILE SECTION.

        * OUTPUT RECORDS ARE FILE1-RECORD, FILE2-RECORD,
        * FILE3-RECORD
(B)       FD  FILE1
              BLOCK CONTAINS 34 RECORDS
              LABEL RECORDS ARE STANDARD.
          01  FILE1-RECORD.
              05 FILLER PIC X(100).
```

```
      FD  FILE2
          BLOCK CONTAINS 34 RECORDS
          LABEL RECORDS ARE STANDARD.
      01  FILE2-RECORD.
          05 FILLER PIC X(100).
      FD  FILE3
          BLOCK CONTAINS 34 RECORDS
          LABEL RECORDS ARE STANDARD.
      01  FILE3-RECORD.
          05 FILLER PIC X(100).
      FD  CUSTOMER-FILE
          BLOCK CONTAINS 34 RECORDS
          LABEL RECORDS ARE STANDARD.
      01  CUSTOMER-FILE-RECORD.
          05 FILLER PIC X(100).

      WORKING-STORAGE SECTION.

      * INPUT RECORD
(C)   01  CUSTOMER-INFO.
          05 FILLER     PIC X(89).
          05 REGION-CODE PIX X.
          05 FILLER     PIC X(10).

      PROCEDURE DIVISION.
      * MODEL-I.

(D)       OPEN INPUT CUSTOMER-FILE
              OUTPUT FILE1
                     FILE2
                     FILE3.

      * FILE PROCESSING PAIR
          PERFORM INPUT-A-RECORD.
          PERFORM SEPARATES
              UNTIL REGION-CODE = HIGH VALUES.

      * TERMINATION ACTIVITY
          CLOSE CUSTOMER-FILE
               FILE1
               FILE2
               FILE3.
          STOP RUN.

      * INPUT PROCEDURE
      INPUT-A-RECORD.
          READ CUSTOMER-FILE INTO CUSTOMER-INFO
              AT END MOVE HIGH-VALUES TO REGION-CODE.

      * RECORD PROCESSING
      SEPARATES.
(E)       IF REGION-CODE = 'A'
              WRITE FILE1-RECORD FROM CUSTOMER-INFO
          ELSE
              IF REGION-CODE = 'B'
                  WRITE FILE2-RECORD FROM CUSTOMER-INFO
              ELSE
                  IF REGION CODE = 'C'
                      WRITE FILE3-RECORD FROM CUSTOMER-INFO.
          PERFORM INPUT-A-RECORD.
```

(A) Since we need one file for each of the regions, we SELECT three utility files. There are actually four utility files available; we only need three.

(B) Along with the usual SELECT statement, we need the file description for each of these files. There is no carriage control feature with a tape or disk file. The carriage control signal is only related to the line printer and its need to advance the paper before writing.

(C) The only field we need to access is the REGION–CODE field, so we account for the other bytes of the record with FILLER. There are still 100 bytes of information in each record. However, we only need to use data names for the fields we will access in the program.

(D) Each file that is used must be OPENed and CLOSEd. We open FILE1, FILE2, and FILE3 for output because we want to write some of the records in CUSTOMER–FILE on each of them.

(E) A Nested IF construction allows us to decide where to put the record currently in memory. The WRITE statement uses the name of the record associated with the file on which we are writing a record. The record name is a user defined name found in the FILE SECTION of the DATA DIVISION. The line printer is not used at all in this program since the output files are FILE1, FILE2, and FILE3.

Generating a Backup Listing

The program we have just examined writes the appropriate three new files for the regional offices. We should make a hard copy listing for backup purposes. Normal operating procedures will probably also require making a copy in machine readable form to protect against the cost of recreating the file if the current version is lost or destroyed. The program to list the records of FILE1 by the PRINTER follows.

```
*
* NAME:                        ID:
* PROGRAM-NUMBER: 5.1-2
* DESCRIPTION:  MAKE A HARD COPY LISTING OF THE RECORDS
*    OF FILE1.
*
      COPY TEXTA.
 WORKING-STORAGE SECTION.
 77 END-OF-FILE   PIC X(3)    VALUE 'NO'.

 PROCEDURE DIVISION.
 * MODEL-I.
     OPEN INPUT FILE1
          OUTPUT PRINTER.

 * FILE PROCESSING PAIR
     PERFORM READ-FILE1.
     PERFORM MAKE-LISTING
         UNTIL END-OF-FILE = 'YES'.

 * TERMINATION ACTIVITY
     CLOSE FILE1
           PRINTER.
     STOP RUN.
```

```
* INPUT PROCEDURE
 READ-FILE1.
     READ FILE1
         AT END MOVE 'YES' TO END-OF-FILE.

* RECORD PROCESSING
 MAKE-LISTING.
     WRITE PRINT-LINE FROM FILE1-RECORD.
     PERFORM READ-FILE1.
```

This program is simple enough to require no special explanation. Realize that similar programs would have to be written for FILE2 and FILE3. Rather than write a different program for each set of output requirements, it is quite common to write a single program that can be used for such tasks regardless of the file used. The program should allow the transfer of a file from one storage medium to another and allow hard copy listings to be created with various formats for the printed line. Clearly, the problem we faced for FILE1, FILE2, and FILE3 is ideally suited for the use of a special utility program. The program developed here can easily be modified to list the contents of the other files created in PROGRAM–NUMBER 5.1-1. A utility program written in COBOL called COPYPROG, which can be used with each of the files defined in TEXTA, is described in Appendix B.

EXERCISES

1. Why is the condition

```
                    IF REGION-CODE = 'C'
```

used in PROGRAM–NUMBER 5.1-1?
2. What is a utility program?
3. What is file-to-file processing? Give some examples.
4. What lines of code from TEXTA are required by PROGRAM–NUMBERs 5.1-1 and 5.1-2?
5. Why is there no carriage control byte in the records for the output files in PROGRAM–NUMBER 5.1-1?

PROGRAM TESTING AND MODIFICATION EXERCISE

1. Modify PROGRAM–NUMBER 5.1-2 so that

   a. the input file is CARD–READER
      the output file is FILE3
   b. the input file is FILE1
      the output file is FILE4
   c. the input file is CUSTOMER–FILE
      the output file is FILE2

PROGRAMMING PROBLEMS

1. Separate the records of the REGISTRAR–FILE into two files. One file should contain the records of all of the students who received an A or a B in PHILOSOPHY–3. The

second file should contain the remaining records. List the NAME and GRADEs of each student in the REGISTRAR–FILE so that all of the students who received an A or a B in PHILOSOPHY–3 are listed before those who received lower grades in that course.

2. Create a file consisting of all customers in NEW–WORLD–FILE who live in Maine or Massachusetts. List the NAME and STATE of each record in this new file.

3. Prepare a report consisting of the NAME, AMOUNT–DUE, and PAYMENT for each customer in the NEW–WORLD–FILE.

4. Prepare a report consisting of the NAME, CREDIT–LIMIT, and REGION–CODE for each customer in the CUSTOMER–FILE.

5. Prepare a report consisting of the NAME, AGE, CLASS, and HOME–STATE for each student in the REGISTRAR–FILE.

5.2 Sorting

Most files are not created with the records in a particular order. Many sequential files are created by adding records to the end of the current file as they occur. A large number of applications require a particular ordering of the records in a file, such as a listing of records in a file so that the names occur in alphabetical order. The CUSTOMER–FILE and the STUDENT–FILE have their records arranged in increasing order by the value of the identification number field. In more complicated situations, we might require a file to have its records organized by zip code, and within a particular zip code to have the names arranged in alphabetical order. For other applications using the same file, different ordering schemes may be appropriate. Rather than maintain many copies of a single file, each with a different ordering of the records, COBOL supplies the verb SORT that is used in programs to carry out the ordering process when it is needed.

The Sorting Process

Before we examine how the sort process works in a program, let's first look at the sorting process.

Sorting requires the programmer to input information concerning the field(s), called **key field(s)**, that are used both to identify a record and to determine if one record is greater than another. The sorting process compares key field values and rearranges records so that the record with the smallest value in the key field is first, the one with the second smallest is next, and so on. Typical key fields are a person's name or an identification number.

There is an important distinction to remember when we sort files. The object of the sorting process is to line up all the records of a file so that the first record listed is the "smallest" record, and the last record listed is the "largest" record. The complete contents of each record are normally not used for determining whether one record is larger or smaller than another record. Only a part of each record—the key field—is used. It is the order among values of the key field that determines the order among records of the file. Figure 5.2.1 shows a file and two different orderings of the records depending on the key field used. In the first, the key field is NAME; in the second it is ID–NO.

EXAMPLE FILE

NAME	AGE	ID	CITY
Zygmund, Alf	18	51816	Bangor
Jones, Peter	16	00468	Portland
Phillips, Gene	17	03571	Springfield
George, Ann	17	09913	Hartford
Prentis, Mary	14	00441	Boston

SORTED BY NAME

NAME	AGE	ID	CITY
George, Ann	17	09913	Hartford
Jones, Peter	16	00468	Portland
Phillips, Gene	17	03571	Springfield
Prentis, Mary	14	00441	Boston
Zygmund, Alf	18	51816	Bangor

SORTED BY ID–NO

NAME	AGE	ID	CITY
Prentis, Mary	14	00441	Boston
Jones, Peter	16	00468	Portland
Phillips, Gene	17	03571	Springfield
George, Ann	17	09913	Hartford
Zygmund, Alf	18	51816	Bangor

Figure 5.2.1 Example of a file sorted by name and ID numbers.

A Simple Form of the SORT Verb

Now that we know what the sorting process can accomplish, let's examine ways that a programmer implements this process in practice.

One implementation is the COBOL SORT verb. It will be helpful to list carefully all the information required for the sorting process. There must be a file of records to sort. There must be a file that will end up containing the records in sorted order. The SORT verb also requires a third file that is used to hold intermediate versions of the original file as it progresses toward being sorted. We will focus on sorting records in ASCENDING order, although DESCENDING order is also possible with SORT. Finally, the key field must be identified. In a program using SORT, we can use the name used in the program to identify the field. In any implementation of the sorting process, all this information must be identified. We can now see how this all fits together in a program using the SORT verb to order the records of the STUDENT–FILE so that NAMEs occur in alphabetical order.

```
IDENTIFICATION DIVISION.
PROGRAM-ID.  SORTEM.
*
* NAME:                        ID:
* PROGRAM-NUMBER: 5.2-1
* DESCRIPTION:  SORT STUDENT-FILE ON KEY FIELD
*   NAME ORDERED IN INCREASING ORDER.  PUT THE SORTED
*   VERSION OF STUDENT-FILE ON FILE1.
*
```

```
           ENVIRONMENT DIVISION.
           CONFIGURATION SECTION.
           SOURCE-COMPUTER.  IBM-370.
           OBJECT-COMPUTER.  IBM-370.
           INPUT-OUTPUT SECTION.
           FILE-CONTROL
               SELECT STUDENT-FILE
                    ASSIGN TO UT-3330-S-FILE03.
               SELECT SORTED-FILE
                    ASSIGN TO UT-3330-S-COBOL1.
               SELECT SORTING-FILE
                    ASSIGN TO UT-3330-S-COBOL2.
           DATA DIVISION.
           FILE SECTION.
(A)        SD  SORTING-FILE.
           01  SORT-RECORD.
               05 FILLER     PIC X(4).
               05 NAME       PIC X(18).
               05 FILLER     PIC X(78).
           FD  STUDENT-FILE
               LABEL RECORDS ARE STANDARD
               BLOCK CONTAINS 34 RECORDS.


         * INPUT RECORD
           01  STUDENT-RECORD.
               05 FILLER     PIC X(4).
               05 KEY-FIELD  PIC X(18).
               05 FILLER     PIC X(78).
           FD  SORTED-FILE
               LABEL RECORDS ARE STANDARD
               BLOCK CONTAINS 34 RECORDS.
         * OUTPUT RECORD
           01  SORTED-RECORD.
               05 FILLER        PIC X(4).
               05 FIELD-IN-ORDER PIC X(18).
               05 FILLER        PIC X(78).


           PROCEDURE DIVISION.

(B)            SORT SORTING-FILE ON ASCENDING KEY
                                   NAME
                   USING STUDENT-FILE
                   GIVING SORTED-FILE.
               STOP RUN.
```

(A)   The file used for storing intermediate versions of the file being sorted has SD as level
       indicator rather than FD. The field NAME in SORT-RECORD will be the key field for
       the sort. No LABEL RECORDS clause is required for a file identified as a sort file.

(B)   The SORT process handles the OPEN and CLOSE for three files: SORTING-FILE,
       STUDENT-FILE, and SORTED-FILE. The records of STUDENT-FILE are first cop-
       ied into SORTING-FILE. The sorting process is then executed. The SORT verb process
       does not put all the records in memory as most files encountered are too large for this.
       Instead, records are moved in and out of memory as required for the sorting process.

When the sorting is accomplished, the sorted version of STUDENT–FILE is copied from SORTING–FILE to SORTED–FILE. Notice that the USING clause identifies the input file, while the GIVING clause identifies the output file. The field in the records of SORTING–FILE used as the key field is identified by the name it was given. The input file looks the same before and after the execution of the sorting process.

Following the SORT process the file identified in the GIVING clause can be OPENed and processed just as any other file. For example, to list the names of students in the STUDENT–FILE the program above could be modified in the following way.

```
OPEN INPUT SORTED-FILE
     OUTPUT PRINTER.
PERFORM READ-SORTED-FILE.
PERFORM LIST-NAMES
     UNTIL FIELD-IN-ORDER = HIGH-VALUES.
CLOSE SORTED-FILE
      PRINTER.
STOP RUN.
```

The paragraphs READ–SORTED–FILE and LIST–NAMES would accomplish the input and record processing requirements. In the next section we will see how processing, both before and after sorting, can be accomplished using some alternate syntax for the SORT verb.

SORT Utility

When a group of programmers can identify a fixed set of files for frequent use, information about these files can be used to prepare utility programs. For the files defined in TEXTA there is a special utility for sorting that can be used in place of the SORT verb. This utility program written in COBOL is called SORTPROG and is explained in Appendix B.

SYNTAX SUMMARY

The simplified version of the SORT verb introduced requires the following new syntax features.

FILE SECTION

```
SD sort-file-name.
  01 record-name.
```

PROCEDURE DIVISION

```
SORT file-name-1
    ON ASCENDING KEY {data-name-1}...
        USING file-name-2
        GIVING file-name-3
```

EXERCISES

1. Why couldn't TEXTA be used in PROGRAM–NUMBER 5.2-1?
2. What is a key field?
3. When the SORT verb is used, how do the files needed get OPENed and CLOSEd?

4. How is the intermediate file used in the sorting process distinguished from other files in the FILE SECTION?

5. What is the difference in the results following the execution of the following sentences:

    a. SORT SORTED-FILE
           ON ASCENDING KEY AGE
           USING STUDENT-FILE
           GIVING FILE2.
    b. SORT SORTED-FILE
           ON DESCENDING KEY AGE
           USING STUDENT-FILE
           GIVING FILE3.

    In each case, what would be the contents of the file identified in the GIVING clause if only the first ten records of STUDENT-FILE are sorted?

6. List the sort key attached to each of the first six records of REGISTRAR-FILE if the sort key is (a) by CUMULATIVE-GPA, (b) by SEX, and (c) by AGE. Determine the different sorted order for these records using these keys if the sort uses descending order.

PROGRAMMING PROBLEMS

1. Modify PROGRAM-NUMBER 5.2-1 so that only NAME, AGE, and SEX are listed by the PRINTER.

2. Sort the records of the STUDENT-FILE by AGE. List the AGE and ALGEBRA grade for each record in the sorted file.

3. Sort the records of the NEW-WORLD-FILE by YEAR of EXPIRATION-DATE. List the NAME and AMOUNT-DUE for each record in the sorted file.

5.3 The SORT Verb

The SORT verb was introduced in a simplified form in the previous section. As we learned, sorting arranges records based on the value of the key. In the case of large files that will not fit in memory, COBOL can still execute a SORT procedure, but it needs a working area of auxiliary storage. This area will hold the file as it is going through various phases of the sorting procedure. Schematically, the sort procedure at the file level for sorting REGISTRAR-FILE can be viewed as shown here.

When using the SORT verb, all files must be defined in the program. The working file must be associated with the sorting procedure, and an SD level indicator rather than an FD level indicator must be used in the FILE SECTION.

The next program sorts records of the REGISTRAR-FILE by CLASS by HOME-STATE. TEXTA is not used in this program.

```
        IDENTIFICATION  DIVISION.
        PROGRAM-ID.     SORTTRY.
       *
       * NAME:                   ID:
       * PROGRAM-NUMBER: 5.3-1
       * DESCRIPTION: SORT REGISTRAR-FILE BY CLASS BY
       *   HOME-STATE USING THE SORT VERB.  THE OUTPUT
       *   FILE IS FILE1.
        ENVIRONMENT DIVISION.
        CONFIGURATION SECTION.
        SOURCE-COMPUTER. IBM-370.
        OBJECT-COMPUTER. IBM-370.
        INPUT-OUTPUT SECTION.
        FILE-CONTROL.
            SELECT REGISTRAR-FILE
                ASSIGN TO UT-3330-S-PROJ3.
            SELECT FILE1
                ASSIGN TO UT-3330-S-COBOL1.
            SELECT FILE2
                ASSIGN TO UT-3330-S-COBOL2.
        DATA DIVISION.
        FILE SECTION.
        FD  REGISTRAR-FILE
            BLOCK CONTAINS 34 RECORDS
            LABEL RECORDS ARE STANDARD.
        01  REGISTRAR-FILE-RECORD.
            05  FILLER   PIC X(100).
        FD  FILE1
            BLOCK CONTAINS 34 RECORDS
            LABEL RECORDS ARE STANDARD.
        01  FILE1-RECORD.
            05  FILLER   PIC X(100).
(A)     SD  FILE2.
        01  FILE2-RECORD.
            05  FILLER              PIC X(30).
            05  CLASS               PIC XX.
            05  FILLER              PIC X(33).
            05  HOME-STATE          PIC XX.
            05  FILLER              PIC X(33).
        PROCEDURE DIVISION.
(B)         SORT FILE2
                ON ASCENDING KEY CLASS
(C)                 USING REGISTRAR-FILE
                    GIVING FILE1.
            STOP RUN.
```

(A)   The SD level indicator is used to define the software characteristics of the file used as the auxiliary file in the SORT procedure. The SD keyword is recognized by the compiler to require making the file available for the SORT verb. Notice that the LABEL RECORDS clause is not present.

(B)   Files in the SORT sentence, when the USING and GIVING options are used, are OPENed and CLOSEd by the code that implements the SORT verb. These functions are not under the programmer's control. The key field for each record is the two-character word consisting of the two characters of CLASS. The SORT will order the records in increasing order by value of the two character key.

(C)   The USING clause identifies the input file for the sort. The GIVING clause identifies the output file for the sort.

The sorting procedure first copies the records of the input file onto the auxiliary file. After sorting, the auxiliary file finally contains the records of the input file in the required order. The records are then copied onto the output file.

SORT With PROCEDUREs

Some applications require processing of the records before they are sorted, and others require processing after the file is sorted; still others require processing at both times. We can, for example, require that the records of the STUDENT-FILE be sorted in decreasing order by the value of the average of each student's grades. Since the average does not exist as a field in the records of that file, we need to calculate that value and include it as a field in the records that are sorted. After listing the records of the sorted file, we would then like to store this file on FILE3 so that it is available for future applications. The SORT verb allows this preprocessing and postprocessing by means of blocks of code in the PROCEDURE DIVISION called SECTIONs. The syntax requires

INPUT PROCEDURE IS section-name-1
OUTPUT PROCEDURE IS section-name-2

rather than the USING and GIVING clauses. The INPUT PROCEDURE is executed before the sort and the OUTPUT PROCEDURE after the sort. Let's now see how the problem just described can be solved using this new syntax.

```
IDENTIFICATION DIVISION.
PROGRAM-ID. SORTRTN.
*
* NAME:              ID:
* PROGRAM-NUMBER: 5.3-2
* DESCRIPTION:  WRITE A REPORT THAT LISTS
*    THE NAME, GRADES, AND AVERAGE FOR EACH
*    STUDENT IN STUDENT-FILE.  PRINT THE
*    RECORDS SO THAT THE AVERAGE FIELD IS
*    IN DECREASING ORDER.  STORE THE SORTED
*    VERSION OF THE STUDENT-FILE WITH THE
*    AVERAGE FIELD ATTACHED ON FILE3.
*
ENVIRONMENT DIVISION.
CONFIGURATION SECTION.
SOURCE-COMPUTER.   IBM-370.
OBJECT-COMPUTER.   IBM-370.
INPUT-OUTPUT SECTION.
FILE-CONTROL.
    SELECT STUDENT-FILE
        ASSIGN TO UT-3330-S-FILE03.
    SELECT FILE3
        ASSIGN TO UT-3330-S-COBOL3.
    SELECT PRINTER
        ASSIGN TO UT-1403-S-SYSOUT.
    SELECT FILE2
        ASSIGN TO UT-3330-S-COBOL2.
```

```
        DATA DIVISION.
        FD  STUDENT-FILE
            LABEL RECORDS ARE STANDARD
            BLOCK CONTAINS 34 RECORDS.
        01  STUDENT-FILE-RECORD.
            05  FILLER        PIC X(100).
        FD  FILE3
            BLOCK CONTAINS 34 RECORDS
            LABEL RECORDS ARE STANDARD.
        01  FILE3-RECORD.
            05  FILLER        PIC X(100).
        FD  PRINTER
            LABEL RECORDS ARE OMITTED.
        01  PRINT-LINE.
            05  FILLER        PIC X(133).
(A)     SD  FILE2.
        01  FILE2-RECORD.
            05  FILLER        PIC X(40).
            05  AVERAGE       PIC 9(3)V99.
            05  FILLER        PIC X(55).


        WORKING-STORAGE SECTION.
        77  END-OF-FILE       PIC X(8) VALUE SPACES.
        77  SUM-GRADES        PIC S9(5).


(B)     01  STUDENT-RECORD.
            05  FILLER        PIC X(4).
            05  NAME          PIC X(18).
            05  FILLER        PIC X(3).
            05  ALGEBRA       PIC 999.
            05  GEOMETRY      PIC 999.
            05  ENGLISH       PIC 999.
            05  PHYSICS       PIC 999.
            05  CHEMISTRY     PIC 999.
            05  AVG           PIC 9(3)V99.
            05  FILLER        PIC X(55).
        01  DETAIL-LINE.
            05  FILLER        PIC X.
            05  DL-NAME       PIC X(30).
            05  DL-ALGEBRA    PIC Z(6).
            05  DL-GEOMETRY   PIC Z(6).
            05  DL-ENGLISH    PIC Z(6).
            05  DL-PHYSICS    PIC Z(6).
            05  DL-CHEMISTRY  PIC Z(6).
            05  DL-AVG        PIC Z(10).9.
            05  FILLER        PIC X(60) VALUE SPACES.


        PROCEDURE DIVISION.
(C)         SORT FILE2
                ON DESCENDING KEY AVERAGE
                    INPUT PROCEDURE IS ADD-AVG
                    OUTPUT PROCEDURE IS IN-ORDER.
            STOP RUN.
      *  INPUT PROCEDURE SECTION
(D)     ADD-AVG SECTION.
            OPEN INPUT STUDENT-FILE.
```

```
       *  FILE PROCESSING PAIR
             PERFORM READ-STUDENT-FILE.
             PERFORM CALL-AVG-RELEASE
                 UNTIL END-OF-FILE = HIGH-VALUES.
             CLOSE STUDENT-FILE.
(E)          GO TO EXIT-PARA.
       *  INPUT PROCEDURE
        READ-STUDENT-FILE.
             READ STUDENT-FILE INTO STUDENT-RECORD
                 AT END MOVE HIGH-VALUES TO END-OF-FILE.
         CALL-AVG-RELEASE.
(F)          ADD ALGEBRA
                 GEOMETRY
                 ENGLISH
                 PHYSICS
                 CHEMISTRY
                         GIVING SUM-GRADES.
             DIVIDE SUM-GRADES BY 5 GIVING AVG.
(G)          MOVE STUDENT-RECORD TO FILE2-RECORD.
             RELEASE FILE2-RECORD.
             PERFORM READ-STUDENT-FILE.
         EXIT-PARA.
             EXIT.
       *  OUTPUT PROCEDURE SECTION
(H)      IN-ORDER SECTION.
             OPEN OUTPUT FILE3
                         PRINTER.
             MOVE SPACES TO END-OF-FILE.
       *  FILE PROCESSING PAIR AND INITIALIZATION
(I)          RETURN FILE2 INTO STUDENT-RECORD
                 AT END MOVE HIGH-VALUES TO END-OF-FILE.
             PERFORM FIX-OUTPUT
                 UNTIL END-OF-FILE = HIGH-VALUES.
             CLOSE FILE3
                   PRINTER.
             GO TO EXIT-RTN.
         FIX-OUTPUT.
             MOVE NAME            TO DL-NAME.
             MOVE AVG             TO DL-AVG.
             MOVE ALGEBRA         TO DL-ALGEBRA.
             MOVE GEOMETRY        TO DL-GEOMETRY.
             MOVE PHYSICS         TO DL-PHYSICS.
             MOVE ENGLISH         TO DL-ENGLISH.
             MOVE CHEMISTRY       TO DL-CHEMISTRY.
             WRITE PRINT-LINE  FROM DETAIL LINE.
             WRITE FILE3-RECORD FROM STUDENT-RECORD.
       *  GET NEXT RECORD
             RETURN FILE2 INTO STUDENT-RECORD
                 AT END MOVE HIGH-VALUES TO END-OF-FILE.
         EXIT-RTN.
             EXIT.
```

(A)   The auxiliary file used for sorting must have the key fields identified. These are the fields identified in the SORT verb as keys. The other fields in the records will play no role in the sorting procedure.

(B)   We really are using the record for two different purposes. One use is as the input area for STUDENT–FILE. In this case, we ignore the field AVG as it becomes just a name for some of the 60 bytes of the unused record area. The second use involves calculating the average of the five grades and storing the value in AVG. We now have a record that can be used by the auxiliary file FILE2 for sorting.

(C)   The DESCENDING KEY option in the SORT sentence allows sorting from largest to smallest value in the field mentioned. ADD–AVG and IN–ORDER are names of SECTIONs. A SECTION can consist of a number of paragraphs. This allows one to organize blocks of code into coherent parts. The SECTION designator can be used in programs that do not use the SORT verb.

(D)   The SORT verb first transfers control to the SECTION called ADD–AVG. This section will prepare records for transfer to FILE2. When this SECTION ends, the records on FILE2 will be sorted. A SECTION is terminated by the EXIT statement. Control then returns to the next clause in the SORT sentence which is

                      OUTPUT PROCEDURE IS IN–ORDER

The section IN–ORDER will deal with records from the sorted file.

(E)   A SECTION is a block of code consisting of one or more paragraphs and having a single entry point and a single exit point. The entry point is the first statement following the section name. The exit point must be a paragraph with the single command EXIT. In structured programming a block of code is organized so that the logic becomes clear at the beginning of the block and the paragraphs that follow the outline will complete the processing. Programs we have written end the outline of the program with the statement STOP RUN. In this case we do not want to halt execution, but merely return to the point in the program that originally passed control to the section. This is accomplished with the command EXIT. We cannot, however, merely substitute EXIT for STOP RUN. The syntax for a SECTION requires an EXIT statement to be the last statement in the section. The syntax of EXIT requires that it be the only statement in the paragraph that contains it. To satisfy the syntax requirements, we substitute an unconditional transfer to the paragraph containing EXIT for the STOP RUN statement and put this paragraph at the end of the code for this section.

(F)   The record in STUDENT–RECORD needs to have a value calculated for AVG. This is the function of the two sentences

```
           * INCLUDE A COMMAND TO ADD THE GRADES TOGETHER
                ADD ALGEBRA
                    ENGLISH
                    GEOMETRY
                    PHYSICS
                    CHEMISTRY
                        GIVING SUM–GRADES.
            DIVIDE SUM–GRADES BY 5 GIVING AVG.
```

(G)   The MOVE sentence has copied the current record from STUDENT–FILE augmented by a value for the AVG field into the record area associated with the sort file. The verb RELEASE acts like a WRITE statement for a record headed for the auxiliary file that will hold the records to be sorted. The action of the RELEASE verb is to cause the record that has been preprocessed to be added as the next record on the sort work file.

(H)   This is the beginning of the SECTION to be executed after the file is sorted.

(I)   We deal with the sorted records one at a time in the sorted order. To make the next record available in memory, the verb RETURN is used. This acts like a READ, but is used in conjunction with returning a sorted record from the auxiliary file to memory. The sort file is not OPENed or CLOSEd by the programmer and so the READ verb is not used. This sentence makes the first of the sorted records available in the record area STUDENT–RECORD.

Multiple SORT Keys

Often, the sorting process cannot distinguish among a set of records on the basis of a single sort key. For example, the STUDENT–FILE contains many records with the same value for AGE or SEX. COBOL takes this into account by allowing *multiple sort keys*. Using the following set of records, it will be easy to demonstrate this feature of COBOL syntax.

NAME	AGE	SEX
JONES,K.	15	F
SMITH,M.	16	M
BROWN,R.	15	M
THOMAS,S.	15	F
LOCK,P.	16	F
BOND,J.	16	M

To SORT this set of records by AGE would result in the following order for the records.

NAME	AGE	SEX
JONES,K.	15	F
BROWN,R.	15	M
THOMAS,S.	15	F
SMITH,M.	16	M
LOCK,P.	16	F
BOND,J.	16	M

Within an AGE group, it would be nice to have either all the female students listed first or all the male students listed first. To list all the female students first, we would use the following COBOL sentence.

```
          SORT SORT-FILE
               ASCENDING KEY AGE
                             SEX
               USING STUDENT-FILE
               GIVING FILE1.
```

For any records with the same value for AGE, the SORT verb orders these records by increasing value of SEX. This will put all the records belonging to females before all records belonging to males because the character F comes before the character M in the collating sequence. To list all the male students before all the female students will require the following COBOL sentence.

```
          SORT SORT-FILE
               ASCENDING KEY AGE
               DESCENDING KEY SEX
               USING STUDENT-FILE
               GIVING FILE1.
```

The DESCENDING KEY option will cause the computer to use the same character set as the ASCENDING KEY clause uses, but will view the characters as being ordered in the opposite way. That is, the smallest character will be 9 and the largest character will be the space. Since M is less than F in this ordering, all the records that belong to females will follow all the records that belong to males.

SYNTAX SUMMARY

FILE SECTION

<u>SD</u> sort-file-name

$$
\text{\underline{DATA}} \left\{ \begin{array}{l} \text{\underline{RECORD} IS} \\ \text{\underline{RECORDS} ARE} \end{array} \right\} \text{data-name-1 [data-name-2]...}
$$

<u>RECORD</u> CONTAINS [integer-1 <u>TO</u>] integer-2 CHARACTERS.

PROCEDURE DIVISION

$$
\text{\underline{SORT} file-name-1 ON} \left\{ \begin{array}{l} \text{\underline{DESCENDING}} \\ \text{\underline{ASCENDING}} \end{array} \right\} \text{KEY \{data-name-1\}...}
$$

$$
\text{[ON} \left\{ \begin{array}{l} \text{\underline{DESCENDING}} \\ \text{\underline{ASCENDING}} \end{array} \right\} \text{KEY \{data-name-2\}...]...}
$$

$$
\left\{ \begin{array}{l} \text{\underline{INPUT} \underline{PROCEDURE} IS section-name-1} \\ \text{\underline{USING} file-name-2} \end{array} \right\}
$$

$$
\left\{ \begin{array}{l} \text{\underline{OUTPUT} \underline{PROCEDURE} IS section-name-2} \\ \text{\underline{GIVING} file-name-3} \end{array} \right\}
$$

<u>RELEASE</u> record-name [<u>FROM</u> identifier]
<u>RETURN</u> sort-file-name <u>RECORD</u>
        [<u>INTO</u> identifier]
        AT <u>END</u> imperative-statement

<u>GO</u> TO paragraph-name

<u>EXIT</u>.

EXERCISES

1. What is a SECTION?
2. What is the purpose of the paragraph EXIT–PARA in PROGRAM–NUMBER 5.3-2?
3. Describe the syntax and the semantics for the verbs RELEASE and RETURN.
4. Using the first ten records of STUDENT–FILE for input, determine the sort key for each of the records if the following sentences are executed. After determining the sort keys, list the NAME in each record in the order they occur after sorting.

```
a. SORT SORT-FILE
      ON ASCENDING KEY AGE
      ON DESCENDING KEY ALGEBRA
         USING STUDENT-FILE
         GIVING FILE1.
b. SORT SORT-FILE
      ON DESCENDING KEY SEX
      ON ASCENDING KEY AGE
         USING STUDENT-FILE
         GIVING FILE1.
```

5. Using the first ten records of NEW–WORLD–FILE for input, determine the sort keys for each of these records if the following sentences are executed. After determining the sort keys, list the NAME in each record in the order they occur after sorting.

```
a. SORT SORT-FILE
       ON ASCENDING KEY STATE
       ON DESCENDING KEY CREDIT-RATING
       ON ASCENDING KEY AMOUNT-DUE
           USING NEW-WORLD-FILE
           GIVING FILE1.
b. SORT SORT-FILE
       ON DESCENDING KEY BILLING-DATE
                          EXPIRATION-DATE
       ON ASCENDING KEY STATE
           USING NEW-WORLD-FILE
           GIVING FILE1.
```

PROGRAMMING PROBLEMS

1. Using the REGISTRAR–FILE for input, write a program that lists the NAME and GRADEs of each student together with the students' CUMULATIVE–GPA. Arrange the records so that the CUMULATIVE–GPAs are in increasing order. Include appropriate headings for the output.
2. Using the NEW–WORLD–FILE for input, write a program that lists the NAME, AMOUNT–DUE, PAYMENT, and balance due. Arrange the records so that the balance due amounts are in decreasing order. Include appropriate headings for the output.
3. Using the CUSTOMER–FILE for input, write a program that first selects those customers with REGION-CODE equal to 'A' and then lists the NAME and AMOUNT–DUE fields for each record in decreasing order of AMOUNT–DUE. Include appropriate headings for the output.

5.4   SORT, MERGE, and File Updating

Many business data processing applications require data collection at various places, and the data must later be combined into a single master file. An example is the grouping of the charges against a single customer number at various branches of a store, that then must be combined at billing time. The programmer's task is to merge these files into a single master file.

In this section we will examine the merge process for two files. Merging more than two files can be handled several different ways, but most applications eventually involve merging files two at a time. We will also examine the problem of making additions and deletions to a file. The merging process underlies the solution to both of these problems. To help your understanding of the programs, we will first examine the process of merging two files.

COBOL provides a powerful capability for merging with the MERGE verb. In the first program in this section we will not use the MERGE verb so that we might gain an understanding of the merge process. This will prepare us for using the options available with the MERGE verb treated later in the section.

Merging Two Files

Suppose we have two files, FILE1 and FILE2, and we want to merge their records onto FILE3, so that the customer numbers are in increasing order. See Figure 5.4.1. We will assume that each record of FILE1 and FILE2 consists of only a four-byte customer number field because other data in the records will not enter into the determination of the order in which records are written on FILE3.

```
                    INPUT              INPUT
                    FILE1              FILE2
                    0318               0218
                    4615               0219
                    7913               7385
                    8002               7391

                         MERGED FILE
                            FILE3
                            0218
                            0219
                            0318
                            4615
                            7385
                            7391
                            7913
                            8002
```

Figure 5.4.1 An example of merging files.

In the following example we assume that the first 50 records of CUSTOMER–FILE have been sorted by NAME and put on a file named CUSTOMER1. A file named CUSTOMER2 holds the last 50 records of CUSTOMER–FILE sorted by NAME. The result of the next program is to load a file named MERGED–FILE with all the records of CUSTOMER–FILE sorted by NAME.

```
IDENTIFICATION DIVISION.
PROGRAM-ID.   MERGED.
*
* NAME:                    ID:
* PROGRAM-NUMBER: 5.4-1
* DESCRIPTION: MERGE THE RECORDS ON FILE1 AND FILE2
*    ONTO FILE3.  FILE1 AND FILE2 ARE IN
*    ALPHABETICAL ORDER BY NAME.
*
ENVIRONMENT DIVISION.
CONFIGURATION SECTION.
SOURCE-COMPUTER. IBM-370.
OBJECT-COMPUTER. IBM-370.
INPUT-OUTPUT SECTION.
FILE-CONTROL.
    SELECT CUSTOMER1
        ASSIGN TO UT-3330-S-COBOL1.
    SELECT CUSTOMER2
        ASSIGN TO UT-3330-S-COBOL2.
    SELECT MERGED-FILE
        ASSIGN TO UT-3330-S-COBOL3.
```

```
     DATA DIVISION.
     FILE SECTION.
     FD  CUSTOMER1
         LABEL RECORDS ARE STANDARD
         BLOCK CONTAINS 34 RECORDS.
* OUTPUT RECORD.
     01  CUSTOMER1-RECORD.
         05 FILLER PIC X(100).
     FD  CUSTOMER2
         LABEL RECORDS ARE STANDARD
         BLOCK CONTAINS 34 RECORDS.
     01  CUSTOMER2-RECORD.
         05 FILLER PIC X(100).
     FD  MERGED-FILE
         LABEL RECORDS ARE STANDARD
         BLOCK CONTAINS 34 RECORDS.
     01  MERGED-FILE-RECORD.
         05 FILLER PIC X(100).

     WORKING-STORAGE SECTION.

* INPUT RECORD
     01  CUSTOMER1-INFO.
         05 FILLER PIC X(8).
         05 NAME1  PIC X(20).
         05 FILLER PIC X(72).
     01  CUSTOMER2-INFO.
         05 FILLER PIC X(8).
         05 NAME2  PIC X(20).
         05 FILLER PIC X(72).

     PROCEDURE DIVISION.
* MODEL-III.

         OPEN INPUT CUSTOMER1
                    CUSTOMER2
              OUTPUT MERGED-FILE.


* FILE PROCESSING PAIR WITH TWO INITIAL READS
         PERFORM READ-CUSTOMER1.
         PERFORM READ-CUSTOMER2.
         PERFORM MERGING
             UNTIL NAME1 = HIGH-VALUES
                OR NAME2 = HIGH-VALUES.
* TERMINATION ACTIVITIES
         PERFORM END-ROUTINE.
         CLOSE CUSTOMER1
               CUSTOMER2
               MERGED-FILE.
         STOP RUN.


* INPUT PROCEDURES
     READ-CUSTOMER1.
         READ CUSTOMER1 INTO CUSTOMER1-INFO
             AT END MOVE HIGH-VALUES TO NAME1.
     READ-CUSTOMER2.
         READ CUSTOMER2 INTO CUSTOMER2-INFO
             AT END MOVE HIGH-VALUES TO NAME2.
```

(A)

(B)

```
     * RECORD PROCESSING
     * SELECTION ROUTINE
       MERGING.
(C)        IF NAME1 > NAME2
               PERFORM CUSTOMER2-OUT
           ELSE
               IF NAME1 < NAME2
                   PERFORM CUSTOMER1-OUT
               ELSE
                   IF NAME1 = NAME2
                       PERFORM CUSTOMER1-OUT
                       PERFORM READ-CUSTOMER2.
       END-ROUTINE.
(D)        IF NAME1 = HIGH-VALUES
               PERFORM CUSTOMER2-OUT
                   UNTIL NAME2 = HIGH-VALUES
           ELSE
(E)            PERFORM CUSTOMER1-OUT
                   UNTIL NAME1 = HIGH-VALUES.
       CUSTOMER1-OUT.
           WRITE MERGED-FILE-RECORD FROM CUSTOMER1-INFO.
           PERFORM READ-CUSTOMER1.
       CUSTOMER2-OUT.
           WRITE MERGED-FILE-RECORD FROM CUSTOMER2-INFO.
           PERFORM READ-CUSTOMER2.
```

(A)   Two files have to be merged into one. Therefore, we need the first record of each of the files, since one of these records will be first in the merged file. This initialization process is familiar; here it involves two files instead of one.

(B)   With two files being merged, we don't want to stop processing until all the records from each file have been put on MERGED-FILE. The routine MERGING will terminate when the first of the two files is exhausted of records. Since we don't know which file this will be, we use an OR in the UNTIL clause and then put the remaining records of the other file on MERGED-FILE in END-ROUTINE.

(C)   The merge process requires that either NAME1 or NAME2 be written next on MERGED-FILE. We want to arrange MERGED-FILE in increasing alphabetical order so that after the comparison of the values contained in NAME1 and NAME2, the smaller value is determined and put next on the merged file. If NAME1 > NAME2, then NAME2 should be written next. If this condition is false and NAME1 < NAME2, then NAME1 should be written next. When the two fields are equal, we can choose which one we want to write and then get a new record from each of the files, provided equality means the two records are identical. This avoids duplicates in the merged file.

(D)   If the file CUSTOMER1 has been exhausted, the rest of the file CUSTOMER2 should be added to the end of the existing contents of the merged file. We don't have to ask any more questions, since we know that the remaining names on CUSTOMER2 are each greater than the last name that was on CUSTOMER1. Any remaining names are in order because CUSTOMER2 was sorted before being used in this program.

(E)   If the file CUSTOMER2 has been exhausted, the rest of the file CUSTOMER1 should be added to the end of the existing contents of the merged file. Here again, we won't have to ask any more questions, since we know that the remaining names on CUSTOMER1 are each greater than the last name that was on CUSTOMER2. Any remaining names are in order because CUSTOMER1 was sorted before being used in this program.

After examining the merge process, it is much easier to understand the syntax and the semantics of the COBOL verb, MERGE. We can rewrite Program 5.4-1 using the MERGE verb.

```
IDENTIFICATION DIVISION.
PROGRAM-ID.  CBLMRG.
*
* NAME:           ID:
* PROGRAM-NUMBER: 5.4-2
* DESCRIPTION: MERGE THE FILES CUSTOMER1 AND CUSTOMER2
*    PUT THE RESULT OF THE MERGE PROCESS ON FILE4
*    THE WORK AREA FILE WILL BE CALLED MERGED-WORK.
*    USE THE COBOL VERB MERGE.
*
ENVIRONMENT DIVISION.
CONFIGURATION SECTION.
SOURCE-COMPUTER. IBM-370.
OBJECT-COMPUTER. IBM-370.
INPUT-OUTPUT SECTION.
FILE-CONTROL.
    SELECT CUSTOMER1
        ASSIGN TO UT-3330-S-COBOL1.
    SELECT CUSTOMER2
        ASSIGN TO UT-3330-S-COBOL2.
    SELECT MERGED-WORK
        ASSIGN TO UT-3330-S-COBOL3.
    SELECT FILE4
        ASSIGN TO UT-3330-S-COBOL4.
DATA DIVISION.
FILE SECTION.
FD  CUSTOMER1
    LABEL RECORDS ARE STANDARD.
01  CUSTOMER1-RECORD.
    05  FILLER     PIC X(8).
    05  NAME1      PIC X(20).
    05  FILLER     PIC X(72).
FD  CUSTOMER2
    LABEL RECORDS ARE STANDARD.
01  CUSTOMER2-RECORD.
    05  FILLER     PIC X(8).
    05  NAME2      PIC X(20).
    05  FILLER     PIC X(72).
FD  FILE4
    LABEL RECORDS ARE STANDARD.
01  FILE4-RECORD.
    05  FILLER     PIC X(8).
    05  NAME4      PIC X(20).
    05  FILLER     PIC X(72).
SD  MERGED-WORK.
01  MERGED-WORK-RECORD.
    05  FILLER     PIC X(8).
    05  NAME       PIC X(20).
    05  FILLER     PIC X(72).
```

```
PROCEDURE DIVISION.
MERGE-ROUTINE.
    MERGE MERGED-WORK ON ASCENDING KEY
        USING CUSTOMER1
              CUSTOMER2
        GIVING FILE4.
    STOP RUN.
```

We see that the MERGE verb shortens and simplifies the process of writing a program to merge two files by comparing this program with the preceding one.

Updating Files

The problem considered next involves the modification of some records in a file. The problem is a very real one in data processing. Any file can have records added, deleted, or changed. For example, suppose two new students must be added to the class list, another student needs a grade change, and three other students depart. We would like the file to reflect all these activities. A program that accomplishes these types of tasks is called a **file update program.**

To clarify what is required in the RECORD PROCESSING section of a file update program, the various possibilities and the action required in each case are summarized in Table 5.1. Assume that the key field is the student's name and the resulting file is FILE3. NAME1 is the student's name in FILE1 and NAME2 is the student's name in FILE2. CODE-FOR-TASK is a special one-character code of A, C, or D, meaning add, change, or delete, respectively. The CODE-FOR-TASK field is in the record of FILE1.

TABLE 5.1   SUMMARY OF REQUIREMENTS FOR UPDATING A FILE.

FILES		CODE-FOR-TASK			ACTION
FILE1 (INPUT)	FILE2 (OLD MASTER)				
NAME1 > NAME2		A			Put NAME2 on FILE3 and get a new record from FILE2.
			C		
				D	
NAME1 = NAME2		A			Put NAME1 on exception report. Put NAME2 on FILE3. Get a new record from both FILE1 and FILE2.
			C		Incorporate changes. Put modified record on FILE3. Get new record from both FILE1 and FILE2.
				D	Get new record from both FILE1 and FILE2.
NAME1 < NAME2		A			Put NAME1 on FILE3 and get a new record from FILE1.
			C		Put NAME1 on the exception report and get a
				D	new record from FILE1.

Table 5.1 will help design the code for the record processing of Program 5.4-3.

```
      IDENTIFICATION DIVISION.
      PROGRAM-ID.   FIXIT.
  *
  * NAME:                 ID:
  * PROGRAM-NUMBER: 5.4-3
  * DESCRIPTION: UPDATE THE RECORDS IN A FILE-CHANGE,
  *   DELETE FROM, OR ADD TO, THE RECORDS OF A MASTER FILE
  *   BASED ON ADD, CHANGE, OR DELETE CODES
  *   IN THE INPUT RECORD OF THE FILE OF
  *   MODIFICATIONS.
  *
      ENVIRONMENT DIVISION.
      CONFIGURATION SECTION.
      SOURCE-COMPUTER. IBM-370.
      OBJECT-COMPUTER. IBM-370.
      INPUT-OUTPUT SECTION.
      FILE-CONTROL.
          SELECT MASTER-FILE
              ASSIGN TO UT-3330-S-COBOL3.
          SELECT FILE1
              ASSIGN TO UT-3330-S-COBOL1.
          SELECT FILE2
              ASSIGN TO UT-3330-S-COBOL2.
          SELECT PRINTER
              ASSIGN TO UT-1403-S-SYSOUT.
      DATA DIVISION.
      FILE SECTION.
      FD  MASTER-FILE
          BLOCK CONTAINS 34 RECORDS
          LABEL RECORDS ARE STANDARD.
  * OUTPUT RECORD
      01  TYPICAL-RECORD.
          05 NAME          PIC X(20).
          05 GRADE         PIC 999.
          05 FILLER        PIC X(77).
      FD  FILE1
          LABEL RECORDS ARE STANDARD.
  * INPUT RECORD OF FILE MODIFICATIONS
      01  NEW-INFO.
          05 CODE-FOR-TASK PIC X.
          05 NAME1         PIC X(20).
          05 NEW-GRADE     PIC 999.
          05 FILLER        PIC X(76).
      FD  FILE2
          BLOCK CONTAINS 34 RECORDS
          LABEL RECORDS ARE STANDARD.
  * INPUT RECORD FROM OLD MASTER FILE
      01  TEMP-PLACE.
          05 NAME2           PIC X(20).
          05 GRADE2          PIC 999.
          05 FILLER          PIC X(77).
      FD  PRINTER
          LABEL RECORDS ARE OMITTED.
      01  PRINT-LINE.
          05  FILLER     PIC X.
          05  EXCEPTIONS PIC X(132).
```

```
        WORKING—STORAGE SECTION.
        77   END—OF—FILE1       PIC X(8).
        77   END—OF—FILE2       PIC X(8).

        PROCEDURE DIVISION.
    *   MODEL—III.

            OPEN INPUT FILE1
                      FILE2
                 OUTPUT MASTER—FILE
                        PRINTER.

    *   INITIALIZATION
            MOVE SPACES TO END—OF—FILE1
                           END—OF—FILE2
                           PRINT—LINE.

    *   FILE PROCESSING PAIR
            PERFORM READ—FILE1.
            PERFORM READ—FILE2.
(A)         PERFORM UPDATE
                UNTIL END—OF—FILE1 = HIGH—VALUES
                    OR END—OF—FILE2 = HIGH—VALUES.

    *   TERMINATION ACTIVITY
(B)         PERFORM END—ROUTINE.
            CLOSE FILE1
                  FILE2
                  MASTER—FILE
                  PRINTER.
            STOP RUN.

    *   INPUT PROCEDURES
     READ—FILE1.
            READ FILE1
                AT END MOVE HIGH—VALUES TO END—OF—FILE1.
     READ—FILE2.
            READ FILE2
                AT END MOVE HIGH—VALUES TO END—OF—FILE2.

    *   RECORD PROCESSING FOR THE MODEL—III PROGRAM
     UPDATE.
(C)         IF NAME2 > NAME1
                PERFORM VALID—IF—ADDITION
            ELSE
(D)             IF NAME2 < NAME1
                    PERFORM NEW—MASTER
                ELSE
(E)                 PERFORM TASKS.
     TASKS.
            IF CODE—FOR—TASK = 'A'
                MOVE SPACES TO TYPICAL—RECORD
                WRITE TYPICAL—RECORD FROM TEMP—PLACE
                PERFORM ERROR—ROUTINE
            ELSE
                IF CODE—FOR—TASK = 'C'
                    PERFORM CHANGE—MASTER
```

```
            ELSE
                IF CODE-FOR-TASK = 'D'
                    PERFORM DELETE-RECORD
                ELSE
                    PERFORM ERROR-ROUTINE.
        PERFORM READ-FILE2.
    VALID-IF-ADDITION.
        IF CODE-FOR-TASK = 'A'
            MOVE SPACES     TO TYPICAL-RECORD
            MOVE NAME1      TO NAME
            MOVE NEW-GRADE  TO GRADE
            WRITE TYPICAL-RECORD
        ELSE
            PERFORM ERROR-ROUTINE.
        PERFORM READ-FILE1.
    DELETE-RECORD.
        PERFORM READ-FILE1.
    NEW-MASTER.
        WRITE TYPICAL-RECORD FROM TEMP-PLACE.
        PERFORM READ-FILE2.
    CHANGE-MASTER.
        MOVE SPACES         TO TYPICAL-RECORD.
        MOVE NEW-GRADE      TO GRADE.
        MOVE NAME2          TO NAME.
        WRITE TYPICAL-RECORD.
        PERFORM READ-FILE1.
      ERROR-ROUTINE.
        MOVE NAME1 TO EXCEPTIONS.
        WRITE PRINT-LINE.
        PERFORM READ-FILE1.
    END-ROUTINE.
        IF END-OF-FILE1 = HIGH-VALUES
            PERFORM NEW-MASTER
                UNTIL END-OF-FILE2 = HIGH-VALUES
        ELSE
            PERFORM VALID-IF-ADDITION
                UNTIL END-OF-FILE1 = HIGH-VALUES.
```

(A)   We cannot anticipate which file of records will be exhausted first, so the termination condition involves the logical connective OR.

(B)   The END-ROUTINE must finish processing the records from the file that has not triggered the AT END with the last read command. If FILE1 has been exhausted, the remaining records from FILE2 will be put on the new master file provided the coded values indicate that the records are to be added to the file. Other records remaining on FILE1 will be listed on the exception report for all the erroneous records. If FILE2 has been exhausted, the remaining records from FILE1 will be put at the end of the new master file.

(C)   In this case the only valid operation to the record with the smaller name is the ADD operation. Consider BAKER to be the value of NAME2 and ADAMS to be the value of NAME1. Clearly ADAMS should be processed next if the resulting file is to receive names in increasing order.

(D)   The logic at this point indicates that the record in the input file is farther along in the alphabetical order than the current record from the old master file. As an example, suppose that NAME2 has a value of ABLE and NAME1 has a value CABLE. It is clear that

ABLE belongs on the new master file before the input record with the name CABLE. It is not clear that CABLE will be put on the new master file, but that will not be known, in any case, until a larger value for NAME2 is processed.

(E)   The case considered arises when NAME1 and NAME2 both have the same value. It will be valid to delete this record or change the value of one of its fields, but it is not valid to add a record that is already in the master file.

SYNTAX SUMMARY

$$\underline{\text{MERGE}} \text{ merge file ON} \begin{Bmatrix} \underline{\text{ASCENDING}} \\ \underline{\text{DESCENDING}} \end{Bmatrix} \text{KEY data-name1[data-name2]...}$$

$$\begin{array}{l} \underline{\text{USING}} \quad \text{file-name1 file-name2} \\ \begin{Bmatrix} \underline{\text{GIVING}} \text{ file-name3} \\ \underline{\text{OUTPUT PROCEDURE}} \text{ IS section-name-1} \end{Bmatrix} \end{array}$$

EXERCISES

1. How is the intermediate file used in the merging process identified in the FILE SECTION if the MERGE verb is used?
2. What functions must a file update program be prepared to implement?
3. What kinds of error conditions must a file update program guard against?

PROGRAM TESTING AND MODIFICATION EXERCISES

1. Modify PROGRAM–NUMBER 5.4-1 so that any time the program finds records from each file with the same key value, both these records are saved on a temporary disk file, in addition to the processing already indicated for this case.
2. Modify PROGRAM–NUMBER 5.4-3 so that any records deleted from the master file are saved on a temporary disk file.
3. Indicate the final form of FILE4 if PROGRAM–NUMBER 5.4-1 is executed, and CUSTOMER1 and CUSTOMER2 have the following forms.

CUSTOMER1	
ANDERSON DAVE	100
BROWN BETH	071
CHAPELLE ROGER	067
GAVETT WILL	086
HUMPHRIES ELAINE	079
JOHNSON JACOB	081

CUSTOMER2	
ALEXANDER GRAHAM	083
BROWN ANDERS	071
BROWN BETSY	080
CHAPELLE MARIE	067
HUMPHRIES ELEANOR	074
SMITH ARTIS	062

4. Indicate the final form of FILE3 if PROGRAM–NUMBER 5.4-3 is executed, and FILE1 and FILE2 have the following records.

FILE1	
ANDERSON DAVE	100
BROWN BETH	071
CHAPELLE ROGER	067
GAVETT WILL	086
HUMPHRIES ELAINE	079
JOHNSON JACOB	081

FILE2		
ALEXANDER GRAHAM	083	ADD
BROWN ANDERS	071	ADD
BROWN BETH	080	CHANGE
CHAPELLE ROGER	067	DELETE
HUMPHRIES ELAINE	074	CHANGE
SMITH ARTIS	062	ADD

PROGRAMMING PROBLEMS

1. Modify PROGRAM–NUMBER 5.4-3 so that when a record is to be deleted, rather than eliminate it entirely, the letter D is put in byte 41 of the record sent to the merged file. For all other records, put the letter G in byte 41 before sending the record to the merged file. Prepare a listing from the merged file of records that contain the code G in byte 41. Prepare a second list of all the other records with a D in byte 41. You should think of this second report as an exception report. In real cases, further checking on these students whose names appear on the exception report would usually be called for to determine why they are being dropped from the file.

2. Using the CUSTOMER–FILE for input, write a program that sorts the records by NAME and then processes the following record modifications:

ACTION	NAME		NEW INFORMATION
DELETE	KENNEDY	JF	
CHANGE	TUPPER	5C	STREET: 39 KING ST
CHANGE	WEINSMEIER	CFR	EXPIRE: 100778
DELETE	GRANT	P	

After processing these changes, list the records in the file.

3. Using the REGISTRAR–FILE for input, write a program that processes the following record updates.

ACTION	NAME		NEW INFORMATION
DELETE	JONES	STEVE A	
DELETE	WYSE	MICHAEL RV	
DELETE	SMITH	MICHAEL WA	
CHANGE	ZEPH	DEBORAH VA	CLASS: SR
CHANGE	HARMON	SHARON JOA	GEOGRAPHY: A

After processing these updates, list the records in the file.

Chapter Review

SUMMARY

In this chapter permanent data files are used for applications in which it is first necessary to separate records according to common characteristics. Rather than create a number of smaller permanent files, it is often the practice to either extract or rearrange records from a permanent file and form temporary files. When processing is completed, the temporary file medium can be reused.

This chapter first shows how a file can be separated into several temporary files so that all the records on a temporary file share a common characteristic. After such file-to-file processing, the programmer usually writes and uses a utility program to list the records on the resulting file. This is for security and backup purposes.

Sorting was introduced next. Rather than extracting records from a file, the sorting process rearranges records in a file into a prescribed order based on a value in each record. This special value in a record is called a key field. The sorting process uses the COBOL verb SORT. The simplest form of the verb uses one file for input, transfers the input file to a work area file, and then returns the records in sorted order to a third file. The work area file used by the SORT verb is identified in the FILE SECTION by an SD level indicator. More complex processing before or after the sorting process can be accomplished using an INPUT or OUTPUT PROCEDURE.

Online collection of data often creates a need to merge files. After explaining the merge process, a program was developed that carried out the process. A second example program using the COBOL verb MERGE was also developed. The work file used by the MERGE verb is identified in the FILE SECTION by an SD level indicator. An OUTPUT PROCEDURE may be used for more extensive processing after the merge process.

The last process studied was file updating. File updating consists of adding, deleting, or changing records in a file. A table was developed that displayed all the options that need to be considered. A program for file updating was then developed that incorporated all of these options. The correctness of the program followed from the correctness of the analysis exhibited in the table.

TEST YOURSELF

1. What is a utility, or scratch, file?
2. Why might a program require a utility file?
3. Explain the sorting process.
4. What is a utility program?
5. What are some examples of file-to-file processing?
6. What is a key field?
7. What is a multiple key?
8. How can preprocessing be accomplished before sorting. How can postprocessing be accomplished after sorting?
9. How is the work area for the SORT verb identified in the FILE SECTION?
10. How are files used with the SORT verb OPENed and CLOSEd?
11. Describe the merging process?
12. Which operations are performed in a file updating program?
13. Explain the syntax and the semantics of the ASCENDING (DESCENDING) KEY clause used with the SORT verb.
14. How is the work area for the MERGE verb identified in the FILE SECTION?
15. For which devices is a carriage control byte used?
16. Explain the syntax and the semantics of the SORT verb and the MERGE verb.

Control Breaks and Stepwise Refinement

Chapter Objectives

After studying this chapter you should be able to

- write a program using a one-way control break;
- apply stepwise refinement techniques by extending one-way control breaks to the solution of a problem requiring a two-way control break;
- write a program using two-way control breaks.

Chapter Outline

6.1   One-Level Control Breaks

The Control Break Feature

At the end of each month a retail business normally looks at sales results by department as well as overall results. As the month goes by, transaction records indicating sales are entered in a file. The transactions are entered as they occur, with no ordering of the records in the file. The output requirement for a sales report includes a listing of the items sold, broken down by department. However, since the sales file has a random order, this listing is difficult to produce without some preprocessing. We can sort the file by department number, so that items from one department are listed and their prices accumulated before those from the next department are reported. Yet, we must be able to identify the last record in a department, so that department's total sales can be printed before proceeding to the first record of the next department. To do this requires a **control break** or a detection of a change in the value of a variable so that this change in value can be used to alter the control of processing. When this change in value is encountered in the program, control is passed to a special block of code that prints the department information. The following sales information illustrates the kind of report that can be generated using a control break.

```
          Shovel      $8.65
          Hammer      $9.15

          DEPT-NO. B          $17.80

          Nails       $6.15
          Paint       $9.95
          Brush       $7.65

          DEPT-NO. D          $23.75

          GRAND TOTAL               $41.55
```

The program we examine next requires preprocessing of the input file. The preprocessing must arrange the records of the file so that all the records that have a fixed value for the control break field occur together. This can be done by sorting the original file using the control break field as the sort key. Although there are other methods that could be used, we assume that the input file for the next program has been appropriately preprocessed.

```
      *
      * NAME:               ID:
      * PROGRAM-NUMBER: 6.1-1
      * DESCRIPTION: USING THE CONTROL BREAK FEATURE (CHANGE
      *    IN THE VALUE OF THE FIELD DEPT-CODE), CALCULATE
      *    DEPARTMENT (DEPT-SUM) SALES AND TOTAL SALES FOR
      *    THE MONTH (GRAND-SUM).
      *
            COPY TEXTA.
         WORKING-STORAGE SECTION.
(A)      77  PREV-DEPT-CODE   PIC X.
(B)      01  ACCUMULATIONS.
             05 DEPT-SUM       PIC  S9(9)V99.
             05 GRAND-SUM      PIC  S9(10)V99.
```

```
* INPUT RECORD
01   CARD-RECORD.
       05 ITEM          PIC X(10).
       05 DEPT-CODE     PIC X.
       05 COST          PIC S9(7)V99.
       05 FILLER        PIC X(60).

* OUTPUT RECORD
01   PRINT-PATTERN-1.
       05 FILLER        PIC X.
       05 ITEM-OUT      PIC X(60).
       05 COST-OUT      PIC $,$$$,$$$.99BCR.
       05 FILLER        PIC X(57) VALUE SPACES.
* TOTAL LINE
01   PRINT-PATTERN-2.
       05 FILLER     PIC X.
       05 FILLER     PIC X(9) VALUE 'DEPT-NO.'.
       05 CODE-OUT   PIC X(4).
       05 FILLER     PIC X(61) VALUE SPACES.
       05 TOT        PIC $,$$$,$$$,$$$.99BCR.
       05 FILLER     PIC X(39) VALUE SPACES.


01   PRINT-PATTERN-3.
       05 FILLER     PIC X.
       05 FILLER     PIC X(92) VALUE 'GRAND-TOTAL'.
       05 GRAND-TOT PIC $$,$$$,$$$.99BCR.
       05 FILLER     PIC X(24)  VALUE SPACES.



    PROCEDURE DIVISION.
* MODEL-III.

*   DISCUSSION OF HOW THIS DIFFERS FROM MODEL II
*     FOLLOWS THIS LESSON
*
        OPEN INPUT CARD-READER
            OUTPUT PRINTER.

* INITIALIZATION
        MOVE ZEROS TO ACCUMULATIONS.

* FILE PROCESSING PAIR
        PERFORM READ-A-RECORD.
        MOVE DEPT-CODE TO PREV-DEPT-CODE.
        PERFORM FANCY
            UNTIL DEPT-CODE = HIGH-VALUES.

* TERMINATION ACTIVITY
        PERFORM GRAND-TOTAL.
        CLOSE CARD-READER
             PRINTER.
        STOP RUN.

* INPUT PROCEDURE
   READ-A-RECORD.
        READ CARD-READER INTO CARD-RECORD
            AT END MOVE HIGH-VALUES TO DEPT-CODE.
```

(C)

(D)

```
      * RECORD PROCESSING
        FANCY.
(E)         MOVE ITEM                TO ITEM-OUT.
            MOVE COST                TO COST-OUT.
            WRITE PRINT-LINE FROM PRINT-PATTERN-1.
            ADD COST                 TO DEPT-SUM
                                        GRAND-SUM.
            PERFORM READ-A-RECORD.
(F)         IF DEPT-CODE NOT EQUAL PREV-DEPT-CODE
                MOVE DEPT-SUM       TO TOT
                MOVE PREV-DEPT-CODE TO CODE-OUT
                WRITE PRINT-LINE FROM PRINT-PATTERN-2
                MOVE ZERO           TO DEPT-SUM
                MOVE DEPT-CODE      TO PREV-DEPT-CODE.
(G)     GRAND-TOTAL.
            MOVE GRAND-SUM           TO GRAND-TOT.
            WRITE PRINT-LINE FROM PRINT-PATTERN-3.
```

(A)   The field PREV-DEPT-CODE is used like a switch. Instead of physically flipping a switch, we set aside a storage location and after processing each record ask what value it contains. We ask if the contents of PREV-DEPT-CODE are the same as the contents of the field DEPT-CODE. These two storage locations will have different values only when the record just read is the first record in a new group of records. When these two storage locations have different values, we signal the program to perform some function, usually to recap the information about the department that has just had all its records processed. Notice the role that the preprocessing plays in preparing the file so that all records with the same value for DEPT-CODE occur together. As long as the two storage locations contain the same value, we proceed to execute the main logic of the program; that is, we print a detail line, accumulate numeric information, and access the next record in the file. When these two storage locations contain different values, the program responds as if an *on* switch has been turned *off*. Some action must be performed before the switch can be turned back *on*. These hardware analogies make the function of a control break field more understandable, but they are just analogies since we are simulating a hardware switch with COBOL software features. More complex programs may contain several such variables that direct the program's flow of control.

(B)   A record (01-level identifier) need not be a pattern for only an input or output record. Here we put the accumulators in a single record. There are two advantages to this. First, we have one place in the program to look for the variables to be used as accumulators. This helps us give these variables the correct picture clauses, since usually they are related in size. Second, it is easier to initialize a set of variables by moving zeros to each storage location in a single record in a single command. The record used to hold the accumulators has two pieces. We can ensure that each of these pieces is initialized to zero by moving zeros to ACCUMULATIONS. When a number of similar variables must be defined in the WORKING-STORAGE SECTION, it is preferable to group them as fields of a record rather than as a number of 77-level variables.

(C)   The initialization requirements for this program are more extensive than we have seen so far. The accumulators must be set to zero. The first record must be accessed, so that the UNTIL clause can be evaluated *prior* to processing the first record. There is an additional initialization here, since PREV-DEPT-CODE must be assigned an initial value. We want to continue accumulating for all the records with the same value of DEPT-CODE as in the first record. By assigning PREV-DEPT-CODE the value of DEPT-CODE in the first record, we will not turn the "switch" off until we encounter a record with a different value for DEPT-CODE.

(D)   The printing of the total of all amounts due cannot be done until the whole file has been processed. Thus, after the record processing is complete, we can use the information accumulated from all the records of the file to finish the report. We have seen rather extensive initialization in the program, as well as some postprocessing. We really can't put out a grand total until the amount due in each record has been accumulated. This processing after the end-of-file adds a degree of complexity to a program's structure. However, this will be a familiar procedure in the design of subsequent programs. We will examine this kind of program further in Model III, which follows this section.

(E)   These four sentences comprise the normal processing of a record. The first three sentences cause a detail line to be printed. The fourth, which is the ADD sentence, will cause COST to be added to the current contents of both DEPT–SUM and GRAND–SUM. The general format of the ADD command in COBOL allows any number of variable names to follow the reserved word TO. The command will add the contents of the storage location that occurs immediately after ADD to the current value of each of these variables.

(F)   When a new record is accessed, we must ask whether or not the switch is turned "*off*," that is, whether or not the new record is the first from the set of records with the next value of DEPT–CODE. When a new DEPT–CODE value is encountered, it is time to print the totals accumulated for all the records in the department whose last record has just been processed. We must print this total and then set the DEPT–SUM accumulator back to zero, so that the records from the next department can generate an appropriate total amount due. We must also set the switch ON by putting the value of DEPT–CODE found in the new record in PREV–DEPT–CODE. This way the output routine will not be performed again until all the records of the new department have been processed. The end of the last department's records will be indicated by DEPT–CODE having the value HIGH–VALUES. Clearly, once DEPT–CODE has a value of HIGH–VALUES, it will no longer be equal to the value in PREV–DEPT–CODE. Therefore, the last department total will be printed as required. The initialization done after printing the last department total is not necessary for subsequent processing. However, the program is simpler if we do the same thing at the end of each department's records. The two extra statements are not a serious problem.

(G)   The processing after end-of-file is straightforward. One reason for isolating it in a separate paragraph is to emphasize this pattern for a program.

EXERCISES

1. What lines of code from TEXTA are required by PROGRAM–NUMBER 6.1-1?
2. What is a control break variable? What variable in PROGRAM–NUMBER 6.1-1 is a control break variable?
3. Explain: A control break variable is a software switch. Have you encountered variables used in a similar manner earlier?
4. Answer the following questions about PROGRAM–NUMBER 6.1-1.
   a. Why is the initialization of PREV–DEPT–CODE after the initial read and not in the INITIALIZATION portion of the program? What would happen if the statement MOVE DEPT–CODE TO PREV–DEPT–CODE were the first statement of the paragraph FANCY?
   b. Why is DEPT–SUM reset to zero in the paragraph FANCY while GRAND–SUM is not?
   c. How does the program cause the summary for the last department in the file to be printed?
   d. What would be missing from the output if the TERMINATION ACTIVITY portion consisted of only a CLOSE and a STOP sentence?

PROGRAM TESTING AND MODIFICATION EXERCISE

1. Using PROGRAM–NUMBER 6.1-1, form a table to indicate the contents of *each* of the listed storage locations each time the sentence

```
PERFORM FANCY
     UNTIL DEPT-CODE = HIGH-VALUES.
```

is executed, if the file processed consists of the following records:

	ITEM	CODE	COST
RECORD1	SHOVEL	X	000020103
RECORD2	CHAIN SAW	X	000236514
RECORD3	BACKHOE	Y	005643215
RECORD4	TRACTOR	Y	008635914
RECORD5	HAMMER	Y	000000675

Here is an example of what your table should look like:

DEPT–CODE	COST	DEPT–SUM	GRAND–SUM

PROGRAMMING PROBLEMS

1. Using the CUSTOMER–FILE for input, prepare a report that lists each customer's NAME and AMOUNT–DUE. Include the total AMOUNT–DUE for each REGION–CODE as soon as the last customer from a REGION has been listed.
2. Using the CUSTOMER–FILE for input, prepare a report that lists each customer's NAME, STREET, CITY, and both the AMOUNT–DUE and the INVOICE–NUMBER. Include the TOTAL–AMOUNT–DUE for each CREDIT–LIMIT as soon as the last customer with a CREDIT–LIMIT has been listed.
3. Using the STUDENT–FILE for input, prepare a report that lists each student's NAME, AGE, and SEX. Include the average for ALGEBRA for each AGE group as soon as the last student in an AGE group has been processed. At the end of the file processing, print the average for all students.
4. Using the STUDENT–FILE for input, prepare a report that lists each student's NAME and GRADEs. Include the number of students in each AGE group as soon as the last student from an AGE group is processed. At the end of the file processing, list the total number of students in the file.

Model III Processing After End of File

The previous section examined a program in which the final output requirement was to print the total of the amount due fields for all records of the file being processed. Only after every record in the file has been processed is it possible to output this value. Although printing such a value is a type of termination activity, there is a difference between this kind of termination activity and the kind described in Model II. The major difference is that not only is the processing of each record in the file required before termination activity, but also, each record in the file contributes to the final value being computed. In Model II the termination activity consisted of only completing the processing left after the last record was processed. There is enough difference in these two types of termination activities that Model III is needed. Although the pseudocode outlines of Model II and Model III are similar, there is a significant difference in how the termination activity is viewed.

The pseudocode outline for Model III follows and indicates a difference in the termination activity by accessing a separate paragraph of code to complete the processing after the file has been processed.

```
        ***   TEXTA

    WORKING-STORAGE SECTION.
    *** AUXILIARY STORAGE LOCATIONS


    *** INPUT RECORD


    *** OUTPUT RECORDS


    PROCEDURE DIVISION.
    *** OPEN FILES

    *** INITIALIZE


    *** FILE PROCESSING PAIR
        PERFORM para-name-1.
        PERFORM para-name-2
            UNTIL end-of-file-flag = HIGH-VALUES.

    *** TERMINATION ACTIVITY
        PERFORM para-name-3.

    *** CLOSE AND STOP

    *** INPUT PROCEDURE
    para-name-1.
        READ input file INTO input record
            AT END MOVE HIGH-VALUES TO end-of-file-flag.
    ***   RECORD PROCESSING
    para-name-2.
    ***   PROCESS RECORD


    ***   ACCESS THE NEXT RECORD
        PERFORM para-name-1.

    *** AFTER END OF FILE PROCESSING
    para-name-3.
    ***   DO WHAT WE WANTED TO DO
    ***   BUT COULDN'T DO UNTIL AFTER END-OF-FILE
```

This Model can be used for a wide variety of applications. A few typical examples include

1. printing headings for accumulated totals and then printing the accumulated totals;
2. printing the average grade for all students in one or more courses;
3. printing a distribution of the grades in a course;
4. printing the total amount due broken down into one or more categories, and printing the total amount due in all records;
5. ordering new inventory after accumulating the total available for a product and determining that more units are needed to meet ordinary demand.

EXERCISES

1. How does Model III differ from Model II?
2. Is Model III a stepwise refinement of the previously introduced models? Explain your answer.
3. Why is Model II not appropriate for PROGRAM–NUMBER 6.1-1?

6.2 Two-Level Control Breaks

Displaying information that clearly portrays what is intended to be emphasized is a major requirement for computer generated reports. In the previous section we saw how the records of a file could be grouped into categories determined by values taken on by some field. The control break feature is one way to recap groups of records that share a common characteristic. That programming feature was required to deal with a situation that only occurred after a new record was accessed. We asked whether the new record belonged to the same group as the previous record or whether the record read was the first record in a new group. If the record belonged to the group being processed, we continued without any special processing. If, however, this was the first record in a new group, we printed the information collected about the group just finished and prepared the fields used to collect information to handle the new group. This technique worked because we preprocessed the file so that all the records in a group followed one after another, and once a record from another group was encountered, we knew we would not find any other record from the previous group.

Another One-Level Control Break Program

Before we take control break a step further, here is another example of a one-level control break (Figure 6.2.1) so you can compare it to the two-level control break technique examined later.

The report in Figure 6.2.1 gives a recap of the amount due from all customers in each of the regions represented by a value of the field DEPT. In the next example, we want to represent total sales by department within a given store as well as the total sales for each store. One quickly realizes that for each store total there will be several department totals to be printed. The preprocessing now must not only group together all sales by store, but also, the sales for each store must be organized by departments. This can be accomplished

```
                          RECORDS TO BE PROCESSED
          NAME                      DEPT               AMT-DUE
          Jones, W.                  2                 41652
          Smith, G.                  2                 31948
          Brown, H.                  3                 41413
          Williams, P.               5                 61824


                      TOTAL AMOUNT DUE BY DEPT
     Jones, W.                        $416.52
     Smith, G.                        $319.48
        Total Amount Due for Dept 2                      $736.00
     Brown, H.                        $414.13
        Total Amount Due for Dept 3                      $414.13
     Williams, P.                     $618.24
        Total Amount Due for Dept 5                      $618.24
```

Figure 6.2.1 *Output for a one-level control break.*

by sorting the file using as the sort key the contents of the field STORE followed by the contents of the field DEPT. This sort key will cause all the records from a single store to be grouped together and within this group of records, to form subgroups, each consisting of the records of a department of the store. Again, a sample of records (Figure 6.2.2) from a file can make this process easier to understand. Observe that not all stores need have all the different departments.

```
                          RECORDS BEFORE SORTING
          NAME            STORE          DEPT          AMT-DUE
          Jones            3              2            41865
          Smith            1              2            91321
          Brown            3              3            41438
          Johnson          1              1            71695
          Williams         1              2            61845
          Mercer           3              3            71214

              RECORDS AFTER SORTING BY STORE BY DEPARTMENT
          NAME            STORE          DEPT          AMT-DUE
          Johnson          1              1            71695
          Smith            1              2            91321
          Williams         1              2            61845
          Jones            3              2            41865
          Brown            3              3            41438
          Mercer           3              3            71214
```

Figure 6.2.2 *Sorted records using multiple keys.*

We can now list the printed report we would like generated from this sorted file. Following careful study of the input, preprocessing, and output steps, we will examine the program that can be used to complete the report. See Figure 6.2.3.

NAME	AMT-DUE	DEPT TOTAL	STORE TOTAL
Johnson,W.	$716.95		
TOTAL FOR DEPT 1		$716.95	
Smith,V.	$913.21		
Williams,J.	$618.45		
TOTAL FOR DEPT 2		$1531.66	
TOTAL FOR STORE 1			$2248.61
Jones,B.	$418.65		
TOTAL FOR DEPT 2		$418.65	
Brown,G.	$414.38		
Mercer,D.	$712.14		
TOTAL FOR DEPT 3		$1126.52	
TOTAL FOR STORE 3			$1545.17

Figure 6.2.3 *Store totals with department recap.*

Stepwise Refinement

To avoid being overwhelmed by the task at hand, we will use this programming problem to explain the process of program development called **stepwise refinement.** This approach to complex problem solving will greatly enhance your ability to handle complex programming assignments. The essential idea is to complete a skeleton version of the complete project and then add additional, required features one at a time.

The program we will develop using the stepwise refinement process creates a report using the NEW-WORLD-FILE for input. The report consists of a breakdown of the amount due by CREDIT-RATING and within each category a breakdown based on the STATE of residence of the customer.

As soon as the file is preprocessed so that the records are grouped by CREDIT-RATING by STATE, we can implement a one-level control break program using the value of CREDIT-RATING to determine the break points. The final program will require this. The problem of how to incorporate the STATE control break can be dealt with as a program modification requirement once the CREDIT-RATING control break program is executing correctly. The program for implementing the CREDIT-RATING control break follows the pattern discussed in Section 6.1.

```
*
* NAME:                 ID:
* PROGRAM-NUMBER: 6.2-1
* DESCRIPTION:  IMPLEMENT A ONE-LEVEL CONTROL
*    BREAK USING THE SORTED VERSION OF THE
*    NEW-WORLD-FILE FOR INPUT AND THE FIELD
*    CREDIT-RATING AS THE BREAK FIELD
*
     COPY TEXTA.
 WORKING-STORAGE SECTION.
* AUXILIARY STORAGE LOCATIONS.
  01  EXTRAS.
      05  END-FILE      PIC X(8) VALUE SPACES.
      05  RATING-TOTAL  PIC S9(7).
      05  RATING-BREAK  PIC 9.
```

```
* INPUT RECORD
 01  NEW-WORLD-RECORD.
     05  FILLER      PIC X(15).
     05  NAME-NE     PIC X(20).
     05  FILLER      PIC X(40).
     05  STATE-NE    PIC XX.
     05  FILLER      PIC X(6).
     05  AMT-DUE-NE  PIC 999V99.
     05  FILLER      PIC XXXXX.
     05  RATING-NE   PIC 9.
     05  FILLER      PIC X(6).

* OUTPUT RECORDS
 01  DETAIL-LINE.
     05  FILLER      PIC X.
     05  NAME-DE     PIC X(30).
     05  AMT-DUE-DE  PIC $$,$$$,$$$,$$$.99.
     05  FILLER      PIC X(85) VALUE SPACES.
 01  RATING-LINE.
     05  FILLER      PIC X.
     05  RATING-RA   PIC X(44).
     05  AMT-DUE-RA  PIC $,$$$,$$$,$$$,$$$.99.
     05  FILLER      PIC X(51) VALUE SPACES.

 PROCEDURE DIVISION.
     OPEN INPUT FILE1
          OUTPUT PRINTER.

* INITIALIZATION
     MOVE ZERO TO RATING-TOTAL.
```
(A)

```
* FILE PROCESSING PAIR
     PERFORM READ-A-RECORD.
     MOVE RATING-NE TO RATING-BREAK.
     PERFORM TIL-THE-END
         UNTIL END-FILE = HIGH-VALUES.
```
(A)

```
* TERMINATION ACTIVITY
     PERFORM RATING-BREAK-RTN.
     CLOSE FILE1
           PRINTER.
     STOP RUN.
```
(B)

```
* INPUT PROCEDURE
 READ-A-RECORD.
     READ FILE1 INTO NEW-WORLD-RECORD
         AT END MOVE HIGH-VALUES TO END-FILE.
```

```
* RECORD PROCESSING
 TIL-THE-END.
     ADD AMT-DUE-NE  TO RATING-TOTAL.
     MOVE NAME-NE    TO NAME-DE.
     MOVE AMT-DUE-NE TO AMT-DUE-DE.
     WRITE PRINT-LINE FROM DETAIL-LINE.
     PERFORM READ-A-RECORD.
     IF RATING-BREAK NOT EQUAL RATING-NE
         PERFORM RATING-BREAK-RTN.
```
(C)

(D)

```
(E)      RATING-BREAK-RTN.
             MOVE RATING-BREAK TO RATING-RA.
             MOVE RATING-TOTAL TO AMT-DUE-RA.
             WRITE PRINT-LINE FROM RATING-LINE.
             MOVE ZERO         TO RATING-TOTAL.
             MOVE RATING-NE    TO RATING-BREAK.
```

(A)   The initialization consists of two parts. The first sets to zero the field that is used to accumulate the values for each record in a group. The second phase of the initialization process involves setting RATING-BREAK to the value of RATING-NE that is in the first record of the sorted version of NEW-WORLD-FILE. The value given to RATING-BREAK is the value of RATING-NE for the first group of records to be processed before printing aggregate information.

(B)   After the file has been processed, the recap information for the last group of records needs to be printed. Since no field but END-FILE changes value when the end-of-file is encountered, composite information for the last group of records will be listed only if the recap routine is invoked as part of the TERMINATION ACTIVITY of the program.

(C)   The code merely accumulates and prints information about the record currently in memory. When this is finished, the next record is accessed.

(D)   After a new record is accessed, we must ask whether or not it belongs to the same RATING-NE group as the previous record. If it does, processing continues with the new record. If it does not, we must trigger the control break routine.

(E)   The control break routine consists of two parts. The first part moves the information about this group of records to RATING-LINE and then prints this line. The second part of this paragraph initializes again the fields needed to accumulate information about the group represented by the value of RATING-NE for the record in memory, which happens to be the first record in the next group.

The program just examined implements a one-level control break. The objective of the program we are trying to write needs a two-level control break because we want to break down the records within a rating category by values of the state field. What we have to do now is to decide how to add the needed code to finish the program. It is clear that we need another field to accumulate values of AMT-DUE-NE for the records from a single state having the same value for RATING-NE. We will also need a routine similar to RATING-BREAK-RTN of the last program to print the recap information when all the records from a state within a rating group have been processed. We also must invoke the routine that recaps a group of records with the same state code as part of the TERMINATION ACTIVITY.

The only feature left to be considered is: How does the program determine whether the record in memory belongs to the same state group as the previous record? A first attempt at determining this would be to use the following code.

```
                    PERFORM READ-A-RECORD.
                    IF STATE-BREAK NOT EQUAL STATE-NE
                        PERFORM STATE-BREAK-RTN.
                    IF RATING-BREAK NOT EQUAL RATING-NE
                        PERFORM RATING-BREAK-RTN.
```

This code will not handle all cases correctly. For example, consider the following two records that could occur one after another in the sorted version of the original file.

	NAME-NE	STATE-NE	RATING-NE	AMT-DUE-FL
RECORD 1	Jones B	VT	1	31645
RECORD 2	Smith V	VT	2	81619

When RECORD 2 is read, the program will recognize that this is a record from a different RATING-NE group than RECORD 1. The code we now have will not give a recap of the records that have STATE-NE equal to VT and RATING-NE equal to 1, since the value of STATE-NE has not changed. It is clear that we do not want to include the VT records with RATING-NE equal to 1 in the category of VT records with RATING-NE equal to 2. In fact, the assumption we make is that if the value of RATING-NE changes, we want to recap the current STATE-NE category whether or not the first record of the next RATING-NE group has the same or a different value for STATE-NE. We often refer to a field such as RATING-BREAK as the **major control break** and a field such as STATE-BREAK as the **minor control break.** The rule is that when a major control break is triggered, *all* minor control breaks related to this control break are automatically triggered. This can be implemented in the code by altering the condition that triggers the STATE-NE control break. The new code follows.

```
        PERFORM READ-A-RECORD.
        IF STATE-BREAK NOT EQUAL STATE-NE
           OR RATING-BREAK NOT EQUAL RATING-NE
              PERFORM STATE-BREAK-RTN.
        IF RATING-BREAK NOT EQUAL RATING-NE
              PERFORM RATING-BREAK-RTN.
```

A Program Using a Two-Level Control Break

We are now ready to see how all this code gets incorporated into PROGRAM-NUMBER 6.2-2.

```
*
* NAME:               ID:
* PROGRAM-NUMBER: 6.2-2
* DESCRIPTION: TWO-LEVEL CONTROL BREAK PROGRAM.
*    THE OUTPUT WILL BE BROKEN DOWN BY CREDIT-RATING
*    AND WITHIN A CREDIT-RATING GROUP BY STATE
*
     COPY TEXTA.
 WORKING-STORAGE SECTION.
* AUXILIARY STORAGE LOCATIONS
 01  EXTRAS.
     05  END-FILE      PIC X(8) VALUE SPACES.
     05  RATING-TOTAL  PIC S9(7).
     05  STATE-TOTAL   PIC S9(7).
     05  STATE-BREAK   PIC XX.
     05  RATING-BREAK  PIC 9.
```

```
     * INPUT RECORD
      01   NEW-WORLD-RECORD.
           05   FILLER      PIC X(15).
           05   NAME-NE     PIC X(20).
           05   FILLER      PIC X(40).
           05   STATE-NE    PIC XX.
           05   FILLER      PIC X(6).
           05   AMT-DUE-NE  PIC 999V99.
           05   FILLER      PIC X(5).
           05   RATING-NE   PIC 9.
           05   FILLER      PIC X(6).

     * OUTPUT RECORD
      01   DETAIL-LINE.
           05   FILLER      PIC X.
           05   NAME-DE     PIC X(30).
           05   AMT-DUE-DE  PIC $$,$$$,$$$,$$$.99.
           05   FILLER      PIC X(85) VALUE SPACES.
      01   STATE-LINE.
           05   FILLER      PIC X.
           05   FILLER      PIC X(10) VALUE SPACES.
           05   STATE-ST    PIC X(44).
           05   AMT-DUE-ST  PIC $$,$$$,$$$,$$$.99.
           05   FILLER      PIC X(61) VALUE SPACES.
      01   RATING-LINE.
           05   FILLER      PIC X.
           05   FILLER      PIC X(10) VALUE SPACES.
           05   RATING-RA   PIC 9.
           05   FILLER      PIC X(50) VALUE SPACES.
           05   AMT-DUE-RA  PIC $,$$$,$$$,$$$,$$$.99.
           05   FILLER      PIC X(51) VALUE SPACES.

      PROCEDURE DIVISION.
           OPEN INPUT FILE1
                OUTPUT PRINTER.

     * INITIALIZATION
(A)        MOVE ZERO TO RATING-TOTAL
                        STATE-TOTAL.

     * FILE PROCESSING PAIR
           PERFORM READ-A-RECORD.
(A)        MOVE STATE-NE TO STATE-BREAK.
           MOVE RATING-NE TO RATING-BREAK.
           PERFORM TIL-THE-END
               UNTIL END-FILE = HIGH-VALUES.

     * TERMINATION ACTIVITY
(B)        PERFORM STATE-BREAK-RTN.
           PERFORM RATING-BREAK-RTN.
           CLOSE FILE1
                 PRINTER.
           STOP RUN.

     * INPUT PROCEDURE
      READ-A-RECORD.
           READ FILE1 INTO NEW-WORLD-RECORD
               AT END MOVE HIGH-VALUES TO END-FILE.
```

```
* RECORD PROCESSING
  TIL-THE-END.
(C)       ADD AMT-DUE-NE  TO STATE-TOTAL
                             RATING-TOTAL.
          MOVE NAME-NE    TO NAME-DE.
          MOVE AMT-DUE-NE TO AMT-DUE-DE.
          WRITE PRINT-LINE FROM DETAIL-LINE.
          PERFORM READ-A-RECORD.
(D)       IF STATE-BREAK NOT EQUAL STATE-NE
             OR RATING-BREAK NOT EQUAL RATING-NE
                PERFORM STATE-BREAK-RTN.
          IF RATING-BREAK NOT EQUAL RATING-NE
                PERFORM RATING-BREAK-RTN.
(E)    RATING-BREAK-RTN.
          MOVE RATING-BREAK TO RATING-RA.
          MOVE RATING-TOTAL TO AMT-DUE-RA.
          WRITE PRINT-LINE FROM RATING-LINE.
          MOVE ZERO          TO RATING-TOTAL.
          MOVE RATING-NE     TO RATING-BREAK.
       STATE-BREAK-RTN.
          MOVE STATE-BREAK TO STATE-ST.
          MOVE STATE-TOTAL TO AMT-DUE-ST.
          WRITE PRINT-LINE FROM STATE-LINE.
          MOVE ZERO          TO STATE-TOTAL.
          MOVE STATE-NE    TO STATE-BREAK.
```

(A)   The initialization includes setting an accumulator for the STATE–NE category total as well as one for the RATING–NE category total. We must also use the initial values of STATE–NE and RATING–NE once they become available to determine the groups that will be processed first.

(B)   After the end of file, we need to recap the information for the final group determined by RATING–NE as before. Now we also recap the information for the last subgroup of records with the last value of RATING–NE. This processing is not triggered by the code (D) that determines whether a control break has occurred since the end-of-file indicator, END–FILE, is the only field to change value when the program tried to READ past the end of the file. No field in NEW–WORLD–RECORD changes when END–FILE is assigned HIGH–VALUES. Thus, even though the last record in the last group has been processed, the value in STATE–NE (RATING–NE) still equals STATE–BREAK (RATING–BREAK).

(C)   The record processing only changes by having two fields to increment by the value of AMT–DUE–NE as found in the record in memory. Each record belongs to two groups— one determined by its value of STATE–NE and one determined by its value of RATING– NE. Of course, the STATE–NE categories are formed from among the records with a given value for RATING–NE. This means that there may be as many groups of Maine records as there are values of the field RATING–NE.

(D)   When a new record is brought into memory, we must find out whether or not it is in the same categories as the previous record or not. The first question deals with the minor control break since we want to print the recap information for each state represented in this rating group before we recap the value of RATING–BREAK itself.

(E)   This also consists of two parts just like the code of RATING–BREAK–RTN. The first part consists of some MOVE instructions that fill the recap line after which the line is written. The second part of the paragraph reinitializes the fields needed to accumulate the information about the next value of STATE–NE as represented by the record currently in memory.

By first completing a portion of the program's requirements using a feature previously studied (in this case a one-level control break), we were able to isolate the important parts of a new feature. Since the first version (PROGRAM–NUMBER 6.2-1) included code that was required in the complete program, we saw that we had only to add code for a two-level control break. The technique used for this style of program development is called stepwise refinement. It helps to focus on one problem at a time rather than trying to do the whole program at once. Clearly, the two-level control break is a natural extension of the one-level control break and not a completely new feature.

EXERCISES

1. What lines of code from TEXTA are required by PROGRAM–NUMBER 6.2-1 and 6.2-2?
2. What is a major control break? A minor control break? Identify both kinds of control breaks in PROGRÅM–NUMBER 6.2-2.
3. What is the purpose of the compound condition in the paragraph TIL–THE–END? What would be the result if the simple condition following the logical operator OR were removed?
4. What would be wrong with the output of PROGRAM–NUMBER 6.2-2 if the TERMINATION ACTIVITY were

   a. ```
   PERFORM RATING–BREAK–RTN.
   PERFORM STATE–BREAK–RTN.
   CLOSE FILE1
         PRINTER.
   STOP RUN.
   ```
   b. ```
   PERFORM RATING–BREAK–RTN.
   CLOSE FILE1
         PRINTER.
   STOP RUN.
   ```

5. What is the importance of stepwise refinement in developing a two-level control break application program?

PROGRAM TESTING AND MODIFICATION EXERCISE

1. Using PROGRAM–NUMBER 6.2-2, form a table to indicate the contents of *each* of the listed storage locations each time the sentence

   ```
   PERFORM TIL–THE–END
         UNTIL END–FILE = HIGH–VALUES
   ```

   is executed, if the file processed consists of the following records:

	STATE–NE	RATING–NE	AMT–DUE–NE
RECORD1	CA	1	38519
RECORD2	CA	1	41632
RECORD3	MA	1	51675
RECORD4	ME	1	61003
RECORD5	NH	2	41918
RECORD6	NH	3	71615

An example of what your table should look like:

STATE	STATE −FL	RATING	RATING −FL	STATE TOTAL	RATING TOTAL

PROGRAMMING PROBLEMS

1. Using the CUSTOMER–FILE for input, use two control breaks to print the total AMOUNT–DUE by REGION–CODE and for each value of REGION–CODE include the total by value of CREDIT–LIMIT. For each record list the NAME, AMOUNT–DUE, REGION–CODE, and CREDIT–LIMIT fields.

2. Using the CUSTOMER–FILE for input, use two control breaks to print the total AMOUNT–DUE by CREDIT–LIMIT and by each value of CREDIT–LIMIT include the total by value of REGION–CODE. For each record list the NAME, AMOUNT–DUE, CREDIT–LIMIT, and REGION–CODE fields.

3. Using the NEW–WORLD–FILE for input, use two control breaks to print the total PAYMENT in the current billing period by STATE and for each value of STATE include the total by value of CREDIT–RATING. For each record list the NAME, PAYMENT, STATE, and CREDIT–RATING fields.

4. Using the STUDENT–FILE for input, use two control breaks to print the average of all ALGEBRA grades by AGE and for each value of AGE include the average by value of SEX. For each record list the NAME, ALGEBRA, AGE, and SEX fields.

5. Use *two* control breaks to print the average of the MATH–13 grades of each student in REGISTRAR–FILE by AGE and within each AGE category further include the average by CLASS. For each record print the NAME of each student as well as each student's MATH–13 grade. *Hint:* Use a stepwise refinement process. For the first step, just solve the simpler problem of breaking down the average by AGE. To average the MATH–13 grades, first convert the letter grades into numbers. Use the scale: A = 4; B = 3; C = 2; D = 1; and E = 0.

Chapter Review

SUMMARY

A report that breaks down a file into groups of records with common characteristics is an important management tool. The programming technique that can be used to complete such a report is called a control break.

A control break program has three distinct phases. The first is preprocessing. In this phase all the records with a common characteristic are grouped together for processing as a unit. If the file is currently in the correct form, there is no programming required to complete the first phase. If, however, preprocessing is required, it may be done using the SORT verb with a USING and a GIVING option. The second phase of a control break program is to process the groups of records by printing a detail line for each record and printing the recap information at the end of each group. The final phase involves any termination activity needed to ensure that the recap for the last group of records is printed. At this step, a recap for all the records in the file may also be completed.

A two-level control break program is best developed as a stepwise refinement of a one-level control break program. In this situation, the major control break defines the primary groupings for records. Within such a group, a recap is required each time the value of a second variable changes. This variable is called a minor control break.

The preprocessing step must group the records of the file by values of the major control break, and within each such group, further arrange the records into subgroups as determined by the values of the minor control break.

TEST YOURSELF

1. What is a control break?
2. When is a control break initialized?
3. Why does a control break variable change values?
4. When should a program test to see if a control break has occurred?
5. What processing is done when the control break variable changes values?
6. What initialization is done when the control break processing is finished?
7. Explain a two-level control break.
8. What preprocessing is required before a control break application program?
9. Explain a major control break. A minor control break.
10. What form must a file have to be used in a two-level control break application?
11. Explain why it is assumed that a minor control break occurs every time a major control break occurs.
12. Was any new syntax required for a control break applications program?
13. Explain stepwise refinement.
14. Explain how stepwise refinement can be used in developing a two-level control break application.

One-Dimensional Tables—An Introduction

Chapter Objectives

After studying this chapter you should be able to

- allocate storage for a table in the DATA DIVISION;
- recognize when a record can be associated directly with a table entry by means of a value of one of its fields;
- recognize when a record can be associated with a table entry by subtracting a fixed value from a field in a record;
- give initial values to entries in a table at compile time;
- write programs using tables to count the number of records in a file that contain each of the values of a code;
- write programs using tables given initial values at compile time.

Chapter Outline

7.1   Introduction to One-Dimensional Tables

The tools developed so far allow us to solve a variety of data processing problems using COBOL programs. There are, however, other capabilities that can facilitate the solution of business data processing problems. One is the ability to deal more easily with problems requiring a large number of similar storage locations. This chapter introduces tables, which are one solution to this problem.

Allocating and Accessing Storage Locations

In the STUDENT–FILE each student has grades for five subjects. To find a student's highest grade or average grade, we are not concerned with knowing the particular course or a specific course grade. Rather, we want to treat each grade as a number and find the highest or compute an average using all five numbers. With what we have learned so far, it would be necessary to give each of the five numbers a name and deal with them as though they were each different in some way. Instead, we can think of the five grades as entries in a **table.** A table is merely a group of related data items that are stored in consecutive storage locations in memory. With all of the grades stored in the computer as a table, we can then step through the entries in the table in an orderly way. This new way of storing data does not allow us to do anything not possible before, as we could already treat each grade separately and still compute an average or find the highest grade among the five grades. The use of tables can, however, increase the efficiency and clarity of programs. Moreover, tables are commonly used in business. You may be familiar with tax tables, freight rate tables, and a telephone book. Even a telephone book is a table: it is a table of telephone numbers ordered alphabetically based on a person's name. Tables can be as simple as a one-dimensional table of related values or have two or three dimensions. This chapter will focus on one-dimensional tables (also called one-way and one-level tables). Chapter 9 will deal with two- and three-dimensional tables.

In order to first understand how the same problem can be solved with or without the use of a table, PROGRAM–NUMBER 7.1-1 and 7.1-2 are both solutions to the same problem. In the first, five counters are used to represent the number of customers with each of the five different values of CREDIT–CODE in CUSTOMER–FILE. Instead of separate counters, the second program uses a one-dimensional table with five entries to represent the number of customers with each of the values of CREDIT–CODE in CUS-TOMER–FILE.

```
*
* NAME:                        ID:
* PROGRAM-NUMBER: 7.1-1
* DESCRIPTION: PREPARE A REPORT THAT LISTS THE
*    NUMBER OF CUSTOMERS WITH EACH CREDIT-CODE
*    (1-2-3-4-5).
*
     COPY TEXTA.
 WORKING-STORAGE SECTION.
* INTERNAL ACCUMULATORS
 01   ACCUMULATORS.
      05  COUNT-FOR-CODE-1 PIC 999.
      05  COUNT-FOR-CODE-2 PIC 999.
      05  COUNT-FOR-CODE-3 PIC 999.
      05  COUNT-FOR-CODE-4 PIC 999.
      05  COUNT-FOR-CODE-5 PIC 999.
```

```
* INPUT RECORD
  01  CUSTOMER-RECORD.
        05 CUSTOMER-NUMBER PIC X(8).
        05 FILLER          PIC X(82).
        05 CREDIT-CODE     PIC 9.
        05 FILLER          PIC X(9).

* OUTPUT RECORD
  01  PRINT-PATTERN.
        05 FILLER          PIC X.
        05 FILLER          PIC XX VALUE SPACES.
        05 CODE-VALUE      PIC 9.
        05 TOTAL           PIC Z(6).
        05 FILLER          PIC X(123) VALUE SPACES.


  PROCEDURE DIVISION.
* MODEL-III.

        OPEN INPUT CUSTOMER-FILE
             OUTPUT PRINTER.
```

(A)

```
* INITIALIZATION.
        MOVE ZEROS TO ACCUMULATORS.

* FILE PROCESSING PAIR
        PERFORM READ-A-RECORD.
        PERFORM COUNT-EM
             UNTIL CUSTOMER-NUMBER = HIGH-VALUES.

* TERMINATION ACTIVITY
* TOTALS AVAILABLE FOR PRINTING AFTER END OF FILE.
        PERFORM PRINT-TOTALS.
        CLOSE CUSTOMER-FILE
              PRINTER.
        STOP RUN.

* INPUT PROCEDURE
  READ-A-RECORD.
        READ CUSTOMER-FILE INTO CUSTOMER-RECORD
             AT END MOVE HIGH-VALUES TO CUSTOMER-NUMBER.

* RECORD PROCESSING
  COUNT-EM.
        IF CREDIT-CODE = 1
           ADD 1 TO COUNT-FOR-CODE-1
        ELSE
           IF CREDIT-CODE = 2
              ADD 1 TO COUNT-FOR-CODE-2
           ELSE
              IF CREDIT-CODE = 3
                 ADD 1 TO COUNT-FOR-CODE-3
              ELSE
                 IF CREDIT-CODE = 4
                    ADD 1 TO COUNT-FOR-CODE-4
                 ELSE
                    IF CREDIT-CODE = 5
                       ADD 1 TO COUNT-FOR-CODE-5.
        PERFORM READ-A-RECORD.
```

(B)

(C)
```
       PRINT-TOTALS.
            MOVE 1                 TO CODE-VALUE.
            MOVE COUNT-FOR-CODE-1 TO TOTAL.
            WRITE PRINT-LINE FROM PRINT-PATTERN.
            ADD 1                 TO CODE-VALUE.
            MOVE COUNT-FOR-CODE-2 TO TOTAL.
            WRITE PRINT-LINE FROM PRINT-PATTERN.
            ADD 1                 TO CODE-VALUE.
            MOVE COUNT-FOR-CODE-3 TO TOTAL.
            WRITE PRINT-LINE FROM PRINT-PATTERN.
            ADD 1                 TO CODE-VALUE.
            MOVE COUNT-FOR-CODE-4 TO TOTAL.
            WRITE PRINT-LINE FROM PRINT-PATTERN.
            ADD 1                 TO CODE-VALUE.
            MOVE COUNT-FOR-CODE-5 TO TOTAL.
            WRITE PRINT-LINE FROM PRINT-PATTERN.
```

(A)   This sentence sets all the counters to ZERO. Since each time a code is encountered we want to add one to the current total for the number of customers with the same code as that in the record being processed, all the counters must be initialized to ZERO. The statement moves ZERO to each byte of the record ACCUMULATORS. This is the procedure that is typically used when initializing a record whose fields are used as accumulators.

(B)   Each record in CUSTOMER–FILE contains one of the numbers 1, 2, 3, 4, or 5 in byte 91. The program is required to count the number of records with each of these codes. We use a Nested IF construction to find out what code is in the record currently in memory and then we add one to the storage location used to count the number of times this code occurs in the file.

(C)   This paragraph looks clumsy, because we have to repeat virtually the same block of code five different times. However, we really have no choice when not using a table. We have the counts stored in five different storage locations, and we need to move the contents of each of these, one at a time, to the output area called TOTAL.

Allocating and Accessing With Tables

Now let's look at a more convenient way to write this program. In place of the five counters named

```
                      COUNT-FOR-CODE-1
                      COUNT-FOR-CODE-2
                      COUNT-FOR-CODE-3
                      COUNT-FOR-CODE-4
                      COUNT-FOR-CODE-5
```

we can picture as a model five post office boxes, each with the same name but different numbers. The difference between the five names and the post office box model is that we use one name for the location of the boxes and qualify the name using the number assigned to the box we want to use. A diagram will help. Suppose the boxes are named CODE–COUNTER.

CODE-COUNTER

By convention, the boxes in any table are numbered consecutively, beginning with 1. We now have

CODE-COUNTER

1	2	3	4	5

To access the contents of one of these boxes, COBOL requires us to use the generic name CODE-COUNTER together with a specific box number in parentheses called a **subscript,** as shown.

```
CODE-COUNTER (1)
CODE-COUNTER (2)
CODE-COUNTER (3)
CODE-COUNTER (4)
CODE-COUNTER (5)
```

Two questions remain to be answered before these names become valid variable names. First, how do we tell COBOL to allocate this set of storage locations? Second, how is each of these storage locations assigned a PICTURE clause? The answer to the first of these questions is the clause

```
OCCURS  integer   TIMES
```

where **integer** is a positive integer indicating the number of boxes or entries we want. When this clause is included in a data description entry with a variable name and a picture clause, at a level other than 01 or 77, the compiler automatically takes the variable name as the name of a post office box area consisting of integer number of boxes, each having this picture clause. For example:

```
05 CODE-COUNTER OCCURS 5 TIMES PIC 9(6).
```

This code allocates 30 bytes of storage divided into five six-byte areas whose names are

```
CODE-COUNTER (1)
CODE-COUNTER (2)
CODE-COUNTER (3)
CODE-COUNTER (4)
CODE-COUNTER (5)
```

COBOL treats a reference to an entry in a table the same way it treats a reference to any other user-generated name for a storage location, i.e., the value in the storage location is used. The reference to a storage location in a table, however, consists of two parts. First, the name is used to indicate an area that contains a number of storage locations. Second, the subscript identifies which location in that area is being referenced. The numbers in parentheses are each a subscript. The picture clause is the *same* for each of these storage locations. We refer to this as the **homogeneous character** of the storage locations. The compiler also allocates consecutive bytes to the entries of a table. We refer to this as the **contiguous character** of the storage locations.

Let's go back to the previous problem and allocate a table with five entries as accumulators for the process of counting the number of records with each of the different values for CREDIT-CODE.

```
*
* NAME:              ID:
* PROGRAM-NUMBER: 7.1-2
* DESCRIPTION: USING A ONE-DIMENSIONAL TABLE,
*    CALCULATE THE NUMBER OF CUSTOMERS WITH EACH
*    CREDIT-CODE VALUE.
*
```

```
            COPY TEXTA.
        WORKING—STORAGE SECTION.
        * AUXILIARY STORAGE LOCATION
        77  I  PIC  S9(4) VALUE ZERO.

        * INPUT RECORD
        01   CUSTOMER—RECORD.
             05 CUSTOMER—NUMBER  PIC X(8).
             05 FILLER           PIC X(82).
             05 CREDIT—CODE       PIC 9.
             05 FILLER           PIC X(9).

        * OUTPUT RECORD
        01   PRINT—PATTERN.
             05 FILLER               PIC X.
             05 NAME—OF—CREDIT—CODE  PIC Z(3).
             05 TOTAL                PIC Z(6).
             05 FILLER               PIC X(123) VALUE SPACES.

        * INTERNAL ACCUMULATORS
(A)     01   ACCUMULATORS.
             05   CODE—CTR OCCURS 5 TIMES PIC S9(5).

        PROCEDURE DIVISION.
        * MODEL—III

            OPEN INPUT CUSTOMER—FILE
                 OUTPUT PRINTER.

        * INITIALIZATION
            MOVE ZEROS TO ACCUMULATORS.

        * FILE PROCESSING PAIR
            PERFORM READ—A—RECORD.
            PERFORM COUNT—EM
                UNTIL CUSTOMER—NUMBER = HIGH—VALUES.

        * TERMINATION ACTIVITY
        * TOTALS AVAILABLE FOR PRINTING
        * ONLY AFTER THE END OF FILE
(B)         PERFORM PRINT—TOTALS
                UNTIL I = 5.
            CLOSE CUSTOMER—FILE
                  PRINTER.
            STOP RUN.

        * INPUT PROCEDURE
        READ—A—RECORD.
            READ CUSTOMER—FILE INTO CUSTOMER—RECORD
                AT END MOVE HIGH—VALUES TO CUSTOMER—NUMBER.

        * RECORD PROCESSING
(C)     COUNT—EM.
            ADD 1 TO CODE—CTR (CREDIT—CODE).
            PERFORM READ—A—RECORD.
(D)     PRINT—TOTALS.
            ADD 1           TO I.
            MOVE I          TO NAME—OF—CREDIT—CODE.
            MOVE CODE—CTR (I) TO TOTAL.
            WRITE PRINT—LINE FROM PRINT—PATTERN.
```

(A)   We allocate storage for the five storage locations.

```
CODE-CTR (1)
CODE-CTR (2)
CODE-CTR (3)
CODE-CTR (4)
CODE-CTR (5)
```

Each of these has the picture clause PIC S9(5). These five storage locations can be used in many ways, but we will use a simple, straightforward interpretation for the values they contain. We want CODE-CTR (n), where n is any one of the values 1, 2, 3, 4, 5, to keep track of the number of customers with CREDIT-CODE value n. A subscript can only be a numeric variable with no decimal part in its picture clause or a numeric constant with no decimal part. The variable or constant must have a value between one and the number of storage locations allocated in the OCCURS clause. Also, the subscript must be enclosed in parentheses and follow the name of the area that is divided into entries. Most compilers require a space between the variable name and the left parenthesis.

(B)   Each of the CODE-CTR (I), where I is between 1 and 5, has been initialized to zero. At this point in the program, that is how many customers have been encountered with each of the various values of CREDIT-CODE.

(C)   We don't ask any questions about the value of CREDIT-CODE. We use it to point directly to the entry in the area CODE-CTR that should be incremented. We use the variable CREDIT-CODE as a subscript. It is a numeric variable, it has no decimal part, and it has a value between one and five. The discussion about the interpretation of the contents of each entry in (A) was very important, as we now see. One must always decide how to use data structures and how to interpret the contents of a storage location, since COBOL can only make storage locations *available*. There is no *a priori* interpretation for the use of these storage locations. As each record is processed, a one is added to the storage location that is keeping track of the number of customers with that value of CREDIT-CODE.

(D)   Here we can see an even greater payoff for using tables. The first time this paragraph is entered, I has a value zero. The paragraph adds one to I giving it a value of one. We now print one, which represents the CREDIT-CODE whose summary information is being printed, and the content of entry I of the area CODE-CTR, which represents the number of customers in the file who had CREDIT-CODE equal to one. Control then returns to (B). Since I is one, and clearly not equal to five, control returns to PRINT-TOTALS where summary information about CREDIT-CODE number two is printed. We keep returning to PRINT-TOTALS and printing summary information about the number of customers with CREDIT-CODE equal to I until we have printed all the information we accumulated. This is signaled by I having a value equal to 5 when the clause UNTIL I = 5 is evaluated.

SYNTAX SUMMARY

<u>OCCURS</u> integer <u>TIMES</u>

The OCCURS clause may not be specified in a data description entry that has a level-01 or level-77 number.

EXERCISES

1. Explain the OCCURS clause. What does it mean to allocate storage that is contiguous and homogeneous?

2. What is a subscript? What kind of picture clause can be used to define the storage for a field used as a subscript?
3. Describe another way to initialize the fields of the record ACCUMULATORS in PROGRAM–NUMBER 7.1-1. Will this work in PROGRAM–NUMBER 7.1-2?
4. List several advantages that result from using tables in a COBOL program.
5. What lines of code from TEXTA are required by PROGRAM–NUMBER 7.1-1 and 7.1-2?

PROGRAM TESTING AND MODIFICATION EXERCISE

1. Form a table and indicate the contents of CODE–CTR and the variable CREDIT–CODE the first ten times PROGRAM 7.1-2 executes the sentence:

```
PERFORM COUNT-EM
    UNTIL CUSTOMER-NUMBER = HIGH-VALUES.
```

CODE–CTR

CREDIT– CODE	1	2	3	4	5

PROGRAMMING PROBLEMS

1. Prepare a report that lists the number of customers in NEW–WORLD–FILE with each CREDIT–RATING.
2. Prepare a report that lists by month the number of customers in CUSTOMER–FILE who have the same month for EXPIRATION–DATE.
3. Prepare a report that lists the number of customers in NEW–WORLD–FILE who have the same day for EXPIRATION–DATE.
4. For each student in REGISTRAR–FILE, move the CUMULATIVE–GPA into a field with no decimal point in its picture clause. Use the value of this variable to count the number of students with CUMULATIVE–GPA in the following ranges: 1.00–1.99; 2.00–2.99; 3.00–3.99; 4.00.

Model IV   Processing With Tables

When tables are used in a program, we must determine the appropriate subscript(s) to use with the record in memory. We will see several methods for doing this. Normally, the best method is to complete this calculation near the beginning of the record processing paragraph. The use of tables is common enough that it is useful to include in a separate Model the processing that is characteristically required when using tables. A pseudocode model for the development of programs that use tables in the record processing paragraph follows.

```
***   TEXTA


   WORKING-STORAGE SECTION.
   *** AUXILIARY STORAGE LOCATIONS


   *** INPUT RECORD


   *** OUTPUT RECORD


   *** ALLOCATE STORAGE FOR TABLES


   PROCEDURE DIVISION
   *** OPEN FILES

   *** INITIALIZE

   *** FILE PROCESSING PAIR
        PERFORM para-name-1.
        PERFORM para-name-2
           UNTIL end-of-file-flag = HIGH-VALUES.
   *** PROCESSING AFTER END OF FILE
        PERFORM para-name-3.


   *** CLOSE AND STOP


   *** INPUT PROCEDURE
   para-name-1.
        READ input file INTO input record
           AT END MOVE HIGH-VALUES TO end-of-file-flag.
   para-name-2.
   ***  DETERMINE THE VALUES FOR THE NEEDED SUBSCRIPTS
   ***        DETERMINE THE SUBSCRIPT(S)


   ***  PROCESS THE RECORD

   *** ACCESS THE NEXT RECORD
        PERFORM para-name-1.

   para-name-3.
   *** DO THE AFTER THE END-OF-FILE PROCESSING
```

EXERCISES

1. How does Model IV differ from the other models?
2. Is Model IV a stepwise refinement of any of the previous models? Explain.
3. What will one typically find in AUXILIARY STORAGE LOCATIONS? Can any of the fields called AUXILIARY STORAGE LOCATIONS be part of a record or must all such fields be defined at the 77-level? What variables might be grouped naturally as fields of a record?

7.2   Numeric Translation for Finding Subscripts

Translating a Range of Numeric Values Into Subscripts

Whenever one-dimensional tables are used, the major programming problem involves associating records that have similar key data values with the same storage location in the table. We must determine a subscript by examining the record or some of its fields. In Section 7.1, the subscript was determined very easily: it was the value in the storage location called CREDIT–CODE. If programmers could decree that all codes representing different variables should be the numbers 1, 2, ..., n, where n is the number of distinct values possible, programming would be simpler. Then, when information had to be collected about a particular variable, the value of the variable used as a code could be used as a subscript. Unfortunately, programming has to be done with the data as it is presented. Consider the example of the year a credit card expires. It is certainly easier at the point of data entry to use the last two digits as the value of a data field in the input record than to figure out a code that translates the years into numbers 1, 2, ..., n, where n is the number of different years in the records. Although this translation can be done, it creates more opportunities for error than letting the person putting the data in the record use a very natural way of representing the information. We can see a tradeoff taking place. We are willing to work harder writing a program in order to have more reliable information to work with. In many cases the programming price we pay is slight, as there are only a few different translation processes we could expect to deal with.

Let's look at one way of translating input values into appropriate subscripts. In the CUSTOMER–FILE the field EXPIRATION–DATE is composed of three two-byte fields. One field represents the day, another represents the month, the third represents the year of expiration. After examining the listing of the file, we see that the two bytes that represent the year contain one of the following three values.

84
85
86

The years have values that follow one after another from a starting point of 84 to the finishing point of 86. Suppose we want to accumulate the AMOUNT–DUE by the year of expiration of the credit card. We will need a table with three entries.

ACCUMULATORS

AREA FOR 84	AREA FOR 85	AREA FOR 86
1	2	3

Looking at what we want more carefully, we see that we need the following translation.

$84 \rightarrow 1$
$85 \rightarrow 2$
$86 \rightarrow 3$

This way we can use the three-entry table to accumulate the AMOUNT–DUE for each of the years. The code to do this is

```
            SUBTRACT 83 FROM YEAR GIVING I.
            ADD AMOUNT-DUE TO ACCUMULATORS (I).
```

As each record is processed, we first calculate the appropriate value for I and then use I as a subscript. We will look at the complete program that uses this feature, but first let's look at what we need to make this translation process work.

1. Data values to be translated are numeric.
2. Data values to be translated are the consecutive integers from N1 to N2

The storage problem is solved by using

$$\text{OCCURS} \quad \text{integer} \quad \text{TIMES}$$

where the value of integer is calculated as

$$N2 - N1 + 1$$

We add 1 to this difference because we need a location for each of the values N1, N1 + 1, N1 + 2, ..., N2. There are N2 − N1 + 1 numbers in this list. Compare this calculation to the similar one done in Section 1.3 to calculate the number of bytes of storage in a field for which we know the byte in which the field begins and the byte in which the field ends.

```
*
* NAME:                     ID:
* PROGRAM-NUMBER: 7.2-1
* DESCRIPTION: WRITE A REPORT THAT GIVES THE TOTAL
*    AMOUNT-DUE FOR EACH OF THE YEARS IN WHICH
*    CREDIT CARDS EXPIRE.
*
      COPY TEXTA.
 WORKING-STORAGE SECTION.
 77  I  PIC  999.

* INPUT RECORD
 01  CHARGE-CUSTOMER.
     05 CUSTOMER-NUMBER PIC X(8).
     05 FILLER          PIC X(64).
     05 YEAR            PIC 99.
     05 FILLER          PIC X(6).
     05 AMOUNT-DUE      PIC S9(7)V99.
     05 FILLER          PIC X(11).

* OUTPUT RECORD
 01  PRINT-PATTERN.
     05 FILLER   PIC X.
     05 FILLER   PIC XX VALUE '19'.
     05 OUT-YEAR PIC 99.
     05 OUT-DUE  PIC Z(12).99.
     05 FILLER   PIC X(113) VALUE SPACES.

* WE NEED 86 - 84 + 1 = 3 ENTRIES IN THE TABLE
 01  BOXES.
     05 ACCUMULATORS PIC S9(11)V99 OCCURS 3 TIMES.
```

```
      PROCEDURE DIVISION.
    * MODEL-III
          OPEN INPUT CUSTOMER-FILE
              OUTPUT PRINTER.

    * INITIALIZATION
          MOVE ZEROS TO BOXES.

    * FILE PROCESSING PAIR
          PERFORM READ-A-RECORD.
          PERFORM BY-YEAR
              UNTIL CUSTOMER-NUMBER = HIGH-VALUES.

    * TERMINATION ACTIVITY
    * INFORMATION WE WANT THAT IS ONLY
    * AVAILABLE AFTER THE END OF THE FILE
          PERFORM PRINT-SUMMARY
              VARYING I FROM 1 BY 1
                  UNTIL I > 3.
          CLOSE CUSTOMER-FILE
              PRINTER.
          STOP RUN.

    * INPUT PROCEDURE
     READ-A-RECORD.
          READ CUSTOMER-FILE INTO CHARGE-CUSTOMER
              AT END MOVE HIGH-VALUES TO CUSTOMER-NUMBER.

    * RECORD PROCESSING
     BY-YEAR.
          SUBTRACT 83 FROM YEAR GIVING I.
          ADD AMOUNT-DUE TO ACCUMULATORS (I).
          PERFORM READ-A-RECORD.
     PRINT-SUMMARY.
          ADD 83 I GIVING OUT-YEAR.
          MOVE ACCUMULATORS (I) TO OUT-DUE.
          WRITE PRINT-LINE FROM PRINT-PATTERN.
```

(A) alongside `PERFORM PRINT-SUMMARY` block.

(B) alongside `SUBTRACT 83 FROM YEAR GIVING I.`

(C) alongside `ADD 83 I GIVING OUT-YEAR.`

(A)   When the file has been processed, we need to print the contents of the three entries.

```
          ACCUMULATORS (1)
          ACCUMULATORS (2)
          ACCUMULATORS (3)
```

To use I as a subscript, we need a method of assigning it the value 1 and printing

```
          ACCUMULATORS (1)
```

Then we must assign I the value 2 and print

```
          ACCUMULATORS (2)
```

Finally, we must assign I the value of 3 and print

```
          ACCUMULATORS (3)
```

Since output of tables is a common task, and since we need to print the values from each of the entries, the syntax of COBOL builds in a clause that facilitates this process. The code

```
PERFORM...
     VARYING...
          UNTIL...
```

consists of three distinct actions. The PERFORM verb causes a paragraph of code to be executed. The UNTIL clause stands as a guard in front of the PERFORM statement, only allowing the PERFORM to be executed when the condition in the UNTIL clause is FALSE. The paragraph to be performed normally uses a value supplied by the VARYING clause. Therefore, execution of the code needed to evaluate the condition in the VARY-ING clause is executed first, followed by the UNTIL clause. When the condition in the UNTIL clause is FALSE, the PERFORM command is executed. The VARYING clause has three parts:

VARYING identifier FROM value1 BY value2

Identifier: any valid variable name that is numeric.

Value1: when the VARYING clause is first encountered, this value is assigned to the identifier then the PERFORM...UNTIL pair is executed.

Value2: after returning from the paragraph named in the PERFORM clause, the identifier is incremented by value2 before the PERFORM...UNTIL pair is again executed.

In our example we have

```
VARYING I FROM 1 BY 1
```

This means that I is initialized to a value of 1 before the clause

```
UNTIL I > 3
```

is tested. Since the condition is FALSE, the program transfers control to PRINT–SUMMARY. After this paragraph is executed using the value 1 for I, control returns to the

```
PERFORM...
     VARYING...
          UNTIL...
```

sentence. Since I has been initialized, the first action is to increment I by 1, giving it a value 2. The UNTIL clause is still FALSE, so PRINT–SUMMARY is executed again using 2 as the value of I. When this paragraph returns control to the sentence

```
PERFORM...
     VARYING...
          UNTIL...
```

I is again incremented by 1 giving it a value of 3. Since the UNTIL clause is still FALSE, PRINT–SUMMARY is executed with I having a value 3. When the paragraph returns control to the

```
PERFORM...
     VARYING...
          UNTIL...
```

the variable I is incremented by 1 giving it a value of 4. This time the condition in the UNTIL clause is TRUE, so control is not passed to PRINT–SUMMARY but to the next sentence in sequence, which is the CLOSE command.

The VARYING clause automatically takes care of initialization and incrementation. The VARYING clause does not test the variable's value. Consequently, an UNTIL clause is needed to ensure that we don't execute a paragraph with the value of the variable larger than the number of entries in the table being processed. Compare the code in PROGRAM-NUMBER 7.1-1 and 7.1-2 used to accomplish the same task.

(B)   We have already discussed the function of the first two sentences in this paragraph. You should examine the CUSTOMER–FILE to verify that the first 10 records cause amounts to be added to boxes in ACCUMULATORS in the following order

2:2:3:1:2:3:1:2:3:1

(C)   It is worth noting that we don't have to worry about the value of I in this paragraph, since it is taken care of in the VARYING clause. The actual output for the program is

```
1984     8822064.30
1985     1873788.67
1986      225666.54
```

It was necessary to describe the AMOUNT–DUE field in the input record as a S9(7)V99 field since some of the values in this field are credits.

SYNTAX SUMMARY

```
PERFORM paragraph

    VARYING identifier-1 FROM  {literal-2
                                identifier-2}

        BY  {literal-3
             identifier-3}

        UNTIL condition-1
```

EXERCISES

1. What fields in the NEW–WORLD–FILE would require coding similar to what was introduced in this section to count the number of records with each of the different values that occur in the field? Answer the same question for REGISTRAR–FILE and STUDENT–FILE.
2. How would the procedure described here be modified if the values of the field were 10,12,14,16,18, and 20?
3. What lines of code from TEXTA are required by PROGRAM–NUMBER 7.2-1?
4. For the COBOL sentence

```
PERFORM PRINT–IT
    VARYING I FROM 2 BY 1
        UNTIL I > 4.
```

Answer the following questions:

a. What is the order in which the clauses of the sentence will be executed?
b. What is the value of I the first time PRINT–IT is executed?
c. What is the first thing done after executing PRINT–IT the first time?
d. What is the value of the increment?
e. What is the condition that causes termination?

f. How many times will PRINT–IT be executed?

g. What is the value of I after PRINT–IT is executed the last time?

PROGRAM TESTING AND MODIFICATION EXERCISE

1. Indicate the contents of the table IN–PLACE after each modification of its contents.

```
*
* NAME:            ID:
* PROGRAM-NUMBER: 7.2-2
* DESCRIPTION:  SAMPLE PROGRAM USING NUMERIC
*    TRANSLATION PROCEDURE TO IDENTIFY THE
*    SUBSCRIPT ASSOCIATED WITH A ECORD
*
      COPY TEXTA.
 WORKING-STORAGE SECTION.
 77  I PIC 99.

* INPUT RECORD
 01  IN-RECORD.
      05  HOW-MANY PIC 9(2).
      05  INFO     PIC X(78).

* OUTPUT RECORD
* DETAIL LINE
 01  OUT-RECORD.
      05  FILLER    PIC X.
      05  INFO-PLACE PIC X(92).
      05  MANY      PIC 9(4).
      05  FILLER    PIC X(36) VALUE SPACES.
* SUMMARY LINE
 01  OUT-AGAIN.
      05  FILLER  PIC X.
      05  SUMMARY PIC 9(3).
      05  FILLER  PIC X(129) VALUE SPACES.

 01  PLACES.
      05  IN-PLACE OCCURS 6 TIMES PIC 999.

 PROCEDURE DIVISION.
* MODEL-III

      OPEN INPUT CARD-READER
           OUTPUT PRINTER.

* INITIALIZATION
      MOVES ZEROS TO PLACES.

* FILE PROCESSING PAIR
      PERFORM READ-CARD.
      PERFORM TOTAL-UP
          UNTIL INFO = HIGH-VALUES.

* TERMINATION ACTIVITY
      PERFORM SUM-UP
          VARYING I FROM 1 BY 1
              UNTIL I > 6.
      CLOSE CARD-READER
            PRINTER.
      STOP RUN.
```

```
* INPUT PROCEDURE
  READ-CARD.
      READ CARD-READER INTO IN-RECORD
           AT END MOVE HIGH-VALUES TO INFO.

* RECORD PROCESSING
  TOTAL-UP.
      SUBTRACT 15 FROM HOW-MANY GIVING I.
      ADD 1          TO IN-PLACE (I).
      MOVE INFO      TO INFO-PLACE.
      MOVE HOW-MANY TO MANY.
      WRITE PRINT-LINE FROM OUT-RECORD.
      PERFORM READ-CARD.
  SUM-UP.
      MOVE IN-PLACE (I) TO SUMMARY.
      WRITE PRINT-LINE FROM OUT-AGAIN.
```

The data is read in the following order. Entries from Column 1 should be processed before the entries in Columns 2 and 3. Each column entry should be considered as a different input record.

Column 1	Column 2	Column 3
16ABCD	21UVWX	21OPQR
18EFGH	20YZAB	18STUV
20IJKL	18CDEF	19WXYZ
19MNOP	19GHIJ	17AABC
17QRST	16KLMN	20DEFG

I	IN-PLACE					
	1	2	3	4	5	6

PROGRAMMING PROBLEMS

1. Modify PROGRAM-NUMBER 7.2-1 so that an error message is printed if YEAR has a value other than 84, 85, or 86. Also include an appropriate heading for the information printed.
2. Using the STUDENT-FILE for input, prepare a report listing the number of students of each AGE.
3. Using the REGISTRAR-FILE for input, prepare a report listing the number of students of each AGE.
4. Using the NEW-WORLD-FILE for input, prepare a report that lists by year of EXPIRATION-DATE the number of customers with CREDIT-RATING greater than 3. Note that not all records in the file will contribute to the count.
5. Using the NEW-WORLD-FILE for input, prepare a report that lists by CREDIT-RATING the number of customers with EXPIRATION-DATE after 1986.
6. Using the NEW-WORLD-FILE for input, prepare a report listing the number of customers with the same value for year in EXPIRATION-DATE.
7. Write a program that performs the following edit check. Each card must contain only alphabetic characters in columns 5 through 10 and in columns 60 through 70. Read and

print each card, and print a message indicating whether or not the card contained only valid characters.

8. Write a program that performs the following edit check. Columns 1 through 10 must contain alphabetic characters; columns 30 through 39 must contain numeric characters; and columns 50 through 55 must contain either alphabetic or numeric characters. An indicator is punched in column 60. If the indicator is an asterisk, columns 70 through 80 must contain numeric characters. Otherwise, columns 70 through 80 must contain alphabetic characters. Your program should read N data cards, and print only those cards that contain errors. *Hint:* These two problems are easier to do if the input record has a record description of the form:

```
05  CARD-COLUMNS OCCURS 80 TIMES PIC X.
```

9. For each student in REGISTRAR-FILE, divide the TOTAL-HOURS by 30 and then add one. Put the answer in a data field with picture clause PIC 99. Use this variable to count the number of students having total credit hour count falling in the categories listed:

Category	Number of Completed Hours
1	0–29
2	30–59
3	60–89
4	90–119
5	120–

7.3 Initial Values for Tables

Before learning another important way of assigning subscripts, we need to learn how COBOL gives initial values to the locations in a table. For simple variables, we often give initial values at compile time by using the VALUE clause. In the case of tables, COBOL syntax does not allow both VALUE and OCCURS clauses in the same data description entry. The OCCURS clause causes several storage locations to be allocated, while the VALUE clause assigns a value to a single storage location. You should begin to see the logical problems the compiler would have to resolve to enable each of the allocated storage locations to receive an appropriate value by means of a VALUE clause. Other languages deal with this problem so often that their compilers have built-in features that make it easy to assign values to each storage location of any table. The COBOL language also has a mechanism for accomplishing this, and we will examine the rules for using it.

New World Airlines pays its hourly employees every two weeks. In this organization there are ten different wage rates ranging from $5.85 to $6.75 per hour. The wage rates have the following hourly pay scale.

WAGE RATE	HOURLY RATE
1	$5.85
2	$5.97
3	$6.01
4	$6.23
5	$6.31
6	$6.42
7	$6.50
8	$6.58
9	$6.63
10	$6.75

The payroll program uses card input. Each employee's work record for the payroll period is read from an input record. The record contains the employee's number, name, number of hours worked, and a code indicating the employee's wage rate. The wage rate is an integer code with values taken from the numbers 1, 2, ..., 10. The program uses the wage rate information as a subscript to access the entry of a table called WAGE–RATES that contains the employee's hourly rate of pay. We would like the program to have the ten locations of a table filled as follows:

WAGE–RATES   PIC 9V99

585	597	601	623	631	642	650	658	663	675
1	2	3	4	5	6	7	8	9	10

Creating a table with ten locations is no problem, since we could use

```
01   PERMANENT-INFORMATION.
     05 WAGE-RATES OCCURS 10 TIMES   PIC 9V99.
```

We now have

WAGE–RATES   PIC 9V99

1	2	3	4	5	6	7	8	9	10

Unfortunately, we have now lost the contents of the locations. We can assign the numbers that represent wages to storage locations using the VALUE clause ten times, as follows:

```
01   NUMBERS-WE-WANT.
     05 FILLER PIC 9V99 VALUE 5.85.
     05 FILLER PIC 9V99 VALUE 5.97.
     05 FILLER PIC 9V99 VALUE 6.01.
     05 FILLER PIC 9V99 VALUE 6.23.
     05 FILLER PIC 9V99 VALUE 6.31.
     05 FILLER PIC 9V99 VALUE 6.42.
     05 FILLER PIC 9V99 VALUE 6.50.
     05 FILLER PIC 9V99 VALUE 6.58.
     05 FILLER PIC 9V99 VALUE 6.63.
     05 FILLER PIC 9V99 VALUE 6.75.
```

Now in storage we have the following:

NUMBERS–WE–WANT

585597601623631642650658663675

In this case, we have lost the ability to access any of the values individually because we used FILLER instead of names for the fields. Clearly we could give each of these locations a variable name and use a Nested IF construction to determine which wage rate to use. For small-scale problems, either option might be satisfactory. To see how more complex problems can be solved, we should become familiar with certain programming techniques by applying them to small problems. What we would really like is for the storage area called NUMBERS–WE–WANT to be identified with the 30-byte storage location named PERMANENT–INFORMATION. If this could be accomplished, the numbers in NUMBERS–WE–WANT would fit correctly into the ten entries of the table called WAGE–RATES. This is exactly what COBOL allows us to do by using the REDEFINES verb as follows:

```
        01   NUMBERS-WE-WANT.
                      .
                      .
                      .

        01   PERMANENT-INFORMATION REDEFINES
                      NUMBERS-WE-WANT.
```

The following picture shows how memory is organized after the REDEFINES clause is implemented.

PERMANENT INFORMATION
NUMBERS-WE-WANT

585	597	601	623	631	642	650	658	663	675
1	2	3	4	5	6	7	8	9	10

WAGE-RATES

In COBOL, the REDEFINES clause causes the starting address of the storage area allocated to the record NUMBERS-WE-WANT to be assigned as the starting address of the storage area allocated to the record PERMANENT-INFORMATION. After the REDEFINES clause is employed, any reference to WAGE-RATES (I), for I between 1 and 10, will be a reference to a storage location with values supplied in NUMBERS-WE-WANT. This two-step process for assigning initial values to a table is required by COBOL. Two important considerations are (1) that the number of bytes of storage allocated in each record must be the same, and (2) that the two areas involved in the REDEFINES procedure must be consecutive areas at the same level in the WORKING-STORAGE SECTION. We normally use the REDEFINES clause with consecutively defined records. Let's now see how we use this technique in a complete program.

```
*
* NAME:                    ID:
* PROGRAM-NUMBER: 7.3-1
* DESCRIPTION: PREPARE THE PAYROLL FOR
*    NEW WORLD CO. USING A TABLE TO HOLD THE
*    HOURLY WAGES ASSOCIATED WITH THE WAGE RATES.
*
      COPY TEXTA.
  WORKING-STORAGE SECTION.

* INPUT RECORD
  01   CARD-INPUT.
       05  EMPL-NO        PIC X(9).
       05  NAME           PIC X(30).
       05  WAGE-SCALE     PIC 99.
       05  HOURS-WORKED   PIC 99V99.
       05  FILLER         PIC X(35).
* OUTPUT RECORD
* DETAIL LINE
  01   PRINT-PATTERN.
       05  FILLER         PIC X.
       05  NAME-OUT       PIC X(30).
       05  CLASS          PIC Z(9).
       05  HRLY-PAY       PIC $(9).99.
       05  GROSS-PAY      PIC $(10).99.
       05  FILLER         PIC X(68) VALUE SPACES.
```

```
        * REPORT HEADER
(A)       01  HEADER.
              05 FILLER   PIC X.
              05 FILLER   PIC X(30) VALUE 'NAME'.
              05 FILLER   PIC X(9)  VALUE 'WAGE RATE'.
              05 FILLER   PIC X(12) VALUE '  HOURLY PAY'.
              05 FILLER   PIC X(81) VALUE '    GROSS PAY'.
        * TABLE
(B)       01  NUMBERS-WE-WANT.
              05 FILLER PIC 9V99 VALUE 5.85.
              05 FILLER PIC 9V99 VALUE 5.97.
              05 FILLER PIC 9V99 VALUE 6.01.
              05 FILLER PIC 9V99 VALUE 6.23.
              05 FILLER PIC 9V99 VALUE 6.31.
              05 FILLER PIC 9V99 VALUE 6.42.
              05 FILLER PIC 9V99 VALUE 6.50.
              05 FILLER PIC 9V99 VALUE 6.58.
              05 FILLER PIC 9V99 VALUE 6.63.
              05 FILLER PIC 9V99 VALUE 6.75.
          01  PERMANENT-INFORMATION
              REDEFINES NUMBERS-WE-WANT.
              05 WAGE-RATES PIC 9V99
                  OCCURS 10 TIMES.


          PROCEDURE DIVISION.
        * MODEL-I.

              OPEN INPUT CARD-READER
                  OUTPUT PRINTER.

        * INITIALIZATION
              WRITE PRINT-LINE FROM HEADER.

        * FILE PROCESSING PAIR
              PERFORM READ-A-RECORD.
              PERFORM PAYROLL
                  UNTIL EMPL-NO = HIGH-VALUES.

        * TERMINATION ACTIVITY
              CLOSE CARD-READER
                    PRINTER.
              STOP RUN.

        * INPUT PROCEDURE
          READ-A-RECORD.
              READ CARD-READER INTO CARD-INPUT
                  AT END MOVE HIGH-VALUES TO EMPL-NO.

        * RECORD PROCESSING
          PAYROLL.
(C)           MULTIPLY HOURS-WORKED BY WAGE-RATES (WAGE-SCALE)
                                GIVING GROSS-PAY.
              MOVE NAME                     TO NAME-OUT.
              MOVE WAGE-SCALE               TO CLASS.
              MOVE WAGE-RATES (WAGE-SCALE)  TO HRLY-PAY.
              WRITE PRINT-LINE FROM PRINT-PATTERN.
              PERFORM READ-A-RECORD.
```

(A)   We have left headings off most programs since they can be added at the next stage of the stepwise refinement process. We include one here to remind you that we are not neglecting to write them.

(B)   We have seen how these two records are used to give initial values to the table called WAGE–RATES.

(C)   We can use the data field WAGE–SCALE as a subscript, because it is numeric, without any digits to the right of the decimal point, and because its value points to the location containing the employee's wage scale. This latter reason is a result of our design of the program, and is the natural correspondence between values in the input record's field and the table of wage rates as defined in the program.

Remember that in learning COBOL we want to examine and use features of the language in a context in which we can see the value of that feature. We must, however, keep in mind that the examples we use are somewhat pared down to a manageable size, although the size of the problem is not intrinsically limited by COBOL. In fact, it shouldn't be hard to imagine a corporation where there are hundreds of wage rates to be considered in producing a payroll. The point of this is to emphasize that the Nested IF construction, used with individual identifier names, is a very inflexible way of approaching even a small problem. It becomes more cumbersome as the size of the problem increases, until we reach a point where the effort needed to solve the problem is way out of proportion to the problem itself. The table approach does not reach such a limitation nearly as quickly, and actually helps us increase the reliability of the program, since certain information is always available in its correct form. Notice that if the wage scales remain the same for a year, we have a program that can run without modification for the entire year. Also, if one or two wage rates change, the program can be easily modified since the only code that needs to be changed is the appropriate VALUE clause(s) in NUMBERS–WE–WANT. We don't have to look at the PROCEDURE DIVISION at all. This feature in itself is a strong argument for using tables.

SYNTAX SUMMARY

```
01 data-name-1.
01 data-name-2
   REDEFINES data-name-1.
```

The REDEFINES clause may be used with fields with level number other than 01. In this text we will only use it with 01-level data items.

EXERCISES

1. Explain the action caused by the REDEFINES verb.
2. What lines of code from TEXTA are required by PROGRAM–NUMBER 7.3-1?
3. For the code

```
01  DATA-FOR-PROGRAM.
    05  FILLER PIC X(4) VALUE '1234'.
    05  FILLER PIC X(3) VALUE '567'.
    05  FILLER PIC X(5) VALUE '89101'.
01  USABLE REDEFINES DATA-FOR-PROGRAM.
    05  ACCT-CODE OCCURS 4 TIMES PIC X(3).
```

Answer the following questions:
a. How many bytes of storage are allocated to USABLE?
b. What value is used for ACCT–CODE (1)? ACCT–CODE (3)?
c. What values would ACCT–CODE (1) and ACCT–CODE (2) have if the picture clause for ACCT–CODE were PIC X(4)?

4. Supply the code needed in the WORKING–STORAGE SECTION to allocate storage for a one-dimensional table with 11 entries each having a value of zero.
5. Supply the code needed in the WORKING–STORAGE SECTION to allocate storage for a one-dimensional table with eleven entries. Include the code needed so that entry one contains three; entry two contains five; ...; and entry eleven contains twenty-three.
6. Repeat Exercise 2 but supply the values to the table at execution time. This means that in the PROCEDURE DIVISION the appropriate values will be MOVEd into the correct entries of the table after reading the values from an input file.

PROGRAM TESTING AND MODIFICATION EXERCISE

1. What changes are needed in the code for PROGRAM–NUMBER 7.3-1 if an additional wage rate of $6.17 were needed? If the $6.75 wage rate were eliminated? If all the original wage rates were increased by ten percent?

PROGRAMMING PROBLEMS

1. Using the STUDENT–FILE for input, prepare a report that indicates the quality of each student's performance. List the NAME and GRADEs for each student. If the student has no grade greater than 70, put SPACES in the field used to indicate the quality of the performance. For quality evaluation use the following scale:

NO. GRADES > 70	EVALUATION
1	GOOD
2	LOW HONORS
3	HONORS
4	HIGH HONORS
5	EXCELLENT

Hint: Put the designators for the quality level in a table. Count the number of grades greater than 70, then use that number to determine which location in the table contains the information you want to print.

2. Modify the solution to Programming Problem 1 so that the total number of students with each level of evaluation is printed after all the records in STUDENT–FILE are processed.
3. Using the REGISTRAR–FILE for input, prepare a report that indicates the quality of each student's performance in the current semester. Use the following scale:

NO. GRADES > D	EVALUATION
0	DISMISSAL
1	DISMISSAL
2	PROBATION
3	MARGINAL
4	PASSING
5	PASSING

Hint: Put the quality designators in a table as initial values. Count the number of C or better grades, set the value for the subscript that points to the message you want to print.

4. Modify the solution to Programming Problem 3 so that the total number of students with each level of evaluation is printed after all the records in REGISTRAR–FILE are processed.
5. Using the CUSTOMER–FILE for input, prepare a report listing the NAME, STREET, CITY, EXPIRATION–DATE, and CREDIT–LIMIT for each customer who owes more than $100.00. Also list the information that describes the range of the CREDIT–LIMIT for each customer. This information is included in Appendix D. *Hint:* Put the information in a table at compile time. Then use the value of CREDIT–LIMIT to point to the information to be printed.

Chapter Review

SUMMARY

Effective use of tables expands the scope of applications. Even though table processing can be simulated with features introduced earlier, program development for large applications is usually much easier when using tables.

The use of tables requires an understanding of how storage is allocated for tables. Storage for tables is characterized as homogeneous and contiguous. This means that a series of storage locations is laid out in memory, one after the other, and that each storage location has the same picture clause description. The number of storage locations allocated is indicated in the OCCURS...TIMES clause included with the PICTURE clause.

Use of a storage location in a table requires a two-part data name. The first part is the name defined when storage is allocated for the table. This name, however, does not differentiate one storage location in the table from another, and so a second part of the name, called a subscript, is needed. A subscript is a variable or a literal that is numeric without a decimal part and having a value between one and the number of storage locations allocated for the table. With these two parts to the name, each storage location in the table can be uniquely identified and used as any other data name in a program.

The main problem in table processing is to determine which subscript is appropriate to use at a given time. Two cases in which the answer is relatively straightforward are the instance in which a variable takes on only the values 1 to the number of entries in a table or when the values of a variable occur in order from some number to a larger number. In the first case, the variable itself can be used as a subscript. In the second case, after a simple arithmetic operation, the range of values for a modified variable fall into the appropriate range between 1 and the number of storage locations in the table.

The problem of providing initial values for a table at compile time is accomplished using the REDEFINES verb. Two consecutive records are defined. The first uses the VALUE clause to supply the needed initial values. The second organizes storage of the same length as a table. The REDEFINES verb links these two records by having the compiler assign the same physical storage area for each, thus providing initial values for the table area.

TEST YOURSELF

1. What are the parts of a data name for a table entry?
2. What is a subscript?
3. How are initial values assigned to the entries of a table at compile time? At execution time?
4. Explain the syntax and the semantics of the REDEFINES verb.
5. What kind of picture clause is allowed for a subscript?
6. Explain two methods for associating a subscript with a value in a field if the values are in the range $1, 2, \ldots, n$ or $m, m + 1, \ldots, m + k$ where m, n, and k are each greater than one.
7. How can all the entries of a table with a numeric picture clause be initialized to zero using one statement at execution time?
8. What would an error message that says ''subscript out of range'' mean?
9. Why is storage for a table described as homogeneous and contiguous?
10. Explain the syntax and the semantics of the OCCURS clause.
11. Explain the syntax and the semantics of the VARYING...FROM...BY clause.
12. Explain the syntax and the semantics of the PERFORM...VARYING...UNTIL statement.

One-Dimensional Tables— Advanced Processing Techniques

Chapter Objectives

After studying this chapter you should be able to

● use a table lookup procedure to find the largest value in a table and a value within some specified range of values;
● match a code in a record with a table entry in order to accumulate information about records with the same code value;
● write a program that uses the value in one table as a subscript to identify the location of an element in a second table.

Chapter Outline

8.1   Sequential Table Lookup

In Section 7.1 the value of CREDIT–CODE in each record of CUSTOMER–FILE was used directly as a subscript. In Section 7.2 we saw how values of a variable could be easily transformed by a simple subtraction into values used as subscripts. In this section the focus will shift from using the values of a field to determine a subscript to finding in a table the value of a field in the input record. The actual processing may depend on the values in the table. A typical example would be finding the state associated with one of a set of zip codes. Clearly, all possible values of the field must be known beforehand so that each possible value occurs in the table used to identify the value in the record. The table that contains all the possible values is given its original values using the REDEFINES procedure explained in Section 7.3. A slightly more general problem will be solved in this section in that an exact match between the value in a record and a value in a table is not required; it is only necessary to determine the range of values which contains the value in the record. A typical example would be to determine the sales tax for a purchase or to determine the state or federal tax owed using tax tables. This technique in both cases is called a **table lookup.** The implementation explained here is a sequential search of the entries of a table starting with the first entry and proceeding to the second, and so on, until the required determination is made. The range search is explained in this section, and the process of looking for an exact match will be explained in Section 8.3.

Using a Tax Table

Before examining a program that deals with computing the income tax for a given amount using a tax table, we need to look at what is involved in calculating taxes.

When a personal income tax return is filed, the first checks made are whether the correct tax table was used and the arithmetic performed correctly. These very simple checks are done before the taxpayer receives any refund. This is not an audit, and the refund does not mean the return will escape audit. Auditing is a much more complicated process and requires more human intervention. Nevertheless, with so many tax returns being processed, programs must be available to do the initial checking quickly and, more importantly, with a high degree of accuracy.

Let's first look at what must be done to calculate the taxes due on some income amount. First, a table is given that breaks down all possible taxable amounts into a number of brackets. We need to develop a *table lookup* procedure to find information stored in a table. We will use Table 8.1.

TABLE 8.1
TAXABLE AMOUNT
BRACKETS

$ 0	–	$ 2,000
$ 2,000	–	$ 4,000
$ 4,000	–	$ 5,000
$ 5,000	–	$ 6,000
$ 6,000	–	$ 8,000
$ 8,000	–	$10,000
$10,000	–	$15,000
$15,000	–	$25,000
$25,000	–	$50,000
$50,000	–	

Suppose the taxable amount is $12,561. The tax will be calculated by breaking up this amount into the following parts.

```
$2,000  in  the  $      0 - $ 2,000  bracket
$2,000  in  the  $ 2,000 - $ 4,000  bracket
$1,000  in  the  $ 4,000 - $ 5,000  bracket
$1,000  in  the  $ 5,000 - $ 6,000  bracket
$2,000  in  the  $ 6,000 - $ 8,000  bracket
$2,000  in  the  $ 8,000 - $10,000  bracket
$2,561  in  the  $10,000 - $15,000  bracket
```

Table 8.2 is the tax schedule.

TABLE 8.2   TAX SCHEDULE

Percent	For amount in bracket
1%	$ 0 - $ 2,000
2%	$ 2,000 - $ 4,000
3%	$ 4,000 - $ 5,000
3.5%	$ 5,000 - $ 6,000
4.5%	$ 6,000 - $ 8,000
5%	$ 8,000 - $10,000
6%	$10,000 - $15,000
6.5%	$15,000 - $25,000
7.5%	$25,000 - $50,000
8%	$50,000 -

Using the example, we calculate the tax as

$$0.01 * 2000 + .02 * 2000 + .03 * 1000 + .035 * 1000 + .045 * 2000 + .05 * 2000 + .06 * 2561$$

This gives a tax liability of $468.66. In practice, we don't calculate the tax for each of the brackets. Instead, we associate with each bracket the sum of the taxes due for all the brackets below. If we have a taxable amount, we want to find the topmost bracket that holds some taxable amount. We then calculate the tax for all brackets under it. Thus, Table 8.3 is the table we really want.

TABLE 8.3

Taxable amount	Percent for bracket	Tax for this bracket	Sum of taxes for all brackets below this one
$ 0 - $ 2,000	1%	$ 20	$ 0
$ 2,000 - $ 4,000	2%	$ 40	$ 20
$ 4,000 - $ 5,000	3%	$ 30	$ 60
$ 5,000 - $ 6,000	3.5%	$ 35	$ 90
$ 6,000 - $ 8,000	4.5%	$ 90	$ 125
$ 8,000 - $10,000	5%	$100	$ 215
$10,000 - $15,000	6%	$300	$ 315
$15,000 - $25,000	6.5%	$650	$ 615
$25,000 - $50,000	7.5%	$875	$ 1,265
$50,000 -	8%	---	$ 2,140

Since we are examining tables in COBOL, you might guess that each of these columns, as needed, will be represented by a table. If, for example, the information about the bottom of the bracket $6000–$8000, which is $6000, is contained in entry six of a table called BRACKET, and entry six of a table called PER–CENT contains .045, and entry six of still another table called CONSTAN contains 125, then for $7135 the tax liability is

$$(7135 - BRACKET (6)) * PER-CENT (6) + CONSTAN (6)$$

The programming problem here becomes one of identifying the subscript 6.

We need a strategy for finding the bracket in which a taxable amount falls. Clearly, we can ask a series of questions like:

```
IF TAXABLE-AMOUNT NOT LESS THAN ZERO
   AND TAXABLE-AMOUNT NOT GREATER THAN 2000
   COMPUTE TAX = TAXABLE-AMOUNT * PERCENT (1)
                              + CONSTAN (1).
IF TAXABLE-AMOUNT NOT LESS THAN 2000
   AND TAXABLE-AMOUNT NOT GREATER THAN 4000
   COMPUTE TAX = (TAXABLE-AMOUNT - 2000) * PER-CENT (2)
                              + CONSTAN (2).
```

This would solve the problem, and after ten such questions we would be finished. An advantage might be gained by using a Nested IF construction or just identifying the correct subscript in the true range of the conditions and doing all the calculations after all the questions have been asked. This final try at solving the problem of identifying the bracket would require that we modify the last question. However, since there is no upper limit to what can be taxed when the TAXABLE-AMOUNT is greater than $50,000, the procedure we want to use is better than either of these alternatives.

Table Lookup

This problem is known as a table lookup problem. We need a programming method for solving this problem so that with tables of various sizes we do not always have to ask as many questions as there are brackets. We are considering the table lookup problem for tables that are ordered in some way from largest to smallest. Notice that we ordered the table smallest to largest when introducing the problem. For the programming solution to this problem, it is more convenient to have the reverse ordering. (Tables organized in other ways require other techniques than the one we will use.) As we have seen, once we know the top bracket for an amount, we can have the corresponding percent and constant available in the same numbered entry in other tables. To find the bracket we are interested in, we first ask if the amount is greater than $50,000, in which case we use .08 and $2,140. If the answer to this question is no, we ask if the amount is greater than $25,000. If the answer is yes, we know this is the bottom of the appropriate bracket, since we already know that the amount is less than $50,000. In this case we use .075 and $1,265. We will continue in this manner until we get the first yes answer to our question, at which time we will know the location of the appropriate percent, as well as the correct constant. The program that solves this problem is very short once we get to the PROCEDURE DIVISION. However, since all these tables must have initial values, the WORKING-STORAGE SECTION is rather long.

```
*
* NAME:                   ID:
* PROGRAM-NUMBER: 8.1-1
* DESCRIPTION: CHECK THE ARITHMETIC ON A
*    STATE INCOME TAX RETURN
     COPY TEXTA.
 WORKING-STORAGE SECTION.
* AUXILIARY STORAGE LOCATIONS
 77  I     PIC 99.
 77  PLACE PIC 999.
```

```
* INPUT RECORD
  01  TAXPAYER.
      05 NAME                        PIC X(30).
      05 SOCIAL-SECURITY-NUMBER PIC X(9).
      05 TAXABLE-AMOUNT              PIC 9(9)V99.
      05 FILLER                      PIC X(30).

* OUTPUT RECORD
  01  PRINT-PATTERN.
      05 FILLER  PIC X.
      05 NAME-PP PIC X(50).
      05 TAX     PIC $,$$$,$$$,$$$.99.
      05 FILLER  PIC X(64) VALUE SPACES.
* TABLES
(A)   01  TAX-BRACKETS.
      05 FILLER PIC 9(5) VALUE 50000.
      05 FILLER PIC 9(5) VALUE 25000.
      05 FILLER PIC 9(5) VALUE 15000.
      05 FILLER PIC 9(5) VALUE 10000.
      05 FILLER PIC 9(5) VALUE  8000.
      05 FILLER PIC 9(5) VALUE  6000.
      05 FILLER PIC 9(5) VALUE  5000.
      05 FILLER PIC 9(5) VALUE  4000.
      05 FILLER PIC 9(5) VALUE  2000.
      05 FILLER PIC 9(5) VALUE  ZERO.
  01  TAXABLES REDEFINES TAX-BRACKETS.
      05 BRACKET OCCURS 10 TIMES PIC 9(5).

(B)   01  PER-CENT-FOR-BRACKETS.
      05 FILLER PIC V999 VALUE  .08.
      05 FILLER PIC V999 VALUE .075.
      05 FILLER PIC V999 VALUE .065.
      05 FILLER PIC V999 VALUE .060.
      05 FILLER PIC V999 VALUE  .05.
      05 FILLER PIC V999 VALUE .045.
      05 FILLER PIC V999 VALUE .035.
      05 FILLER PIC V999 VALUE  .03.
      05 FILLER PIC V999 VALUE  .02.
      05 FILLER PIC V999 VALUE  .01.
  01  PERCENTAGES REDEFINES PER-CENT-FOR-BRACKETS.
      05 PER-CENT PIC V999 OCCURS 10 TIMES.

(C)   01  FIXED-AMOUNTS.
      05 FILLER PIC 9(4) VALUE 3140.
      05 FILLER PIC 9(4) VALUE 1265.
      05 FILLER PIC 9(4) VALUE  615.
      05 FILLER PIC 9(4) VALUE  315.
      05 FILLER PIC 9(4) VALUE  215.
      05 FILLER PIC 9(4) VALUE  125.
      05 FILLER PIC 9(4) VALUE   90.
      05 FILLER PIC 9(4) VALUE   60.
      05 FILLER PIC 9(4) VALUE   20.
      05 FILLER PIC 9(4) VALUE ZERO.
  01  CONSTANT-AMOUNT REDEFINES FIXED-AMOUNTS.
      05 CNSTNT OCCURS 10 TIMES PIC 9(4).

  PROCEDURE DIVISION.
* MODEL-I.
      OPEN INPUT CARD-READER
           OUTPUT PRINTER.
```

```
* FILE PROCESSING PAIR
      PERFORM READ-A-RECORD.
      PERFORM CALCULATE-TAXES
          UNTIL NAME = HIGH-VALUES.

* TERMINATION ACTIVITY
      CLOSE CARD-READER
            PRINTER.
      STOP RUN.

* INPUT PROCEDURE
 READ-A-RECORD.
      READ CARD-READER INTO TAXPAYER
          AT END MOVE HIGH-VALUES TO NAME.

* RECORD PROCESSING
 CALCULATE-TAXES.
```

(D)
```
      MOVE ZERO TO PLACE.
      PERFORM FIND-BRACKET
          VARYING I FROM 1 BY 1
              UNTIL PLACE NOT EQUAL ZERO.
```
(E)
```
      COMPUTE TAX = (TAXABLE-AMOUNT - BRACKET (PLACE))
              * PER-CENT (PLACE) + CNSTNT (PLACE).
      MOVE NAME TO NAME1.
      WRITE PRINT-LINE FROM PRINT-PATTERN.
      PERFORM READ-A-RECORD.
* TABLE LOOK-UP
```
(F)
```
 FIND-BRACKET.
      IF TAXABLE-AMOUNT GREATER THAN BRACKET (I)
          MOVE I TO PLACE.
```

(A), (B)   We want to establish three tables with initial values. We do this by using the REDEFINES clause.

(C)   You should verify that the information contained in CONSTANT (I), PER-CENT (I), and BRACKET (I) is correct for calculating the taxes for a person with a taxable amount in this bracket, where I = 1, 2, ..., 10.

(D)   This is the initialization of the variable PLACE that is tested in the UNTIL clause in the next sentence. When the next sentence has been executed, not only will PLACE contain a nonzero value; the value in PLACE will be the value for the subscript needed to calculate the tax for the TAXABLE-AMOUNT being processed. PLACE is a software switch.

(E–F)   For some first value of I, this condition (F) will have a value of TRUE. The value of I when the condition is TRUE points to the entry number we need for the calculation (E). Once we have found this bracket, we don't want to examine any other entry in the table BRACKET. To avoid looking in any other entries, we use the assignment of a nonzero value to PLACE as the condition in the UNTIL that governs whether or not to pass control to FIND-BRACKET.

We will now examine a second table lookup problem that includes a review of the SORT verb with both an INPUT PROCEDURE and an OUTPUT PROCEDURE. The program is a refinement of the program presented when the full syntax of the SORT verb was introduced. This refinement will not only list the NAME, GRADEs, and AVERAGE for each student in the STUDENT-FILE, but will also determine the letter grade that goes with the student's average.

The table lookup procedure is needed to determine the letter grade for the given average, and it requires that the program know the lowest grade in each bracket. When a grade is lower than the lowest grade in a bracket, the program must search one or more brackets to find out where this average occurs. The sorting procedure will guarantee that once the average is lower than the lowest grade in a bracket there will not be any more occurrences of an average in that bracket.

```
        IDENTIFICATION DIVISION.
        PROGRAM-ID. LETTERS.
        *
        * NAME:              ID:
        * PROGRAM-NUMBER: 8.1-2
        * DESCRIPTION:  SORT STUDENT-FILE IN
        *   DECREASING ORDER ON THE AVERAGE
        *   FIELD.  DISPLAY THE NAME.
        *   AVERAGE AND GRADE FOR THE AVERAGE.
        *   STORE THE SORTED FILE ON FILE3.
        *
        ENVIRONMENT DIVISION.
        CONFIGURATION SECTION.
        SOURCE-COMPUTER.  IBM-370.
        OBJECT-COMPUTER.  IBM-370.
        INPUT-OUTPUT SECTION.
        FILE-CONTROL.
            SELECT STUDENT-FILE
                ASSIGN TO UT-3330-S-FILE03.
            SELECT FILE3
                ASSIGN TO UT-3330-S-COBOL3.
            SELECT PRINTER
                ASSIGN TO UT-1403-S-SYSOUT.
            SELECT FILE2
                ASSIGN TO UT-3330-S-COBOL2.
        DATA DIVISION.
        FILE SECTION.
        FD  STUDENT-FILE
            LABEL RECORDS ARE STANDARD
            BLOCK CONTAINS 34 RECORDS.
        01  STUDENT-FILE-RECORD.
            05  FILLER        PIC X(100).
        FD  FILE3
            BLOCK CONTAINS 34 RECORDS
            LABEL RECORDS ARE STANDARD.
        01  FILE3-RECORD.
            05  FILLER        PIC X(100).
        FD  PRINTER
            LABEL RECORDS ARE OMITTED.
        01  PRINT-LINE.
            05  FILLER        PIC X(133).
(A)     SD  FILE2.
        01  FILE2-RECORD.
            05  FILLER        PIC X(40).
            05  AVERAGE       PIC 9(3)V99.
            05  FILLER        PIC X(55).
```

```
      WORKING-STORAGE SECTION.
    * AUXILIARY STORAGE LOCATIONS
      77  EOF         PIC X(8) VALUE SPACES.
      77  SUM-GRADES  PIC S9(5).
    * STORAGE LOCATIONS NEEDED TO PROCESS
    * THE TABLES
      01  TABLE-HELPERS.
          05  I               PIC 999.
          05  J               PIC 999.
          05  IN-RANGE        PIC XXX.
          05  NOT-FOUND       PIC XXX VALUE 'NO'.
          05  FOUND           PIC XXX VALUE 'YES'.
          05  RANGE-NO        PIC 999.
    * INPUT RECORD
(B)   01  STUDENT-RECORD.
          05  FILLER          PIC X(4).
          05  NAME            PIC X(18).
          05  FILLER          PIC X(3).
          05  GRADES          PIC 999 OCCURS 5 TIMES.
          05  AVG             PIC 9(3)V99.
          05  LTR-GRADE       PIC X.
          05  FILLER          PIC X(54).
    * OUTPUT RECORD
      01  DETAIL-LINE.
          05  FILLER          PIC X.
          05  DL-NAME         PIC X(30).
          05  DL-AVG          PIC Z(10).9.
          05  FILLER          PIC X(10) VALUE SPACES.
          05  LETTER-GRADE    PIC X(80).
    * TABLES
      01  GRADE-RANGE-VALUES.
          05  FILLER          PIC 99 VALUE 75.
          05  FILLER          PIC 99 VALUE 65.
          05  FILLER          PIC 99 VALUE 55.
          05  FILLER          PIC 99 VALUE 49.
          05  FILLER          PIC 99 VALUE ZERO.
      01  USEABLE-GRADES REDEFINES GRADE-RANGE-VALUES.
          05  BOT-OF-RANGE    PIC 99 OCCURS 5 TIMES.
      01  GRADE-DESIGNATORS.
          05  FILLER          PIC X(5) VALUE 'ABCDE'.
      01  LETTER-GRADES REDEFINES GRADE-DESIGNATORS.
          05  EARNED-GRADE    PIC X OCCURS 5 TIMES.

      PROCEDURE DIVISION.
(C)       SORT FILE2
              ON DESCENDING KEY AVERAGE
                  INPUT PROCEDURE IS ADD-AVG
                  OUTPUT PROCEDURE IS ADD-LETTER.
          STOP RUN.

    *  INPUT PROCEDURE SECTION
(D)   ADD-AVG SECTION.
          OPEN INPUT STUDENT-FILE.
    *  FILE PROCESSING PAIR
          PERFORM READ-STUDENT-FILE.
          PERFORM FIND-AVG-RELEASE
              UNTIL EOF = HIGH-VALUES.
```

```
               CLOSE STUDENT-FILE.
               GO TO EXIT-RTN.


           *   INPUT PROCEDURE
             READ-STUDENT-FILE.
                   READ STUDENT-FILE INTO STUDENT-RECORD
                       AT END MOVE HIGH-VALUES TO EOF.


           *RECORD PROCESSING
             FIND-AVG-RELEASE.
(E)                MOVE ZERO TO SUM-GRADES.
                   PERFORM TOTAL-GRADES
                       VARYING I FROM 1 BY 1
                           UNTIL I > 5.
                   DIVIDE SUM-GRADES BY 5 GIVING AVG.
(F)                MOVE STUDENT-RECORD TO FILE2-RECORD.
                   RELEASE FILE2-RECORD.
                   PERFORM READ-STUDENT-FILE.
             TOTAL-GRADES.
                   ADD GRADE (I) TO SUM-GRADES.
             EXIT-RTN.
                   EXIT.


           *   OUTPUT PROCEDURE SECTION
(G)          ADD-LETTER SECTION.
                   OPEN OUTPUT FILE3
                               PRINTER.
                   MOVE SPACES TO EOF.
           *   FILE PROCESSING PAIR AND INITIALIZATION
(H)                RETURN FILE2 INTO STUDENT-RECORD
                       AT END MOVE HIGH-VALUES TO EOF.
(I)                MOVE NOT-FOUND TO IN-RANGE.
                   MOVE 1         TO RANGE-NO.
                   PERFORM FIND-RANGE
                       UNTIL IN-RANGE = FOUND.
                   PERFORM FIX-OUTPUT
                       UNTIL EOF = HIGH VALUES.
                   CLOSE FILE3
                         PRINTER.
                   GO TO FINAL-EXIT.
             FIND-RANGE.
                   IF AVG > BOT-OF-RANGE (RANGE-NO)
                       MOVE FOUND TO IN-RANGE
                   ELSE
                       ADD 1 TO RANGE-NO.
             FIX-OUTPUT.
                   MOVE NAME                    TO DL-NAME.
                   MOVE AVG                     TO DL-AVG.
                   MOVE EARNED-GRADE (RANGE-NO) TO LETTER-GRADE
                                                   LTR-GRADE.
                   WRITE PRINT-LINE FROM DETAIL-LINE.
                   WRITE FILE3-RECORD FROM STUDENT-RECORD.
           *   GET NEXT RECORD
                   RETURN FILE2 INTO STUDENT-RECORD
                       AT END MOVE HIGH-VALUES TO EOF.
```

(J)
```
          IF EOF NOT EQUAL HIGH-VALUES
              AND AVG LESS THAN BOT-OF-RANGE (RANGE-NO)
              ADD 1        TO RANGE-NO
              MOVE NOT-FOUND TO IN-RANGE
              PERFORM FIND-RANGE
                  UNTIL IN-RANGE = FOUND.
      FINAL-EXIT.
          EXIT.
```

(A)   The file used for sorting must have the key field identified. This is the field identified in the SORT verb as a key. The other fields in the records will play no role in the sorting procedure.

(B)   We really are using the record for three different purposes. The first is as the input area for STUDENT-FILE. In this case, we ignore the fields AVG and LTR-GRADE as they become just names for some of the 60 bytes of unused area. The second use involves calculating the average of the five grades and storing the value in AVG. We now have a record that can be used by the auxiliary file FILE2 for sorting. In this case, we just ignore the field LTR-GRADE as it just becomes a name for one of the 55 unused bytes in a record of the kind we want to sort. The third use involves calculating a value for LTR-GRADE and then writing a copy of this record on FILE3 so this record with 56 bytes of usable information will be available for other applications.

(C)   The DESCENDING KEY option in the SORT sentence allows sorting from largest to smallest value in the field mentioned. ADD-AVG and ADD-LETTER are names of SECTIONs. A SECTION can consist of a number of paragraphs. This allows one to organize blocks of code into coherent parts. The SECTION designator can be used in programs that do not use the SORT verb.

(D)   The SORT verb first transfers control to the SECTION called ADD-AVG. This section will prepare records for transfer to FILE2. When this SECTION ends, the records on FILE2 will be sorted. A SECTION is terminated by the EXIT statement. Control then returns to the next clause in the SORT sentence which is

```
          OUTPUT PROCEDURE IS ADD-LETTER
```

The section ADD-LETTER will deal with records being returned from the sorted file.

(E)   The record in STUDENT-RECORD needs to have a value calculated for AVG. This is the function of the two sentences beginning with

```
          MOVE ZERO TO SUM-GRADES.
          PERFORM TOTAL-GRADES
              VARYING I FROM 1 BY 1
                  UNTIL I > 5.
```

Also notice that the five grades in STUDENT-RECORD have been defined as entries of a table. It is often useful to consider some, but not all, of the entries in a record to be organized as a table.

(F)   The MOVE sentence has copied the current record from STUDENT-FILE augmented by a value for the AVG field into the record area associated with the sort file. The verb RELEASE acts like a WRITE statement for a record headed for the auxiliary file that will hold the records to be sorted.

(G)   This is the beginning of the SECTION to be executed after the file is sorted.

(H)   We deal with the sorted records one at a time in the sorted order. To make the next record available in memory the verb used is RETURN. This acts like a READ, but is used in conjunction with returning a sorted record from the auxiliary file to memory. The sort file is not OPENed or CLOSEd by the programmer, and so the READ verb is not used. This sentence makes the first of the sorted records available in the record area STUDENT–RECORD.

(I)   To attach a letter grade to the first record in the sorted file, we need to determine what grade range contains it. There is no guarantee that the first average is necessarily in the A range. We test the current value of AVG against the smallest value in a grade range beginning with the highest grade range. Eventually, we will find a smallest value in a grade range that is less than AVG. Clearly every average will fall into one of the ranges as we have all the values from zero to one hundred broken into groups.

(J)   When a new record is put in STUDENT–RECORD, we have to check to see if its AVG is in the same grade range as the range of the previous value. We use AVG much like a control break, but we are not concerned when the value in the field changes unless the new value no longer falls in the grade range of the previous value. Here again we must be careful because there is no guarantee that if one average is an A and the next record has an average from another grade range the new grade range will be the B range. We keep comparing the bottom values of lower grade ranges until the value of AVG becomes bounded below by the smallest value in a grade range.

EXERCISES

1. What is the purpose of a sequential table lookup?
2. What is the purpose of the field PLACE in PROGRAM–NUMBER 8.1-1? Of the field IN–RANGE in PROGRAM–NUMBER 8.1-2?
3. Why are all the picture clauses in FIXED–AMOUNTS the same in PROGRAM–NUMBER 8.1-1? What would happen if the picture clauses were of the form $X(n)$ where n was the number of digits in the value for that location?
4. What lines of code from TEXTA are required by PROGRAM–NUMBER 8.1-1?
5. Are the following blocks of code semantically equivalent?

    a.
```
        MOVE 'NO' TO IN-RANGE.
        MOVE 1 TO RANGE-NO.
        PERFORM FIND-RANGE.
            UNTIL IN-RANGE = 'YES'.
              .
              .
              .
    FIND-RANGE.
        IF AVG > BOT-OF-RANGE (RANGE-NO)
            MOVE 'YES' TO IN-RANGE
        ELSE
            ADD 1 TO RANGE-NO.
```

    b.
```
        MOVE ZERO TO RANGE-NO.
        PERFORM FIND-RANGE
            VARYING I FROM 1 BY 1
                UNTIL RANGE-NO NOT = ZERO.
              .
              .
              .
```

```
FIND-RANGE.
    IF AVG > BOT-OF-RANGE (I)
       MOVE I TO RANGE-NO.
```

Is one block of code preferable to the other?

PROGRAM TESTING AND MODIFICATION EXERCISE

1. For the following taxable amounts, determine the values of the following variables after the line labeled (E) in PROGRAM–NUMBER 8.1-1 is executed.

TAXABLE-AMT	12561	37615	4613	2195	8651	29365
PLACE						
BRACKET (PLACE)						
PERCENT (PLACE)						
CONSTANT (PLACE)						
TAX						

PROGRAMMING PROBLEMS

1. Modify PROGRAM–NUMBER 8.1-1 to incorporate the 1984 rates for the State Income Tax. Each of the three rate tables given below should be used in a different version of PROGRAM–NUMBER 8.1-1. Do not try to incorporate all three rate tables into one program.

a. *Tax Rate Schedule* 1—for Single Individuals and Married Persons Filing Separate Returns

If taxable income is:	The tax is:
Not over $2,000	1% of the taxable income
$ 2,000 – $ 4,000	$ 20 plus 2% of excess over $ 2,000
$ 4,000 – $ 6,000	$ 60 plus 3% of excess over $ 4,000
$ 6,000 – $ 8,000	$ 120 plus 6% of excess over $ 6,000
$ 8,000 – $10,000	$ 240 plus 7% of excess over $ 8,000
$10,000 – $15,000	$ 380 plus 8% of excess over $10,000
$15,000 – $25,000	$ 780 plus 9.2% of excess over $15,000
$25,000 or more	$1,700 plus 10% of excess over $25,000

b. *Tax Rate Schedule* 2—for Unmarried or Legally Separated Taxpayers who Qualify as Heads of Household

If taxable income is:	The tax is:
Not over $3,000	1% of the taxable income
$ 3,000 – $ 6,000	$ 30 plus 2% of excess over $ 3,000
$ 6,000 – $ 9,000	$ 90 plus 3% of excess over $ 6,000
$ 9,000 – $12,000	$ 180 plus 6% of excess over $ 9,000
$12,000 – $15,000	$ 360 plus 7% of excess over $12,000
$15,000 – $22,500	$ 570 plus 8% of excess over $15,000
$22,500 – $37,500	$1,170 plus 9.2% of excess over $22,500
$37,500 or more	$2,550 plus 10% of excess over $37,500

c. *Tax Rate Schedule* 3—for Married Taxpayers and Widows and Widowers Filing Joint Returns

If taxable income is:	The tax is:
Not over $4,000	1% of the taxable income
$ 4,000 – $ 8,000	$ 40 plus 2% of excess over $ 4,000
$ 8,000 – $12,000	$ 120 plus 3% of excess over $ 8,000
$12,000 – $16,000	$ 240 plus 6% of excess over $12,000
$16,000 – $20,000	$ 480 plus 7% of excess over $16,000
$20,000 – $30,000	$ 760 plus 8% of excess over $20,000
$30,000 – $50,000	$1,560 plus 9.2% of excess over $30,000
$50,000 or more	$3,400 plus 10% of excess over $50,000

2. Most states have either a sales tax, an income tax, or both. Using a local sales tax table, implement the calculation of the tax for transactions that may involve the purchase of more than a single item.

8.2 Finding the Largest Value in a Table

As another application of the use of tables, this section examines the problem of finding the largest element occurring among the values in a table. This problem differs from the one considered in Section 8.1 since in this instance, each entry in the table must be examined before the largest element can be correctly identified. In Section 8.1 the sequential search through the values in the table was terminated as soon as the required information was found.

The application examined in this section involves finding the highest grade earned by each student in STUDENT–FILE. Once the problem of finding the largest element in a table is solved, it is easy to modify this solution to find the smallest value in a table. After finding the distinguished element in a table, that element must be indicated in the output. This is accomplished by having a table as part of the output line so that no matter which element is distinguished, it can be indicated when the values in the table are printed.

Each record in the STUDENT–FILE contains grades for five different subjects. As part of a report on student performance, each student's best subject must be indicated by placing an * next to the highest grade. Two programming problems must be solved here. First, the highest grade must be identified. Second, an output pattern must be laid out so that the highest grade can be identified as required.

Normally when a program needs to refer to several fields, the programmer must generate a name for each field and use the names at the appropriate places in a record description. In the case that all the fields occur one after another and can each be described by the same picture clause, an alternative strategy is available. The five grades of the STUDENT–FILE are a case in point. We can access them using the following record description.

```
01    STUDENT-RECORD.
      05   FILLER        PIC X(25).
      05   GRADES        PIC 999 OCCURS 5 TIMES.
      05   FILLER        PIC X(60).
```

The OCCURS clause may occur at any point of a record description for which it is appropriate. We saw an example of this in PROGRAM–NUMBER 8.1–2. The program in this section will use this method for accessing these fields in the records of the STUDENT–FILE.

In the general case, suppose we have a table with N elements, where N is a positive integer. To find the largest of these N items we must at least examine the contents of each of the N entries. Only after examining each entry will we know for certain which element is the largest. If we think a little more about the solution to this problem, we realize that what we really need to know is the number of the entry containing the largest element so that when we finish looking in each of the N entries, we will have determined the number of the entry containing the largest element in the table. We can then access this entry and use the value stored there as needed.

At any point in the process after we have examined M of the N entries, where $1 \leq M \leq N$, we will know the subscript of the entry containing the largest element so far encountered. Continuing this process until M = N will give the required answer. In any process of this sort we need to have some initial candidate for the element we are seeking. To keep the process simple, we usually start out with an initial guess that the WINNER is entry number 1. If we find an entry containing a larger value, we update the value of the storage location WINNER that contains the entry number of the highest grade encountered so far. Let's look at the code to do this for a table called GRADES that contains N elements.

```
MOVE 1 TO WINNER.
PERFORM BEST-YET
    VARYING I FROM 2 BY 1
        UNTIL I > N.
            .
            .
            .

BEST-YET.
    IF GRADES (I) > GRADES (WINNER)
        MOVE I TO WINNER.
```

When PERFORM BEST-YET is entered the first time, we have an initial guess that the largest element is in entry number 1. When the UNTIL clause is true, and this sentence has been completed, the storage location WINNER will contain the number that points to the entry in GRADES that contains the largest of the N elements. The paragraph BEST-YET tests the next element, GRADES (I), against the largest of the elements found in entries 1, 2, ..., I − 1. If the current largest element is greater than this next element, WINNER is not altered because the entry pointed to by WINNER contains an element larger than any other element found not just in entries 1 to I − 1 but 1 to I. If the current largest element is not greater than this next element, the value of WINNER is changed to I to reflect this. In any case, after BEST-YET the value of WINNER points to the largest element found in entries 1, 2, ..., I.

To put an * next to

```
GRADES (WINNER)
```

and not next to any of the other grades, we use an OCCURS clause in the pattern for the output lines. Notice we must return to our real file now, because we have to use a constant in the OCCURS clause to indicate the number of entries being allocated.

```
01  PRINT-PATTERN.
    05  FILLER PIC X.
    05  GRADES-OUT OCCURS 5 TIMES.
        10 GRADE-AREA   PIC 999.
        10 STAR-AREA    PIC X(5).
    05  FILLER PIC X(92) VALUE SPACES.
```

The code to fill up this pattern could be

```
(1)     MOVE SPACES TO PRINT-PATTERN.
(2)     MOVE '*'   TO STAR-AREA (WINNER).
(3)     PERFORM MOVE-GRADES
            VARYING I FROM 1 BY 1
                UNTIL I > 5.
            .
            .
            .


    MOVE-GRADES.
        MOVE GRADES (I) TO GRADE-AREA (I).
```

The first sentence (1) ensures that the * from the last record does not appear on the current record. We actually move spaces to each of the 40 bytes allocated by

```
GRADES-OUT OCCURS 5 TIMES.
```

The data area we have looks like

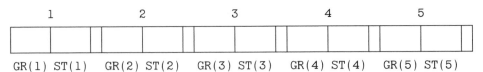

When we refer to

```
GRADES-OUT (I)
```

we are referring to an eight-byte area. We can access two separate parts of this eight-byte area by using GRADE-AREA (I), which is the first three of these eight bytes, and STAR-AREA (I), which is the last five of these eight bytes.

Since each of the 40 bytes contains a blank, we can put the * on the correct grade by means of the second sentence (2):

```
MOVE '*' TO STAR-AREA (WINNER).
```

Finally, we have to move the five grades in the input record to the five data areas of the output record. This is easily accomplished by using the third sentence (3):

```
PERFORM MOVE-GRADES
    VARYING I FROM 1 BY 1
        UNTIL I > 5.
        .
        .
        .

    MOVE-GRADES.
        MOVE GRADES (I) TO GRADE-AREA (I).
```

The complete program that we will now examine does the two tasks just described for each record in the file.

```
*
* NAME:                    ID:
* PROGRAM-NUMBER: 8.2-1
* DESCRIPTION:  LIST EACH STUDENT'S GRADES MARKING
* THE BEST OF THE FIVE GRADES.  IN CASE OF TIES,
* MARK THE FIRST OF THE BEST GRADES.
*
```

```
        COPY TEXTA.
WORKING-STORAGE SECTION.
* AUXILIARY STORAGE LOCATIONS
77  WINNER PIC 999.
77  I      PIC 999.

* INPUT RECORD
01  STUDENT-INFO.
    05 FILLER PIC X(4).
    05 NAME   PIC X(18).
    05 FILLER PIC X(3).
    05 GRADES PIC 999 OCCURS 5 TIMES.
    05 FILLER PIC X(60).

* OUTPUT RECORD
01  PRINT-PATTERN.
    05 FILLER         PIC X.
    05 PP-NAME        PIC X(30).
    05 GRADES-OUT OCCURS 5 TIMES.
       10 GRADE-AREA PIC Z(3).
       10 STAR-AREA  PIC X(5).
    05 FILLER         PIC X(62) VALUE SPACES.

PROCEDURE DIVISION.
* MODEL-I
    OPEN INPUT STUDENT-FILE
         OUTPUT PRINTER.

* FILE PROCESSING PAIR
    PERFORM READ-A-RECORD.
    PERFORM LIST-GRADES
        UNTIL NAME = HIGH-VALUES.

* TERMINATION ACTIVITY
    CLOSE STUDENT-FILE
          PRINTER.
    STOP RUN.

* INPUT PROCEDURE
READ-A-RECORD.
    READ STUDENT-FILE INTO STUDENT-INFO
        AT END MOVE HIGH-VALUES TO NAME.

* RECORD PROCESSING
LIST-GRADES.
    MOVE SPACES TO PRINT-PATTERN.
    MOVE NAME   TO PP-NAME.
    MOVE 1      TO WINNER.
    PERFORM BEST-YET
        VARYING I FROM 1 BY 1
            UNTIL I > 5.
    MOVE '*'    TO STAR-AREA (WINNER).
    WRITE PRINT-LINE FROM PRINT-PATTERN.
    PERFORM READ-A-RECORD.
BEST-YET.
    IF GRADES (I) > GRADES (WINNER)
        MOVE I      TO WINNER.
    MOVE GRADES (I) TO GRADE-AREA (I).
```

This program follows a very simple pattern: process each record in the file, then STOP. The processing itself consists of two steps:

1. Find the distinguished element in the record being processed.
2. Print certain information in the record with a special mark for the distinguished element.

You should think about how important an appropriate data structure is in making the program understandable. The care and attention given to a program before any code is written always pays off in the quality of the finished product. This is particularly true in designing efficient algorithms to solve parts of the problem and in deciding on the appropriate structures for the program.

EXERCISES

1. Why must all entries in the table be examined in finding the largest or smallest element in a table?
2. Define a pattern for the printed line that can be used to list the five grades of a student with a letter grade equivalent following each numeric score. Also print a star next to any letter grade that is an A.
3. Is there any difference in the result when the following two blocks of code are executed?

```
a. MOVE 1 TO WINNER.              b. MOVE 1 TO WINNER.
   PERFORM BEST                      PERFORM BEST
        VARYING I FROM 1 BY 1             VARYING I FROM 2 BY 1
           UNTIL I > 8.                      UNTIL I > 8.
                      .
                      .
                      .
                  BEST.
                     IF GRADE (I) > GRADE (WINNER)
                         MOVE I TO WINNER.
```

Which block is better code?

4. For the COBOL code

```
               MOVE 1 TO BIGGEST.
               PERFORM BIG-YET
                    VARYING I FROM 2 BY 1
                       UNTIL I > N.
                          .
                          .
                          .
               BIG-YET.
                  IF CROP (I) > CROP (BIGGEST)
                      MOVE I TO BIGGEST.
```

answer the following questions.

a. What is the initial guess as to the storage location in the table CROP that contains the largest element?
b. When the sentence PERFORM BIG-YET is executed for the first time, what value will I have?
c. When will the PERFORM sentence terminate?
d. If N has a value of 13, how many times will the paragraph BIG-YET be executed?

e. When the sentence PERFORM BIG–YET terminates what value does I have?
f. When the sentence PERFORM BIG–YET terminates what does the value of BIG-GEST tell you?

PROGRAM TESTING AND MODIFICATION EXERCISE

1. Using the code of PROGRAM–NUMBER 8.2-1, determine the different values put in the storage location WINNER for each of the given sets of GRADES. You won't need to fill all the boxes under WINNER in most cases.

GRADES					WINNER					
1	2	3	4	5						
65	63	85	56	76	1	3				
65	86	85	84	74						
75	72	70	68	65						
70	58	90	64	83						
85	80	80	75	74						
72	74	75	75	75						
73	72	72	73	84						
72	70	70	74	72						
53	56	58	59	58						
58	56	54	62	63						

PROGRAMMING PROBLEMS

1. Modify PROGRAM–NUMBER 8.2-1 so that the appropriate headings are printed and the smallest GRADE is distinguished.
2. Modify PROGRAM–NUMBER 8.2-1 so that an * is printed next to the highest GRADE and the lowest GRADE of each student. In case of ties, mark only one occurrence of the highest or lowest GRADE.
3. Using the REGISTRAR–FILE for input, list the NAME and GRADEs of each student. Put a distinguishing mark next to the student's highest and lowest GRADEs. Break ties in some way.

8.3 Associating Subscripts With Code Values

Data is often stored in a record using abbreviations and codes. For example, states are usually represented by a two-character code and years by using the last two digits. Since some codes may not even be numeric, the problem of associating a location in a table with each different value of the code cannot be solved using the techniques described so far. The technique to solve this new problem is a combination of the methods we examined earlier. We will have to define a table having as initial values all possible values of the code and then perform a table lookup to match the input value with one of the values in the table.

Matching Values of REGION

The problem examined next has successive letters of the alphabet as values for the code, but this should be considered a coincidence. The solution presented does not depend on this in any way. Suppose we must count the number of customers for each of the different values of REGION. The values for this field are A, B, and C. Using our models, it would be nice to write

```
ADD 1 TO ACCUMULATE (REGION)
```

and have three entries ready to keep track of the number of occurrences of A, B, and C. Subscripts, however, must be numeric variables or positive integer constants, without decimal parts, having values in an appropriate range. The programmer's job is to turn the values of a variable into appropriate numeric values for use as subscripts. For the example just described, we can make the following association.

$$A \rightarrow 1$$
$$B \rightarrow 2$$
$$C \rightarrow 3$$

Now, whenever a record with A as the value for REGION is read, we add 1 to entry number 1. When a record with B as the value for REGION is read, we add 1 to entry number 2. Finally, when a record with C as the value for REGION is read, we add 1 to entry number 3. The code for this could be

```
IF REGION = 'A'
    ADD 1 TO ACCUMULATE-BY-REGION (1)
ELSE
    IF REGION = 'B'
        ADD 1 TO ACCUMULATE-BY-REGION (2)
    ELSE
        IF REGION = 'C'
            ADD 1 TO ACCUMULATE-BY-REGION (3).
```

This really puts us back at the start of the table sections, since we don't need tables with the code as now written. When the number of values is small, it is hard to be convinced that tables are really necessary. However, just think about what would be needed if there were 100 values for the REGION code!

Let's write comments for what we want the code to do, and then see if we can accomplish it.

```
* FOR A, B, & C VALUES OF REGION, SUBSTITUTE THE
* NUMERIC VALUES 1, 2, AND, 3, RESPECTIVELY, AND PUT
* THIS ASSOCIATED VALUE IN THE VARIABLE CALLED PLACE.
* FOR THE CURRENT RECORD, INCREMENT THE CONTENTS OF
* ENTRY NUMBER PLACE IN COUNT-BY-REGION THAT HAS JUST
* BEEN ASSOCIATED WITH THE VALUE REGION

    ADD 1 TO COUNT-BY-REGION (PLACE).
```

We can use the model given in the tax problem to find an appropriate value for PLACE. The code is

```
MOVE ZERO TO PLACE.
PERFORM TRANSLATE
    VARYING I FROM 1 BY 1
        UNTIL PLACE NOT EQUAL ZERO.
```

We still have more to do for a complete solution of the problem, but all the code needed will be in the paragraph TRANSLATE. To model the code after the tax problem, we will need a table in the WORKING–STORAGE SECTION that looks like:

REGIONS

We can write

```
TRANSLATE.
    IF REGION = REGIONS (I)
        MOVE I TO PLACE.
```

Trace the execution of this code with the value of REGION being A and see that PLACE is assigned a value of 1. Then try the same code with the other values of REGION to see that the correct value for PLACE is determined. It should be clear that this procedure does not depend on the code having three values, but on knowing ahead of time how many different values there are for the code and what each of the different values is. It should also be clear that the programmer has the freedom to decide which entry contains which code. There is no reason why A must be in entry 1 and B in entry 2. This determination is made by the programmer when setting up the code value table in the WORKING–STORAGE SECTION. This will seem like a routine programming tool after we examine the complete program to solve this problem and work on a similar problem independently.

```
*
* NAME:              ID:
* PROGRAM-NUMBER: 8.3-1
* DESCRIPTION: PREPARE A REPORT THAT LISTS THE
*    NUMBER OF CUSTOMERS IN CUSTOMER-FILE
*    IN EACH OF THE THREE DIFFERENT REGIONS.
*
     COPY TEXTA.
 WORKING-STORAGE SECTION.
 77  PLACE PIC S9(4).
 77  I     PIC S9(4).

* INPUT RECORD
 01  CHARGE-INFO.
     05 CUSTOMER-NUMBER PIC X(8).
     05 FILLER          PIC X (81).
     05 REGION          PIC X.
     05 FILLER          PIC X(10).

* OUTPUT RECORD
 01  PRINT-PATTERN.
     05 FILLER          PIC X.
     05 CODE-OUT        PIC X(18).
     05 COUNT-BY-CODE   PIC Z(10).
     05 FILLER          PIC X(104) VALUE SPACES.
* TABLES
 01  VALUE-OF-CODE.
     05 FILLER PIC X VALUE 'A'.
     05 FILLER PIC X VALUE 'B'.
     05 FILLER PIC X VALUE 'C'.
 01  ARRAY-OF-VALUES REDEFINES VALUE-OF-CODE.
     05 CODED PIC X OCCURS 3 TIMES.
```

(A)

(B)
```
       01  COUNTER.
           05 COUNT-BY-REGION PIC 999 OCCURS 3 TIMES.

       PROCEDURE DIVISION.
     * MODEL-III
           OPEN INPUT CUSTOMER-FILE
               OUTPUT PRINTER.

     * INITIALIZATION
```
(C)
```
           MOVE ZEROS TO COUNTER.

     * FILE PROCESSING PAIR
           PERFORM READ-A-RECORD.
           PERFORM COUNT-EM
               UNTIL CUSTOMER-NUMBER = HIGH-VALUES.

     * TERMINATION ACTIVITY
```
(D)
```
           PERFORM PRINT-SUMMARY
               VARYING I FROM 1 BY 1
                   UNTIL I > 3.
           CLOSE CUSTOMER-FILE
               PRINTER.
           STOP RUN.

     * INPUT PROCEDURE
       READ-A-RECORD.
           READ CUSTOMER-FILE INTO CHARGE-INFO
               AT END MOVE HIGH-VALUES TO CUSTOMER-NUMBER.

     * RECORD PROCESSING
       COUNT-EM.
```
(E)
```
           MOVE ZERO TO PLACE.
           PERFORM TRANSLATE
               VARYING I FROM 1 BY 1
                   UNTIL PLACE NOT EQUAL ZERO.
           ADD 1 TO COUNT-BY-REGION (PLACE).
     * GET THE NEXT RECORD
           PERFORM READ-A-RECORD.
       PRINT-SUMMARY.
```
(F)
```
           MOVE CODED (I)              TO CODE-OUT.
           MOVE COUNT-BY-REGION (I) TO COUNT-BY-CODE.
           WRITE PRINT-LINE FROM PRINT-PATTERN.
       TRANSLATE.
           IF REGION = CODED (I)
               MOVE I TO PLACE.
```

(A) We want to match the value of the variable REGION in the record being processed with one of the possible values for that variable. We know ahead of time what the possible values are, so we set up a table with these as initial values. The REDEFINES clause allows us to access the codes individually by means of the table CODED. Once we match the code in the record with the contents of one of these entries, we use the entry number of the entry that has its value matched as a subscript. The subscript points to the entry in the table where we accumulate information about that value of the code. In this case, all the information about region A will be in entry number 1 of the tables CODED and COUNT-BY-REGION. We try to keep the code as simple as possible. The following picture illustrates how we are setting up our tables.

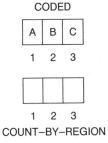

CODED

COUNT–BY–REGION

(B)   The table COUNT–BY–REGION will be used to keep track of the number of records with each of the values of the variable REGION. Entry 1 will keep track of region A, entry 2 will keep track of region B, and entry 3 will keep track of region C. This correspondence follows naturally from the picture we set up in (A). Since this would not be a complicated problem to solve by hand, we want to keep the COBOL code as simple as the problem itself.

(C)   At this point in the program no records have been processed, so the correct value for each of the counters is zero. With this initialization we know the final value in each of the entries in the table COUNT–BY–REGION will be the actual number of records in the file with the corresponding value in the code field.

(D)   This processing must be done after the end–of–file. Only at that point is the correct count of the number of records with each value of the code available. We have three values, one for each of the regions. We want to print the contents of each of the entries, one at a time. This is handled by the construction:

```
PERFORM...
    VARYING...
        UNTIL...
```

(E)   These two sentences translate a region code into an appropriate numeric value that can be used as a subscript in the counting process. The process will stop as soon as PLACE is assigned a nonzero value. We won't have any problem with subsequent records, since we start PLACE with a value of zero each time a record is processed.

(F)   The output again is very simple. On line 1 we want to print an A and the number of records that have this value for REGION. Notice we are using the subscript I to point to one of the entries in the table CODED, so we can print A, the actual region code, rather than printing the value of I to indicate the region number.

This section has examined how to translate character codes into subscripts. The problem studied used the codes A, B, and C. The method employed does not depend on the codes being in any particular order or even of one particular type, such as all letters or all digits. Further, the same procedure works regardless of the number of values. The important criteria is that *all* possible values of the code must be known ahead of time, so that a table look-up can be used to find the match.

EXERCISES

1. What lines of code from TEXTA are required by PROGRAM–NUMBER 8.3-1?
2. Identify the field(s) in NEW–WORLD–FILE that would need to use the method introduced in this section for identifying subscripts if a program were required to count the number of records that had each value of the field.
3. Can this method of identifying a subscript be used if the values of the field were 14, 15, 16, 17, 18, and 19? Why would you not want to use this method in such a case?

4. Can this method of identifying a subscript be used if the values of the field were 1, 2, 3, 4, and 5? Why would you not want to use this method in such a case?

5. Define the storage locations needed to count the number of students in REGISTRAR–FILE with each different HOME–STATE.

6. Suppose a table called MAIL–BOXES has 7 entries whose contents are

MAIL–BOXES

A	B	Q	Z	R	S	U
1	2	3	4	5	6	7

a. Indicate the value of I at the end of the block of code listed below, for the following values of SPECIAL–CODE:

```
            MOVE 'NO' TO FLAG.
            PERFORM LOOK-UP
                VARYING I FROM 1 BY 1
                    UNTIL FLAG = 'ZEBRA'.
            SUBTRACT 1 FROM I
                    .
                    .
                    .
        LOOK-UP.
            IF SPECIAL-CODE = MAIL-BOXES (I)
                MOVE 'ZEBRA' TO FLAG.
```

SPECIAL-CODE	I
U	
Z	
B	
A	
Q	
S	
S	
R	
Z	
A	
U	
Q	

b. Indicate the value of J at the end of the block of code listed below, for the following values of SPECIAL–CODE:

```
            MOVE 'NO' TO FLAG.
            PERFORM SEEK
                VARYING I FROM 1 BY 1
                    UNTIL FLAG = 'YES'.
                    .
                    .
                    .
        SEEK.
            IF SPECIAL-CODE = MAIL-BOXES (I)
                MOVE 'YES' TO FLAG
                MOVE I TO J.
```

SPECIAL-CODE	J
U	
Z	
B	
A	
Q	
S	
S	
R	
Z	
A	
U	
Z	

PROGRAM TESTING AND MODIFICATION EXERCISE

1. Using the code of PROGRAM–NUMBER 8.3-1, indicate the value of the listed variables each time the sentence

```
        PERFORM COUNT-EM
            UNTIL CUSTOMER-NUMBER = HIGH-VALUES.
```

is executed. Do this for the first 12 records in CUSTOMER–FILE by forming a table such as the following.

		COUNT–BY–REGION		
PLACE	REGION	1	2	3

PROGRAMMING PROBLEMS

1. Using the REGISTRAR–FILE for input, prepare a report that counts the number of each grade for MATH–13.
2. Using the REGISTRAR–FILE for input, list each student's NAME, GRADEs, and semester average. *Hint:* Use the following table to identify the value that grade contributes to the calculation of the average.

MARKS

1 2 3 4 5

To calculate the average, suppose the grade is found in location I. That grade contributes $3 * (I - 1)$ to the sum that is divided by 15 to find the average.

3. Using the REGISTRAR–FILE for input, determine the average grade for all students in each course. Use the letter-to-number translation scheme explained in Problem 2.
4. Using the REGISTRAR–FILE for input, determine the number of students from each HOME–STATE.
5. Using the NEW–WORLD–FILE for input, determine the number of customers from each STATE.

8.4   Indirect Addressing

The next technique examined for determining an appropriate subscript is called **indirect addressing.** This technique is used when a value in one table is used as a subscript to identify the location of an element in a second table. COBOL does not allow a subscripted variable to be a subscript. So when indirect addressing is needed, we must assign the value in a table to a variable that can be used as a subscript *before* accessing the entry in the second table. In this section, a special case is described in which the elements of one table are to be printed in an order different from the way they are stored in the table.

The OCCURS clause can be used at any point in the description of a record. For example, as we saw before, the record in the STUDENT–FILE can be

```
01   STUDENT-INFO.
     05 STU-NUMBER            PIC X(4).
     05 NAME                  PIC X(18).
     05 SEX                   PIC X.
     05 AGE                   PIC 99.
     05 GRADES OCCURS 5 TIMES PIC 999.
     05 FILLER                PIC X(60).
```

Now the fields we use have the following names

```
ALGEBRA    → GRADES (1)
GEOMETRY  → GRADES (2)
ENGLISH    → GRADES (3)
PHYSICS    → GRADES (4)
CHEMISTRY → GRADES (5)
```

This way of describing these fields makes it easy for us to calculate the average of all the grades for each subject. The code for this has two parts. The first part occurs when the record is being processed. It accumulates the sum of all the grades in each course in the locations of a table that we will call ADD–UP–AREA, as well as the number of records being processed in a field called NO–STUDENTS that has been initialized to zero.

```
ADD 1 TO NO-STUDENTS.
PERFORM ADD-UP
     VARYING I FROM 1 BY 1
        UNTIL I > 5.
              .
              .
              .

ADD-UP.
     ADD GRADES (I) TO ADD-UP-AREA (I)
```

The second part of the code occurs when the end–of–file is encountered. We divide the contents of each entry in ADD–UP–AREA by NO–STUDENTS to obtain the average for each course. The answers will be put in the entries of a table called AVG–GR.

```
PERFORM CALCULATE-AVERAGES
     VARYING I FROM 1 BY 1
        UNTIL I > 5.
            .
            .
            .
CALCULATE-AVERAGES.
     DIVIDE ADD-UP-AREA (I) BY NO-STUDENTS GIVING AVG-GR (I).
```

This is straightforward. Now suppose that for output we want the answers displayed:

AVG–GR (3)   AVG–GR (2)   AVG–GR (5)   AVG–GR (1)   AVG–GR (4)

To display the information this way, we will use a table as part of the output record.

```
01   PRINTED-LINE.
     05 FILLER  PIC X.
     05 OUT-AVG PIC Z(10).99 OCCURS 5 TIMES.
     05 FILLER  PIC X(67)     VALUE SPACES.
```

We can meet our objective by the following code.

```
MOVE AVG-GR (1) TO OUT-AVG (4)
MOVE AVG-GR (2) TO OUT-AVG (2)
MOVE AVG-GR (3) TO OUT-AVG (1)
MOVE AVG-GR (4) TO OUT-AVG (5)
MOVE AVG-GR (5) TO OUT-AVG (3).
```

By now you should be uncomfortable with all these lines of code for moving the contents of one table into the fields of another table. We can simplify the code by using an intermediate step: set up a table called RIGHT–PLACE such that the contents of location I of this table tells the location in AVG–GR that contains the information that must be printed in OUT–AVG (I). This idea can be illustrated as follows:

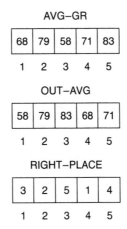

AVG–GR

68	79	58	71	83
1	2	3	4	5

OUT–AVG

58	79	83	68	71
1	2	3	4	5

RIGHT–PLACE

3	2	5	1	4
1	2	3	4	5

We can cause this shifting around of the values by the code:

```
MOVE RIGHT-PLACE (I) TO J.
MOVE AVG-GR (J)     TO OUT-AVG (I).
```

The table RIGHT–PLACE will be allocated space and have initial values in its entries as:

```
01  STEP-ONE.
    05 FILLER PIC 9 VALUE 3.
    05 FILLER PIC 9 VALUE 2.
    05 FILLER PIC 9 VALUE 5.
    05 FILLER PIC 9 VALUE 1.
    05 FILLER PIC 9 VALUE 4.
01  STEP-TWO REDEFINES STEP-ONE.
    05 RIGHT-PLACE PIC 9 OCCURS 5 TIMES.
```

This looks quite complicated, so let's look at what this code does when I equals 1, 2, 3, 4, and 5.

I	RIGHT-PLACE (I)	J	AVG-GR (J)	OUT-AVG (I)
1	3	3	AVG-GR (3)	OUT-AVG (1)
2	2	2	AVG-GR (2)	OUT-AVG (2)
3	5	5	AVG-GR (5)	OUT-AVG (3)
4	1	1	AVG-GR (1)	OUT-AVG (4)
5	4	4	AVG-GR (4)	OUT-AVG (5)

Now let's look at the complete program.

```
*
* NAME:                ID:
* PROGRAM-NUMBER: 8.4-1
* DESCRIPTION: FIND THE AVERAGE GRADE FOR EACH
*    SUBJECT IN THE STUDENT-FILE. ARRANGE
*    THE OUTPUT IN THE ORDER ENGLISH, GEOMETRY,
*    CHEMISTRY, ALGEBRA, AND PHYSICS
*
     COPY TEXTA.
 WORKING-STORAGE SECTION.
* AUXILIARY STORAGE LOCATIONS
 77  I PIC 999.
 77  J PIC 999.
 77  NO-STUDENTS PIC 9(5).
```

```
      * INPUT RECORD
        01  STUDENT-INFO.
            05 STU-NO  PIC X(4).
            05 NAME    PIC X(18).
            05 SEX     PIC X.
            05 AGE     PIC 99.
            05 GRADES  PIC 999 OCCURS 5 TIMES.
            05 FILLER  PIC X(60).
      *  OUTPUT RECORD
        01  PRINT-PATTERN.
            05 FILLER  PIC X.
            05 OUT-AVG PIC Z(10).99 OCCURS 5 TIMES.
            05 FILLER  PIC X(67)     VALUE SPACES.
      *  TABLES
(A)     01  STEP-ONE.
            05 FILLER  PIC 9 VALUE 3.
            05 FILLER  PIC 9 VALUE 2.
            05 FILLER  PIC 9 VALUE 5.
            05 FILLER  PIC 9 VALUE 1.
            05 FILLER  PIC 9 VALUE 4.
        01  STEP-TWO REDEFINES STEP-ONE.
            05 RIGHT-PLACE PIC 9 OCCURS 5 TIMES.
        01  ACCUMULATORS.
            05 ADD-UP-AREA PIC 9(7) OCCURS 5 TIMES.

        PROCEDURE DIVISION.
      * MODEL-III.
            OPEN INPUT STUDENT-FILE
                 OUTPUT PRINTER.

      * INITIALIZATION
(B)         MOVE ZERO TO ACCUMULATORS
                        NO-STUDENTS.

      * FILE PROCESSING PAIR
            PERFORM READ-A-RECORD.
            PERFORM SUM-UP
                UNTIL STU-NO = HIGH-VALUES.

      * TERMINATION ACTIVITY
(C)         PERFORM PRINT-SUMMARY.
            CLOSE STUDENT-FILE
                  PRINTER.
            STOP RUN.

      * INPUT PROCEDURE
        READ-A-RECORD.
            READ STUDENT-FILE INTO STUDENT-INFO
                AT END MOVE HIGH-VALUES TO STU-NO.

      * RECORD PROCESSING
        SUM-UP.
(D)         ADD 1 TO NO-STUDENTS.
            PERFORM INCREMENT
                VARYING I FROM 1 BY 1
                    UNTIL I > 5.
      *  GET THE NEXT RECORD
            PERFORM READ-A-RECORD.
        INCREMENT.
            ADD GRADES (I) TO ADD-UP-AREA (I).
```

```
                PRINT-SUMMARY.
(E)                 PERFORM FILL-UP
                        VARYING I FROM 1 BY 1
                            UNTIL I > 5.
                    WRITE PRINT-LINE FROM PRINT-PATTERN.
                FILL-UP.
                    MOVE RIGHT-PLACE (I) TO J.
                    DIVIDE ADD-UP-AREA (J) BY NO-STUDENTS
                        GIVING OUT-AVG (I).
```

(A)   To give a table initial values, we use the REDEFINES clause. In STEP–ONE and STEP–TWO we set up a table with the appropriate initial values.

(B)   The MOVE statement can have several receiving fields for the same value. Here we move the value ZERO to the five accumulators as well as to the variable that counts the number of records processed.

(C)   Only after the complete file has been processed can we calculate and print averages. These two tasks are accomplished in PRINT–SUMMARY.

(D)   The processing for a record is very simple: count the record and add each of the five grades to the appropriate total.

(E)   FILL–UP calculates the averages and puts them into entries in the table OUT–AVG, which is part of the output pattern. The averages must be printed in the order indicated in RIGHT–PLACE, so the dividend for the DIVIDE operation is not entry I of ADD–UP–AREA but entry J, which has RIGHT–PLACE (I) as its value.

EXERCISES

1. What is meant by indirect addressing?
2. Can a subscripted variable be used as a subscript? How does a program simulate this if the answer is no?
3. What lines of code from TEXTA are required by PROGRAM–NUMBER 8.4-1?
4. Change the values in STEP–ONE so that the grades are printed in the order:
    a. CHEMISTRY, ALGEBRA, PHYSICS, ENGLISH, GEOMETRY
    b. PHYSICS, ALGEBRA, GEOMETRY, CHEMISTRY, ENGLISH
    c. CHEMISTRY, ENGLISH, PHYSICS, ALGEBRA, GEOMETRY

PROGRAM TESTING AND MODIFICATION EXCERCISES

1. For the following sets of grades and values for a table RIGHT–PLACE, determine the values that will be in the table OUT–GRADE after execution of the block of code listed.

```
                    PERFORM ZIP1
                        VARYING I FROM 1 BY 1
                            UNTIL I > 5.
                                .
                                .
                                .

                ZIP1.
                    MOVE RIGHT-PLACE (I) TO J.
                    MOVE GRADE (J) TO OUT-GRADE (I).
```

GRADE					RIGHT–PLACE					OUT–GRADE				
1	2	3	4	5	1	2	3	4	5	1	2	3	4	5
73	72	75	81	94	3	1	4	2	5					
76	68	57	70	80	1	3	5	2	4					
80	75	76	73	74	4	3	2	1	5					
80	83	84	91	93	1	2	3	4	5					
53	56	78	64	52	5	4	3	2	1					
49	67	75	62	81	3	5	4	1	2					

2. For the following sets of grades, determine the values that will be in table OUT–GRADE after execution of the block of code listed.

```
PERFORM ZIP2.
    VARYING I FROM 1 BY 1
        UNTIl I > 7.
            .
            .
            .

ZIP2.
    MULTIPLY I BY 2 GIVING J.
    IF J > 7
        SUBTRACT 7 FROM J.
    MOVE GRADE (J) TO OUT-GRADE (I).
```

GRADE							OUT–GRADE						
1	2	3	4	5	6	7	1	2	3	4	5	6	7
68	71	70	74	74	80	58							
69	72	74	75	72	68	59							
69	70	72	74	53	69	56							
69	69	71	76	69	73	53							
68	74	70	70	68	76	75							
59	75	58	68	71	74	72							
72	72	69	65	70	70	71							

PROGRAMMING PROBLEMS

1. Using the REGISTRAR–FILE for input, prepare a report that lists the NAME and GRADEs of each student. Indicate each student's lowest and highest grade. List the GRADEs in the order: ENGLISH–2, PHILOSOPHY–3, MATH–13, GOVERN-MENT–3, and GEOGRAPHY–10.

2. Using the REGISTRAR–FILE for input, prepare a report that lists the NAME and GRADEs of each student. Indicate by a special mark each GRADE that is an A or B. List the courses in alphabetical order.

3. Using the REGISTRAR–FILE for input, prepare a report that lists the NAME, GRADEs, and HOME–STATE of each student from Maine, New Hampshire, or Vermont. In addition, put ** after the state when it is not Maine. List the grades in the order: PHILOSOPHY–3, GOVERNMENT–3, MATH–13, ENGLISH–2, and GEOGRAPHY–10.

Chapter Review

SUMMARY

Applications programs that use a table lookup are very common. Two forms of table lookup are examined. The first form is used in applications such as finding the largest element in a table where every element in the table must be examined before the answer is known. The second form of table lookup is used in applications such as tax calculations in which an input value has to be found within a range of values. In this case, as soon as the appropriate range is identified, the table lookup can be terminated.

The PERFORM...VARYING...UNTIL statement facilitates the lookup process. When every entry in the table needs to be examined, the termination condition will occur once the variable in the VARYING clause has a value greater than the number of entries in the table. When an early exit from the lookup process is possible, the termination condition requires additional coding. A software switch is initialized before the PERFORM statement to a value not tested for in the UNTIL clause. When the lookup is completed, this software switch is reset so that termination occurs.

The table lookup process is a key ingredient in the process of using coded fields to determine categories of records for accumulation purposes. When the field does not have values $(1,2, ..., n$ or $m, m + 1, ..., m + n)$ the techniques for identifying appropriate subscripts explained earlier cannot be used.

In this case, each possible value for the code is contained in a table. Thus, to process a record, we first identify the storage location of the table that contains the coded value in the input record. The program will then use the value of the subscript that identified the storage location where the coded value was matched as a subscript for the record in memory.

The last section dealt with the problem of rearranging values in a table to conform to output requirements. This technique is called indirect addressing. Indirect addressing normally involves three tables. The first table contains the values that are to be put into the third table in some order other than the natural order (first element in the first table goes into the first element of the third table, ..., the last element in the first table goes into the last element of the third table). The second table has a value in location I that indicates where the element to be put in location I of the third table is to be found in the first table.

TEST YOURSELF

1. What is a sequential table lookup?
2. What is meant by an early exit for a sequential table lookup?
3. How does the determination of a tax bracket use a table with initial values?
4. Explain the syntax and the semantics of the VARYING...FROM...BY clause.
5. Explain the syntax and the semantics of the PERFORM...VARYING...UNTIL statement.
6. How are coded values of a variable associated with the entries of a table for tallying purposes?
7. What is meant by indirect addressing?
8. What are the functions of each of the three tables used in indirect addressing?
9. What is a software switch?
10. How is a software switch used to terminate a table search before all elements in the table have been examined?

Multidimensional Tables

Chapter Objectives

After studying this chapter you should be able to

- write a program using two-dimensional tables;
- write a program that prints data from a two-dimensional table;
- after analysis of a problem, select Model I, Model II, Model III, or Model IV as the appropriate pseudocode outline for program development;
- write a program that uses a three-dimensional table;
- use the PERFORM verb with an AFTER clause.

Chapter Outline

9.1   Two-Dimensional Tables

When displaying information in a report, it is often necessary to show the relationship that exists between the values of two different variables. For example, grades may be broken into categories determined by the value of the variable sex and within these categories by value of the variable age. As another example, the customer's amount due may be separated by region of residence and further broken down by credit limits. Even simpler might be a breakdown of the number of customers in CUSTOMER–FILE by REGION by CREDIT–LIMIT. This final breakdown would be

NUMBER OF CUSTOMERS BROKEN DOWN BY REGION BY CREDIT–LIMIT

		CREDIT–LIMIT			
	1	**2**	**3**	**4**	**5**
A	31	12	13	10	6
REGION B	10	3	1	1	1
C	7	1	3	1	0

The information shown is displayed by means of a data structure consisting of rows (labeled A, B, and C) broken down into a number of columns (labeled 1, 2, 3, 4, and 5). Each of the rows looks like a one-dimensional table. The allocation of such a structure mirrors this intuitive view:

```
01  DATA–STRUCTURE.
    05 ROWS–IN–TABLE OCCURS 3 TIMES.
       10 ENTRY–IN–ROW OCCURS 5 TIMES PIC 999.
```

The data name at the 05-level represents three storage areas.

```
                ROWS–IN–TABLE (1)
                ROWS–IN–TABLE (2)
                ROWS–IN–TABLE (3)
```

The data name at the 10-level represents 15 storage areas, since each of the three rows consists of five entries. Each row is subdivided because the 10-level storage areas indicate how the 05-level areas are organized. If we take the rows apart, we can see our data areas as the following:

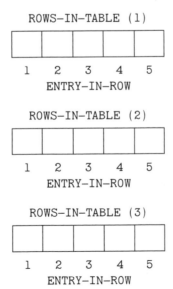

The obvious problem is how to reference a particular part of one of the rows. Since each row has the same organization, a single subscript attached to ENTRY–IN–ROW would be ambiguous, since it does not specify which row's entry is being referenced. **Two-dimensional tables** use two subscripts when referencing a particular entry in one of the rows. The first subscript refers to the row containing the storage location. The second subscript refers to the entry in the row being used. For our structure we can reference the elementary areas as

```
ENTRY–IN–ROW (1,1)
ENTRY–IN–ROW (1,2)
ENTRY–IN–ROW (1,3)
ENTRY–IN–ROW (1,4)
ENTRY–IN–ROW (1,5)
ENTRY–IN–ROW (2,1)
ENTRY–IN–ROW (2,2)
ENTRY–IN–ROW (2,3)
ENTRY–IN–ROW (2,4)
ENTRY–IN–ROW (2,5)
ENTRY–IN–ROW (3,1)
ENTRY–IN–ROW (3,2)
ENTRY–IN–ROW (3,3)
ENTRY–IN–ROW (3,4)
ENTRY–IN–ROW (3,5)
```

Now that we know how the storage areas in a two-dimensional table are referenced using two subscripts, we can find the row we want and then determine within that row the entry to be referenced. The next program shows how the two-dimensional table of output for the CUSTOMER–FILE example can be generated by a program.

```
*
* NAME:              ID:
* PROGRAM-NUMBER: 9.1-1
* DESCRIPTION: DISPLAY THE NUMBER OF RECORDS IN THE
* CUSTOMER FILE BROKEN DOWN BY REGION BY CREDIT LIMIT
*
      COPY TEXTA.
 WORKING-STORAGE SECTION.
* AUXILIARY STORAGE LOCATIONS
 01   SUBSCRIPT-NAMES.
      05   I                PIC S9(4).
      05   J                PIC S9(4).
      05   ROW-NAME         PIC S9(4).
      05   COL-NAME         PIC S9(4).
 01   SWITCH-VARIABLES.
      05   END-OF-FILE      PIC X(7) VALUE SPACES.
      05   REGION-FOUND     PIC X(3).

* INPUT RECORD
 01   CUSTOMER-INFO.
      05 CUSTOMER-NO        PIC X(8).
      05 FILLER             PIC X(81).
      05 REGION             PIC X.
      05 CREDIT-LIMIT       PIC X.
      05 FILLER             PIC X(9).
```

```
      * OUTPUT RECORD
      * DETAIL LINE
        01   PRINT-PATTERN.
             05 FILLER                   PIC X.
             05 OUT-REGION               PIC X.
(A)          05 OUT-REGION-BY-CLIMIT     PIC Z(6)9 OCCURS 5 TIMES.
             05 FILLER                   PIC X(96) VALUE SPACES.
        01   HEADER.
             05 FILLER PIC X.
             05 FILLER PIC X(7) VALUE SPACES.
             05 FILLER PIC X(125) VALUE
                '1        2        3        4        5'.
      * TABLES
(B)     01   REGION-CODE-TABLE-DATA   PIC X(3)   VALUE 'ABC'.
        01   REGION-CODE-TABLE
               REDEFINES REGION-CODE-TABLE-DATA.
             05 CF-REGION-CODE            PIC X OCCURS 3 TIMES.
(C)     01   SUMMARY-TABLE.
             05 COUNT-BY-REGION OCCURS 3 TIMES.
                10 COUNT-CR-CODE OCCURS 5 TIMES   PIC 999.


        PROCEDURE DIVISION.
      * MODEL IV.
             OPEN INPUT CUSTOMER-FILE
                  OUTPUT PRINTER.


      * INITIALIZE TABLE
             MOVE ZEROS TO SUMMARY-TABLE.


      * FILE PROCESSING PAIR
             PERFORM READ-A-RECORD.
             PERFORM SUMMARY-CALCULATIONS
                 UNTIL END-OF-FILE = HIGH-VALUES.


      * TERMINATION ACTIVITY
      * PRINT THE TABLE
             WRITE PRINT-LINE FROM HEADER.
(D)          PERFORM PRINT-SUMMARY
                 VARYING I FROM 1 BY 1
                     UNTIL I > 3.
             CLOSE CUSTOMER-FILE
                   PRINTER.
             STOP RUN.


      * INPUT PROCEDURE
        READ-A-RECORD.
             READ CUSTOMER-FILE INTO CUSTOMER-INFO
                 AT END MOVE HIGH-VALUES TO END-OF-FILE.


      * RECORD PROCESSING
        SUMMARY-CALCULATIONS.
      *
      * FIND THE ROW INDICATOR WHICH GOES WITH
      * THIS RECORD'S VALUE OF REGION-CODE
      *
```

(E)
```
          MOVE 'NO' TO REGION-FOUND.
          PERFORM TRANSLATE-REGION-CODE
              VARYING I FROM 1 BY 1
                  UNTIL REGION-FOUND = 'YES'.
     *
     * FIND THE COLUMN INDICATOR WHICH GOES
     * WITH THIS RECORD'S VALUE OF CREDIT-LIMIT
     *
```
(F)
```
          MOVE CREDIT-LIMIT TO COL-NAME.
     *
     * INCREMENT THE (ROW-NAME, COL-NAME) ENTRY SINCE THIS
     * RECORD CONTRIBUTES TO THAT LOCATION IN THE
     * COUNTER TABLE
     *
          ADD 1 TO COUNT-CR-CODE (ROW-NAME, COL-NAME).
     *
     * GET THE NEXT RECORD
     *
          PERFORM READ-A-RECORD.
     *
     TRANSLATE-REGION-CODE.
          IF REGION = CF-REGION-CODE (I)
              MOVE I TO ROW-NAME
              MOVE 'YES' TO REGION-FOUND.
     *
     PRINT-SUMMARY.
     * WHEN WE GET HERE WE HAVE A ROW VALUE
     * I TO WORK WITH - MUST PRINT THAT ROW
     * BEFORE EXITING THIS PARAGRAPH
          MOVE CF-REGION-CODE (I) TO OUT-REGION.
```
(G)
```
          PERFORM MOVE-C-L-COUNTS
              VARYING J FROM 1 BY 1
                  UNTIL J > 5.
          WRITE PRINT-LINE  FROM PRINT-PATTERN.
     MOVE-C-L-COUNTS.
          MOVE COUNT-CR-CODE (I,J) TO
              OUT-REGION-BY-CLIMIT (J).
```

(A)   Each output line displays the number of customers from one REGION broken down by the CREDIT-LIMIT of these customers. The output line needs a place for each of the five numbers associated with a REGION, so we define a table as part of the typical output line. We can only print lines, so if we want to print a two-dimensional table, we have to arrange to represent the table as a series of lines. This is done by printing the contents of one row of the two-dimensional table at a time. Each row looks like a one-dimensional table, so that is how we model the output record.

(B)   The two records defined here translate information about a particular customer's REGION to a subscript. The subscript points to the row keeping track of the number of customers from that REGION. Notice that

REGION-CODE-TABLE-DATA

has a picture clause X(3), while the record having these same storage locations has the description of

```
PIC X OCCURS 3 TIMES
```

Each of these records describes the same number of bytes of storage, but in a different way. In each case we use a picture clause that is appropriate for that record. The REDEFINES clause only refers to where the storage location of these two records begins and how many bytes are involved, not how each record has its area organized.

(C)   This record gives us a two-dimensional table consisting of the rows named

```
COUNT-BY-REGION (1)
COUNT-BY-REGION (2)
COUNT-BY-REGION (3)
```

Each of these is subdivided into five entries which, for row I where I = 1, 2, 3, are called

```
COUNT-CR-CODE (I,1)
COUNT-CR-CODE (I,2)
COUNT-CR-CODE (I,3)
COUNT-CR-CODE (I,4)
COUNT-CR-CODE (I,5)
```

(D)   The paragraph

```
PRINT-SUMMARY
```

prints the contents of a row of the two-dimensional table that was given values by the processing of the file. The sentence

```
PERFORM PRINT-SUMMARY
    VARYING I FROM 1 BY 1
        UNTIL I > 3
```

causes this block of code to be repeated for each row of the two-dimensional table.

(E)   These two sentences translate the value of REGION in a record into an appropriate row indicator. This procedure was the main point of Section 8.3.

(F)   We use this extra step to identify the column that represents information about the CREDIT–LIMIT of this customer. The next sentence in the program combines the row we have identified in (E) and the column we just identified (F) to increment the count for customers with these two characteristics.

(G)   This paragraph prints the information in a row of the two-dimensional table. We must move the five counts in this row to the output areas. Since I points to the row we are dealing with, we need another subscript to move through this row in an orderly fashion. In this case, we use J as the column indicator. The Jth entry in row I will be displayed in the Jth box in the table

```
OUT-REGION-BY-CLIMIT
```

This was defined in PRINT–PATTERN.

The output for this program is

	1	2	3	4	5
A	31	12	13	10	6
B	10	3	1	1	1
C	7	1	3	1	0

Since we are familiar with the file, we have little trouble interpreting the numbers as they appear. For an actual report we would want this information to be more carefully labeled. In the next section we will focus on refining this program so that the output is easy for the user to understand.

EXERCISES

1. If BOX (I,J) is well defined when I is between one and three and J is between one and five, is BOX (J,I) well defined for the same values?
2. What lines of code from TEXTA are required by PROGRAM–NUMBER 9.1-1?
3. In PROGRAM–NUMBER 9.1-1 how many storage locations have COUNT–BY–REGION as part of their name?
4. What would the output for PROGRAM–NUMBER 9.1-1 look like if the following changes were made?

```
        01  PRINT-PATTERN.
              .
              .
              .
        05  OUT-REGION-BY-CLIMIT PIC Z(6)9
                    OCCURS 3 TIMES.
              .
              .
        PERFORM PRINT-SUMMARY
            VARYING I FROM 1 BY 1
                UNTIL I > 5.
              .
              .
    PRINT-SUMMARY.
              .
              .
        PERFORM MOVE C-L-COUNTS
            VARYING J FROM 1 BY 1
                UNTIL J > 3.
```

5. In a two-dimensional table is the first (second) subscript identified with a row or a column of the table?

PROGRAM TESTING AND MODIFICATION EXERCISE

1. Form a table that indicates the contents of COUNT–CR–CODE and the variables REGION and CREDIT–LIMIT after the first 14 times PROGRAM–NUMBER 9.1-1 executes the following sentence:

```
        PERFORM SUMMARY-CALCULATIONS
            UNTIL FLAG = HIGH-VALUES.
```

CREDIT-LIMIT	REGION	COUNT-CR-CODE (1, _)					COUNT-CR-CODE COUNT-CR-CODE (2, _)					COUNT-CR-CODE (3, _)				
		1	2	3	4	5	1	2	3	4	5	1	2	3	4	5

Use the values below COUNT–CR–CODE (I, _) for the underscored position where I = 1, 2, 3.

PROGRAMMING PROBLEMS

1. Using the REGISTRAR–FILE for input, write a program that prints the number of times each GRADE was earned in each course.
2. Using the REGISTRAR–FILE for input, write a program that prints the number of times each GRADE was earned by all the students of each AGE.
3. Using the NEW–WORLD–FILE for input, write a program that prints how many customers from each STATE have EXPIRATION–DATE in the same year.
4. Using the NEW–WORLD–FILE for input, write a program that prints the number of customers broken down by CREDIT–RATING by STATE.

9.2   Printing Two-Dimensional Tables

Previous sections dealing with tables focused on how we can identify the subscript to be used at a particular point in a program. We also need to focus on how the information generated by tables can be presented to the user in a manner that conveys the information effectively. With a two-dimensional table, the user expects the information to be displayed as a two-dimensional table. We can't, however, print output other than one line at a time because the output device is a *line* printer. So we must view a two-dimensional table as a sequence of lines that form a pattern to look like a two-dimensional table. In the last section, a very elementary output pattern was used to display the entries of a two-dimensional table. This section focuses on making the output of a two-dimensional table look like the user would expect it to appear when printed.

In the last lesson we tabulated a count of the number of customers in the CUSTOMER–FILE broken down by REGION by CREDIT–LIMIT. The output was very rudimentary in form:

```
        1    2    3    4    5
  A    31   12   13   10    6
  B    10    3    1    1    1
  C     7    1    3    1    0
```

We would really like the following:

```
                CUSTOMER COUNT
           BY REGION BY CREDIT-LIMIT

                  CREDIT-LIMIT

              1    2    3    4    5
           ┌────┬────┬────┬────┬────┐
        A  │ 31 │ 12 │ 13 │ 10 │  6 │
           ├────┼────┼────┼────┼────┤
 REGION B  │ 10 │  3 │  1 │  1 │  1 │
           ├────┼────┼────┼────┼────┤
        C  │  7 │  1 │  3 │  1 │  0 │
           └────┴────┴────┴────┴────┘
```

Printing the report in this form requires establishing a large number of print patterns in the WORKING–STORAGE SECTION.

If we look at this two-dimensional table of output, we see that we can break the output problem into one of printing headings (you can figure that out) and of printing the two-dimensional table. Printing the two-dimensional table breaks into four parts:

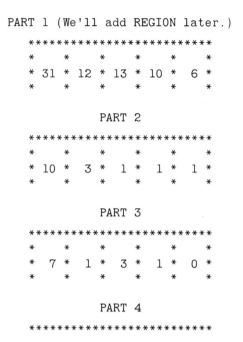

```
            PART 1 (We'll add REGION later.)

            **************************
            *     *     *     *     *     *
            * 31 * 12 * 13 * 10 *  6 *
            *     *     *     *     *     *

                        PART 2

            ****************************
            *     *     *     *     *     *
            * 10 *  3 *  1 *  1 *  1 *
            *     *     *     *     *     *

                        PART 3

            **************************
            *     *     *     *     *     *
            *  7 *  1 *  3 *  1 *  0 *
            *     *     *     *     *     *

                        PART 4

            **************************
```

When we carefully examine PART 1, PART 2, and PART 3, we see that each part consists of four lines. The four lines are similar in each part. Let's break down PART 1 into its pieces and just use these lines three times. PART 4 consists of the first line of PART 1, so after we have figured out how to print PART 1, we will have taken care of PART 4.

```
                      LINE 1
            ************************
```

```
      01  LINE1.
          05 FILLER PIC X.
          05 FILLER PIC X( )  VALUE SPACES.
          05 FILLER PIC X(25) VALUE ALL '*'.
          05 FILLER PIC X( )  VALUE SPACES.
```

We leave the two picture clauses with VALUE SPACES alone for now, since the number of spaces needed will depend on where the heading is placed on the page. We also have to ensure that we save enough space to write REGION to the left of the table. Right now we want to print the table itself, so we will ignore the other minor spacing problems.

```
               LINE 2 = LINE 4
            *____*____*____*____*____*
```

```
      01  LINE2.
          05 FILLER PIC X.
          05 FILLER PIC X( )  VALUE SPACES.
          05 FILLER PIC X(26) VALUE ALL '*____'.
          05 FILLER PIC X( )  VALUE SPACES.
```

We want to repeat the pattern *____ five times and finish that pattern with another * at the end. By using the VALUE ALL clause and PIC X(26), we repeat the pattern five times and then have one space left in the 26-byte field. The VALUE ALL clause puts the first character of the pattern, which is *, in this byte and thus completes the initialization as required. The next line involves data from the table. We indicate the spaces to be used for data with X's.

```
                              LINE 3
                X_*_XX_*_XX_*_XX_*_XX_*_XX_*

       01  LINE3.
             05 FILLER           PIC X.
             05 FILLER           PIC X( ) VALUE SPACES.
             05 REGION-OUT       PIC X.
             05 FILLER           PIC X    VALUE SPACES.
             05  PATTERN OCCURS 5 TIMES.
                 10 STAR-AREA  PIC XX.
                 10 DATA-AREA  PIC Z9.
                 10 BLANK-AREA PIC X.
             05 FILLER           PIC X( ) VALUE '*'.
```

The data structure used for LINE3 will be clearer when we see the code that replaces PRINT–SUMMARY in the program started in Section 9.1.

```
           PRINT-SUMMARY.
               MOVE CF-REGION-CODE (I) TO REGION-OUT.
               PERFORM MOVE-IT
                   VARYING J FROM 1 BY 1
                       UNTIL J > 5.
               WRITE PRINT-LINE FROM LINE1.
               WRITE PRINT-LINE FROM LINE2.
               WRITE PRINT-LINE FROM LINE3.
               WRITE PRINT-LINE FROM LINE2.
           MOVE-IT.
               MOVE COUNT-CR-CODE (I,J)TO DATA-AREA  (J).
               MOVE '*'                TO STAR-AREA  (J).
               MOVE SPACES             TO BLANK-AREA (J).
```

The only step left is to write LINE1 before closing the files. This completes the bottom line of the box.

One important feature illustrated in this section is that the revised code can be put directly in place in the previous program. This method of refining a program leads to more efficient use of time when developing a large system.

EXERCISES

1. How does one build a two-dimensional table with the line printer as the output device?
2. In the paragraph called MOVE–IT why does COUNT–CR–CODE have two subscripts and STAR–AREA have only one?
3. Explain why this section of Chapter 9 could also be titled Stepwise Refinement—Step Two.
4. Fill in the blanks in the picture clauses so that the code can be incorporated into PROGRAM–NUMBER 9.1-1.
5. Indicate how the code developed in this section would have to be modified if the report required:

   a. a listing of the number of customers in NEW–WORLD–FILE broken down by YEAR of EXPIRATION–DATE by STATE;
   b. a listing of the number of each grade given this semester broken down by AGE of student by course. Use the REGISTRAR–FILE for input.

PROGRAMMING PROBLEMS

1. Modify one of the Programming Problems of Section 9.1 to include the output feature explained in this section.
2. A complex problem is best solved by incorporating a series of refinements into a basic program. Such a procedure will make a problem much easier to solve. You should do the following tasks in the order listed, only going on to the next task when the previous ones are incorporated into the basic program. Use the STUDENT–FILE for input.

   a. Calculate the average grade for each student. Create a record description for FILE1 that includes this information in bytes 41–43.
   b. Sort by average the records put on FILE1 in Part a.
   c. Prepare a report that lists each student's NAME, GRADEs, and AVERAGE.
   d. Include in the report described in Part c a mark next to each student's highest grade.
   e. At the end of the detail listing, print the average of all the grades for each subject.
   f. Modify Part (b) so that the sort is by AGE by AVERAGE.
   g. In addition to the output of Part (e), use AGE as a control break to list the average grades at the end of each AGE category.

9.3   Three-Dimensional Tables

One-dimensional and two-dimensional tables are used for a variety of applications. Typically, two-dimensional tables are used to show how values in one field of a record are related to the values of another field in a record. For example, a breakdown of grades by courses or customers broken down by region by credit limit. There are cases when this representation of the relation between values of two variables is not sufficient. In COBOL, a **three-dimensional table** allows representation of relationships that involve values of three different fields. For example, with a sales report it might be important to represent sales by day of the week, by branch of the store, and by product. To represent this data structure in COBOL, we allocate the following record.

```
01  THREE-WAY.
    05  DAY-WEEK OCCURS 5 TIMES.
        10  DAY-BY-STORE OCCURS 4 TIMES.
            15  DAY-STORE-PRODUCT OCCURS 5 TIMES PIC 9(5).
```

Observe that this record contains 100 storage locations, each with a picture clause of the form PIC 9(5). Since there are three OCCURS clauses, the DAY–STORE–PRODUCT storage locations must be referenced using three subscripts. Figure 9.3.1 explains how storage is arranged for three-dimensional tables. The levels of organization are represented from left to right to mean that a name to the left of a brace is organized to include all the locations named within the brace. Identifying a storage location requires that we first identify which of the DAY–WEEK contains the entry sought. The second subscript is needed to identify which DAY–BY–STORE contains the entry. There are four DAY–BY–STORE in each DAY–WEEK. Finally, the third subscript identifies which of the four elements in the DAY–BY–STORE identified by the second subscript is needed. There are five DAY–STORE–PRODUCT in each DAY–BY–STORE. All the techniques used to identify the appropriate subscript in a one-dimensional table can be used three

```
                                      ┌DAY-STORE-PRODUCT(I, 1, 1)
                                      │DAY-STORE-PRODUCT(I, 1, 2)
                    DAY-BY-STORE(I,1) ┤DAY-STORE-PRODUCT(I, 1, 3)
                                      │DAY-STORE-PRODUCT(I, 1, 4)
                                      └DAY-STORE-PRODUCT(I, 1, 5)

                                      ┌DAY-STORE-PRODUCT(I, 2, 1)
                                      │DAY-STORE-PRODUCT(I, 2, 2)
                    DAY-BY-STORE(I,2) ┤DAY-STORE-PRODUCT(I, 2, 3)
                                      │DAY-STORE-PRODUCT(I, 2, 4)
                                      └DAY-STORE-PRODUCT(I, 2, 5)
  DAY-WEEK(I) ┤
                                      ┌DAY-STORE-PRODUCT(I, 3, 1)
                                      │DAY-STORE-PRODUCT(I, 3, 2)
                    DAY-BY-STORE(I,3) ┤DAY-STORE-PRODUCT(I, 3, 3)
                                      │DAY-STORE-PRODUCT(I, 3, 4)
                                      └DAY-STORE-PRODUCT(I, 3, 5)

                                      ┌DAY-STORE-PRODUCT(I, 4, 1)
                                      │DAY-STORE-PRODUCT(I, 4, 2)
                    DAY-BY-STORE(I,4) ┤DAY-STORE-PRODUCT(I, 4, 3)
                                      │DAY-STORE-PRODUCT(I, 4, 4)
                                      └DAY-STORE-PRODUCT(I, 4, 5)
```

Figure 9.3.1 *Storage for a three-dimensional table.*

times to identify the entry of a three-dimensional table needed at a particular point in a program. The product by store by day example would interpret DAY-STORE-PRODUCT (2,4,3) as the number of units of product 3 sold by store 4 on day 2.

Printing Three-Dimensional Tables

To output the entries of a three-dimensional table by the printer usually involves printing a series of two-dimensional tables, one for each of the different values of the first subscript. For example, the two-dimensional table that represents the breakdown by store by product for sales on Wednesday could be printed as:

		WEDNESDAY				
			PRODUCT			
		1	2	3	4	5
	1	3	3	1	9	5
STORE	2	0	5	7	4	9
	3	0	6	5	7	4
	4	5	2	0	6	6

This output pattern could be repeated for each of the days. We see above that DAY-STORE-PRODUCT (3,2,4) has a value of four. That is, four units [contents of DAY-STORE-PRODUCT (3,2,4)] of product 4 (third subscript) were sold in store 2 (second subscript) on Wednesday (first subscript).

We now examine this concept in an application using the REGISTRAR–FILE.

```
*
* NAME:                   ID:
* PROGRAM-NUMBER: 9.3-1
* DESCRIPTION: COUNT THE NUMBER OF RECORDS IN
*    REGISTRAR-FILE BY CLASS BY AGE BY HOME-STATE
*
      COPY TEXTA.
 WORKING-STORAGE SECTION.
*  AUXILIARY STORAGE LOCATIONS
 77  END-OF-FILE     PIC X(8) VALUE SPACES.
 01  SUBSCRIPTS.
     05  I     PIC 9(5).
     05  J     PIC 9(5).
     05  K     PIC 9(5).
     05  L     PIC 9(5).

*  INPUT RECORD
 01  REGISTRAR-RECORD.
     05  FILLER      PIC X(9).
     05  NAME        PIC X(20).
     05  FILLER      PIC X.
     05  CLASS       PIC XX.
     05  AGE         PIC 99.
     05  FILLER      PIC X(31).
     05  HOME-STATE  PIC XX.
     05  FILLER      PIC X(33).

*  ALLOCATION OF STORAGE FOR TABLES
 01  THREE-WAY.
     05  CLASS-LOCATIONS OCCURS 5 TIMES.
         10  CLASS-BY-AGE  OCCURS 8 TIMES.
             15  CL-AG-HS  PIC 9(5)   OCCURS 5 TIMES.
 01  CLASS-TITLES.
     05  FILLER  PIC X(10) VALUE 'FRSOJRSRUN'.
 01  CLASSES REDEFINES CLASS-TITLES.
     05  CLASS-ABBR  PIC X(2) OCCURS 5 TIMES.
 01  H-STATE-ABBR.
     05  FILLER PIC X(10) VALUE 'MAMEVTCANH'.
 01  USEABLE-STATE-NAMES REDEFINES H-STATE-ABBR.
     05  STATE-ABBR  PIC XX  OCCURS 5 TIMES.

*  OUTPUT RECORDS
 01  LAYER-HEADING.
     05  FILLER         PIC X.
     05  FILLER         PIC X(6) VALUE 'CLASS'.
     05  CL-ABBR        PIC X(126).
 01  TABLE-HEADING.
     05  FILLER     PIC X
     05  FILLER     PIC X(132)
         VALUE 'AGE BY HOME-STATE'.
 01  STATE-HEADER.
     05  FILLER     PIC X.
     05  FILLER     PIC X(132) VALUE
       'MA   ME   VT   CA   NH'.
```

(A)

(B)

(C)

```
      01   AGE-LINE.
           05  FILLER   PIC X.
           05  OUT-AGE  PIC 99.
           05  OUT-VAL  PIC Z(4)9 OCCURS 5 TIMES.
           05  FILLER   PIC X(105) VALUE SPACES.
(D)   01   CL-TOTALS.
           05  CL-TOT   PIC 9(5) OCCURS 5 TIMES.
      01   CLASS-LINE.
           05  FILLER       PIC X.
           05  NO-BY-CLASS  PIC Z(9)9 OCCURS 5 TIMES.
           05  FILLER       PIC X(82) VALUE SPACES.


      PROCEDURE DIVISION.
  *   MODEL IV
          OPEN INPUT REGISTRAR-FILE
               OUTPUT PRINTER.

  *   INITIALIZATION
          MOVE ZEROS TO THREE-WAY.

  *   FILE PROCESSING PAIR
          PERFORM PROCESS-REGISTRAR.
          PERFORM TALLY-RECORDS
              UNTIL END-OF-FILE = HIGH-VALUES.

  *   TERMINATION ACTIVITY
(E)       PERFORM AT-THE-END.
          CLOSE REGISTRAR-FILE
                PRINTER.
          STOP RUN.

  *   INPUT PROCEDURE
      PROCESS-REGISTRAR.
          READ REGISTRAR-FILE INTO REGISTRAR-RECORD
              AT END MOVE HIGH-VALUES TO END-OF-FILE.

  *   RECORD PROCESSING
      TALLY-RECORDS.
          PERFORM IDENTIFY-CLASS
              VARYING L FROM 1 BY 1
                  UNTIL L > 5.
          SUBTRACT 16 FROM AGE GIVING J.
          PERFORM IDENTIFY-HOME-STATE
              VARYING L FROM 1 BY 1
                  UNTIL L > 5.
          ADD 1 TO CL-AG-HS (I,J,K).
          PERFORM PROCESS-REGISTRAR.
      IDENTIFY-HOME-STATE.
          IF HOME-STATE = STATE-ABBR (L)
              MOVE L TO K.
      IDENTIFY-CLASS.
          IF CLASS = CLASS-ABBR (L)
              MOVE L TO I.

  *   AFTER END-OF-FILE PROCESSING
      AT-THE-END.
```

```
(F)                PERFORM OUT-LAYERS
                       VARYING I FROM 1 BY 1
                           UNTIL I > 5.
(G)                MOVE ZEROS TO CL-TOTALS.
                   PERFORM BY-CLASS
                       VARYING I FROM 1 BY 1
                           UNTIL I > 5.
                   PERFORM RECAP.
           OUT-LAYERS.
               MOVE CLASS-ABBR (I) TO CL-ABBR.
               WRITE PRINT-LINE FROM LAYER-HEADING
                   AFTER 1.
               WRITE PRINT-LINE FROM TABLE-HEADING
                   AFTER ADVANCING 5 LINES.
               WRITE PRINT-LINE FROM STATE-HEADER.
               PERFORM FILL-CLASS-BY-AGE
                   VARYING J FROM 1 BY 1
                       UNTIL J > 8.
           FILL-CLASS-BY-AGE.
               ADD J 16 GIVING OUT-AGE.
               PERFORM FILL-ROW
                   VARYING K FROM 1 BY 1
                       UNTIL K > 5.
               WRITE PRINT-LINE FROM AGE-LINE
                   AFTER 1.
           FILL-ROW.
               MOVE CL-AG-HS (I,J,K) TO OUT-VAL (K).
           BY-CLASS.
(H)                PERFORM TALLY-UP
                       VARYING J FROM 1 BY 1
                           UNTIL J > 8
                       AFTER K FROM 1 BY 1
                           UNTIL K > 5.
           TALLY-UP.
               ADD CL-AG-HS (I,J,K) TO CL-TOT (I).
           RECAP.
               PERFORM FILL-ROWS
                   VARYING I FROM 1 BY 1
                       UNTIL I > 5.
               WRITE PRINT-LINE FROM CLASS-LINE
                   AFTER 1.
           FILL-ROWS.
               MOVE CL-TOT (I) TO NO-BY-CLASS (I).
```

(A)   A three-dimensional table is allocated storage by means of three nested OCCURS clauses. The 05-level sentence causes the record to be subdivided into five pieces called

CLASS-LOCATIONS (1)
CLASS-LOCATIONS (2)
CLASS-LOCATIONS (3)
CLASS-LOCATIONS (4)
CLASS-LOCATIONS (5)

Each of these is subdivided into eight pieces called

CLASS–BY–AGE (I,1)
CLASS–BY–AGE (I,2)
CLASS–BY–AGE (I,3)
CLASS–BY–AGE (I,4)
CLASS–BY–AGE (I,5)
CLASS–BY–AGE (I,6)
CLASS–BY–AGE (I,7)
CLASS–BY–AGE (I,8)

where I ranges from 1 to 5 to indicate which of the areas called CLASS–LOCATIONS is being subdivided. Finally, each of the forty CLASS–BY–AGE pieces is subdivided into five pieces called

CL–AG–HS (I,J,1)
CL–AG–HS (I,J,2)
CL–AG–HS (I,J,3)
CL–AG–HS (I,J,4)
CL–AG–HS (I,J,5)

where the value of J indicates which of the eight CLASS–BY–AGE is being subdivided and the value of I indicates which CLASS–LOCATIONS contains this CLASS–BY–AGE. All together there are 200 elementary storage locations allocated in THREE–WAY.

(B)   The next four records are used to identify the correct subscript to use with the value of CLASS and HOME–STATE that are found in a record.

(C)   The next four records are used to print the five two-dimensional tables associated with CLASS–LOCATIONS (I) where I ranges from 1 to 5. Each two-dimensional table represents a breakdown of all students in one CLASS by AGE by HOME–STATE.

(D)   The next two records are used to accumulate and print the number of students in each CLASS. The accumulation will be accomplished by adding all the entries in a particular CLASS–LOCATIONS which is a two-dimensional table.

(E)   The termination activity consists of two phases. First, the two-dimensional tables associated with CLASS–LOCATIONS (I) where I ranges from 1 to 5 must be printed. When that is finished, each of the two-dimensional tables printed must have all its entries totaled and printed as the value of the number of students in the CLASS represented by that two-dimensional table.

(F)   This sentence will cause the two-dimensional tables that represent the breakdown of the records by AGE by HOME–STATE to be printed. The value of I will be the first subscript and will remain the same for each execution of OUT–LAYERS.

(G)   The next two sentences cause the values in the two-dimensional tables that represent the number of students by AGE by HOME–STATE to be totaled by CLASS. This process could be incorporated with other code in the program, but it is clearer to isolate this distinct function from other parts of the code. It may also have been the case that this additional information was the result of modifying an earlier version of the program. In that case, it is helpful to be able to leave the original code as it is and add the new code as a separate part of the program.

(H)   When totaling a two-dimensional table, we can make use of a new feature in the COBOL syntax. We can arrange that both J and K range over their appropriate values by means of a nesting of the VARYING feature. The code used here is equivalent to the following more familiar code, where control is passed to Paragraph (W) five times with I having a value 1 the first time, ..., and I having a value 5 the fifth time.

```
W.
    PERFORM X
        VARYING J FROM 1 BY 1
            UNTIL J > 8.
            .
            .
            .

X.
    PERFORM Y
        VARYING K FROM 1 BY 1
            UNTIL K > 5.
            .
            .
            .
Y.
    ADD CL-AG-HS (I,J,K) TO CL-TOT (I).
```

This new feature is very useful. Notice that the VARYING only occurs once. The syntax is described at the end of the section.

The program just written contains many familiar blocks of code such as identifying a value in a field or filling a table in the output record. It is instructive to see how all the pieces fit together. Figure 9.3.2 represents the relationship among paragraphs of code.

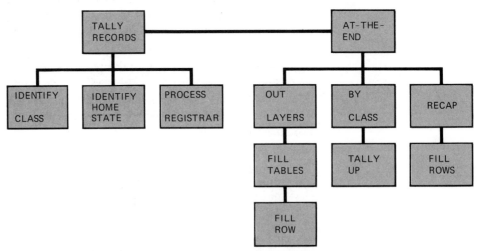

Figure 9.3.2 *Relationship among the paragraphs of PROGRAM–NUMBER 9.3-1.*

After studying the diagram, the program seems to be a relatively straightforward problem. This is relatively complex and only seems simple because of the use of good programming practices.

SYNTAX SUMMARY

```
PERFORM procedure-name-1

     VARYING {identifier-1}   FROM   {literal-2    }
                                     {identifier-2 }

     BY      {literal-3    }   UNTIL condition-1
             {identifier-3 }

     [AFTER   {identifier-4}  FROM   {literal-5    }
                                     {identifier-5 }

     BY      {literal-6    }   UNTIL condition-2
             {identifier-6 }

     [AFTER   {identifier-7}  FROM   {literal-8    }
                                     {identifier-8 }

     BY      {literal-9    }   UNTIL condition-3]]
             {identifier-9 }
```

EXERCISES

1. What lines of code from TEXTA are required by PROGRAM–NUMBER 9.3–1?
2. How many subscripts must be used with the CL–AG–HS, CLASS–LOCATIONS, CLASS–BY–AGE, CL–TOT, CLASS–ABBR?
3. Rewrite

```
             PERFORM TALLY-UP
                 VARYING J FROM 1 BY 1
                     UNTIL J > 8
                 AFTER K FROM 1 BY 1
                     UNTIL K > 5.
```

   without using the AFTER clause.
4. Which code of PROGRAM–NUMBER 9.1–3 causes the contents of the record THREE–WAY to be printed?

PROGRAM TESTING AND MODIFICATION EXERCISE

1. Using the code of PROGRAM–NUMBER 9.3–1 form a table and trace the execution of the program for the first twelve records of REGISTRAR–FILE. As a check point for the trace, determine the value of I, J, and K each time the statement

```
             ADD 1 TO CL-AG-HS (I, J, K)
```

   is executed.

NAME	AGE	CLASS	HOME-STATE	I	J	K

PROGRAMMING PROBLEMS

1. Using the REGISTRAR–FILE for input, write a program that prints for each value of STATE the number of times each grade was earned in each course.
2. Using the REGISTRAR–FILE for input, write a program that prints for each value of CLASS the number of times each grade was earned by all students of each AGE.
3. Using the NEW–WORLD–FILE for input, write a program that prints for each value of CREDIT–RATING how many customers from each STATE have the same year in the field EXPIRATION–DATE.
4. Using the NEW–WORLD–FILE for input, write a program that prints for each value of year in the field EXPIRATION–DATE the number of customers with the same value for CREDIT–RATING and STATE.
5. Using the NEW–WORLD–FILE for input, write a program that prints for each value of STATE the number of customers with the same values for CREDIT–RATING and year of EXPIRATION–DATE.
6. Using the REGISTRAR–FILE for input, write a program that prints for each value of CLASS the number of students from a dorm with CUMULATIVE–GPA in the same range. Use the following information to define the ranges.

RANGE	GPA
1	0.00–0.99
2	1.00–1.99
3	2.00–2.99
4	3.00–3.99
5	4.00

A student's dorm is identified by the last 16 bytes of the field CAMPUS–ADDRESS.

7. Using the REGISTRAR–FILE for input, write a program that prints for each value of AGE the number of students in a CLASS with the TOTAL–HOURS in each of the ranges:

RANGE	TOTAL–HOURS
1	0– 29
2	30– 59
3	60– 89
4	90–119
5	120

Chapter Review

SUMMARY

The programming techniques learned in dealing with one-dimensional tables can be used with two- and three-dimensional tables. Many problems are naturally represented by a two-dimensional table or a series of two-dimensional tables organized as a three-dimensional table.

Allocation of storage for a two-dimensional table is a two-step process. Each step involves an OCCURS clause. The first step is to give a name to each row of the table and describe how many rows will be in the table. No picture clause appears with the first OCCURS clause because each row will be subdivided further. The second step is to indicate with the second OCCURS clause how each row is organized. The picture clause is written at this step because these are elementary items.

Referring to a storage location in a two-dimensional table requires two subscripts. The first subscript identifies the row containing the element and the second indicates the storage location within that row that is being referenced.

A three-dimensional table is allocated using three OCCURS clauses and a storage location is accessed using three subscripts. The process described for two-dimensional tables is merely extended for three-dimensional tables.

The display of a two-dimensional table is accomplished by building up a pattern line-by-line until the result looks like a two-dimensional table. In the case of three dimensional tables, the best a programmer can do is to print a series of two-dimensional tables with the understanding that the three-dimensional table can be decomposed in this way.

TEST YOURSELF

1. How is a two-dimensional table defined?
2. How many subscripts are needed to identify a row of a two-dimensional table?
3. How many subscripts are needed to identify an elementary item in a two-dimensional table? Explain the purpose of each subscript.
4. What kind of a data structure can be accessed using one subscript if a record contains only the allocation of a three-dimensional table?
5. In a three-dimensional table what kind of a data structure can be accessed using two subscripts? Using three subscripts?
6. How can output be organized so that a two-dimensional table looks like a table on the printed page?
7. In a three-dimensional table with five rows and seven columns occurring ten times, how many elementary items are there? What element is accessed as elementary item (3,2,5)?
8. What is a typical way of displaying the elements of a three-dimensional table?

10

COBOL SEARCH Feature

Chapter Objectives

After studying this chapter, you should be able to

- explain how the SEARCH verb accomplishes a sequential search;
- explain how the SEARCH ALL verb works, as implemented using a binary search;
- write programs using the SEARCH and SEARCH ALL syntax.

Chapter Outline

10.1   The SEARCH Verb

Table lookups are used in a variety of applications. We have seen examples that use the technique to determine which subscript is associated with the count of all records with a fixed value for a code. We also saw a table lookup used to determine whether or not a value in a field of a record was a valid value. There is a verb in COBOL that will cause a table to be searched until a condition is satisfied. Before examining the syntax of this verb, we need to review the code used thus far to accomplish a table lookup. In this way, we can see how all the pieces of the new syntax fit together. The code follows:

```
* TABLE VALUES INITIALIZED AT COMPILE TIME
*     THREE LETTER ABBREVIATIONS FOR MONTHS
  01  RAW-VALUES.
      05  FILLER  PIC X(9) VALUE 'JANFEBMAR'.
      05  FILLER  PIC X(9) VALUE 'APRMAYJUN'.
      05  FILLER  PIC X(9) VALUE 'JULAUGSEP'.
      05  FILLER  PIC X(9) VALUE 'OCTNOVDEC'.
  01  USEFUL-VALUES REDEFINES RAW-VALUES.
      05  MO-ABBR OCCURS 12 TIMES PIC XXX.
                    .
                    .
                    .
* MATCH THE VALUE OF MONTH-DUE FROM THE INPUT
* RECORD WITH A VALUE IN THE TABLE
      MOVE 'NO' TO FOUND-YET.
      PERFORM CHECK-MO
          VARYING I FROM 1 BY 1
              UNTIL I > 12 OR FOUND-YET = 'YES'.
                    .
                    .
                    .
* ACTUAL TABLE COMPARISON
  CHECK-MO.
      IF MONTH-DUE = MO-ABBR (I)
          MOVE 'YES' TO FOUND-YET
          MOVE I TO J.
```

This code has several parts that belong to any table lookup procedure. These are

1. Initialization of the table.

   Accomplished at compile time.

2. A variable that contains the value to be matched.

   ```
   MONTH-DUE
   ```

3. An orderly way to proceed through the entries of the table

   ```
   VARYING I FROM 1 BY 1
   ```

4. A condition that has the value TRUE only when a match is found and a command to execute when the condition is TRUE.

   ```
   MONTH-DUE = MO-ABBR (I)
   MOVE 'YES' TO FOUND-YET
   ```

5. A termination condition for the search process

   ```
   I > 12 OR FOUND-YET = 'YES'
   ```

The SEARCH verb incorporates Items 3, 4, and 5 in two sentences as follows:

```
SET INDX TO 1.
SEARCH MO-ABBR
    WHEN MONTH-DUE = MO-ABBR (INDX)
        MOVE 'YES' TO FOUND-YET.
```

The SEARCH verb is followed by the name of the table to be searched. Rather than an IF condition syntax, the syntax here prescribes WHEN followed by a condition. As soon as the condition is evaluated as TRUE, the statement following the condition will be executed and then control will be passed to the next sentence.

Indexing

The only feature left to explain is the SET verb and INDX. The SEARCH verb does not use a subscript to indicate the table entry to be used in the comparison. The SEARCH verb uses an **index,** which is a system variable and is not defined like a normal variable. It does act like a subscript inasmuch as it is used to reference an entry in a table. An index is associated with a particular table by using the

```
INDEXED BY
```

clause. Table 10.1 will help explain the difference between a subscript and an index. The table is called MO-ABBR and has 12 entries. Each entry is a three-letter abbreviation for the name of a month. The numbers below the entries indicate which bytes of this storage area contain the first letter of an abbreviation.

TABLE 10.1

MO-ABBR											
JAN	FEB	MAR	APR	MAY	JUN	JUL	AUG	SEP	OCT	NOV	DEC
1 —	4 —	7 —	1 0	1 3	1 6	1 9	2 2	2 5	2 8	3 1	3 4

To access 'MAY' we could use a subscript with a value 5 and the name MO-ABBR (5). We could also access this information by instructing the program to get the next three bytes of MO-ABBR beginning with byte 13. This is actually what happens when an index is used. The byte that contains the beginning of the information to be processed can be determined as the value of the calculation:

$$(index\ value - 1) * length\ of\ individual\ entry + 1$$

In the case of using 'MAY' from the table MO-ABBR this is

$$(5 - 1) * 3 + 1 = 13.$$

The operating system will automatically calculate the appropriate value for the starting byte of the information needed. Notice that there are not 13 entries in the table. So if INDX has a value 13, it cannot be a subscript.

The **SEARCH verb** uses an index to proceed in a sequential manner through the table looking for a value that makes the WHEN condition TRUE. Since a SEARCH may terminate at any place in the table, subsequent executions of the sentence must be sure that the search begins with the first entry. The SET verb acts like a MOVE, but acts on indexes rather than variables that are completely under the control of the programmer. With the SET verb the index is assigned an initial value prior to the search.

PROGRAM-NUMBER 8.3-1 calculated the number of customers in CUSTOMER-FILE from each of the three different regions. This program will be rewritten incorporating the SEARCH and SET verbs.

```
*
* NAME:              ID:
* PROGRAM-NUMBER: 10.1-1
* DESCRIPTION: PREPARE A REPORT THAT LISTS THE
*    NUMBER OF CUSTOMERS IN CUSTOMER-FILE
*    IN EACH OF THE THREE DIFFERENT REGIONS.
      COPY TEXTA.
 WORKING-STORAGE SECTION.
* AUXILIARY STORAGE LOCATIONS
 77  I              PIC S9(4).
 77  END-OF-FILE    PIC X(8) VALUE SPACES.


* INPUT RECORD
 01   CHARGE-INFO.
      05 CUSTOMER-NUMBER PIC X(8).
      05 FILLER          PIC X(81).
      05 REGION-CODE      PIC X.
      05 FILLER          PIC X(10).


* OUTPUT RECORD
 01   PRINT-PATTERN.
      05 FILLER          PIC X.
      05 CODE-OUT         PIC X(18).
      05 COUNT-BY-CODE    PIC Z(10).
      05 FILLER          PIC X(104) VALUE SPACES.
* TABLES
 01   VALUE-OF-CODE.
      05 FILLER PIC X VALUE 'A'.
      05 FILLER PIC X VALUE 'B'.
      05 FILLER PIC X VALUE 'C'.
 01   ARRAY-OF-VALUES REDEFINES VALUE-OF-CODE.
      05 CODED PIC X OCCURS 3 TIMES INDEXED BY PLACE.
 01   COUNTER.
      05 COUNT-BY-REGION PIC 999 OCCURS 3 TIMES
            INDEXED BY FOUND.


 PROCEDURE DIVISION.
* MODEL IV.
      OPEN INPUT CUSTOMER-FILE
          OUTPUT PRINTER.


* INITIALIZATION
      MOVE ZEROS TO COUNTER.


* FILE PROCESSING PAIR
      PERFORM READ-A-RECORD.
      PERFORM COUNT-EM
          UNTIL END-OF-FILE = HIGH-VALUES.


* TERMINATION
      PERFORM PRINT-SUMMARY
          VARYING I FROM 1 BY 1
              UNTIL I > 3.
      CLOSE CUSTOMER-FILE
          PRINTER.
      STOP RUN.
```

(A)

(A)

(B)

```
      * INPUT PROCEDURE
        READ-A-RECORD.
              READ CUSTOMER-FILE INTO CHARGE-INFO
                  AT END MOVE HIGH-VALUES TO END-OF-FILE.

      * RECORD PROCESSING
        COUNT-EM.
(C)           SET PLACE FOUND TO 1.
(D)           SEARCH CODED
(C)               VARYING FOUND
(E)                   WHEN CODED (PLACE) = REGION-CODE
                      ADD 1 TO COUNT-BY-REGION (FOUND).
              PERFORM READ-A-RECORD.
        PRINT-SUMMARY.
              MOVE CODED (I)            TO CODE-OUT.
              MOVE COUNT-BY-REGION (I) TO COUNT-BY-CODE.
              WRITE PRINT-LINE FROM PRINT-PATTERN.
```

(A)   Both the table of values and the table consisting of the accumulators for the different regions are indexed. The indexes have their storage allocated and managed by the operating system. The only feature under user control is the name given to the indexes. A table that has an index can also have its entries accessed by means of a subscript. We see this in the paragraph PRINT-SUMMARY. The role of FOUND will be clear when we examine the SEARCH verb sentence.

(B)   When the program executes this sentence, all the records in the file have been processed. The total number of customers from each region is contained in the table COUNT-BY-REGION. We use a subscript to step through the entries of this table in order to print the REGION-CODE and the number of customers from that region. There is an index for each of these tables, but we can only use an index with the table it is associated with. We can, however, use the same subscript with more than one table as we do in this case.

(C)   The table lookup involves the table CODED. When a match is found, we want to add one to the entry in the table COUNT-BY-REGION that keeps track of the number of customers with that REGION-CODE. The SET sentence initializes both the indexes to point to the first entry of the tables they index. The SEARCH verb automatically increments the index for the table it searches. The VARYING clause causes the index for the table COUNT-BY-REGION to be incremented along with the index for CODED. Without these two clauses, we would find a match in the table CODED, but have no way to access the corresponding entry in COUNT-BY-REGION that we want to increment. An index can only be used with the table it is associated with. This coding implies that if the match is found in entry I of table CODED the entry I of the table COUNT-BY-REGION is used to count the number of customers with this value of REGION-CODE.

(D)   The sentence begins with the verb indicating the action to be executed. The name of the table to be searched is the second entry in the statement.

(E)   The SEARCH terminates in the case that the condition CODED (PLACE) = REGION-CODE is TRUE. At that time the entry in table COUNT-BY-REGION that keeps track of the number of customers with the value of REGION-CODE just matched is pointed to by the current value of the index FOUND. This correspondence is a result of the SET and VARYING statements explained in (C). The variable FOUND is an index and not a subscript.

Indexes With Two-Dimensional Tables

Indexes can be used with two-dimensional tables as well as one-dimensional tables. The important thing to remember is that both the row indicator and the column indicator must be indexes or they must both be subscripts. It is not permitted to use one subscript and one index. This use of indexes with two-dimensional tables is shown in the following program.

```
*
* NAME:              ID:
* PROGRAM-NUMBER: 10.1-2
* DESCRIPTION: COUNT THE NUMBER OF STUDENTS
*   IN THE REGISTRAR-FILE BY HOME-STATE BY
*   CLASS.
*
      COPY TEXTA.
  WORKING-STORAGE SECTION.
* AUXILIARY STORAGE LOCATIONS
  77  I           PIC 999.
  77  J           PIC 999.
  77  END-OF-FILE PIC X(8) VALUE SPACES.

* INPUT RECORD
  01  REGISTRAR-RECORD.
      05  FILLER      PIC X(30).
      05  CLASS       PIC XX.
      05  FILLER      PIC X(33).
      05  HOME-STATE  PIC XX.
      05  FILLER      PIC X(33).

* OUTPUT RECORD
  01  OUT-LINE.
      05  FILLER      PIC X.
      05  OL-CLASS    PIC X(20).
      05  OL-ACCUM    PIC Z(10) OCCURS 5 TIMES.
      05  FILLER      PIC X(62) VALUE SPACES.
  01  HEADER.
      05  FILLER PIC X.
      05  FILLER PIC X(25) VALUE SPACES.
      05  FILLER PIC X(10) VALUE 'MA'.
      05  FILLER PIC X(10) VALUE 'ME'.
      05  FILLER PIC X(10) VALUE 'VT'.
      05  FILLER PIC X(10) VALUE 'CA'.
      05  FILLER PIC X(65) VALUE 'NH'.

* STORAGE ALLOCATION FOR TABLES
(A)   01  ACCUMULATORS.
          05  BY-CLASS OCCURS 5 TIMES
                  INDEXED BY IND-CL.
              10  BY-HOME-STATE OCCURS 5 TIMES
                      INDEXED BY H-STATE PIC 9(5).
(B)   01  FIXED-ST-INFO.
          05  FILLER PIC X(10) VALUE 'MAMEVTCANH'.
      01  STATES REDEFINES FIXED-ST-INFO.
          05  STATE-ABBR OCCURS 5 TIMES
                  INDEXED BY ABBR-ST PIC XX.
```

```
(C)       01  FIXED-CL-INFO.
              05  FILLER PIC X(10) VALUE 'FRSOJRSRUN'.
          01  CLASSES REDEFINES FIXED-CL-INFO.
              05  CLASS-ABBR OCCURS 5 TIMES
                     INDEXED BY ABBR-CL PIC XX.

      PROCEDURE DIVISION.
      * MODEL IV.

              OPEN INPUT REGISTRAR-FILE
                   OUTPUT PRINTER.

      * INITIALIZATION
              MOVE ZEROS TO ACCUMULATORS.

      * FILE PROCESSING PAIR
              PERFORM READ-REGISTRAR-FILE.
              PERFORM TALLY-UP
                 UNTIL END-OF-FILE = HIGH-VALUES.

      * TERMINATION ACTIVITY
              WRITE PRINT-LINE FROM HEADER.
              PERFORM PRINT-SUMMARY
                 VARYING I FROM 1 BY 1
                    UNTIL I > 5.
              CLOSE REGISTRAR-FILE
                    PRINTER.
              STOP RUN.

      * INPUT PROCEDURE
       READ-REGISTRAR-FILE.
              READ REGISTRAR-FILE INTO REGISTRAR-RECORD
                 AT END MOVE HIGH-VALUES TO END-OF-FILE.

      * RECORD PROCESSING
       PRINT-SUMMARY.
              MOVE CLASS-ABBR (I) TO OL-CLASS.
              PERFORM FILL-ROWS
                 VARYING J FROM 1 BY 1
                    UNTIL J > 5.
              WRITE PRINT-LINE FROM OUT-LINE.
       FILL-ROWS.
              MOVE BY-HOME-STATE (I,J) TO OL-ACCUM (J).
       TALLY-UP.
      * FIND THE ROW INDICATOR
(D)           SET  H-STATE ABBR-ST TO 1.
              SEARCH STATE-ABBR
                    VARYING H-STATE
                       WHEN HOME-STATE = STATE-ABBR (ABBR-ST)
                       NEXT SENTENCE.

      * FIND THE COLUMN INDICATOR
(E)           SET IND-CL ABBR-CL TO 1.
              SEARCH CLASS-ABBR
                    VARYING IND-CL
                       WHEN CLASS = CLASS-ABBR (ABBR-CL)
                       NEXT SENTENCE.
```

```
      * INCREMENT THE STORAGE LOCATION FOR THE ROW AND
      *    COLUMN JUST IDENTIFIED FOR THIS RECORD
(F)         ADD 1 TO BY-HOME-STATE (IND-CL,H-STATE).
      * GET THE NEXT RECORD
            PERFORM READ-REGISTRAR-FILE.
```

(A–C)   The tables used to count the students by CLASS by HOME–STATE have both the 05-level and the 10-level entries indexed. The two tables being searched are indexed by ABBR–CL and ABBR–ST. When matches are found, the two indexes needed to identify an entry in the two-dimensional table will have the correct values. As far as the programmer is concerned, indexes are used just like subscripts. The advantage of indexes involves the way the compiler translates statements into machine language when indexes are used.

(D)   The table STATE–ABBR is searched to find a match for the current value of HOME–STATE. Because of the VARYING clause, as the value of ABBR–ST changes to advance through the table, the value of H–STATE is advanced accordingly. Although only the equality relation is used in this condition, it is not necessary that the condition used to terminate the search be restricted to this test.

(E)   The table CLASS–ABBR is searched to find a match for current value of CLASS. Because of the VARYING clause, as the index ABBR–CL changes to advance through the table, the value of IND–CL is also advanced accordingly. When a match is found, the index IND–CL will have a value that can be used to indicate the entry in the row pointed to by H–STATE that keeps track of information about this value of CLASS.

(F)   To increment an entry in a two-dimensional table requires identifying both a row and a column. Either both the row and the column indicators must be subscripts or they must both be indexes. In this case they are both indexes. The values of IND–CL and H–STATE were determined by the SEARCH sentences.

SYNTAX SUMMARY

```
SEARCH identifier-1

[           {identifier-2}]
[VARYING    {           }]
[           {index-name-1}]

[; AT END imperative-statement-1]

                 {imperative-statement-2}
;WHEN condition-1{                      }
                 {NEXT SENTENCE         }

    {identifier-1 [,identifier-2]...}    {identifier-3}
SET {                               } TO {index-name-3}
    {index-name-1 [,index-name-2]...}    {integer-1   }


OCCURS integer TIMES
    [INDEXED BY index-name]
```

```
PERFORM procedure-name-1

    VARYING  {index-name-1}  FROM  {index-name-2}
             {identifier-1}         {literal-2   }
                                    {identifier-2}

    BY  {literal-3   }  UNTIL condition-1
        {identifier-3}

    [AFTER  {index-name-4}  FROM  {index-name-5}
            {identifier-4}        {literal-5   }
                                  {identifier-5}

    BY  {literal-6   }  UNTIL condition-2
        {identifier-6}

    [AFTER  {index-name-7}  FROM  {index-name-8}
            {identifier-7}        {literal-8   }
                                  {identifier-8}

    BY  {literal-9   }  UNTIL condition-3]]
        {identifier-9}
```

EXERCISES

1. What are the parts of the algorithm used for a table lookup?

2. What is an index? How is the value of an index determined by the compiler?

3. How is an index defined? How is an index given a value?

4. Explain the syntax and the semantics of the sentences:

```
SET H-INDEX K-INDEX TO 1.
SEARCH H-TABLE
    VARYING K-INDEX
        WHEN INPUT-NO = H-TABLE (H-INDEX)
            NEXT SENTENCE.
```

5. If a one-dimensional or two-dimensional table is defined to have an index, must every access of the table be accomplished by using the index?

PROGRAM TESTING AND MODIFICATION EXERCISES

1. Using the code of PROGRAM-NUMBER 10.1-2, determine the contents of the table BY-HOME-STATE each time the sentence

```
PERFORM TALLY-UP
    UNTIL EOF = HIGH-VALUES
```

is executed. Do this for the first twelve records of REGISTRAR-FILE. Indicate the final values in the following table.

BY–HOME–STATE

	1	2	3	4	5
1					
2					
3					
4					
5					

2. Suppose each record in a file has a field called CODE–VALUE that has for a value one of the entries of the table MAIL–BOXES.

MAIL–BOXES

A	B	Q	Z	R	S	U
1	2	3	4	5	6	7

Determine the values to be found in a table COUNT–CODE that keeps track of how many times each code has occurred after the following block of code is executed. Also determine how many entries of MAIL–BOXES are examined before each match is found.

```
SET I TO 1.
SEARCH MAIL-BOXES
    WHEN CODE-VALUE = MAIL-BOXES (I)
        ADD 1 TO COUNT-CODE (I).
```

CODE–VALUE	COUNT–CODE							No. of entries examined
	1	2	3	4	5	6	7	
U								
Z								
B								
A								
Q								
S								
S								
R								
Z								
A								
U								
Q								

PROGRAMMING PROBLEMS

1. Using the REGISTRAR–FILE for input, write a program that uses the SEARCH verb and prints the number of students broken down by value of the grade in GOVERN-MENT–3.
2. Using the REGISTRAR–FILE for input, write a program that uses the SEARCH verb and prints the average grade in MATH–13 broken down by value of HOME–STATE.
3. Using the REGISTRAR–FILE for input, write a program that uses the SEARCH verb and prints the average grade in PHILOSOPHY–3 broken down by value of the grade in ENGLISH–2. To calculate the averages, translate the letter grades into numeric equivalents using the scale: A = 4; B = 3; C = 2; D = 1; E = 0.

4. Using the CUSTOMER–FILE for input, write a program that uses the SEARCH verb and prints the total AMOUNT–DUE for each of the values of REGION.
5. Do one of the Programming Problems of Section 8.3 using the SEARCH verb to identify the table entry associated with a particular record.
6. Do one of the Programming Problems of Section 9.1 using the SEARCH verb to identify the table entry associated with a particular record.
7. Do one of the Programming Problems of Section 9.3 using the SEARCH verb to identify the table entry associated with a particular word.

10.2   SEARCH ALL

The SEARCH verb implements a sequential search of the entries of a table starting with the first entry in the table looking for a value that will make a condition TRUE. If the table being searched is very large, a sequential search is not particularly efficient.

A normal assumption about input records is that the data is random, that is, one element has no bearing on the next or subsequent elements. It is also assumed that each element is equally likely to be the next item. These assumptions can be used to analyze a sequential search process and conclude that on the average, $n/2$ probes or examinations of different elements in the table will be required to find a match. For a file with 100,000 records, a sequential search can take a considerable amount of time. Fortunately, there are other search procedures that will save time. The one we will examine is called a **binary search.** The idea of the binary search is to eliminate from further consideration one-half of the unsearched elements each time a probe or examination of an entry in a table is made. We will go through an example in detail to see how a binary search works.

Suppose we want to identify a three-letter month code that is included in a record in a field called MONTH–DUE.

MONTH–DUE						MO–ABBR						
AUG	APR	AUG	DEC	FEB	JAN	JUL	JUN	MAR	MAY	NOV	OCT	SEP
	1	2	3	4	5	6	7	8	9	10	11	12

The first thing to notice is that the entries of MO–ABBR are stored in alphabetical order. We will soon see the importance of this. The first probe compares MONTH–DUE with an entry that is a middle value. In this case, that entry is 6 and the month is 'JUL'. Since MO–ABBR (6), which is 'JUL', does not equal MONTH–DUE which is 'AUG', we must continue the search. The value of MONTH–DUE is less than MO–ABBR (6) and not equal to MO–ABBR (6) ('AUG' is less than 'JUL'). We now take advantage of the fact that the entries of MO–ABBR are in alphabetical order and observe that since MONTH–DUE is less than MO–ABBR (6) it must also be less than MO–ABBR (7), MO–ABBR (8), ..., MO–ABBR (12). If there is a match, it must occur among the elements MO–ABBR (1), ..., MO–ABBR (5). We can repeat the procedure focusing only on the elements of the table that can still hold a match.

MONTH–DUE		MO–ABBR			
AUG	APR	AUG	DEC	FEB	JAN
	1	2	3	4	5

We now compare MONTH–DUE with the middle element, MO–ABBR (3) = 'DEC', which is the middle element remaining. Since MONTH–DUE is less than 'DEC', we repeat the procedure with the entries of MO–ABBR that can still hold a match.

MONTH–DUE	MO–ABBR	
AUG	APR	AUG
	1	2

The middle element in this case is MO–ABBR (1) = 'APR'. Since 'AUG' is greater than 'APR', the match, if it exists, must be in a higher numbered entry than entry one. Since all the entries of MO–ABBR have been eliminated except MO–ABBR (2), we now continue the search by asking whether MONTH–DUE is equal to MO–ABBR (2). Since the answer is yes, we know that

MONTH–DUE = MO–ABBR (2) = 'AUG'.

We have needed four probes into the table MO–ABBR to find the match. If the months were stored in their natural order, we would have needed eight probes to find the match.

Although the implementation of a faster search method is an implementor responsibility, it is usually implemented using a binary search. We will assume that this is the case. The syntax that causes the binary search method to be used has two differences from the syntax discussed in Section 10.1. In order to use a binary search, the SEARCH ALL command is required before identifying the table to be searched. The second difference is that the SET verb is not required to give an initial value to an index since the index used is calculated by the operating system when it determines which portion of the entries of the table are still possibilities for a match. One additional syntactical requirement is that the OCCURS clause that defines a table to be used with the SEARCH ALL command must have a clause indicating whether the values are ordered in ascending or descending order as determined by the values of a key field.

Using SEARCH ALL

We now see this feature used in a program that matches the four-letter dorm abbreviation in a campus address with one of the twenty-nine four-letter dorm abbreviations that represent all the campus address fields in REGISTRAR–FILE. The actual implementation of the SEARCH ALL procedure is dependent on the operating system used. It is not uncommon, though, for the procedure to be implemented with a binary search algorithm. Whatever algorithm is used is transparent to the user. We can assume that a binary search procedure or some efficient procedure is being used.

```
*
* NAME:        ID:
* PROGRAM-NUMBER: 10.2-1
* DESCRIPTION:  USING REGISTRAR-FILE FOR INPUT
*    CALCULATE THE NUMBER OF RESIDENTS IN EACH
*    DORM.  LIST THE COUNT FOR EACH DORM AND
*    DETERMINE THE TWO MOST POPULOUS DORMS.
*    USE THE SEARCH ALL CLAUSE TO IDENTIFY THE
*    DORM OF A STUDENT.
*
     COPY TEXTA.
 WORKING-STORAGE SECTION.
```

```
*   AUXILIARY STORAGE LOCATIONS
77  END-OF-FILE  PIC X(8) VALUE SPACES.
77  I           PIC 9(5).
77  WINNER      PIC 9(5).


*   INPUT RECORD
01  REGISTRAR-RECORD.
    05  FILLER     PIC X(49).
    05  DORM-ABBR  PIC X(4).
    05  FILLER     PIC X(47).


*   OUTPUT RECORD
01  COUNT-LINE.
    05  FILLER    PIC X.
    05  CL-ABBR   PIC X(10).
    05  CL-COUNT  PIC Z(10).
    05  FILLER    PIC X(112) VALUE SPACES.
01  MOSTEST.
    05  FILLER  PIC X.
    05  FILLER  PIC X(32)
            VALUE 'THE TWO MOST POPULOUS DORMS ARE'.
    05  PLACE1  PIC X(5).
    05  FILLER  PIC X(4) VALUE 'AND'.
    05  PLACE2  PIC X(4).
    05  FILLER  PIC X(87) VALUE '.'.


*   STORAGE ALLOCATION FOR TABLES
01  DORM-ABBREVIATIONS.
    05  FILLER PIC X(16) VALUE 'ANDRAROOAUGUBALE'.
    05  FILLER PIC X(16) VALUE 'BELFCHADCOLVCORB'.
    05  FILLER PIC X(16) VALUE 'CROSCUMBDUNNELLS'.
    05  FILLER PIC X(16) VALUE 'ESTAGANNHANCHANN'.
    05  FILLER PIC X(16) VALUE 'HARTJENEKAPPKENN'.
    05  FILLER PIC X(16) VALUE 'KNOXLEWIOXFOPENO'.
    05  FILLER PIC X(16) VALUE 'OAK ROCKSOMESTOD'.
    05  FILLER PIC X(4)  VALUE 'YORK'.
(A) 01  DORM-NAMES REDEFINES DORM-ABBREVIATIONS.
    05  DORM-NAME PIC X(4) OCCURS 29 TIMES
            ASCENDING KEY DORM-NAME
            INDEXED BY D-NAME.
(A) 01  COUNTERS.
    05  DORM-COUNT PIC 9(5) OCCURS 29 TIMES
            INDEXED BY D-COUNT.


PROCEDURE DIVISION.
* MODEL IV
    OPEN INPUT REGISTRAR-FILE
        OUTPUT PRINTER.


*   INITIALIZATION
    MOVE ZEROS TO COUNTERS.


*   FILE PROCESSING PAIR
    PERFORM READ-REGISTRAR-FILE.
    PERFORM TALLY-UP
        UNTIL END-OF-FILE = HIGH-VALUES.
```

```
      *   TERMINATION ACTIVITY
             PERFORM END-ROUTINE.
             CLOSE REGISTRAR-FILE
                   PRINTER.
             STOP RUN.


      *   INPUT PROCEDURE
          READ-REGISTRAR-FILE.
             READ REGISTRAR-FILE INTO REGISTRAR-RECORD
                   AT END MOVE HIGH-VALUES TO END-OF-FILE.


      *   RECORD PROCESSING
          TALLY-UP.
(B)          SEARCH ALL DORM-NAME
                   WHEN DORM-ABBR = DORM-NAME (D-NAME)
                        SET D-COUNT TO D-NAME
                        ADD 1 TO DORM-COUNT (D-COUNT).
             PERFORM READ-REGISTRAR-FILE.
          END-ROUTINE.
(C)          MOVE 1 TO WINNER.
             PERFORM LARGEST
                   VARYING I FROM 2 BY 1
                        UNTIL I > 29.
             MOVE DORM-NAME (WINNER) TO PLACE1.
(D)          MULTIPLY -1 BY DORM-COUNT (WINNER).
(E)          MOVE 1 TO WINNER.
             PERFORM LARGEST
                   VARYING I FROM 2 BY 1
                        UNTIL I > 29.
             MOVE DORM-NAME (WINNER) TO PLACE2.
             WRITE PRINT-LINE FROM MOSTEST.
             PERFORM PRINT-COUNTS
                   VARYING I FROM 1 BY 1
                        UNTIL > 29.
          LARGEST.
             IF DORM-COUNT (WINNER) < DORM-COUNT (I)
                   MOVE I TO WINNER.
          PRINT-COUNTS.
             MOVE DORM-COUNT (I) TO CL-COUNT.
             MOVE DORM-NAME (I) TO CL-ABBR.
             WRITE PRINT-LINE FROM COUNT-LINE.
```

(A)   The two tables DORM-NAME and DORM-COUNT are defined with indexes. This will facilitate the search process and the subsequent incrementation of an appropriate counter. The table DORM-NAME also includes the ASCENDING KEY clause since this table is used with the SEARCH ALL command. It should be clear that this clause is necessary so that the search process can know whether the larger elements are above or below an element of a table that is being used in a comparison.

(B)   The search process uses the binary search. We will need no more than five probes of the table DORM-NAME to identify the DORM-ABBR value. When a match is found, we increment the corresponding entry of DORM-COUNT. Even though D-COUNT gets the same value as D-NAME, in DORM-COUNT (D-COUNT), we access the five bytes of DORM-COUNT beginning with byte

$$(D-COUNT - 1) * 5 + 1$$

The only condition allowed with SEARCH ALL is equality.

(C)   This is just the code we saw in Section 8.2. We make an initial guess at the location of the largest element. As we proceed through the table, we update the value of WINNER whenever we find an entry that is larger than the value in DORM–COUNT. At the end of this PERFORM sentence, WINNER holds the box number of the entry of DORM–COUNT with the largest value.

(D–E)   We need to repeat the process of finding the largest value in the table after we somehow eliminate the value just found that is the largest value in the table. Count is a positive integer, so if we multiply the largest element by minus one, we will turn a largest value into a smallest value. Thus if we repeat the process of finding the largest entry in the table after this multiplication, the previous winner has been eliminated. This means that the value found next will actually be the second largest value of the table we started with. If we needed the third largest element also, we could repeat this process one more time.

SYNTAX SUMMARY

There are so many options in the syntax for SEARCH, SEARCH ALL, and SET that a formal listing will be helpful.

```
level-number data-name

        {PICTURE}
        {        } IS character-string
        {PIC    }

        [OCCURS integer-1 TIMES]

        [ {ASCENDING }  KEY IS data-name-4 ]
        [ {DESCENDING}                     ]

             SEARCH ALL identifier-1

   [;AT END imperative-statement-1]


                {data-name-1
        ;WHEN   {
                {condition-name-1

                {IS EQUAL TO} {identifier-3               }}
                {           } {literal-1                  }}
                {IS =       } {arithmetic-expression-1    }}

        [       {data-name-2                ]
        [ AND   {                           ]
        [       {condition-name-2           ]

                {IS EQUAL TO} {identifier-4               }}]
                {           } {literal-2                  }}] ...
                {IS =       } {arithmetic-expression-2    }}]

        {imperative-statement-2}
        {                      }
        {NEXT SENTENCE         }
```

The AT END clause indicates what is to be done if no match is found. If the clause is not present, control passes directly to the next sentence in the normal order of execution of the program. In the WORKING–STORAGE SECTION any table that is to be searched using the SEARCH ALL command must have one of the reserved words ASCENDING or DESCENDING present to indicate how the values in the table are ordered.

EXERCISES

1. What is meant by a probe of a table?
2. What is a binary search?
3. Explain the difference between the SEARCH command and the SEARCH ALL command.
4. Explain the differences between the rules for defining a table used with the SEARCH command and the rules for defining a table used with the SEARCH ALL command.
5. What lines of code from TEXTA are required by PROGRAM–NUMBER 10.2-1?

PROGRAM TESTING AND MODIFICATION EXERCISES

1. Using the code of PROGRAM–NUMBER 10.2-1, determine the contents of the table DORM–COUNT each time the sentence

```
PERFORM TALLY-UP
    UNTIL EOF = HIGH-VALUES
```

is executed. Do this for the first twenty records of REGISTRAR–FILE. Indicate the final values in the following table.

DORM–COUNT

ANDR	AROO	AUGU	BALE	BELF	CHAD	COLV	CORB	CROS	CUMB
1	2	3	4	5	6	7	8	9	10

DUNN	ELLS	ESTA	GANN	HANC	HANN	HART	JENE	KAPP	KENN
11	12	13	14	15	16	17	18	19	20

KNOX	LEWI	OXFO	PENO	OAK	ROCK	SOME	STOD	YORK
21	22	23	24	25	26	27	28	29

2. Suppose each record in a file has a field called CODE–VALUE, and that field has for a value one of the entries of the table MAIL–BOXES.

MAIL–BOXES

A	B	Q	R	S	U	Z
1	2	3	4	5	6	7

Determine the values to be found in a table COUNT–CODE that keeps track of how many times each code has occurred after the following block of code is executed. Also determine how many entries of MAIL–BOXES are examined before each match is found.

```
SEARCH ALL MAIL-BOXES
     VARYING J
          WHEN CODE-VALUE = MAIL-BOXES (I)
               ADD 1 to COUNT-CODE (J).
```

CODE-VALUE	COUNT-CODE							No. of entries examined
	1	2	3	4	5	6	7	
U								
Z								
B								
A								
Q								
S								
S								
R								
Z								
A								
U								
Q								

PROGRAMMING PROBLEMS

1. Using the NEW-WORLD-FILE for input, write a program that uses the SEARCH ALL syntax and prints the total amount due for each value of STATE.
2. Using the REGISTRAR-FILE for input, write a program that uses the SEARCH ALL syntax and prints the average student grade point average broken down by HOME-STATE.
3. Using the REGISTRAR-FILE for input, write a program that uses the SEARCH ALL syntax and prints the average CUMULATIVE-GPA broken down by value of CLASS by value of HOME-STATE.
4. Using the CUSTOMER-FILE for input, write a program that uses the SEARCH ALL syntax and prints the total amount due for each value of REGION.
5. Do one of the Programming Problems of Section 8.3 using the SEARCH ALL syntax to identify the table entry associated with a particular record.
6. Do one of the Programming Problems of Section 9.1 using the SEARCH ALL syntax to identify the table entry associated with a particular record.
7. Do one of the Programming Problems of Section 9.3 using the SEARCH ALL syntax to identify the table entry associated with a particular record.

Chapter Review

SUMMARY

Table lookups are an integral part of many business applications programs. The VARYING clause is one example of incorporating both initialization and incrementation of a variable in a single clause. The searching of a table for a particular value is another example. The SEARCH verb implements a search of a table and automatically exits from the search when an answer is determined.

For large tables, a sequential search is often time consuming. To speed up the process, the SEARCH ALL verb is used. A search algorithm faster than a sequential search may be used. When the faster search is a binary search, the improvement in performance for a table with two hundred entries can be the difference between two hundred probes of the table when using a sequential search and eight probes of the table when using a binary search.

Syntax for the SEARCH verb incorporates the use of an index rather than a subscript. An index is a user-generated name associated with a table. The allocation of storage for an index is under the program's control. Values may be assigned to an index using the SET verb. For the SEARCH verb, the index used is set to an initial value to indicate the location in the table where the search should begin. In the SEARCH ALL option, the index is not set, as the system determines the value appropriate for each probe of the table. In a binary search, the next position to be examined depends not only on the current location in the table but also on the result of the current comparison. Because a binary search requires the elements of a table to be ordered, any table used with the SEARCH ALL option must have its entries ordered and the ordering must be defined when defining the table.

TEST YOURSELF

1. What is an index?
2. How is an index defined?
3. How is storage managed for an index?
4. What is the difference between an index and a subscript?
5. Can an index be used any time a subscript can be used? Can a subscript be used any time an index can be used?
6. When must an index be used?
7. Explain the syntax and the semantics of the SET verb.
8. Explain the syntax and the semantics of the SEARCH...WHEN statement.
9. Explain the syntax and the semantics of the SEARCH...VARYING...WHEN statement.
10. What is a binary search?
11. Explain the syntax and the semantics of the SEARCH ALL...VARYING...WHEN statement.
12. What condition can be tested for in the SEARCH ALL statement? Can other conditions be tested for in the SEARCH statement?
13. What syntax is required when defining a table to be used with the SEARCH ALL statement?

Stepwise Refinement and the REPORT WRITER

Chapter Objectives

After studying this chapter you should be able to

- write a program using stepwise refinement techniques to produce a report with a fixed number of lines printed on each page of the report;
- use the control features of the REPORT WRITER;
- write a program using the REPORT WRITER.

Chapter Outline

11.1   Using Stepwise Refinement in Report Writing

This section introduces new COBOL features that allow more programmer control over the spacing of printed pages. The remainder of the discussion is intended to show stepwise refinement used as a program design tool. The final report written will lay the groundwork for looking at the REPORT WRITER of COBOL.

The Form of a Report

Files are often used to generate reports. Typically, a report will involve some detailed listing of fields of each record. In addition, it is often important to provide information based on all the information in the file about one item. For example, the average of all the ALGEBRA grades in the STUDENT–FILE or the total of each of the values in the AMOUNT–DUE field of the records of CUSTOMER–FILE. A last kind of feature commonly found in a report is headings for (1) the beginnings of the report itself, (2) each page of the detailed listings, and (3) the information found at the bottom of the page or the end of the report. The listing on a single line of field(s) from a single record of the input file is called a **detail line.** An important consideration under the programmer's control is the number of detail lines that will be printed on a page. All these features will be incorporated into the solution of the following problem.

> Using the STUDENT–FILE for input, prepare a report that lists the NAME, AGE, and ALGEBRA grade for each record in the file. The records should be listed by AGE in increasing order. Within each AGE group, the ALGEBRA grades should be listed in decreasing order. Each page should include the records of no more than 40 students. Each page of the report, as well as the report itself, should have a heading. Finally, at the end of the detail lines, the average of all the ALGEBRA grades should be listed with an appropriate heading.

Parts of the Report Requirements

There are several parts to this program and rather than tackle them all at once, let's first list the major requirements and then decide on a strategy for accomplishing them in some order. The requirements are

> 1. Sort the STUDENT–FILE in increasing order by AGE and within each AGE group in decreasing order by ALGEBRA grade.
> 2. Using the sorted file for input, list the NAME, AGE, and ALGEBRA fields of each record.
> 3. Modify the listing in Step 2 so that only 40 records are listed on a page.
> 4. Prepare a heading for the report and for each page of the report.
> 5. Calculate the sum of all the ALGEBRA grades and the number of records processed while accomplishing Step 2 so that the average and a suitable heading for the average can be completed as the TERMINATION ACTIVITY part of the program.

This outline could be accomplished step-by-step, but it seems reasonable to write this program in the following three steps.

> 1. SORT the file and list the records of the sorted file with a heading for the report.
> 2. Incorporate into Step 1 the listing of at most 40 records per page together with appropriate page headings.
> 3. Incorporate into Step 2 the calculation of the sum of all ALGEBRA grades and the number of records in the file as well as the listing of the average ALGEBRA grade at the end of the report.

Phase One of the Stepwise Refinement

The programming strategy that we are illustrating is called **stepwise refinement.** This is a fundamental tool for use with the control structures of sequence, selection, and repetition. We will write and test a program that accomplishes Step 1; then test the program that results from incorporating Step 2; and finally test the program that incorporates Step 3 into the program accomplishing Steps 1 and 2.

```
IDENTIFICATION DIVISION.
PROGRAM-ID. PHASEONE.
*
* NAME:                ID:
* PROGRAM-NUMBER: 11.1-1
* DESCRIPTION: SORT STUDENT-FILE BY AGE IN
*    INCREASING ORDER AND WITHIN EACH AGE GROUP
*    BY ALGEBRA GRADE IN DECREASING ORDER.  LIST
*    THE NAME, AGE, AND ALGEBRA FIELDS OF THE
*    SORTED FILE.
*
ENVIRONMENT DIVISION.
CONFIGURATION SECTION.
SOURCE-COMPUTER. IBM-370.
OBJECT-COMPUTER. IBM-370.
INPUT-OUTPUT SECTION.
FILE-CONTROL.
    SELECT STUDENT-FILE
        ASSIGN TO UT-3330-S-FILE03.
    SELECT PRINTER
        ASSIGN TO UT-1403-S-SYSOUT.
    SELECT FILE1
        ASSIGN TO UT-3330-S-COBOL1.
    SELECT FILE2
        ASSIGN TO UT-3330-S-COBOL2.
DATA DIVISION.
FILE SECTION.
FD  PRINTER
    LABEL RECORDS ARE OMITTED.
01  PRINT-LINE.
    .05  FILLER    PIC X(133).
FD  STUDENT-FILE.
    LABEL RECORDS ARE STANDARD
    BLOCK CONTAINS 34 RECORDS.
01  STUDENT-FILE-RECORD.
    05  FILLER        PIC X(100).
```

```
(A)       SD   FILE1.
          01   FILE1-RECORD.
               05   FILLER     PIC X(4).
               05   NAME       PIC X(18).
               05   FILLER     PIC X.
               05   AGE        PIC XX.
               05   ALGEBRA    PIC 999.
               05   FILLER     PIC X(72).
          FD   FILE2
               LABEL RECORDS ARE STANDARD
               BLOCK CONTAINS 34 RECORDS.
          01   FILE2-RECORD.
               05   FILLER        PIC X(100).


          WORKING-STORAGE SECTION.
     * AUXILIARY STORAGE LOCATION
          77   END-OF-FILE  PIC X(8) VALUE SPACES.
     * INPUT RECORD
          01   STUDENT-RECORD.
               05   FILLER        PIC X(4).
               05   S-NAME        PIC X(18).
               05   FILLER        PIC X.
               05   S-AGE         PIC XX.
               05   S-ALGEBRA     PIC 999.
               05   FILLER        PIC X(72).
     * OUTPUT RECORDS
          01   DETAIL-LINE.
               05   FILLER        PIC X.
               05   DL-NAME       PIC X(30).
               05   DL-AGE        PIC X(10).
               05   DL-ALGEBRA    PIC Z(10).
               05   FILLER        PIC X(82) VALUE SPACES.
          01   REPORT-HEADER.
               05   FILLER        PIC X.
               05   FILLER        PIC X(132) VALUE
                    'THIS IS THE REPORT HEADER'.


          PROCEDURE DIVISION.
(A)            SORT FILE1
                   ON ASCENDING KEY AGE
                   ON DESCENDING KEY ALGEBRA
                       USING STUDENT-FILE
                       GIVING FILE2.
     *  MODEL I
(B)            OPEN INPUT FILE2
                    OUTPUT PRINTER.

     *  INITIALIZATION
               WRITE PRINT-LINE FROM REPORT-HEADER.

     *  FILE PROCESSING PAIR
               PERFORM READ-FILE2.
               PERFORM DETAIL-LISTING
                   UNTIL END-OF-FILE = HIGH-VALUES.

     * TERMINATION ACTIVITY
               CLOSE FILE2
                       PRINTER.
               STOP RUN.
```

```
*   INPUT PROCEDURE
 READ-FILE2.
        READ FILE2 INTO STUDENT-RECORD
            AT END MOVE HIGH-VALUES TO END-OF-FILE.


*   RECORD PROCESSING
 DETAIL-LISTING.
        MOVE S-NAME        TO   DL-NAME.
        MOVE S-AGE         TO   DL-AGE.
        MOVE S-ALGEBRA     TO   DL-ALBEGRA.
        WRITE PRINT-LINE   FROM DETAIL-LINE.
        PERFORM READ-FILE2.
```

(A)   The SD level indicator tells the operating system this is the work area for the sorting procedure. All the sort keys occur as named fields in the record description associated with this file. These names occur in the SORT sentence in the PROCEDURE DIVISION.

(B)   The remainder of the program is merely an application in the use of Model I. Certainly a simple model is a good place to start as we will be confident of getting this part of the coding done quickly and correctly. Further refinements will build on code that is correct and solves some portion of the problem at hand.

Phase Two of the Stepwise Refinement

The basic program is now complete. The report includes the required output fields for each detail line. Until this point, there is no concern for how many records are printed on a page; also missing is the page heading that will identify each page of detail lines. These features will be incorporated in the following program.

```
 IDENTIFICATION DIVISION.
 PROGRAM-ID. PHASE TWO.
*
* NAME:                  ID:
* PROGRAM-NUMBER: 11.1-2
* DESCRIPTION: SORT STUDENT-FILE BY AGE IN
*   INCREASING ORDER AND WITHIN EACH AGE GROUP
*   BY ALGEBRA GRADE IN DECREASING ORDER. LIST
*   NAME, AGE, AND ALGEBRA OF EACH RECORD
*   WITH 40 DETAIL LINES PER PAGE.
*
 ENVIRONMENT DIVISION.
 CONFIGURATION SECTION.
 SOURCE-COMPUTER. IBM-370.
 OBJECT-COMPUTER. IBM-370.
 SPECIAL-NAMES.   C01 IS TOP-OF-PAGE.
 INPUT-OUTPUT SECTION.
 FILE-CONTROL.
        SELECT STUDENT-FILE
            ASSIGN TO UT-3330-S-FILE03.
        SELECT PRINTER
            ASSIGN TO UT-1403-S-SYSOUT.
        SELECT FILE1
            ASSIGN TO UT-3330-S-COBOL1.
        SELECT FILE2
            ASSIGN TO UT-3330-S-COBOL2.
```

(A)

```
        DATA DIVISION.
        FILE SECTION.
        FD  PRINTER
            LABEL RECORDS ARE OMITTED.
        01  PRINT-LINE.
            05  FILLER     PIC X(133).
        FD  STUDENT-FILE
            LABEL RECORDS ARE STANDARD
            BLOCK CONTAINS 34 RECORDS.
        01  STUDENT-FILE-RECORD.
            05  FILLER        PIC X(100).
        SD  FILE1.
        01  FILE1-RECORD.
            05  FILLER     PIC X(4).
            05  NAME       PIC X(18).
            05  FILLER     PIC X.
            05  AGE        PIC XX.
            05  ALGEBRA    PIC 999.
            05  FILLER     PIC X(72).
        FD  FILE2
            LABEL RECORDS ARE STANDARD
            BLOCK CONTAINS 34 RECORDS.
        01  FILE2-RECORD.
            05  FILLER        PIC X(100).
        WORKING-STORAGE SECTION.

       * AUXILIARY STORAGE LOCATIONS
        77  END-OF-FILE        PIC X(8) VALUE SPACES.
        77  RECORDS-THIS-PAGE  PIC 9(5).
       * INPUT RECORD
        01  STUDENT-RECORD.
            05  FILLER     PIC X(4).
            05  S-NAME     PIC X(18).
            05  FILLER     PIC X.
            05  S-AGE      PIC XX.
            05  S-ALGEBRA  PIC 999.
            05  FILLER     PIC X(72).
       * OUTPUT RECORDS
        01  DETAIL-LINE.
            05  FILLER     PIC X.
            05  DL-NAME    PIC X(30).
            05  DL-AGE     PIC X(10).
            05  DL-ALGEBRA PIC Z(10).
            05  FILLER     PIC X(82) VALUE SPACES.
(A)     01  PAGE-HEADER.
            05  FILLER     PIC X.
            05  FILLER     PIC X(30) VALUE 'NAME'.
            05  FILLER     PIC X(15) VALUE 'AGE'.
            05  FILLER     PIC X(87) VALUE 'ALGEBRA'.
        01  REPORT-HEADER.
            05  FILLER     PIC X.
            05  FILLER     PIC X(132) VALUE
                'THIS IS THE REPORT HEADER'.

        PROCEDURE DIVISION.
            SORT FILE1
                ON ASCENDING KEY AGE
                ON DESCENDING KEY ALGEBRA
                    USING STUDENT-FILE
                    GIVING FILE2.
```

```
* MODEL I
      OPEN INPUT FILE2
            OUTPUT PRINTER.


* INITIALIZATION
      WRITE PRINT-LINE FROM REPORT-HEADER
            AFTER 1.
      MOVE ZERO TO RECORDS-THIS-PAGE.
      WRITE PRINT-LINE FROM PAGE-HEADER
            AFTER 1.


* FILE PROCESSING PAIR
      PERFORM READ-FILE2.
      PERFORM DETAIL-LISTING
            UNTIL END-OF-FILE = HIGH-VALUES.


* TERMINATION ACTIVITY
      CLOSE FILE2
            PRINTER.
      STOP RUN.


* INPUT PROCEDURE
  READ-FILE2.
      READ FILE2 INTO STUDENT-RECORD
            AT END MOVE HIGH-VALUES TO END-OF-FILE.


* RECORD PROCESSING
  DETAIL-LISTING.
      MOVE S-NAME        TO  DL-NAME.
      MOVE S-AGE         TO  DL-AGE.
      MOVE S-ALGEBRA     TO  DL-ALGEBRA.
      WRITE PRINT-LINE   FROM DETAIL-LINE
            AFTER 1.
      ADD 1 TO RECORDS-THIS-PAGE.
      IF RECORDS-THIS-PAGE = 40
            WRITE PRINT-LINE FROM PAGE-HEADER
                  AFTER ADVANCING TOP-OF-PAGE
            MOVE ZERO TO RECORDS-THIS-PAGE.
      PERFORM READ-FILE2.
```

(B)

(C)

(A)   The carriage control feature used to this point has been to allow the first byte of the output record to be used by the operating system to supply the printer with a message. When we want special messages sent to the printer so that spacing is appropriate, we can give user-generated names to the codes the operating system uses in the SPECIAL-NAMES paragraph of the CONFIGURATION SECTION and then use these user-generated names in the AFTER ADVANCING clause of the WRITE statement. The operating system's name represents the instruction to advance to the top of a new page. Other signals can be used to position the printer at various points of the record.

(B)   We have to keep track of how many records are printed on a page so that when we reach a count of 40, we can start a new page. At this point, the correct record count is zero, which is the value we use to initialize the counter.

(C)   As each record is printed, we increment the line count and ask if we have the output for 40 records on this page. The output for a record is called a *detail line*. If the answer is no, we continue to process records. If the answer is yes, we want to put a page heading at the top of the next page so that the detailed listings on the next page have a heading. When the answer is yes, we must also reset RECORDS–THIS–PAGE to zero to indicate the current number of records on this new page. The name TOP–OF–PAGE in the AFTER ADVANCING clause is defined in the CONFIGURATION SECTION, see (A). This is a mnemonic for the carriage control setting that causes the printer to advance the continuous form to the top of the next page. We assume that the number of records in the file is not a multiple of 40. What modifications would we need in order to prevent the printing of a heading on a page with no detail lines if the number of records in the file *were* a multiple of 40?

Phase Three of the Stepwise Refinement

The report is beginning to look more respectable. Report and page headings are now in place. There are now, at most, 40 detail lines on a page. Each page of detail lines has an appropriate heading to identify the output for the reader. The feature we still have to incorporate is the recap information at the end of the report. The average for all the ALGEBRA grades must be calculated and included at the end of the report. The calculation and printing of the average will now be incorporated.

```
    IDENTIFICATION DIVISION.
    PROGRAM-ID. PHSTHR.
*
*   NAME:                   ID:
*   PROGRAM-NUMBER: 11.1-3
*   DESCRIPTION: SORT STUDENT-FILE BY AGE IN
*      INCREASING ORDER AND WITHIN EACH AGE GROUP
*      BY ALGEBRA GRADE IN DECREASING ORDER.  LIST
*      NAME, AGE, AND ALGEBRA OF EACH RECORD
*      WITH 40 DETAIL LINES PER PAGE. GIVE OVERALL
*      ALGEBRA AVERAGE AFTER THE LAST DETAIL LINE.
*
    ENVIRONMENT DIVISION.
    CONFIGURATION SECTION.
    SOURCE-COMPUTER. IBM-370.
    OBJECT-COMPUTER. IBM-370.
    SPECIAL-NAMES. C01 IS TOP-OF-PAGE.
    INPUT-OUTPUT SECTION.
    FILE-CONTROL.
        SELECT STUDENT-FILE
            ASSIGN TO UT-3330-S-FILE03.
        SELECT PRINTER
            ASSIGN TO UT-1403-S-SYSOUT.
        SELECT FILE1
            ASSIGN TO UT-3330-S-COBOL1.
        SELECT FILE2
            ASSIGN TO UT-3330-S-COBOL2.
    DATA DIVISION.
    FILE SECTION.
    FD  PRINTER
        LABEL RECORDS ARE OMITTED.
    01  PRINT-LINE.
        05  FILLER    PIC X(133).
    FD  STUDENT-FILE
        LABEL RECORDS ARE STANDARD
        BLOCK CONTAINS 34 RECORDS.
```

```
        01   STUDENT-FILE-RECORD.
             05  FILLER         PIC X(100).
        SD   FILE1.
        01   FILE1-RECORD.
             05  FILLER   PIC X(4).
             05  NAME     PIC X(18).
             05  FILLER   PIC X.
             05  AGE      PIC XX.
             05  ALGEBRA  PIC 999.
             05  FILLER   PIX X(72).
        FD   FILE2
             LABEL RECORDS ARE STANDARD
             BLOCK CONTAINS 34 RECORDS.
        01   FILE2-RECORD.
             05  FILLER         PIC X(100).


        WORKING-STORAGE SECTION.
        * AUXILIARY STORAGE LOCATIONS
        77   END-OF-FILE         PIC X(8) VALUE SPACES.
        77   RECORDS-THIS-PAGE   PIC 9(5).
        77   NO-OF-RECORDS       PIC 9(5).
        77   SUM-OF-ALGEBRA      PIC 9(5).
        * INPUT RECORD
        01   STUDENT-RECORD.
             05  FILLER         PIC X(4).
             05  S-NAME         PIC X(18).
             05  FILLER         PIC X.
             05  S-AGE          PIC XX.
             05  S-ALGEBRA      PIC 999.
             05  FILLER         PIC X(72).
        * OUTPUT RECORDS
        01   DETAIL-LINE.
             05  FILLER         PIC X.
             05  DL-NAME        PIC X(30).
             05  DL-AGE         PIC X(10).
             05  DL-ALGEBRA     PIC Z(10).
             05  FILLER         PIC X(82) VALUE SPACES.
        01   PAGE-HEADER.
             05  FILLER         PIC X.
             05  FILLER         PIC X(30) VALUE 'NAME'.
             05  FILLER         PIC X(15) VALUE 'AGE'.
             05  FILLER         PIC X(87) VALUE 'ALGEBRA'.
        01   REPORT-HEADER.
             01  FILLER         PIC X.
             05  FILLER         PIC X(132) VALUE
                 'THIS IS THE REPORT HEADER'.
(A)     01   RECAP-HEADER.
             05  FILLER   PIC X.
             05  AVERAGE  PIC Z(3).99.
             05  FILLER   PIC X(126) VALUE
                 ' AVERAGE OF ALL ALGEBRA GRADES'.


        PROCEDURE DIVISION.
            SORT FILE1
                ON ASCENDING KEY AGE
                ON DESCENDING KEY ALGEBRA
                    USING STUDENT-FILE
                    GIVING FILE2.
```

```
                * MODEL III
                      OPEN INPUT FILE2
                           OUTPUT PRINTER.


                * INITIALIZATION
                      WRITE PRINT-LINE FROM REPORT-HEADER
                           AFTER 1.
                      MOVE ZERO TO RECORDS-THIS-PAGE
(A)                                  NO-OF-RECORDS
                                     SUM-OF-ALGEBRA.
                      WRITE PRINT-LINE FROM PAGE-HEADER
                           AFTER 1.


                * FILE PROCESSING PAIR
                      PERFORM READ-FILE2.
                      PERFORM DETAIL-LISTING
                           UNTIL END-OF-FILE = HIGH-VALUES.


                *   TERMINATION ACTIVITY
(B)                   PERFORM SUMMARY.
                      CLOSE FILE2
                            PRINTER.
                      STOP RUN.


                * INPUT PROCEDURE
                  READ-FILE2.
                      READ FILE2 INTO STUDENT-RECORD
                           AT END MOVE HIGH-VALUES TO END-OF-FILE.


                * RECORD PROCESSING
                  DETAIL-LISTING.
(C)                   ADD 1              TO   NO-OF-RECORDS
                                              RECORDS-THIS-PAGE.
                      ADD S-ALGEBRA      TO   SUM-OF-ALGEBRA.
                      MOVE S-NAME        TO   DL-NAME.
                      MOVE S-AGE         TO   DL-AGE.
                      MOVE S-ALGEBRA     TO   DL-ALGEBRA.
                      WRITE PRINT-LINE FROM DETAIL-LINE
                           AFTER 1.
                      IF RECORDS-THIS-PAGE = 40
                           WRITE PRINT-LINE FROM PAGE-HEADER
                                AFTER ADVANCING TOP-OF-PAGE
                           MOVE ZERO TO RECORDS-THIS-PAGE.
                      PERFORM READ-FILE2.
(D)               SUMMARY.
                      DIVIDE SUM-OF-ALGEBRA BY NO-OF-RECORDS
                           GIVING AVERAGE.
                      WRITE PRINT-LINE FROM RECAP-HEADER
                           AFTER 1.
```

(A)   To calculate the average ALGEBRA grade, we need to accumulate both the sum of all the ALGEBRA grades and the number of records contributing to the sum. At this point, both of these accumulators should have a value of zero and so they are initialized to that value.

(B)   This paragraph extends the general form of the program to be one that uses Model III. The termination activity is just the calculation of the average ALGEBRA grade and the printing of a line of output indicating the value.

(C)   The two ADD sentences are used so that the NO–OF–RECORDS and SUM–OF–RECORDS fields always have a current value representing the sum of all the ALGEBRA grades from all the records as well as the current number of records read so far.

(D)   The final output line includes the average ALGEBRA grade. This is calculated by dividing SUM–OF–ALGEBRA by NO–OF–RECORDS. We get the average from this calculation because the value in these fields at this point represents the total of all ALGEBRA grades and the total number of records in the file.

EXERCISES

1. What is a detail line?
2. Why can TEXTA not be used in PROGRAM–NUMBER 11.1-1?
3. What is the purpose of the SPECIAL–NAMES paragraph?
4. Why is RECORDS–THIS–PAGE in PROGRAM–NUMBER 11.1-3 set to zero whenever it reaches a value of 40?
5. Complete the record descriptions for a report having at most 35 detail lines to a page and the following form.

```
REPORT  HEADING
       THE  NEW-WORLD  INSURANCE CO.
         WILLIAM  COLES,  PRESIDENT

PAGE  HEADING

CUSTOMER  NAME          CUSTOMER  ADDRESS          INSURANCE  AMOUNT


DETAIL  LINE
   ---20-----      ---10-----   ---10-----
   XX-------X      XXX------X   XXX------X             $,$$$,$$$
     (NAME)         (STREET)     (CITY)

PAGE  NUMBERING
Center the numbers on a line after skipping one line after the last detail line
printed on the page. The number should start with 1 and increase by 1 for
each additional page in the report.
```

PROGRAMMING PROBLEMS

1. Using the STUDENT–FILE for input, prepare a report listing the NAME, AGE, and GEOMETRY grade for each student. Include an appropriate heading for the report and list no more than 40 detail lines on a page.
2. Using the NEW–WORLD–FILE for input, prepare a report listing the NAME, AMOUNT–DUE, PAYMENT, and the resulting balance due. Include a total for the three numeric fields at the end of the report. List at most 35 detail lines on a page.
3. Using the STUDENT–FILE for input, prepare a report listing the NAME, GRADEs, and the average for the five grades for each student. List the students in order of increasing average. Include at most 30 records on a page. Include a heading for the report as well as a heading for each page of detail lines.
4. Using the NEW–WORLD–FILE for input, prepare a report that lists by STATE the NAME and AMOUNT–DUE for each customer. Include an average amount due for

each state as soon as the records from a STATE are listed. Also include the average for all records at the end of the report. Include at most 40 detail lines on a page. Include a report heading as well as a heading for each page of detail lines.

11.2 The REPORT WRITER

To understand the REPORT WRITER, it is first necessary to have an idea of what a business report is likely to include; then we can see how COBOL makes these features available. In some cases, we will see that the automated features of the REPORT WRITER are not sufficient, so we must write a special program. However, in a great number of the familiar cases, we will find the automatic formatting and accumulating features of the REPORT WRITER adequate.

Parts of a Report

The simplest report has a heading for the report itself and then a detail line for each record in the file. A pseudocode outline of such a report would be

```
***   REPORT HEADING
***   DETAIL LINE FOR EACH RECORD
```

Throughout the exercises in this book, listings have usually included a heading for the kinds of information included in the detail line. This is reflected in the following refinement of the previous outline.

```
***   REPORT HEADING
***   HEADING FOR DETAIL LINES
***   DETAIL LINES
```

Since most files contain more records than will fit on a single page, we see that the heading for the detail line really needs to be printed at the top of each page that lists records of the file. The report outline now becomes

```
***   REPORT HEADING
***   HEADING FOR PAGE OF DETAIL LINES
***   PAGE OF DETAIL LINES
***   HEADING FOR PAGE OF DETAIL LINES
***   PAGE OF DETAIL LINES
              .
              .
              .
***   HEADING FOR PAGE OF DETAIL LINES
***   PAGE OF DETAIL LINES
```

It is now easy to see that the next piece that may be needed is some indication on the last page of the report that the report is finished. This expands the outline:

```
***   REPORT HEADING
***   HEADING FOR PAGE OF DETAIL LINES
***   PAGE OF DETAIL LINES
              .
              .
              .
***   HEADING FOR PAGE OF DETAIL LINES
***   PAGE OF DETAIL LINES
***   FOOTING FOR END OF REPORT
```

A heading printed at the bottom of a group of records or at the end of the report is called a *footing*. In addition to the footing at the end of the report, we often want special information at the end of each page. Typically, this will include a page-numbering scheme. We can now represent a report with the following outline.

```
***    REPORT HEADING
***    HEADING FOR PAGE OF DETAIL LINES
***    PAGE OF DETAIL LINES
***    FOOTING FOR PAGE OF DETAIL LINES
             .
             .
             .

***    HEADING FOR PAGE OF DETAIL LINES
***    PAGE OF DETAIL LINES
***    FOOTING FOR PAGE OF DETAIL LINES
***    FOOTING FOR END OF REPORT
```

We have indicated the major features in the packaging of the detail lines on a page and in the report. The next automatic feature that is useful is a control break to indicate categories within the records in a file. A feature often associated with a control break is a sum of some field over all the records in a category. The control break and accumulation feature are both available in the REPORT WRITER. The features just described are available and are identified by the key words defined below:

Report Heading:	lines that form the heading for the report.
Page Heading:	heading lines for each page of detailed listings.
Detail Line:	format for record listing.
Control Footing:	record description for the end of a control break group.
Page Footing:	record description for lines at the bottom of a page.
Report Footing:	record description for lines at end of the report.

In describing the report, each page will be broken down by indicating the starting and finishing line for the various kinds of lines. The portions of the page are split among lines for the report header, the detail lines, and the various footing lines. This information is incorporated in COBOL by indicating in the code that a record description has one of the following types:

```
REPORT HEADING
         .
PAGE HEADING
         .
DETAIL LINE
         .
PAGE FOOTING
         .
REPORT FOOTING
```

Using REPORT WRITER

We will now see how these features are described by COBOL. The syntax will formally describe the portions of the report that normally are included. The first report incorporates a REPORT HEADING, PAGE HEADING, and DETAIL LINE features of the REPORT WRITER. Other features will be shown in PROGRAM-NUMBER 11.2-2.

```
          IDENTIFICATION DIVISION.
          PROGRAM-ID. RPRTONE.
        * PROGRAM-NUMBER: 11.2-1
        * DESCRIPTION: SORT STUDENT-FILE BY AGE IN
        *    INCREASING ORDER AND WITHIN EACH AGE GROUP
        *    BY ALGEBRA GRADE IN DECREASING ORDER. LIST
        *    THE NAME, AGE, AND ALGEBRA FIELDS OF EACH
        *    RECORD OF THE SORTED FILE.
        *
          ENVIRONMENT DIVISION.
          CONFIGURATION SECTION.
          SOURCE-COMPUTER. IBM-370.
          OBJECT-COMPUTER. IBM-370.
          INPUT-OUTPUT SECTION.
          FILE-CONTROL.
              SELECT STUDENT-FILE
                  ASSIGN TO UT-3330-S-FILE03.
              SELECT PRINTER
                  ASSIGN TO UT-1403-S-SYSOUT.
              SELECT FILE1
                  ASSIGN TO UT-3330-S-COBOL1.
              SELECT FILE2
                  ASSIGN TO UT-3330-S-COBOL2.
          DATA DIVISION.
          FILE SECTION.
(A)       FD  PRINTER
              REPORT IS ALGEBRA-REPORT
              LABEL RECORDS ARE OMITTED.
          FD  STUDENT-FILE
              LABEL RECORDS ARE STANDARD
              BLOCK CONTAINS 34 RECORDS.
          01  STUDENT-FILE-RECORD.
              05  FILLER        PIC X(100).
          SD  FILE1.
          01  FILE1-RECORD.
              05  FILLER  PIC X(4).
              05  NAME    PIC X(18).
              05  FILLER  PIC X.
              05  AGE     PIC 99.
              05  ALGEBRA PIC 999.
              05  FILLER  PIC X(60).
          FD  FILE2
              LABEL RECORDS ARE STANDARD
              BLOCK CONTAINS 34 RECORDS.
          01  FILE2-RECORD.
              05  FILLER        PIC X(100).

          WORKING-STORAGE SECTION.
        * AUXILIARY STORAGE LOCATION
          77  END-OF-FILE PIC X(8) VALUE SPACES.
        * INPUT RECORD
          01  STUDENT-RECORD.
              05  FILLER    PIC X(4).
              05  S-NAME    PIC X(18).
              05  FILLER    PIC X.
              05  S-AGE     PIC XX.
              05  S-ALGEBRA PIC 999.
              05  FILLER    PIC X(60).
          REPORT SECTION.
```

```
(B)        RD   ALGEBRA-REPORT
                PAGE 59 LINES
                HEADING 1
                FIRST DETAIL 9
                LAST DETAIL 48.
(C)        01   TYPE REPORT HEADING.
                05  LINE 1 COLUMN 30 PIC X(26)
                    VALUE 'THIS IS THE ALGEBRA REPORT'.
(D)        01   PAGE-HEAD TYPE PAGE HEADING LINE 7.
                05  COLUMN 10 PIC X(20) VALUE 'NAME'.
                05  COLUMN 40 PIC X(20) VALUE 'AGE'.
                05  COLUMN 60 PIC X(10) VALUE 'ALGEBRA'.
(E)        01   DETAIL-INFO TYPE DETAIL LINE PLUS 1.
                05  COLUMN 10 PIC X(20) SOURCE S-NAME.
                05  COLUMN 40 PIC X(5)  SOURCE S-AGE.
                05  COLUMN 60 PIC Z(5)  SOURCE S-ALGEBRA.

           PROCEDURE DIVISION.
(F)            SORT FILE1
                   ON ASCENDING KEY AGE
                   ON DESCENDING KEY ALGEBRA
                       USING STUDENT-FILE
                       GIVING FILE2.
         * MODEL I
               OPEN INPUT FILE2
                    OUTPUT PRINTER.
         * INITIALIZATION
(G)            INITIATE ALGEBRA-REPORT.
         * FILE PROCESSING PAIR
               PERFORM READ-FILE2.
               PERFORM DETAIL-LISTING
                   UNTIL END-OF-FILE = HIGH-VALUES.
         * TERMINATION ACTIVITY
(G)            TERMINATE ALGEBRA-REPORT.
               CLOSE FILE2
                     PRINTER.
               STOP RUN.

         * INPUT PROCEDURE
          READ-FILE2.
               READ FILE2 INTO STUDENT-RECORD
                   AT END MOVE HIGH-VALUES TO END-OF-FILE.

         * RECORD PROCESSING
          DETAIL-LISTING.
(H)            GENERATE DETAIL-INFO.
               PERFORM READ-FILE2.
```

(A) Among the software characteristics of a file is included whether or not it is used by the REPORT WRITER. For a report to be output to a file the clause

                    REPORT IS report-name

must be included in the FD level indicator. Notice that no record description is used. All the different record descriptions used with this file to complete the report are defined in the REPORT SECTION.

(B) Each report is defined in the REPORT SECTION. More than one report may be created within a single program. Each different report is identified by the RD level indicator that defines the general form of the report. The size of the page is given as well as the line numbers of the lines that will contain the first and last detail line. In this report there will be 40 detail lines per page of the report. The page heading will be printed on line 1 of the page. The headings for the detail lines will occur on line 7. The first detail line will occur on line 9 and the last detail line will appear on line 48. The page size need not be the size of the continuous form used by the output device.

(C)   A record description is needed for the heading. In the statement

```
LINE 1 COLUMN 30 PIC X(26)
```

the COLUMN 30 identifies where the field begins in the output record while the PIC X(26) indicates how wide the field is. The 26 bytes will be filled with the literal constant found in the VALUE clause. There is no name for the record since a name is optional. A name is required if the record is directly referenced in the PROCEDURE DIVISION. REPORT HEADING identifies the TYPE of this record. LINE 1 indicates that the records should be printed on line 1 of the page. If the heading consisted of more than one line, the other lines would be identified by the line on which they would be printed. Heading lines must end before line 7, as the detail line heading is printed on that line.

(D)   This line of the output will be printed at the top of each page that includes the listing of records of the file. LINE 7 indicates that when this line is printed, it should appear on line 7 of the page.

(E)   The purpose of any report is to list information from records in a file. The TYPE of such output is a DETAIL LINE. The program will reference this record, so it needs a name which appears before the TYPE clause. The PLUS 1 clause indicates that before a record is printed, the carriage control should cause the output device to advance to its next record. The values are supplied to the fields of this record by means of the SOURCE clause. The SOURCE clause acts like a MOVE statement. The field identified following SOURCE will have its contents moved to this field in the output record. In this case, S–NAME, S–AGE, and S–ALGEBRA which are fields defined in the STUDENT–RECORD in the WORKING–STORAGE SECTION are listed. The column clause indicates the location of the first byte of the receiving field.

(F)   It is unlikely that the STUDENT–FILE or any input file for the REPORT WRITER will necessarily have the records ordered as required by the report. Because it is not necessary to keep extra copies of a file available for an occasional report, a preprocessing step using the SORT verb works well. If the file to be processed has the required order, then this sentence can be removed and the report can be prepared as required. The column clause indicates the location of the first byte of receiving field.

(G)   At execution time the report process is begun with an INITIATE statement. The end of the report is indicated by a TERMINATE statement. These sentences activate the code needed to implement the report as described in the REPORT SECTION. The headings will be printed and all appropriate variables used by the report writing code will be initialized. For example, a line counter will be needed to make sure that detail lines occur on appropriate lines of the page.

(H)   As soon as all the fields referenced in the SOURCE clauses that may be needed for the next line of the report are ready, a detail line with this information is printed by means of a statement of the form

```
GENERATE detail-line
```

This statement will be repeated for every record to be listed.

The program just examined creates the same report as PROGRAM–NUMBER 11.1-2. It is instructive to compare the code of each of these programs to understand what is being accomplished by the syntax of REPORT WRITER.

Control Breaks and Automatic Summing Features

In the next program we examine the control break and automatic summing feature of the REPORT WRITER. The control break feature is identified by print patterns that include the CONTROL FOOTING clause in the 01-level portion of the record description. The summing feature is identified in the description of the field that will include the sum by means of the SUM clause. The report will also include a FINAL FOOTING for an indication that the report is finished.

```
          IDENTIFICATION DIVISION.
          PROGRAM-ID. RPRTTW.
      *
      * NAME:                ID:
      * PROGRAM-NUMBER: 11.2-2
      * DESCRIPTION: PREPARE A REPORT USING THE REPORT
      *    WRITER.  BREAK DOWN THE AMOUNT-DUE BY REGION
      *    BY YEAR.  INCLUDE A RECAP TOTAL AT THE END.
      *
          ENVIRONMENT DIVISION.
          CONFIGURATION SECTION.
          SOURCE-COMPUTER. IBM-370.
          OBJECT-COMPUTER. IBM-370.
          INPUT-OUTPUT SECTION.
          FILE-CONTROL.
              SELECT CUSTOMER-FILE
                  ASSIGN TO UT-3330-S-CONSUM3.
              SELECT FILE1
                  ASSIGN TO UT-3330-S-COBOL1.
              SELECT FILE2
                  ASSIGN TO UT-3330-S-COBOL2.
              SELECT PRINTER
                  ASSIGN TO UT-1403-S-SYSOUT.
          DATA DIVISION.
          FILE SECTION.
(A)       FD  PRINTER
              REPORT IS CUSTOMER-OWES
              LABEL RECORDS ARE OMITTED.
          FD  CUSTOMER-FILE
              LABEL RECORDS ARE STANDARD
              BLOCK CONTAINS 34 RECORDS.
          01  CUSTOMER-FILE-RECORD.
              05  FILLER  PIC X(100).
          FD  FILE1
              LABEL RECORDS ARE STANDARD
              BLOCK CONTAINS 34 RECORDS.
          01  FILE1-RECORD.
              05  FILLER PIC X(100).
          SD  FILE2.
          01  FILE2-RECORD.
              05  FILLER  PIC X(72).
              05  YEAR    PIC XX.
              05  FILLER  PIC X(15).
              05  REGION  PIC X.
              05  FILLER  PIC X(10).
```

```
            WORKING-STORAGE SECTION.
          * AUXILIARY STORAGE LOCATIONS
            77  END-OF-FILE    PIC X(8)  VALUE SPACES.
            77  SAVED-REGION   PIC X.
            77  SAVED-YEAR     PIC XX.
          * INPUT RECORD.
            01  CUSTOMER-RECORD.
                05  CR-CUST-ID   PIC X(8).
                05  CR-NAME      PIC X(20).
                05  FILLER       PIC X(44).
                05  CR-YEAR      PIC XX.
                05  FILLER       PIC X(6).
                05  CR-AMT-DUE   PIC 9(7)V99.
                05  CR-REGION    PIC X.
                05  FILLER       PIC X(10).


            REPORT SECTION.
(A)         RD  CUSTOMER-OWES
(B)             CONTROLS ARE FINAL, CR-REGION, CR-YEAR
                PAGE 58 LINES
                    HEADING 1
                    FIRST DETAIL 7
                    LAST DETAIL 46
                    FOOTING 52.
            01  TYPE REPORT HEADING.
                05  LINE 1 COLUMN 27 PIC X(60) VALUE
                    'CUSTOMER-FILE AMOUNT DUE BY REGION BY YEAR'.
                05  LINE 2 COLUMN 40 PIC X(20) VALUE
                    'JANUARY 3, 1985'.
            01  PAGE-HEAD TYPE PAGE HEADING LINE 6.
                05  COLUMN 5  PIC X(2)  VALUE 'ID'.
                05  COLUMN 20 PIC X(4)  VALUE 'NAME'.
                05  COLUMN 50 PIC X(6)  VALUE 'REGION'.
                05  COLUMN 60 PIC X(4)  VALUE 'YEAR'.
                05  COLUMN 70 PIC X(10) VALUE 'AMOUNT DUE'.
            01  DETAIL-INFO TYPE DETAIL LINE PLUS 1.
                05  COLUMN 5  PIC X(8)  SOURCE CR-CUST-ID.
                05  COLUMN 20 PIC X(20) SOURCE CR-NAME.
                05  COLUMN 50 PIC X     SOURCE CR-REGION.
                05  COLUMN 60 PIC XX    SOURCE CR-YEAR.
                05  COLUMN 70 PIC $$,$$$,$$$.99
                                        SOURCE CR-AMT-DUE.
(C)         01  TYPE CONTROL FOOTING CR-REGION LINE PLUS 2.
                05  COLUMN 30          PIC X(25)
                        VALUE 'TOTAL AMT-DUE FOR REGION'.
                05  COLUMN 56          PIC X
                        SOURCE SAVED-REGION.
                05  TOTAL-REG COLUMN 90 PIC $$,$$$,$$$.99BCR
                        SUM CR-AMT DUE.
(D)         01  TYPE CONTROL FOOTING CR-YEAR LINE PLUS 2.
                05  COLUMN 30          PIC X(23)
                        VALUE 'TOTAL AMT-DUE FOR YEAR'.
                05  COLUMN 54          PIC XX
                        SOURCE SAVED-YEAR.
                05  TOTAL-YEAR COLUMN 60 PIC $$,$$$,$$$.99 BCR
                        SUM CR-AMT-DUE.
```

```
(E)      01  TYPE CONTROL FOOTING FINAL LINE PLUS 3.
             05  COLUMN 30  PIC X(31)
                 VALUE 'TOTAL AMT-DUE FOR ALL CUSTOMERS'.
             05  COLUMN 110 PIC $$$,$$$,$$$.99BCR
                 SUM CR-AMT-DUE.


         PROCEDURE DIVISION.
(F)          SORT FILE2
                 ON ASCENDING KEY REGION
                                     YEAR
                 USING CUSTOMER-FILE
                 GIVING FILE1.
         * MODEL I
             OPEN INPUT FILE1
                  OUTPUT PRINTER.


         * INITIALIZATION
(G)          INITIATE CUSTOMER-OWES.


         * FILE PROCESSING PAIR
             PERFORM READ-FILE1.
             PERFORM DETAIL-REGION-YEAR
                UNTIL END-OF-FILE = HIGH-VALUES.


         * TERMINATION ACTIVITY
(G)          TERMINATE CUSTOMER-OWES.
             CLOSE FILE1
                   PRINTER.
             STOP RUN.


         * INPUT PROCEDURE
         READ-FILE1.
             READ FILE1 INTO CUSTOMER-RECORD
                 AT END MOVE HIGH-VALUES TO END-OF-FILE.


         * RECORD PROCESSING
         DETAIL-REGION-YEAR.
(G)          GENERATE DETAIL-INFO.
(H)          MOVE CR-YEAR   TO SAVED-YEAR.
             MOVE CR-REGION TO SAVED-REGION.
             PERFORM READ-FILE1.
```

(A)   In the FILE SECTION the name of the report described in the REPORT SECTION is given. The description of the various formats for records associated with that file are given in the REPORT SECTION where the report name is again used in an RD (report description) clause.

(B)   In addition to the description of how the lines and the page are divided among headings, detail lines, and footings, the control breaks that give additional form to the report are given in decreasing order of importance. This means that when a particular control break occurs, all following control breaks are assumed to happen also. A break in CR-REGION will imply that there is also a break in CR-YEAR. In this case a recap for the current value of CR-YEAR will be printed followed by a recap for the current value of CR-REGION.

(C)   This output record will be printed when the value of CR–REGION changes. The output will consist of appropriate headings as well as the sum of all the values of CR–AMT–DUE for records with the same value of CR–REGION. The variable TOTAL–REG will be initialized to zero automatically before the first record is processed as well as after the sum for one value of the variable CR–REGION has been recapped.

(D)   This output record will be printed when the value of CR–YEAR changes. The output will consist of appropriate headings as well as the sum of all the values of CR–AMT–DUE for records with the same value of CR–YEAR. The variable TOTAL–YEAR is used to accumulate all the values of CR–AMT–DUE from records with a fixed value of CR–YEAR. The program logic is of the form:

```
IF CR-REGION NOT EQUAL OLD-CR-REGION
   OR  CR-YEAR NOT EQUAL OLD-CR-YEAR
      PERFORM YEAR-RECAP.
```

The compound condition is needed in the first case because the value of CR–REGION does not have to change even though the more important control break does. For example, the values of CR–REGION and CR–YEAR could be the following:

CR–REGION	CR–YEAR
A	86
B	86
B	87

The variable TOTAL–YEAR is used to accumulate the values of CR–AMT–DUE in all records with the same value for CR–YEAR. This must be a separate variable from TOTAL–REG as TOTAL–REG printed may be the sum of several different printed values of TOTAL–YEAR. TOTAL–YEAR is only reset to zero when the value of CR–YEAR changes and the appropriate control break is executed.

(E)   This output record is printed when an end-of-file is encountered. The value printed is the sum of the value of CR–AMT–DUE in all the records in the file. The accumulation is automatically managed by the REPORT WRITER. This accumulator is initialized to zero at the beginning of the report. The other accumulators need to be distinct from this one, as it is possible for them to be reinitialized to zero several times while the file is being processed.

(F)   Preprocessing is needed so that the control breaks will operate correctly. The SORT will be by REGION by YEAR. The actual report will use the output file of the sort as its input file. If a report is needed and the file has the required ordering for the records, this SORT step may not be necessary. In this text, the SORT is necessary because the CUSTOMER–FILE is not ordered based on these fields. By using this preprocessing step, the programmer knows that the file will be organized in the way required for this application.

(G)   These two sentences are required to activate the REPORT WRITER. The name of the report is the same as the name identified in the report file and the RD level indicator of the REPORT SECTION.

(H)   When the control breaks are triggered, the value of CR–YEAR and CR–REGION are the values of the next category to use for accumulation purposes. The recap information is about a value of these variables that is no longer in these fields. In order to correctly identify the recap information, it is necessary to save the value of these fields as they existed before the next record is accessed. For this purpose, we allocate storage for two variables to hold the values. The SOURCE clause in the output records that recap the values of these variables use the special storage locations rather than the current value of CR–REGION and CR–YEAR.

SYNTAX SUMMARY

<u>FILE</u> <u>SECTION</u>
<u>FD</u> file-name

$$\left\{ \begin{array}{l} \underline{REPORT} \ \underline{IS} \\ \underline{REPORTS} \ \underline{ARE} \end{array} \right\} \ \text{report-name-1 [report-name-2]...}$$

[BLOCK CONTAINS clause]

$$\underline{LABEL} \ \underline{RECORDS} \ ARE \ \left\{ \begin{array}{l} \underline{OMITTED} \\ \underline{STANDARD} \end{array} \right\}$$

<u>REPORT</u> <u>SECTION</u>
<u>RD</u> report-name

$$\left[\left\{ \begin{array}{l} \underline{CONTROL} \ \underline{IS} \\ \underline{CONTROLS} \ \underline{ARE} \end{array} \right\} \left\{ \begin{array}{l} \underline{FINAL} \\ [\underline{FINAL}] \end{array} \right\} \ \text{identifier-1 [identifier-2]...} \right]$$

$$\left[\underline{PAGE} \left\{ \begin{array}{l} \underline{LIMIT} \ \underline{IS} \\ \underline{LIMITS} \ \underline{ARE} \end{array} \right\} \ \text{integer-1} \left\{ \begin{array}{l} \underline{LINE} \\ \underline{LINES} \end{array} \right\} \right.$$

$$[\underline{HEADING} \quad \text{integer-2}]$$
$$[\underline{FIRST} \ \underline{DETAIL} \ \text{integer-3}]$$
$$[\underline{LAST} \ \underline{DETAIL} \quad \text{integer-4}]$$
$$[\underline{FOOTING} \qquad \text{integer-5}]]$$

01 [data-name]

$$\underline{TYPE} \ IS \left[\begin{array}{l} \left\{ \begin{array}{l} \underline{REPORT} \ \underline{HEADING} \\ \underline{RH} \end{array} \right\} \\ \left\{ \begin{array}{l} \underline{PAGE} \ \underline{HEADING} \\ \underline{PH} \end{array} \right\} \\ \left\{ \begin{array}{l} \underline{CONTROL} \ \underline{HEADING} \\ \underline{CH} \end{array} \right\} \left\{ \begin{array}{l} \underline{FINAL} \\ \text{identifier-n} \end{array} \right\} \\ \left\{ \begin{array}{l} \underline{DETAIL} \\ \underline{DE} \end{array} \right\} \\ \left\{ \begin{array}{l} \underline{CONTROL} \ \underline{FOOTING} \\ \underline{CF} \end{array} \right\} \left\{ \begin{array}{l} \text{identifier-}n \\ \underline{FINAL} \end{array} \right\} \\ \left\{ \begin{array}{l} \underline{PAGE} \ \underline{FOOTING} \\ \underline{PF} \end{array} \right\} \\ \left\{ \begin{array}{l} \underline{REPORT} \ \underline{FOOTING} \\ \underline{RF} \end{array} \right\} \end{array} \right.$$

$$\left[\underline{LINE} \ NUMBER \ IS \ \left\{ \begin{array}{l} \text{integer-1} \\ \underline{PLUS} \ \text{integer-2} \\ \underline{NEXT} \ \underline{PAGE} \end{array} \right\} \right]$$

EXERCISES

1. What are the major classifications for printed lines in a report?

2. What code in a program using the REPORT WRITER makes it impossible to use TEXTA?

3. Explain the syntax and the semantics of the verbs INITIATE, TERMINATE, and GENERATE.

4. Explain the syntax and the semantics for field descriptions using SOURCE or SUM clauses.

5. Is there a difference between a control break and a TYPE CONTROL FOOTING clause?

6. Complete the REPORT SECTION for a report having at most 35 detail lines to a page and the form as indicated below.

```
REPORT HEADING
      THE NEW-WORLD INSURANCE CO.
        WILLIAM COLES, PRESIDENT

PAGE HEADING

CUSTOMER NAME          CUSTOMER ADDRESS          INSURANCE AMOUNT


DETAIL LINE
   ---20-----    ---10-----  ---10-----
  XX-------X    XXX------X  XXX------X          $,$$$,$$$
     (NAME)       (STREET)    (CITY)              AMOUNT

PAGE NUMBERING
Center the numbers on a line after skipping one line after the last detail line
printed on the page. The number should start with 1 and increase by 1 for
each additional page in the report.
```

PROGRAMMING PROBLEMS

Use the REPORT WRITER feature of COBOL to generate each of the reports described.

1. Using the CUSTOMER-FILE for input, list the NAME, AMOUNT-DUE, and REGION for each customer. Include both report and page headings. List 40 detail lines on a page.

2. Using the CUSTOMER-FILE for input, list the total AMOUNT-DUE by REGION. Also include the total for all regions at the end of the report. Include at most 40 detail lines on a page. Use appropriate report, detail page, and end-of-report headings.

3. Using the NEW-WORLD-FILE for input, list the AMOUNT-DUE by CREDIT-RATING. Include at most 40 detail lines on a page. Use headings for the report and the detail line pages. Include the total amount due for all records at the end of the report.

4. Using the NEW-WORLD-FILE for input, list the AMOUNT-DUE by CREDIT-RATING by STATE. Include at most 40 detail lines on a page. Include the total amount due for all records at the end of the report. Include appropriate headings for the report and the pages of detail lines.

Chapter Review

SUMMARY

Using the REPORT WRITER effectively depends on learning the special names for features that can be included in a report. The syntax can then be associated with a function and the whole programming process made easier.

By listing the features of a report, you can begin to see why all the syntax is needed. A report needs a heading. This heading, like a title page in a book, appears once at the beginning. In a report each page also needs a heading. Each page may also have a heading for the detail lines that are to be printed. The bottom of a page normally has page numbers. These all give an overall form to the report and require one or more record descriptions.

The next part of the report is the detail line for each record of the file. The detail line is filled with information from storage by means of the GENERATE verb in the PROCEDURE DIVISION. Detail lines are filled by indicating in the SOURCE clauses where information is found that is to be displayed in a particular field of the output record.

Two additional features are used in many reports. These features are use of a control break and accumulation of the values in one field of a record. The control break recap record is identified by the TYPE CONTROL clause in the REPORT SECTION. COBOL automatically tests for the control break and writes the appropriate recap information when a control break occurs. TYPE CONTROL records are also used to recap information at the bottom of a page or at the end of a report. The automatic accumulation of values from a single field is caused by the SUM clause which indicates that the field being described should be given the value of the sum of the values found in the field whose name appears after SUM.

This chapter began with a detailed description of the stepwise refinement process used for constructing a report. This introduction introduced features that are available in REPORT WRITER. REPORT WRITER is very useful because of the number of options normally needed in a report. A good strategy for using REPORT WRITER is to apply stepwise refinement in building a report. The detail lines should be completed, then the report should have the headings added, and finally the control breaks should be incorporated. Using this three-step process increases the utility of REPORT WRITER.

TEST YOURSELF

1. What is stepwise refinement?
2. What is a detail line in a report?
3. What is a report heading?
4. What is a page heading?
5. What sections of the DATA DIVISION have entries pertaining to a report written by REPORT WRITER?
6. How is the number of detail lines to be printed on a page indicated when using REPORT WRITER? When not using REPORT WRITER?
7. What is the role of a TYPE CONTROL FOOTING clause?
8. How is a control break incorporated into a report using REPORT WRITER?
9. Explain the syntax and the semantics of the verb GENERATE.
10. Explain the syntax and the semantics of the verbs INITIATE and TERMINATE.
11. Explain the syntax and the semantics of the SOURCE clause.
12. Explain the syntax and the semantics of the SUM clause.

12

Direct Access Processing

Chapter Objectives

After studying this chapter you should be able to

- describe the different methods of file organization and know how to access records using each method;
- write a program to access, update, and replace records on a file with an indexed sequential file organization;
- write a program to access, update, and replace records on a file with a relative file organization.

Chapter Outline

12.1   Introduction to Direct Access Processing

Direct Access Storage on a Disk or Disk Pack

We have previously dealt with files organized sequentially; records in the file are stored and processed one after the other. Records in a sequential file are usually kept on magnetic tape, magnetic disk, or punched cards. To access these records, the computer must read the file in sequence from the beginning. To locate a particular record, the computer program must read and test each record in sequence. If only one record in a sequential file is needed, the computer would read, on the average, about half of the file before finding the record wanted. Figure 12.1.1 shows a disk and a tape organized sequentially.

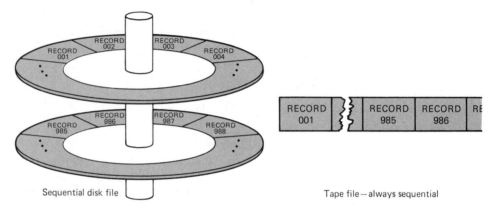

Sequential disk file

Tape file—always sequential

Figure 12.1.1 Sequential file organization on disk and tape.

Obviously, a sequential file organization with sequential (batch) processing is efficient when a high percentage of the records need to be accessed. Applications such as payroll, billing, student registration, and preparation of mailing labels are examples where sequential processing is efficient. However, there are many applications that do not meet these conditions. The sequential file organization is not an efficient method when only small numbers of records from a large file are required for processing, when the records need to be accessed in some sequence other than the one in which the file is organized, and when input is entered randomly to update a file or make inquiries about a particular record on a file. Suppose, for example, that management needs to make frequent daily inquiries about the status of customers in the CUSTOMER–FILE. If such inquiries are of a significant number and are made randomly, then the time to read each record one after the other could be excessive. Clearly, alternative methods of file organization are needed to meet these and other similar user needs. Three commonly used methods of file organization are **indexed, random (direct),** and **relative.**

These methods permit direct access processing—processing of records directly or randomly without accessing each record from the beginning of the file to the end. So far in this discussion, we have used terms such as direct access processing and direct file organization without explaining the terminology. Figure 12.1.2 summarizes the relationship between the way a file is organized and the resulting methods used to access the records and process the program.

Direct access processing using direct, indexed, or relative file organizations requires a storage medium suited for these types of file organizations. Magnetic disks are the most popular medium for direct-access secondary storage. All magnetic disks are round platters coated with a surface that is magnetized, but the similarities end there. As Figure 12.1.3 shows, they come in different sizes and configurations, they can be portable (removable)

Type of file organization	A record can be accessed	Method of processing is called
Sequential	Sequentially	Batch (sequential)
Indexed	Sequentially, or randomly via index	Sequential, Indexed, or Direct Access
Relative	Sequentially, or randomly via relative key	Sequential or Direct Access
Direct (random)	Randomly via hashing function	Direct Access

Figure 12.1.2 *File organizations and accessing methods.*

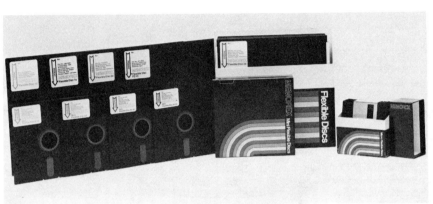

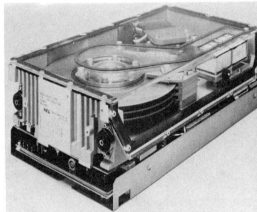

(a)   *(b)*

(c)   *(d)*

Figure 12.1.3 *Types of disks and disk drives. (a) Floppy disks. Small portable, flexible disks or diskettes packed in protective envelopes. Currently the most popular online secondary storage medium for microcomputers and intelligent terminals. (b) Winchester disks. Small rigid disks permanently housed in Winchester disk drives. (c) Large- and medium-sized disks in permanent cabinets. These are used in most types of large main-frames and minicomputers but not microcomputer systems. (d) Medium-sized disks packaged in removable disk packs. These are also used in all but the smallest systems. Photo (a) courtesy of Memorex Corporation. Photo (b) courtesy of NEC Information Systems, Inc. Photos (c) and (d) courtesy of Digital Equipment Corporation.*

or permanently mounted in their devices (called disk drives), and they can be constructed of rigid or flexible materials.

Figure 12.1.4 illustrates a typical disk pack with eleven platters, and shows how data is read or written on the surfaces with multiple read/write heads. The read/write heads are moved in and out together by the access mechanism. Data is stored on the surfaces and each surface is divided into tracks as Figure 12.1.5 illustrates. The track number is also called a track index.

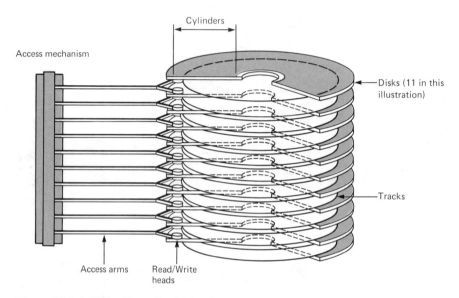

Figure 12.1.4 *Disk with read/write heads.*

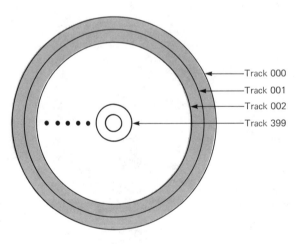

Figure 12.1.5 *Tracks on a disk surface.*

The amount of data that can be stored on each track varies from manufacturer to manufacturer. Typically, each track can store thousands and even tens of thousands of bytes. Storage capacity of a disk pack is usually millions of bytes (megabytes).

The cylinder concept is an important feature of disk packs. Visualize all tracks numbered 050 on the pack as shown in Figure 12.1.6.

The stack of tracks can then be thought of as a **cylinder.** A disk pack with 800 tracks would have 800 cylinders as illustrated in Figure 12.1.7.

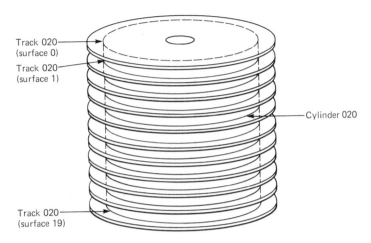

Figure 12.1.6 Cylinder of a disk pack.

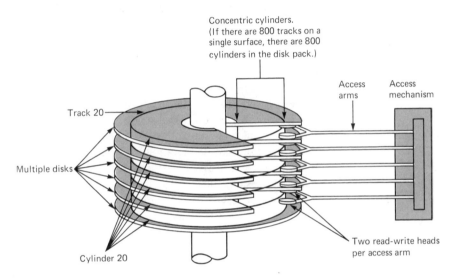

Figure 12.1.7 Tracks and cylinders.

Fortunately, the COBOL programmer can rely on the operating system to assign storage locations based on track and cylinder numbers. Nevertheless, an understanding of how disks are physically organized should prove helpful in later problems.

With this brief but essential introduction to direct access storage on a disk or disk packs, we will now work through an example of what is called a hashing technique for direct (random) file organization.

Direct (Random) File Organization Using the Hashing Technique

In this type of file, records are accessed by a record key that uses some arithmetic calculations based on values in the record to determine the actual physical address (cylinder and track numbers). Suppose that a disk area could be laid out with 100 areas, each of which could hold one record of the file. Furthermore, suppose that we have a file of 100 records that are stored in these 100 disk locations. Now suppose a particular record needs to be accessed. Provided that we know which of the 100 areas holds this record, we can directly access it. Two problems need to be resolved. First, how do we decide which record goes into which area? Second, how does the program know which area is to be accessed? The first problem is resolved by means of a function defined on a field or fields of a record that gives a value indicating which area should hold this record. As a simple example, the CUSTOMER–FILE has customer identification numbers ranging from 51900000 to 51909900 by increments of 100. By isolating the fifth and sixth digit of the CUSTOMER–ID we can associate a unique storage area with a record of CUSTOMER–FILE. We use the fifth and sixth digits as a number between zero and ninety-nine. By adding one to the value of these two digits we obtain a number between one and one hundred which will then be used to identify the storage location for that record. A function that associates a record with a storage area by means of a calculation based on a field or fields of the record is called a **hashing function.** It is a very fortunate occurrence when a function can be found that will uniquely distribute the records of a file among a set of storage locations. In case two records have the same value for the hashing function, a **collision** is said to occur. There are various strategies for resolving collisions, but a detailed discussion of collision resolution strategies is beyond the scope of this brief overview of file organization.

Let us assume for the sake of simplicity that there is a function that uniquely associates a record of a file with a storage location on disk. Knowing the physical location of the record needed allows us to instruct the operating system to access it directly and then to process that record. Similarly, if we are storing records of a file so that they can be accessed later using this method, we first use the field or fields of the record to calculate the value of an appropriate function that indicates the storage location to use for storing this record and then put the record in the corresponding location.

To familiarize you with the direct access method using hashing, we will work through loading and using a file with five records. We assume that the storage area for the file can hold seven records. Allowing for extra space reduces the likelihood of collisions. The records we process consist of two fields, an identification number field and a name field. The hashing function to indicate the storage location for a record will use the remainder that results from dividing the identification number by seven. When there is zero remainder, we use 7 as the hashing value. (This is a common type of function; but there are other methods possible for a programmer to use.)

RECORD	HASHING VALUE
816 JONES, WILLIAM	$4 = 816 - 116 * 7$

SECONDARY STORAGE

1	
2	
3	
4	816 JONES, WILLIAM
5	
6	
7	

RECORD	HASHING VALUE
983 SMITH, PHIL	$3 = 983 - 140 * 7$

SECONDARY STORAGE

1	
2	
3	983 SMITH, PHIL
4	816 JONES, WILLIAM
5	
6	
7	

	RECORD	HASHING VALUE
586	BROWN, GEORGE	$5 = 586 - 83 * 7$

SECONDARY STORAGE

1		
2		
3	983	SMITH, PHIL
4	816	JONES, WILLIAM
5	586	BROWN, GEORGE
6		
7		

	RECORD	HASHING VALUE
391	CYR, MARY	$6 = 391 - 55 * 7$

SECONDARY STORAGE

1		
2		
3	983	SMITH, PHIL
4	816	JONES, WILLIAM
5	586	BROWN, GEORGE
6	391	CYR, MARY
7		

	RECORD	HASHING VALUE
635	WILLIAMS, SUE	$5 = 635 - 90 * 7$

SECONDARY STORAGE

1			
2			
3	983	SMITH, PHIL	
4	816	JONES, WILLIAM	
5	586	BROWN, GEORGE	COLLISION
6	391	CYR, MARY	
7			

Since storage location five already contains the record belonging to BROWN, there is a collision to resolve. A simple strategy for collision resolution is just to proceed in order through the rest of the storage areas looking for the first empty storage location. When an empty storage location is found, put the new record there. If this search starts toward the end of the storage area, it may be necessary to continue at the top of the area if no empty location is found at the bottom of the storage area. In this case the first empty location encountered is storage location seven. The final storage configuration will be

SECONDARY STORAGE

1		
2		
3	983	SMITH, PHIL
4	816	JONES, WILLIAM
5	586	BROWN, GEORGE
6	391	CYR, MARY
7	635	WILLIAMS, SUE

Once the file is loaded into secondary storage, processes such as file updating can be executed. Because deletions can cause special problems, we will go through a file updating cycle that deletes the record belonging to CYR and changes the first name in WILLIAMS' record to SUSAN.

UPDATE CYCLE

DELETE	HASHING VALUE
391 CYR, MARY	$6 = 391 - 55 * 7$

Check to see if the record in location six belongs to CYR. Since it does, proceed with the deletion.

SECONDARY STORAGE

1	
2	
3	983 SMITH, PHIL
4	816 JONES, WILLIAM
5	586 BROWN, GEORGE
6	
7	635 WILLIAMS, SUE

UPDATE	HASHING VALUE
635 WILLIAMS, SUSAN	$5 = 635 - 90 * 7$

SECONDARY STORAGE

1	
2	
3	983 SMITH, PHIL
4	816 JONES, WILLIAM
5	586 BROWN, GEORGE
6	
7	635 WILLIAMS, SUE

The record needed is not in location five. Since there may have been a collision when the record was first added, we must continue the search until an empty location is found or the record itself is found. Since this record was added in location seven and we have deleted the record at location six, the program will think that there is no record in the file with identification number 635. One way to resolve this problem is to add a one-byte field to each storage location. The storage location contains a value 'E' if the location has never contained a record, an 'F' if it contains a record, and a 'D' if it did contain a record before a delete operation. The secondary storage for the sample file then becomes

SECONDARY STORAGE

1		E
2		E
3	983 SMITH, PHIL	F
4	816 JONES, WILLIAM	F
5	586 BROWN, GEORGE	F
6		D
7	635 WILLIAMS, SUE	F

We now know that when looking for the record with identification number 635 we should continue the search past storage location six. We find the needed record in storage location seven. The final configuration of the file is

SECONDARY STORAGE

1		E
2		E
3	983 SMITH, PHIL	F
4	816 JONES, WILLIAM	F
5	586 BROWN, GEORGE	F
6		D
7	635 WILLIAMS, SUSAN	F

If the next operation involves the addition of a record that had a hashing value 3, 4, 5, or 6, we could use storage location six for the new record. The capability to reuse a storage location immediately after the deletion of a record is one feature not available with some other file organizations.

EXERCISES

1. Briefly define the following terms:

   a. track   e. hashing
   b. cylinder   f. collision
   c. removable disk   g. hashing function
   d. floppy disk   h. collision resolution

2. Suppose BOXES is a table with thirteen entries. Using the remainder when a number is divided by 13 (use 13 as the value when the remainder is zero) as a hashing function defined on the ID field for the records listed below, indicate the contents of each location in BOXES after the file given below is processed. The value in the field called CODE should be put in the entry of BOXES. Resolve collisions by finding the first empty location following the location given by the hashing function. Process the records in the order indicated.

ID	CODE		ID	CODE
1. 24	A	8. 37	B
2. 41	C	9. 56	D
3. 73	E	10. 91	F
4. 82	G	11. 77	H
5. 69	I	12. 71	J
6. 83	K	13. 97	L
7. 38	M		

3. Determine the contents of the file shown below after the indicated modifications are made.

CURRENT STATUS OF FILE

1		E
2		E
3	983 SMITH, PHIL	F
4	816 JONES, WILLIAM	F
5	586 BROWN, GEORGE	F
6		D
7	635 WILLIAMS, SUSAN	F

Process records in the order they are listed.

```
                RECORD MODIFICATIONS
        DELETE   983   SMITH, PHIL
        ADD      716   JONES, GRETA
        ADD      918   BILLS, ALLAN
        DELETE   816   JONES, WILLIAM
        ADD      777   GREEN, GEORGE
        ADD      784   BLUE, VIVIAN
```

Remember that the deletion process is more than just replacing data with blanks.

12.2   Introduction to Indexed File Organization

Indexed files use a file organization that allows both sequential and random access to records of a file. Recall that a disk pack normally looks like a number of phonograph records stacked one on top of another with room between consecutive recording surfaces so that a read/write mechanism can be placed at any point on the surface. The grooves on which information is recorded are concentric circles called **tracks.** The tracks are numbered consecutively beginning with zero. All the tracks with the same number form a **cylinder.** The records of an indexed file are loaded by filling the tracks of one cylinder at a time.

The records of a file can be organized as an indexed file provided the values of one field in each record can be used uniquely to determine the record. This field, called a **key field,** is used to order the records. If the indexed file is accessed as a sequential file, the records are in increasing order as determined by the key field. As the file is loaded, indexes are created that will be used for subsequent direct access to the records of the file. The chief index is a **cylinder index.** The value of this index consists of an entry for each cylinder that contains records of the file and is the largest key value that occurs in a record in the cylinder. These values are stored in increasing order. By a sequential search of this index it is possible to identify the cylinder that contains the record sought. For each cylinder a similar index is constructed that contains as values the largest key value that occurs in a record in each track of the cylinder. These values are also stored in sequential order. By a sequential search of this index it is possible to identify the track within the cylinder that contains the record sought. Both the cylinder index and each cylinder's **track index** are assigned values by the operating system when the file is organized and created.

The fact that the records of the file are ordered in increasing order by value of the key field means that if two consecutive entries in the cylinder index are 318 and 596, then one knows immediately that a record with key value ranging from 319 to 596 is contained on the track of the cylinder with cylinder index 596. Before exploring an example in detail, we need to see how records are handled when added to an indexed file.

Adding Records to an Indexed File

Suppose a track contains at most three records from a file. A particular track contains records that have key values

318   325   331

If a record with key value 321 is added to the file, then this clearly is the track on which it belongs. If we put the new record in place and shift following records forward, the track becomes

318   321   325

The record with key value 331 cannot be placed on the track. It is inappropriate to advance all the remaining records in the file to make room for a record with key value 321. To handle this problem an indexed file consists of two storage areas called the **prime area** and the **overflow area.** The prime area consists of the cylinders that contain the file when it is first loaded. The overflow area is reserved to hold records (like the one with key value 331) that are removed from a track to make room for the addition of a new record. A track can be thought of as a certain physical space on a cylinder or it can be thought of as a logical entity consisting of all the records that should occur on a single physical track. We saw a similar distinction when examining blocked records, earlier in the text. The records in a block are one physical record, but logically may be a number of records. As with blocking, the linking of records in the overflow area with tracks of the prime area is done by the operating system and does not involve direct coding by the programmer. In Section 12.4 we will study the COBOL commands that cause the operating system to add records to an indexed file. The discussion which follows is designed to give an understanding of what happens without direct programmer intervention.

The detailed example we will examine shows how the indexes are modified as a result of adding records to an indexed file. The example will consist of a file occupying three cylinders that consist of three tracks containing three records per track. We use this small example to see how the operating system manages an indexed file. We will represent records in this file by their unique key value. Although different manufacturers have different schemes for storing indexed files, the one described here is widely used and exhibits all the problems any scheme must resolve.

INDEXED FILE

TRACK	CYLINDER 1			CYLINDER 2			CYLINDER 3		
1	34	49	56	484	501	518	833	878	890
2	101	187	269	526	646	765	903	930	1016
3	273	289	482	776	778	830	1049	1111	

The cylinder index is easy to form as it is.

CYLINDER INDEX

CYLINDER	KEY
1	482
2	830
3	1111

We assume that the overflow area consists of one cylinder that is located apart from the prime area. The track indexes are also easy to form when the file is loaded and the overflow area is empty.

TRACK INDEXES

CYLINDER 1				CYLINDER 2				CYLINDER 3			
PRIME		OVERFLOW		PRIME		OVERFLOW		PRIME		OVERFLOW	
TRACK	KEY	TRACK	KEY	TRACK	KEY	TRACK	KEY	TRACK	KEY	TRACK	KEY
1	56	1	56	1	518	1	518	1	890	1	890
2	269	2	269	2	765	2	765	2	1016	2	1016
3	482	3	482	3	830	3	830	3	1111	3	1111

The prime and overflow index entries are the same when no record that belongs on that track is found in the overflow area. The complete picture of the prime and overflow area as well as the indexes follow.

INDEXED FILE

PRIME AREA

TRACK	CYLINDER 1			CYLINDER 2			CYLINDER 3		
1	34	49	56	484	501	518	833	878	890
2	101	187	269	526	646	765	903	930	1016
3	273	289	482	776	778	830	1049	1111	

OVERFLOW AREA

TRACK	CYLINDER 70		
1			
2			
3			

CYLINDER INDEX

CYLINDER	KEY
1	482
2	830
3	1111

TRACK INDEXES

CYLINDER 1				CYLINDER 2				CYLINDER 3			
PRIME		OVERFLOW		PRIME		OVERFLOW		PRIME		OVERFLOW	
TRACK	KEY	TRACK	KEY	TRACK	KEY	TRACK	KEY	TRACK	KEY	TRACK	KEY
1	56	1	56	1	518	1	518	1	890	1	890
2	269	2	269	2	765	2	765	2	1016	2	1016
3	482	3	482	3	830	3	830	3	1111	3	1111

We next see how the picture changes after adding to the file records with key values 165, 1103, and 681.

INDEXED FILES

PRIME AREA

TRACK	CYLINDER 1			CYLINDER 2			CYLINDER 3		
1	34	49	56	484	501	518	833	878	890
2	101	165	187	526	646	681	903	930	1016
3	273	289	482	776	778	830	1049	1103	1111

OVERFLOW AREA

TRACK	CYLINDER 70		
1	269 ***	765 ***	
2			
3			

CYLINDER INDEX

CYLINDER	KEY
1	482
2	830
3	1111

TRACK INDEXES

CYLINDER 1				CYLINDER 2				CYLINDER 3			
PRIME		OVERFLOW		PRIME		OVERFLOW		PRIME		OVERFLOW	
TRACK	KEY	TRACK	KEY	TRACK	KEY	TRACK	KEY	TRACK	KEY	TRACK	KEY
1	56	1	56	1	518	1	518	1	890	1	890
2	187	T1,R1	269	2	681	T1,R2	765	2	1016	2	1016
3	482	3	482	3	830	3	830	3	1111	3	1111

The notation T1,R1 indicates that the next record on this logical track is found as record 1 on track 1 of the overflow area. The 187 entry indicates the largest key on physical track number 2 of cylinder 1. The value 269 indicates the largest key on logical track 2.

The next representation of the file shows what the file and its indexes contain after adding records with key values 659 and 987.

INDEXED FILES

PRIME AREA

TRACK	CYLINDER 1			CYLINDER 2			CYLINDER 3		
1	34	49	56	484	501	518	833	878	890
2	101	165	187	526	646	659	903	930	987
3	273	289	482	776	778	830	1049	1103	1111

OVERFLOW AREA

TRACK	CYLINDER 70		
1	269 ***	765 ***	681 T1,R2
2	1016 ***		
3			

CYLINDER INDEX

CYLINDER	KEY
1	482
2	830
3	1111

TRACK INDEXES

CYLINDER 1				CYLINDER 2				CYLINDER 3			
PRIME		OVERFLOW		PRIME		OVERFLOW		PRIME		OVERFLOW	
TRACK	KEY	TRACK	KEY	TRACK	KEY	TRACK	KEY	TRACK	KEY	TRACK	KEY
1	56	1	56	1	518	1	518	1	890	1	890
2	187	T1,R1	269	2	659	T1,R3	765	2	987	T2,R1	1016
3	482	3	482	3	830	3	830	3	1111	3	1111

The notation 681 T1,R2 on track 1 of the overflow area indicates that the next entry on this logical track after 681 is found as record 2 of track 1 of the overflow area. The *** notation indicates that there is currently no next entry in the overflow area for this logical track.

As one observes, the linkages between tracks and the overflow area become increasingly complex. This complexity must be handled with software routines that eventually can cause deterioration in the level of performance. This can further necessitate reading the file sequentially by increasing key value and storing it on a utility file. When the file is completely on the utility file, the creation of an indexed file is executed using this file for input. This will create a new indexed file and associated indexes with the same records as in the previous indexed file, but now the overflow area will again be empty.

EXERCISES

1. Briefly define the following terms:

   a. indexed file   d. track index
   b. prime storage area   e. cylinder index
   c. overflow storage area

2. Can an indexed file be processed sequentially?
3. How must a file be preprocessed before being organized as an indexed file?

4. How does the operating system determine where a record is stored if the file is organized as an indexed file?
5. What strategy is used to improve the performance of random access once the overflow area of an indexed file is nearly full.
6. Compare and contrast relative file organization and indexed file organization. List advantages and disadvantages for each.
7. Determine the contents of the indexed file shown below after the indicated modifications are made.

CURRENT STATUS FOR INDEXED FILE

PRIME AREA

TRACK	CYLINDER 1			CYLINDER 2			CYLINDER 3		
1	34	49	56	484	501	518	833	878	890
2	101	165	187	526	646	659	903	930	987
3	273	289	482	776	778	830	1049	1103	1111

OVERFLOW AREA

TRACK	CYLINDER 70		
1	269 ***	765 ***	681 T1,R2
2	1016 ***		
3			

CYLINDER INDEX

CYLINDER	KEY
1	482
2	830
3	1111

TRACK INDEXES

CYLINDER 1				CYLINDER 2				CYLINDER 3			
PRIME		OVERFLOW		PRIME		OVERFLOW		PRIME		OVERFLOW	
TRACK	KEY	TRACK	KEY	TRACK	KEY	TRACK	KEY	TRACK	KEY	TRACK	KEY
1	56	1	56	1	518	1	518	1	890	1	890
2	187	T1,R1	269	2	659	T1,R3	765	2	987	T2,R1	1016
3	482	3	482	3	830	3	830	3	1111	3	1111

RECORD MODIFICATIONS

OPERATION	KEY
ADD	87
DELETE	890
DELETE	765
ADD	1105
ADD	783
DELETE	289

Indicate deleted records by placing a D following the key value. Remember that with an indexed file organization, deletions are really detected when the record is read and the status field is checked.

12.3   Programming With Relative Files

A relative file allows direct access to any record in the file. If necessary, it is also possible to process a relative file as a sequential file. In the processing of record updates, it is convenient to be able to access directly just the records needed. On the other hand, if all the records are to be listed, there is no advantage to direct access as opposed to sequential access. The relative file organization allows the access method to be chosen to suit the application.

The programs we will examine process a file that will be loaded with the records of the CUSTOMER–FILE, but organized as a relative file. We are able to use a relative file organization conveniently for this file because the CUSTOMER–NUMBER field of each record can uniquely be associated with a number between one and one hundred. Using this uniquely determined value will give a way to determine where to store the record in the relative file. Also by means of this number, a record can be accessed directly from the relative file. The computation to calculate the value associated with a record takes advantage of the fact that the CUSTOMER–NUMBER is of the form 5190XX00 where the two digits represented by XX have a value that ranges between zero and ninety-nine. By adding one to the value of these digits in a record, we can get a number between one and one hundred. This calculation will be used as the hashing function for locating records of the relative file. This hashing function will not cause any collisions.

We assume that any records added to the file are handled by another file maintenance procedure that also does the data verification before including a record in the file. In this application we will not do any physical deletion of records from this file, even though it is possible in COBOL. The assumption that leads to this decision is that periodically it is necessary to make a report of all the records that have been deleted during a particular time period. By using a deletion by marking procedure, we will be able to determine at a later date all the records that have been deleted. At that time it will be a normal procedure to physically delete these records marked as deleted and reorganize the file.

Creating a Relative File
Using Sequential Access

The first program must load the CUSTOMER–FILE onto the file CREATE–RELA organized as a relative file. This program will only write records to the relative file so we can use the relative file as a sequential file.

```
IDENTIFICATION DIVISION.
PROGRAM-ID. RELALOAD.
*
* NAME:            ID:
* PROGRAM-NUMBER: 12.3-1
* DESCRIPTION:  LOAD THE CUSTOMER-FILE ONTO FILE1
*    SO THAT CREATE-RELA IS ORGANIZED AS A RELATIVE FILE.
*
ENVIRONMENT DIVISION.
CONFIGURATION SECTION.
SOURCE-COMPUTER. IBM-370.
OBJECT-COMPUTER. IBM-370.
INPUT-OUTPUT SECTION.
FILE-CONTROL.
    SELECT PRINTER
        ASSIGN TO UT-1403-S-SYSOUT.
    SELECT CUSTOMER-FILE
        ASSIGN TO UT-3330-S-CONSUM3.
    SELECT CREATE-RELA
        ASSIGN TO UT-3330-I-COBOL1
        ORGANIZATION IS RELATIVE
        ACCESS IS SEQUENTIAL.
```

(A)

```
          DATA DIVISION.
          FILE SECTION.
          FD  CUSTOMER-FILE
              LABEL RECORDS ARE STANDARD
              BLOCK CONTAINS 34 RECORDS.
          01  CUSTOMER-FILE-RECORD.
              05  FIELDS-OF-INFORMATION    PIC X(91).
              05  FILLER                   PIC X(9).
          FD  PRINTER
              LABEL RECORDS ARE OMITTED.
          01  PRINT-LINE.
              05  FILLER           PIC X.
              05  DATA-AREA-OUT    PIC X(132).
          FD  CREATE-RELA
              LABEL RECORDS ARE STANDARD.
          01  CREATE-RELA-RECORD.
              05  DATA-AREA            PIC X(99).
              05  STATUS-CODE          PIC X.


          WORKING-STORAGE SECTION.
        * AUXILIARY STORAGE LOCATIONS.
          77  END-OF-FILE     PIC X(8) VALUE SPACES.
          77  A-CODE          PIC X    VALUE 'A'.



          PROCEDURE DIVISION.
        * MODEL I
              OPEN INPUT CUSTOMER-FILE
                   OUTPUT CREATE-RELA.


        * FILE PROCESSING PAIR
              PERFORM READ-CUSTOMER-FILE.
              PERFORM LOAD-RELATIVE-FILE
                  UNTIL END-OF-FILE = HIGH-VALUES.


        * TERMINATION ACTIVITY
              CLOSE CUSTOMER-FILE
                    CREATE-RELA
                    PRINTER.
              STOP RUN.


        * INPUT PROCEDURE
          READ-CUSTOMER-FILE.
              READ CUSTOMER-FILE
                  AT END MOVE HIGH-VALUES TO END-OF-FILE.


        * RECORD PROCESSING
          LOAD-RELATIVE-FILE.
(B)           MOVE FIELDS-OF-INFORMATION    TO DATA-AREA.
              MOVE A-CODE                   TO STATUS-CODE.
(C)           WRITE CREATE-RELA-RECORD
                  INVALID KEY PERFORM ERROR-RTN.
              PERFORM READ-CUSTOMER-FILE.
          ERROR-RTN.
              MOVE CUSTOMER-FILE-RECORD TO DATA-AREA-OUT.
              WRITE PRINT-LINE.
```

(A)   The SELECT clause has more functions to perform in the case of a direct access file. The kind of file organization and the way that the records of the file will be accessed must be identified. This allows the system to process the file in an appropriate manner. When no special organization or access mode is noted, the system assumes that the file is organized as a sequential file and is going to be accessed sequentially. The I in the ASSIGN clause indicates that the file organization is either indexed or relative.

(B)   The CUSTOMER–FILE has 91 bytes of information and 9 extra bytes of space for future use. The information portion of the CUSTOMER–FILE–RECORD is put in the first 99 bytes of the record that will be written onto the relative file. The 100th byte of each record in the relative file will hold the status code for the record. The code will be either 'A' for active records, 'E' for empty record areas, or 'D' for records marked deleted.

(C)   The first time the WRITE command is executed, record number one of the relative file is loaded. Since the access to the file CREATE–RELA is sequential, the records will be put on the relative file in the same order as they are read from the CUSTOMER–FILE. This will accomplish what is required because the records of CUSTOMER–FILE are already sequenced by the values in the field CUSTOMER–NUMBER. The INVALID KEY clause is required when writing to a relative file. The code that follows it is only executed when an invalid value for the relative key is used.

Direct Access of a Relative File

The next program will show how direct access is accomplished. The file maintenance will be limited to changing the amount due field or changing the status code to represent deletion. The appropriate action will be determined by examining the code contained in byte one of the input record.

```
      IDENTIFICATION DIVISION.
      PROGRAM-ID.  RELACORD.
*
* NAME:              ID:
* PROGRAM-NUMBER: 12.3-2
* DESCRIPTION: PROCESS CHANGES TO THE AMOUNT-DUE
*   FIELD OR CHANGE THE STATUS OF A RECORD
*   ON CREATED-RELA TO DELETE.  CREATED-RELA IS
*   ORGANIZED AS A RELATIVE FILE.
*
      ENVIRONMENT DIVISION.
      CONFIGURATION SECTION.
      SOURCE-COMPUTER. IBM-370.
      OBJECT-COMPUTER. IBM-370.
      INPUT-OUTPUT SECTION.
      FILE-CONTROL.
          SELECT CREATE-RELA
              ASSIGN TO UT-3330-I-COBOL1
              ORGANIZATION IS RELATIVE
              ACCESS IS RANDOM
              RELATIVE KEY IS WORK-VALUE.
          SELECT CARD-READER
              ASSIGN TO UT-2540-S-SYSIN.
          SELECT PRINTER
              ASSIGN TO UT-1403-S-SYSOUT.
      DATA DIVISION.
      FILE SECTION.
      FD  CREATE-RELA
          LABEL RECORDS ARE STANDARD.
```

```
* OUTPUT RECORD
  01   CREATE-RELA-RECORD.
       05   FILLER       PIC X(80).
       05   AMT DUE       PIC S9(7)V99.
       05   FILLER       PIC X(10).
       05   STATUS-CODE  PIC X.
  FD   CARD-READER
       LABEL RECORDS ARE OMITTED
* INPUT RECORD
  01   CARD-IMAGE.
       05   ACTION-CODE        PIC X.
       05   CUSTOMER-NUMBER.
            10   FILLER         PIC X(4).
            10   DIGITS-WE-WANT  PIC 99.
            10   FILLER         PIC XX.
       05   AMT-CA             PIC S9(7)V99.
       05   FILLER             PIC X(62).
  FD   PRINTER
       LABEL RECORDS ARE OMITTED.
  01   PRINT-LINE.
       05   FILLER PIC X(133).


  WORKING-STORAGE SECTION.
* AUXILIARY STORAGE LOCATIONS
  77   END-OF-FILE      PIC X(3) VALUE SPACES.
  77   WORK-VALUE       PIC 999.
  77   REWRITE-RECORD   PIC X(8).
  77   C-CODE           PIC X VALUE 'C'.
  77   D-CODE           PIC X VALUE 'D'.


* OUTPUT RECORD FOR ERROR ROUTINE
  01   ERROR-MSGS.
       05   FILLER  PIC X.
       05   FILLER  PIC X(132)
            VALUE 'SOMETHING IS WRONG'.


  PROCEDURE DIVISION.
* MODEL I
       OPEN INPUT CARD-READER
            OUTPUT PRINTER
            I-O CREATE-RELA.


* FILE PROCESSING PAIR
       PERFORM READ-CARD-INPUT.
       PERFORM FILE-UPDATE
            UNTIL END-OF-FILE = HIGH-VALUES.


* TERMINATION ACTIVITY
       CLOSE CARD-READER
             PRINTER
             CREATE-RELA.
       STOP RUN.


* INPUT PROCEDURE
  READ-CARD-INPUT.
       READ CARD-READER
            AT END MOVE HIGH-VALUES TO END-OF-FILE.
```

(A)

(B)

```
     * RECORD PROCESSING
       FILE-UPDATE.
(C)         ADD 1 DIGITS-WE-WANT GIVING WORK-VALUE.
            MOVE SPACES TO REWRITE-RECORD.
            READ CREATE-RELA
                INVALID KEY PERFORM ERROR-RTN.
            IF REWRITE-RECORD = SPACES
                PERFORM FILE-FIXES.
            PERFORM READ-CARD-INPUT.
       FILE-FIXES.
            IF ACTION-CODE = C-CODE
                ADD AMT-CA TO AMT-DUE
            ELSE
                IF ACTION-CODE = D-CODE
                    MOVE D-CODE TO STATUS-CODE
                ELSE
(D)                 PERFORM ERROR-RTN.
(E)         REWRITE CREATE-RELA-RECORD
                INVALID KEY PERFORM ERROR-RTN.
       ERROR-RTN.
            WRITE PRINT-LINE FROM ERROR-MSGS.
            MOVE HIGH-VALUES TO REWRITE-RECORD.
```

(A)   The SELECT clause must identify the field that will hold the location of the record to be accessed from the relative file. This field must have a picture clause that represents an unsigned integer. The field must be defined in the WORKING-STORAGE SECTION. In this program it is called WORK-VALUE. We will assign the field the value calculated by adding one to the value represented by the fifth and sixth digits of the CUSTOMER-NUMBER field as found in the input record currently in memory. The two digits needed in this calculation are isolated by defining the CUSTOMER-NUMBER field as being composed of three parts, the second of which will be the digits needed for the calculation.

(B)   A file that is to be accessed randomly is identified in the OPEN statement by the designation of I-O rather than INPUT or OUTPUT. Neither INPUT nor OUTPUT alone will suffice as both functions are needed for this file.

(C)   This calculation supplies a value for WORK-VALUE that will identify the storage location that should hold the record that belongs to the customer with the CUSTOMER-NUMBER that occurs on the input record. This is the first step in accessing a record from the relative file. The second step is a READ command. The READ command uses the current value of WORK-VALUE to determine which record in the relative file is to be brought into the memory area CREATE-RELA-RECORD. The INVALID KEY option is activated when the value in WORK-VALUE does not correspond to a storage area in the relative file.

(D)   The error routine for both an incorrect action code and an error in reading from or writing to the relative file will simply indicate that something is wrong. More extensive output for an error condition can be incorporated as a next step in the stepwise refinement of the program.

(E)   Since the record from the relative file that was last read into memory comes from the record area on that file that this modified record is to occupy, the REWRITE command is issued. The REWRITE command must be the next access to the relative file after a read from the record area that is the target of the REWRITE command.

Sequential Access of a Relative File

The last program processed the relative file as if it were a direct file. In the next program, the name, identification number, and status code fields of each record in the relative file will be listed. Notice that deleted records will be accessed the same as any other record and only by having the program check the value of the status code field will they be identified as deleted records.

```
    IDENTIFICATION DIVISION.
    PROGRAM-ID.  RLTVLIST.
*
*  NAME:                  ID:
*  PROGRAM-NUMBER: 12.3-3
*  DESCRIPTION:  LIST THE RECORDS STORED ON THE
*     CREATE-RELA ORGANIZED AS A RELATIVE FILE.  ACCESS
*     THE RECORDS IN THE ORDER IN WHICH THEY
*     OCCUR IN THE FILE.
*
    ENVIRONMENT DIVISION.
    CONFIGURATION SECTION.
    SOURCE-COMPUTER. IBM-370.
    OBJECT-COMPUTER. IBM-370.
    INPUT-OUTPUT SECTION.
    FILE-CONTROL.
        SELECT PRINTER
            ASSIGN TO UT-1403-S-SYSOUT.
        SELECT RELATIVE-FILE
            ASSIGN TO UT-3330-S-COBOL1
            ORGANIZATION IS RELATIVE
            ACCESS IS SEQUENTIAL
            RELATIVE KEY IS RELA-KEY-HOLDER.
    DATA DIVISION.
    FILE SECTION.
    FD  PRINTER
        LABEL RECORDS ARE OMITTED
        DATA RECORD IS PRINT-LINE.
    01  PRINT-LINE.
        05  FILLER PIC X(133).
    FD  CREATE-RELA
        LABEL RECORDS ARE STANDARD
        DATA RECORD IS RELATIVE-RECORD.
    01  CREATE-RELA-RECORD.
        05  R-ID-NO        PIC 9(8).
        05  R-NAME         PIC X(20).
        05  FILLER         PIC X(71).
        05  STATUS-CODE    PIC X.

    WORKING-STORAGE SECTION.
*  AUXILIARY STORAGE LOCATIONS
    77  RELA-KEY-HOLDER  PIC 9(4).
    77  END-OF-FILE      PIC X(8) VALUE SPACES.
    77  A-CODE           PIC X VALUE 'A'.
*  OUTPUT RECORD
    01  PRINT-PATTERN.
        05  FILLER        PIC X.
        05  PP-ID-NO      PIC 9(8).
        05  FILLER        PIC X(10) VALUE SPACES.
        05  PP-NAME       PIC X(30).
        05  PP-STATUS     PIC X(89).
```

```
   PROCEDURE DIVISION.
* MODEL I
     OPEN INPUT CREATE-RELA
          OUTPUT PRINTER.

* FILE PROCESSING PAIR
     PERFORM READ-A-RECORD.
     PERFORM PRINT-RELATIVE
          UNTIL END-OF-FILE = HIGH VALUES.

* TERMINATION ACTIVITY
     CLOSE CREATE-RELA
           PRINTER.
     STOP RUN.

* INPUT PROCEDURE
 READ-A-RECORD.
     READ CREATE-RELA
          AT END MOVE HIGH-VALUES TO END-OF-FILE.

* RECORD PROCESSING
 PRINT-RELATIVE.
     IF STATUS-CODE = A-CODE
          MOVE ACTIVITY-FLAG     TO PP-STATUS
          MOVE R-ID-NO           TO PP-ID-NO
          MOVE R-NAME            TO PP-NAME
          WRITE PRINT-LINE FROM PRINT-PATTERN.
     PERFORM READ-A-RECORD.
```

The relative file organization was easy to implement for the CUSTOMER–FILE because the values of the CUSTOMER–NUMBER field occurred in a recognizable order. A more extensive case of organizing a relative file would involve including some strategy to resolve any collisions that occur. Even without extensive collision resolution coding, the special case considered gave an insight into the value of this type of file organization.

SYNTAX SUMMARY

```
SELECT
     ASSIGN TO system-name
     ORGANIZATION IS RELATIVE

                            ⎧SEQUENTIAL⎫
     ACCESS MODE IS        ⎨          ⎬
                            ⎩RANDOM    ⎭

     RELATIVE KEY IS data-name-1

WRITE record-name [FROM identifier]

     [INVALID KEY imperative statement]

REWRITE record-name [FROM identifier]
     [INVALID KEY imperative-statement]
```

EXERCISES

1. How does the SELECT clause for a file with relative organization differ from the SELECT clause for a sequentially organized file?

2. What is the purpose of the RELATIVE KEY clause? How is the value in the data name found in the RELATIVE KEY clause used in accessing a record?

3. If a file with relative organization is processed sequentially, are the records in the same order as they were entered? Are they in any predictable order?

4. What storage location is used to store the value of the hashing function?

5. Describe the syntax and semantics of the REWRITE verb as used with a relative file. What is an INVALID KEY clause used to signal?

6. How many collisions will result from using the TOTAL–HOURS field of REGIS-TRAR–FILE for determining the location of the record if 100 storage locations are allocated; 123 storage locations are allocated; 197 storage locations are allocated?

7. How many collisions will result from using the CHARGE–ID field of NEW–WORLD–FILE to determine the location of a record by adding up the digits in CHARGE–ID to determine which storage location allocated should be used to store the record. Is this a good function for this file?

8. For alphabetic fields associate with each letter a numeric value as follows: A = 1; B = 2; . . . ; Z = 26. Use the procedure of Exercise 2 after making this translation on the letters of the last name of each customer in the NEW–WORLD–FILE to organize NEW–WORLD–FILE as a relative file. How many collisions occur? Is there a better way to associate letters with numbers so that fewer collisions occur?

PROGRAMMING PROBLEMS

1. Using the STUDENT–FILE for input, create a new file that uses these records and has a relative file organization. Associate with a student the storage location given by the remainder after dividing the ID–NUMBER by 137. Resolve collisions using the technique described in Section 12.1. After forming this file prepare a report that lists the contents of each of the 137 storage locations.

2. Using the CUSTOMER–FILE for input, use PROGRAM–NUMBER 12.3-1 as a model to create a new file that uses these records and has a relative file organization. Use this new file to process the following record changes:

ACTION	CUSTOMER–NUMBER	NEW INFORMATION
CHANGE	51902200	STREET: 39 OAK STREET
CHANGE	51909600	CITY: BOSTON, MASS
DELETE	51901600	
DELETE	51905800	

After processing these changes, list the contents of each of the 100 storage locations in the file. How difficult is it to add a record to this file?

3. Using the REGISTRAR–FILE for input, create a new file that uses these records and has a relative file organization. Associate with a record the storage location given by considering the CUMULATIVE–GPA field as having all its digits to the left of the decimal point. Initialize 400 storage locations. Resolve collisions using the technique described in Section 12.1. After forming this file, prepare a report that lists the contents of each of the 400 storage locations.

12.4   Indexed Files

The earlier discussion about indexed files focused attention on how the operating system manages the file on secondary storage. Most of those actions of the operating system are transparent to the programmer; that is, they are accomplished without direct user intervention. Different operating systems will use different file storage techniques. Whatever technique is used will be transparent to the user, as standard COBOL code will be the same regardless of the physical organization of the file. In this section we introduce the COBOL code that is used by the programmer to create and access an indexed file.

Since an indexed file organization involves a secondary storage device, a considerable amount of JCL will be needed to identify both the device used for setting up a communications channel and the specific part of the storage area of the device containing the file. A typical disk pack has a storage capacity that enables it to hold several large files simultaneously. Consequently, the operating system must know the exact part of the disk pack that contains a particular file. In the discussion that follows, we assume that appropriate JCL is used when a program is executed. Since the JCL is dependent on the operating system, it is necessary for you to inquire at the installation where the program will be executed to find out what JCL is needed. Fortunately, there are only minor differences in COBOL code for execution under different operating systems. These differences are usually limited to the form of the SELECT clause.

When creating an indexed file, the programmer merely reads records from the presorted file and writes them on the indexed file area. The operating system manages the creation of the indexes without direct user intervention.

Access of a record from an indexed file really consists of two steps. The first step requires the programmer to have the key of the record sought made available to the operating system. The storage location is identified in one of the clauses in the SELECT sentence. In 1968 ANSI COBOL a separate area is allocated in the WORKING–STORAGE SECTION which will hold this key. In 1974 ANSI COBOL this field is contained in the record description area for the indexed file as given in the FILE SECTION. In the second step, the operating system uses the value in this field to search the index(es) to find the physical location of the record with the given key value. When the record is located, it is read into the record storage area for the indexed file allocated in the FILE SECTION. Once the record is put in this record area, the information in that record is available for use by the program.

The file update cycle can be accomplished by accessing just the records that need modification. The change procedure is similar to the way a change is accomplished with a relative file. The record to be changed is brought into memory, changed and then written back onto the secondary storage area that it originally occupied. Normally the deletion process is accomplished by changing the value in a code field of the record that indicates whether the record is to be considered as deleted. When reading the file as a sequential file, it will be necessary to find out the value in this special field to know how to process it. The advantage to deletion by marking is that at a later time the deleted records can be identified because they are not physically removed from the file. On the other hand, though additional coding effort is needed to distinguish active records from these marked as deleted.

Creating and Using an Indexed File

The next programming example consists of three distinct programs. The first reads a presorted file and causes the operating system to organize the records of this file as an indexed file. The second program accesses the indexed file records in random order and updates the file. In this application file updates will be restricted to modifying one field or marking the record as deleted. Finally, the third program reads the indexed file sequentially and lists the records as they exist after the update cycle. Figure 12.4.1 (next page) illustrates how the job stream can be viewed.

You should follow through the logic of these programs using the data that is listed. At the end of the execution of each program be sure you agree with the list of the records of the file as given in the text.

Figure 12.4.1 *Program schematic.*

```
 IDENTIFICATION DIVISION.
 PROGRAM-ID. TRYNDXD.
*
* NAME:                    ID:
* PROGRAM-NUMBER = 12.4-1
* DESCRIPTION: LOAD THE RECORDS OF A CARD FILE
*    ONTO DISK AS AN INDEXED FILE.  THE KEY FIELD
*    IS THE NAME.
*
 ENVIRONMENT DIVISION.
 CONFIGURATION SECTION.
 SOURCE-COMPUTER.  IBM-370.
 OBJECT-COMPUTER.  IBM-370.
 INPUT-OUTPUT SECTION.
 FILE-CONTROL.
     SELECT PRINTER
         ASSIGN TO UT-1403-S-SYSOUT.
     SELECT CARD-READER
         ASSIGN TO UT-2540-S-SYSIN.
     SELECT INDEXEDFILE
         ASSIGN TO UT-2314-I-COBOL1
         ACCESS IS SEQUENTIAL
         RECORD KEY IS NAME.
 DATA DIVISION.
 FILE SECTION.
 FD  CARD-READER
     LABEL RECORDS ARE OMITTED
     DATA RECORD IS CARD-IMAGE.

* INPUT RECORD
 01  CARD-IMAGE.
     05  NAME-IN   PIC X(9).
     05  PLACE-IN  PIC X(15).
     05  FILLER    PIC X(56).
 FD  INDEXEDFILE
     LABEL RECORDS ARE STANDARD
     DATA RECORD IS DISK-IN.

* OUTPUT RECORD
 01  DISK-IN.
     05  ACTIVE-OR-NOT   PIC X.
     05  PLACE           PIC X(15).
     05  NAME            PIC X(9).
     05  FILLER          PIC X(55).
 FD  PRINTER
     LABEL RECORDS ARE OMITTED
     DATA RECORD IS PRINT-LINE.
 01  PRINT-LINE.
     05  FILLER  PIC X.
     05  ERRORS  PIC X(132).
```

(A)

```
      WORKING-STORAGE SECTION.
    * AUXILIARY STORAGE LOCATION
      77   END-OF-FILE PIC X(9) VALUE SPACES.
      77   A-CODE       PIC X    VALUE 'A'.

      PROCEDURE DIVISION.
    * MODEL I
          OPEN INPUT CARD-READER
               OUTPUT PRINTER
                      INDEXEDFILE.

    *   FILE PROCESSING PAIR
          PERFORM READ-CARD-FILE.
          PERFORM FORM-FILE
              UNTIL END-OF-FILE = HIGH-VALUES.

    * TERMINATION ACTIVITY
          CLOSE CARD-READER
                INDEXEDFILE
                PRINTER.
          STOP RUN.

    * INPUT PROCEDURE
     READ-CARD-FILE.
          READ CARD-READER
              AT END MOVE HIGH-VALUES TO END-OF-FILE.

    * RECORD PROCESSING
     FORM-FILE.
          MOVE SPACES TO DISK-IN.
          MOVE PLACE-IN TO PLACE.
          MOVE A-CODE   TO ACTIVE-OR-NOT.
          MOVE NAME-IN  TO NAME.
          WRITE DISK-IN
              INVALID KEY PERFORM ERROR-RTN.
          PERFORM READ-CARD-FILE.
     ERROR-RTN.
          MOVE CARD-IMAGE TO ERRORS.
          WRITE PRINT-LINE.
```

(A) — appears beside the OPEN statement block

(B) — appears beside the WRITE DISK-IN block

(A)   The ACCESS clause in the SELECT clause indicated that the file should be treated as a sequential file. In this case the OPEN statement is the same as for a normal sequential file. If this clause is not included, COBOL assumes that ACCESS is sequential.

(B)   The records that will form the indexed file are supposed to be ordered by increasing value of the KEY field. If a record is out of order and the indexed file building process attempts to put a record with a lower key after a record with a higher key value, the INVALID KEY clause indicates what to do. In this case the paragraph ERROR-RTN is executed. This INVALID KEY clause acts very much like the AT END clause used with a READ statement. The INVALID KEY stands guard preventing execution of the statement PER-FORM ERROR-RTN unless the WRITE is not to be allowed. We will see the INVALID KEY clause later when we try to randomly access a record that we think is in the file but in fact is not there.

Random Access of an Indexed File

As an aid in understanding these programming examples, we will list a small number of records that can be considered as the input file and see how they are processed. In the program just examined, suppose that the input file consists of the following records:

NAME–IN	PLACE–IN
BENDER, A.	OAK HALL
DOER, S.	SMITH HALL
FINE, L.	COLBY HALL
KNIGHT, G.	RASTER HALL
MOORE, V.	EAST HALL
OWEN, R.	SOUTH HALL
RAY, W.	QUAD HALL
THOM, S.	SIMS HALL

With the file organized for random access using an indexed technique, we will examine a program now that does file updates using direct access.

```
IDENTIFICATION DIVISION.
PROGRAM-ID. NDXDADD.
*
* NAME:               ID:
* PROGRAM-NUMBER: 12.4-2
* DESCRIPTION: UPDATE AN INDEXED FILE.  THE ACCESS
*    MODE IS RANDOM.  INDICATE DELETIONS BY PUTTING
*    A 'D' IN THE STATUS FIELD OF SUCH RECORDS.
*
ENVIRONMENT DIVISION.
CONFIGURATION SECTION.
SOURCE-COMPUTER. IBM-370.
OBJECT-COMPUTER. IBM-370.
INPUT-OUTPUT SECTION.
FILE-CONTROL.
    SELECT INDEXEDFILE
        ASSIGN TO UT-3330-I-COBOL1
        RECORD KEY IS NAME
        ACCESS IS RANDOM.
    SELECT CARD-READER
        ASSIGN TO UT-2540R-S-SYSIN.
    SELECT PRINTER
        ASSIGN TO UT-1403-S-SYSOUT.
DATA DIVISION.
FILE SECTION.
FD  INDEXEDFILE
    LABEL RECORDS ARE STANDARD
    DATA RECORD IS DISK-IN.
* INPUT FROM INDEXED FILE
01  DISK-IN.
    05  ACTIVE-OR-NOT   PIC X.
    05  PLACE           PIC X(15).
    05  NAME            PIC X(9).
    05  FILLER          PIC X(55).
FD  CARD-READER
    LABEL RECORDS ARE OMITTED
    DATA RECORD IS CARD-IMAGE.
```

```
* INPUT FROM CARD READER
 01   CARD-IMAGE.
      05 INDICATOR PIC 9.
      05 NAME-IN   PIC X(9).
      05 PLACE-IN  PIC X(15).
      05 FILLER    PIC X(55).
 FD   PRINTER
      LABEL RECORDS ARE OMITTED
      DATA RECORD IS PRINT-LINE.
* OUTPUT RECORD FOR ERROR CONDITION
 01   PRINT-LINE.
      05  FILLER     PIC X.
      05  PRINT-DATA PIC X(132).


     WORKING-STORAGE SECTION.
* AUXILIARY STORAGE LOCATIONS
 77   END-OF-FILE  PIC X(9) VALUE 'YES'.
 77   CORRECT-READ PIC X(8).
 77   VALID-DISK-OP PIC X(8).


     PROCEDURE DIVISION.
* MODEL I
     OPEN INPUT CARD-READER
          OUTPUT PRINTER
          I-O INDEXEDFILE.


* FILE PROCESSING PAIR
     PERFORM READ-CARD-IN.
     PERFORM UPDATE
         UNTIL END-OF-FILE = HIGH-VALUES.


* TERMINATION ACTIVITY
     CLOSE CARD-READER
           PRINTER
           INDEXEDFILE.
     STOP RUN.


* INPUT PROCEDURE
 READ-CARD-IN.
     READ CARD-READER
         AT END MOVE HIGH-VALUES TO END-OF-FILE.


* RECORD PROCESSING
 UPDATE.
     MOVE NAME-IN  TO NAME.


*  CODE FOR INDICATION OF ACTION
*     1       ADD NEW RECORD
*     2       DELETE CURRENTLY EXISTING RECORD
*     3       CHANGE A CURRENTLY EXISTING RECORD
     IF INDICATOR = 1
         PERFORM NEW-RECORD
     ELSE
         IF INDICATOR = 2
             PERFORM DEACTIVATE
         ELSE
             IF INDICATOR = 3
```

(B)

(C)

(D)

```
(E)                              PERFORM DOIT
                         ELSE
                              PERFORM MSGS.
                 PERFORM READ-CARD-IN.
             DOIT.
                 MOVE 'YES' TO VALID-DISK-OP.
                 READ INDEXEDFILE
                     INVALID KEY PERFORM MSGS.
                 IF VALID-DISK-OP = 'YES'
(F)                  REWRITE DISK-IN
                         INVALID KEY PERFORM MSGS.
             DEACTIVATE.
                 MOVE 'YES' TO VALID-DISK-OP.
                 READ INDEXEDFILE
                     INVALID KEY PERFORM MSGS.
                 IF VALID-DISK-OP = 'YES'
                     MOVE 'D' TO ACTIVE-OR-NOT
                     REWRITE DISK-IN
                         INVALID KEY PERFORM MSGS.
             NEW-RECORD.
                 MOVE PLACE-IN   TO PLACE.
                 MOVE 'A'        TO ACTIVE-OR-NOT.
                 WRITE DISK-IN
                     INVALID KEY PERFORM MSGS.
             MSGS.
                 MOVE CARD-IMAGE TO PRINT-DATA.
                 WRITE PRINT-LINE.
                 MOVE 'NO' TO VALID-DISK-OP.
```

(A)   The ACCESS clause indicates that the file will have records accessed in RANDOM order. The clause is reflected in the OPEN sentence.

(B)   An indexed file can be both read from and written to. Since this is neither exclusively INPUT or OUTPUT, the OPEN sentence identifies this as I–O.

(C)   After a record is read from the CARD-READER, the NAME1 field is moved to the RECORD KEY field so that the record can be found in the indexed file if updating is required. Updating will be required whenever the field INDICATOR has a value of one. If this is a record to be added to the indexed file, the value in the RECORD KEY field will be used to determine the correct location for this record in the indexed file.

(D)   Card records represent either information to be changed in a record currently in the indexed file or a new record to be added to the indexed file. If INDICATOR has a value 1, a new record is being added to the file. In this case the INVALID KEY clause will be executed only if there already is a record in the indexed file with the KEY value that is in NAME.

(E)   In the case that a currently existing record in the indexed file is to be updated, the process has two parts which are found in the paragraphs DOIT and MSGS. The REWRITE verb must be used to return a record to the area that the last READ accessed.

(F)   The record with KEY equal to the value in NAME is found and brought into the record area associated with the file. At that point any changes that need to be made can be made. Provided the next access to the indexed file involves the record with the KEY value used in the last seek, a direct REWRITE to the same area in the indexed file is possible. This will put the updated record in the storage location from which a record was just read. If the record written to the indexed file has any KEY value other than the KEY of the last record read, the write process will involve either moving records or using the overflow area for storing the new record.

With the use of the input file listed before this program, we will be able to understand the random processing better by tracing the execution of the program using the following records:

INDICATOR	NAME-IN	PLACE-IN
1	BLACK, W.	ST. HELENS HALL
3	THOM, S.	STELLAR HALL
3	FINE, L.	COLVAN HALL
2	MOORE, V.	EAST HALL
1	DOXEN, T.	NESSOR HALL
2	OWEN, R.	SOUTH HALL

To find out what the file contains after these updates, we process the file as if it were a sequential file and list the records as they occur in the file. The program to do this is given next and is followed by the output it would generate. We list the deleted records with a 'D' in the status field since this is how they exist in the file. If only active records were to be listed, the records marked as deleted could be eliminated by adding a command to select for printing only those records with status code 'A'.

```
       IDENTIFICATION DIVISION.
       PROGRAM-ID. READNDXD.
      *
      * NAME:                   ID:
      * PROGRAM-NUMBER: 12.4-3
      * DESCRIPTION: LIST ON THE PRINTER THE RECORDS
      *    OF AN INDEXED FILE.  THE INDEXED FILE IS TO BE
      *    PROCESSED AS A SEQUENTIAL FILE.
      *
       ENVIRONMENT DIVISION.
       CONFIGURATION SECTION.
       SOURCE-COMPUTER. IBM-370.
       OBJECT-COMPUTER. IBM-370.
       INPUT-OUTPUT SECTION.
       FILE-CONTROL.
           SELECT PRINTER
               ASSIGN TO UT-1403-S-SYSOUT.
           SELECT INDEXEDFILE
               ASSIGN TO UT-3330-I-COBOL1
               RECORD KEY IS NAME.
       DATA DIVISION.
       FILE SECTION.
       FD  PRINTER
           LABEL RECORDS ARE OMITTED
           DATA RECORD IS PRINT-LINE.
      * OUTPUT RECORD
       01  PRINT-LINE.
           05  FILLER       PIC X.
           05  STATUS-CODE  PIC X(5).
           05  PLACE-OUT    PIC X(20).
           05  NAME-OUT     PIC X(107).
```

(A)

```
FD   INDEXEDFILE
     LABEL RECORDS ARE STANDARD
     DATA RECORD IS DISK-IN.
* INPUT RECORD
01  DISK-IN.
     05  ACTIVE-OR-NOT   PIC X.
     05  PLACE           PIC X(15).
     05  NAME            PIC X(9).
     05  FILLER          PIC X(55).

WORKING-STORAGE SECTION.
* AUXILIARY STORAGE LOCATION
77  END-OF-FILE PIC X(9) VALUE SPACES.

PROCEDURE DIVISION.
* MODEL-I
     OPEN INPUT INDEXEDFILE
          OUTPUT PRINTER.

* FILE PROCESSING PAIR
     PERFORM READ-INDEXEDFILE.
     PERFORM LISTING
          UNTIL END-OF-FILE = HIGH-VALUES.

* TERMINATION
     CLOSE INDEXEDFILE
          PRINTER.
     STOP RUN.

* INPUT PROCEDURE
 READ-INDEXEDFILE.
     READ INDEXEDFILE
          AT END MOVE HIGH-VALUES TO END-OF-FILE.

* RECORD PROCESSING
 LISTING.
     MOVE NAME           TO NAME-OUT.
     MOVE PLACE          TO PLACE-OUT.
     MOVE ACTIVE-OR-NOT TO STATUS-CODE.
     WRITE PRINT-LINE.
     PERFORM READ-INDEXEDFILE.
```

(A)   This program simply lists the records in the file that was created by the updating process. The program treats the indexed file as a sequential file. Each record of the file is read and listed by the printer. This really is a kind of utility program that gives a hard copy listing of the file.

The final version of the file will be

STATUS CODE	NAME	PLACE
A	BENDER, A.	OAK HALL
A	BLACK, W.	ST. HELENS HALL
A	DOER, S.	SMITH HALL
A	FINE, L.	COLVAN HALL
A	KNIGHT, G.	RASTER HALL
D	MOORE, V.	EAST HALL
D	OWEN, R.	SOUTH HALL
A	RAY, W.	QUAD HALL
A	THOM, S.	STELLAR HALL

After a period of time the deleted records will need to be physically deleted from the file. At that point this file should be read as a sequential file and act as the input file for a program like PROGRAM–NUMBER 12.4-1, which loads an indexed file.

SYNTAX SUMMARY

```
SELECT file-name
    ASSIGN to system-name
    ORGANIZATION IS INDEXED

    [                        (SEQUENTIAL) ]
    [ ACCESS MODE IS        {RANDOM     } ]
    [                        (DYNAMIC    ) ]

    RECORD KEY is data-name-1

OPEN I-O file-name-1 [file-name-2]...

WRITE record-name [FROM identifier]
    INVALID KEY imperative-statement

REWRITE record-name [FROM identifier]
    [INVALID KEY imperative-statement]
```

EXERCISES

1. How does the SELECT clause for a file with indexed organization differ from the SELECT clause for a sequential file? A file with relative organization?
2. What is the purpose of the RECORD KEY clause? Where is the storage location referred to in the RECORD KEY clause found? How is the value in this storage location used in accessing a record from an indexed file?
3. If a file with indexed organization is processed sequentially, are the records in any particular order? If so, what order?
4. Describe the syntax and semantics of the REWRITE verb as used with an indexed file? What is the purpose of the INVALID KEY clause? What condition will cause the statement following INVALID KEY to be executed?
5. What are some advantages of deletion by marking?
6. Determine which fields can be used as key fields in organizing the following files as indexed files.

   a. STUDENT–FILE   c. REGISTRAR–FILE
   b. CUSTOMER–FILE   d. NEW–WORLD–FILE

   Will each of the possible key fields be useful?

PROGRAM TESTING AND MODIFICATION EXERCISE

1. Modify PROGRAM–NUMBER 12.4-3 so that only the active records will be listed.

PROGRAMMING PROBLEMS

1. Using the NEW–WORLD–FILE for input and the NAME field as the key field, create a new file that uses these records and is organized as an indexed file. Process the following records using the new file:

ACTION	NAME		NEW INFORMATION
ADD	SMITH	HARRY	All other fields blank
CHANGE	NOLET	LINDA LOUI	CLASS: SO
CHANGE	HEATH	RICHARD DA	AGE: 21
DELETE	JOHNSON	CLARENCE S	

After processing these records, list all the active records in the order in which they are stored.

2. Using the REGISTRAR–FILE for input and the NAME field as the key field, create a new file that uses these records and is organized as an indexed file. Prepare a report that lists the NAME, GRADEs and CUMULATIVE–GPA for the following students:

```
RODGERS TIMOTHY
JOHNSON SUZANNE AL
BARRY   DONNA JEAN
ROBERTS BENJAMIN J
BAKER   ERIC
```

Include appropriate headings for the report and the page(s) of detail lines.

3. Using the REGISTRAR–FILE for input and the SOC–SEC–NUMBER field as the key field, create a new file that uses these records and is organized as an indexed file. Prepare a report using this new file that lists the NAME and CAMPUS–ADDRESS of the students with the following values for SOC–SEC–NUMBER:

```
495166352
324666739
241636262
877768237
428577007
188201869
302082262
845083349
456437820
123456789
```

The last number does not belong to any record. Make sure your program handles such a data item.

Chapter Review

SUMMARY

Until this chapter, file processing was sequential. There are applications, however, in which relatively few of the records of a file are actually examined or quick access of a record is required without reading each preceding record. In cases like this, sequential file processing is slow and inefficient. What is needed is a file organization that allows direct access of any record in a file.

Before examining two typical physical organizations for files that allow direct access, it is necessary to understand that the storage medium should not be a tape, since tapes must be processed sequentially. The storage medium typically used for direct access is the magnetic disk, either floppy or hard.

The next point to understand is how files are organized for direct access processing. Two major direct access file organizations are used in COBOL applications: relative file organization and indexed file organization. In a relative file organization, each record is associated with a number that indicates the relative position of that record in the file. By knowing the starting location for the records of the file and the size of a record, the operating system can use this number to calculate the location of the record needed. For an indexed file, each record has a key value that uniquely identifies it. The largest key for a record on a cylinder is kept in a cylinder index. In addition, there is an index for each track. When a record is needed, the cylinder index is searched first to identify the cylinder that should contain the record. Second, the cylinder's track index is searched to determine which track of that cylinder contains the record. Finally, the track identified is searched sequentially to determine if the record is present.

The sample programs with these file organizations use familiar READ and WRITE commands; but before these commands are executed, the key that identifies the record or the relative number of the record must be made available in a predetermined storage location named in the SELECT clause for the file. There is also an INVALID KEY clause that describes the action to be taken if the record is not found or if the key for the record is not appropriate.

In each type of file organization, the deletion of a record can be done in different ways. For purposes of simplicity, deletion by marking process is used in the example programs. In this case, a byte in the record is used to indicate whether the record is valid or not. The deletion process allows subsequent processing of all the records marked as deleted.

TEST YOURSELF

1. Explain what is meant by cylinder and track on a disk drive.
2. Name three kinds of disk drives. Explain how they differ.
3. What is meant by relative file organization?
4. What is a collision?
5. What is meant by an indexed file organization?
6. What is meant by deletion by marking? How does a program recognize a record deleted by marking?
7. What information is kept in a cylinder index?
8. What information is kept in a track index?
9. What is a prime storage area? An overflow storage area? Explain the functions of each.
10. How does a track index change when an element from the track is put in the overflow area?
11. Explain the syntax and the semantics of the INVALID KEY clause.
12. Explain the syntax and the semantics of the REWRITE verb.

13

Subprograms

Chapter Objectives

After studying this chapter you should be able to

- write COBOL programs using subprograms;
- understand how programs can CALL one another and share data;
- use structure charts as a program design tool;
- explain the usefulness of chief programmer teams, structured walkthroughs, and development support libraries as software development tools.

Chapter Outline

13.1   Using Subprograms

Considering the number of lines in the PROCEDURE DIVISION, the programs we have studied and written so far are short and consist of one main program. In this section we will learn the use of **subprograms** with a main program to solve a problem. This will allow us to build up a larger program out of subprograms. The purpose of having subsidiary programs is so that a larger programming problem can be divided into parts. In this way, we can "divide and conquer" an otherwise complex problem. Important reasons for using subprograms include the following:

1. Divide a large problem into parts which can be solved and coded by different programmers.
2. Divide a large program into parts that can be worked on over a period of time.
3. Make a large program easier to understand and maintain by building it out of simpler parts.
4. Use a subprogram for solving a particular problem in various programs without having to recode the solution.

As a rule of thumb, consider a PROCEDURE DIVISION larger than one page of output as a prime candidate for subdivision into modules or subprograms. We will design the final solution of a long program as consisting of a series of subprograms, each of which solves a part of the original problem. These separate programs will then be joined together by a main program to form a solution to the original problem.

Subprograms in COBOL

COBOL has a special facility that enables us to break a problem into subprograms and pass control of execution from the main program to a subprogram or from one subprogram to another. This is accomplished by one program calling another. The **called program** is referred to as a subprogram; the program that calls it is usually a **main program,** although a subprogram can call another subprogram as long as it does not try to call itself either directly or indirectly.

Figure 13.1.1 (following page) illustrates these concepts. In this illustration the main program calls three different subprograms in its PROCEDURE DIVISION. The three subprograms have PROGRAM–ID paragraphs of EDITCK, SALES, and DISPLAYD. As the arrows indicate, when a subprogram is called, the main program branches to the subprogram, the instructions in the subprogram are executed, and then the subprogram branches back to continue execution of the program that called it. This procedure is repeated for execution of the other two subprograms.

Let us now look at an example that uses three subprograms and a main program to solve an inventory control problem for a hardware company with multiple stores.

The Thrifty Hardware Company has five branch stores. They have just had a thirty-day special on four items: shovels, hammers, chisels, and saws. As a first step toward analyzing the success of this promotion, management would like a report that gives a breakdown of sales by item by store. The data to be processed has been transmitted from point-of-sale input devices and stored at company headquarters on disk. Weather conditions can affect the integrity of the data transmitted, so the first task is to create an exception report listing all the records with incorrect data and to create a disk file of all valid records for use as the input file.

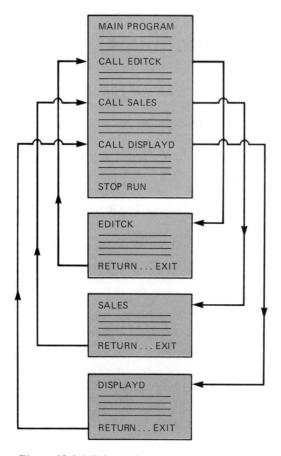

Figure 13.1.1 *Relationship of main program to subprograms.*

Two problems must be solved:

1. Edit the data file, create an exception report, and create an input file of valid records.
2. Use the file of valid records as input to accumulate sales totals by item by store and print an appropriate report for management.

If we examine Problem 2 more carefully, we can see that it has two parts:

a. Accumulate total sales in a table by item by store using for input the valid file created in Problem 1.
b. Use the table in which totals were accumulated to create a printed report.

Thus, the complete problem can be solved by sequentially solving the following three problems:

1. Process the raw data to create a file of valid records and an exception report.
2. Process the file of valid records to produce a two-dimensional table with sales totals by item by store.
3. Use the two-dimensional table created in Step 2 to produce the final sales report.

Unfortunately, management wants the report immediately. Fortunately, we have Excellent Programmers 1, 2, and 3 ready and eager to tackle the task. The problem is how to manage the work so that the programmers don't get in each other's way, but work together to solve the complete problem. We can do this as follows:

> **Assignment For Excellent Programmer 1 (E.P.1)**
> Process the file and create a disk file of valid records. Put the file of valid
> records on a disk area known to the system as COBOL1.
>
> **Assignment For Excellent Programmer 2 (E.P.2)**
> Process the valid records, creating a two-dimensional table whose rows
> represent the items sold and columns represent the stores. The contents of
> the storage locations of this table are the total sales by item by store found
> by processing all the records of the file on COBOL1.
>
> **Assignment For Excellent Programmer 3 (E.P.3)**
> Assume a program has a two-dimensional table with rows representing the
> items sold and columns representing the stores. The contents of the storage
> locations of this table are the total sales by item by store, as calculated
> correctly by Excellent Programmer 2. Print a suitable report using this
> information.

E.P.1 and E.P.2 must know what a typical record in the input file should look like. E.P.2
and E.P.3 must know what the picture clause for the two-dimensional table they are using
is supposed to be.

Let's suppose that E.P.1, E.P.2, and E.P.3 have now finished their assignments.
Now, only by combining these subprograms can we immediately solve the original problem. In COBOL we accomplish this by passing control from one program to another.
After the called program is completed, control is returned to the calling program and
execution in the calling program is continued with its next instruction. Furthermore, in
some cases data areas in the calling program are made available for use by the called
program. When control returns to the calling program, this shared data has the value that
exists when the called program is finished.

We have used the words *called* and *calling* because these are the keys to COBOL's
syntax. If we are executing a statement in a program called PROGRAM1 and want to pass
control to a program called PROGRAM2, we use the sentence

```
CALL 'PROGRAM2'
```

at the appropriate point in PROGRAM1. The operating system then looks for a program
that has

```
PROGRAM-ID.  PROGRAM2.
```

and starts executing PROGRAM2 with the first statement of its PROCEDURE DIVI-
SION. The return to PROGRAM1 from PROGRAM2 is caused by the command

```
EXIT PROGRAM.
```

When this command is encountered, control is returned to the command that follows

```
CALL 'PROGRAM2'
```

in PROGRAM1.

Finally, when we have shared data areas, we tell the called program which data areas
of the calling program are available for its use. Suppose we want a program called PROG1
to call a program called PROG2. In addition, we want PROG2 to use the following two
data areas of PROG1: (1) a 77-level variable called FLAG with PIC X(8), and (2) a
one-dimensional table called BANGOR, with 25 entries having PIC 9(3) as the picture
clause for the elementary items. This is done in two steps.

```
Step 1.   In the PROCEDURE DIVISION of the calling program we use

                    CALL 'PROG2' USING FLAG
                                       BANGOR.

Step 2.   In the DATA DIVISION of the called program (PROG2) we use


          WORKING-STORAGE SECTION
                    .
                    .
                    .

          LINKAGE SECTION.
          77  AREA-CALLED-FLAG-IN-PROG1  PIC X(8).
          01  ARRAY-CALLED-BANGOR-IN-PROG1.
              05 BOXES OCCURS 25 TIMES   PIC 999.
          PROCEDURE DIVISION USING
                  AREA-CALLED-FLAG-IN-PROG1
                  ARRAY-CALLED-BANGOR-IN-PROG1.
                    .
                    .
                    .

          RETURN-COMMAND.
              EXIT PROGRAM.
```

After USING in Step 1 we list the data areas used in PROG1 that are to be made available to PROG2: FLAG and BANGOR. PROG2 does not allocate new storage areas to these variables but uses the storage areas allocated in PROG1. This is done by listing in PROG2 the variables that use the storage areas of FLAG and BANGOR in the statement

```
          PROCEDURE DIVISION USING
                  AREA-CALLED-FLAG-IN-PROG1.
                  ARRAY-CALLED-BANGOR-IN-PROG1.
```

The storage area of FLAG is used by the first variable in the list following USING. The storage of BANGOR is used by the second variable in the list following USING. This assignment is positional, so order is important. Since these variables are using pre-existing storage areas, we can't put them in the FILE SECTION or the WORKING-STORAGE SECTION because new storage areas would be allocated. The problem is solved by having a new section present in the DATA DIVISION. This new section (LINKAGE SECTION) contains only the description of variables listed after USING. The location of a storage area in the calling program is conveyed to the called program, but the name of this storage location in the calling program is not conveyed. Therefore, we are free to use any name we want for these variables in the called program.

We now have all the pieces needed to solve our problem. We let our three programmers independently solve the three parts of the problem, then we link these parts together with the main program that follows:

```
IDENTIFICATION DIVISION.
PROGRAM-ID.  BOSS.
ENVIRONMENT DIVISION.
CONFIGURATION SECTION.
SOURCE-COMPUTER.  IBM-370.
OBJECT-COMPUTER.  IBM-370.
```

```
DATA DIVISION.
WORKING-STORAGE SECTION.
01  ITEM-BY-STORE.
    05 COUNT-OF-ITEM OCCURS 4 TIMES.
       10 COUNT-BY-STORE OCCURS 5 TIMES PIC 9(5).

PROCEDURE DIVISION.
*
* EDITCK TAKES THE RAW FILE AND CREATES A FILE
* OF VALID RECORDS AND PRINTS AN EXCEPTION REPORT
* FOR INCORRECT RECORDS
*
      CALL 'EDITCK'.
*
* SALES TAKES THE FILE OF VALID RECORDS AND
* TABULATES THE SALES TOTALS BY ITEM BY STORE.
* THESE TOTALS ARE STORED IN ITEM-BY-STORE.
*
      CALL 'SALES' USING ITEM-BY-STORE.
*
* DISPLAYD CREATES THE REQUIRED REPORT USING
* THE INFORMATION IN ITEM-BY-STORE
*
      CALL 'DISPLAYD' USING ITEM-BY-STORE.
      STOP RUN.
```

Before examining the subprograms that accomplish the preceding main program, we should discuss two alternatives for executing subprograms, since not every operating system uses the same conventions for connecting a main program and subprograms together to make a complete job.

One way commonly used is a two-step process. First, the main program and the subprograms are compiled separately. Second, a program called a linkage editor is invoked to arrange communication between the parts of the job. Special job control language (JCL) is needed to define the blocks of code to be compiled separately and to invoke the linkage editor.

Another method is to stack the main program and all required subprograms one after another with the main program first and the subprograms in any order. The job control language indicates the beginning and end of this collection of programs. The subprograms are not compiled as separate jobs, but the complete program is compiled as a single job.

To find out what job control language is required to run your program, you will need a description of the JCL required for the computer system you are using.

In the following program, the JCL issue is avoided by omitting all JCL and merely listing the main program and the required subprograms one after another. Also omitted is any JCL needed to access the disk file used to temporarily hold the file of records being processed. The complete program needed to solve the original problem follows. It consists of the main program followed by the three subprograms.

```
IDENTIFICATION DIVISION.
PROGRAM-ID. BOSS
*
* NAME:              ID:
* PROGRAM-NUMBER: 13.1-1
* DESCRIPTION:  THIS IS THE MAIN PROGRAM WHICH
* CALLS SUBPROGRAMS.
*
```

```
          ENVIRONMENT DIVISION.
          CONFIGURATION SECTION.
          SOURCE-COMPUTER.  IBM-370.
          OBJECT-COMPUTER.  IBM-370.
          DATA DIVISION.
          WORKING-STORAGE SECTION.
          01  ITEM-BY-STORE.
              05 COUNT-OF-ITEM OCCURS 4 TIMES.
                 10 COUNT-BY-STORE OCCURS 5 TIMES PIC 9(5).
          PROCEDURE DIVISION.
          *
          * EDITCK TAKES THE RAW FILE AND CREATES A FILE
          * OF VALID RECORDS AND PRINTS AN EXCEPTION
          * REPORT FOR INCORRECT RECORDS.
          *
(A)           CALL 'EDITCK'.
          *
          * SALES TAKES THE FILE OF VALID RECORDS AND
          * TABULATES THE SALES TOTALS BY ITEM BY STORE.
          * THESE TOTALS ARE STORED IN ITEM-BY-STORE.
          *
(B)           CALL 'SALES' USING ITEM-BY-STORE.
          *
          * DISPLAYD CREATES THE REQUIRED REPORT USING THE
          * INFORMATION IN ITEM-BY-STORE.
          *
              CALL 'DISPLAYD' USING ITEM-BY-STORE.
              STOP RUN.
          *
          *
          *
          *   THE SUBPROGRAM EDITCK
          *
          IDENTIFICATION DIVISION.
(C)       PROGRAM-ID. EDITCK.
          *
          * NAME:                 ID:
          * PROGRAM-NUMBER: 13.1-2
          * DESCRIPTION: CHECK THE ITEM NAME FIELD
          *    (COLUMNS 11-16) TO SEE THAT THESE
          *    COLUMNS ONLY CONTAIN LETTERS OR BLANKS
          *    CHECK THE FIELDS QUANTITY (COLUMN 21-23)
          *    AND STORE (COLUMN 24-25) TO SEE THAT THESE
          *    ONLY CONTAIN DIGITS.
          *
          ENVIRONMENT DIVISION.
          SOURCE-COMPUTER.  IBM-370.
          OBJECT-COMPUTER.  IBM-370.
          INPUT-OUTPUT SECTION.
          FILE-CONTROL.
             SELECT CARD-READER
                 ASSIGN TO UT-2540R-S-SYSIN.
             SELECT LINE-PRINTER
                 ASSIGN TO UT-1403-S-SYSOUT.
(D)          SELECT TEMP-FILE
                 ASSIGN TO UT-3330-S-COBOL1.
          DATA DIVISION.
          FILE SECTION.
```

```
FD   CARD-READER
     LABEL RECORDS ARE OMITTED.
01   CARD-IMAGE.
     05 FILLER PIC X(80).
FD   LINE-PRINTER
     LABEL RECORDS ARE OMITTED.
01   LINE-PATTERN.
     05 FILLER PIC X(133).
FD   TEMP-FILE
     LABEL RECORDS ARE STANDARD
     BLOCK CONTAINS 34 RECORDS.
01   TEMP-FILE-RECORD.
     05 FILLER PIC X(80).


     WORKING-STORAGE SECTION.
*    AUXILIARY STORAGE LOCATIONS
77   I       PIC 999.
77   FLAG    PIC X(8) VALUE SPACES.
*    INPUT RECORD
01   DATA-IN.
     05 CARD-COLUMN  PIC X OCCURS 80 TIMES.
*    OUTPUT RECORD
01   DATA-CHECK.
     05  FILLER         PIC X.
     05  ERROR-OUTPUT.
         10 ERROR-CARD PIC X OCCURS 80 TIMES.
     05  FILLER         PIC X(52) VALUE SPACES.
*    TABLES
01   NAMES-FOR-SPECIAL-CHARACTERS.
     05  ALPHA  PIC X    VALUE 'A'.
     05  ZETA   PIC X    VALUE 'Z'.
     05  NINE   PIC X    VALUE '9'.
     05  STAR   PIC X    VALUE '*'.
     05  OOH    PIC X    VALUE '0'.
     05  BLANKS PIC X    VALUE SPACES.
01   DATA-GOOD.
     05 COLUMN-CORRECT PIC X OCCURS 80 TIMES.


     PROCEDURE DIVISION.
*    MODEL I.


         OPEN INPUT CARD-READER
              OUTPUT TEMP-FILE
                     LINE-PRINTER.


*    FILE PROCESSING PAIR
         PERFORM READ-A-CARD.
         PERFORM EDIT
             UNTIL FLAG = HIGH-VALUES.


*    TERMINATION ACTIVITY
         CLOSE CARD-READER
               LINE-PRINTER
               TEMP-FILE.
     RETURN-COMMAND.
(E)      EXIT PROGRAM.
```

```
       * INPUT PROCEDURE FOR SUBPROGRAM EDITCK
         READ-A-CARD.
             READ CARD-READER INTO DATA-IN
                 AT END MOVE HIGH-VALUES TO FLAG.


       *  RECORD PROCESSING FOR SUBPROGRAM EDITCK
         EDIT.
 (F)         MOVE SPACES TO DATA-GOOD.
             PERFORM LETTERS
                 VARYING I FROM 11 BY 1
                     UNTIL I > 16.
             PERFORM DIGITS
                 VARYING I FROM 21 BY 1
                     UNTIL I > 25.
 (G)         IF DATA-GOOD = SPACES
                 WRITE TEMP-FILE-RECORD FROM DATA-IN
             ELSE
                 MOVE DATA-IN TO ERROR-OUTPUT
                 WRITE LINE-PATTERN FROM DATA-CHECK
                 MOVE DATA-GOOD TO ERROR-OUTPUT
                 WRITE LINE-PATTERN FROM DATA-CHECK.
       * GET THE NEXT RECORD
             PERFORM READ-A-CARD.
 (H)     DIGITS.
             IF(CARD-COLUMN (I) NOT LESS THAN OOH
                 AND
                 CARD-COLUMN (I) NOT GREATER THAN NINE)
                   NEXT SENTENCE
             ELSE
                 MOVE STAR TO COLUMN-CORRECT (I).
 (I)     LETTERS.
             IF ((CARD-COLUMN (I) NOT LESS THAN ALPHA
                 AND
                 CARD-COLUMN (I) NOT GREATER THAN ZETA
                 OR
                 CARD-COLUMN (I) = BLANKS)
                   NEXT SENTENCE
             ELSE
                 MOVE STAR TO COLUMN-CORRECT (I).
       *
       *
       *
       * SUBPROGRAM SALES
       *
       *

         IDENTIFICATION DIVISION.
 (J)     PROGRAM-ID. SALES.
       * NAME:                 ID:
       * PROGRAM-NUMBER: 13.1-3
       * DESCRIPTION: USING THE VALID RECORDS FOUND IN
       *   PROGRAM-NUMBER 13.1-2 DETERMINE HOW MANY UNITS
       *   OF EACH PRODUCT WAS SOLD BY EACH STORE.  THE
       *   INFORMATION IS PUT IN A TWO-DIMENSIONAL TABLE THAT
       *   HAS THE ROWS LABELED BY ITEMS AND THE COLUMNS
       *   LABELED BY STORE NUMBERS.
       *
```

```
         ENVIRONMENT DIVISION.
         CONFIGURATION SECTION.
         SOURCE-COMPUTER.  IBM-370.
         OBJECT-COMPUTER.  IBM-370.
         INPUT-OUTPUT SECTION.
         FILE-CONTROL.
(K)          SELECT GOOD-RECORDS
                 ASSIGN TO UT-3330-S-COBOL1.
         DATA DIVISION.
         FILE SECTION.
         FD  GOOD-RECORDS
             LABEL RECORDS ARE STANDARD
             BLOCK CONTAINS 34 RECORDS.
         01  TYPICAL-RECORD.
             05 FILLER PIC X(80).

         WORKING-STORAGE SECTION.
        * AUXILIARY STORAGE LOCATIONS
         77  FLAG  PIC X(8).
         77  I     PIC 999.
         77  J     PIC 999.
         77  FOUND PIC XXX.


        * INPUT RECORD
         01  RECORD-IN.
             05 FILLER   PIC X(10).
             05 TITLE    PIC X(6).
             05 FILLER   PIC X(4).
             05 QUANTITY PIC 999.
             05 STORE    PIC 99.
             05 FILLER   PIC X(55).
        * TABLE
(L)      01  KINDS-OF-STUFF.
             05 FILLER  PIC X(6) VALUE 'SHOVEL'.
             05 FILLER  PIC X(6) VALUE 'HAMMER'.
             05 FILLER  PIC X(6) VALUE 'CHISEL'.
             05 FILLER  PIC X(6) VALUE 'SAW'.
         01  IDENTIFY REDEFINES KINDS-OF-STUFF.
             05 WHAT-IS-IT OCCURS 4 TIMES PIC X(6).
(M)      LINKAGE SECTION.
         01  BREAK-DOWN.
             05  BY-PRODUCT OCCURS 4 TIMES.
                 10 BY-PRODUCT-BY-STORE  OCCURS 5 TIMES PIC 9(5).


(N)      PROCEDURE DIVISION USING BREAK-DOWN.
        * MODEL I.

             OPEN INPUT GOOD-RECORDS.


        * INITIALIZATION
             MOVE ZEROS  TO BREAK-DOWN.
             MOVE SPACES TO FLAG.

        * FILE PROCESSING PAIR
             PERFORM READ-A-GOOD-RECORD.
             PERFORM ACCUMULATE
                 UNTIL FLAG = HIGH-VALUES.
```

```
*  TERMINATION ACTIVITY
      CLOSE GOOD-RECORDS.
 RETURN-COMMAND.
      EXIT PROGRAM.


* INPUT PROCEDURE FOR SUBPROGRAM SALES
 READ-A-GOOD-RECORD.
      READ GOOD-RECORDS INTO RECORD-IN
          AT END MOVE HIGH-VALUES TO FLAG.


*  RECORD PROCESSING FOR SUBPROGRAM SALES
 ACCUMULATE.
      MOVE SPACES TO FOUND.
      PERFORM FIND
          VARYING I FROM 1 BY 1
              UNTIL FOUND = HIGH-VALUES.
      ADD QUANTITY TO BY-PRODUCT-BY-STORE (J,STORE).
* GET THE NEXT RECORD
      PERFORM READ-A-GOOD-RECORD.
 FIND.
      IF TITLE = WHAT-IS-IT (I)
          MOVE I TO J
          MOVE HIGH-VALUES TO FOUND.
*
*
* SUBPROGRAM DISPLAYD
*
 IDENTIFICATION DIVISION.
 PROGRAM-ID. DISPLAYD.
*
*
* NAME:                 ID:
* PROGRAM-NUMBER: 13.1-4
* DESCRIPTION: PRINT THE CONTENTS OF THE
*    TWO-DIMENSIONAL TABLE THAT HOLDS THE
*    SALES RECAP INFORMATION.
*
 ENVIRONMENT DIVISION.
 CONFIGURATION SECTION.
 SOURCE-COMPUTER.  IBM-370.
 OBJECT-COMPUTER.  IBM-370.
 INPUT-OUTPUT SECTION.
 FILE-CONTROL.
      SELECT LINE-PRINTER
          ASSIGN TO UT-1403-S-SYSOUT.
 DATA DIVISION.
 FILE SECTION.
 FD  LINE-PRINTER
      LABEL RECORDS ARE OMITTED.
 01  PRINT-PATTERN.
      05 FILLER PIC X(133).
 WORKING-STORAGE SECTION.
* AUXILIARY STORAGE LOCATIONS
 77  I  PIC 99.
 77  J  PIC 999.
```

(O)

```
         * OUTPUT RECORD
           01  DETAIL-LINE.
               05 FILLER     PIC X.
               05 FILLER     PIC X(20)  VALUE SPACES.
               05 INVEN-AMT  PIC Z(6)9  OCCURS 5 TIMES.
               05 FILLER     PIC X(77)  VALUE SPACES.

(P)        LINKAGE SECTION.
           01  INVENTORY-DATA.
               05 COUNT-BY-ITEM OCCURS 4 TIMES.
                  10 COUNT-ITEM-STORE OCCURS 5 TIMES PIC 9(5).

           PROCEDURE DIVISION USING INVENTORY-DATA.

               OPEN OUTPUT LINE-PRINTER.

         *   TERMINATION ACTIVITY
(Q)            PERFORM LOAD-OUT-ROWS
                   VARYING I FROM 1 BY 1
                       UNTIL I > 4.
               CLOSE LINE-PRINTER.
           RETURN-COMMAND.
               EXIT PROGRAM.


         *   RECORD PROCESSING
           LOAD-OUT-ROWS.
               PERFORM LOAD-COLUMNS-IN-ROWS
                   VARYING J FROM 1 BY 1
                       UNTIL J > 5.
               WRITE PRINT-PATTERN FROM DETAIL-LINE.
           LOAD-COLUMNS-IN-ROWS.
               MOVE COUNT-ITEM-STORE (I,J) TO INVEN-AMT (J).
```

(A)   The main program BOSS calls a subprogram EDITCK. The CALL command causes control to pass to the block of code with a PROGRAM-ID of EDITCK.

(B)   The main program BOSS calls the subprogram SALES. In addition to passing control to the subprogram SALES, we want to calculate values of the entries for the 4 by 5 table called ITEM-BY-STORE. The values put in these storage locations are later used by the program DISPLAYD. DISPLAYD is called by the main program after SALES is finished. The program DISPLAYD uses the values put in the storage locations of ITEM-BY-STORE. The allocation of storage for this table is done in the program called BOSS (see the WORKING-STORAGE SECTION of BOSS). The location of this allocated storage is made known to both SALES and DISPLAYD by means of the USING clause in the CALL statements.

(C)   This is one of the subprograms called by BOSS. This paragraph of a COBOL program is important because it is used to identify to other programs and the operating system where this block of code resides in memory after compilation.

(D)   The records that are correct when received at company headquarters are stored on the temporary file called TEMP-FILE. This is actually on a disk area that the system calls COBOL1. Information put on a peripheral device does not necessarily go away when a program terminates execution. The file we create can be made available for later use. We can think of this as being like a recording on a record. We can play back the record as often as we want to use the information stored there. Since a disk file is permanent storage, we can use this file in another program without having to pass information in a formal way from one program to the next. The names that different programs give this file need not be the same. The system name COBOL1 will be the same in different programs.

(E)   EXIT PROGRAM causes control to return to the code that called EDITCK. Upon return, execution in the calling program proceeds normally with the next command following the CALL command.

(F)   We want to know if there are letters in bytes 11–16 and digits in columns 21–25. DATA–GOOD will be used to point out incorrect characters in these two sets of columns. Each time we process a record, we want to start with a clean slate in DATA–GOOD. When we find errors, we want to put a symbol in one of its bytes.

(G)   When the checking process is finished, we can ask if we have put anything in one or more of the bytes of DATA–GOOD. Remember that this data area started out containing SPACES. If it no longer contains SPACES, we have found at least one column of DATA–IN that contains the wrong kind of symbol. For the correct records, we merely write the records onto the disk file called TEMP–FILE. For the incorrect records, we create an exception report.

(H)–(I)   In the collating sequence, we line up special characters, letters, and digits to form an extended alphabet. Thus, DIGITS checks to see if the symbols in columns 21–25 of DATA–IN fall in the range of the digits in the collating sequence. LETTERS checks to see if the symbols in columns 11–16 of DATA–IN are letters. Rather than use the class checks that were introduced in Section 4.4, we independently examine each byte of the fields. This is a first step in turning this subprogram into a general purpose utility program in which the type of character required and the beginning and ending bytes of the field are passed to the subprogram. The subprogram can then be kept in the user's library and used in a variety of programs when this task needs to be accomplished.

(J)   This is the beginning of the subprogram SALES that is called by BOSS.

(K)   This file was called TEMP–FILE in EDITCK. The name is not important, but its physical location is. By means of this system name (COBOL1) and the JCL we gain access to the disk file created in the previous program regardless of the particular name this subprogram uses to refer to the area on the disk.

(L)   In EDITCK we just asked if the right kind of symbol occurred in certain columns of the data record. Here we want to ask if the item that was sold was one of the items we want to tally. We will use a table with initial values that are the names of the items to check this before adding any number on the data card to the table of totals.

(M)   In the calling statement we made available to this program the storage area allocated to

```
ITEM-BY-STORE
```

in BOSS. In the LINKAGE SECTION we list the attributes of all the storage locations made available to this program by the calling program. The attributes are those appropriate for this program and do not always match the attributes of this same area when it is used elsewhere. No storage is allocated to BREAK–DOWN by this subprogram.

(N)   When storage is shared by two or more subprograms, we not only have a LINKAGE SECTION in the DATA DIVISION but also a listing of the names of the shared storage locations in the heading for the PROCEDURE DIVISION. Remember the first data area mentioned in the CALL statement has its address assigned to the first data area listed in the PROCEDURE…USING… statement.

(O)   DISPLAYD is another subprogram called by BOSS.

(P)   ITEM–BY–STORE in this subprogram uses the storage allocated in BOSS to the table of the same name.

(Q)   To print a two-dimensional table, we print one row at a time. In LOAD–OUT–ROWS we move each entry in row I to the appropriate output area before writing a row. By repeating this process for each row, we end up with output that appears two-dimensional.

SYNTAX SUMMARY

LINKAGE SECTION

```
[77-level-description-entry]
[                          ] ...
[record-description-entry  ]
```

PROCEDURE DIVISION
```
    [USING data-name-1
           [data-name-2]...]
```

```
        {identifier-1}
CALL    {           }  [USING data-name-1
        {literal-1  }
                              [,data-name-2]...]
```

EXIT PROGRAM

EXERCISES

1. Find out from your local computer installation what job control language is required to execute a COBOL program that involves a main program and one or more subprograms.
2. What is the difference between a program and a subprogram?
3. List the sections of the DATA DIVISION that we have discussed so far in the order which they occur in a program.
4. What is the purpose of the LINKAGE SECTION? Explain why the LINKAGE SECTION does not have any storage allocated for its elements.
5. How is control returned from a subprogram to the calling program? What values will the variables in the USING clause of the CALL statement have?
6. Explain the syntax and semantics of the following sentence:

```
                CALL 'WORKER' USING WAGES
                                    RATES
                                    SWITCH.
```

7. Explain the syntax and semantics of the following sentence:

```
                PROCEDURE DIVISION USING ZONE-1
                                        ZONE-2
                                        INFO.
```

8. Is the following reorganization of data by the LINKAGE SECTION valid?

```
         IDENTIFICATION DIVISION.
         PROGRAM-ID.  BOSS.
                    .
                    .
                    .
         01  GOOD-RECORDS PIC X(80).
                    .
                    .
                    .
         PROCEDURE DIVISION.
                    .
                    .
                    .
             CALL 'RECORD-CHECK' USING GOOD-RECORDS.
                    .
                    .
                    .
         IDENTIFICATION DIVISION.
         PROGRAM-ID. RECORD-CHECK.
                    .
                    .
                    .
         LINKAGE SECTION.
         01  CHECK-INFO.
             05  BYTE-BY-BYTE PIC X OCCURS 80 TIMES.
         PROCEDURE DIVISION USING CHECK-INFO.
                    .
                    .
                    .
```

Why will this be a useful technique?

PROGRAM TESTING AND MODIFICATION EXERCISE

1. Modify PROGRAM-NUMBER 13.1-2 so that the bytes of the numeric fields may have either a zero or a blank to the left of the most significant digit.

PROGRAMMING PROBLEMS

Use a main program and subprograms for each of the following problems.

1. Using REGISTRAR-FILE for input, calculate the number of students with the same value for AGE, HOME-STATE, and CLASS. Prepare a report that lists for each value of AGE the two-dimensional table that breaks down the number of students of that AGE by HOME-STATE by CLASS.
2. Using STUDENT-FILE for input, prepare a report that lists for each grade for each student whether the grade is greater than the average grade for all students that are the same age as the student.
3. Using STUDENT-FILE for input, create a new file that includes for each record a new field that contains the average for all grades in the record. Create a file that contains the records of all students with an average at least five points higher than the average of all the students' averages. Also create a file that contains the records of all students with an average at least five points lower than the average of all the students' averages.

4. Using the REGISTRAR–FILE for input, first create a new file consisting of all students with HOME–STATE being Maine. Using this new file, calculate the average grade by CAMPUS–ADDRESS. Prepare a report that lists for each dormitory the names and the average for students in the dormitory in decreasing order of the average. To calculate the average use the scale: A = 4; B = 3; C = 2; D = 1; E = 0.

13.2   Top-Down Design

So far you have designed and developed programs that gradually increased in size and difficulty. You have made effective use of pseudocode, applied stepwise refinement, and adhered to good programming style. You have found various pseudocode models useful in helping to design the logic of a program solution. However, you have typically dealt with relatively small, self-contained programs. Now, you have advanced to the point where you can begin using subprograms to design and develop larger, more complex application programs. This section, therefore, introduces and discusses top-down design and software development techniques that have proven effective in a variety of professional software projects that involve large programming problems.

The overall structure of a program is important in producing software that is reliable, easily maintained, and easily modified. Top-down design is a methodology for designing the overall structure of a program or a system of programs from a top-down view. The overall structure is represented by a collection of functional components that together solve the problem.

Pseudocode is useful for designing the logic of a program and then depicting that logic as comments easy to read and follow within a program. Program flowcharts can also be used to visualize the control flow and logic of a program. Traditional flowcharts, however, tend to hide the structure of complex programs. Similarly, pseudocode is not ideally suited for depicting the relationships that exist among a system of related programs, subprograms, and parts of programs.

Two widely used top-down design and documentation tools that aid the programmer in dealing with complexity are structure charts and HIPO diagrams. HIPO is an acronym for Hierarchy plus Input-Process-Output.

Structure Charts and HIPO Charts

Structure charts and HIPO charts are used to develop and depict the overall structure and relationships of the parts of a program. Unlike pseudocode and program flowcharts, control flow and logic are not shown.

Coding should not be the first step in program development. Rather, coding should be preceded by careful design. There are two aspects of designing a program. One is the *program structure*, or how the components are built and related to each other. The second is the actual *logic* of the program solution. Structure charts and HIPO diagrams are tools for the first; pseudocode and flowcharts are techniques for the second.

Dealing With Complexity

A key to successful software design and development is to master complexity somehow. As programs grow in size, complexity increases at an exponential rate. This relationship of size to complexity is shown in Figure 13.2.1. It is not unusual for application programs in business organizations to have lines of code numbering thousands or even tens of

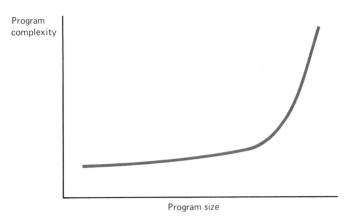

Figure 13.2.1 *Program size and complexity.*

thousands. This is considerably different from the smaller problems typically assigned in college textbooks.

The best way to handle complexity is to break down a problem into pieces that can be understood and solved. A large program cannot be created in a single step. Rather, the problem has to be decomposed into functional modules and related components at ever-lower levels of detail. This decomposition might be visualized as moving from the abstract statement of a problem to a detailed solution. From a high level design, the programmer proceeds to attack the problem with lower levels of detail. As the programmer moves from the high level conceptualization, more insight can be gained about the intricate details of a solution. The term used to describe this process is *top-down design*.

A **module** is the basic unit of a program's structure. A module is a group of program statements that solves a part of the overall problem. A well-designed module consists only of statements functionally related to each other and that collectively solve a single, specific part of the problem. The following example of a payroll problem illustrates the top-down approach first using structure charts and then HIPO diagrams.

A Payroll Example

The XYZ Company wants to computerize its payroll for wage earners. Wages are paid according to a formula that includes hours worked and job classification. The calculation includes tax computations, accumulation of year-to-date figures, and deductions for voluntary contributions withheld from the paycheck. Assume that the input records, output records and the employee files have already been designed. All that remains is to design the program(s).

The first top-down design step would be to portray the overall program in terms of its major functions. That is shown in Figure 13.2.2(a). Note that no details are given at this point about how the program will accomplish the tasks. Instead, the entire program is shown as a single box that processes input data into output data.

The next step is to subdivide the one box into even more detail. Again, there is still no concern with the details as to what initialization activities and termination activities entail. Moreover, no attempt is yet made to show the sequence of each part of the program. The purpose at this level is to identify and depict what makes up the next level of detail in the Payroll Program. See Figure 13.2.2(b).

Top-down decomposition continues with further elaboration of the Process Each Employee box as shown in Figure 13.2.2(c). The same principles apply—simple statements that tell what each box is to accomplish. Details as to how are still avoided.

Figure 13.2.3(a) illustrates the next level of detail for the box Compute Payroll. In like manner, each of the boxes would require decomposition into the lowest practical levels of detail. Figure 13.2.3 (a), (b), and (c) show the principle of proceeding level by

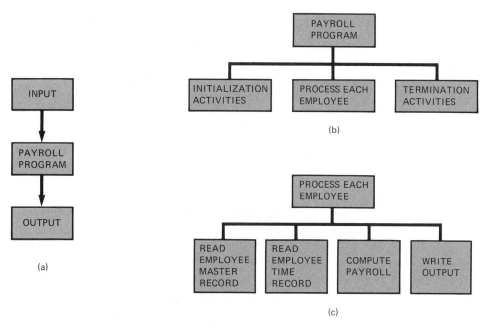

Figure 13.2.2 *Structure charts for payroll problem.*

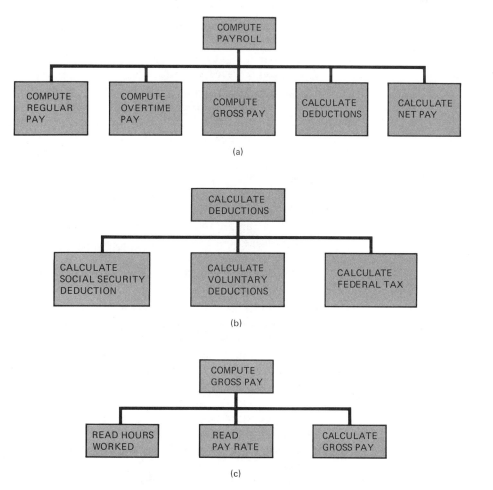

Figure 13.2.3 *Top-down design with structure charts.*

level. These figures also illustrate another important principle of top-down design; that is, deal with each component on its own level without introducing sublevel details. For example, notice the box Calculate Federal Tax. At that level, there is no concern as to how an appropriate rate is actually determined. The process of rate determination is left to the boxes at lower levels. This concept of separation of levels is a major strength of top-down design. Separation of levels permits the human mind to deal with the problem in smaller pieces without undue concern for detail. Also, it simplifies program maintenance and modification. For instance, if the government later changes the withholding tax formula, only one box would be affected. Similarly, if the city later levies an income tax, the required modification would be a new box (and new module) under Calculate Deductions.

Advantages of Top-Down Design

The most important advantages of top-down design using structure charts and program modularity are:

1. The overall problem is easier to understand because it is decomposed into pieces.
2. It is easier to debug and correct program errors because an output error can easily be traced back to the module that caused it.
3. Program modifications can be made with less difficulty and have less impact on the overall program because all other modules need not be changed to include a new module.
4. Modules in other programs can be lifted out and included in the program. Many routines are common to several programs. Searching and sorting routines in system libraries are good examples. Considerable time and effort can be saved since these require no additional coding and testing effort.
5. Structure charts help document the program design because they are developed before the detailed logic. After a program is decomposed into modules, each module can then be designed and documented with tools such as pseudocode and program flowcharts.

HIPO Diagrams

HIPO diagrams share the advantage of structure charts. Some professional programmers prefer to use the IBM-developed design and documentation tool known as HIPO charts. A HIPO package normally includes a visual table of contents (VTOC), overview diagrams, and detail diagrams. The VTOC is referred to as a hierarchy chart and is very similar to the structure chart; they differ only with respect to labeling schemes. In fact, it is common for some professional programmers to mix and match features of the two to create their own useful tools. The overview and detail diagrams depict the input, process, and output operations of each function at successive levels of detail.

HIPO was conceived at IBM because of the recognition that documentation that emphasized a program's functions could simplify program maintenance and modification. In the traditional bottom-up approach that predated the top-down approach, documentation was often delayed because programmers waited for an operational program before trying to document the code. As a result, documentation was frequently inadequate due to tight project schedules or programmer neglect. Moreover, past methods of documentation often consisted only of program flowcharts or narrative descriptions. These early flowcharts and narratives usually showed or explained what a program *did* but not *how* a program did it or how its parts were *related*.

Over the years, HIPO charts have evolved from being used for program documentation to an aid for expressing program specifications. Today, HIPO diagrams are used effectively as both a design and documentation tool.

Figure 13.2.4 shows a VTOC, an overview diagram, and a detail diagram. Collectively these constitute a HIPO package.

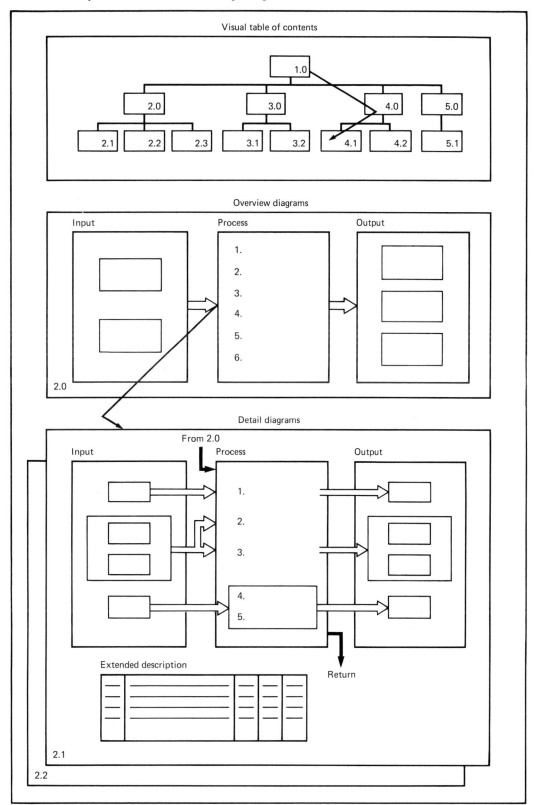

Figure 13.2.4 HIPO *package.*

Like a structure chart, a VTOC provides a general picture of the modules in a program. An **overview diagram** describes the major functions given in the VTOC, references the detail diagrams, and when necessary, explains functions. The overview diagram is divided into input, process, and output sections. The input section identifies the input files, records, and tables used; the process section describes major processing steps; and the output section reflects the files, records, and data items that are modified or created in the process steps.

Detail diagrams describe the specific functions that will be coded as modules in the program. Detail diagrams also reference other detail diagrams with a solid arrow coming into and out of the diagram. An extended description is also contained on most detail diagrams in order to clarify process steps further, refer to other record layouts, explain logic, and so forth.

Figures 13.2.5 through 13.2.7 depict a VTOC, an overview diagram, and a detail diagram for the XYZ payroll problem discussed earlier. Notice that the VTOC shows only the first level in a fashion similar to the structure chart. However, unlike the structure

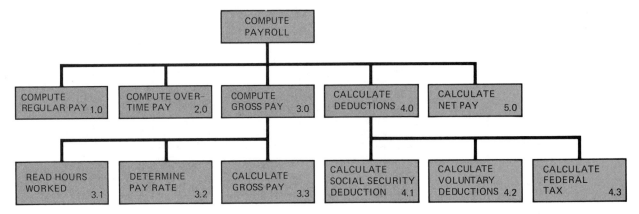

Figure 13.2.5 VTOC for payroll program.

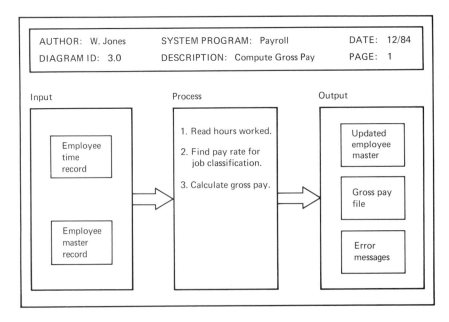

Figure 13.2.6 HIPO overview diagrams for calculating gross pay.

chart, the VTOC shows identification numbers in the lower right-hand corner. These identification numbers point to the corresponding overview diagrams.

An overview diagram for module 3.0 of the VTOC is shown in Figure 13.2.6. The overview diagram indicates that an employee record and an employee master record are read by this module. Gross pay is calculated with data from the employee record, such as employee identification and hours worked; and data from the master record. The master file is updated with a new year-to-date gross pay figure, a gross pay record is written to a gross pay file, and appropriate messages are written if errors are detected.

Figure 13.2.7 is a detail diagram for Module 3.2. The detail diagram shows the fields from the employee master record, employee record, and the rate table used to determine the correct pay based on the job classification of an employee.

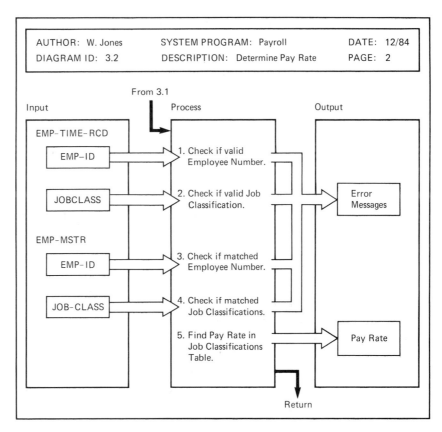

Figure 13.2.7 Detail diagrams.

Software Development Techniques

Structure charts, HIPO diagrams, and well-structured, modular programs are useful during program design and maintenance. A variety of other techniques are also used in commercial programming. Three that have proven invaluable for managing software projects are discussed in the remainder of this section. The three are chief programmer teams, structured walkthroughs, and development support libraries.

Chief Programmer Team

The **chief programmer team** is a technique for effectively managing a software development project. The team typically consists of a *chief programmer,* a *senior backup programmer,* a *program librarian,* and other *programmers* with varying levels of expertise and experience.

A senior programmer is the team chief, supervisor, and guide. The chief programmer is selected based on his or her skill and experience and is responsible for the design of all programs. The chief programmer writes high-level modules, codes critical parts of a program, and defines the lower-level modules written by other members of the team. The chief programmer directs, supervises, and guides the other programmers.

A second senior programmer serves as a backup for the chief programmer. The backup programmer works closely with the chief programmer and assumes the duties of the chief programmer when necessary. The backup programmer acts as a sounding board for the chief programmer, contributes to design and development decisions, writes significant parts of the code, and also provides guidance to other team members.

The program librarian relieves programmers of tedious and time-consuming clerical tasks. The librarian is responsible for maintaining the current status of programs and test data. The librarian also manages the development support library that contains source and object program listings, source and object programs on storage media, test data files, and other important listings, documents, and diagrams pertaining to the software project. The librarian also typically handles the compilation and testing of programs in order to free the team to work on programs.

Structured Walkthrough

A **structured walkthrough** is an informal examination of a programmer's design and logic by his or her peers and others. It is used to review a proposed design, coded solutions, and testing and implementation plans. A typical structured walkthrough takes place with the programmer who developed the design or code and peer reviewers in attendance. Users also may attend the review. Prior to the review, those who will attend are given copies of the proposed design or code. This permits the reviewers time to study the problem and proposed solution.

To be most effective, a walkthrough should be brief. The review should concentrate on error detection rather than error correction. The main objective is to detect errors. One reviewer records what is found, and a few days after the meeting, the programmer provides a report on corrections made. Depending on the outcome and criticality of the reviewed code or design, subsequent walkthroughs may be scheduled to review the changes made.

Development Support Library

A **development support library** serves as a central repository of information related to the project. It is used to organize and control the software development project. A development support library is important because it helps to separate design and coding functions from clerical tasks. The library is maintained by a program librarian. A development support library typically consists of an **internal library** and an **external library.** The former, stored on magnetic tapes or disks, contains source and object programs, job control language for running the programs, and test data. The latter contains source program listings, testing results, job control listings, and related printed documents and listings.

From your programming experience so far, you can appreciate the positive impact on programmer productivity that can result from the use of a program librarian, a development support library, structured walkthroughs, and a well-managed team effort. Large, complex program development projects that produce correct, easily-maintained programs have successfully applied one or more of these methodologies.

This section has introduced and briefly examined techniques for designing, documenting, and managing complex software development projects. Both structure charts and HIPO diagrams are useful for breaking a seemingly complex problem into understandable pieces and functionally-related modules. After decomposition to the lowest sensible levels, the logic of individual modules can be designed using pseudocode and/or program flowcharts. Finally, the solutions are converted to COBOL code.

From design at the higher levels through the coding and testing of COBOL programs, the chief programmer team, structured walkthroughs, and the use of a development support library can prove immensely effective for managing a software development project.

EXERCISES

1. Contrast the use of structure charts and HIPO diagrams with the use of pseudocode and program flowcharts.
2. Explain what is meant by a module. What are the features of a well-designed module?
3. Refer to Figure 13.2.3. Which boxes still require further decomposition? List them.
4. Draw a VTOC or structure chart for the table of contents of this book. Do you think that a structure chart or VTOC would improve a student's understanding of the contents of any book?
5. What does the acronym HIPO mean?
6. What three diagrams constitute a complete HIPO package?
7. Which HIPO diagram is most similar to a structure chart?
8. Explain the chief programmer team. Why is it used?
9. Explain what a structured walkthrough is. Why do you think this is also called egoless programming?
10. Why is the use of a development support library important?
11. Why should top-down design make programs easier to understand and modify?
12. Draw a structure chart for a noncomputer problem such as making a telephone call or planning a party. Decompose it to the lowest practical levels.

PROBLEMS

1. Your city has passed a levy on the income of all employees. Modify Figure 13.2.3(b) to show where this new module would appear.
2. The Federal Government permits employees to withhold an additional amount of money for income tax purposes. What modifications would you make to Figure 13.2.3(b) to provide for this new function?
3. Convert the structure chart of Figure 13.2.3(a) to a VTOC diagram.
4. Draw a structure chart for PROGRAM–NUMBER 13.1-1.

13.3   A Payroll System

The previous section introduced two similar techniques for program design and documentation, and discussed methodologies for managing software development projects. This final section presents a large, complex problem that requires you to apply those principles. The problem is similar to what might be expected in a professional programming setting. The problem involves more than one program and requires you to deal with file and program design issues. In addition, you are expected to solve interfaces and decompose problems using top-down design techniques. You may be assigned to programming teams and the various subproblems may be solved by different teams. Within each team, you may have the opportunity to use structured walkthroughs, a chief programmer organization, and development support library techniques. The problem is to automate a payroll system.

Payroll is one of the oldest and most common computer applications. Payroll preparation at the basic level involves recording and collecting employee hours worked, converting hours worked to gross pay, calculating deductions, computing net pay, and preparing payroll checks. Other byproduct functions are often performed along with payroll processing. These include keeping year-to-date figures, printing quarterly and year-end statements, and reporting job performance measurements. A payroll system might also include personnel operations such as sick leave, vacation time accounting, and time-in-grade accrual. Organizations may initially develop and implement a payroll system with a few of the above activities and add additional functions later. A basic payroll application with only a few personnel operations will be the desired system for this problem.

Assume that you are a programmer recently hired for a programming project. You and your colleagues are assigned to develop a computerized payroll system. Your employer experienced a rapid growth in business and number of employees in recent months. As a result, the manual payroll system is too slow and cumbersome. Some weeks ago, the president directed that a payroll system be designed and developed. A system analyst was hired and given the task of designing the system. You are now at a briefing where the analyst is describing the payroll system as designed so far. Assume that the following descriptions and figures are what the analyst describes and presents to you and your fellow programmers.

Your team is to design and develop a payroll system with the following capabilities:

1. Payroll Master File Updating. This program is executed when updates to the master file are required.
2. Payroll Editing and Processing. Preliminary analysis indicates that this should consist of at least three programs run weekly: Payroll Edit, Payroll Register, and Payroll Check Writing.
3. Periodic Reports Processing. This process includes a quarterly federal tax return, W-2 statement, and end-of-year processing.

Payroll Master File Updating

The master file is updated on a regular basis to ensure that accurate and timely data on each employee is in the employee master file. The personnel office maintains data on current and new employees. Personnel will obtain this data and run the payroll master update program to keep the master file current. Data to identify a new employee and corrections for existing employees are entered. Examples of the type of data are correct spellings of names, social security numbers, number of tax exemptions, and marital status. Changes for existing employees and data for new employees are manually prepared on an employee change form. Prior to running the weekly payroll, these changes and additions to the master file are keyed by the personnel office to make sure that the latest data is in the master file. The data is entered into the master file as either a change or addition transaction. These corrections and additions are randomly entered to the most recent version of the master file. In addition to updating the master file, a temporary file is created that records all of the changes and additions to the master file. This ensures that copies of both the original and updates of the master file are available. An employee change report for existing employees and a report of new employees are also produced by the master file update program. The output for both reports are identical in format except that one is entitled the New Employee Report and the second is entitled the Employee Change Report. Figure 13.3.1 shows a system flowchart of the payroll master file update program. Figure 13.3.2 is the format of the New Employee Report.

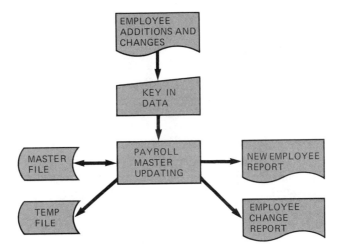

Figure 13.3.1 *System flowchart of payroll master file updating.*

12/31/84	NEW EMPLOYEE REPORT	PAGE _____

EMPLOYEE NAME	ADDRESS	WAGES REG	WAGES OVER	SOCIAL SECURITY NUMBER

Figure 13.3.2 *Format of New Employee Report.*

Payroll Editing and Processing

Payroll processing each week is accomplished with an up-to-date master file that Personnel keeps current. Employees manually prepare time cards, approved by supervisors, that reflect the employee name, social security number, regular hours worked, overtime hours worked, job classification, sick time used, and vacation time taken. Salaried employees are not paid overtime; salary data is in the master file. Figure 13.3.3 shows the data elements keyed in to the payroll editing program from the manually-prepared time cards.

EMPL ID	LAST NAME	FIRST NAME	MIDDLE INITIAL		
(9 Numeric)	(12 Alpha)	(12 Alpha)	(1 Alpha)		
Reg Hours	Overtime	Job Class	Sick Time	Vacation	
(4 Numeric)	(4 Numeric)	(3 Alpha-Numeric)	(2 Numeric)	(2 Numeric)	

Figure 13.3.3 *Employee input data.*

A lead (heading) record is keyed in preceding the batched input of employee time data. This lead record indicates how many employees are in the batch and includes a total of hours worked by all employees. This lead record is used as a batch check to make certain that all records are processed and that totals match after all employee records have been processed.

Figure 13.3.4 shows a system flowchart for weekly payroll editing and processing. As this system flowchart depicts, inputs consist of the keyed data from employee time cards, a batch control lead record, and the latest master file.

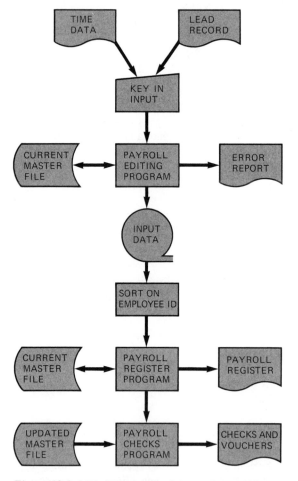

Figure 13.3.4 *Weekly payroll editing and processing system.*

Outputs are an updated master file with new year-to-date figures and various reports. Preliminary analysis indicates that payroll editing and processing should consist of three programs: payroll editing, payroll register, and payroll check writing.

Payroll Editing Program. The payroll editing program accepts data from the batch lead record and the employee time records. The first function of the edit program is to check the validity of the employee's social security number (use the social security number as an employee ID and record key). It will also check to ensure that hours worked is not a zero or negative number and that hours worked does not exceed 80 hours. Current company policy is that no employee will be paid for more than 80 hours per week. When an error is detected, an appropriate error message line is printed on the edit report. As each record is read, total hours worked and number of employee records read are accumulated. If the accumulated figures do not match the lead record, then an error condition is also printed on the error report. If any errors are detected, further processing is suspended until the errors are corrected and the edit program is again executed. Once an error-free run of the edit program is executed, the lead record and employee time records are written to a magnetic tape or disk, and the final, correct version of the employee input and lead records are processed next as an input file to the payroll register program as shown in Figure 13.3.4.

Payroll Register Program. Before being input to the payroll register program, the employee data file previously written to a tape or disk file is sorted from lowest to highest employee ID. As each record of this file is read, an employee master file record is accessed. The register program converts hourly information to gross pay, totals gross pay for an employee, and computes net pay after subtracting taxes, social security withholdings, and voluntary deductions. These current pay figures are then written to the master file.

Having computed current pay, the register program computes year-to-date figures for each employee. New year-to-date figures are the current figures plus the year-to-date figures already in the master file from the previous weekly payroll run. Year-to-date figures are used to ensure that social security withholding does not exceed $3500 during the year used by the check printing program to produce an employee's pay voucher. After the register program has been executed, the master file contains information extracted from the employee time records such as vacation time and hours worked. Additionally, the master file contains year-to-date data updated by the register program. Once all payroll records have been processed the payroll register is printed. The payroll register contains employee social security number, name, and all current and year-to-date figures from the latest updates to the master file. The register is produced as a printed output record that can be used officially for the current pay period. A continuing set of payroll registers provides complete documentation of payroll activities during the year and is stored for internal review and reference. Total gross pay, total net pay of all employees, and other data for the weekly pay period are printed on the register. A sample output is shown in Figure 13.3.5.

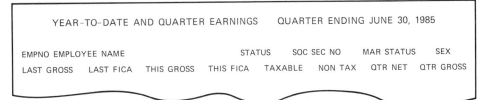

Figure 13.3.5 Payroll register.

Payroll Check Program. The last program in Figure 13.3.4 is the payroll check program that prints employee checks and vouchers. Since the register program computed figures needed to write an employee's check and voucher, the payroll check program makes no calculations. However, it does accumulate total gross pay and net pay figures for manual comparison to the total figures printed on the register. It accomplishes this by printing the last check with the accumulated figures and overprints the last check with "void" so it cannot be cashed. Preprinted check and voucher forms are used to produce the checks and vouchers. Figure 13.3.6 shows the payroll check and voucher forms.

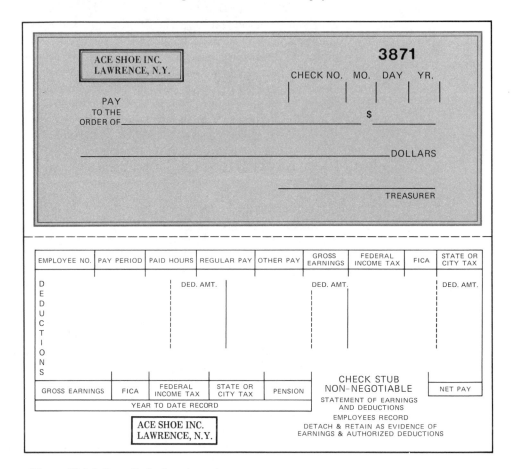

Figure 13.3.6 Payroll check and voucher.

Periodic Reports Processing

In addition to weekly payroll processing, government regulations require periodic reports on payroll activities. A special form is submitted to the federal government each quarter. The format of the form is shown in Figure 13.3.7, opposite. This government report is prepared by a program run quarterly that uses the master file current as of the end of the quarter and the master file of the previous quarter (January through March is the first quarter, April through May is the second, and so on). Figure 13.3.8 shows a system flowchart for quarterly processing.

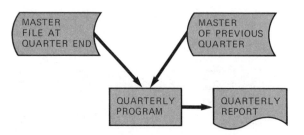

Figure 13.3.8 Quarterly program.

Form **941**
(Rev. January 1984)
Department of the Treasury
Internal Revenue Service

Employer's Quarterly Federal Tax Return
▶ For Paperwork Reduction Act Notice, see page 2.

OMB No. 1545-0029

| T |
| FF |
| FD |
| FP |
| I |
| T |

Your name, address, employer identification number, and calendar quarter of return. (If not correct, please change.)

Name (as distinguished from trade name)   Date quarter ended

Trade name, if any   Employer identification number

Address and ZIP code

If address is different from prior return, check here ▶

Record of Federal Tax Liability
(Complete if line 13 is $500 or more)

See the instructions under rule 4 on page 4 for details before checking these boxes.

Check only if you made eighth-monthly deposits using the 95% rule. . . . . ▶ ☐

Check only if you are a first-time 3-banking-day depositor. . . . . ▶ ☐

If you are not liable for returns in the future, write "FINAL" . . . . ▶

Date final wages paid . . . . ▶

Complete for First Quarter Only

1 **a** Number of employees (except household) employed in the pay period that includes March 12th . . ▶

b If you are a subsidiary corporation AND your parent corporation files a consolidated Form 1120, enter parent corporation's employer identification number (EIN) ▶

Date wages paid		Tax liability
Day		
1st-3rd	A	
4th-7th	B	
8th-11th	C	
12th-15th	D	
16th-19th	E	
20th-22nd	F	
23rd-25th	G	
26th-last	H	
I Total . . ▶		
1st-3rd	I	
4th-7th	J	
8th-11th	K	
12th-15th	L	
16th-19th	M	
20th-22nd	N	
23rd-25th	O	
26th-last	P	
II Total . . ▶		
1st-3rd	Q	
4th-7th	R	
8th-11th	S	
12th-15th	T	
16th-19th	U	
20th-22nd	V	
23rd-25th	W	
26th-last	X	
III Total . . ▶		
IV Total for quarter (add lines I, II, and III) . .		

(First month of quarter: A–H) (Second month of quarter: I–P) (Third month of quarter: Q–X)

2 Total wages and tips subject to withholding, plus other compensation . . . . ▶

3 **a** Income tax withheld from wages, tips, pensions, annuities, sick pay, gambling, etc. . . . . . ▶

b Backup withholding . . . . ▶

c Total income tax withheld (add lines 3a and 3b) . ▶

4 Adjustment of withheld income tax for preceding quarters of calendar year:

a From wages, tips, pensions, annuities, sick pay, gambling, etc. . . . . ▶

b From backup withholding . . . . ▶

c Total adjustments (add lines 4a and 4b) . . . . ▶

5 Adjusted total of income tax withheld (line 3c as adjusted by line 4c) . . . . ▶

6 Taxable social security wages paid:
$ _____ X 13.7% (.137) . .

7 **a** Taxable tips reported:
$ _____ X 6.7% (.067) . .

b Tips deemed to be wages (see instructions):
$ _____ X 7% (.07) . .

8 Total social security taxes (add lines 6, 7a, and 7b) . .

9 Adjustment of social security taxes (see instructions) ▶

10 Adjusted total of social security taxes . . . . .

11 Total taxes (add lines 5 and 10) . . . . ▶

12 Advance earned income credit (EIC) payments, if any ▶

13 Net taxes (subtract line 12 from line 11). This must equal line IV (plus line IV of Schedule A (Form 941) if you have treated backup withholding as a separate liability.) . . . .

14 Total deposits for quarter, including any overpayment applied from a prior quarter, from your records . . . . . . ▶

15 Undeposited taxes due (subtract line 14 from line 13). Enter here and pay to Internal Revenue Service . . . . . ▶

16 If line 14 is more than line 13, enter overpayment here ▶ $ _____ and check if to be: ☐ Applied to next return, or ☐ Refunded.

Under penalties of perjury, I declare that I have examined this return, including accompanying schedules and statements, and to the best of my knowledge and belief it is true, correct, and complete.

Signature ▶   Title ▶   Date ▶

Please file this form with your Internal Revenue Service Center (see instructions on "Where to File").

Form **941** (Rev. 1-84)

Figure 13.3.7 Employer's Quarterly Federal Tax Return.

The quarterly program uses the payroll master file from the preceding quarter as an additional input to the program. Quarter-to-date figures are the difference between the year-to-date (YTD) figures on these two payroll master files. The government also requires end-of-year printing of employee W-2 forms as shown in Figure 13.3.9.

1 Control number		OMB No. 1545-0008		
2 Employer's name, address, and ZIP code		3 Employer's identification number		4 Employer's State number
		5 Stat. employee ☐ Deceased ☐ Legal rep. ☐ 942 emp. ☐ Subtotal ☐ Void ☐		
		6 Allocated tips		7 Advance EIC payment
8 Employee's social security number	9 Federal income tax withheld	10 Wages, tips, other compensation		11 Social security tax withheld
12 Employee's name, address, and ZIP code		13 Social security wages		14 Social security tips
		16		
		17 State income tax	18 State wages, tips, etc.	19 Name of State
		20 Local income tax	21 Local wages, tips, etc.	22 Name of locality

Form **W-2 Wage and Tax Statement** **1984**   Copy 1 For State, City, or Local Tax Department ☐
Employee's and employer's copy compared

Figure 13.3.9 W-2 Wage and Tax Statement.

In addition, the master file is reset to zero for year-to-date figures at the end of each fiscal year. We use a calendar year as the fiscal year. The system flowchart for end-of-year processing is shown in Figure 13.3.10.

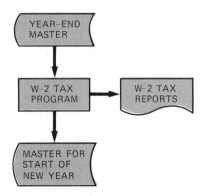

Figure 13.3.10 Year-end processing.

Some of the fields that would be in the payroll master file and their recommended format are listed below.

EMPLOYEE NUMBER	9 Numeric
LAST NAME	12 Alpha
FIRST NAME	12 Alpha
MIDDLE INITIAL	1 Alpha
ADDRESS	22 Alpha-numeric
SEX	1 Alpha
BIRTH DATE	10 Alpha-numeric
NUMBER OF DEPENDENTS	2 Numeric
MARITAL STATUS	1 Alpha
DATE EMPLOYMENT BEGAN	10 Alpha-numeric
NUMBER OF TAX EXEMPTIONS	2 Numeric
SALARY FOR WEEK	6 Numeric
REGULAR WAGE	6 Numeric
OVERTIME WAGE	6 Numeric
VACATION ACCUMULATION RATE	3 Numeric
SICK LEAVE ACCUMULATION RATE	3 Numeric
ACCUMULATED VACATION	3 Numeric
ACCUMULATED SICK LEAVE	2 Numeric
VACATION USED CURRENT YEAR	3 Numeric
SICK LEAVE USED CURRENT YEAR	3 Numeric
CURRENT GROSS PAY	6 Numeric
CURRENT FEDERAL TAX	6 Numeric
CURRENT SOC SEC WITHHOLDING	6 Numeric
CURRENT NET PAY	6 Numeric
CURRENT REGULAR HOURS	4 Numeric
CURRENT OVERTIME HOURS	4 Numeric
YTD GROSS PAY	7 Numeric
YTD FEDERAL TAX	7 Numeric
YTD SOC SEC WITHHOLDING	7 Numeric
YTD NET PAY	7 Numeric
YTD HOURS REGULAR	7 Numeric
YTD HOURS OVERTIME	7 Numeric

Figure 13.3.11 *Partial payroll master file.*

QUESTIONS FOR DISCUSSION

1. Did you feel that the analyst left out some important details about the system's design? What questions do you still have?
2. Would you recommend a sequential, relative, or indexed file organization for the master file? Why?
3. What data elements would be required on the manually prepared employee change form for existing employees. Do you agree that the same form could be used for new employees? Why?
4. What other fields are needed to complete the quarterly tax return and W-2 statement that are not included in Figure 13.3.11?
5. The analyst has chosen batch processing for the payroll system. Is this the best approach? Why or why not?
6. Do you have the information necessary to compute income tax withholding?
7. The maximum social security withholding is now $3,500. Assuming that it will increase in future years, how would you prepare for this without having to modify program code each time it changes?

8. Did the analyst explain all potential update procedures for the master file? For example, how is social security withholding rate updated in the master file?

9. As a further check and record for control purposes, do you recommend that the system produce any other output in the year-end processing of W-2 forms?

10. Are there any fields in the quarterly report that are not in the master file? Can you think of a way to process the quarterly report without adding more fields to the master file?

11. If your company later decided to permit employees to deduct contributions to a fund for the purchase of company common stock, would you add more fields to the master record or to the employee time record? Explain your choice.

12. Should the payroll system be developed as separate programs, subprograms, or a combination of the two? Defend your answer.

13. If the city later levies a city income tax, how can you plan for that possibility? Which program should compute the city income tax? Where would you store the city tax data?

14. Assume that management later wants to keep a record of the average overtime hours worked in each department and produce a report showing these figures each week. Which programs and records would you modify at that time?

15. Anticipating that management may eventually expand the payroll system to other capabilities such as job classification, union dues, and so forth, how can you prepare now?

16. Assume that you heard a manager boast that the company will soon have a completely computerized payroll system. Would you agree? Why or why not?

EXERCISES

1. Develop a structure chart that shows each of the programs in the payroll system. Do not decompose below the level of showing each program.

2. Develop structure charts that decompose the payroll edit program into functionally related modules down to the lowest practical level. Do not forget to include reading the lead record and showing any initialization and termination activities.

3. Design the payroll master file on paper. (If available, a COBOL coding form or printer layout form can be helpful for this.)

4. Write a pseudocode solution for the PROCEDURE DIVISION of the payroll edit program.

5. Develop structure charts for the payroll register program. Decompose into functionally related modules down to the lowest level. Include the sort as a module in this program and again provide for appropriate initialization and termination activities you consider necessary.

6. Design the payroll register output from the register program.

7. Write a pseudocode solution for the payroll register program.

8. Develop structure charts that show the payroll check-writing program decomposed into the lowest levels.

9. Write a pseudocode solution for the PROCEDURE DIVISION of the check-writing program.

10. Develop a structure chart for the quarterly report program.

11. Develop a structure chart for year-end processing.

12. Write a pseudocode solution for processing the quarterly report program.

13. Write a pseudocode solution for the PROCEDURE DIVISION of the year-end report.

Chapter Review

SUMMARY

Large-scale applications must include features that allow programs to communicate with one another. COBOL uses subprograms and the CALL verb to permit subdividing large applications into subprograms.

Subprograms contain all the divisions required of any COBOL program. The difference between a program and a subprogram is that a subprogram begins execution as the result of a command in another COBOL program and a subprogram can use the contents of storage locations allocated in the calling program.

The actual mechanics of using a subprogram require the calling program to issue a CALL 'program–name' command with or without the USING option. The CALL statement causes control to pass to the first statement of the PROCEDURE DIVISION of the program that has 'program–name' in its PROGRAM–ID paragraph. The called program returns control (after executing) to the statement in the calling program which follows the CALL command. The USING clause lists the storage locations in the calling program that will be available for use in the subprogram. The called program describes these fields in the LINKAGE SECTION and lists the names given them in the called program in a USING clause that follows the PROCEDURE DIVISION entry in the called program.

The use of subprograms allows large problems to be broken down into manageable parts that can be developed independently. Provided the interfaces are well defined (i.e., a clear specification of which variables are being sent to the subprogram and which variables have values created by the subprogram), the development of large applications can proceed with concurrent development activities.

Section 13.2 explains some of the modern design tools and methodologies used to solve more advanced, complex programming problems. The top-down approach encourages the programmer to decompose a larger problem into functionally related parts, called *modules*. This approach not only permits the programmer to deal more effectively with complexity at ever-lower levels of detail, but it also makes programs easier to understand and maintain.

Being limited by the number of details and relationships that our minds can handle, we must control complexity by dividing a problem into parts and subparts that can be understood. Top-down design has been shown to be an effective tool for dividing problems into manageable parts. Two similar tools used in implementing top-down design— structure charts and HIPO charts—were introduced.

A structure chart is not intended to show program logic as are pseudocode statements and program flowcharts. Rather, a structure chart depicts the modules required to solve the overall problem at various levels of detail. Similarly, HIPO diagrams show graphically what a program does, what data is processed, and what data is created. HIPO is a useful design as well as documentation tool. A typical HIPO package consists of a visual table of contents (VTOC) diagram, overview diagrams, and detail diagrams.

Like a structure chart, a VTOC (also called a hierarchy chart) shows the hierarchical structure of the program solution. An overview diagram and the detail diagram are divided into input, process, output sections and show what data is read, processed, and created in each module. A detail diagram is more specific than an overview diagram and often includes extensive explanatory information.

In addition to structure charts and HIPO diagrams, a variety of other techniques are used by software development professionals. Three discussed in this chapter are the chief programmer team, structured walkthroughs, and the development support library. A chief programmer leads a team that usually consists of an assistant leader, expert and less experienced programmers, a librarian, and others, depending on the size of a particular project. A structured walkthrough is a group review of a programmer's design or code to detect faulty design or coding errors. Structured walkthroughs can be conducted at various stages in the software development process. A development support library serves as a central repository of information related to the project.

Section 13.3 presented a problem that involved a number of interrelated programs that together solve an organization's payroll processing and reporting problems. This application provided an opportunity to deal with complexity and apply any or all of the techniques introduced in Section 13.2.

TEST YOURSELF

1. Explain the syntax and the semantics of the CALL 'program–name' statement.
2. Explain the syntax and the semantics of the CALL 'program–name' USING... statement.
3. Explain the syntax and the semantics of the PROCEDURE DIVISION USING... statement.
4. Explain the function of the LINKAGE SECTION.
5. Where is storage allocated for a field defined in the LINKAGE SECTION of a subprogram?
6. Why are subprograms especially useful in large applications? How can they be just as useful in smaller applications?
7. What does it mean that the name of a storage location is a local phenomenon?
8. How does a subprogram know that it is time to return to its calling program?
9. If you were a chief programmer, why would you recommend the use of subprograms instead of a single main program?
10. List four reasons for using subprograms.
11. Control is passed from one subprogram or from the main program to another subprogram with which statement?
12. Which subprogram can a subprogram not call in COBOL?
13. Explain two possible methods for handling subprograms that are generally available with different operating systems.
14. Where does control return to in a calling program after the called program has been executed?
15. When storage locations are shared by two or more subprograms, what is required in the PROCEDURE DIVISION in addition to the LINKAGE SECTION in the DATA DIVISION?
16. Explain why the top-down approach is recommended for large, complex programs.
17. Why is a structure chart easier to use than HIPO diagrams? If you were a manager, why would you prefer HIPO over a structure chart?
18. Programmers often avoid using structure and HIPO charts and go directly to a logic design of a program. If you were a manager, what could you say to encourage programmers to first design the solution with structure or hierarchy charts?
19. If you were a manager, why would you encourage a complete HIPO package?
20. After a program or system of programs has been designed using structure or HIPO charts and diagrams, why use pseudocode or a program flowchart?
21. Why are well-documented program designs so important?
22. Pseudocode solutions converted to comments in the program are often referred to as internal documentation while program flowcharts, structure charts, and HIPO diagrams are referred to as external documentation. Explain why those terms are appropriate descriptions.

23. Why use a structured walkthrough?
24. Do you prefer to use pseudocode or program flowcharts? Defend your choice.
25. Why is a development support library useful in team projects?
26. If you were in charge of a large software development project, how could you defend the assignment of someone to your team who was not a programmer?

Appendix A

Flowcharts

Figure A.1

Figure A.2

Figure A.3

The most common program flowchart symbols approved by the National Standards Institute are

1. Terminal. The terminal symbol represents the beginning (START) and the end (STOP) of a program's logic. (Figure A.1)

2. Input/Output. Special symbols for cards, tapes, etc., that are used in system flowcharts are usually not used in program flowcharts. Instead, the parallelogram is used for all I/O operations. (Figure A.2)

3. Processing. A processing step causes a change in the value of a storage location. It may represent a more general process in a macro flowchart such as Compute Net Pay, or a more specific process, such as MOVE NAME TO PRINT–LINE. (Figure A.3)

4. Decision. The diamond illustrates a decision for alternate paths in a program. The decision is a test that determines which path to follow. Two examples are shown as Figure A.4.

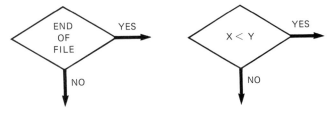

Figure A.4

5. Flowlines. Lines with arrowheads link the various symbols and show the sequence of operations. (Figure A.5)

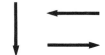

Figure A.5

6. Logic connector. A small circle is used (1) as an exit and entry point from another part of a flowchart to another page; (2) to avoid drawing lines that cross; (3) to avoid drawing very long links. Figure A.6 shows two examples.

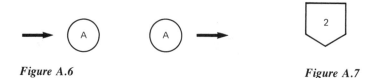

Figure A.6   *Figure A.7*

The page connector symbol shown in Figure A.7 is used as a logic connector to another page.

7. Annotation. The symbol of a three-sided rectangle with a broken line is used to add comments to a flowchart. Broken lines extend toward the symbol to which the comment pertains. (Figure A.8)

8. Predefined process. Certain operations, modules, and routines are repeated throughout a program. It can be defined once, and then this symbol can be used subsequently. (Figure A.9)

Figure A.8   *Figure A.9*

There are no set rules regarding how much detail to provide in a program flowchart. A general (macro) flowchart might be suitable to provide an overview for management. A macro flowchart for computing employee pay might simply show: (1) compute gross pay; (2) compute deductions; (3) compute net pay. A detailed (micro) flowchart is normally what programmers draw.

Flowcharts have certain advantages for program design. A flowchart aids in communicating to others the solution of a problem; it provides a permanent record of the solution, which can be consulted later in order to understand a program's logic; it serves as a blueprint to guide the development process; and it may be presented in any desired degree of detail. On the other hand, there are certain limitations and disadvantages. Complex flowcharts can be laborious to draw and difficult to follow especially when a large number of decision paths are included. For this reason, there is a tendency for programmers (and programming students) to avoid drawing a flowchart until *after* the program is developed. While an after-the-fact flowchart does not detract from its utility as a documented description of a final design, it does keep it from serving as a tool for program planning. An even more serious disadvantage is that too often flowcharts are not updated when a program is changed. As a result, it no longer serves as an accurate description of the program when someone is later faced with trying to understand the logic. Because of these limitations, flowcharts are not emphasized in this book. Instead, pseudocode outlines and models are used.

The flowchart given as Figure A.10 shows the logic for processing student grades to compute a student's average, to determine if the student passed or failed, and to print the student's name and the pass or fail information. After all the records have been processed, a class average grade is computed and printed. For instructional purposes, initialization, input, process, output, and termination activities are highlighted. These activities are not normally shown as distinct parts on a flowchart.

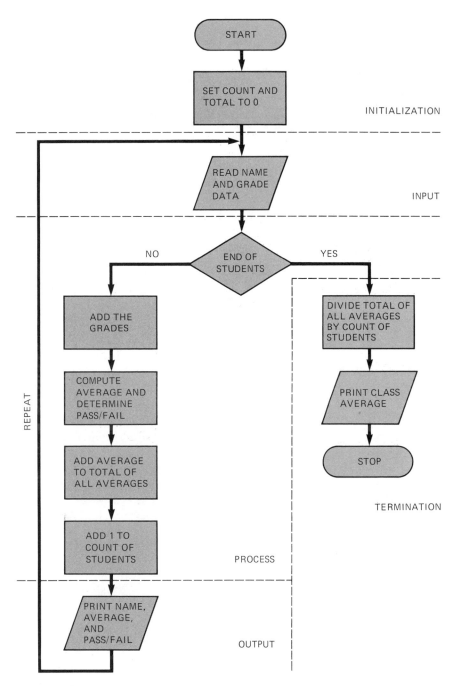

Figure A.10 *Student grade program.*

Appendix B

WATBOL System

This appendix explains features of the WATBOL compiler for ANSI standard COBOL. The WATBOL compiler is used in many student and development environments. Two COBOL programs often used with WATBOL—COPYPROG and SORTPROG—are also discussed in detail.

A number of different COBOL compilers exist and are in use today. Standard COBOL can be executed on a wide variety of machines. Except for minor parts of a COBOL program, the language is designed so that the code written is highly portable and can be used easily in different environments with little or no change to the source program. It is not unusual for the same computer installation to have more than one COBOL compiler. For example, one compiler might provide clearer error messages, but have slower execution. This compiler would be used to compile during program or system development. Another compiler may have fewer of the possible capabilities of a complete COBOL compiler, but may be executed on a smaller computer, may be better suited for student use, or may have other advantages. Still other compilers may minimize execution time.

WATBOL, a compiler developed at the University of Waterloo in Ontario, Canada, is especially well suited for students who are learning to code COBOL programs. WATBOL supports Standard COBOL with additional student-oriented features: (1) It can be implemented in a manner that excludes certain standard COBOL capabilities not normally needed in an introductory COBOL course, for example, the SORT verb need not be implemented; (2) It provides more assistance than most other COBOL compilers during compilation; (3) It implements some COBOL features differently than standard COBOL, but the use of these features seems standard to the programmer. WATBOL is one of several widely used student-oriented compilers. Others include WATFIV (a FORTRAN compiler also developed by the University of Waterloo) and PLC (a subset of PL/I that was developed at Cornell University) and the UCSD Pascal System.

When a program is submitted to a computer for compilation and execution, the program must be accompanied by special instructions for the operating system. A sample program setup is shown in Figure B.1. These special instructions include who should be charged for the time and resources used, which compiler is required, and which part of the input is the instruction set and which is the program's data. All this is accomplished with Job Control Language (JCL). There is not one standard JCL for all systems. The JCL depends on the computing environment used by the program. The WATBOL compiler supports 1974 ANSI standard COBOL code, but also includes some features that facilitate

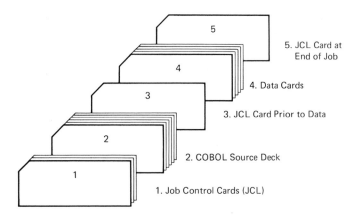

Figure B.1 *Blocks of cards in a program deck for batch processing.*

student use of COBOL in the learning environment. The special features include in-line error messages for errors detected at compile time, a program in the COPY library that simulates the SORT verb, and a program in the COPY library that is a utility for file-to-file processing. The WATBOL compiler also provides a convenient way to execute programs that include subprograms. A final feature of WATBOL is the ease with which it can be used with many microcomputers currently on the market. These features will be discussed in detail in this Appendix.

Your instructor will provide you with specific instructions on the form of the JCL that must occur in a program. Once you have assembled the source program correctly and submitted the job for compilation and execution (some or all of the data will be read if there are no compilation errors), the next WATBOL feature you will need to understand is the printed output. See Figure B.2 on the following page.

As part of the printed output, the WATBOL system may generate a number of possible messages. These include the following.

1. $NOSOURCE
2. ***WARNING***
3. ***ERROR***
4. A message may appear that says the compilation process was successfully completed.
5. The program started to execute, but failed to produce all expected output.

With any or all of these likely to happen, a few words of explanation are in order so you can assess the seriousness of each of these possibilities.

1. $NOSOURCE indicates that the code referred to in the COPY sentence just above this notation will not be listed as part of your source program. The code in TEXTA is included as part of the program to be compiled and executed at the point the COPY verb occurs. However, all the lines in TEXTA are not going to be listed as they would have appeared if you had typed them in the program and had not used the COPY verb. This is an option that is set by the local computer installation when WATBOL is implemented.

2. The ***WARNING*** clause is hard to describe because sometimes nothing can be done but to note its existence. Other times, specific action must be taken to eliminate the warning. For example, a READ statement with no AT END clause will cause a WARNING to be issued. Some compilers require this clause and signal an ERROR if the clause is not present. The WATBOL compiler accepts this extension to COBOL. A warning may also note that a

```
TIME=03:17:46    VERSION=V3L0.1     * * *  WATBOL  * * *  ID=UMO   DATE=THU, OCT. 11, 1984
            $JOB   WATBOL  RCS370,TT=15 HAGGARD BOX801
               *
               * NAME:              ID:
               * PROGRAM-NUMBER: 2.3-1
               * DESCRIPTION:  THE FIRST THREE RECORDS
               *  OF THE CUSTOMER-FILE ARE TO BE LISTED BY
               *  THE PRINTER.
               *
                    COPY TEXTA.
         $NOSOURCE
               WORKING-STORAGE SECTION.
               01  CHARGE-CUSTOMER PICTURE X(100).
               01  PRINT-PATTERN   PICTURE X(133).
       1       PROCEDURE DIVISION.
       2           OPEN INPUT CUSTOMER-FILE
                        OUTPUT PRINTER.

       3           READ CUSTOMER-FILE INTO CHARGE-CUSTOMER AT END.
       4           MOVE CHARGE-CUSTOMER TO PRINT-PATTERN.
       5           WRITE PRINT-LINE FROM PRINT-PATTERN.

       6           READ CUSTOMER-FILE INTO CHARGE-CUSTOMER AT END.
       7           MOVE CHARGE-CUSTOMER TO PRINT-PATTERN.
       8           WRITE PRINT-LINE FROM PRINT-PATTERN.

       9           READ CUSTOMER-FILE INTO CHARGE-CUSTOMER AT END.
      10           MOVE CHARGE-CUSTOMER TO PRINT-PATTERN.
      11           WRITE PRINT-LINE FROM PRINT-PATTERN.

      12           CLOSE CUSTOMER-FILE,
                        PRINTER.
      13           STOP RUN.

***** THERE ARE NO STATEMENTS FLAGGED IN THIS COMPILE


1900000WEINSMEIER CFR    44 BERTA PLACE     TORONTO ONT        0906750000050000000123A2
1900100MENZIES RG        17 BERTA PLACE     OSHAWA ONT         0906750000065000001254A2
1900200BAYLESS GF        15 SAMSON CR       BLUE RIDGE MANITOBA 1711760000066000000432A2


COMPILE TIME      0.04 SECONDS TASK;    1.00 SECONDS REAL
EXECUTION TIME    0.00 SECONDS TASK;    0.00 SECONDS REAL
CARDS READ DURING COMPILE       31 DURING EXECUTION        0
LINES PRINTED DURING COMPILE    36
PAGES PRINTED DURING COMPILE     1 DURING EXECUTION        0
CORE UNUSED AT COMPILE TIME 364040 BYTES
CORE AVAILABLE AT ENTRY TO EXECUTION 371280 BYTES

FOR INFORMATION ABOUT WATBOL PLACE THE WORD HELP ON THE $JOB CARD
```

Figure B.2 *Typical output from WATBOL.*

period was missing at the end of a sentence or that characters were punched to the left of margin B when they should have been punched in margin B. In the case of missing punctuation, the program can be modified so that it will run without the warnings. The presence of a warning will not make successful compilation impossible, and normally a program will execute even though a warning was noted at compile time.

3. An ***ERROR*** condition at compile time will not necessarily cause the compilation process to stop. However, no effort will be made to execute the results of compilation if an error was detected. Before execution begins the compilation must be successfully completed. Any compile time error message will be printed immediately under the line of code in the source program that caused the error. Misspelled words are often the source of compile time errors the first time the program is submitted for execution. Often an error at the beginning of a program can cause errors later in the program. Thus, it is not always necessary to change every line that is flagged as being in error. In WATBOL the first word in the sentence that triggers the ERROR message will have a $ printed underneath it.

4. This message, included with the source listing, indicates that the code was written using proper syntax. It verifies that you apparently gave the machine correct instructions.

5. A program you write will go through two levels of scrutiny: at *compile time* and then at *execution time*. If the program does not compile, the source program and the compilation errors will appear on the terminal screen or printed listing and the execution phase will not be attempted. Even if the program compiles and execution begins, run time errors may exist. Moreover, certain errors during execution cause the machine to stop executing the program although a logical error in the program itself may not cause an error even at execution time. A message at the bottom of the output indicates the line of code that is the apparent cause of the program's termination. There is usually some indication of what went wrong. You must then review the program and correct the error condition before submitting the program again.

Utility Programs (COPYPROG and SORTPROG)

In any computing environment, there are a number of file-to-file processing activities that many different programs use. Typically, these activities include listing the records of a file or transferring a file from one storage medium to another. Sometimes the only difference between two applications is the files used. Customarily, a local computer installation will have an applications programmer write a single application program for file-to-file processing that accepts as data the names of the files being processed. The program is made available through one of the installation's libraries so that all programmers may use it when it is needed. Programs of this type are called **utility programs.** WATBOL includes two application programs in its COPY library. The first, called COPYPROG, allows file-to-file processing for all the files defined in TEXTA. The second, called SORTPROG, simulates features of the SORT verb. The SORT simulation is very helpful for students since the sorting process can be explained and used without all the usual problems associated with the JCL for sort work files. In addition, the simulation allows much faster turnaround for student jobs that require a sort.

Both COPYPROG and SORTPROG are COBOL programs. The algorithms they use depend on having all the file names in a table. This makes it easy to extend these programs to different environments where files other than the ones in the TEXTA may be used.

The COBOL program COPYPROG is a utility program written to handle typical file-to-file processing requirements. In order to use COPYPROG in an application we must supply it with data that indicates the input and output files to be used as well as any special requirements for the format of the records of the output file. The program is brought on-line from the COPY library by the command:

```
COPY COPYPROG.
```

This one sentence makes a complete program available for execution. The input and output files are identified on the first two data cards used. These cards have the following form.

```
FILE-IN  = input file name
FILE-OUT = output file name
```

The file names used are the file names defined in TEXTA. If no FILE-OUT card is included, COPYPROG assumes that the line printer is the intended output file.

Suppose we have put all the Canadian customers from CUSTOMER–FILE on FILE1. To list the records on FILE1, we use the following program.

```
       *
       * NAME:               ID:
       * PROGRAM-NUMBER: B-1
       * DESCRIPTION:  LIST THE RECORDS IN FILE1
               COPY COPYPROG.
  $ENTRY
  FILE-IN=FILE1
```

Since no file is identified for the output, the output is automatically sent to the printer. When we list the contents of a file there is no separation between successive data fields unless the space is already there as part of each record. Obviously, COPYPROG would be more useful if the information displayed could be formatted as it is done in business reports. This feature is available by means of the statement

$$FORMAT=(I,J,K)$$

The parameter I indicates the location in the input record of the first byte of information we want to list. The parameter J indicates how many bytes in the input record we want to access beginning with byte I. The parameter K indicates the first of the J bytes in the output record that will contain this information. As an example let's look at

```
    INPUT RECORD        OUTPUT RECORD

    1 2 3 4 5 6 7 8 9    1 2 3 4 5 6
    A B C D E F G H I        E F G
```

Displaying the output can be accomplished by

$$FORMAT=(5,3,3)$$

This statement directs the computer to take the three bytes of the input record beginning with byte five and display these in successive bytes of the output record beginning with its byte three.

Up to ten FORMAT data cards may be included in a program following the two data records that identify the input and output files. Processing of the format records will be done in the order of occurrence of the FORMAT cards.

The second utility simulates parts of the syntax of the SORT verb. This utility is particularly useful for preparing files for a control break or report writer application. The sorting process is simulated in WATBOL by means of a COBOL program called SORTPROG, which is in the COPY library. The COBOL verb SORT is also available in WATBOL, but with SORTPROG, we can avoid the special coding needed in the DATA DIVISION and the JCL needed for the special sort work file that the SORT verb requires. Since SORTPROG was written to sort the files designed for use with this book, we can focus attention on the use of the sorting process rather than on the details of implementation. As in the case of COPYPROG, we supply SORTPROG with the names of input and output files as well as the locations of the key fields as input data rather than as part of the source listing (as is done when using the SORT verb). The first two data cards for SORTPROG identify the input and output files using the file names defined in TEXTA.

```
    SORT-IN  = name of file to be sorted
    SORT-OUT = name of file to receive sorted records
```

SORTPROG only sorts in ASCENDING order so the only remaining information needed is the location of the key field in a record. This is supplied on a data card that has the form:

$$SORT-KEY=(I,J)$$

where I is the number of the byte in a record that indicates the starting position of that key field, and J is the number of bytes starting at byte I that comprises the key field. Multiple field keys will be explained after an example using a single key field is shown. Figure B.3 is an example that will help illustrate the use of SORTPROG. Using SORTPROG to sort the STUDENT-FILE alphabetically by student NAME follows:

```
      *
      * NAME:                              ID:
      * PROGRAM-NUMBER: B-2
      * DESCRIPTION: ORDER THE STUDENT-FILE
      *    ALPHABETICALLY BY STUDENT NAME. PUT THE
      *    SORTED FILE ON FILE1.
      *
              COPY SORTPROG.
$ENTRY
SORT-IN=STUDENT-FILE
SORT-OUT=FILE1
SORT-KEY=(5,18)
```

The program SORTPROG is driven by a table lookup scheme that includes the names of all the files in the computing environment. Using this program in other environments only requires slight adjustments to the tables.

```
            1   2   3   4   5   6   7   8   9  10  11  12  13  14
 Record 1   A   B   C   D   E   F   G   H   I   J   K   L   M   N
 Record 2   O   P   Q   R   S   T   U   V   W   X   Y   Z   A   B
 Record 3   C   D   E   F   G   H   I   J   K   L   M   N   O   P


                        SORT-KEY=(7,3)
                           GHI
                           UVW
                           IJK
                        SORT-KEY=(10,5)
                          JKLMN
                          XYZAB
                          LMNOP
```

Figure B.3 *An example of SORT KEYs using SORTPROG.*

Sometimes several records have a key field with the same value, such as AGE in STUDENT-FILE. When this occurs we may want to refine the ordering within each category determined by the first key field. Suppose we want to list the NAMEs of students in alphabetical order within each AGE category. To do this, we form a longer word for use in the dictionary ordering process. The first part of the key word should be the two digits of the student's AGE, and the next 18 bytes of the key word should be the letters in the student's NAME. When the sort procedure is executed, and the AGEs in two records are the same, the ordering procedure moves on to compare the next 18 letters in the key word. We generate this key word by using an additional SORT-KEY data card. In this case we would have

$$SORT-KEY=(24,2)$$
$$SORT-KEY=(5,18)$$

When there are multiple SORT–KEY cards, the key word is generated using the bytes of the first SORT–KEY as the leftmost bytes of the key word. The next SORT–KEY statement will have the bytes referred to used as the next bytes of the key word. Up to ten such records are allowed by SORTPROG. Figure B.4 illustrates an example of using a key field composed of several different fields in the record. The sort of the records shown in Figure B.4 is by SEX by AGE by NAME.

```
                    ORIGINAL ORDER

        BYTE              2 2 2 2     3
                  5       0 1 2 3 4   5
                  STEVENS       M 17  056
                  ROTH          M 17  074
                  ELLIS         M 17  085
                  COOK          M 17  058
                  WHITE         F 17  070
                  SHELL         F 18  067

                    REQUIRED ORDER

        AGE   SEX      NAME      PHYSICS
        17     F      WHITE        070
        18     F      SHELL        067
        17     M      COOK         058
        17     M      ELLIS        085
        17     M      ROTH         074
        17     M      STEVENS      056

                    SORT WORD
                  M17STEVENS
                  M17ROTH
                  M17ELLIS
                  M17COOK
                  F17WHITE
                  F18SHELL

                      CODE
                  SORT-KEY=(23,1)
                  SORT-KEY=(24,2)
                  SORT-KEY=(5,18)
```

Figure B.4 *An example of multiple SORT KEYs.*

The next program with WATBOL JCL included uses SORTPROG to sort STUDENT–FILE by AGE, by SEX, by NAME.

```
$JOB WATBOL
       *
       * NAME:       ID:
       * PROGRAM-NUMBER: B-3
       * DESCRIPTION: SORT THE RECORDS OF THE STUDENT-
       *   FILE BY SEX BY AGE BY NAME.
       *
            COPY SORTPROG.
```

```
$ENTRY
SORT-IN=STUDENT-FILE
SORT-OUT=FILE1
SORT-KEY=(23,1)
SORT-KEY=(24,2)
SORT-KEY=(5,18)
```

The sorted version of the file is now on FILE1, which doesn't help much if we want to see how it looks. We can now use the COPYPROG utility to obtain a listing of the file.

```
     *
     * NAME               ID:
     * PROGRAM-NUMBER: B-4
     * DESCRIPTION: LIST THE RECORDS ON FILE1 WHICH
     *   ARE THE RECORDS OF THE STUDENT-FILE ORDERED
     *   BY SEX BY AGE BY NAME.
     *
            COPY COPYPROG.
$ENTRY
FILE-IN=FILE1
```

WATBOL JCL for Subprograms

A complete program that includes a main program and one or more subprograms plays a fundamental role in the development of large-scale application programs. WATBOL makes the execution of such a job particularly easy. The JCL for a program with subprograms is simply

```
$JOB WATBOL xxx
  any required file definition cards for the main program and all
subprograms

    MAIN PROGRAM

    CALLED PROGRAM 1

        -                     ⎫   IN ANY
                              ⎬
        -                     ⎬   ORDER
                              ⎭
        -

    CALLED PROGRAM N
$ENTRY
DATA
```

The subprograms are not compiled as separate programs and then linked together by the operating system. Rather, they are all treated as a single job.

WATBOL Reserved Words

The WATBOL compiler has incorporated a number of reserved words not on the ANSI 1974 list of reserved words. They are listed on the following page.

ACTUAL	ETI	SEEK
ADDRESS	EXAMINE	SELECTED
ALPHANUMERIC	EXCEEDS	SERVICE
ALPHANUMERIC–EDITED	EXHIBIT	SKIP1
APPLY	EXTENDED–SEARCH	SKIP2
BASIS	FILE–LIMIT	SKIP3
BEGINNING	FILE–LIMITS	SORT–CORE–SIZE
CHANGED	GOBACK	SORT–FILE–SIZE
COMP–REG	HOLD	SORT–MESSAGE
COMP–1	ID	SORT–MODE–SIZE
COMP–2	INITIALIZE	SORT–RETURN
COMP–3	INSERT	SUPERVISOR
COMP–4	KEYS	SUSPEND
COMPUTATIONAL–1	LABEL–RETURN	SYSIN
COMPUTATIONAL–2	LEAVE	SYSIPT
COMPUTATIONAL–3	LIBRARY	SYSLST
COMPUTATIONAL–4	LOWER–BOUND	SYSOUT
CONSOLE	LOWER–BOUNDS	SYSPCH
CONSTANT	MASTER–INDEX	SYSPUNCH
CORE–INDEX	MORE–LABELS	S01
CSP	NAMED	S02
CURRENT–DATE	NOMINAL	TALLY
CYL–INDEX	NOTE	THEN
CYL–OVERFLOW	NSTD–REELS	TIME–OF–DAY
C01	NUMERIC–EDITED	TOTALED
C02	OBJECT–PROGRAM	TOTALING
C03	OH	TRACE
C04	OTHERWISE	TRACK
C05	OV	TRACK–AREA
C06	POSITIONING	TRACK–LIMIT
C07	PREPARED	TRACKS
C08	PRINT–SWITCH	TRANSFORM
C09	PRIORITY	UNEQUAL
C10	PROCESS	UPPER–BOUND
C11	PROCESSING	UPPER–BOUNDS
C12	RANGE	UPSI–0
DAY–OF–WEEK	READY	UPSI–1
DEBUG	RECORD–OVERFLOW	UPSI–2
DEPTH	RECORDING	UPSI–3
DISP	RELOAD	UPSI–4
DISPLAY–ST	REMARKS	UPSI–5
EJECT	REORG–CRITERIA	UPSI–6
ENDING	REREAD	UPSI–7
ENTRY	RETURN–CODE	WRITE–ONLY
EQUALS	SA	WRITE–VERIFY

Appendix C

STUDENT–FILE

The STUDENT–FILE consists of 100 records. Each record contains 100 bytes of information about a single student. The records are organized as follows:

STUDENT-RECORD

ID-NO	NAME	SEX	AGE	ALG	GEO	ENG	PHY	CHE	FILLER
1 4	5 22	23	24 25	26 28	29 31	32 34	35 37	38 40	41 100

Figure C.1 *Record layout for STUDENT–FILE.*

	Begins in Byte	Length	Description
ID–NUMBER	1	4	This is a four-digit code. The codes are in increasing order, but this order is determined by the sequence in which records are added to the file.
NAME	5	18	There is space for 18 characters. The form of the field is last name followed by two or three initials in left-justified bytes 16–18 of the field.
SEX	23	1	The code is M for male students and F for female students.
AGE	24	2	This is a two-digit field. The ages range from 14 to 19.
ALGEBRA	26	3	Each field contains three digits which represent a grade in this particular course. The grading scale is 75 = honors and 55 = failing.
GEOMETRY	29	3	
ENGLISH	32	3	
PHYSICS	35	3	
CHEMISTRY	38	3	
Extra Space	41	60	The end of each record is left blank so that additional fields can be added to each record at a later date.

STUDENT–FILE is the same file as the one of this name created at the University of Waterloo for use with the WATBOL compiler.

ID–NO.	NAME		SEX	AGE	ALG	GEO	ENG	PHY	CHE
0110	STEVENS	TK	M	17	065	063	085	056	076
0297	WAGNER	YL	M	15	065	086	085	084	074
0317	RANCOURT	FU	F	16	075	072	070	068	065
0364	WAGNER	DT	M	16	070	058	090	064	083
0617	HAROLD	FB	M	17	085	080	080	075	074
0998	WEICKLER	EF	M	16	072	074	075	075	075
1203	WILLS	KE	F	16	073	072	072	073	084
1232	ROTH	KM	M	17	072	070	070	074	072
1234	GEORGE	LI	M	18	070	070	071	058	069
1265	MAJOR	LK	M	16	065	065	068	068	069
1568	POLLOCK	CKK	M	17	089	088	085	092	063
1587	PEARSON	MJK	F	15	055	050	049	061	060
1617	REITER	KJ	M	17	100	068	069	075	089
2028	SCHULTZ	MF	M	18	069	068	075	074	053
2036	BROOKS	KJ	M	18	065	068	069	070	065
2039	ELLIS	RE	M	17	085	085	085	085	085
2049	BECKER	JL	F	15	065	065	065	068	069
2055	ASSLEY	ER	M	16	065	063	060	063	065
2087	STECKLEY	AS	M	15	056	053	085	084	072
2093	WEBER	IOU	M	15	075	072	071	070	058
2108	COOK	LK	M	17	052	070	070	058	069
2165	MAJOR	KL	M	16	068	069	072	072	070
2238	HORST	BG	M	17	074	072	070	075	074
2282	SPARLING	DKL	M	18	055	056	092	042	068
2283	WAGLER	RB	F	16	073	072	076	065	069
2302	PRESTON	SK	M	17	072	075	074	078	076
2313	LESSARD	AC	F	17	062	063	058	057	055
2320	MACDONALD	HK	M	18	075	072	071	075	074
2444	KOCH	EW	F	15	070	072	074	068	063
2469	MUNDT	CG	F	16	072	053	062	061	072
2485	YOST	TY	M	17	056	059	074	072	073
2503	SCHENDEL	YF	M	16	080	085	072	073	084
2555	TATTERSALL	JH	M	16	082	079	075	076	074
2646	ZETTLER	HL	F	16	073	069	065	080	070
2657	LAAS	RT	M	17	080	085	086	084	082
2725	YANTZI	WR	M	18	056	053	052	045	052
2751	THIBIDEAU	FK	F	17	063	069	071	075	058
2873	ELLIS	TR	M	17	053	056	052	053	052
2875	OWENS	RT	F	14	078	074	081	062	080
2883	ALBRECHT	WL	M	18	045	065	063	055	052
2888	MCNAUGHTON	DJ	F	17	068	069	085	083	076
2975	APPELL	JK	F	15	072	071	056	085	085
2985	HABER	LH	M	17	082	075	069	068	068
3137	ARISS	LK	M	18	065	063	062	069	068
3258	LOGAN	GH	M	17	065	063	068	069	045
3431	KLASSEN	MB	M	15	085	089	075	085	059
3573	EDGAR	BJK	F	15	075	074	079	081	069
3608	ASHBURY	LK	M	17	070	075	074	075	074
3621	KNACK	YU	M	17	058	056	054	062	063
3742	ARMSTRONG	KL	M	16	056	058	059	074	070
3889	VOGEL	PK	M	17	056	058	059	085	062
4039	MINKE	AJK	F	17	073	072	075	081	092
4235	BROWN	KJ	M	16	058	056	056	045	072
4253	PETTY	HG	M	17	054	056	075	072	070
4259	REIST	SD	M	15	080	081	085	092	090
4301	MERCER	ER	M	15	072	068	057	080	070
4567	BROWN	GJ	M	16	068	069	065	063	068
4603	LOGOZNY	IK	F	17	080	075	076	074	072
4631	CANDENBORN	TN	M	16	065	063	063	068	069
4735	KUNTZ	RH	M	16	089	083	085	092	068
4783	ANGUS	CJ	M	17	072	070	068	072	059
4944	TAYLOR	FL	M	18	045	055	053	065	064
4969	MEYER	PS	M	17	074	072	073	072	071
4988	MACEWEN	WL	F	17	070	070	070	071	069
5171	PRESTON	ED	M	17	085	072	082	075	074
5178	HARDING	VM	M	16	080	083	084	091	079
5214	MOSER	RT	F	15	045	042	043	032	051
5236	SMITH	WR	M	16	070	070	057	087	082

ID—NO.	NAME		SEX	AGE	ALG	GEO	ENG	PHY	CHE
5277	MAJORS	KLJ	M	16	053	056	058	059	058
5279	CARON	PL	M	16	053	056	058	058	058
5321	KNOWLES	WD	M	17	074	072	071	064	082
5432	ALLEN	TU	M	16	053	056	072	070	071
5435	ANTLER	YO	M	16	072	070	070	073	072
5465	WHITE	QHJ	F	17	068	069	069	070	075
5527	ARMSTRONG	GF	M	16	053	056	059	086	085
5597	COXON	RY	M	16	070	058	070	071	072
6159	CANDLER	PJW	F	18	069	065	063	065	075
6415	HARRISSON	JM	M	17	042	075	078	074	072
6491	SHANTZ	RF	M	18	075	075	074	078	079
6665	TURNBULL	SK	M	18	056	096	098	053	084
6701	RIVERS	KJ	M	16	068	069	070	075	074
6986	CARTER	JL	M	16	085	083	068	069	085
7191	ANTONISON	TMK	M	16	049	051	053	046	076
7256	CARDY	WF	M	18	075	078	087	089	097
7272	SHELL	YA	F	18	090	086	053	067	084
7336	NEVILL	TY	F	16	063	065	068	072	053
7354	ARNOLD	WR	M	18	072	070	072	075	074
7504	ELLIOT	HK	M	17	068	067	065	063	062
7607	CARROLL	TY	M	16	075	078	076	084	056
7716	CROSS	KE	F	16	081	072	065	051	075
7942	CAMPBELL	LKK	M	16	053	056	059	058	057
8255	WILSON	WE	M	17	075	072	071	070	074
8388	LANTZ	TY	M	19	080	068	069	073	070
8556	WHITE	RH	M	18	070	071	068	069	053
9407	CAPP	AS	M	16	074	075	074	074	072
9517	SAUNDERS	PK	M	16	076	070	068	065	069
9612	ROSS	KJ	M	17	074	072	071	070	058
9706	ROOT	KH	M	18	070	071	072	070	069
9760	DUNKLEY	RS	F	16	059	072	072	075	074
9768	CALLINGHAM	LO	M	16	068	069	069	069	068

Appendix D

CUSTOMER–FILE

The CUSTOMER–FILE consists of 100 records. Each record contains 100 bytes of information about a single customer. The records are organized as follows:

CUSTOMER–RECORD

ID-NO	NAME	STREET	CITY	EXPIRE	INVOICE	AMT DUE	REGION	C-LIMIT	FILLER
1 8	9 28	29 48	49 68	69 74	75 80	81 89	90	91	92 100

Figure D.1 *Record layout for CUSTOMER–FILE.*

CUSTOMER–FILE has the same format as the file of the same name that was created at the University of Waterloo for use with the WATBOL compiler. Some dates, names, and addresses have been changed.

	Begins in byte	Length	Description
CUSTOMER–NUMBER	1	8	This is an eight-digit code. The codes range from 51900000 to 51909900 in increments of 100.
NAME	9	20	Each of these fields contains 20 characters.
STREET	29	20	The three fields together supply the mailing
CITY	49	20	address for the customer.
EXPIRATION–DATE	69	6	These six bytes are organized in the form ddmmyy. This gives the day (dd), month (mm), and year (yy) this customer's account number expires.
INVOICE–NUMBER	75	6	A six-digit code that gives the number of the last invoice sent to this customer.
AMOUNT–DUE	81	9	The number has nine digits. The two rightmost digits of this field represent cents and the other digits represent from 0 to $9999999.
REGION–CODE	90	1	There are three values for this code: A: Canadian customer, B: United States customer, C: All other customers.
CREDIT–LIMIT	91	1	This code has five different values. Before a charge is made, the current balance due is added to the possible new charge. This total must be less than or equal to the dollar amount associated with the value of the code: 1: $100 2: $300 3: $500 4: $1,000 5: $3,000
Extra Space	92	9	Available for new information as it becomes available.

ID–NO.	NAME	STREET
51900000	WEINSMEIER CFR	44 BERTA PLACE
51900100	MENZIES RG	17 BERTA PLACE
51900200	BAYLESS GF	15 SAMSON CR
51900300	GRAY MJ	2906 DOUGLASS ROAD
51900400	MATHEWS B	1525 SUNSET LANE
51900500	BATTISTAS LB	768 STIRLING AVE
51900600	SAMUELS HR	17 W 34TH ST
51900700	MITCHELL JE	120 ROSEMONT AVE
51900800	COOPER RH	10 PUDGET DRIVE
51900900	GRAHAM JW	84 SUSSEX DR
51901000	DYCK TA	NO 12 DOWNING ST
51901100	FISCHER R	1600 PENN AVE
51901200	VARNEY JC	1 KREMLIN ROAD
51901300	EVANS L	4 STARK ST
51901400	LARSEN B	12 ARM ST
51901500	DEMMONS DE	4 FINCH RD
51901600	KASHDAN I	40 WONDER RD
51901700	MORPHY P	36 14th STREET
51901800	WORCESTER HL	15 RUNNING RD
51901900	LASKER E	40 WEST RD
51902000	DAY L	5168 YONGE ST
51902100	GRINDLE LS	55 421 BEAVER RD
51902200	EVANS HL	4 MINSK BLVD
51902300	BYRNE D	4 ROCHESTER RD
51902400	KORPOV A	6 RAINY RD
51902500	LOPEZ R	4 MUDDY RD
51902600	REINFIELD F	4 MUDDY RD
51902700	BAFFI L	6 YONGE ST
51902800	GABLER W	4 ARGO RD
51902900	ROTH FR	32 RAINY BROOK
51903000	BARTON G	86 WONDER ROAD
51903100	ALLEN E	45 SILVER RD
51903200	KENNY RB	321 CALIFORNIA DR
51903300	OLIVER JT	4 BRIDGE ST
51903400	LEARY PJ	75 RING RD
51903500	BELL TW	4 DUSTY LANE
51903600	NEWCOMB RS	6 DAISY LANE
51903700	STILES HW	5 BEAR CR RD
51903800	HALEY JA	63215 MAIN ST
51903900	ANDREWS EE	965 POND LANE RD
51904000	THOMAS AH	44 DINNER LANE RD
51904100	PEASE JF	65 DO LANE
51904200	BENNETT RB	65 URANIUM BLVD
51904300	ST LAURENT L	4 MARKET BLVD
51904400	FARRIS BN	65 CONNING RD
51904500	CARTER DE	532 IRISH RD
51904600	BORDEN R	532 BRADLEY RD
51904700	UPTON TM	44 RANCH TRAIL RD
51904800	RIST S	53 LOWE STREET
51904900	TUPPER C	45 KING ST

CITY	EXPIRE	INVOICE	AMT DUE	REGION	C-LIMIT
TORONTO ONT	090685	000050	000000123	A	2
OSHAWA ONT	090685	000065	000001254	A	2
BLUE RIDGE MANITOBA	171186	000066	000000432	A	2
RICHMOND ALTA	250484	000067	000154374	A	4
RICHMOND MANITOBA	050985	000068	000015435	A	3
GALT ONT	130286	000069	000002323	A	2
MONTREAL QUEBEC	210784	000070	000056782	A	3
QUEBEC QUEBEC	011285	000071	000567845	A	4
OTTAWA ONT	090586	000072	000056745	A	3
OTTAWA ONT	171084	000073	000043567	A	3
LONDON ENGLAND	250385	000074	00000456P	C	2
WASHINGTON DC	050886	000075	000345686	B	4
MOSCOW USSR	130184	000076	000456743	C	4
EDMONTON ALTA	210685	000077	000564324	A	4
LONDON ONT	011186	000078	009456757	A	5
VANCOUVER BC	090484	000079	000000000	A	1
CLARKSON ONT	170985	000080	000000000	A	1
GENERAL MILLS ONT	250286	000081	000000000	A	1
SUNTER SASK	050784	000082	000010000	A	3
KINGSTON ONT	131285	000083	000075000	A	3
TORONTO ONT	210586	000453	000000100	A	2
KING CITY ALTA	011084	000342	000340000	A	4
KITCHENER ONT	090385	003476	000000213	A	2
VICTORIA BC	170886	000096	00000347Q	A	2
SUNNY CITY YUKON	250184	000010	000000234	A	2
RAINY RIVER ONT	050685	000150	000567800	A	4
SNOWY RIVER NWT	131186	000155	000000000	A	1
TORONTO ONT	210484	000160	000000000	A	1
TORONTO ONT	010985	000165	000000000	A	1
THREE RIVERS QUE	090286	000170	000034000	A	3
CRUMMY CITY BC	170784	000175	000000000	A	1
GOLD ONT	211285	000180	000045000	A	3
TORONTO ONT	050586	000185	000000000	A	1
TORONTO ONT	131084	000190	000000000	A	1
WATERLOO ONT	210385	000195	000340000	A	4
VACUUM BC	010886	000200	000000000	A	1
FLOWER CITY NS	090184	000205	000000000	A	1
HUNTING NWFD	170684	000000	000000000	A	1
OCEAN CITY PEI	251186	000215	000000000	A	1
ELMIRA ONT	010484	000220	000001200	A	2
LUNCH NB	130986	000300	003400000	A	5
NOT BC	210286	000295	000000000	A	1
RICH QUEBEC	010784	000280	000000000	A	1
FREE PEI	091285	000900	000002300	A	2
GREAT ALBERTA	170586	000895	000000000	A	1
MARVELOUS NB	250184	000880	000000000	A	1
CLEVER TOWN BC	050385	000875	000003400	A	2
SPRING CITY NS	130886	000869	000000000	A	1
BRONTE ONT	210184	000567	000000000	A	1
QUEEN CITY NFLD	010685	000123	000000000	A	1

ID–NO.	NAME	STREET
51905000	THOMPSON R	54 RUNNINGTON RD
51905100	STEEVES RT	RETRACE RD
51905200	TERRILL RD	1 JAMESON
51905300	FAHEY MH	10 PENOBSCOT BLVD
51905400	PATTERSON TW	SHADOW LANE
51905500	KIMBALL RT	MARTIN MINK RANCH
51905600	BEARS TJ	121 INDIAN PLACE
51905700	ENFIELD RJ	KENNEBEC RD
51905800	PECK PM	TAYLOR ST
51905900	AMES NA	GRAND AVE
51906000	GANDEN H	632 ODLIN RD
51906100	KAMPBELL RS	STARLIGHT DR
51906200	GUNN JE	26 WEBSTER AVE
51906300	DEARBORN TM	321 STICKS ROAD
51906400	ROUND ES	999 SAGE AVE
51906500	HACKETT JE	103 PEARL
51906600	OAKES CM	86 BENNOCH
51906700	LEONARD TW	123 ESSEX ST
51906800	MICHAUD TS	7812 PINE ST
51906900	MATTHEWS BC	36 SUNSET BLVD
51907000	NICHOLS JF	618 COLLEGE AVE
51907100	CARR GL	PRESIDENTIAL AVE
51907200	PELLETIER AJ	123 GLAMOUR AVE
51907300	HALLS R	111 WILLOW
51907400	UNRUH RJ	459 BROADWAY
51907500	HALL B	THIRD MAIN ST
51907600	SANDERSON D	6 WAIN ST
51907700	PARENT B	56 LESLIE ST
51907800	STANFIELD F	54 OHIO ST
51907900	VALLEY DE	654 JAMES ST
51908000	YORK PJ	218 HANCOCK BLVD
51908100	GUEST J	4 MOORE AVE
51908200	MARTIN J	3 JASPER CR
51908300	POWER G	4 EDMUND ST
51908400	GREENE G	348 DUKE ST
51908500	MCCOY S	184 LOUISA ST
51908600	SMITH A	5 COLLEGE ST
51908700	EDWARDS C	75 QUEEN ST
51908800	KING E	32 KING ST
51908900	STRONG RE	45 DUCK POND LANE
51909000	COLE H	103 LAWRENCE AVE
51909100	EVANS S	258 YORK ST
51909200	GRANT P	2 JOHN ST
51909300	WALKER R	22 YOUNG ST
51909400	WARD G	1 CRESCENT AVE
51909500	FINLEY W	9 DOON ST
51909600	WATSON C	12 WARD ST
51909700	ADAMS Z	2 MAIN ST
51909800	HALL ST	300 WATER STREET
51909900	GARDNER P	3 KARN ST

CITY	EXPIRE	INVOICE	AMT DUE	REGION	C-LIMIT
SCARED CITY SASK	091186	001000	000000000	A	1
LONDON ONT	170484	001100	000013400	A	3
HALLING STIX	250985	001200	000012000	C	3
SOME PLACE PEI	050286	001300	000120000	A	4
PUNKYDOODLE ONT	130784	001700	000000000	A	1
WALLENSTEIN ONT	211285	002000	134000000	A	5
HIGHBALL LAKE NWT	010586	003000	000000000	A	1
SLETHIN BELGIUM	091084	000479	000000000	C	1
REYKJAVIK ICELAND	170385	000391	000000000	C	1
PARRY SOUND ONT	250886	005000	000000000	A	1
NOVOSIBIRSK SIBERIA	010584	000003	000000000	C	1
ANGEGIN PQ	130685	090000	000000000	A	1
RUSSIA CAN	211186	091000	000000000	A	1
HAWKESVILLE ONT	010484	920000	000000000	A	1
ROSEMARY SASK	090985	930000	000000000	A	1
WOLF ISLAND NFLD	170286	940000	000000000	A	1
WATERLOO ONT	250784	950000	000340000	A	4
GORGEVILLE MAN	051285	960000	045000000	A	5
ROME ITALY	130586	970000	000000000	C	1
UNIWAT ONT	211084	045678	000078000	A	3
PEKING CHINA	010385	980000	000000000	C	1
NGO TOC N VIETNAM	090886	981000	000000000	C	1
HOLLYWOOD CALIF	170184	008888	880000000	B	5
SAIGON VIET NAM	250685	982000	000000000	C	1
PEANUTS OHIO	051186	983000	000000000	B	1
WINNIPEG MAN	130484	987000	000000000	A	1
PHILADELPHIA PENN	210985	990000	000000000	B	1
PHILADELPHIA PENN	010286	991000	000004500	B	2
ANTIGONISH NS	090784	992000	000046000	A	3
SPORTSTOWN BC	171285	996000	005703400	A	5
DODGE CITY KANS	250586	995000	000000000	B	1
LAWRENCE ILL	051084	995001	000000000	B	1
LOS ANGELES CAL	130385	995002	000000000	B	1
TORONTO ONT	210886	995003	000000000	A	1
OSHAWA ONT	010184	995004	000045600	A	3
VANCOUVER BC	090685	995005	000346000	A	4
CALGARY ALTA	171186	995006	000000500	A	2
DUBLIN EIRE	250484	995007	000056030	C	3
LONDON ENG	050985	995008	000078000	C	3
MYRTLE BEACH SC	130286	995009	000079089	B	3
SAN FRANCISCO CAL	210784	995010	000000000	B	1
DENVER COL	011285	995011	000005300	B	2
NEW YORK NY	090586	995012	000000000	B	1
RALEIGH NC	171084	895013	000000000	B	1
HANG TOWN NEV	250385	895002	000000000	B	1
HOUSTON TEX	050886	895003	000000000	B	1
MIAMI FLA	130784	895100	000004500	B	2
KENORA ONT	210685	895200	000056040	A	3
ORILLIA ONT	011186	895300	009070000	A	5
HALIFAX NS	090484	999999	000560000	A	4

Appendix E

REGISTRAR-FILE

The REGISTRAR-FILE consists of 100 records. Each record contains 100 bytes of information about a single student. The records are organized as follows:

REGISTRAR-FILE

SOC SEC NUMBER	NAME	SEX	CLASS	AGE	MATH	ENG	GVT	GEOG	PHIL	CUM GPA	TOTAL HOURS	CAMPUS-ADDRESS	HOME ST.	FILLER
1 9	10 29	30	31 32	33 34	35	36	37	38	39	40 42	43 45	46 65	66 67	68 100

Figure E.1 Record layout for REGISTRAR-FILE.

	Begins in Byte	Length	Description
SOC–SEC–NUMBER	1	9	Nine digits is the standard form.
NAME	10	20	There is space for 20 characters. The form of the field is last name in the first 10 bytes followed by the first name beginning in byte 11.
SEX	30	1	The code has values M for male and F for female.
CLASS	31	2	Indicates one of the usual designations: 　FR: freshman 　SO: sophomore 　JR: junior 　SR: senior 　UN: unclassified or special student
AGE	33	2	This is a two-digit field. The values of this variable range from 17 to 24.
MATH–13	35	1	The value for each of these is a letter grade A, B, C, D, or E.
ENGLISH–2	36	1	
GOVERNMENT–3	37	1	
GEOGRAPHY–10	38	1	
PHILOSOPHY–3	39	1	
CUMULATIVE–GPA	40	3	The values for this variable range from 1.86 to 4.00
TOTAL–HOURS	43	3	This is a three-digit number. 120 approved hours are required for graduation.
CAMPUS–ADDRESS	46	20	The on-campus dormitory address of each student. The information is of the form ddd DORM NAME where ddd is the three-digit room number in the dormitory whose name is given.
HOME–STATE	66	2	The values are standard two-letter codes for the states represented. 　MA 　ME 　VT 　CA 　NH
Extra space	68	33	Available for new information as it becomes available.

SOC. SECURITY NUMBER	NAME		SEX	CLASS	AGE
945708384	JONES	SUSAN MARI	F	JR	24
495166352	MOLL	ANNA MAE	F	FR	17
397886434	BARNES	ROSELLE GR	F	SR	22
119289762	BAKER	ERIC	M	JR	23
241636262	VARNEY	LAWRENCE J	M	JR	20
408985763	SMITH	LAURIE LEI	F	UN	20
418745203	GEORGE	JANET LEE	F	JR	24
134049461	MITCHELL	SARAH LYNN	F	JR	18
194912780	DAY	LAURIE JEA	F	JR	23
711032574	FLINT	RAY	M	UN	21
969395233	FORD	JANET LYNN	F	JR	21
373477189	NOLET	LINDA LOUI	F	FR	21
748709349	GATES	MARK HAYES	M	UN	21
324666739	REYNOLDS	SCOTT LAWR	M	UN	17
746517820	ADAMS	LLOYD RAYM	M	SO	23
879788435	OLSEN	PATRICIA A	F	SR	21
594095555	WILLIAMS	SHERRIE AN	F	UN	18
248907449	STEVENS	MAUREEN AN	F	FR	18
318301485	CROSS	CINDY LEA	F	FR	21
701061555	GERAGHTY	GERALD ALA	M	FR	18
322417517	WILSON	PAMELA ANN	F	FR	24
558496688	MEAD	KEVIN JOSE	M	UN	21
906705267	THURSTON	STEVEN JOE	M	SR	17
311109310	FORD	CRAIG STEP	M	UN	20
268709346	ROBERTS	BENJAMIN J	M	UN	19
523912722	FLEMING	CHERYL LYN	F	SR	24
668202992	OLIVER	RACHEL ROS	F	UN	21
428577007	JONES	STEVE A	M	UN	17
944446839	WILLIAMS	JAMES PAUL	M	JR	20
992705475	MAHON	JOHN JOSEP	M	SO	17
154605824	HAYNES	KARLA	F	FR	19
307586325	CROKE	LISA JO	F	UN	19
774715404	BRUCE	CHRISTINA	F	SR	21
755302979	WOOD	EDWARD WAY	M	UN	22
997479548	HENRY	JUDITH LUC	F	UN	18
360414683	YORK	MARK DAVID	M	JR	23
877768237	RODGERS	EMERSON W	M	JR	17
156365091	BIRD	MONICA ALE	F	SR	22
362542590	NORBURG	SCOT WEBB	M	FR	17
565399894	GAUVIN	LINDA ANN	F	FR	18
173547550	RICHARDS	BRIAN DAVI	M	UN	19
326481967	WOODARD	LIANE SHEV	F	UN	20
250728427	MALONE	DAVID ROSS	M	SO	19
519625638	CRANE	EDWARD HEN	M	SO	19
161898669	CHABOT	RHONDA LEE	F	UN	21
762336975	CAULKINS	CRISTINE C	F	SR	18
962799319	HEBERT	CATHERINE	F	SR	23
725028461	YOUNG	ANDREW PHI	M	UN	24
865789888	WYSE	MICHAEL RV	M	UN	18
178693305	BROWN	JERRY MICH	M	FR	20

MS	EN	GO	GE	PH	GPA	TOTAL HOURS	CAMPUS ADDRESS	STATE
A	D	B	E	D	347	079	403 GANNETT HALL	ME
D	E	C	A	A	395	016	321 SOMERSET HALL	MA
B	C	C	B	D	233	101	209 HART HALL	MA
D	B	D	A	A	361	068	342 HANCOCK HALL	CA
D	B	D	B	B	331	067	405 SOMERSET HALL	MA
C	A	E	E	D	397	125	233 ANDROSCOGGIN HAL	CA
C	A	A	C	B	393	087	202 JENESS HALL	CA
A	C	E	E	B	345	062	308 ANDROSCOGGIN HAL	VT
B	A	B	C	C	298	088	341 HANCOCK HALL	CA
A	D	E	A	E	399	126	110 OXFORD HALL	ME
E	C	D	C	D	213	086	233 KNOX HALL	MA
B	C	E	B	B	355	015	224 GANNETT HALL	VT
B	A	A	C	C	234	144	142 HANCOCK HALL	VT
A	C	E	C	D	260	145	437 KNOX HALL	VT
B	D	B	D	B	203	031	201 AUGUSTA HALL	NH
E	B	A	C	E	279	092	308 ROCKLAND HALL	MA
A	B	B	C	C	366	142	123 CORBETT HALL	VT
E	A	C	A	A	390	008	241 CROSBY HALL	ME
E	E	C	B	C	384	007	404 DUNN HALL	ME
D	E	C	B	C	201	024	314 STODDER HALL	NH
D	E	E	E	D	243	021	411 DUNN HALL	CA
D	D	B	B	E	192	125	123 CUMBERLAND HALL	MA
A	E	E	C	E	321	106	322 AROOSTOOK HALL	VT
B	D	B	B	E	371	124	123 HART HALL	VT
C	C	A	E	D	294	013	410 HANNIBAL-HAMLIN	CA
E	A	C	E	D	349	109	403 PENOBSCOT HALL	VT
C	D	A	E	E	289	136	433 SOMERSET HALL	ME
E	E	E	D	C	259	137	208 KENNEBEC HALL	CA
B	C	D	E	E	354	069	224 COLVIN HALL	MA
B	C	C	E	B	389	046	317 BELFAST HALL	MA
A	B	A	A	C	379	006	303 LEWISTON HALL	MA
B	C	B	D	B	335	129	103 OAK HALL	CA
E	D	E	A	A	335	094	209 CORBETT HALL	MA
E	A	E	E	D	250	149	145 YORK HALL	NH
D	C	D	A	A	388	148	303 OAK HALL	MA
B	D	D	B	A	308	086	322 KENNEBEC HALL	ME
E	B	B	C	A	377	080	207 DUNN HALL	CA
E	D	B	E	C	332	091	101 HART HALL	VT
B	B	D	B	E	241	015	112 AROOSTOOK HALL	VT
D	C	C	C	D	309	008	203 ROCKLAND HALL	CA
D	E	C	D	B	320	137	340 HANCOCK HALL	MA
A	B	D	D	C	295	149	408 KNOX HALL	CA
D	A	B	D	C	381	053	118 ELLSWORTH HALL	CA
B	D	D	E	D	336	053	313 KENNEBEC HALL	ME
A	B	A	D	B	353	144	415 KENNEBEC HALL	CA
E	C	D	D	A	306	116	430 KNOX HALL	VT
A	A	D	C	D	266	094	109 OXFORD HALL	MA
B	D	E	E	A	262	129	412 CHADBOURNE HALL	ME
E	A	E	C	B	293	130	411 DUNN HALL	CA
B	C	A	E	E	385	020	265 ESTABROOKE HALL	ME

SOC. SECURITY NUMBER	NAME		SEX	CLASS	AGE
605506440	HARMON	SHARON JOA	F	SO	24
995109987	THOMAS	CAROL ANNE	F	UN	19
574637828	REED	GREGORY AL	M	SR	23
633091980	THORNTON	SCOTT ABBO	M	FR	24
943925229	O'BRIEN	JILL SUZAN	F	SO	24
275329599	THORN	JOANNE ELI	F	SR	20
662045380	DAVIS	THOMAS ALA	M	FR	24
966344509	KAPLAN	ERNEST JOH	M.	SO	23
463506686	THORNE	WILLIAM JA	M	FR	22
456437820	MORIN	SUSAN ANNE	F	UN	20
740109363	NORTON	LINDA JEAN	F	JR	23
388408710	WINSLOW	ELLEN VIVI	F	SO	19
779242093	FORSYTH	DOUGLAS L	M	UN	23
954263515	BIGGART	WILLIAM ED	M	UN	24
799259000	CROCKETT	KAREN ELLE	F	SO	20
221316973	CYR	NICHOLAS S	M	UN	22
465982820	WISE	JEAN-LOUIS	M	JR	23
250707230	DUMAS	WILFORD CA	M	FR	18
167966904	OLSON	BARRY ADAM	M	SR	22
567376791	MADDEN	TRACI ELIZ	F	FR	21
441253536	ROGERS	TIMOTHY	M	FR	19
519073137	ADLER	JULIE N	F	FR	24
892464836	ROBINSON	TOOD STEWA	M	JR	18
173875176	VALLEY	KIM LURINE	F	FR	18
317111475	RICE	SHARON L	F	FR	20
709867273	YATES	JOSEPH PAU	M	SO	24
294686107	VAN DRESS	BRENDA MAR	F	JR	17
356276460	KAVANAUGH	ANGELA SUS	F	UN	20
263418300	HEATH	RICHARD DA	M	FR	19
567306489	HERBERT	DAVID WILL	M	JR	19
243381305	ZEPH	DEBORAH NA	F	JR	20
986336002	HANNIGAN	DANIEL FRE	M	FR	21
188201869	JOHNSON	SUZANNE AL	F	JR	21
112662090	WRIGHT	GARY WILLI	M	SO	18
782345905	STAPLES	MARK CHRIS	M	JR	21
302082262	YOUNGS	REBECCA SU	F	FR	19
189092597	FORSYTHE	JAMES PAUL	M	JR	20
144194528	WINTLE	ANN PIERS	F	SR	19
868373230	VICKERS	DEBBIE LYN	F	JR	20
969602355	ROLLINS	NANCY CATH	F	FR	19
543665995	MILLER	DAVID ALAN	M	UN	24
779225158	BROWN	RICHARD PA	M	SO	17
166895790	BARRY	DONNA JEAN	F	UN	18
590131900	CRAIG	JOHN MICHA	M	SR	17
653408277	STEWAET	THOMAS HUN	M	SO	22
898937127	BRYANT	WENDY LEE	F	FR	18
145133708	JOHNSON	CLARENCE S	M	FR	21
441949609	JONES	AMY JEANNE	F	FR	20
845083349	SMITH	MICHAEL WA	M	SO	21
716983186	RICHARDS	JOHN BAUGH	M	UN	24

MS	EN	GO	GE	PH	GPA	TOTAL HOURS	CAMPUS ADDRESS	STATE
B	C	E	C	A	226	032	238 OXFORD HALL	ME
C	B	D	C	D	196	121	239 YORK HALL	CA
E	B	E	C	A	327	110	216 LEWISTON HALL	MA
D	C	E	A	D	354	018	408 HANNIBAL-HAMLIN	NH
B	C	B	A	B	233	031	413 OXFORD HALL	VT
D	C	E	C	D	313	097	265 HANCOCK HALL	MA
D	D	D	D	E	372	011	435 YORK HALL	MA
C	D	D	A	E	191	047	309 HANNIBAL-HAMLIN	VT
D	A	A	D	C	322	010	102 OXFORD HALL	ME
E	A	A	A	B	203	147	428 SUMERSET HALL	NH
D	D	B	A	D	383	062	311 HANCOCK HALL	MA
B	A	E	A	E	227	040	338 DUNN HALL	MA
D	A	E	E	E	348	122	206 CHADBOURNE HALL	ME
B	C	B	D	D	304	134	254 ESTABROOKE HALL	ME
B	E	E	E	E	301	039	133 CUMBERLAND HALL	VT
D	E	B	A	A	273	140	325 SOMERSET HALL	VT
C	B	B	C	B	247	086	336 OXFORD HALL	ME
E	C	A	C	E	199	010	219 PENOBSCOT HALL	ME
D	E	A	A	B	197	106	323 CORBETT HALL	NH
D	B	B	D	A	333	003	111 OXFORD HALL	ME
B	E	B	B	D	317	014	317 ROCKLAND HALL	ME
E	D	B	E	C	240	010	234 HART HALL	ME
D	B	B	E	D	200	070	237 HANCOCK HALL	VT
C	B	C	B	A	329	021	101 OAK HALL	MA
C	B	E	B	A	232	027	323 COLVIN HALL	MA
C	B	A	D	B	394	032	213 ANDROSCOGGIN HAL	VT
B	A	B	A	C	308	080	338 KNOX HALL	CA
E	D	A	D	B	349	125	115 ROCKLAND HALL	ME
D	C	A	C	A	313	017	208 LEWISTON HALL	NH
B	B	E	B	D	398	088	322 HANCOCK HALL	ME
E	A	D	C	D	269	077	314 ROCKLAND HALL	CA
C	E	E	B	D	280	017	410 CHADBOURNE HALL	NH
E	A	A	B	E	394	069	362 ESTABROOKE HALL	VT
E	A	E	D	D	248	031	211 AROOSTOOK HALL	NH
D	E	C	C	A	280	069	106 CUMBERLAND HALL	MA
B	D	E	C	E	207	004	411 SOMERSET HALL	VT
B	B	D	C	A	200	073	435 CUMBERLAND HALL	CA
D	C	C	A	B	300	102	319 OXFORD HALL	CA
A	D	D	B	D	211	085	203 BALENTINE HALL	MA
E	E	C	E	A	336	008	412 HANNIBAL-HAMLIN	CA
D	B	B	C	B	222	127	218 AROOSTOOK HALL	VT
A	A	A	E	C	205	035	234 CUMBERLAND HALL	MA
A	C	E	E	A	301	142	205 YORK HALL	NH
C	B	B	B	A	348	109	202 CORBETT HALL	CA
B	C	C	A	A	186	034	248 YORK HALL	VT
B	B	E	D	E	272	020	222 STODDER HALL	NH
B	E	C	C	B	381	003	113 STODDER HALL	CA
E	D	B	A	A	380	012	105 SOMERSET HALL	VT
D	D	B	D	A	256	038	TAU KAPPA EPSILON	ME
C	E	E	C	E	264	144	107 GANNETT HALL	CA

Appendix F

NEW–WORLD–FILE

The NEW–WORLD–FILE consists of 100 records. Each record contains 100 bytes of information about a single customer. The records are organized as follows:

NEW–WORLD–FILE

CHARGE-ID	EXPIRATION DATE	NAME	HOME ADDRESS	CITY	STATE	BILLING DATE	AMT DUE	PAYMENT	CREDIT RATING	FILLER
1 9	10 15	16 35	36 55	56 75	76 77	78 83	84 88	89 93	94	95 100

Figure F.1 *Record layout for NEW–WORLD–FILE.*

	Begins in Byte	Length	Description
CHARGE–ID	1	9	Nine-digit identification code. The value is different for each customer. There is no ordering of the records by this number.
EXPIRATION–DATE	10	6	This field is of the form ddmmyy. The value indicates the expiration date for the customer's credit card. The value for yy ranges from 85 to 90.
NAME HOME–ADDRESS CITY	16 36 56	20 20 20	Each field contains 20 characters. The three fields together supply the mailing address for each customer. The name field is of the form: last name followed by two initials in the last two bytes of this field. The home address is a 20-byte field with the information beginning in byte 1 of the field. The city field has a form like the form of the home address field.

STATE	76	2	The standard two-letter code for the states represented:
			    MA VT
			    ME NY
			    NH CA

BILLING–DATE	78	6	This field is of the form ddmmyy. The value indicates the date the last invoice was sent for payment.
AMOUNT–DUE	84	5	This is a five-digit field with the decimal point assumed to be between the second and third digit counting backward from the right of the field. This field represents the amount due on the last bill sent to the customer.
PAYMENT	89	5	Same form as the AMOUNT–DUE field. This field represents the amount received in response to the last billing.

CREDIT–RATING	94	1	This is a code with values: 1,2,3,4,5,6. The credit limits associated with the codes are
			   code limit
			    1 $200
			    2 $400
			    3 $600
			    4 $700
			    5 $900
			    6 $1,000

Extra space	95	6	Available for new information as it becomes available.

CHARGE–ID	EX. DATE	NAME	ADDRESS
753498417	250987	ENGLE	JC 1300 FRANKLIN ST
444526390	240785	EISNER	WL 1911 JOPLIN ST
162608679	110590	SHERIFF	NL 1816 STONEGATE DR
362623609	290986	SNIDER	RC 1751 SUNSET BLVD
415301971	120486	PARKER	CH 280 MASS AVE
322955523	021086	PRINCE	KP 171 DEAN ST
639648209	160688	VINCENT	RT 790 HARTWELL ST
700958186	031087	FULLER	HG 6306 STAGHORN CT
433086794	230485	ZELLER	HG 4981 DENTON RD
793501604	010689	JONES	HE 1368 MILBURN
648264657	250686	KEARNS	ST 2103 CLIFFORD
896592747	140188	HARMAN	JF 2103 CEDAR LANE DR
352606811	010286	WALKER	FC 1682 ADAMS ST
345266733	130288	BORDEN	KR 94 BROADWAY ST
891289390	020787	TORRES	SK 1103 RUBY DR
520528534	161190	DANA	RD 2110 TERRACE DR
334095204	100890	RICHARDSON	CE 1861 NEW RODGERS RD
818591641	060189	LAMBERT	EH 5112 CAROL LANE
825431781	120286	OSTER	DG 3750 HANLEY ROAD
585141533	110686	YATES	FF 689 EASTWOOD DR
944491915	191086	SNOW	GS 4050 GREENLEAF ST
137103193	080585	FURMAN	RJ 331 JAY ST
411336713	061088	MILLER	CM 413 CIRCULAR DR
294238808	140785	KING	EA 767 RADCLIFF AVE
360311142	110788	KELLER	DH 913 MOUNTAIN ST
113601886	080686	MAYS	AJ 316 NORWOOD ST
863532076	230990	CARR	GA 3640 MONROE ST
793001553	090289	GLICK	GF 1521 DELWOOD RD
704288842	070689	RICHMOND	EI 2108 YACHT ST
208699351	101186	GAVETT	MM 2981 AMBOY RD
400476268	271185	HATCHER	KD 15609 OTTAWA ST
918068529	090487	ORSON	PF 3105 NW TAFT
478062292	021090	RAUSEN	TR 1570 OAK AVE
692705850	240190	VEST	FE 4830 RICHARD RD
994505694	310887	JENKINS	GL 12 APPLETON RD
947435878	131089	ZIMMERMAN	RF 2613 DITHRIDGE ST
312197274	131188	JONES	WE 2099 ATLANTIC AVE
873067780	291286	ASHBY	RE 381 OAKVILLE RD
121882268	180387	JORDAN	WR 1184 E GRAND
350534623	011288	WHEELER	RV 2605 CARMELO DR
716146209	121188	ANDERSEN	KD 8013 ASHWORTH AVE
466455169	270489	WALL	LW 4561 OAKHURST ST
512779118	301186	FISCHER	LE 61 COLEMAN PL
538188172	180588	NICHOLAS	DJ 133 SNOWDEN AVE
828275050	111188	BAVER	RP 513 JOHN MUIR DR
122009178	020788	BEAN	CD 191 MULLINS ST
901257053	090488	INGLE	RA 2161 NATREBA DR
612629817	080990	WEAVER	WE 769 CHESTNUT DR
165879529	220487	WATSON	KE 5909 NORTH HILLS DR
739529603	080387	QUIRK	RH 119 TURTLE CREEK RD

CITY	STATE	BILL–DATE	AMT–DUE	PAYMENT	RATING
RUMFORD	ME	060681	40170	83378	1
PARIS	ME	240181	69026	22365	3
SEEKONK	MA	280185	28572	95668	6
BRIGHTON	MA	210482	46690	37642	1
NEW YORK	NY	220682	34634	16443	6
JOHNSON	VT	070380	71375	30590	4
LATHAM	NY	040184	27410	18410	5
READING	MA	300380	71766	49126	5
KEENE	NH	020383	59600	64339	6
ARLINGTON	MA	070185	68663	38349	2
SAN FRANCISCO	CA	201081	54817	28160	6
SYRACUSE	NY	010481	92950	75638	5
GORHAM	ME	051081	24455	41050	4
BILLERICA	MA	060385	28561	26247	5
MEXICO	ME	100181	36762	62535	3
PORTLAND	ME	010983	80450	29893	1
UNIONDALE	NY	290685	15503	76575	6
RANDOLPH	NH	240481	67564	78560	1
AUGUSTA	ME	120683	41793	12666	6
MERRIMACK	NH	240180	40805	96869	3
ORONO	ME	040785	34566	91928	5
LYNDONVILLE	VT	190183	26001	77130	2
CHICO	CA	261283	56039	98201	1
BOSTON	MA	170682	91877	88110	2
MOUNTAIN VIEW	CA	060280	42186	74139	2
MARLBORO	VT	070980	43023	34821	4
ENFIELD	NH	211081	58203	42302	6
WALPOLE	MA	220185	37861	20230	4
SAN DIEGO	CA	251081	78981	51253	1
PLYMOUTH	NH	180385	31615	57948	6
LINCOLN	ME	110983	94569	46648	4
FAIRFAX	VT	170880	44279	82902	6
EXETER	NH	270584	40648	67332	1
BURLINGTON	VT	310685	53586	80628	4
BATAVIA	NY	220982	53997	66433	2
HANOVER	NH	021285	12978	20869	5
ALBION	NY	011081	52963	57454	5
MANCHESTER	NH	250780	94574	16161	4
BENNINGTON	VT	300785	42927	85367	6
NORTHFIELD	VT	190982	57137	54370	1
PARIS	ME	171080	46778	22709	1
BREWSTER	NY	031281	39046	62612	4
LEWISTON	NY	070881	60377	90674	5
MIDDLEBURY	VT	231180	76262	30180	2
AMHERST	MA	030584	33026	52070	5
DURHAM	NH	150382	45297	77811	6
DOVER	NH	081181	72941	48097	3
SUNNYVALE	CA	270480	31186	85937	6
MEADE	NH	120380	77715	63072	2
SALEM	MA	300385	20450	54355	5

CHARGE-ID	EX. DATE	NAME	ADDRESS
775284129	300788	DAVEY	DM 3612 STORY ST
117482307	310387	NOBLE	JP 561 GOLDEN LAKE RD
375098011	221089	BROWN	DM 3609 WALKER DR
693982370	050888	SMITH	JK 2106 GARRICK ST
126761086	211187	CHABOT	KR 218 WILLOW ST
787824967	011288	MERCHANT	GM 421 GRACE AVE
981044455	021287	ZORN	DW 1586 MILLPOINT ST
487607039	050286	UNDERWOOD	JP 178 OAKHURST DR
201469874	280385	NORMAN	TR 2651 MASSACHUSETTS A
300091968	211288	GAVIN	RT 1103 POLK ST
137713050	240289	HAMMOND	WJ 5316 CROSSLEES AVE
487704302	070890	RICHARDS	RA 5 WELLINGS DR
249092956	270290	LIDDLE	RW 2431 ONEIDA RD
221509053	020685	ADAMS	DW 420 ELDORADO DR
377984836	300289	NORDON	GL 2006 VIRGINIA AVE
372303486	130885	CANTWELL	KM 2160 CEDAR VALLEY DR
273247984	050885	TOLAN	EA 6145 LINDELL AVE
763261427	310586	YOUNG	DW 513 METOMEN ST
363674084	131185	DANIELS	JR 561 MONTGOMERY ST
269434970	270685	FICKETT	AJ 1915 LEHIGH AVE
781439377	180886	JOHNSON	DH 91 HALES HOLLOW
524099178	170486	ULMAN	CN 639 N REBECCA
635498341	170585	KING	DJ 4413 CHERRY ST
117773082	120886	GRAY	HR 1056 W CORNELIA
535067676	251186	BOWSER	RW 6718 AGEE RD
246724775	311090	MARSHALL	LC 2190 VALLEY GREEN DR
363059658	010386	PARSON	FG 1056 83RD ST
611342809	081289	VERNER	MJ 19024 COLFFIELD PL
299465188	051287	HARRISON	RE 861 ALBION RD
564635721	101086	INGRAHAM	BL 54 PARK ST
948709341	160689	HENNING	LH 160 BANBURY ROAD
510608086	310388	CHAMBERS	DR 6420 ROCKSHIRE ST
593859411	120786	DODGE	DR 1103 NOTTINGHAM ST
552726304	080990	TOLL	RD 2561 BROGAN RD
508405457	170790	LEECH	FI 1809 MEADOWBROOK DR
392383904	030889	SMYTH	JW 2106 SHENANDOAH DR
441373352	120587	LOSER	JH 516 LANDFAIR AVE
477286589	230990	SLOAN	JE 3401 N COLUMBUS
159953298	030985	PENROSE	GB 61 HEMLOCK LANE
399938884	241289	JOHNS	RS 916 ALVARADO RD
119053028	010388	ELLIS	MA 2209 TOPEKA ST
546028430	281286	PARK	DJ 36 ADAMS ST
234778040	151090	THOMAS	BH 7350 GOFF AVE
992912783	220189	MCCARTER	PH 10 ADAMS LN
907834959	230389	MILES	HT 5011 ROCKMERE ST
658038710	221286	ROGERS	RJ 3679 HAINESVILLE RD
297011927	030685	GLASS	LM 520 WACO LANE
697373988	240988	ELLISON	WJ 2185 DUMAS ST
842583678	140186	QUINN	DJ 1037 PALOMAS DR
153851696	211088	ANDERSON	BA 1816 PRAIRIE VIEW DR

CITY	STATE	BILL–DATE	AMT–DUE	PAYMENT	RATING
ACTON	MA	140485	89793	76891	3
CONCORD	NH	040485	19071	35812	2
DELMAR	NY	300780	76934	45442	1
OAKLAND	CA	140985	95455	94696	4
TAUNTON	MA	080983	37685	24829	1
HUDSON	NY	010784	48406	90174	6
BELMONT	MA	021084	31847	67472	6
AUBURN	NY	230483	92000	85692	3
CASTLETON	VT	080880	35946	43198	5
OLD TOWN	ME	071183	14011	81660	5
BINGHAMTON	NY	040780	23700	85335	3
COREA	ME	031080	37967	74505	3
STOW	MA	190183	71486	61803	4
PORTSMOUTH	NH	101181	72031	40170	6
PRESQUE ISLE	ME	261281	88813	71215	5
MONTPELIER	VT	020781	61516	42706	3
BANGOR	ME	021284	73789	63962	2
ANDOVER	MA	170881	14941	67871	4
BAYSIDE	NY	200185	93588	88314	1
MILLINOCKET	ME	090981	47003	81719	1
HEMPSTEAD	NY	150580	89920	61510	2
VEAZIE	ME	101082	46543	14196	2
LEWISTON	ME	180784	95020	65851	2
JAMESTOWN	NY	051183	69518	67733	3
WALTHAM	MA	251184	59522	69796	5
NEWTON	MA	061283	56968	50842	2
PEACHAM	VT	031280	88112	74057	4
NATICK	MA	180784	77983	36705	1
HERMON	ME	200782	89814	82689	6
AMHERST	NH	060681	97674	46773	3
BOONVILLE	NY	200983	36052	99183	1
WABAN	MA	240484	70144	59355	1
BEDFORD	MA	020581	30596	47567	6
AMHERST	NY	270685	56449	43218	1
REVERE	MA	200783	90035	18493	6
NORWICH	VT	310581	67577	16172	2
SAN JOSE	CA	120683	49244	40330	4
SAUSALITO	CA	030384	32407	28672	6
AMSTERDAM	NY	010980	91852	75265	4
ALFRED	NY	080283	90686	72408	5
HOULTON	ME	280781	57120	40390	1
NASHUA	NH	240284	10992	13897	2
ANTRIM	NH	020485	63371	53797	1
HENNIKER	NH	050180	33705	53080	1
FARMINGDALE	NY	190982	17535	56750	2
SANTA CRUZ	CA	250680	38975	69170	2
MINEOLA	NY	060683	81540	54400	4
CHELSEA	VT	170382	39692	17974	6
BRATTLEBORO	VT	300285	84822	47630	2
UTICA	NY	220285	99454	88024	1

Appendix G

Reserved Words, Reserved Symbols, and Glossary

The following are COBOL reserved words and symbols. They should only be used where permitted by the rules of the COBOL language. The meanings of many of these may not be clear. Nevertheless, their use must be in accordance with the expectations of the compiler, since any misuse will be noted at compile time.

Reserved Words and Reserved Symbols

ACCEPT	CF	DATE
ACCESS	CH	DATE–COMPILED
ADD	CHARACTER	DATE–WRITTEN
ADVANCING	CHARACTERS	DAY
AFTER	CLOCK–UNITS	DE
ALL	CLOSE	DEBUG–CONTENTS
ALPHABETIC	COBOL	DEBUG–ITEM
ALSO	CODE	DEBUG–LINE
ALTER	CODE–SET	DEBUG–NAME
ALTERNATE	COLLATING	DEBUG–SUB–1
AND	COLUMN	DEBUG–SUB–2
ARE	COMMA	DEBUG–SUB–3
AREA	COMMUNICATION	DEBUGGING
AREAS	COMP	DECIMAL–POINT
ASCENDING	COMPUTATIONAL	DECLARATIVES
ASSIGN	COMPUTE	DELETE
AT	CONFIGURATION	DELIMITED
AUTHOR	CONTAINS	DELIMITER
BEFORE	CONTROL	DEPENDING
BLANK	CONTROLS	DESCENDING
BLOCK	COPY	DESTINATION
BOTTOM	CORR	DETAIL
BY	CORRESPONDING	DISABLE
CALL	COUNT	DISPLAY
CANCEL	CURRENCY	DIVIDE
CD	DATA	DIVISION

DOWN	JUST	PICTURE
DUPLICATES	JUSTIFIED	PLUS
DYNAMIC	KEY	POINTER
EGI	LABEL	POSITION
ELSE	LAST	POSITIVE
EMI	LEADING	PRINTING
ENABLE	LEFT	PROCEDURE
END	LENGTH	PROCEDURES
END–OF–PAGE	LESS	PROCEED
ENTER	LIMIT	PROGRAM
ENVIRONMENT	LIMITS	PROGRAM–ID
EOP	LINAGE	QUEUE
EQUAL	LINAGE–COUNTER	QUOTE
ERROR	LINE	QUOTES
ESI	LINE–COUNTER	RANDOM
EVERY	LINES	RD
EXCEPTION	LINKAGE	READ
EXIT	LOCK	RECEIVE
EXTEND	LOW–VALUE	RECORD
FD	LOW–VALUES	RECORDS
FILE	MEMORY	REDEFINES
FILE–CONTROL	MERGE	REEL
FILLER	MESSAGE	REFERENCE
FINAL	MODE	RELATIVE
FIRST	MODULES	RELEASE
FOOTING	MOVE	REMAINDER
FOR	MULTIPLE	REMOVAL
FROM	MULTIPLY	RENAMES
GENERATE	NATIVE	REPLACING
GIVING	NEGATIVE	REPORT
GO	NEXT	REPORTING
GREATER	NO	REPORTS
GROUP	NOT	RERUN
HEADING	NUMBER	RESERVE
HIGH–VALUE	NUMERIC	RESET
HIGH–VALUES	OBJECT–COMPUTER	RETURN
I–O	OCCURS	REVERSED
I–O–CONTROL	OF	REWIND
IDENTIFICATION	OFF	REWRITE
IF	OMITTED	RF
IN	ON	RH
INDEX	OPEN	RIGHT
INDEXED	OPTIONAL	ROUNDED
INDICATE	OR	RUN
INITIAL	ORGANIZATION	SAME
INITIATE	OUTPUT	SD
INPUT	OVERFLOW	SEARCH
INPUT–OUTPUT	PAGE	SECTION
INSPECT	PAGE–COUNTER	SECURITY
INSTALLATION	PERFORM	SEGMENT
INTO	PF	SEGMENT–LIMIT
INVALID	PH	SELECT
IS	PIC	SEND

SENTENCE	SUM	UPON
SEPARATE	SUPPRESS	USAGE
SEQUENCE	SYMBOLIC	USE
SEQUENTIAL	SYNC	USING
SET	SYNCHRONIZED	VALUE
SIGN	TABLE	VALUES
SIZE	TALLYING	VARYING
SORT	TAPE	WHEN
SORT–MERGE	TERMINAL	WITH
SOURCE	TERMINATE	WORDS
SOURCE–COMPUTER	TEXT	WORKING–STORAGE
SPACE	THAN	WRITE
SPACES	THROUGH	ZERO
SPECIAL–NAMES	THRU	ZEROES
STANDARD	TIME	ZEROS
STANDARD–1	TIMES	+
START	TO	–
STATUS	TOP	*
STOP	TRAILING	/
STRING	TYPE	**
SUB–QUEUE–1	UNIT	>
SUB–QUEUE–2	UNSTRING	<
SUB–QUEUE–3	UNTIL	=
SUBTRACT	UP	

Glossary

The terms in this appendix are defined in accordance with their meaning as given in the American National Standards Institute document that defines COBOL. These terms may not have the same meaning as in other languages. The definitions are intended to be reference material. For this reason, they are in most instances brief, and do not include detailed syntactical rules.

Abbreviated Combined Relation Condition.   The combined condition that results from the explicit omission of a common subject or a common subject and common relational operator in a consecutive sequence of relation conditions.

Access Mode.   The manner in which records are to be operated upon within a file.

Actual Decimal Point.   The physical representation—using either of the decimal point characters period (.) or comma (,)—of the decimal point position in a data item.

Alphabet–Name.   A user-defined word in the SPECIAL–NAMES paragraph of the Environment Division that assigns a name to a specific character set and/or collating sequence.

Alphabetic Character.   A character that belongs to the following set of letters: A,B,C,D,E,F,G,H,I,J,K,L,M,N,O,P,Q,R,S,T,U,V,W,X,Y,Z, and the space.

Alphanumeric Character.   Any character in the computer's character set.

Alternate Record Key.   A key, other than the prime record key, whose contents identify a record within an indexed file.

Arithmetic Expression.   An arithmetic expression can be an identifier or a numeric elementary item, a numeric literal, such identifiers and literals separated by arithmetic operators, two arithmetic expressions separated by an arithmetic operator, or an arithmetic expression enclosed in parentheses.

Arithmetic Operator.   A single character or a fixed two-character combination that belongs to the following set:

Character	Meaning
+	addition
−	subtraction
*	multiplication
/	division
**	exponentiation

Ascending Key.   A key upon the values of which data is ordered, starting with the lowest value of key up to the highest value of key, in accordance with the rules for comparing data items.

Assumed Decimal Point.   A decimal point position that does not involve the existence of an actual character in a data item. The assumed decimal point has logical meaning but no physical representation.

At End Condition.   A condition caused

1. During the execution of a READ statement for a sequentially accessed file.
2. During the execution of a RETURN statement, when no next logical record exists for the associated sort or merge file.
3. During the execution of a SEARCH statement, when the search operation terminates without satisfying the condition specified in any of the associated WHEN phrases.

Block.   A physical unit of data that is normally composed of one or more logical records. For mass storage files, a block may contain a portion of a logical record. The size of a block has no direct relationship to the size of the file within which the block is contained or to the size of the logical record(s) that are either continued within the block or that overlap the block. The term is synonymous with physical record.

Body Group.   Generic name for a report group of TYPE DETAIL, CONTROL HEADING, or CONTROL FOOTING.

Called Program.   A program which is the object of a CALL statement combined at object time with the calling program to produce a run unit.

Calling Program.   A program that executes a CALL to another program.

Cd–Name.   A user–defined word that names an MCS interface area described in a communication description entry within the Communication Section of the DATA DIVISION.

Character.   The basic indivisible unit of the language.

Character Position.   A character position is the amount of physical storage required to store a single standard data format character described as usage in DISPLAY. Additional characteristics of the physical storage are defined by the implementor.

Character–String.   A sequence of contiguous characters that form a COBOL word, a literal, a PICTURE character–string, or a comment–entry.

Class Condition.   The proposition, for which a truth value can be determined, that the content of an item is wholly alphabetic or is wholly numeric.

Clause.   A clause is an ordered set of consecutive COBOL character-strings whose purpose is to specify an attribute of an entry.

COBOL Character Set.   The complete COBOL character set consists of the following 51 characters.

Character	Meaning
0,1, . . . ,9	digit
A,B, . . . ,Z	letter
	space (blank)
+	plus sign
−	minus sign (hyphen)
*	asterisk
/	stroke (virgule, slash)
=	equal sign
$	currency sign
,	comma (decimal point)
;	semicolon
.	period (decimal point)
"	quotation mark
(	left parenthesis
)	right parenthesis
>	greater than symbol
<	less than symbol

COBOL Word.   (See *Word.*)

Collating Sequence.   The sequence in which the characters that are acceptable in a computer are ordered for purposes of sorting, merging, and comparing.

Column.   A character position within a print line. The columns are numbered from 1, by 1, starting at the leftmost character position of the print line and extending to the rightmost position of the print line.

Combined Condition.   A condition that is the result of connecting two or more conditions with the "AND" or the "OR" logical operator.

Comment–Entry.   An entry in the IDENTIFICATION DIVISION that may be any combination of characters from the computer character set.

Comment Line.   A source program line represented by an asterisk in the indicator area of the line and any characters from the computer's character set in area A and area B of that line. The comment line serves only for documentation in a program. A special form of comment line represented by a stroke (/) in the indicator area of the line and any characters from the computer's character set in area A and area B of that line causes page ejection prior to printing the comment.

Communication Description Entry.   An entry in the Communication Section of the DATA DIVISION that is composed of the level indicator CD, followed by a CD–name, and then followed by a set of clauses as required. It describes the interface between the Message Control System (MCS) and the COBOL program.

Communication Device.   A mechanism (hardware or hardware/software) capable of sending data to a queue and/or receiving data from a queue. This mechanism may be a computer or a peripheral device. One or more programs containing communication description entries and residing within the same computer define one or more of these mechanisms.

Communication Section.   The section of the DATA DIVISION that describes the interface areas between the MCS and the program, composed of one or more CD description entries.

Compile Time.   The time at which a COBOL source program is translated, by a COBOL compiler, to a COBOL object program.

Compiler Directing Statement.   A statement, beginning with a compiler directing verb, that causes the compiler to take a specific action during compilation.

Complex Condition. A condition in which one or more logical operators act upon one or more conditions. (See *Negated Simple Condition, Combined Condition, Negated Combined Condition.*)

Computer–Name. A system–name that identifies the computer upon which the program is to be compiled or run.

Condition. A status of a program at execution time for which a truth value can be determined. Where the term "condition" (condition–1, condition–2, . . .) appears in these language specifications in or in reference to "condition" (condition–1, condition–2, . . .) of a general format, it is a conditional expression consisting of either a simple condition optionally parenthesized, or a combined condition consisting of the syntactically correct combination of simple conditions, logical operators, and parentheses, for which a truth value can be determined.

Condition–Name. A user-defined word assigned to a specific value, set of values, or range of values, within the complete set of values that a conditional variable may possess; or the user-defined word assigned to a status of an implementor–defined switch or device.

Condition–Name Condition. The proposition, for which a truth value can be determined, that the value of a conditional variable is a member of the set of values attributed to a condition–name associated with the conditional variable.

Conditional Expression. A simple condition or a complex condition specified in an IF, PERFORM, or SEARCH statement. (See *Simple Condition* and *Complex Condition.*)

Conditional Statement. A conditional statement specifies that the truth value of a condition is to be determined and that the subsequent action of the object program is dependent on this truth value.

Conditional Variable. A data item one or more values of which has a condition–name assigned to it.

Configuration Section. A section of the ENVIRONMENT DIVISION that describes overall specifications of source and object computers.

Connective. A reserved word that is used to

1. Associate a data–name, paragraph–name, condition–name, or text–name with its qualifier.
2. Link two or more operands written in a series.
3. Form conditions (logical connectives). (See *Logical Operator.*)

Contiguous Items. Items that are described by consecutive entries in the DATA DIVISION, and that bear a definite hierarchic relationship to each other.

Control Break. A change in the value of a data item that is referenced in the CONTROL clause. More generally, a change in the value of a data item that is used to control the hierarchical structure of a report.

Control Break Level. The relative position within a control hierarchy at which the most major control break occurred.

Control Data Item. A data item, a change in whose contents may produce a control break.

Control Data–Name. A data–name that appears in a CONTROL clause and refers to a control data item.

Control Footing. A report group that is presented at the end of the control group of which it is a member.

Control Group. A set of body groups that is presented for a given value of a control data item or of FINAL. Each control group may begin with a CONTROL HEADING, end with a CONTROL FOOTING, and contain DETAIL report groups.

Control Heading.   A report group that is presented at the beginning of the control group of which it is a member.

Control Hierarchy.   A designated sequence of report subdivisions defined by the positional order of FINAL and the data–names within a CONTROL clause.

Counter.   A data item used for storing numbers or number representations in a manner that permits these numbers to be increased or decreased by the value of another number, or to be changed or reset to zero or to an arbitrary positive or negative value.

Currency Sign.   The character "$" of the COBOL character set.

Currency Symbol.   The character defined by the CURRENCY SIGN clause in the SPECIAL–NAMES paragraph. If no CURRENCY SIGN clause is present in a COBOL source program, the currency symbol is identical to the currency sign.

Current Record.   The record which is available in the record area associated with the file.

Current Record Pointer.   A conceptual entity that is used in the selection of the next record.

Data Clause.   A clause that appears in a data description entry in the DATA DIVISION and provides information describing a particular attribute of a data item.

Data Description Entry.   An entry in the DATA DIVISION that is composed of a level–number followed by a data–name, if required, and then followed by a set of data clauses, as required.

Data Item.   A character or a set of contiguous characters (excluding literals in either case) defined as a unit of data by the COBOL program.

Data–Name.   A user–defined word that names a data item described in a data description entry in the DATA DIVISION. When used in the general formats, "data–name" represents a word that cannot be subscripted, indexed, or qualified unless specifically permitted by the rules for that format.

Debugging Line.   A debugging line is any line with "D" in the indicator area of the line.

Debugging Section.   A debugging section is a section that contains a USE FOR DE-BUGGING statement.

Declaratives.   A set of one or more special purpose sections, written at the beginning of the PROCEDURE DIVISION, the first of which is preceded by the key word DE-CLARATIVES and the last of which is followed by the key words END DECLARA-TIVES. A declarative is composed of a section header, followed by a USE compiler directing sentence, followed by a set of zero, one, or more associated paragraphs.

Declarative–Sentence.   A compiler–directing sentence consisting of a single USE statement terminated by the separator period.

Delimiter.   A character or a sequence of contiguous characters that identify the end of a string of characters and separates that string of characters from the following string of characters. A delimiter is not part of the string of characters that it delimits.

Descending Key.   A key upon the values of which data is ordered, starting with the highest value of key down to the lowest value of key, in accordance with the rules for comparing data items.

Destination.   The symbolic identification of the receiver of a transmission from a queue.

Digit Position.   A digit position is the amount of physical storage required to store a single digit. This amount may vary depending on the usage of the data item describing the digit position. Further characteristics of the physical storage are defined by the implementor.

Division.   A set of zero, one, or more sections of paragraphs, called the division body, that are formed and combined in accordance with a specific set of rules. There are four (4) divisions in a COBOL program: IDENTIFICATION, ENVIRONMENT, DATA, and PROCEDURE.

Division Header.   A combination of words followed by a period and a space that indicates the beginning of a division. The division headers are

```
IDENTIFICATION DIVISION.
ENVIRONMENT DIVISION.
DATA DIVISION.
PROCEDURE DIVISION [USING data-name-1 [data-name-2] . . . ].
```

Dynamic Access.   An access mode in which specific logical records can be obtained from or placed into a mass storage file in a nonsequential manner (see *Random Access*) and obtained from a file in a sequential manner (see *Sequential Access*), during the scope of the same OPEN statement.

Editing Character.   A single character or a fixed two-character combination belonging to the following set.

Character	Meaning
B	space
0	zero
+	plus
–	minus
CR	credit
DB	debit
Z	zero suppress
*	check protect
$	currency sign
,	comma (decimal point)
.	period (decimal point)
/	stroke (virgule, slash)

Elementary Item.   A data item that is described as not being further logically subdivided.

End of PROCEDURE DIVISION.   The physical position in a COBOL source program after which no further procedures appear.

Entry.   Any descriptive set of consecutive clauses terminated by a period and written in the IDENTIFICATION DIVISION, ENVIRONMENT DIVISION, or DATA DIVISION of a COBOL source program.

Environment Clause.   A clause that appears as part of an ENVIRONMENT DIVISION entry.

Execution Time.   (See *Object Time.*)

Extend Mode.   The state of a file after execution of an OPEN statement, with the EXTEND phrase specified, for that file and before the execution of a CLOSE statement for that file.

Figurative Constants.   A compiler-generated value referenced through the use of certain reserved words.

File.   A collection of records.

File Clause.   A clause that appears as part of any of the following DATA DIVISION entries.

```
File description (FD)
Sort-merge file description (SD)
Communication description (CD)
```

FILE–CONTROL.   The name of an ENVIRONMENT DIVISION paragraph in which the data files for a given source program are declared.

File Description Entry.   An entry in the File Section of the DATA DIVISION that is composed of the level indicator FD, followed by a file–name, and then followed by a set of file clauses as required.

File–Name.   A user-defined word that names a file described in a file description entry or a sort–merge file description entry within the File Section of the DATA DIVISION.

File Organization.   The permanent logical file structure established at the time that a file is created.

File Section.   The section of the DATA DIVISION that contains file description entries and sort–merge file description entries together with their associated record descriptions.

Format.   A specific arrangement of a set of data.

Group Item.   A named contiguous set of elementary or group items.

High Order End.   The leftmost character in a string of characters.

I–O–CONTROL.   The name of an ENVIRONMENT DIVISION paragraph in which object program requirements for specific input–output techniques, rerun points, sharing of same areas by several data files, and multiple file storage on a single input–output device are specified.

I–O Mode.   The state of a file after execution of an OPEN statement with the I–O phrase specified for that file and before the execution of a CLOSE statement for that file.

Identifier.   A data–name, followed (as required), by the syntactically correct combination of qualifiers, subscripts, and indices necessary to make unique reference to a data item.

Imperative Statement.   A statement that begins with an imperative verb and specifies an unconditional action to be taken. An imperative statement may consist of a sequence of imperative statements.

Implementor–Name.   A system–name that refers to a particular feature available on that implementor's computing system.

Index.   A computer storage position or register, the contents of which represent the identification of a particular element in a table.

Index Data Item.   A data item in which the value associated with an index–name can be stored in a form specified by the implementor.

Index–Name.   A user-defined word that names an index associated with a specific table.

Indexed Data–Name.   An identifier that is composed of a data–name, followed by one or more index–names enclosed in parentheses.

Indexed File.   A file with indexed organization.

Indexed Organization.   The permanent logical file structure in which each record is identified by the value of one or more keys within that record.

Input File.   A file that is opened in the input mode.

Input Mode.   The state of a file after execution of an OPEN statement, with the INPUT phrase specified, for that file and before the execution of a CLOSE statement for that file.

Input–Output File.   A file that is opened in the I–O mode.

Input–Output Section.   The section of the ENVIRONMENT DIVISION that names the files and the external media required by an object program and provides information required for transmission and handling of data during execution of the object program.

Input Procedure.   A set of statements that is executed each time a record is released to the sort file.

Integer.   A numeric literal or numeric data that does not include any character positions to the right of the assumed decimal point. Where the term integer appears in general formats, integer must not be a numeric data item, must not be signed, and must not be zero unless explicitly allowed by the rules of that format.

Invalid Key Condition.   A condition, at object time, caused when a specific value of the key associated with an indexed or relative file is determined to be invalid.

Key.   A data item that identifies the location of a record, or a set of data items that serves to identify the ordering of data.

Key of Reference.   The key, either prime or alternate, currently being used to access records within an indexed file.

Key Word.   A reserved word whose presence is required when the format in which the word appears is used in a source program.

Language–Name.   A system–name that specifies a particular programming language.

Level Indicator.   Two alphabetic characters that identify a specific type of file or a position in hierarchy.

Level–Number.   A user-defined word that indicates the position of a data item in the hierarchical structure of a logical record or that indicates special properties of a data description entry. A level–number is expressed as a one- or two-digit number. Level–numbers in the range 1 through 49 indicate the position of a data item in the hierarchical structure of a logical record. Level–numbers in the range 1 through 9 may be written either as a single digit or as a zero followed by a significant digit. Level–numbers 66, 77, and 88 identify special properties of a data description entry.

Library–Name.   A user–defined word that names a COBOL library that is to be used by the compiler for a given source program compilation.

Library Text.   A sequence of character–strings and/or separators in a COBOL library.

Line.   (See *Report Line.*)

Line Number.   An integer that denotes the vertical position of a report line on a page.

Linkage Section.   The section in the DATA DIVISION of the called program that describes data items available from the calling program. These data items may be referred to by both the calling and called program.

Literal.   A character–string whose value is implied by the ordered set of characters comprising the string.

Logical Operator.   One of the reserved words AND, OR, or NOT. In the formation of a condition, both or either AND and OR can be used as logical connectives. NOT can be used for logical negation.

Logical Record.   The most inclusive data item. The level–number for a record is 01. (See *Report Writer Logical Record.*)

Low Order End.   The rightmost position of a string of characters.

Mass Storage.   A storage medium on which data may be organized and maintained in both a sequential and nonsequential manner.

Mass Storage Control System (MSCS).   An input–output control system that directs or controls the processing of mass storage files.

Mass Storage File.   A collection of records that is assigned to a mass storage medium.

MCS.   (See *Message Control System.*)

Merge File.   A collection of records to be merged by a MERGE statement. The merge file is created and can be used only by the merge function.

Message.   Data associated with an end–of–message indicator or an end–of–group indicator. (See *Message Indicators.*)

Message Control System (MCS).   A communication control system that supports the processing of messages.

Message Count.   The count of the number of complete messages that exist in the designated queue of messages.

Message Indicators.   EGI (end–of–group indicator), EMI (end–of–message indicator), and ESI (end–of–segment indicator) are conceptual indications that serve to notify the MCS that a specific condition exists (end–of–group, end–of–message, end–of–segment). Within the hierarchy of EGI, EMI, and ESI, an EGI is conceptually equivalent to an ESI, EMI, and EGI. An EMI is conceptually equivalent to an ESI and EMI. Thus, a segment may be terminated by an ESI, EMI, or EGI. A message may be terminated by an EMI or EGI.

Message Segment.   Data that forms a logical subdivision of a message normally associated with an end–of–segment indicator. (See *Message Indicators.*)

Mnemonic–Name.   A user–defined word that is associated in the ENVIRONMENT DIVISION with a specified implementor–name.

MSCS.   (See *Mass Storage Control System.*)

Native Character Set.   The implementor-defined character set associated with the computer specified in the OBJECT–COMPUTER paragraph.

Native Collating Sequence.   The implementor-defined collating sequence associated with the computer specified in the OBJECT–COMPUTER paragraph.

Negated Combined Condition.   The NOT logical operator immediately followed by a parenthesized combined condition.

Negated Simple Condition.   The NOT logical operator immediately followed by a simple condition.

Next Executable Statement.   The next statement to which control will be transferred after execution of the current statement is complete.

Next Record.   The record that logically follows the current record of a file.

Noncontiguous Item.   Elementary data items, in the Working–Storage and Linkage Sections, that bear no hierarchic relationship to other data items.

Nonnumeric Item.   A data item whose description permits its contents to be composed of any combination of characters taken from the computer's character set. Certain categories of nonnumeric items may be formed from more restricted character sets.

Nonnumeric Literal.   A character–string bounded by quotation marks. The string of characters may include any character in the computer's character set. To represent a single quotation mark character within a nonnumeric literal, two contiguous quotation marks must be used.

Numeric Character.   A character that belongs to the following set of digits: 0, 1, 2, 3, 4, 5, 6, 7, 8, 9.

Numeric Item: A data item whose description restricts its contents to a value represented by characters chosen from the digits "0" through "9"; if signed, the item may also contain "+", "−", or other representation of an operational sign.

Numeric Literal.   A literal composed of one or more numeric characters that also may contain either a decimal point, or an algebraic sign, or both. The decimal point must not be the rightmost character. The algebraic sign, if present, must be the leftmost character.

OBJECT–COMPUTER.   The name of an ENVIRONMENT DIVISION paragraph in which the computer environment, within which the object program is executed, is described.

Object of Entry.   A set of operands and reserved words, within a DATA DIVISION entry, that immediately follows the subject of the entry.

Object Program.   A set or group of executable machine language instructions and other material designed to interact with data to provide problem solutions. In this context, an object program is generally the machine language result of the operation of a COBOL compiler on a source program. Where there is no danger of ambiguity, the word ''program'' alone may be used in place of the phrase ''object program''.

Object Time.   The time at which an object program is executed.

Open Mode.   The state of a file after execution of an OPEN statement for that file and before the execution of a CLOSE statement for that file. The particular open mode is specified in the OPEN statement as either INPUT, OUTPUT, I–O, or EXTEND.

Operand.   Whereas the general definition of operand is ''that component which is operated upon'', for the purposes of defining the meaning in COBOL, any lowercase word or words that appear in a statement or entry format may be considered to be an operand and, as such, is an implied reference to the data indicated by the operand.

Operational Sign.   An algebraic sign, associated with a numeric data item or a numeric literal, to indicate whether its value is positive or negative.

Optional Word.   A reserved word that is included in a specific format only to improve readability of the language and whose presence is optional to the user when the format in which the word appears is used in a source program.

Output File.   A file that is opened in either the output mode or extend mode.

Output Mode.   The state of a file after execution of an OPEN statement, with the OUTPUT or EXTEND phrase specified, for that file and before the execution of a CLOSE statement for that file.

Output Procedure.   A set of statements to which control is given during execution of a SORT statement after the sort function is completed, or during execution of a MERGE statement after the merge function has selected the next record in merged order.

Page.   A vertical division of a report representing a physical separation of report data, the separation being based on internal reporting requirements and/or external characteristics of the reporting medium.

Page Body.   That part of the logical page in which lines can be written and/or spaced.

Page Footing.   A report group that is presented at the end of a report page as determined by the Report Writer Control System.

Page Heading.   A report group that is presented at the beginning of a report page as determined by the Report Writer Control System.

Paragraph.   In the PROCEDURE DIVISION, a paragraph–name followed by a period and a space and by zero, one, or more sentences. In the IDENTIFICATION and ENVIRONMENT DIVISIONS, a paragraph header followed by zero, one, or more entries.

Paragraph Header.   A reserved word, followed by a period and a space that indicates the beginning of a paragraph in the IDENTIFICATION and ENVIRONMENT DIVISIONs. The permissible paragraph headers are

1. In the IDENTIFICATION DIVISION:

PROGRAM–ID.
AUTHOR.
INSTALLATION.
DATE–WRITTEN.
DATE–COMPILED.
SECURITY.

2. In the ENVIRONMENT DIVISION:

SOURCE–COMPUTER.
OBJECT–COMPUTER.
SPECIAL–NAMES.
FILE–CONTROL.
I–O–CONTROL.

Paragraph–Name.   A user-defined word that identifies and begins a paragraph in the PROCEDURE DIVISION.

Phrase.   A phrase is an ordered set of one or more consecutive COBOL character–strings that form a portion of a COBOL procedural statement or of a COBOL clause.

Physical Record.   (See *Block.*)

Prime Record Key.   A key whose contents uniquely identify a record within an indexed file.

Printable Group.   A report group that contains at least one print line.

Printable Item.   A data item, the extent and contents of which are specified by an elementary report entry. This elementary report entry contains a COLUMN NUMBER clause; a PICTURE clause; and a SOURCE, SUM, or VALUE clause.

Procedure.   A paragraph or group of logically successive paragraphs, or a section or group of logically successive sections, within the PROCEDURE DIVISION.

Procedure–Name.   A user-defined word that names a paragraph or section in the PROCEDURE DIVISION. It consists of a paragraph–name (which may be qualified), or a section–name.

Program–Name.   A user-defined word that identifies a COBOL source program.

Pseudo–Text.   A sequence of character–strings and/or separators bounded by, but not including, pseudo–text delimiters.

Pseudo–Text Delimiter.   Two contiguous equal sign (=) characters used to delimit pseudo–text.

Punctuation Character.   A character that belongs to the following set.

Character	Meaning
,	comma
;	semicolon
.	period
"	quotation mark
(	left parenthesis
)	right parenthesis
	space
=	equal sign

Qualified Data–Name.   An identifier that is composed of a data-name followed by one or more sets of either of the connectives OF and IN followed by a data–name qualifier.

Qualifier.

1. A data–name that is used in a reference together with another data name at a lower level in the same hierarchy.

2. A section–name that is used in a reference together with a paragraph-name specified in that section.

3. A library–name that is used in a reference together with a text–name associated with that library.

Queue.   A logical collection of messages awaiting transmission or processing.

Queue Name.   A symbolic name that indicates to the MCS the logical path by which a message or a portion of a completed message may be accessible in a queue.

Random Access.   An access mode in which the program-specified value of a key data item identifies the logical record that is obtained from, deleted from, or placed into a relative or indexed file.

Record.   (See *Logical Record.*)

Record Area.   A storage area allocated for the purpose of processing the record described in a record description entry in the File Section.

Record Description.   (See *Record Description Entry.*)

Record Description Entry.   The total set of data description entries associated with a particular record.

Record Key.   A key, either the prime record key or an alternate record key, whose contents identify a record within an indexed file.

Record–Name.   A user–defined word that names a record described in a record description entry in the Data Division.

Reference Format.   A format that provides a standard method for describing COBOL source programs.

Relation.   (See *Relational Operator.*)

Relation Character.   A character that belongs to the following set.

Character	Meaning
>	greater than
<	less than
=	equal to

Relation Condition.   The proposition, for which a truth value can be determined, that the value of an arithmetic expression or data item has a specific relationship to the value of another arithmetic expression or data item. (See *Relational Operator.*)

Relational Operator.   A reserved word, a relation character, a group of consecutive reserved words, or a group of consecutive reserved words and relation characters used in the construction of a relation condition. The permissible operators and their meanings are

Relational Operator	Meaning
IS [NOT] GREATER THAN IS [NOT] >	Greater than *or* not greater than
IS [NOT] LESSS THAN IS [NOT] <	Less than *or* not less than
IS [NOT] EQUAL TO IS [NOT] =	Equal to *or* not equal to

Relative File.   A file with relative organization.

Relative Key.   A key whose contents identify a logical record in a relative file.

Relative Organization.   The permanent logical file structure in which each record is uniquely identified by an integer value greater than zero, which specifies the record's logical ordinal position in the file.

Report Clause.   A clause, in the Report Section of the DATA DIVISION, that appears in a report description entry or a report group description entry.

Report Description Entry.   An entry in the Report Section of the DATA DIVISION that is composed of the level indicator RD, followed by a report name, followed by a set of report clauses as required.

Report File.   An output file whose file description entry contains a REPORT clause. The contents of a report file consist of records that are written under control of the Report Writer Control System.

Report Footing.   A report group that is presented only at the end of a report.

Report Group.   In the Report Section of the DATA DIVISION, a 01 level–number entry and its subordinate entries.

Report Group Description Entry.   An entry in the Report Section of the DATA DIVI-

SION that is composed of the level–number 01, the optional data–name, a TYPE clause, and an optional set of report clauses.

Report Heading.   A report group that is presented only at the beginning of a report.

Report Line.   A division of a page representing one row of horizontal character positions. Each character position of a report line is aligned vertically beneath the corresponding character position of the report line above it. Report lines are numbers from 1, by 1, starting at the top of the page.

Report–Name.   A user-defined word that names a report described in a report description entry within the Report Section of the DATA DIVISION.

Report Section.   The section of the DATA DIVISION that contains one or more report description entries and their associated report group description entries.

Report Writer Control System (RWCS).   An object time control system, provided by the implementor, that accomplishes the construction of reports.

Report Writer Logical Record.   A record that consists of the Report Writer print line and associated control information necessary for its selection and vertical positioning.

Reserved Word.   A COBOL word specified in the list of words which may be used in COBOL source programs, but which must not appear in the programs as user–defined words or system–names.

Routine–Name.   A user–defined word that identifies a procedure written in a language other than COBOL.

Run Unit.   A set of one or more object programs that function, at object time, as a unit to provide problem solutions.

RWCS.   (See *Report Writer Control System.*)

Section.   A set of zero, one, or more paragraphs or entries, called a section body, the first of which is preceded by a section header. Each section consists of the section heading and the related section body.

Section Header.   A combination of words followed by a period and a space that indicates the beginning of a section in the ENVIRONMENT, DATA, and PROCEDURE DIVISIONs.

In the ENVIRONMENT and DATA DIVISIONs, a section header is composed of reserved words followed by a period and a space. The permissible section headers are

1. In the ENVIRONMENT DIVISION:

    CONFIGURATION SECTION.
    INPUT–OUTPUT SECTION.

2. In the DATA DIVISION:

    FILE SECTION.
    WORKING–STORAGE SECTION.
    LINKAGE SECTION.
    COMMUNICATION SECTION.
    REPORT SECTION.

In the PROCEDURE DIVISION, a section header is composed of a section–name, followed by the reserved word SECTION, followed by a segment–number (optional), followed by a period and a space.

Section–Name.   A user–defined word that names a section in the PROCEDURE DIVISION.

Segment–Number.   A user–defined word that classifies sections in the PROCEDURE DIVISION for purposes of segmentation. Segment–numbers may contain only the characters ''0'', ''1'', . . . , ''9''. A segment–number may be expressed either as a one- or two-digit number.

Sentence.   A sequence of one or more statements, the last of which is terminated by a period followed by a space.

Separator.   A punctuation character used to delimit character–strings.

Sequential Access.   An access mode in which logical records are obtained from or placed into a file in a consecutive predecessor–to–successor logical record sequence determined by the order of records in the file.

Sequential File.   A file with sequential organization.

Sequential Organization.   The permanent logical file structure in which a record is identified by a predecessor–successor relationship established when the record is placed into the file.

Sign Condition.   The proposition, for which a truth value can be determined, that the algebraic value of a data item or an arithmetic expression is either less than, greater than, or equal to zero.

Simple Condition.   Any single condition chosen from the following set.

    Relation condition
    Class condition
    Condition–name condition
    Switch–status condition
    Sign condition
    (Simple–condition)

Sort File.   A collection of records to be sorted by a SORT statement. The sort file is created and can be used by the sort function only.

Sort–Merge File Description Entry.   An entry in the File Section of the DATA DIVISION that is composed of the level indicator SD, followed by a file–name, and then followed by a set of file clauses as required.

Source.   The symbolic identification of the originator of a transmission to a queue.

SOURCE–COMPUTER.   The name of an ENVIRONMENT DIVISION paragraph in which the computer environment, within which the source program is compiled, is described.

Source Item.   An identifier designated by a SOURCE clause that provides the value of a printable item.

Source Program.   Although it is recognized that a source program may be represented by other forms and symbols, in this book it always refers to a syntactically correct set of COBOL statements beginning with an IDENTIFICATION DIVISION and ending with the end of the PROCEDURE DIVISION. In contexts where there is no danger of ambiguity, the word "*program*" alone may be used in place of the phrase "*source program.*"

Special Character.   A character that belongs to the following set.

Character	Meaning
+	plus sign
–	minus sign
*	asterisk
/	stroke (virgule, slash)
=	equal sign
$	currency sign
,	comma (decimal point)
;	semicolon
.	period (decimal point)
"	quotation mark
(	left parenthesis
)	right parenthesis
>	greater than symbol
<	less than symbol

Special–Character Word.   A reserved word that is an arithmetic operator or a relation character.

SPECIAL–NAMES.   The name of an ENVIRONMENT DIVISION paragraph in which implementor–names are related to user-specified mnemonic–names.

Special Register.   Compiler–generated storage areas whose primary use is to store information produced in conjunction with the use of specific COBOL features.

Standard Data Format.   The concept used in describing the characteristics of data in a COBOL DATA DIVISION under which the characteristics or properties of the data are expressed in a form oriented to the appearance of the data on a printed page of infinite length and breadth, rather than a form oriented to the manner in which the data is stored internally in the computer, or on a particular external medium.

Statement.   A syntactically valid combination of words and symbols written in the PROCEDURE DIVISION beginning with a verb.

Subqueue.   A logical hierarchical division of a queue.

Subject of Entry.   An operand or reserved word that appears immediately following the level indicator or the level–number in a DATA DIVISION entry.

Subprogram.   (See *Called Program.*)

Subscript.   An integer whose value identifies a particular element in a table.

Subscripted Data–Name.   An identifier that is composed of a data–name followed by one or more subscripts enclosed in parentheses.

Sum Counter.   A signed numeric data item established by a SUM clause in the Report Section of the DATA DIVISION. The sum counter is used by the Report Writer Control System to contain the result of designated summing operations that take place during production of a report.

Switch–Status Condition.   The proposition, for which a truth value can be determined, that an implementor-defined switch, capable of being set to an ''on'' or ''off'' status, has been set to a specific status.

System–Name.   A COBOL word that is used to communicate with the operating environment.

Table.   A set of logically consecutive items of data that are defined in the DATA DIVISION by means of the OCCURS clause.

Table Element.   A data item that belongs to the set of repeated items comprising a table.

Terminal.   The originator of a transmission to a queue or the receiver of a transmission from a queue.

Text–Name.   A user–defined word that identifies library text.

Text–Word.   Any character–string or separator, except space, in a COBOL library or in pseudo–text.

Truth Value.   The representation of the result of the evaluation of a condition in terms of one of two values—true or false.

Unary Operator.   A plus (+) or a minus (−) sign that precedes a variable or a left parenthesis in an arithmetic expression and that has the effect of multiplying the expression by +1 or −1, respectively.

Unit.   A module of mass storage, the dimensions of which are determined by each implementor.

User–Defined Word.   A COBOL word that must be supplied by the user to satisfy the format of a clause or statement.

Variable. A data item whose value may be changed by execution of the object program. A variable used in an arithmetic expression must be a numeric elementary item.

Verb. A word that expresses an action to be taken by a COBOL compiler or object program.

Word. A character–string of not more than 30 characters that forms a user–defined word, a system–name, or a reserved word.

Working–Storage Section. The section of the DATA DIVISION that describes working storage data items, composed either of noncontiguous items, working storage records, or both.

77–Level–Description–Entry. A data description entry that describes a noncontiguous data item with the level–number 77.

Appendix H

Section 2.1

EXERCISES

```
6. a. 01  STUDENT-INFO.
          05 ID-NO      PIC X(4).
          05 NAME       PIC X(18).
          05 SEX        PIC X.
          05 AGE        PIC X(2).
          05 ALGEBRA    PIC X(3).
          05 GEOMETRY   PIC X(3).
          05 ENGLISH    PIC X(3).
          05 PHYSICS    PIC X(3).
          05 CHEMISTRY  PIC X(3).
          05 FILLER     PIC X(60).
   b. 01  STUDENT-RECORD.
          05 ID-NUMBER        PIC X(4).
          05 NAME             PIC X(18).
          05 FILLER           PIC X(12).
          05 PHYSICS-GRADE    PIC X(3).
          05 CHEMISTRY-GRADE  PIC X(3).
          05 FILLER           PIC X(60).
   c. 01  STUDENT-INFORMATION.
          05 FILLER PIC X(4).
          05 NAME   PIC X(18).
          05 SEX    PIC X.
          05 FILLER PIC X(2).
          05 ALG    PIC X(3).
          05 FILLER PIC X(3).
          05 ENG    PIC X(3).
          05 FILLER PIC X(66).
7. a. 01  CUSTOMER-INFO.
          05 ID-NUMBER    PIC X(8).
          05 NAME         PIC X(20).
          05 STREET       PIC X(20).
          05 CITY         PIC X(20).
          05 EXPIRATION   PIC X(6).
          05 INVOICE-NO   PIC X(6).
```

```
        05  AMOUNT-DUE   PIC X(9).
        05  REGION       PIC X.
        05  CREDIT-LIMIT PIC X.
        05  FILLER       PIC X(9).
  b. 01  CUSTOMER-RECORD.
        05  FILLER PIC X(8).
        05  NAME   PIC X(20).
        05  STREET PIC X(20).
        05  CITY   PIC X(20).
        05  FILLER PIC X(32).
  c. 01  CUSTOMERS.
        05  FILLER       PIC X(80).
        05  AMOUNT-DUE   PIC X(9).
        05  REGION-CODE  PIC X.
        05  CREDIT-LIMIT PIC X.
        05  FILLER       PIC X(9).
```

Section 2.2

EXERCISES

1. See Figure 2.2.1
2. IDENTIFICATION DIVISION
   ENVIRONMENT DIVISION
   DATA DIVISION
   PROCEDURE DIVISION
3. The compiler recognizes this line as a comment. A comment has no effect on the compilation or execution phases of a program.
4. TEXTA allows programmers to write programs in a computing environment without having to deal with the hardware dependencies. Each programmer will not have to write this portion of code for each program, but merely access it from the COPY library.

5.

USER-GENERATED NAMES	RESERVED WORDS
CMMNPRT	IDENTIFICATION
CARD-READER	DIVISION
PRINTER	PROGRAM-ID
FILE1	ENVIRONMENT
FILE2	CONFIGURATION
FILE3	SECTION
FILE4	SOURCE-COMPUTER
CUSTOMER-FILE	OBJECT-COMPUTER
STUDENT-FILE	INPUT-OUTPUT
NEW-WORLD-FILE	FILE-CONTROL
REGISTRAR-FILE	SELECT
CARD-IMAGE	ASSIGN
PRINT-LINE	TO
FILE1-RECORD	DATA
FILE2-RECORD	FILE
FILE3-RECORD	FD
FILE4-RECORD	LABEL
CUSTOMER-FILE-RECORD	RECORDS
STUDENT-FILE-RECORD	ARE
NEW-WORLD-FILE-RECORD	OMITTED
REGISTRAR-FILE-RECORD	BLOCK
	CONTAINS

6. If a file is blocked with a blocking factor greater than one, the logical record will not be identical to the physical record.
7. A library of programs and portions of programs that can be incorporated in any program using the compiler by means of the verb COPY. Usually the entries are portions of code used by a large number of different programs.

Section 2.3

EXERCISES

5. a. READ—WRITE—ROUTINE.
```
        READ CARD—READER INTO CARD—RECORD AT END.
        MOVE CARD—RECORD TO PRINT—RECORD.
        WRITE PRINT—LINE FROM PRINT—RECORD.
        READ CARD—READER INTO CARD—RECORD.
```
   b. READ—WRITE—ROUTINE.
```
        READ CARD—READER INTO CARD—RECORD AT END.
        READ CARD—READER INTO CARD—RECORD AT END.
        MOVE CARD—RECORD TO PRINT—PATTERN RECORD.
        WRITE PRINT—LINE FROM PRINT—RECORD.
```
   c. READ—WRITE—ROUTINE.
```
        READ CARD—READER INTO CARD—RECORD AT END.
        MOVE CARD—RECORD TO PRINT—RECORD.
        WRITE PRINT—LINE FROM PRINT—RECORD.
        WRITE PRINT—LINE FROM PRINT—RECORD.
```

PROGRAM TESTING AND MODIFICATION

1.

HERO	PRINT—PATTERN
CARNER, JOANNE	undefined
DI MAGGIO, JOE	undefined
MANTLE, MICKEY	undefined
BERRA, YOGI	BERRA, YOGI
NAMATH, JOE	NAMATH, JOE
EVERT-LLOYD, CHRIS	EVERT-LLOYD, CHRIS

Section 2.4

EXERCISES

```
3. a. 01  INPUT—RECORD.
          05 NAME             PIC X(30).
          05 FILLER           PIC X(6).
          05 CREDIT—RATING    PIC X(2).
          05 FILLER           PIC X(29).
          05 STREET—ADDRESS   PIC X(26).
          05 FILLER           PIC X(2).
          05 ZIP—CODE         PIC X(5).
          05 FILLER           PIC X(57).
          05 CURRENT—BALANCE  PIC X(12).
          05 FILLER           PIC X(29).
          05 PERCENT—INTEREST PIC X(3).
          05 FILLER           PIC X(10).
          05 LAST—LOAN        PIC X(10).
          05 FILLER           PIC X(28).
          05 LENGTH—OF—LOAN   PIC X(5).
          05 FILLER           PIC X(15).
   b. 01  PRINT—PATTERN—A.
          05 FILLER           PIC X.
          05 NAME             PIC X(40).
          05 ZIP—CODE         PIC X(50).
          05 CURRENT—BALANCE PIC X(42).
```

```
c. 01  PRINT-PATTERN-B.
       05 FILLER           PIC X.
       05 CREDIT-RATING    PIC X(30).
       05 CURRENT-BALANCE  PIC X(30).
       05 PERCENT-INTEREST PIC X(72).
d. 01  PRINT-PATTERN-C.
       05 FILLER           PIC X.
       05 NAME             PIC X(40).
       05 CURRENT-BALANCE  PIC X(20).
       05 LAST-LOAN        PIC X(15).
       05 LENGTH-OF-LOAN   PIC X(57).
```

Section 2.5

PROGRAM TESTING AND MODIFICATION

```
1. a. 01  PRINT-RECORD.
          05 FILLER             PIC X.
          05 OUT-CUSTOMER-NUMBER PIC X(30).
          05 OUT-NAME           PIC X(30).
          05 OUT-STREET         PIC X(30).
          05 OUT-CITY           PIC X(42).

       READ-WRITE-ROUTINE.
           READ CUSTOMER-FILE INTO CUSTOMER-RECORD.
           MOVE CUSTOMER-NUMBER TO OUT-CUSTOMER-NUMBER.
           MOVE NAME            TO OUT-NAME.
           MOVE STREET          TO OUT-STREET.
           MOVE CITY            TO OUT-CITY.
           WRITE PRINT-LINE FROM PRINT-RECORD.
   b. 01  HEADER-LINE.
          05 FILLER PIC X.
          05 FILLER PIC X(30) VALUE 'CUSTOMER-NUMBER'.
          05 FILLER PIC X(30) VALUE 'NAME'.
          05 FILLER PIC X(30) VALUE 'STREET'.
          05 FILLER PIC X(42) VALUE 'CITY'.

       PROCEDURE DIVISION.
           OPEN INPUT CUSTOMER-FILE
                OUTPUT PRINTER.
           WRITE PRINT-LINE FROM HEADER-LINE.
           PERFORM READ-WRITE-ROUTINE 100 TIMES.
           CLOSE CUSTOMER-FILE
                 PRINTER.
           STOP RUN.
   c. 01  PRINT-RECORD.
          05 FILLER           PIC X.
          05 CUSTOMER-NUMBER  PIC X(30).
          05 NAME             PIC X(30).
          05 STREET           PIC X(30).
          05 CITY             PIC X(42).

       READ-WRITE-ROUTINE.
           READ CUSTOMER-FILE INTO CUSTOMER-RECORD AT END.
           MOVE CORRESPONDING CUSTOMER-RECORD TO
                PRINT-RECORD.
           WRITE PRINT-LINE FROM PRINT-RECORD.
```

Section 2.6

PROGRAM TESTING AND MODIFICATION

1. Insert the following record descriptions at the end of the WORKING–STORAGE SECTION:

```
01 REPORT-HEADER.
   05 FILLER PIC X.
   05 FILLER PIC X(132) VALUE 'STUDENT FILE 6/5/82'.
01 DETAIL-HEADER.
   05 FILLER PIC X.
   05 FILLER PIC X(132) VALUE 'NAME'.
```

Insert the following two sentences after the OPEN sentence:

```
WRITE PRINT-LINE FROM REPORT-HEADER.
WRITE PRINT-LINE FROM DETAIL-HEADER.
```

2.
```
1234
ABLE
1243
CAIN
9999
ERROR
```

3.
```
1234
ABLE
1243
CAIN
```

Section 3.1

EXERCISES

2. a.
```
(1) ASHBY  RE        (4) CARR   GA
(2) BEAN   CD        (5) EISNER WL
(3) BORDEN KR        (6) ENGLE  JC
```

b.
```
(1) 818591641        (4) 863532076
(2) 828275050        (5) 873067780
(3) 842583678        (6) 896592747
```

c.
```
(1) 2 BEAN   CD      (4) 3 BORDEN KR
(2) 2 CARR   GA      (5) 4 ENGLE  JC
(3) 3 ASHBY  RE      (6) 5 EISNER WL
```

d.
```
(1) EISNER WL   863532076   5   ACTON
(2) ASHBY  RE   896592747   3   ALFRED
(3) ENGLE  JC   818591641   4   AMHERST
(4) CARR   GA   828275050   2   ANDOVER
(5) BEAN   CD   842583678   2   ANTRIM
(6) BORDEN KR   873067780   3   AUBURN
```

e.
```
(1) CARR   GA   828275050   2   ANDOVER
(2) BEAN   CD   842583678   2   ANTRIM
(3) ASHBY  RE   896592747   3   ALFRED
(4) BORDEN KR   873067780   3   AUBURN
(5) ENGLE  JC   818591641   4   AMHERST
(6) EISNER NL   863532076   5   ACTON
```

If two records have the same value for RATING, the record that occurred first in the original file was considered smaller.

If two records have the same value for RATING the record that has the smaller value in another field is considered smaller. If ties still remain, one can use a third field or resort to the first alternative.

Section 3.2

PROGRAM TESTING AND MODIFICATION

1.

TIME-EXECUTED	OUT-AGE	OUT-ALGEBRA-GRADE	NAME
1	—	—	STEVENS
2	—	—	WAGNER Y
3	—	—	RANCOURT
4	16	075	WAGNER D
5	16	075	HAROLD
6	16	075	WEICKLER
7	16	075	WILLS
8	16	073	ROTH
9	16	073	GEORGE
10	16	073	MAJOR

Section 3.3

PROGRAM TESTING AND MODIFICATION

1. 3 4 8 5 10 11 13 15 17 18 19 12 8 5 10 11 13 15 17 18 19
   12 8 5 10 11 13 15 17 18 19 12 8 5 10 11 13 15 16 18 19
   12 8 5 10 11 13 15 16 18 19 12 8 5 10 11 13 15 17 18 19
   12 8 5 10 11 13 15 16 18 19 12 8 5 10 11 13 15 16 18 19
   12 8 5 10 11 15 16 18 19 12 8 5 10 11 13 15 16 18 19
   12 8 5 10 12

   Note: The 12 8 5 sequence is deceptive because control returns to 12 after 8 before control is passed back to 5.

   ```
   OUTPUT
   51900000    WEINSMEIER          ***
   51900100    MENZIES             ***
   51900200    BAYLESS             ***
   51900300    GRAY                001544374
   51900400    MATHEWS             000015435
   51900500    BATTISTAS           ***
   51900600    SAMUELS             000056782
   51900700    MITCHELL            000567845
   51900800    COOPER              000056745
   51900900    GRAHAM              000043567
   ```

Section 3.4

EXERCISES

4. a. 85 86 75 90 85 75
   b. 85 86 75 83 80 74
   c. 85 86 75 83 85 74

5.
```
01  REGISTRAR-DATA.
    05  FILLER              PIC X(9).
    05  NAME-IN-ONE-PIECE.
        10  LAST-NAME       PIC X(10).
        10  FIRST-NAME      PIC X(10).
    05  FILLER              PIC X(71).
```

Section 3.5

EXERCISES

4.	2883	7.	0317	10.	JONES	SUSAN MARI
	2975		0617		MOLL	ANNA MAE
	3137		1234		BARNES	ROSELLE GR
	3608		2028		SMITH	LAURIE LEA
	3742		2093		GEORGE	JANET LEE
5.	0110	8.	0317	11.	JONES	SUSAN MARI
	0297		0617		MOLL	ANNA MAE
	0317		1203		BARNES	ROSELLE GR
	0364		1234		BAKER	ERIC
	0617		1587		VARNEY	LAWRENCE J
6.	0317	9.	0110			
	0617		0297			
	1234		0317			
	2028		0364			
	2093		0617			

Section 3.6

EXERCISES

```
6. IDENTIFICATION DIVISION.
   PROGRAM-ID. NOTEXTA.
   ENVIRONMENT DIVISION.
   CONFIGURATION SECTION.
   SOURCE-COMPUTER. IBM-370.
   OBJECT-COMPUTER. IBM-370.
   INPUT-OUTPUT SECTION.
   FILE-CONTROL.
       SELECT STUDENT-FILE
           ASSIGN TO UT-3330-S-FILE03.
       SELECT PRINTER
           ASSIGN TO UT-1403-S-SYSOUT.
   DATA DIVISION.
   FILE SECTION.
   FD  STUDENT-FILE
       LABEL RECORDS ARE STANDARD
       BLOCK CONTAINS 34 RECORDS.
   01  STUDENT-RECORD.
       05 STUDENT-ID-SR    PIC X(4).
       05 NAME-SR          PIC X(18).
       05 SEX-SR           PIC X.
       05 AGE-SR           PIC X(2).
       05 ALGEBRA-SR       PIC X(3).
       05 GEOMETRY-SR      PIC X(3).
       05 ENGLISH-SR       PIC X(3).
       05 PHYSICS-SR       PIC X(3).
       05 CHEMISTRY-SR     PIC X(3).
       05 FILLER           PIC X(60).
   FD  PRINTER
       LABEL RECORDS ARE OMITTED.
```

```
01  PRINT-PATTERN.
    05 FILLER           PIC X.
    05 NAME-PP          PIC X(20).
    05 ALGEBRA-PP       PIC X(10).
    05 GEOMETRY-PP      PIC X(10).
    05 ENGLISH-PP       PIC X(10).
    05 PHYSICS-PP       PIC X(10).
    05 CHEMISTRY-PP     PIC X(72).
```

Section 4.1

EXERCISES

1. 95.5
   83.1
   178.6
2. 385.12
   4613.12
   4228.00
3. 39.75
   4.18
   166.15

4.   319
   318514.12
      998.47
5. 95.5
   178.6
6. 385.12
   4228.00

7. 39.75
   166.15
8.   998.47
   318514.12

Section 4.2

EXERCISES

5.   1.2
     456.7
   90123
      56.78
   34
   67
       .9012
       .34567

6. a. 0955
       0831
       01786
   b. 38512
       461312
       042280

c.   3975
      418
     16615
d. 31851412
        319
     099847

Section 4.3

EXERCISES

5. a. 148.97
      190.71
      769.34
   b. 3,007.80
        809.83
      2,304.83
   c. $212.84
       $909.81
       $1,807.84
          $50.20
          $79.83
   d. $**109.80
      $2,807.81
      $**606.83
      $2,202.85

e. 300,380
   70,185
   2,906CR
   $2,401.80
   $602.81CR
f. +4,017.08
   −6,902.62
   +2,857.29
   −4,669.03
   +3,463.48
   +2,445.10

g. −31.54
   539.97
   −66.48
   8.11
h. 781,100
   180.00
   307,200CR
   $4,345.00
i. 982 CR
   11 12 81
   318 542

Section 4.4

EXERCISES

```
4. IF CREDIT-RATING = 1
       PERFORM PROCESS-1
   ELSE
       IF CREDIT-RATING = 3
           PERFORM PROCESS-3
       ELSE
           IF CREDIT-RATING = 5
               PERFORM PROCESS-5.

5. IF GEOGRAPHY-10 = 'A'
       PERFORM A-ROUTINE
   ELSE
       IF GEOGRAPHY-10 = 'B'
           PERFORM B-ROUTINE.

6. IF CREDIT-LIMIT = 1 AND
       AMOUNT-DUE > 100
       PERFORM TOO-MUCH-1
   ELSE
       IF CREDIT-LIMIT = 2 AND
           AMOUNT-DUE > 300
           PERFORM TOO-MUCH-2
       ELSE
           IF CREDIT-LIMIT = 3 AND
               AMOUNT-DUE > 500
               PERFORM TOO-MUCH-3
           ELSE
               IF CREDIT-LIMIT = 4 AND
                   AMOUNT-DUE > 1000
                   PERFORM TOO-MUCH-4
           ELSE
               IF CREDIT-LIMIT = 5 AND
                   AMOUNT - DUE > 3000
                   PERFORM TOO-MUCH-5.
```

This is probably as much nesting as you would ever want. We will soon see other ways of handling this and other problems where there are more categories to deal with.

Section 5.1

PROGRAM TESTING AND MODIFICATION

```
1. a. *
      * NAME:                        ID:
      * PROGRAM-NUMBER: 5.1-2
      * DESCRIPTION:  MAKE A LISTING OF THE RECORDS
      *   OF A CARD FILE ON FILE3.
      *
          COPY TEXTA.
       WORKING-STORAGE SECTION.
       77 END-OF-FILE   PIC X(3)   VALUE 'NO'.
       PROCEDURE DIVISION.
      * MODEL I
          OPEN INPUT CARD-READER
               OUTPUT FILE3.
```

```
      * FILE PROCESSING PAIR
            PERFORM READ-CARD-READER.
            PERFORM MAKE-LISTING
                UNTIL END-OF-FILE = 'YES'.
      * TERMINATION ACTIVITY
            CLOSE CARD-READER
                  FILE3.
            STOP RUN.
      * INPUT PROCEDURE
       READ-CARD-READER.
            READ CARD-READER
                AT END MOVE 'YES' TO END-OF-FILE.
      * RECORD PROCESSING
       MAKE-LISTING.
            WRITE FILE3-RECORD FROM CARD-IMAGE.
            PERFORM READ-CARD-READER.
   b. *
      * NAME:                                 ID:
      * PROGRAM-NUMBER: 5.1-2 MODIFIED
      * DESCRIPTION:  COPY THE RECORDS ON FILE1 TO
      *    FILE4.
      *
            COPY TEXTA.
       WORKING-STORAGE SECTION.
       77  END-OF-FILE   PIC X(3)   VALUE 'NO'.
       PROCEDURE DIVISION.
      * MODEL I
            OPEN INPUT FILE1
                 OUTPUT FILE4.
      * FILE PROCESSING PAIR
            PERFORM READ-FILE1.
            PERFORM MAKE-LISTING
                UNTIL END-OF-FILE = 'YES'.
      * TERMINATION ACTIVITY
            CLOSE FILE1
                  FILE4.
            STOP RUN.
      * INPUT PROCEDURE
       READ-FILE1.
            READ FILE1
                AT END MOVE 'YES' TO END-OF-FILE.
      * RECORD PROCESSING
       MAKE-LISTING.
            WRITE FILE4-RECORD FROM FILE1-RECORD.
            PERFORM READ-FILE1.
   c. *
      * NAME:                                 ID:
      * PROGRAM-NUMBER: 5.1-2
      * DESCRIPTION:  MAKE A LISTING OF THE RECORDS
      *    OF CUSTOMER-FILE.
      *
            COPY TEXTA.
       WORKING-STORAGE SECTION.
       77  END-OF-FILE   PIC X(3)   VALUE 'NO'.
       PROCEDURE DIVISION.
      * MODEL I.
            OPEN INPUT CUSTOMER-FILE
                 OUTPUT FILE2.
```

```
* FILE PROCESSING PAIR
      PERFORM READ-CUSTOMER-FILE.
      PERFORM MAKE-LISTING
          UNTIL END-OF-FILE = 'YES'.
* TERMINATION ACTIVITY
      CLOSE CUSTOMER-FILE
            FILE2.
      STOP RUN.
* INPUT PROCEDURE
 READ-CUSTOMER-FILE.
      READ CUSTOMER-FILE
          AT END MOVE 'YES' TO END-OF-FILE.
* RECORD PROCESSING
 MAKE-LISTING.
      WRITE FILE2-RECORD FROM CUSTOMER-FILE-RECORD.
      PERFORM READ-CUSTOMER-FILE.
```

Section 5.2

EXERCISES

6.

a.	b.	c.
347	F	24
395	F	17
233	F	22
361	M	23
331	M	20
397	F	20
SMITH	BAKER	JONES
MOLL	VARNEY	BAKER
BAKER	JONES	BARNES
JONES	MOLL	VARNEY
VARNEY	BARNES	SMITH
BARNES	SMITH	MOLL

Section 5.3

EXERCISES

4. a.

SORT KEY	FINAL ORDER	
17065	9	WAGNER
15065	1	RANCOURT
16075	2	WILLS
16070	5	WEICKLER
17085	7	WAGNER
16072	4	MAJOR
16073	3	HAROLD
17072	8	ROTH
18070	10	STEVENS
16065	6	GEORGE

b.

SORT KEY	FINAL ORDER	
M17	5	WAGNER
M15	1	WAGNER
F16	9	WEICKLER
M16	2	MAJOR
M17	6	STEVENS
M16	3	HAROLD
F16	10	ROTH
M17	7	GEORGE
M18	8	RANCOURT
M16	4	WILLS

5. a.

SORT KEY	FINAL ORDER	
ME140170	6	SHERIFF
ME369026	5	FULLER
MA628572	7	JONES
MA146690	10	SNIDER
NY634634	2	EISNER
VT471375	1	ENGLE
NY527410	3	ZELLER
MA571766	8	PARKER
NH659600	4	VINCENT
MA268663	9	PRINCE

b.

SORT KEY	FINAL ORDER	
060681250987ME	7	FULLER
240181240785ME	3	SHERIFF
280185110590MA	2	EISNER
210482290986MA	5	PARKER
220682120486NY	4	SNIDER
020380160688VT	10	PRINCE
040184031087NY	8	JONES
300380230485MA	1	ENGLE
020383010689NH	9	VINCENT
070185250686MA	6	ZELLER

Section 5.4

PROGRAM TESTING AND MODIFICATION

```
3. ALEXANDER GRAHAM      083
   ANDERSON DAVE         100
   BROWN ANDERS          071
   BROWN BETH            071
   BROWN BETSY           071
   CHAPELLE MARIE        067
   CHAPELLE ROGER        067
   GAVETT WILL           086
   HUMPHRIES ELAINE      079
   HUMPHRIES ELEANOR     074
   JOHNSON JACOB         081
   SMITH ARTIS           062

4. ALEXANDER GRAHAM      083
   ANDERSON DAVE         100
   BROWN ANDERS          071
   BROWN BETH            080
   GAVETT WILL           086
   HUMPHRIES ELAINE      074
   JOHNSON JACOB         081
   SMITH ARTIS           062
```

Section 6.1

PROGRAM TESTING AND MODIFICATION

1.

DEPT–CODE	COST	DEPT–SUM	GRAND–SUM
X	$201.03	0	0
X	$2,365.14	$201.03	$201.03
Y	$56,432.15	0	$2,566.17
Y	$86,359.14	$56,432.15	$58,998.32
Y	$6.75	$142,791.29	$145,357.46
Y	$6.75	0	$145,364.21

Section 6.2

PROGRAM TESTING AND MODIFICATION

1.

STATE BREAK	STATE –NE	RATING BREAK	RATING –NE	STATE TOTAL	RATING TOTAL
CA	CA	1	1	0	0
CA	CA	1	1	38519	38519
MA	MA	1	1	0	80151
ME	ME	1	1	0	131826
NH	NH	2	2	0	0
NH	NH	3	3	0	0
NH	NH	3	3	71615	71615

Section 7.1

PROGRAM TESTING AND MODIFICATION

1.

CREDIT–CODE	CODE–CTR				
	1	2	3	4	5
2	0	0	0	0	0
2	0	1	0	0	0
2	0	2	0	0	0
4	0	3	0	0	0
3	0	3	0	1	0
2	0	3	1	1	0
3	0	4	1	1	0
4	0	4	2	1	0
3	0	4	2	2	0
3	0	4	3	2	0

Section 7.2

PROGRAM TESTING AND MODIFICATION

1.

I	IN–PLACE					
	1	2	3	4	5	6
–	0	0	0	0	0	0
1	1	0	0	0	0	0
3	1	0	1	0	0	0
5	1	0	1	0	1	0
4	1	0	1	1	1	0
2	1	1	1	1	1	0
6	1	1	1	1	1	1
5	1	1	1	1	2	1
3	1	1	2	1	2	1
4	1	1	2	2	2	1
1	2	1	2	2	2	1
6	2	1	2	2	2	2
3	2	1	3	2	2	2
4	2	1	3	3	2	2
2	2	2	3	3	2	2
5	2	2	3	3	3	2

Section 7.3

EXERCISES

```
5. 01  STORAGE-SPACE.
       05 BOXES  PIC 9(4) OCCURS 11 TIMES.
```

```
01   STEP-ONE.
     05 FILLER PIC 99 VALUE 3.
     05 FILLER PIC 99 VALUE 5.
     05 FILLER PIC 99 VALUE 7.
     05 FILLER PIC 99 VALUE 9.
     05 FILLER PIC 99 VALUE 11.
     05 FILLER PIC 99 VALUE 13.
     05 FILLER PIC 99 VALUE 15.
     05 FILLER PIC 99 VALUE 17.
     05 FILLER PIC 99 VALUE 19.
     05 FILLER PIC 99 VALUE 21.
     05 FILLER PIC 99 VALUE 23.
01   STEP-TWO REDEFINES STEP-ONE.
     05 BOXES  PIC 99 OCCURS 11 TIMES.

6. 01   STORAGE-SPACE.
        05 BOXES  PIC 99 OCCURS 11 TIMES.

   PROCEDURE DIVISION.
        OPEN INPUT CARD-READER.
        READ CARD-READER INTO STORAGE-SPACE.

   $ENTRY
   0305070911131517192123
```

PROGRAM TESTING AND MODIFICATION

```
1. a. 01   NUMBERS-WE-WANT.
           05 FILLER PIC 9V99 VALUE 5.85.
           05 FILLER PIC 9V99 VALUE 5.97.
           05 FILLER PIC 9V99 VALUE 6.01.
           05 FILLER PIC 9V99 VALUE 6.17.
           05 FILLER PIC 9V99 VALUE 6.23.
           05 FILLER PIC 9V99 VALUE 6.31.
           05 FILLER PIC 9V99 VALUE 6.42.
           05 FILLER PIC 9V99 VALUE 6.50.
           05 FILLER PIC 9V99 VALUE 6.58.
           05 FILLER PIC 9V99 VALUE 6.63.
           05 FILLER PIC 9V99 VALUE 6.75.
      01   PERMANENT-INFORMATION
           REDEFINES NUMBERS-WE-WANT.
           05 WAGE-RATES PIC 9V99
               OCCURS 11 TIMES.

   b. 01   NUMBERS-WE-WANT.
           05 FILLER PIC 9V99 VALUE 5.85.
           05 FILLER PIC 9V99 VALUE 5.97.
           05 FILLER PIC 9V99 VALUE 6.01.
           05 FILLER PIC 9V99 VALUE 6.23.
           05 FILLER PIC 9V99 VALUE 6.31.
           05 FILLER PIC 9V99 VALUE 6.42.
           05 FILLER PIC 9V99 VALUE 6.50.
           05 FILLER PIC 9V99 VALUE 6.58.
           05 FILLER PIC 9V99 VALUE 6.63.
      01   PERMANENT-INFORMATION
           REDEFINES NUMBERS-WE-WANT.
           05 WAGE-RATES PIC 9V99
               OCCURS 9 TIMES.
```

```
c. 01  NUMBERS-WE-WANT.
       05 FILLER PIC 9V99 VALUE 6.44.
       05 FILLER PIC 9V99 VALUE 6.57.
       05 FILLER PIC 9V99 VALUE 6.61.
       05 FILLER PIC 9V99 VALUE 6.85.
       05 FILLER PIC 9V99 VALUE 6.94.
       05 FILLER PIC 9V99 VALUE 7.06.
       05 FILLER PIC 9V99 VALUE 7.15.
       05 FILLER PIC 9V99 VALUE 7.24.
       05 FILLER PIC 9V99 VALUE 7.29.
       05 FILLER PIC 9V99 VALUE 7.43.
   01  PERMANENT-INFORMATION
       REDEFINES NUMBERS-WE-WANT.
       05 WAGE-RATES PIC 9V99
          OCCURS 10 TIMES.
```

Section 8.1

PROGRAM TESTING AND MODIFICATION

1.

12561	37615	4613	2195	8651	29365
4	2	8	9	5	2
10000	25000	4000	2000	8000	25000
.060	.075	.03	.02	.05	.075
315	1265	60	20	215	1265
468.66	2211.12	78.39	23.90	247.55	1592.37

Section 8.2

PROGRAM TESTING AND MODIFICATION

WINNER

1	3		
1	2		
1			
1	3		
1			
1	2	3	
1	5		
1	4		
1	2	3	4
1	4	5	

Section 8.3

EXERCISES

6. a. 7 4 2 1 3 6 6 5 4 1 7 3
   b. 7 4 2 1 3 6 6 5 4 1 7 4
   The first block of code is more efficient because you don't check any additional locations in MAIL-BOXES once a match is found. In the second block you check all the locations in MAIL-BOXES for each value of SPECIAL-CODE.

PROGRAM TESTING AND MODIFICATION

1.

PLACE	REGION	COUNT–BY–REGION 1	2	3
—	A	0	0	0
1	A	1	0	0
1	A	2	0	0
1	A	3	0	0
1	A	4	0	0
1	A	5	0	0
1	A	6	0	0
1	A	7	0	0
1	A	8	0	0
1	A	9	0	0
1	C	10	0	0
3	B	10	0	1
2	C	10	1	1

Section 8.4

PROGRAM TESTING AND MODIFICATION

1.   **OUT–GRADE**

75	73	81	72	94
76	57	80	68	70
73	76	75	80	74
80	83	84	91	93
52	64	78	56	53
75	81	62	49	67

2.   **OUT–GRADE**

71	74	80	68	70	74	58
72	75	68	69	74	72	59
70	74	69	69	72	53	56
69	76	73	69	71	69	53
74	70	76	68	70	68	75
75	68	74	59	58	71	72
72	65	70	72	69	70	71

Section 9.1

PROGRAM TESTING AND MODIFICATION

1.

CREDIT LIMIT	REGION	ROW1 1	2	3	4	5	ROW2 1	2	3	4	5	ROW3 1	2	3	4	5
2	A	0	0	0	0	0	0	0	0	0	0	0	0	0	0	0
2	A	0	1	0	0	0	0	0	0	0	0	0	0	0	0	0
2	A	0	2	0	0	0	0	0	0	0	0	0	0	0	0	0
4	A	0	3	0	0	0	0	0	0	0	0	0	0	0	0	0
3	A	0	3	0	1	0	0	0	0	0	0	0	0	0	0	0
2	A	0	3	1	1	0	0	0	0	0	0	0	0	0	0	0
3	A	0	4	1	1	0	0	0	0	0	0	0	0	0	0	0
4	A	0	4	2	1	0	0	0	0	0	0	0	0	0	0	0
3	A	0	4	2	2	0	0	0	0	0	0	0	0	0	0	0
3	A	0	4	3	2	0	0	0	0	0	0	0	0	0	0	0
2	C	0	4	4	2	0	0	0	0	0	0	0	0	0	0	0
4	B	0	4	4	2	0	0	0	0	0	0	0	1	0	0	0
4	C	0	4	4	2	0	0	0	0	1	0	0	1	0	0	0
4	A	0	4	4	2	0	0	0	0	1	0	0	1	0	1	0

Section 9.2

EXERCISES

```
6. a.  01   LINE3.
             05 FILLER          PIC X.
             05 FILLER          PIC X( ) VALUE SPACES.
             05 EXPIRATION-OUT PIC XX.
             05 FILLER          PIC X VALUE SPACES.
             05 PATTERN OCCURS 6 TIMES.
                10 STAR-AREA     PIC XX.
                10 DATA-AREA     PIC Z9.
                10 BLANK-AREA    PIC X.
             05 FILLER          PIC X( ) VALUE '*'.
         PRINT-SUMMARY.
             MOVE CF-EXPIRATION-DATE TO EXPIRATION-OUT.
        * THE PERFORM PRINT-SUMMARY MUST BE CHANGED
        * SO THAT THE CONDITION IS I > 6. THE REST OF
        * THE CODE IS THE SAME.
   b.  01   LINE1.
             05 FILLER          PIC X.
             05 FILLER          PIC X( ) VALUE SPACES.
             05 FILLER          PIC X(35) VALUE ALL '*'.
             05 FILLER          PIC X( ) VALUE SPACES.
       01   LINE2.
             05 FILLER          PIC X.
             05 FILLER          PIC X( ) VALUE SPACES.
             05 FILLER          PIC X(36) VALUE ALL '*
             05 FILLER          PIC X( ) VALUE SPACES.
       01   LINE3.
             05 FILLER          PIC X.
             05 FILLER          PIC X( ) VALUE SPACES.
             05 EXPIRATION-OUT PIC 99.
             05 FILLER          PIC X VALUE SPACES.
             05 PATTERN OCCURS 6 TIMES.
                10 STAR-AREA     PIC XX.
                10 DATA-AREA     PIC Z9.
                10 BLANK-AREA    PIC X.
             05 FILLER          PIC X( ) VALUE '*'.
         PRINT-SUMMARY.
             MOVE CF-EXPIRE (I) TO EXPIRATION-OUT.
             PERFORM MOVE-IT
                VARYING J FROM 1 BY 1
                   UNTIL J > 8.
        *   THE REST OF THE CODE IS UNCHANGED.
```

Section 9.3

PROGRAM TESTING AND MODIFICATION

1.

NAME	AGE	CLASS	HOME STATE	I	J	K
JONES	24	JR	ME	3	8	2
MOLL	17	FR	MA	1	1	1
BARNES	22	SR	MA	4	6	1
BAKER	23	JR	CA	3	7	4
VARNEY	20	JR	MA	3	4	1
SMITH	20	UN	CA	5	4	4
GEORGE	24	JR	CA	3	8	4
MITCHELL	18	JR	VT	3	2	3
DAY	23	JR	CA	3	7	4
FLINT	21	UN	ME	5	5	2
FORD	21	JR	MA	3	5	1
NOLET	21	FR	VT	1	5	3

Section 10.1

PROGRAM TESTING AND MODIFICATION

1.

	1	2	3	4	5
1	1	0	0	0	1
2	0	0	0	0	0
3	2	1	3	0	1
4	1	0	0	0	0
5	0	1	1	0	0

2.

CODE-VALUE	COUNT-CODE							No. of entries examined
	1	2	3	4	5	6	7	
U	0	0	0	0	0	0	1	7
Z	0	0	0	1	0	0	1	4
B	0	1	0	1	0	0	1	2
A	1	1	0	1	0	0	1	1
Q	1	1	1	1	0	0	1	3
S	1	1	1	1	0	1	1	6

Section 10.2

PROGRAM TESTING AND MODIFICATION

1.

DORM—COUNT

ANDR	AROO	AUGU	BALE	BELF	CHAD	COLV	CORB	CROS	CUMB
2	0	1	0	0	0	0	1	1	0
1	2	3	4	5	6	7	8	9	10

DUNN	ELLS	ESTA	GANN	HANC	HANN	HART	JENE	KAPP	KENN
1	0	0	2	3	0	1	1	0	0
11	12	13	14	15	16	17	18	19	20

KNOX	LEWI	OXFO	PENO	OAK	ROCK	SOME	STOD	YORK
2	0	1	0	0	1	2	1	0
21	22	23	24	25	26	27	28	29

2.

CODE-VALUE	COUNT-CODE							No. of entries examined
	1	2	3	4	5	6	7	
U	0	0	0	0	0	0	0	2
Z	0	0	0	0	0	1	1	3
B	0	1	0	0	0	1	1	2
A	1	1	0	0	0	1	1	3
Q	1	1	1	0	0	1	1	3
S	1	1	1	0	1	1	1	3

Section 11.1

EXERCISES

```
5. 01  HEADER-1.
        05 FILLER PIC X.
        05 FILLER PIC X(51) VALUE SPACES.
        05 FILLER PIC X(14) VALUE 'THE NEW-WORLD'.
        05 FILLER PIC X(67) VALUE 'INSURANCE CO.'.
```

```
01  HEADER-2.
    05 FILLER PIC X.
    05 FILLER PIC X(56) VALUE SPACES.
    05 FILLER PIC X(15) VALUE 'WILLIAM COLES,'.
    05 FILLER PIC X(61) VALUE 'PRESIDENT'.
01  DETAIL-HEADER.
    05 FILLER PIC X.
    05 FILLER PIC X(33) VALUE SPACES.
    05 FILLER PIC X(25) VALUE 'CUSTOMER NAME'.
    05 FILLER PIC X(25) VALUE 'CUSTOMER ADDRESS'.
    05 FILLER PIC X(82) VALUE 'INSURANCE AMOUNT'.
01  DETAIL-LINE.
    05 FILLER     PIC X.
    05 FILLER     PIC X(33) VALUE SPACES.
    05 DL-NAME    PIC X(25).
    05 DL-STREET  PIC X(12).
    05 DL-CITY    PIC X(16).
    05 DL-INS-AMT PIC $,$$$,$$$.
    05 FILLER     PIC X(66) VALUE SPACES.
01  PAGE-NUMBERING-LINE.
    05 FILLER  PIC X.
    05 FILLER  PIC X(65) VALUE SPACES.
    05 PAGE-NO PIC ZZ.
    05 FILLER  PIC X(65) VALUE SPACES.
```

Section 11.2

EXERCISES

```
6. RD    INSURANCE-REPORT
         PAGE 59 LINES
         HEADING 3
         FIRST DETAIL 8
         LAST DETAIL 50
         FOOTING 56.
   01  TYPE REPORT HEADING.
       05 LINE 3 COLUMN 52
          VALUE 'THE NEW WORLD INSURANCE CO.'.
       05 LINE 4 COLUMN 57
          VALUE 'WILLIAM COLES, PRESIDENT'.
   01  TYPE PAGE HEADING LINE 7.
       05 COLUMN 34 VALUE 'CUSTOMER NAME'.
       05 COLUMN 59 VALUE 'CUSTOMER ADDRESS'.
       05 COLUMN 84 VALUE 'INSURANCE AMOUNT'.
   01  TYPE DETAIL LINE PLUS 1.
       05 COLUMN 34 PIC X(20) SOURCE NAME.
       05 COLUMN 59 PIC X(10) SOURCE STREET.
       05 COLUMN 71 PIC X(10) SOURCE CITY.
       05 COLUMN 89 PIC $,$$$,$$$ SOURCE INS-AMOUNT.
   01  TYPE PAGE FOOTING LINE 58.
       05 COLUMN 66 PIC ZZ SOURCE PAGE-NO.
```

Section 12.1

EXERCISES

3. CURRENT STATUS OF FILE

1	918	BILLS, ALLAN	F
2	716	JONES, GRETA	F
3	777	GREEN, GEORGE	F
4	784	BLUE, VIVIAN	F
5	586	BROWN, GEORGE	F
6			D
7	635	WILLIAMS, SUSAN	F

Section 12.2

EXERCISES

7. **CURRENT STATUS FOR INDEXED FILE**

PRIME AREA

TRACK	CYLINDER 1			CYLINDER 2			CYLINDER 3		
1	34	49	56	484	501	518	833	878	890D
2	101	165	187	526	646	659	903	930	987
3	273	289D	482	776	778	783	1049	1103	1105

OVERFLOW AREA

TRACK	CYLINDER 70		
1	269 ***	765D***	681 T1,R2
2	1016 ***	87 ***	1111 ***
3	830 ***		

CYLINDER INDEX

CYLINDER	KEY
1	482
2	830
3	1111

TRACK INDEXES

CYLINDER 1				CYLINDER 2				CYLINDER 3			
PRIME		OVERFLOW		PRIME		OVERFLOW		PRIME		OVERFLOW	
TRACK	KEY	TRACK	KEY	TRACK	KEY	TRACK	KEY	TRACK	KEY	TRACK	KEY
1	56	T2,R3	87	1	518	1	518	1	890	1	890
2	187	T1,R1	269	2	659	T1,R3	765	2	987	T2,R1	1016
3	482	3	482	3	783	T3,R1	830	3	1105	T2,R3	1111

Section 12.3

EXERCISES

6. Following each number is the count of records that would hash to the location when there are 100 storage locations. Numbers with a count of zero are omitted.

1 1	21 3	41	61	81
2 1	22 1	42 2	62 2	82
3 2	23	43	63	83
4 1	24 2	44 3	64	84
5	25 3	45 1	65	85 1
6 3	26 1	46 1	66	86 3
7 1	27 2	47 2	67 1	87 1
8 3	28	48 1	68 1	88 2
9 2	29 2	49 2	69 3	89
10 4	30 1	50	70 1	90
11 1	31 3	51	71	91 1
12 1	32 2	52	72	92 1
13 1	33	53 2	73 1	93
14 1	34 2	54	74	94 2
15 2	35 1	55	75	95
16 2	36 1	56	76	96
17 2	37 2	57	77 1	97 1
18 1	38 1	58	78	98
19	39 1	59	79 1	99
20 2	40 2	60	80 2	100

Following each number is a count of records that would hash to that location when there are 123 storage locations.

1 1	26 2	51	76	101 1
2 3	27 1	52	77 1	102 1
3 3	28	53 2	78	103
4 2	29	54	79 1	104
5	30	55	80 2	105
6 3	31 3	56	81	106 2
7 2	32 2	57	82	107
8 3	33	58	83	108
9	34 1	59	84	109 2
10 3	35 1	60	85 1	110 1
11 2	36	61	86 3	111
12 1	37	62 2	87 1	112
13 2	38 1	63	88 2	113
14 3	39 1	64	89	114
15 2	40 1	65	90	115
16 1	41	66	91 1	116 1
17 3	42	67 1	92 1	117
18 1	43	68 1	93	118
19 2	44	69 3	94 2	119
20 2	45	70 1	95	120
21 5	46 1	71	96	121 1
22 1	47 1	72	97 1	122 1
23	48	73 1	98	123
24 2	49	74	99	
25 1	50	75	100	

Following each number is the count of records that would hash to that location when there are 197 storage locations.

1	31 3	61	91 1	121 1
2	32 2	62 2	92 1	122 1
3 2	33	63	93	123
4 1	34 1	64	94 2	124 1
5	35 1	65	95	125 3
6 1	36	66	96	126 1
7 1	37	67 1	97 1	127 1
8 3	38 1	68 1	98	128
9	39 1	69 3	99	129 2
10 3	40 1	70 1	100	130 1
11 1	41	71	101 1	131
12 1	42	72	102 1	132
13 1	43	73 1	103	133
14 1	44	74	104	134 1
15 2	45	75	105	135
16 1	46 1	76	106 2	136 1
17 2	47 1	77 1	107	137 2
18 1	48	78	108	138
19	49	79 1	109 2	139
20 2	50	80 2	110 1	140 1
21 2	51	81	111	141
22	52	82	112	142 2
23	53 2	83	113	143
24 1	54	84	114	144 3
25	55	85 1	115	145 1
26	56	86 3	116 1	146
27 1	57	87 1	117	147 1
28	58	88 2	118	148 1
29	59	89	119	149 2
30	60	90	120	150

7. Following each number is the count of records that would hash to that location when there are 123 storage locations.

1	17	33 2	49 2	65
2	18	34 6	50 1	66
3	19	35 4	51 3	67
4	20	36 6	52 2	68
5	21 1	37 5	53	69
6	22	38 5	54 1	70
7	23	39 3	55 2	71
8	24	40 3	56 1	72
9	25	41 4	57 1	73
10	26	42 2	58 1	74
11	27 2	43 5	59	75
12	28 1	44 8	60 1	76
13	29 2	45 7	61 1	77
14	30 2	46 5	62	78
15	31 2	47 2	63	79
16	32 4	48 3	64	80

8. Following each number is the count of records that would hash to that location when there are 123 storage locations.

1		26		51 1		76 3		101
2		27		52		77 1		102 1
3		28		53 1		78 2		103
4		29		54		79		104
5		30		55 2		80 3		105
6		31		56		81 3		106
7		32		57 2		82 6		107
8		33 1		58 4		83 1		108
9		34		59 1		84 2		109 1
10		35 1		60		85 1		110
11		36		61 2		86 1		111
12		37		62 2		87 1		112 1
13		38 1		63 4		88		113
14		39		64 1		89		114
15		40 1		65 1		90 2		115
16		41 2		66 2		91		116
17		42 1		67		92 2		117
18		43 1		68 3		93		118
19		44		69 6		94		119 1
20 1		45		70 3		95 2		120
21		46 2		71 5		96		121
22 1		47 1		72 1		97		122
23		48 3		73 2		98		123
24		49 1		74 3		99		
25		50		75 3		100		

Section 12.4

EXERCISES

```
6. STUDENT-FILE
        ID-NUMBER
        NAME
   CUSTOMER-FILE
        CUSTOMER-NUMBER
        NAME
        INVOICE-NUMBER
   REGISTRAR-FILE
        SOC-SEC-NUMBER
        NAME
   NEW-WORLD-FILE
        CHARGE-ID
        NAME
        HOME-ADDRESS
        AMOUNT-DUE
        PAYMENT
```

Fields such as AMOUNT-DUE and PAYMENT should be viewed as normally varying overtime and thus cannot be expected to identify a unique record with the same information for a long period of time. In fact, it should be viewed as a coincidence that each record has a different value in these two fields.

PROGRAM TESTING AND MODIFICATION

```
1. LISTING
        IF  ACTIVE-OR-NOT = 'A'
            MOVE NAME          TO NAME-OUT
            MOVE PLACE         TO PLACE-OUT
            MOVE ACTIVE-OR-NOT TO STATUS-CODE
            WRITE PRINT-LINE.
```

Section 13.1

PROGRAM TESTING AND MODIFICATION

```
1. MOVE SPACES TO SIGNIFICANT-YET
   PERFORM DIGITS
        VARYING I FROM 21 BY 1
             UNTIL I > 25.
                 .
                 .
                 .

   DIGITS.
       IF SIGNIFICANT-YET = SPACES
           PERFORM CK-DIGIT-SPACE-ZERO
         ELSE
           PERFORM CHECK-DIGIT.
   CK-DIGIT-SPACE-ZERO.
           IF CARD COLUMN (I) = SPACE
              OR CARD-COLUMN (I) = 00H
                  NEXT SENTENCE
           ELSE
               MOVE 'YES' TO SIGNIFICANT-YET
               PERFORM CHECK-DIGIT.
   CHECK-DIGIT.
       IF CARD-COLUMN (I) NOT LESS THAN ONE
          AND CARD-COLUMN (I) NOT GREATER THAN NINE
           NEXT SENTENCE
         ELSE
           MOVE STAR TO COLUMN-CORRECT (I).
```

Appendix I

COBOL: 1968, 1974, and 198X

1968 and 1974 COBOL

Programs illustrated in this text conform to 1974 COBOL standards. All programs have been run on one or more of the following systems: IBM, DEC VAX-11, and PRIME-850.

It should be noted that not all computer installations have upgraded their COBOL compilers from the 1968 to the 1974 standards. Recent estimates are that no more than sixty percent of U.S. installations have the 1974 standard compilers. Moreover, many manufacturer-enhanced compilers have extensions of one or both standards.

In reality, from the point of view of the beginning programmer, the differences between 1968 and 1974 standards are not substantial. Only some minor program changes might be required before a COBOL program could be run on another system. The major differences are summarized here.

1968	1974
In the WRITE statement, the word LINES is used; LINE is not permitted.	The word LINE is equivalent to LINES, both may be used.
The editing symbol slash is not available.	The editing symbol slash may be used in both numeric and alphanumeric fields.
The SIGN clause is not available.	The SIGN clause is available.
MULTIPLE answer fields may not be specified for any arithmetic statement.	Multiple answer fields may be specified for ADD, SUBTRACT, MULTIPLY, DIVIDE, and COMPUTE statements.
The INSPECT statement is not available.	The EXAMINE statement has been replaced with the INSPECT.
Multiple subscripts and indexes must be separated by commas when they appear within parentheses.	The commas may be omitted from multiple subscripts and indexes when they appear within parentheses.
77-level items, if used, must appear at the beginning of WORKING-STORAGE.	77-level items do not have to be placed at the beginning of WORKING-STORAGE.
The PAGE option of the WRITE statement is not available.	The PAGE option may be used in the WRITE statement to eject to the top of a new page.

After learning how to write COBOL programs as illustrated in this text, it is likely that you would have no difficulty following a COBOL program written in any version. The fact is that COBOL has changed only gradually over the years.

Proposed ANSI COBOL 198X Standards

It is possible that still another new COBOL standard will be approved. However, any of the changes will be of little consequence to you unless you become a professional COBOL programmer or use COBOL concepts far in advance of the material studied in this text.

The proposed standard was initially called COBOL 80 because its specifications were laid down in 1980. Later it has been known as COBOL 198X in recognition of the fact that its approval is likely to occur in the eighties. There has been some serious opposition to COBOL 198X. One major cause of resistance is the addition of several new reserved words. The problem with this is that programs already written under an earlier standard may contain user–defined words that would become reserved words in COBOL 198X. As a result, conversion of these programs could be prohibitively costly, given that there are thousands and thousands of COBOL programs already in use that might require revision to be compatible with COBOL 198X.

COBOL 198X as proposed will include features that:

1. Permit programmers to delimit a statement in the PROCEDURE DIVISION with a whole new set of reserved words that begin with END.
2. Increase the maximum number of subscripts from three to some larger number. The original proposal was forty-eight!
3. Permit STOP RUN to close all files without the programmer having to remember to close them.
4. Permit the command ADD...TO...GIVING.... The present form is ADD... ...GIVING....
5. Ease the use of structured programming techniques to make the programming process more enjoyable.

Following is a list of new proposed reserved words. Compilers of some computer manufacturers have already adopted some of these features.

ADDING	END–PERFORM
ALPHABET	END–READ
ALPHABETIC–LOWER	END–RECEIVE
ALPHABETIC–UPPER	END–RETURN
ALPHANUMERIC	END–REWRITE
ALPHANUMERIC–EDITED	END–SEARCH
ANY	END–START
COMMON	END–STRING
CONTENT	END–SUBTRACT
CONTINUE	END–UNSTRING
CONVERSION	END–WRITE
CONVERTING	EVALUATE
DAY–OF–WEEK	EXTERNAL
DEBUG–LENGTH	FALSE
DEBUG–NUMERIC–CONTENTS	GLOBAL
DEBUG–SIZE	GOBACK
DEBUG–START	INITIALIZE
DEBUG–SUB	NUMERIC–EDITED
DEBUG–SUB–N	ORDER
DEBUG–SUB–ITEM	OTHER
DEBUG–SUB–NUM	PURGE
END–ADD	REFERENCE
END–CALL	REFERENCE–MODIFIER
END–COMPLETE	REPLACE
END–DELETE	STANDARD–2
END–DIVIDE	TEST
END–EVALUATE	THEN
END–IF	TRUE
END–MULTIPLY	

Index